Inflation & the Nixon Administration

Volume 1

1969-71

Inflation & the Nixon Administration

Volume 1
1969-71

Edited by Lester A. Sobel

Contributing editors: Joseph Fickes, Joanne Edgar,
Susan J. Shoch

FACTS ON FILE, INC.   NEW YORK, N.Y.

Inflation & the Nixon Administration

Volume 1

1969-71

Library of Congress Catalog Card No. 74-75153
ISBN 0-87196-275-6

9 8 7 6 5 4 3 2 1
PRINTED IN
THE UNITED STATES OF AMERICA

Contents

Introduction

INFLATION IS AN ECONOMIC ailment that exacts a toll from almost every facet of domestic and international activity. It reduces the buying power of the worker's pay, the businessman's profits and the government's revenues. Foreign trade and relations between governments are profoundly troubled by the changes in currency values and trading patterns caused by inflation. Because of inflation, businesses may fail, workers lose jobs, governments fall.

The purpose of this book is to describe the inflation that faced the Nixon Administration and the efforts made to deal with it during 1969–71, Richard M. Nixon's first three years as President of the U.S.

The current period of inflation is the fourth to beset the U.S. economy since World War II ended the depression of the 1930s.

The high level of employment of the war and the pent-up demand brought on by war-caused shortages had spurred an upsurge of prices and wages during 1945–48. The wholesale price index rose by 52% and the consumer price (cost-of-living) index by 34%. This trend was accelerated by government efforts to avert unemployment and economic dislocation that, it was feared, might accompany the sharp decrease in war spending and the conversion of industry from war to civilian requirements. Relative stability was not achieved until mid-1948 and was followed by a brief, mild recession.

The Korean War brought a new inflationary period, which began in June 1950 and continued through March 1951. A buying wave pushed prices up. Truman Administration policies that in-

1

cluded a tax increase and cuts in nondefense spending helped curtail the spiral, but the most effective brake was, probably, the Defense Production Act of 1950, which allowed the Administration to freeze prices and wages.

Another minor recession took place during 1953–54, but conditions improved after about mid-1954.

A condition described as "creeping inflation" stretched from April 1956 to July 1958 despite a general slackness in production and demand during the period. The Eisenhower Administration reacted with restrictive budgetary and monetary policies.

Prices began to level off after mid-1958 and remained relatively stable until the latest inflationary trend in 1965. During this stable period, considerable attention centered on avoidance of inflation, and the Kennedy Administration in 1962 proposed wage-price "guideposts" that would key labor costs and price movements to increases in productivity.

The period of inflation that began in 1965 was spurred by a high rate of employment, greatly increased federal spending (both military and nonmilitary as the Vietnam conflict heated up), lowered taxes and the Johnson Administration's application of monetary stimulation to the economy. An Administration request for a tax surcharge was rejected by Congress in 1967, and the federal budget deficit rose to $12.4 billion. Congress finally passed the Administration's tax requests in 1968 but demanded budget cuts.

This book chronicles the troubled economic events of the period in which the Nixon Administration assumed office and developed its "game plan" for dealing with inflation. The book records the economy's ups and downs and the changes of Nixon policy—from the initial rejections of economic controls to the wage-price freeze of Phase One and the follow-up controls of Phase Two, the imposition of trade curbs and the devaluation of the dollar. The material in this volume is almost exclusively from the record compiled by Facts on File. Where changes or additions were made, the purpose was usually to clarify or to provide necessary amplification. A conscientious effort was made to record all events without bias.

1969

The departing Johnson Administration and the incoming Nixon Administration used budget, tax and international monetary policies in efforts to halt steadily growing inflation. Nixon policy called for slowing the economy during 1969's second half. Nixon ordered cuts in the Johnson budget. He "ruled out wage and price controls . . . under conditions that are now foreseeable." His Administration termed the 4% unemployment rate of October "acceptable" and indicated that its anti-inflation policies might result in even more unemployment. Nixon appealed to business and labor for restraint on prices and wages. Some labor spokesmen, rejecting the plea, demanded "equity." Pay raises were negotiated and price increases announced during 1969. U.S. trade and international payments problems added to the inflationary pressures by causing a loss of monetary gold reserves. Other countries were also affected. International gold speculation battered foreign currencies. Interest rates went up in the U.S. and other countries. France devalued the franc, and West Germany allowed its mark to "float," free from its fixed exchange rate. Wheat surpluses led to an international wheat price war.

Government Policy

The Johnson Legacy

When he took office as the 37th President of the U.S. Jan. 20, 1969, Richard M. Nixon was faced with the need to act against the increasingly serious problem of mounting inflation. Some anti-inflationary steps had already been taken by his predecessor, outgoing President Lyndon B. Johnson, and additional actions were proposed by Johnson and his aides in their final reports and messages in the early days of 1969.

Johnson Budget Proposals. The federal budget is a major tool in national economic policy-making. In his sixth and last federal budget, sent to Congress Jan. 15, President Johnson proposed a $3½ billion reduction in spending for the war in Vietnam. He called for federal outlays totaling a record $195.272 billion in fiscal 1970 and estimated fiscal 1970 receipts at a record $198.686 billion. The resulting $3.414 billion surplus, the President said, was needed "to relieve the inflationary pressures in the economy and to reduce the strains that federal borrowing would place on financial markets and interest rates."

The anti-inflationary effect was listed by the President as one of three major goals of the fiscal 1967 budget. The other two goals: (1) Support "for our commitments in Southeast Asia" and "necessary improvements" in overall military capabilities; (2) "continued emphasis on domestic programs which help disadvantaged groups obtain a fairer share of the nation's economic and cultural advancements."

The budget surplus was predicated in part on Mr. Johnson's request for an extension of the 10% income tax surcharge beyond its June 30 expiration date.

Mr. Johnson said Congress should give "serious consideration" to granting the President discretionary authority to remove or reduce the surcharge if "warranted by developments." He urged consideration for establishing, "as a permanent part of our tax system," discretionary Presidential authority to raise or lower income tax rates within certain limits, possibly 5%. Both powers would be subject to Congressional veto.

The President criticized "devices" enacted by Congress in 1967 and 1968 to control the level of federal spending. He held that these "devices"—"a reduction in agency obligations" and "an arbitrary ceiling on total [federal] outlays"—conflicted "with the normal appropriations process" and with planning and execution. He assailed the spending ceiling in particular because "in some cases, national priorities are arbitrarily distorted by the fact that the outlays for some federal programs are sheltered in basic law from meaningful annual control, and, consequently, compensating reductions have to be made elsewhere." Mr. Johnson said it was necessary to "reach an agreement on which of these conflicting budgetary approaches will be used in the future."

In summarizing the six budgets presented during his Administration, Pres. Johnson said that in fiscal 1965–70 the federal government would have provided $969 billion "for programs to improve the lives of our citizens and to protect the nation's security" and would have received $936 billion in revenues. He said the total deficit in those years, an estimated $33½ billion, "is more than offset by over $35 billion in lower taxes returned to individuals, families, and corporations." The tax reduction, he said, "takes into account" increases in social security taxes, extension of the income tax surcharge and automobile and phone excise tax rates.

Growth with Restraint Urged. The Johnson Administration Jan. 16 submitted to Congress two major economic reports advocating both economic restraint and continued growth for 1969. President Johnson's annual Economic Report to Congress was accompanied by the lengthier report of his Council of Economic Advisers. In addition, a report of the Cabinet Coordinating Committee on Economic Planning for the End of Vietnam Hostilities was appended to the Economic Report. The Congressional Joint Economic Committee began hearings on the three reports Jan. 17.

President's report—Calling for a "decisive step toward price stability" as the economy's "immediate task in 1969," the President's Economic Report proposed policies to provide "enough restraint . . . to permit a cooling-off of the economy and a waning of inflationary forces." "But the restraint must also be tempered to ensure continued economic growth," it added. "We must adopt a carefully balanced program that curbs inflation and preserves prosperity."

The report stressed that a balance in fiscal and monetary policy was necessary to achieve this goal without a major rise in unemployment. Johnson specifically referred to the intended effect of his latest budget and called on the Federal Reserve Board to moderate the economy's expansion without subjecting credit-sensitive areas "to the sharp and uneven pressures

of a credit squeeze." "Monetary policy," he said, "should be flexible and prepared to lessen restraint as the economy cools off."

Johnson rejected price stability through "an overdose of fiscal and monetary restraint," since such a policy would inevitably mean "stumbling into recession and slack, losing precious billions of dollars of output, suffering rising unemployment, with growing distress and unrest." He excluded the use of "mandatory controls on prices and wages" on grounds that such action was "a dead end for economic freedom and progress." Johnson's report repudiated a third possibility, that the country's leaders should "throw up our hands and allow the price-wage spiral to turn faster and faster." Such inaction, he said, "would eventually undermine our prosperity and our financial system. . . ."

To carry out his program of restraining monetary-fiscal policies in a growing economy, Johnson recommended a continued rise in productivity and industrial efficiency, but he warned business and labor that they must exercise "utmost" restraint in wage and price decisions. He said: "A decisive step toward price stability in 1969 requires labor and business to accept some mutual sacrifices in the short run to preserve their enormous long-term interest in prosperity and a stable value of the dollar."

The report advocated that the government's fiscal-monetary administrative structure be reinforced. In order to provide more coordination of Congressional budgetary decisions, it recommended that Congress "review its procedures for acting on the annual budget and . . . consider ways that may improve the coordination of decisions among federal programs and on federal revenues in relation to expenditures." He asked that Congress consider giving the President "discretionary authority to inititiate limited changes in tax rates, subject to Congressional veto"; such a procedure, he said, would eliminate "costly delays" in benefiting from tax legislation.

On international monetary matters, the report hailed the achievement of a U.S. balance of payments surplus in 1968, but emphasized that it had been aided by the imposition of temporary restraints on capital outflows. Warning that these

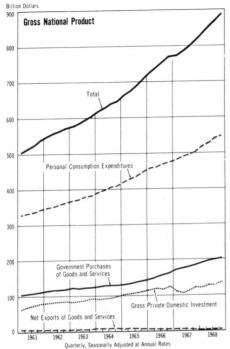

Billion Dollars

Gross National Product

Total

Personal Consumption Expenditures

Government Purchases of Goods and Services

Gross Private Domestic Investment

Net Exports of Goods and Services

1961 1962 1963 1964 1965 1966 1967 1968

Quarterly, Seasonally Adjusted at Annual Rates

restraints could not yet be relaxed, it advocated the renewal of the interest equalization tax before its expiration July 31, maintenance of the direct-investment control program in its current form, and continuation of the Federal Reserve's "program of voluntary restraint of foreign lending."

On the controversial question of the price of gold, the report asserted that "there is clearly no need to change" the current price of $35 an ounce. It proposed that the U.S. "actively participate" in discussions to improve the international monetary system, but it stressed that the problem could not "be resolved in a summit meeting or by a superplan."

A large part of the Economic Report was devoted to economic advances made by the U.S. during the Johnson Administration. It also predicted an increase of 3% in the Gross National Product to $921 billion in 1969. [See graph for 1961–1968 GNP statistics.] For the coming year it envisaged an increase in state and local government spending but little rise in federal purchases; a decrease in consumer spending and homebuilding activity; and maintenance of the unem-

ployment rate at a level below 4%. Summing up its projections for 1969, the report said that the "overall gains will not and should not be as large as those in 1968, but they will still make for a highly prosperous year."

Economic advisers' report—Longer and more specific in content than the Economic Report, the report of the Council of Economic Advisers reemphasized the goal of price stability with little unemployment, analyzed the current U.S. economic situation and discussed in detail several controversial issues.

The CEA report predicted a "real" growth in Gross National Product of less than 3% in 1969 (compared with 5% in 1968), with unemployment remaining below 4% and inflation dropping from about 4% to "a little more than 3%." The 1969 forecast predicted a $7 billion–$8 billion increase in business investment, an increase in federal spending of $10 billion (compared with an increase of $19 billion in 1968), with little of the increase going to defense; an increase in state and local government spending of $10 billion; an increase in consumer building of about $35 billion; and a slight decline in inventory growth and the level of housing starts.

In examining ways to achieve price stability, the council attacked the trend toward large corporate mergers and suggested key changes in antitrust laws to force greater corporate competition that would benefit price stability. The report explained that if a particular industry's production was concentrated in a few companies, an "inflationary bias" could be created because such companies "often maintain prices in the face of declining demand" by reducing output, and raise prices when demand increases. The council suggested that large firms in industries of critical economic importance could be divested of part of their operations to create new competitors. It also urged action to prevent large firms in one industry from purchasing large firms in another. "The major route for entry into a concentrated industry by a very large firm would then be to build a new capacity or to buy an existing smaller firm. When a very large firm buys a small firm in a concentrated industry, it has the resources to expand that firm's capacity and to try to increase its share of the market. Such a merger can infuse new vigor and ideas in that market."

Suggesting that business and labor make "mutual sacrifices" to help achieve price stability, the council supported a proposal by the President's Cabinet Committee on Price Stability that businesses absorb increases of up to 1% in unit costs and hold profit margins to 1967–68 levels and that labor accept less than 5% in annual wage increases. The council also suggested that the formulation of the government's voluntary wage-price policy, currently handled by the CEA alone, should include business and labor groups and members of the public.

The CEA report proposed reexamination of three laws that it felt led to higher prices—the two federal laws authorizing states to enact "fair-trade" laws and the Robinson-Patman Act, originally designed to aid small businesses against competition from large businesses. The fair-trade laws, according to the CEA, had often increased retailers' costs and prices; and the Robinson-Patman Act "has had the unintended effect of accentuating price rigidities" and has conflicted "with the development of more efficient methods of distribution."

The report examined the controversial issue of money supply and in effect rejected the theory that the rate of growth or decline in the supply of money determined the economic situation and that the Federal Reserve System should concentrate on achieving a growth of the money supply without regard to interest rates. "Given the complex role of interest rates in affecting various demand categories and the likely variations in so many other factors," the report declared, "any such simple policy guide could prove to be quite unreliable."

In the area of international monetary theory the CEA discussed proposed reforms and recommended more study of the idea for a flexible exchange rate. A free "floating" exchange-rate policy was rejected, but proposals for "wider bands" or a "crawling peg," both of which would permit a wider fluctuation of a currency's value, were viewed more sympathetically. The CEA concluded, however, that "modifications in the exchange rate system raise many difficult technical issues" and require "a great deal of careful study."

In discussing the International Monetary Fund's Special Drawing Rights or "paper gold" program, the council suggested that the proposed reserve plan should aim at several times the $1 billion to $2 billion per year usually mentioned; if reserves only grew at the lower rate, the program "might fail to achieve its objective of avoiding a destructive competition" for reserves and could hamper world trade.

Concurring with the Economic Report, the CEA rejected mandatory wage and price controls. The council said: "Such controls freeze the market mechanism which guides the economy in responding to the changing pattern and volume of demand; they distort decisions on production and employment; they require a huge and cumbersome bureaucracy; they impose a heavy and costly burden on business; they perpetrate inevitable injustices. They are incompatible with a free enterprise economy and must be regarded as a last resort appropriate only in an extreme emergency such as all-out war."

In what appeared to be an argument for some form of minimum income plan, the council asserted that poverty in the U.S. could be eliminated within six to eight years, without any substantial sacrifice, if "only a relatively small redistribution" of income growth were undertaken. The CEA said: "If the increase in real income for nonpoor [85% of the households receiving 95% of the total income] is lowered merely from 3% to 2½% a year and if that differential of about $2.8 billion annually is effectively transferred to those in poverty, then family incomes for those now poor can grow about 12% annually" and the $9.7 billion poverty gap could be eliminated in less than four years. Practically speaking, the council said that six to eight years was a more realistic goal. The redistribution would not be unfair, the council said, because proportionately "higher taxes are paid by households in the lower income classes than by those with incomes between $6,000 and $15,-000." The council's report discussed several specific methods of redistributing income—including the negative income tax proposal—and concluded that

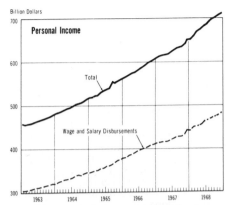

Billion Dollars

Personal Income

Total

Wage and Salary Disbursements

1963   1964   1965   1966   1967   1968

INCOME RECORD IN 1968. The Commerce Department reported Jan. 16 that U.S. personal incomes had risen from a record $628.8 billion total in 1967 to $685.8 billion in 1968. Total wage and salary disbursements rose from a record $423.4 billion to $463½ billion in the period, and farm incomes rose from a record $19½ billion to $20½ billion. The graph, adapted from the Commerce Department (Office of Business Economics), shows the monthly rise in U.S. personal incomes, seasonally adjusted, at annual rates, during the period 1963–68. Total personal incomes in December 1968, seasonally adjusted, were at a record annual rate of $713.4 billion. Wage and salary disbursements, seasonally adjusted, reached a record annual rate of $483.1 billion in the same month.

"a number of good alternatives are available."

The council noted that while minimum wage laws generally protected the lowest-paid employes, "excessively rapid and general increases in the minimum can hurt these workers by curtailing their employment opportunities." The report suggested that Congress seek other ways of helping low-wage workers.

Post-Vietnam economic report—The report submitted by the Cabinet Co-ordinating Committee on Economic Planning for the End of Vietnam Hostilities declared that the war was a burden for the U.S. economy and not a "supporting 'prop'" as many contended. The committee said that the nation's "prosperity has not depended on the defense buildup and will not need high military spending to support it." "On the contrary, peace will provide the nation with welcome opportunities to channel into civilian use manpower and material resources now being devoted to war."

The report warned, however, that if no special programs were undertaken to offset the problems caused by demobilization, the economy could fall into a recession within two years of a Vietnam truce. The committee said that about 600,000 returning servicemen and 750,000 laid-off defense workers would need to be reintegrated into the economy over a period of 1½ years, "a significant—but not enormous—addition to the normal amount of job-shifting."

Assuming that the war ended early in 1969, the committee predicted that a "peace and growth dividend" of $22 billion would be available to the economy by 1972. The committee suggested that the 10% income surtax be ended after fighting stopped, but it opposed any other major tax cuts, recommending instead that federal education and social programs be fully funded. The committee concluded that the main emphasis of the immediate postwar period should be on general measures to keep the economy growing, so that only a relatively small amount of special aid would be needed for the reintegration of servicemen and defense workers.

'Moderate' Income: $9,076. The Bureau of Labor Statistics (BLS) reported March 16 that it would have cost an urban family of four $9,076 a year to maintain a "moderate" standard of living, based on the price level in the spring of 1967. The bureau also issued budgets for a "lower" standard for a family of four that would have required $5,915 and for a "higher" standard that required $13,050. The BLS said that all the budgets included taxes, and it did not claim that the budgets were "typical" or "average."

The most expensive of the 39 areas computed was Honolulu, with $10,902 for the moderate budget, $7,246 for the lower budget and $16,076 for the higher one. The cheapest area was Austin, Tex., with budgets of $7,952, $5,237 and $11,299, respectively. The bureau said that all the budgets "share the basic assumption that maintenance of health and social well-being, the nurture of children, and participation in community activities are desirable and necessary goals."

The Internal Revenue Service reported Feb. 11 that individual incomes, as reported on 1967 tax returns, had surpassed the $500 billion mark for the first time. The incomes reported totaled $505 billion, up 8% or $36 billion above 1966. Seventy-two million taxpayers filed returns for 1967, 1½ million more than for the previous year. The number of persons reporting incomes above $15,000 rose by 900,000, while the number of people reporting income of less than $500 declined by 600,000. One out of every five returns reported an income of more than $10,000.

GNP Rose During 1968. According to revised figures reported by the Department of Commerce Feb. 14, the U.S.' gross national product (GNP) had risen by $16.5 billion in the fourth quarter of 1968 to a seasonally adjusted annual rate of $887.5 billion. The fourth quarter increase compared with an $18.1 billion increase in the third quarter. The department said that the latest advance was attributable to increases of 1% in prices and slightly under 1% in the physical volume of production.

Corporate Profits Rise. A Wall Street Journal tabulation Feb. 12 revealed an aggregate profit of $5,996,052,000 for 521 major U.S. companies during 1968's final quarter. The total was 7.3% above the profits of the fourth quarter of 1967, but it was the smallest gain in 1968 (the quarterly increases in 1968: 11.1% over 1967 in the first quarter, 10.2% in the second and 13.6% in the third). Of the 25 industry groupings in the survey, 23 showed increases above 1967's fourth quarter, and 10 had gains of more than 10%. Declines in profits were reported in 1968's fourth quarter by distillers (14.1%) and steel manufacturers (23%).

The Commerce Department reported March 17 that 1968 fourth-quarter corporate profits (before taxes) had reached a record seasonally adjusted annual rate of $95.8 billion. The advance was $3.1 billion above the gain in 1968's third quarter. In 1968 as a whole, corporate profits before taxes were estimated at $92.3 billion; after-tax profits were placed at $51 billion, up $2.9 billion over 1967.

Nixon Administration Takes Charge

First News Conference. Problems of foreign affairs dominated his first week in office, Richard M. Nixon told newsmen Jan. 27 at his first news conference as President. Nixon responded to questions on various topics. *Among his comments:*

Inflation—His Administration would try, without "too much managing of the economy," to "have some fine tuning of our fiscal and monetary affairs in order to control inflation." "I do not go along with the suggestion that inflation can be effectively controlled by exhorting labor and management and industry to follow certain guidelines." While that was "a very laudable objective for labor and management to follow," he was "aware" that, "much as they might personally want to do what was in the best interests of the nation," labor and business leaders "have to be guided by the interests of the organizations that they represent."

"The primary responsibility for controlling inflation rests with the national Administration and its handling of fiscal and monetary affairs. ... We assume that responsibility. We think ... we can control inflation without an increase in unemployment."

Budget reductions—Instructions had been sent Jan. 24 to all departments to examine their budgets "very closely and to give us recommendations as to where budget cuts might be made." "We would like to cut the over-all budget and ... have room for some of the new programs that this Administration—and the new approaches that this Administration—would like to implement. ... We are taking a fresh look at all of the programs, and we shall attempt to make cuts in order to carry out the objectives that I set forth during the campaign."

Postwar Economy Study. President Nixon Feb. 3 created a study group to investigate the problems that would arise for the economy and the federal budget after the end of the war in Vietnam. The study group was headed by Herbert Stein, a member of the President's Council of Economic Advisers.

The group was created during a meeting of the Cabinet-level Urban Affairs Council.

Economic Planning. An economic growth rate slower than forecast by the Johnson Administration was favored by top Nixon Administration economic planners for the second half of 1969. This proposed slow-down and other details of the Nixon Administration's economic planning were disclosed in testimony before the Joint Economic Committee of Congress Feb. 17–20.

Administration witnesses insisted that a budget surplus was essential in the fight against inflation. Other major proposals in the anti-inflation effort were a probable extension of the 10% income surtax and a "tight" monetary policy. The value of wage and price guideposts was discounted. Administration spokesmen emphasized the need to expand the effort to aid the poor, disadvantaged and jobless.

The committee heard testimony from the President's Council of Economic Advisers (CEA) Feb. 17, Budget Director Robert P. Mayo. Feb. 18, Treasury Secretary David M. Kennedy Feb. 19 and Labor Secretary George P. Shultz Feb. 20. *Among highlights of their testimony:*

Feb. 17—The Administration's goal of a growth rate slightly slower than that projected by the Johnson Administration was outlined by CEA Chairman Paul W. McCracken and his two fellow council members, Herbert Stein and Hendrik S. Houthakker. The policy of restraint was to be extended through the second half of the year in order to try to maintain an economic growth rate well below the rate of 5% in 1968. The council members forecast that unemployment would "average less than 4%" (current level: 3.3%).

The council recommended that the Federal Reserve Board follow a "tight" monetary policy throughout the year. The witnesses stressed the need to attain a federal budget surplus and suggested the probable necessity for extending the 10% income tax surcharge. They discounted the effectiveness of wage-price guide-posts, which, they said, applied "only to a limited segment of the economy." They favored a continued lower-

ing of trade barriers and exploration of ways to improve the international monetary system.

The council said that increased aid for the poor would be high "in our scale of national priorities" but would necessitate "rigorous trimming of those budget flows which serve purposes of lower priority." The council members also recommended efforts to lessen the "concentration" of unemployment, which was especially high for the unskilled, the non-white and the aging. A "great many programs" for manpower and training were undergoing review, the council members said, and there was "intense" interest in "well-designed tax incentives" to "promote the training and employment of hard-to-place workers." But they cautioned that, "at the same time, no one can assure that the distortions from three years of economic overheating and price inflation can be corrected with no effect on unemployment."

Feb. 18—Budget Director Mayo affirmed that no area of the budget was "sacrosanct" and immune from review. He said he would take a "skeptical look" at all proposals for military spending. Mayo disclosed these developments that could affect the predicted $2.4 billion budget surplus: (a) payments on the national debt had risen "significantly" because of higher-than-expected interest rates; (b) a lower volume of farm-price support loans probably would be held by private banks because of the tight credit situation; (c) the Nixon Administration had already increased advance payments to farmers by $168 million for the feed-grain program on the ground that the cut-off had been too abrupt and an "unjust burden" on farmers; (d) receipts from offshore oil leasing "appear to be falling short" of estimates.

Feb. 19—Treasury Secretary Kennedy emphasized that the policy of "firm restraint" would be pursued until there were "unmistakable signs that we are headed back on a noninflationary path." He cautioned against a repetition of the experience of 1967, when there had been an economic slowdown and easing of the pace of inflation early in the year but when "expansionary policies were pressed so vigorously as the economy slowed that the inflationary trend was never broken." There were risks in trying "to stop inflation too abruptly" and "in doing too little," he warned. "If the economy were to be halted in its tracks, unemployment would rise prohibitively. Even though the inflationary psychology might be broken, the cost would be too high. . . . Insufficient restraint would mean only a brief slowing down of the economy and no lasting reduction in inflationary pressures."

Kennedy stressed the need for a budget surplus and said the surtax would have to be continued for another year "unless fiscal 1970 federal expenditures can be cut back appreciably from the levels now apparently in prospect."

Treasury Undersecretary Charls E. Walker testified that the Treasury was working on reforms to bring about an "equitable distribution of the income tax burden."

Feb. 20—Labor Secretary Shultz testified that there was "substantial evidence" that inflation could be reduced without large increases in unemployment. The prime factor in such effort might be the efficiency of the manpower programs, he said. He reported that these programs were being scrutinized for refocusing on specific groups, especially the young Negro unemployed. Special efforts were also necessary to provide skills useful to the economy, to develop a job-vacancy information system to speed up placements and to improve the unemployment insurance system, he said. Shultz called the minimum wage a "useful device" but said "a pause is called for, and we should not push it too far."

(Outgoing Treasury Secretary Joseph W. Barr, in testimony before the committee Jan. 17, had warned of "the possibility of a taxpayer revolt if we do not soon make major reforms in our income taxes." The revolt would come, he said, not from the poor but from "middle-class" taxpayers with $7,000–$20,000 incomes because of their concern and anger "about the high-income recipients who pay little or no federal income tax." He estimated that more than $50 billion in revenue would be lost to the federal government in 1969 because of "loopholes" [special provisions] in the tax laws.)

Appeal to Labor. The AFL-CIO Executive Council, meeting in Bal Harbour, Fla., received a Nixon Administration appeal for restraint in wage demands. But the council, in a statement on the national economy, put the emphasis on lower profit margins rather than on wage curbs as the essential ingredient in price stability.

Labor Secretary George P. Shultz met members of the council Feb. 21 and delivered a letter from President Nixon to AFL-CIO President George Meany. It appealed for a cooperative effort to "find ways to curb inflation . . . without asking the wage-earners to pay for the cost of stability with their jobs."

One of the subjects Shultz discussed with the labor leaders was the minimum wage; the federation was advocating an increase from the current $1.60 an hour to $2.00. After their meeting, Meany told newsmen he was convinced Shultz had an open mind on the issue. Shultz reported his desire for a study to determine whether there was any relationship between minimum wage rises and high unemployment among young workers. This study should be made, before any "bold step" was taken to increase the minimum wage, Shultz said.

In its policy statement on the national economy Feb. 23, the council said: Price stability could be achieved without an increase in unemployment and with "substantial improvements in workers' earnings." This could be accomplished if there were "lower profit margins and reduced profit rates of return on investment," expanded manpower training programs, including a federal program to create jobs for the hard-core unemployed, and an effective nationwide employment service.

Declaring that "the lag of real wages and salaries must be ended," the council cited increases between 1960 and 1968 of 91% for after-tax profits, of 84% for dividend payments to stockholders but of only 31% for the weekly after-tax take-home pay of the average non-supervisory worker.

The council urged a drive toward full employment as a primary economic goal and said the trend of unemployment should be a determining factor in federal decisions on whether to ease monetary policy in case of a general economic slowdown and on whether to continue or end the 10% income surtax.

Prices Soar. U.S. consumer prices rose in January to a record 124.1% of the 1957–59 average and in February to a record 124.6%. The monthly increases in the consumer-price (cost-of-living, or COL) index, reported by the Bureau of Labor Statistics Feb. 25 and March 26, were .3% in January (4.6% above January 1968) and .4% in February (4.7% above February 1968). (In the N.Y. Metropolitan area, consumer prices rose .5% during January to 127.8% of the 1957–59 average and .4% in February. February was the 22d month in which they rose.) The increases were attributed to higher prices for automobiles, homes, apparel and food. (The COL index had risen .2% to 123.7% of the 1957–59 average in December 1968.)

In January, the wholesale price index jumped to 110.7%; the .8% rise was the largest increase in three years. The February rise was only .4%, or 2.9% above the 108% of February 1968.

The Agriculture Department reported that prices received by farmers rose by 1.5% in the month ended Feb. 15 and by 2% in the month ended March 15. Prices paid by farmers for services and commodities rose .5% during the month ended Feb. 15 and by 1% in the following month. The parity ratio, rising a point each month, reached 74 in the month ended March 15. The "adjusted" parity ratio, also rising a point a month, was 80 in the latter period. Consumers had spent a record $101 billion for food during 1968. The average American family spent 17.2% of after-tax earnings for food in 1968. Compared with 1957–59 prices, food prices were up 19.3% in 1968.

Consumer Credit. The Federal Reserve Board reported March 5 that outstanding consumer installment credit, showing the smallest expansion since April 1968, had risen in January, on a seasonally adjusted basis, by $641 million, compared with $775 million in December 1968. (The rise, however, was much greater than the $399 million increase for January 1968.) The extension of consumer installment credit rose from $8.28 billion in December 1968 to

$8.37 billion in January, but the increase was offset, the board said, by an unusually large increase of repayments from the $7.5 billion (seasonally adjusted) of December 1968 to a record $7.53 billion in January. The net increase of $641 million raised the amount of consumer installment credit outstanding to $89.492 billion as of Jan. 31.

The board reported April 2 that the growth of installment credit had accelerated to a seasonally adjusted rate of $798 million in February. The extension of credit rose to $8.41 billion. The board said that a "moderate increase" in loans extended and a drop in repayments had caused the acceleration. Total consumer installment credit outstanding as of Feb. 28 was $89.38 billion.

Total consumer credit outstanding (including non-installment) declined from $112.117 billion Jan. 31 to $111.-569 billion Feb. 28.

Rise in Personal Incomes. The Commerce Department reported March 18 that U.S. personal incomes had risen by $5.3 billion in February to a record $721.4 billion seasonally adjusted annual rate. Personal income had increased $2.6 billion (originally estimated at $1.6 billion) in January from December's $713.5 billion seasonally adjusted annual rate, but the rise had been well below December's $5.5 billion increase. Economists attributed January's small increase primarily to dock strikes and to increased Social Security taxes (at a $1.75 billion annual rate of increase). Most of February's increase was due to a $4.2 billion rise in wages and salaries in "almost all major industry divisions."

Factory Orders Set Record. The Commerce Department reported April 3 that new factory orders had increased by 1.8% in February to a record $54.04 billion seasonally adjusted. (The previous high was October 1968's $53.93 billion.) The February total compared with January's $53.02 billion and the $48.53 billion of February 1968.

Orders for new machinery and equipment rose by $140 million in February to a $6.34 billion total after declining in January by $33 million. Defense industry orders increased by $370 million to a

$2.21 billion total. In January they had fallen by $33 million.

GNP Continues Rise. The U.S. gross national product (GNP)—the total output of the nation's goods and services—rose at an annual rate of $16 billion to a total annual rate of $904–$905 billion in the first quarter of 1969, the Commerce Department reported April 17. This was the first time the rate had exceeded $900 billion. A $16.4 billion rate of increase in the GNP had been reported for the final quarter of 1968. The 1969 gain was 1.8%, of which 1% represented higher prices and .8% was "real." The rise in prices as measured for the GNP was at a faster pace than in the four quarters of 1968.

Andrew F. Brimmer, a member of the Federal Reserve Board, said April 17 that "it has become increasingly evident that inflationary pressures in the American economy are much stronger than was anticipated even a few months ago." "We will need more over-all fiscal and monetary restraint—and it should last for a longer period of time—than was foreseen at the beginning of the year," he said in a speech before the American Bankers Association in White Sulphur Springs, W. Va.

Debt Limit Raised. A bill (HR8508) raising the permanent public debt limit from $358 billion to $365 billion was passed by 313–93 House vote March 19 and 67–18 Senate vote March 26. The bill was signed by President Nixon April 7. A temporary debt limit of an additional $12 billion, or a total of $377 billion, effective until June 30, 1970, was provided by the bill.

President Nixon's proposal to revise the debt ceiling to apply only to the amount held by the general public had been rejected by the House Ways & Means Committee March 6. The committee authorized the introduction of the measure later adopted by both houses. In reporting its version March 10, the committee warned that "tight control of expenditures must remain a matter of high priority by both Congress and the Executive for the entire fiscal year 1970 for this limitation to be adequate."

President Nixon's support of the committee bill was relayed to the House March 19 by House Speaker John W. McCormack (D, Mass.). The House vote March 19 was the first since 1958 in which a majority of Republicans supported a rise in the debt limit. The vote breakdown: 173 D & 140 R vs. 52 D & 41 R.

In a Senate Finance Committee hearing on the bill March 24, Treasury Secretary David M. Kennedy and Budget Director Robert P. Mayo pledged the Nixon Administration to hold fiscal 1970 federal spending below the $195.3 billion forecast by the Johnson Administration. Kennedy also indicated his opposition to suspension of the tax credit permitting businesses a deduction of 7% of investment expenditures. The question came up in light of a federal study reporting March 13 the possibly inflationary plans of business to increase capital spending by 13.9% during calendar 1969. (The 1968 rise was 4%.) Commenting on the report March 14, Kennedy had said he was "frankly disturbed" by the inflationary aspect of the business investment plans. He said there were "not many indications that the slowdown [in the economy] has begun," but he expressed confidence that the budgetary and monetary "restraints now in effect will not fail to do their work." He said that he was "aware of the risk of slamming on the brakes too hard" but that the Administration would "apply them firmly" until there was "positive evidence" of an economic slowdown.

Tax Program. President Nixon asked Congress March 26 to extend the 10% income tax surcharge for a year and to postpone scheduled reductions in the phone and automobile excise taxes. (But less than a month later Nixon revised his surcharge proposal and requested a 50% cut in the tax.)

The President also called for significant reductions in the fiscal 1970 budget. He said he would submit budget revisions "which will reduce federal spending in fiscal 1970 significantly below the amount recommended in January [$195.-272 billion]." Mr. Nixon said he would also send Congress later specific proposals for tax reform.

"Clearly this nation must come to grips with the problem of an inflation that has been allowed to run into its fourth year," Mr. Nixon said in his message. "This is far too long. . . . Inflation is a form of economic aggression against the very young and the very old, the poor and the thrifty. It is these Americans who are largely defenseless against the kind of price increases for food, clothing, medicine, housing and education that have swept over the nation in the last few years."

Mr. Nixon asserted that the January estimates of budget surpluses in fiscal 1969 and 1970 were overestimates. Instead of the $2.4 billion surplus projected for fiscal 1969 and the $3.4 billion surplus for fiscal 1970, he said, "current analysis . . . shows a reduction in the surplus of $1.3 billion for this fiscal year and $1.7 billion for the fiscal year 1970." The revised figures reflected higher interest on the federal debt than originally estimated, "an underestimate of farm price support payments and a substantial overestimate of off-shore oil lease receipts."

Surplus & Tax Reform Urged. Members of the Congressional Joint Economic Committee stressed in their annual report April 1 the need to lessen inflationary pressures and to reform taxation.

Republican and Democratic members of the committee agreed on the necessity of achieving a "significant" federal budget surplus as an anti-inflation move. They also agreed on the need to extend the 10% income tax surcharge. But the Republicans, in their minority report, suggested giving the President authority to reduce the rate unless Congress objected within a specific time period. The Democratic majority said the surtax was necessary unless the same effect on the economy could be achieved by reducing federal expenditures "at least $12 billion" or by enacting "quick and drastic" tax reform.

There was bipartisan agreement that tax reform was "long overdue" and should be a "major objective." There was disagreement over the 7% investment tax credit for business. Democrats, identifying the tax credit as "one of the most important sources of the recent inflation," advocated repeal. Republicans called repeal unwise.

The committee members agreed that the monetary policy of Federal Reserve Board should be one of "restraint," that

the nation's money supply should be permitted to grow at the "lower end" of a recommended range of 2% to 6%, about the same rate as U.S. productive capacity.

While the majority and minority reports agreed on the necessity for "voluntary restraint on wages and prices," the Democrats supported a revival of "guidelines" whereas the Republicans backed the Administration's proposal to abandon them.

There was bipartisan backing for a "liberalization" of trade policy, for continuation of the "dual" price system for gold and for the creation of the new "paper gold" or special drawing rights in the International Monetary Fund.

Surtax Cut Proposed. President Nixon sent Congress April 21 a tax message proposing both a 50% reduction in the 10% income tax surcharge, effective January 1970, and the repeal of the 7% business investment tax credit, effective immediately (April 21). The recommendation of a 5% surtax was a surprise and a sudden change in policy; Mr. Nixon March 26 had requested the extension of the 10% surtax for a year.

The message made several other tax-reform proposals. The most important reforms would exempt "persons or families in poverty" from payment of the federal income tax and would subject to the tax at least 50% of the income of citizens with "substantial incomes."

Other reform proposals would: (a) liberalize provisions for deductions for persons having to move because of their jobs; (b) tighten provisions pertaining to tax-exempt organizations (including foundations), charitable deductions, farm losses sustained by "gentlemen farmers," the "multiple surtax exemption" enjoyed by corporations with subsidiaries, non-business deductions of persons with certain non-taxable income, and mineral production payments. Mineral production payments, Mr. Nixon said, "would be treated in a way that would stop artificial creation of net operating losses in these industries." A Treasury official said this meant that such payments should be treated as "basically a loan transaction."

The federal revenue loss and gain from the President's surtax and investment tax proposals were expected to balance out for fiscal 1970, and Mr. Nixon warned that "reduction of the surtax without repeal of the investment tax credit would be imprudent." The 50% cut in the surtax would cost the government some $1.9 billion in fiscal 1970, but repeal of the investment credit was expected to add $1.8 billion to federal revenues.

The other tax-reform proposals were expected to result in a net gain of $150 million in fiscal 1970.

The President said that "the gradual increase in federal revenues resulting from repeal of the investment tax credit and the growth of the economy will also facilitate a start during fiscal 1971 in funding two high-priority programs to which this Administration is committed: revenue sharing with state and local government; tax credits to encourage investment in poverty areas and hiring and training of the hard-core unemployed."

Mr. Nixon's "low-income allowance" proposal was expected to apply to more than two million families. The poverty line, below which income would not be taxable, would be $1,700 for a single person, $2,300 for a married couple with no children and $3,500 for a family of four.

The "minimum income tax" proposal for those with "substantial incomes" would impose a 50% limitation "on the use of the principal tax preferences which are subject to change by law." The plan did not cover the excluded half of long-term capital gains nor tax-exempt interest on municipal bonds; these items were still being studied by the Administration.

(House Democrats at a party caucus April 16 had resolved to call for immediate repeal of the 7% business investment tax credit if a pending House Ways & Means Committee study "reaches the same conclusion." Conditioning the call on the study was done at the suggestion of committee Chairman Wilbur D. Mills [Ark.]. While Mills agreed with the other Democrats that the tax credit was inflationary, he said he wanted "to find out what impact" repeal would have on the economy. Mills had said April 15 he regarded the Administration's budget reductions as inadequate; he indicated that unless stronger revisions were im-

posed to offset inflationary pressures, his committee would not approve extension of the 10% surtax and would seek a Congressional reduction of $5 billion more in the federal budget. Mills had been the dominant figure in the 1968 Congressional decision to couple the surtax with a mandatory $6 billion budget cut. He said April 16 that "the circumstances" "are exactly the same as they were last year.")

Interest & Reserve Requirement Up. The U.S. Federal Reserve Board announced April 3 that it had raised its discount rate—the rate at which the 6,000 member banks borrow from the Federal Reserve System—from 5½% to 6%, the highest rate in 40 years. The increased rate affected 11 of the 12 district banks; the exception was the Boston bank. At the same time, the board raised the reserve requirement on the system's city banks from 16½% to 17% on net demand deposits of less than $5 million and from 17% to 17½% on checking-account-type deposits of more than $5 million. The board said that this action would reduce the lending power of 182 banks by about $375 million. For the other 5,790 member banks—the system's "country banks"—the board raised the reserve requirement from 12% to 12½% on deposits of less than $5 million and to 13% on larger deposits. The new reserve requirements, to become effective April 17, "froze" about $650 million in lending ability. The board described both actions as a "further move against inflation."

Led by the Morgan Guaranty Trust Co. of New York, the nation's major commercial banks had raised their prime rates March 17 from 7% to 7½%, a record high. Economists said that the increase should "cool" the economy by dampening the demand for goods and services. The increase in prime rates was the fourth since early December 1968. The last increase had come Jan. 7, when major U.S. banks had increased their prime rates from 6¾% to 7%. News of the increase had touched-off a sharp decline in stock and bond prices, and the Dow-Jones industrial stock average had dropped 10.94 points Jan. 7.

Budget Cuts Announced. President Nixon April 12 announced federal budget revisions that would result in a $5.8 billion surplus for fiscal 1970.

The revisions included reductions of $1.1 billion in defense outlays and $2.9 billion in domestic outlays from a revised Johnson Administration budget. The original Johnson budget total of $195.3 billion was revised upward to $196.9 billion because of increases in such "uncontrollable" items as interest on the national debt and farm price supports. The new estimate of federal outlays, with the $4 billion reduction, therefore, was $192.9 billion. Defense and military aid outlays were projected at $79.4 billion, non-defense outlays at $113½ billion. The Johnson estimate of receipts —$198.7 billion—was left unchanged pending later revisions.

In announcing the reduction, Mr. Nixon said: "Our actions now, we believe, have brought an end to the era of the chronic budget deficit. We believe that a surplus of this magnitude will speak louder than any words to the business and labor communities in this country and to the world that the United States is determined to bring a halt to the inflationary spiral which has seriously affected our economy these last four years."

The budget changes included a $5½ billion reduction—to $204.6 billion—in requests for appropriations. "Our proposals mean not only a substantial cutback in the spending of tax dollars in the coming year but a substantial reduction in claims against future tax dollars and future budgets," the President said. "With this approach, we believe we have made a necessary and significant beginning toward bringing the federal budget under control."

Mr. Nixon pointed out that despite the reductions, domestic spending would rise $6½ billion in fiscal 1970 over 1969 and "will far exceed that for any other year in American history."

Details of the proposed budget revisions were disclosed by the Nixon Administration April 15. The largest item was a $1.23 billion reduction stemming from a proposal to increase Social Security benefits only 7% instead of the 10% sought by Mr. Johnson. Largely as a result of this, Health, Education & Welfare Department outlays were re-estimated at $50.55 billion for fiscal 1970 (compared to $46.26 billion for fiscal

1969). But the request for funds to relieve hunger was raised by $15 million over the Johnson request to a $1.461 billion total.

(The President had revealed at his press conference March 14 that the preliminary revision of the defense budget had cut approximately $2½ billion from the request submitted in the January budget. Defense Secretary Melvin R. Laird, appearing March 19 before the Senate Armed Services Committee, put the saving in actual expenditures for fiscal 1970 at $500 million. The reduction resulted largely from the abandonment of a proposal to seek a $1.2 billion military pay increase as the first step toward a volunteer army. Treasury Secretary David M. Kennedy estimated that the Nixon Administration budget revisions "should give us a surplus larger" than the $3½ billion surplus forecast in January for fiscal 1970. For fiscal 1969, Kennedy said, the estimated surplus would be smaller, but "there will be a surplus." He made the appraisals on ABC's "Issues & Answers" program March 23.)

Domestic Program. President Nixon sent Congress April 14 a message outlining the ten broad domestic programs he intended to submit in detail for the current session. Mr. Nixon noted that his first 12 weeks in office had been preoccupied with foreign policy. "Peace has been the first priority," he said. Also high in priority was the need for a reduced budget as part of the fight against "the ruinous rise of inflationary pressures."

The President said there had been "long and hard" deliberation on the legislative proposals because it was his Administration's goal "to propose only legislation that we know we can execute once it becomes law." "Merely making proposals takes only a typewriter," he said. "Making workable proposals takes time. We have taken this time."

If "more time is needed, we will take more time," Mr. Nixon said. "I urge the Congress to join with this Administration in this careful approach to the most fundamental issues confronting our country. Hasty action or a seeking after partisan advantage . . . can only be self-defeating and aggravate the very ills we seek to remedy."

Among proposals the President outlined: (1) "An increase in Social Security benefits" (Administration sources said increases of 7% had been planned). (2) "A program of tax credits, designed to provide new incentives for the enlistment of additional private resources in meeting our urgent social needs." (3) A partial tax reform plan "to prevent several specific abuses this year" (a broader program would be readied for later submission).

Mr. Nixon described his immediate proposals as only a "beginning." He said they would not "carry large price tags for the coming fiscal year."

Silverless Coins Requested. The Treasury announced May 12 its decision to request legislation authorizing the production of non-silver half-dollars and dollars. The purpose was to return coins of those denominations to circulation. The current half-dollars of 40% silver and 60% copper currently went out of circulation almost as soon as they were minted. In Nevada, where silver dollars were in demand for the gambling industry, dollar "tokens" were being used.

The Treasury May 12 also ended the ban on the melting and export of old silver coins no longer in production because it "no longer either keeps silver coins in circulation or contributes to the Treasury's supply of silver coins." It reduced the weekly Treasury sales of surplus silver to industry from two million ounces to 1½ million to prepare the market for the eventual adjustment when, "at some point, the government will cease to be a silver supplier."

Wage-Price Controls Barred. White House Press Secretary Ronald L. Ziegler asserted July 16 that the Nixon Administration "has ruled out wage and price controls as a way of dealing with inflation under conditions that are now foreseeable." The statement resolved apparently conflicting statements by Administration officials on the issue.

In Senate Finance Committee hearings on the income tax surcharge bill (HR 12290) July 8, Treasury Secretary David M. Kennedy had said that he

strongly opposed wage and price controls "in principle," but he said if the surtax extension were defeated, "in my judgment [wage and price controls] would have to be considered." However, in an interview published in the U.S. News & World Report July 14, Arthur E. Burns, counselor to the President, repeated what he and other Administration officials had said before: "There is no support for direct controls of prices or wages within the executive establishment—none whatever."

Ziegler said the President "is not for wage and price controls" and "he had consistently taken that position" in the past. Ziegler said he had discussed the statement with Mr. Nixon, Kennedy, Burns and Paul W. McCracken, chairman of the President's Council of Economic Advisers.

Congress Approves Spending Ceiling. Congress completed action July 9 on a supplemental appropriations bill (HR 11400) providing $4.3 billion in additional funds for fiscal 1969 programs. The measure placed a $191.9 billion flexible limitation on federal spending for fiscal 1970, which began July 1. The bill was a compromise worked out by House-Senate conferees between a House measure passed May 21 and a Senate version of the same bill passed June 19. The House adopted the final measure as reported by the joint conference committee by a roll-call vote of 348–49. Shortly afterward the Senate approved the bill by voice vote. The spending restriction was the first such curb ever imposed by Congress, which in 1968 had imposed a $6 billion spending reduction on the Administration.

The May 21 House version of the bill would have imposed a $192.9 billion limit on fiscal 1970 federal spending. The total was the Nixon Administration's estimate of spending in its revised budget.

The Senate version had appropriated $4.5 billion in additional funds and set a ceiling of $191 billion for fiscal 1970.

The fiscal 1970 ceiling in the final measure was $1 billion less than President Nixon's spending estimates for the year, but a $2 billion "cushion" was provided for "uncontrollable" items such as interest on the national dept, Social Security and other specified domestic social measures and farm price supports. The ceiling would automatically rise or fall depending on Congressional action on spending bills.

$3.5 Billion Cut Ordered. President Nixon July 22 ordered a $3.5 billion cut in federal expenditures to offset spending increases expected as a result of "uncontrollable" items in the budget and actions of Congress. The President said he was ordering the reductions to "hold the line" on the $192.9 billion figure proposed in April for fiscal 1970 spending. He said the April proposal still reflected "a responsible fiscal policy in our highly inflationary environment."

Mr. Nixon said increases in "uncontrollable" budget items such as the national debt, medicare and veterans' benefits indicated that spending would be $2.5 billion higher than anticipated in the April budget review. He said "at least another billion dollars" would be needed because of Congressional actions—such as failure to approve a postal rate increase and expenditures required in farm appropriations.

Budget Director Robert P. Mayo said he expected "very substantial" cuts in outlays for defense. He said defense spending reductions probably would account for "more than half" of the $3.5 billion cut. Distribution of the rest of the reductions among various government agencies would be worked out by August, Mayo said.

The cuts were announced in connection with Presidential approval of the catchall supplemental appropriations bill (HR 11400) setting a $191.9 billion ceiling on fiscal 1970 federal spending. Nixon said the ceiling "will be of little help in keeping federal spending under control if the Congress that imposed it does not cooperate fully with the Administration in meeting it."

Budget Surplus Surprisingly Large. A $3.1 billion federal budget surplus for fiscal 1969 was reported by the Nixon Administration July 28. The surplus was $2.2 billion more than the amount predicted May 20 by Budget Director Robert P. Mayo. The difference between Mayo's estimate and the final figure a month later surprised Administration officials as well as members of Congress, where it was seen as a blow to the Administra-

tion contention that the surtax was vital to achieve the projected $6.3 billion surplus for fiscal 1970.

President Johnson had predicted in January 1968 a fiscal 1969 deficit of $8 billion, later revising the estimate to a $2.4 billion surplus. President Nixon first predicted a surplus of $1.2 billion before it was reduced in May to a projected $900 million.

The final variation was said to have resulted primarily from a $1.8 billion underestimate of anticipated tax revenue and a $100 million decrease in federal spending.

The surplus resulted from $187,843,-000,000 in total receipts and expenditures of $184,769,000,000.

The surplus—which contrasted with the $25.4 billion deficit in fiscal 1968—was the first since fiscal 1960 ($240 million) and the biggest since fiscal 1957 ($3.2 billion).

Congress Criticized on Spending. President Nixon Aug. 12 criticized Congress for "disappointing" action on Administration revenue recommendations. He said Congressional policies so far in the session "add up to taxing less and spending more." While this might currently be appealing, he said, "it promises long-term grief for the people."

The President emphasized his intention of keeping to a $192.9 federal budget ceiling. The ceiling, Mr. Nixon said, reflected citizen concern "with inflation and excessive federal expenditures." He specifically objected to the House's addition of more than $1.1 billion to Administration proposals for a $15.5 million budget for the Department of Health, Education & Welfare in fiscal 1970. The addition was "inconsistent" with Congress' earlier intent in imposing the spending ceiling, he said.

The HEW appropriation castigated by Mr. Nixon was passed by the House July 31 by 293–120 vote. It would provide $4.2 billion for education, the largest sum Congress had ever earmarked for education. The President also warned of increases of some $2.5 billion in "uncontrollable" budget programs, such as interest on the national debt, plus "another billion dollars of added expenditures arising from Congressional action or inaction to date other than on HEW." He said the $3.5 billion total increase required an offsetting reduction in other programs. He added: "I have ordered that cut."

Defense Spending Cut. Defense Secretary Melvin R. Laird Aug. 21 announced plans to reduce fiscal 1970 defense expenditures by up to $3 billion. The reduction would lower the defense spending estimate for the period to $74.9 billion. The move was part of the $3.5 billion budget reduction ordered by President Nixon to offset budgetary increases.

Laird said the reduction was necessitated by the "economic needs in our country" and by Congressional actions in imposing federal spending limits. He also spoke of "anticipated budget cuts by the Congress."

Laird cautioned that the cuts "will reduce our capability to meet current commitments," weaken "our defense readiness" and cause "an inevitable weakening of our worldwide military posture."

Laird said he had already approved specific cuts totaling $1.5 billion. These initial reductions included: (a) cuts of 100,000 men in total military personnel (from 3.4 million to 3.3 million) and of 50,000 men in Defense Department civilian employment; (b) a $500 million cut in the Army's non-Southeast Asia operations; (c) deactivation of more than 100 Navy ships; (d) a 300,000-hour reduction of planned Air Force training flights; (e) the closing of "some" military bases.

Postwar Budget Views. The large funds being spent on the Vietnam war would not be available for domestic programs at the war's end, Daniel P. Moynihan, Presidential assistant for urban affairs, said Aug. 25. Moynihan based his findings on a study prepared by a Nixon Administration committee headed by Herbert Stein, a member of the President's Council of Economic Advisers. "It is clearly the conclusion of the analysis," Moynihan said, "that the so-called peace dividend forecast" by a similar study in the Johnson Administration "was simply not realistic." The Johnson Administration study had projected a potential $16 billion fund for new projects a year and a

half after the war's end and a $19 billion fund after two and a half years.

Moynihan's interpretation of the' Nixon Administration report, however, was discounted Aug. 26 by other Administration sources (unnamed), who said that while "we have mortgaged the melon," there would always be "some room for new programs."

Moynihan, briefing newsmen after a meeting of the Urban Affairs Council at President Nixon's Western White House in San Clemente, Calif., said: "I'm afraid that the peace dividend tends to become evanescent like the morning clouds around San Clemente"; any budgetary savings from an end to the war would be preempted through the mid-1970's by current and proposed military and domestic programs; some current programs that would help absorb such post-war funds were the President's recently proposed welfare and revenue-sharing projects.

Moynihan described the budget for fiscal 1971 as "very tight" and said "it's going to be a very hard year." It "will undoubtedly be the most difficult budget the President will face," he said. "The combination of revenues and expenditures is going to make it difficult in the next budget to make it much higher than this year's."

Other Administration sources did not deny that the fiscal 1971 budget would be tight, but they contended Aug. 26 that Moynihan had exaggerated the post-1971 budgetary problems. They also stressed the demands on the post-war budgets proposed by Mr. Nixon, such as revenue sharing, in which large increases were projected following a small-scale initial funding. The fiscal picture also would be shaded, they indicated, by Congress' resolution of the tax-reform issue; if it included a decrease in federal revenues, the tax cut could be construed as a form of peace dividend.

Surtax Extended 6 Months. A compromise six-month extension of the 10% income surtax was passed by the Senate July 31 and House Aug. 4. The Senate vote was 70–30 and the House vote was 237–170. The compromise (President Nixon had requested extension at a 10% rate through Dec. 31 and a reduced 5% rate through June 30, 1970) was effected after Senate Democrats balked at the longer extension in the absence of parallel action on tax reform.

The House had passed June 30 an Administration-backed bill to extend the surtax as requested by the President. The bill had incorporated several tax reforms demanded by the Democrats. The Senate did not act directly on the House-passed measure and instead offered the surtax legislation as an amendment to another bill.

The legal authority for the surtax had expired June 30 and a temporary extension of income tax withholding rates reflecting the surtax expired July 31, but employers had been advised to continue the withholding tax at the previous levels in expectation of its probable extension.

A tax reform measure was moving through Congress at the same time, largely in response to the pressures generated by the surtax extension bill. The House Ways and Means Committee approved July 31, a few hours after Senate approval of the surtax compromise, a bill that included extension of the surtax at 5% through June 30, 1970, repeal of the 7% investment tax credit, postponement of scheduled reductions in the telephone and automobile excise taxes and tax relief for the poor.

The Senate Democratic position, insisting on a delay of the surtax legislation until a tax reform plan was ready, was ratified during meetings of the Senate Democratic Policy Committee. The committee had met July 24 with Democratic members of the Senate Finance Committee and had decided to support extension of the 10% surtax only through November to give the Finance Committee time to work on a reform bill.

Republican opposition to the Democratic stand was immediately expressed. Senate GOP leader Everett M. Dirksen (Ill.) said July 24 the Democratic plan "would do nothing with respect to the inflation fever that is plaguing the country today." Treasury Secretary David M. Kennedy said a four-month surtax extension would "not do the job" of combating inflation.

Sen. Mike Mansfield (Mont.) explained the Democratic position July 25. He warned that "enthusiasm for a year's extension of the surtax is rapidly dimin-

ishing." "Indeed," he continued, "if it is to pass at all it may well have to be accompanied by assurances of very substantial tax reform." He said Democrats were aware of the Administration view that the surtax was a necessary anti-inflation measure, but he said they were also aware "of a gathering public view that the surtax has been an inequitable and ineffective way to fight inflation and [of] a public demand for changes in the present tax structure in the direction of greater equity."

As the July 31 deadline for expiration of the withholding legislation drew near, Mansfield said July 28 that the surtax "would be most difficult to revive" if the withholding rates died.

Vice President Spiro Agnew met July 29 with the Senate leadership and relayed word that President Nixon intended to discuss the surtax issue "frankly and fully with the American people" on his return from a current foreign tour. Agnew said Democratic insistence on limitation of the measure to a four-month extension was "unacceptable." He indicated that the President would blame Senate Democrats for blocking the surtax extension and that failure to extend it threatened to bring "injury to every citizen."

Mansfield defended the Democratic stand and announced he would reject a plan to extend the withholding rates at their current levels for an additional 15 days. (The House July 30 passed a stopgap bill to provide a 15-day extension of the current withholding rates.)

A compromise was affected July 30 by the Democratic and Republican Senate leadership. Under it, the Senate would vote on a Democratic plan to extend the 10% surtax through Dec. 31, on a GOP plan for an additional extension at a 5% rate through June 30, 1970, and on the proposal to repeal the 7% investment tax credit.

The Senate votes were taken July 31. The vote approving the Democratic plan for a six-month extension of the 10% surtax, in the form of an amendment, was 51–48. The vote rejecting the Republican amendment to extend the surtax at 5% for another six months was 59–41. The vote on the 7% investment tax credit was 66–34 in favor of tabling it after Mansfield promised that the issue would be brought before the body again. The final 70–30 Senate vote was for passage of the measure (HR9951) —a bill requiring federal unemployment taxes in quarterly rather than annual payments—to which the surtax provision had been attached.

House approval Aug. 4 sent the bill to the President, who signed the measure Aug. 7. Nixon simultaneously urged a further extension of the surcharge through 1970's first half at a 5% rate.

AFL-CIO Vs. High Interest Rates. The AFL-CIO Executive Council expressed concern Aug. 7 that "skyrocketing" interest rates—"the highest" in 100 years— were "leading to a collapse of home construction, cutbacks in production and rising unemployment." The council said the 8½% prime rate, representing an increase of 31% over the 1968 rate and an 89% increase since 1960, constituted the "biggest price increase of them all." It suggested a Justice Department antitrust probe of the nation's big banks and their "price-fixing actions" and a Congressional examination of the nation's monetary policies for action toward "much-needed reform."

AFL-CIO President George Meany, at a news conference after the Aug. 7 meeting, advocated a permanent 6% interest rate ceiling.

Meeting in New York in a two-day quarterly session, the council Aug. 8 approved a statement characterizing the Congressional tax reform plan as a major step toward tax justice but one that had not gone far enough.

In an economic report Sept. 30, the Executive Council said the Administration's anti-inflation policy was ineffective and inflicting hardship on workers, consumers, small businesses and farmers while having only a marginal effect on big corporations, which it cited as the major source of "inflationary demand pressure." The council recommended a surtax on corporate profits at twice the rate of the surtax on personal income, repeal of the tax credit for business equipment and of the fast depreciation permitted for real estate investment, action to curb the trend toward business mergers, public focus on pricing policies, and moves to depress the upward thrust of specific prices, such as medical

charges, automobile and property insurance rates and housing costs.

Treasury Offers 8% on Notes. The Treasury Department announced Sept. 17 that it would pay 8% interest on a 19½-month note to be issued Oct. 1—the highest rate since 1859. The Treasury also offered a three year, 7½-month note at 7¾% interest and a six year, 10½-month note at 7½% interest. The three issues were offered in exchange for $8.9 billion in bonds and notes maturing later in 1969, most of which the government had paid 2½–4% interest. Only holders of the maturing notes would be allowed to purchase the new notes.

The 8% interest rate topped a 7¾% 18-month note offered July 31, and designed to refinance $3.2 billion of 6% securities maturing Aug. 15. The Treasury Department had offered a seven-year, 6.5% note May 10 in exchange for $6.8 billion of securities maturing in May and June.

(The department July 11 announced an increase from 4¼% to 5% in the interest rate on U.S. savings bonds. The new rate, retroactive to June 1, was finally authorized under legislation passed by the House of Representatives Oct. 23 and by the Senate Nov. 26 and signed by the President Dec. 1.)

Governors Back Nixon Cutbacks. President Nixon met Sept. 22 with a delegation of governors on the Administration's request for a 75% cutback on federally-aided state construction projects. Gov. John A. Love (R, Colo.), who led the group, said his colleagues agreed "without exception" to support the President's action to combat inflationary prices in construction. Vice President Spiro T. Agnew, who attended the meeting, also indicated that the Administration had softened its threat of withdrawing the federal share of project costs if the states did not act to cut back on projects. Agnew said there were no longer any "enforcer roles" or "deadline" involved in the request.

Nixon on Inflation. At his press conference Sept. 26, Mr. Nixon made these comments on his anti-inflationary policy:

"We've attacked the source of the problem" by cutting the budget, exercising monetary restraints and seeking an extension of the surtax. These "basic policies" were "beginning to work" and "anybody who bets on a continuing inflation will lose that bet."

He did not believe in "jawboning"—to "put the blame on" business for price increases and labor for wage increases. ". . .When government, which is the primary agent for increasing prices, fails to do its job, government asking labor and management to do theirs simply won't work. It's hypocritical, it's dishonest; but most important, it's ineffective." But, "labor that asks for exorbitant wage increases, management that raises prices too high—will be pricing themselves out of the market."

4% Joblessness Called 'Acceptable.' The Bureau of Labor Statistics (BLS) reported Oct. 6 that the unemployment rate had increased in September by 0.5% to a seasonally adjusted rate of 4%, the highest level in nearly two years. The increase in the actual number of unemployed was 89,000, while on a seasonally adjusted rate the increase was 365,000; total unemployment was placed at 2,958,000 individuals. The increase in unemployment was highest among blue-collar workers as their rate jumped from 3.8% to 4.4%; white-collar unemployment held steady at 2.2%. The BLS said nearly all the increase was among whites.

Treasury Secretary David M. Kennedy, testifying before the Joint Economic Committee of Congress Oct. 7, said the 4% unemployment rate was "acceptable" and added that the Nixon Administration believed it was necessary to continue restrictive policies that might force unemployment even higher. He declined, however, to say what maximum unemployment level would be tolerated before the Administration would reverse its present economic policies designed to slow the business boom as a means to restrain inflation. Under questioning, Kennedy replied that the Administration's intent was to "strive for unemployment at the lowest possible level consistent with price stability," and that it was not planning a recession to reduce inflation. Rather, Kennedy said, the Administration intended to request a six-month extension of the tax surcharge at 5% beginning Jan. 1, 1970 and a repeal of the investment tax credit as means to curb inflation. Sen. William Proxmire (D, Wis.) indicated that both requests were in jeopardy unless the Administration gave assurances it would act "decisively and effectively" against possible substantial increases in unemployment.

The Treasury Department issued a statement Oct. 8 in an attempt to make "crystal clear" the Administration's policy that "any unemployment in our country, however small, is an unhappy condition and one that we will constantly seek to correct." The statement further said that the Administrations' anti-inflation program "must be continued because it is designed to head off what would otherwise develop into a renewed boom that would almost certainly lead to a later economic bust and mass unemployment." It also asserted that the Administration "has already taken vigorous steps to increase the employability of people without jobs," such as in manpower training programs and the computer job-bank program.

On a seasonally adjusted annual basis, the unemployment rate had been 3.5% in August, 3.6% in July, 3.4% in June, 3.5% in May and April, and 3.4% in March.

Pentagon to Cut 212,000 Jobs. Defense Department Controller Robert C. Moot said Oct. 20 that 212,000 of the two million employes in the defense industry would lose their jobs by the spring of 1970 as part of the department's defense spending cuts of $4.1 billion. (The department already had announced it would cut 220,000 men from the 3.45 million in the military services and 68,000 civilian employes from the 1.2 million in the Defense Department.) Moot said the 10% cutback in defense industries' employment was part of President Nixon's anti-inflation campaign, noting that defense spending accounted for "75-80% of all goods and services purchased by the federal government" and any defense cutbacks would have an important effect on inflationary spending.

Moot emphasized that the employment cutback could be accomplished without widespread dismissals or an "induced recession." He said the reduction could be achieved through transfers and normal attrition.

Jobless Rate Down. The nation's unemployment rate declined in November to 3.4% of the labor force from its 3.9% rate in October, according to the Labor Department Dec. 5. Despite the drop, the sharpest in 10 years, the department read a continuing slowdown of the economy from other employment indicators.

The decline itself was attributed mainly to a decline in the number of persons seeking work, largely "secondary workers" such as teen-agers, adult women and young men. There was a continued slowdown in the expansion of the civilian labor force—from a seasonally adjusted 81,486,000 in October to 81,295,000 in November, and a slow growth in total employment—from (seasonally adjusted) 78,325,000 in October to 78,497,000 in November. Nonfarm payroll employment rose in November by 26,000. The monthly payroll employment advances averaged 80,000 in the June-November period contrasted with a 240,000 figure for the November 1968-June 1969 period.

The November decline in unemployment was about 360,000 to 2.8 million. The jobless rate among white workers was 3.1%, among nonwhites 6.2%.

For 1969 as a whole, total employment increased by 2 million to 77.9 million (largely in the first half), unemployment declined to 3.5% from a 3.6% rate in 1968, the civilian labor force rose by 2 million, the largest gain since 1947 on an annual basis (again largely reflecting the increases early in the year).

Congress' Cooperation Sought. President Nixon appealed to Congress Oct. 11 to join him in a "working partnership" to enact legislation to meet "the needs of a nation in distress." "Neither the Democratic Congress nor the Republican Administration is without fault for the delay of vital legislation," the President said. His special message was formally sent to Congress Oct. 13.

The President said the American people were not interested in "political posturing" between the executive and legislative branches of the government. These branches were "co-equal," he said, and "elected not to maneuver for partisan advantage but to work together to find hopeful answers to problems that confound the people all of us serve."

Mr. Nixon spoke of detecting a rising "spirit of party" in political remarks concerning the legislative record, that the Democratic-controlled Congress was being accused of "dragging its feet" and the Administration of being "laggard" in submitting its program. "There may be merit in both charges," Mr. Nixon noted, but the legislative issue for the 1970 campaign, he said, would be "the question of who deserves greater credit for the 91st Congress' record of accomplishment, not which of us should be held accountable because it did nothing."

The message mentioned about 30 legislative proposals of the Administration and said a "great majority" of them could be enacted by the end of the year.

Nixon Asks Restraints. President Nixon called on the American people Oct. 17 to help in the fight against inflation. In a half hour radio address, the President said "we are on the road to recovery from the disease of runaway prices," but he cautioned that prices would continue to rise, although at a slower rate. He said: "Prices are still going up; they may continue to do so for a while—a five-year momentum is not easy to stop. But now prices are no longer increasing faster and faster. . . . Without shock treatment, we're curing the causes of the rising cost of living."

Mr. Nixon blamed the previous Administration for the spiraling wage and price increases. "To put it bluntly," he said, "the frequent failure to balance the federal budget over the past five years has been the primary cause for unbalancing the family budgets of millions of Americans."

The President declared that he considered wage and price controls "bad for business, bad for the working man and bad for the consumer," and he said wage and price guidelines "failed to get to the root of the problem." Rather, Mr. Nixon said, he planned to call on labor unions "to base their wage demands on the new prospect of a return toward price stability" and to call on business "to base their investment and price decisions on that new economic climate, keeping in mind it is in their private interests to be realistic in their planning and to help build a strong economy."

He appealed to all Americans "to bear the burden of restraint in their personal credit and purchasing decisions, so as to reduce the pressures that help drive prices out of sight."

The President admitted that his policies to curb inflation would result in some "slowing pains" for some industries and individuals. But he added: "There are some who say that a high rate of unemployment can't be avoided. I don't agree. In our leveling-off process, we intend to do everything we can to resist increases in unemployment, to help train and place workers in new jobs, to cushion the effect of readjustment."

Reporting on what his Administration had accomplished to curb inflation, the President cited proposed cuts in federal spending of more than $7 billion, the extension of the 10% income tax surcharge at a reduced rate of 5% from Jan. 1 to June 30, 1970 (the extension had been approved by the Senate Finance Committee Oct. 16), and a continuation of the Federal Reserve Board's policy of restricting money and credit. Mr. Nixon also appealed to state and local governments to postpone "spending that can appropriately be delayed." (In a meeting with Congressional leaders Oct. 16, the President had warned against adding to appropriation bills money that had not been requested.)

Appeal to Unions and Business. In a letter to 2,200 business and labor leaders Oct. 18, President Nixon appealed to the private sector to join the Administration in the fight against inflation. Asserting that the "government's house is now in order," Mr. Nixon said: "A sense of responsibility must be part of every prudent judgment concerning prices and wages, now that the government has repudiated the previous inflationary policies. Price and wage decisions that anticipate inflation's continuing at or near present levels would be shortsighted, imprudent and unprofitable."

To business, the President warned: "The business that commits errors in pricing on the up side, expecting to be bailed out by inflation, is going to find itself in a poor competitive position."

To labor, he said: "It is in the interest of every union leader and workingman to avoid wage demands that will reduce the purchasing power of his dollar and reduce the number of job opportunities."

UAW to Seek Wage 'Equity.' In a special convention in Detroit Nov. 8–9, the United Auto Workers union (UAW) served notice it would not be bound by pleas from business or the Nixon Administration for wage restraint. The delegates also approved a donation of $5 million to the 11 unions (non-UAW) striking the General Electric Co. and a $10-a-week increase in UAW strike-benefit payments (to $30 for single workers, $40 for married workers with families).

UAW President Walter P. Reuther told the delegates Nov. 8 "we are going to the bargaining table in 1970 to get our equity and we don't care what business's attitude may be or the attitude of the Nixon Administration may be." The Administration's anti-inflation policies, he said, "put the economic burden of fighting inflation upon workers and their families, the very economic group least able to carry that burden." Reuther accused the Administration of "openly encouraging corporations to resist labor's legitimate wage demands."

The UAW would seek to cooperate with the AFL-CIO in GE strike aid. Reuther proposed a $50 million strike fund and told newsmen he hoped the AFL-CIO would "rise above" its differences with his union and help "in disciplining General Electric into a sense of responsibility." However, he said, the UAW would "move without" the AFL-CIO if necessary. Collections were to be sought by the UAW at plant gates to aid the GE strikers. The $5 million contribution was to come from the UAW's $95.6 million strike fund.

AFL-CIO action—The AFL-CIO Executive Council Oct. 29 pledged to "raise all necessary funds" to support the GE strikers. A council panel was named to "mobilize" union financial resources for the GE strike effort. The AFL-CIO also was promoting a $13.5 million GE strike fund to be obtained from a $1 collection from all federation members. A nationwide boycott against GE products was begun Nov. 28 by the federation, the first such boycott initiated from its international headquarters.

Nixon Aides on Inflation Policy. Murray L. Weidenbaum, assistant secretary of the Treasury for economic policy, had said in late August that fiscal restraints should remain until inflationary pressures had been reduced. He said the economy had cooled down from its 1968 pace, but he warned that "the cooling down process needs to continue until it is clearly reflected in a much slower rate of advance in costs and prices."

Arthur M. Okun, former chairman of the CEA, urged the Administration Sept. 25 to revive wage-price guideposts. Testifying before the House Government Operations subcommittee, Okun conceded that restrictive monetary and fiscal policies "are our first and most important lines of defense against inflation," but he argued that these policies could lead to cuts in output, profits and jobs. Okun said use of Administration pressure for "improving price-wage behavior" could be effective in holding price inflation "administered" by major industries.

Paul W. McCracken, chairman of the President's Council of Economic Advisers (CEA), testifying before the same committee Sept. 23, opposed reviving wage-price guideposts. He argued that such devices were of "unproven" effectiveness, might divert public and official attention from the need to fight monetary and fiscal causes of inflation, and were often unfair.

The testimony involved a House bill introduced by Rep. Henry A. Reuss (D, Wis.) that would require the Administration to create new voluntary guideposts. Reuss had argued that "inflation is out of control" and that monetary and fiscal restraints were not enough because "major companies and unions in highly concentrated industries have substantial discretion in their price and wage decisions." (Until abandoned in 1967, the old guideposts had called for wages and prices to increase no faster than productivity, usually estimated as a 3.2% rise annually in output per man hour.)

McCracken said Oct. 1 that there was "some early evidence that present fiscal and monetary policies of restraint" were beginning to cool the economy. He said he was "encouraged by the slowdown in the rise of the Consumer Price Level Index" and that the "important thing is to reach a new stability in price levels."

Andrew F. Brimmer, a Federal Reserve Board governor, said Oct. 4 that he thought the present tight credit policy with its consequent high interest rates should be continued. He said, "We should not run the risk of relaxing credit restraint until it is clear that we have a reasonable chance of making a noticeable dent in inflationary expectations." Brimmer admitted that the rate of growth had slowed during the third quarter, but he said that economic activity in terms of real and current dollars had been brisker than anticipated. "The national economy," he said, "has expanded more rapidly, resources have been used more fully and inflationary pressures have been intense."

Treasury Secretary David M. Kennedy told the Business Council in Hot Springs, Va. Oct. 17 that he expected the current decline in the gross national product (GNP) "to continue for some time." But he insisted that until there were clear signs that the economy had shifted from inflation to recession "We must and shall resist the all-too tempting route of moving into an expansionary policy too soon." Kennedy also admonished business to heed the Administration's demand for restraint in raising prices.

Labor Secretary George P. Shultz predicted Oct. 18 that there would be many strikes soon and lasting into 1970. Shultz, interviewed after he had addressed the council, said: "There will be a lot of tension, there will be strikes. It's all part of the process of sorting out and rearranging the economy." He asserted that the only proper role for the government to play would be to bring full use of the Federal Mediation and Conciliation Service and to show a willingness "to be helpful in every way," adding that it was up to both sides to mediate the problems themselves "so we won't be intervening right and left in these disputes." Shultz also cautioned that increased prices might force some markets for business to disappear; he cited construction as an industry that was pricing itself out of the market.

Tax Reform Enacted. The Tax Reform Act of 1969 (HR13270) was cleared by Congress Dec. 22 and signed into law by

President Nixon Dec. 30. It was passed by votes of 381–2 in the House and 71–6 in the Senate. The opposing votes, all Republican, were cast by Sens. Henry Bellmon (Okla.), Carl T. Curtis (Neb.), Jacob K. Javits and Charles E. Goodell (N.Y.), William B. Saxbe (Ohio) and John J. Williams (Del.) and Reps. John M. Ashbrook (Ohio) and Earl F. Landgrebe (Ind.).

The total individual income tax reductions provided by the bill, once all of its provisions were in effect in 1973, was estimated at $9.1 billion annually; in the same period, tax collections would be increased by $6.6 billion annually.

The bill's major provisions were a 15% rise in Social Security benefits, an increase in the personal exemption and standard deduction, a reduction in the oil depletion allowance to 22%, extension of the income tax surcharge at a 5% rate through June 1970, postponement of scheduled reductions in telephone and automobile excise taxes and repeal of the 7% business investment tax credit.

The bill also contained a "minimum tax" designed to cover large incomes heretofore escaping federal tax (except for interest on bonds of state and local governments, which remained tax exempt), plus stiffer provisions for foundations, those with capital-gain income and real estate operators.

The final version of the bill, as worked out by the House-Senate conferences— the 14 senior members of the House Ways and Means and Senate Finance Committees—was close to Administration recommendations in its net revenue effects, excluding those of the Social Security increase. The Administration version had called for a net revenue increase of $7.1 billion in 1970, $615 million in 1971 and a net revenue decrease of $2.3 billion in 1972; the final version provided for a net increase of $6.5 billion in 1970, $288 million in 1971 and a $1.8 billion loss in 1972. After 1972, the final version would cost the government from $500 million to $1 billion a year more than the Administration proposals. The figures excluded the effects of the 15% rise in Social Security benefits provided by the bill, which would cost about $1.5 billion more a year than the 10% increase requested by President Nixon.

The conferees revised the Senate version, which would have reduced tax collections from individuals by $1.2 billion a year, to conform largely to the net effects of the House version, which would have raised collections from individuals by $1.4 billion.

Prior to the bill's passage many observers had speculated that, in its pre-compromise versions, the measure was more than likely to be vetoed by the President, but Senate Republican leader Hugh Scott (Pa.) said after a meeting with President Nixon Dec. 20 that the inflationary effect of the Senate bill, against which Mr. Nixon had directed his threat, had been "considerably reduced" by the conferees' version.

The conferees revised the personal exemption from its current $600 to $650 on July 1, 1970, to $700 in 1972 and to $750 in 1973. On the Social Security provision, the 15% increase in benefits was retained but the Senate's increase in the minimum monthly benefit payment to $100 was deleted.

Among other final provisions:

(a) A minimum standard deduction was set at $1,100 for 1970, $1,050 for 1971 and $1,000 for 1972; (b) the standard deduction was increased from 10% of income or $1,000 (whichever was lower) to 13% or $1,500 for 1971, 14% or $2,000 for 1972 and 15% or $2,000 for 1973; (c) a special new tax rate for single persons would begin in 1971 to keep them from paying more than 20% more tax than married couples with the same taxable income; (d) a maximum tax on earned income was set at 60% for 1971 and 50% thereafter; a "minimum tax" provision would apply to heretofore tax-sheltered income in excess of $30,000—from this the taxpayer would subtract the tax paid on his regularly taxable income and be taxed 10% on the remainder; (e) the depletion allowance for minerals currently at more than 22% rate, such as sulphur and uranium, was reduced, like the allowance for the oil and gas industry, to 22%; molybdenum, currently at 15%, was raised to 22%, most now at 15% were cut to 14% except for gold, silver, copper, oil shale and iron ore; depletion allowance for foreign operations of oil firms was retained at its current level; (f) the capital gains holding period was retained at six months, the amount of capital gains that could be taxed on the alternative tax rate of 25%, was set at $50,000, above that the rate would rise as high as 35%; (g) the first income tax on private foundations was set at 4% of investment income, and foundations would be required to distribute an amount equal to at least 6% of their income; restrictions were set on a foundation's financing of voter registration drives, on controlling interests in business corporations and on lobbying activities; (h) on real estate, the double depreciation, currently available for all new construction, would be limited to new housing; other new building could be depreciated at a 150% rate, all used construction would be permitted only straight-line depreciation except residences with a useful life of more than 20 years, which were permitted a 125% rate; a new provision was written for "recapture" of excess depreciation, permitting a 1%-a-month phaseout of the recapturable amount after an 8¼-year period; (i) individuals with an extraordinary income in a single year (exceeding 120% of the five-year average) would ce allowed to pay lower rates on the excess by treating it as if it were earned over five years; (j) certain deductions were permitted for direct costs of moving not reimbursed by an employer.

When he signed the bill Dec. 30, President Nixon complained that the measure had elements of "both good and bad" in it. He considered the tax reforms, on the whole, good but its effect on the budget and cost of living bad. It "unduly favors spending at the expense of saving," he said, "at a time when demands on our savings are heavy." And it would make the anti-inflation effort "more difficult." He chided Congress about its "reluctance . . . to face up to the adverse impact of its tax and spending decisions." Tax reduction must be accompanied by corresponding expenditure reduction, he cautioned, pointing out that in this session Congress had not done this but had cut revenues by $3 billion while increasing spending $3 billion over his recommendations.

Mr. Nixon said a budget deficit at this time would be "irresponsible and intolerable" and he pledged to "take the action I consider necessary to present a balanced budget for the next fiscal year."

Secretary of the Treasury David M. Kennedy had complained to the Senate Finance Committee Sept. 4 that the original House version of the bill was "weighted in favor of consumption to the potential detriment of the nation's productive investment." The "bias in the bill against investment in favor of consumption," he said, could "impede economic growth . . . by curtailing the incentive to make productive investments."

Nixon Urges Spending Restraint. President Nixon appealed to Congress Dec. 17 to join with him in fighting inflation by holding down spending and maintaining revenue. "We stand at the crossroads of credibility," Mr. Nixon said in a letter to House and Senate leaders. By persevering for "a strong" budget and fiscal policy, "we can build on the growing evidence that policies of 1969 are beginning to exert a stabilizing effect," he said. "But

if we miss this opportunity it will be a long time before the public will ever believe that government can manage its finances in any way other than to produce sustained and serious inflation. . . . At stake is nothing less than the future of the American economy."

The President spoke of "tangible evidence" of progress in the Administration's anti-inflation efforts. But he pointed out some budgetary problems—some $6 billion in spending increases since January in "uncontrollable" areas, such as interest on the national debt, and some $6.6 billion potential additional expenditures in Congressional spending and tax decisions. The latter included the tax bill, increased educational aid, a "premature" civilian and military pay raise, a 15% increase in Social Security benefits and new legislation, "worthy though it may be, to benefit veterans, children and others." The President also cited potential revenue loss through Congressional inaction on postal reform and legislation to permit sales of certain financial assets of the Farmers Home Administration and Veterans Administration.

"The responsible path toward protecting the buying power of the consumer's dollar is clear," he said. "But the Congress has not appeared to be willing to take that path." As for taxes, he said "Congress appears to be well on its way to substituting tax reduction for tax reform. This will harm rather than help the average taxpayer." Inflation, he said, "the hole in everybody's pocket, is the most unfair tax of all."

6% Savings Bank Rate Backed. The Federal Home Loan Bank Board Dec. 19 authorized savings and loan associations to pay a record-breaking 6% interest rate to savers willing to buy certificates called Housing Certificates of Deposit worth at least $10,000 and running for at least two years. The previous maximum rate on certificates was 5¼% and for regular passbook accounts, 4¾%.

Preston Martin, board chairman, said that if the new interest rate succeeded in heading off heavy withdrawals expected at the end of 1969 and in April 1970 after quarterly interest was credited, the flow of mortgage funds into housing would be correspondingly greater.

Savings institutions, supplying the bulk of money for home mortgages, were particularly hard hit by tight-money conditions. According to a New York Times report Dec. 31, the nation's savings and loan associations had a net outflow of lendable funds in the first 11 months of 1969 of $609 million compared with a net inflow of $2.6 billion during the same months of 1968.

Burns on Relaxing Monetary Policy. Arthur F. Burns told Congress Dec. 18 he favored relaxation of the current extremely restrictive monetary policy in "normal conditions." Such a condition, he said, would be a balanced budget in both the current and next fiscal year. However, Burns stressed that the current time was not "normal" and was marked by the lack of "credibility" in the business and financial community in the government's determination to combat inflation through the budget process.

Burns made the comments to the Senate Banking Committee the same day he was confirmed by the Senate as a member (and chairman) of the Federal Reserve Board, effective Feb. 1, 1970, to succeed William McChesney Martin Jr.

Burns' remarks favoring eventual easing of monetary restrictions appeared to have had an ebullient repercussion on the stock market Dec. 18—the Dow-Jones industrial average jumped 13.86 points to 783.79, the largest gain since April 30, and volume on the New York Stock Exchange rose to 15.95 million shares, the heaviest turnover in almost two months. The tight monetary policy was considered to have been a major factor in depressing stock prices for the past 12 months.

Federal Reserve Board member Andrew F. Brimmer had told a Pittsburgh audience Dec. 2 the 12 months of monetary restraint had not as yet accomplished its goal and should be continued.

A summary of the Federal Reserve Board's Open Market Committee meeting Sept. 9, released Dec. 8, confirmed that two board members, George W. Mitchell and Sherman J. Maisel, had dissented from the board's restrictive monetary policy. According to the summary, the two held that the restrictive policy should be relaxed and the board should shift from its emphasis on short-term interest rates and other "money market conditions" to an emphasis on "aggregates" such as bank reserves and money supply.

The summary said the two members "favored maintaining the overall posture of restraint measured in terms of such aggregates and interest rates, and permitting more flexibility in money-market conditions in order to do so." In an interview Dec. 8, Maisel said the board might provoke a "financial crisis" unless its monetary policy was relaxed, and he endorsed a policy of rapid shinkage of financial liquidity.

Inflation & Administration Policy. Commerce Secretary Maurice H. Stans predicted Dec. 30 that 1970 would bring "significant progress" toward ending the nation's worst inflation in 19 years. In an end-of-the-year statement, Stans warned, however, that the fight against inflation would require "continued fiscal and monetary restraint," and he said that real growth in 1970 "should be modest, less than in 1969, although possibly more rapid in the second half of 1970 than in the first."

Stans' statement was issued together with the Commerce Department's review of the economy for 1969. It said that the nation's gross national product (GNP), reflecting total output of goods and services, reached about $932 billion in 1969, an increase of 7.75% over 1968. The report said, however, that increases in prices accounted for 4.75% of the advance, the worst price inflation since 1951. Stans said that actual output of goods and services had increased only by about 3% in 1969, compared with 5% in 1968.

In an address at the annual convention of the Investment Bankers Association of America Dec. 8, Stans had warned that the U.S. economy faced some "bad, bitter medicine" before it would begin to grow solidly again. Stans declared that "just about the right pressures" had been applied by the Administration to bring a decrease in the growth of inflation without causing a recession. At a news conference after his address Stans said that wage and price controls were "farthest from the thoughts of the Administration."

Paul W. McCracken, chairman of the President's Council of Economic Advisers (CEA), had warned Oct. 30 that business conditions were likely to be "rather uncomfortable" during most of 1970. Predicting a continued slow growth and a stiffening of management resistance to wage demands, McCracken asserted, "If we are ever to regain a more stable price level, there will have to be a transition period in which gains become less than they have been." He added that 1970 "may well be" that difficult transition time. He also said that the economy's "real" or physical output increase in 1970 "might well be below" the historic annual average of 3% to 3½%.

Herbert Stein, a CEA member, said Nov. 11 that proposals for a revival of voluntary wage-price controls were "unlikely to be effective" and "out of fashion." Stein argued that inflation could decrease even while a number of economic indicators, such as GNP, investment, spending, wages and prices, continued to increase. Arthur Okun, former chairman of the CEA, said Nov. 11 that he was "distressed" with the Administration's attitude toward voluntary controls, arguing that such controls had proved helpful.

Pierre A. Rinfret, a former economic adviser to President Nixon, charged Dec. 9 that the Administration did not have an effective anti-inflation policy. He said that not only would there be no recession in 1970, "but I think we will smash every economic record that has been established in the history of the world." Rinfret assailed the President's Oct. 18 appeal to unions and business for their help in the fight against inflation, and he denounced proposals for the extension of the 10% surtax at half its rate, cuts in federal spending, cuts in construction outlays and a budget surplus. ("Magnificent," he said, ". . . Never have so many lied to so few so successfully.") Rinfret proposed instead an increase to 15% in the surtax, a ban on bank credit cards, reimposition of controls on consumer credit, and an increase in the investment tax credit.

Stock Market: *1969 D-J Averages.* The Dow-Jones industrial stock average (30 stocks) moved up 5.68 points Dec. 31 to close at 800.36 as the New York Stock Exchange ended its 1969 trading year. The closing figure was up from the lowest mark in three years, registered Dec. 16 when it fell to 777.83. The previous record low was reached Oct. 14, 1966, when the D-J industrial average had closed at 771.71. The industrial average had soared to the highest point of 1969 on May 14, closing at 968.85. The high

reflected the enthusiastic anticipation of President Nixon's May 14 speech proposing a gradual withdrawal of most troops from Vietnam.

The 1969 monthly D-J industrial average in January was 934.999, followed by a fluctuating but generally downward trend through November. The other monthly figures: February, 931.29; March, 916.52; April 927.38; May, 954.86; June, 896.61; July, 844.02; August, 825.46; September, 826.71; and November, 841.09.

1969 price rise 6.1%. A 6.1% rise in consumer prices during 1969 was reported by the Labor Department. It was the sharpest annual increase in consumer prices since the Korean war year of 1951.

Price increases were registered in every category of goods and services, the largest being 9.5% for household services, 8.5% for transportation services, 7.2% for food, 7.1% for medical care services (not counting drugs), and 5.3% for apparel. Price rises in services constituted 40% of the 1969 increase.

Consumer prices rose at an annual rate of 6.3% in the first half of the year, 5.8% in the second half.

The December 1969 consumer price rise was .6%, with a 1.4% hike in food prices leading the way.

GNP Climb Slowed. During 1969's final quarter the gross national product (GNP) registered its first "real" decline (measured in 1958 dollar terms) since the "mini-recession" of 1957's first quarter. The rate of this physical decline was .4%. But in current (inflated) dollars, there was a $9.4 billion rise (the smallest in 2½ years) to a $952.2 billion annual rate for the quarter. The increase for all 1969 was $65.7 billion to a $931.4 billion level. The annual increase was 7% above the 1968 level, but 4¾% of the rise was attributed to price increases, the sharpest since 1951, and the remaining 3% represented increase in real output.

Industrial production declined in each of the final five months of 1969. The drop from August through December was estimated by the Federal Reserve Board at 2.1%.

A major factor of the fourth quarter slowdown was a decrease in the rate of accumulation of business inventories, down to an annual rate of $7.8 billion (based on figures of two months of the quarter) from the third quarter's $10.7 billion. Also in 1969's fourth quarter, consumer outlays rose $9.4 billion to a $589.2 billion annual rate, while the rate of savings declined to 6.4% of disposable income from 6.7% in the third quarter. The savings rate for 1969 was 6% compared with 1968's 6.5%.

The fourth quarter price index for the overall GNP revealed a 4.4% annual rate increase contrasted to a 5.6% rate in the third quarter and a 4.9% rate for the first half of 1969.

Wage Disputes & Agreements

Employers and employes conducted normal wage negotiations during 1969. The settlements achieved, sometimes after strikes or under the threat of strike, frequently were for pay increases that exceeded those of previous years.

Median Wage Rise 7%. The Labor Department reported July 25 a 7.1% median wage and benefit increase in major labor settlements in the first six months of 1969. The six-month average for wage increases alone was 6.1% (5.2% in 1968).

In commenting on the data July 25, Labor Secretary George P. Shultz cautioned both labor and management not to price themselves out of the market in wages or prices. He pointed out "that we think the economic environment is going to be quite different two or three years from now," and it would be "in the self-interest" of labor and management in the negotiation of multiple-year contracts "not to assume the current rate of inflation several years hence."

Pressure for higher wages continued, however, and by the time the year had ended, major labor union settlements achieved during 1969 covered nearly 2.5 million workers and called for a record median increase in wages and fringe benefits of 8.2% annually. The figure for 1968 was 6.6%, for 1967, 5.5%. Wage increases alone in 1969 averaged 7.1%, compared with 5.2% in 1968 and 5% in 1967. The median first-year wage increase was 8.2% (7.2% in 1968, 5.6% in 1967).

Among examples of specific pay disputes and settlements during 1969:

AP Strike. Editorial employes of the Associated Press (AP) went on strike Jan. 9. They settled Jan. 16 for a three-year contract providing a $43 increase in the top minimum salary.

The new top minimum for newsmen and related classifications was $250 a week, effective at the start of the third year of the contract. The previous minimum was $207 a week.

The new contract also reduced the work week from 40 hours to 37½ for employes on night, overnight and Sunday duty and provided: (a) an additional holiday, raising the total to eight; (b) a cost-of-living allowance, effective in 1971, based on any rise of more than 4.7% in the Consumer Price Index during 1970; (c) a $2 increase in monthly contributions for hospital and medical benefits; (d) three weeks' vacation after four years' service and four weeks after nine years' service.

N.J. Teacher Strike. A Jersey City (N.J.) teachers' strike closed the city's 35 public schools to 35,000 pupils for five school days beginning Jan. 23. The strike ended Jan. 29 when the Jersey City Education Association agreed to a two-day cooling-off period. The 1,200 striking teachers voted Feb. 3 to accept a new contract, offered by the board of education, that provided a salary schedule ranging from $7,000 a year to $10,750. The previous scale ran from $6,200 to $9,750.

N.Y. Police Pact. N.Y. City policemen ratified a new contract that would raise the annual pay of first-grade patrolmen from $9,383 to $10,425, retroactive to Oct. 1, 1968, and to $10,950 Oct. 1, 1969. Other grades would receive corresponding raises.

Results of a mail referendum among the 23,000 members of the Patrolmen's Benevolent Association (PBA) were announced Feb. 11. Acceptance of the pact had been recommended by PBA delegates Jan. 29.

A basic agreement for firemen and sanitationmen as well as for policemen had been negotiated in 1968 and accepted by the other two services. The final policemen's pact differed somewhat from the original agreement in that the policemen gained $200 more in basic salary, a night-shift differential of 5%, time and one-half pay for overtime after 40 hours a week, and cash or time off (a total of seven days' compensation) for work during the 1966 transit strike and the 1968 funerals of the Rev. Dr. Martin Luther King Jr. and Sen. Robert F. Kennedy.

Dock Workers. *N. Y. strike*—A 57-day dock strike, the longest in the history of the Port of New York, ended Feb. 14 when striking dock workers, by a vote of 9,328 to 3,213, approved a new three-year contract. The settlement covered about 22,000 members of the AFL-CIO International Longshoremen's Association (ILA).

The strike had started after the expiration of an 80-day cooling-off period imposed under the Taft-Hartley Act. The new contract for the New York area was retroactive to Oct. 1, 1968. It provided a $1.60-an-hour package increase over the life of the contract. The wage raise was 98¢ an hour (38¢ immediately), and this would increase the wage base from $3.62 an hour to $4.60. Ancillary benefits would rise from $3.00 an hour to $3.62.

An important provision of the new contract was a paid-work guarantee of 2,080 hours a year (full employment), compared with the current guarantee of 1,600 hours.

Other provisions increased the monthly pension from $175 to $300 and provided for six weeks of vacation annually (an increase of two weeks) and for 13 paid holidays (an increase of one).

The New York dockers also gained the right to unpack and repack all cargo containers with consolidated shipments of less than full trailer loads.

***Texas strike ends*—**The nation's longest maritime strike ended in its 103d day April 2 when longshoremen in Galveston and Houston, Tex. ratified a new contract for 8,000 members in 26 union locals from Lake Charles, La. to Brownsville, Tex. The container clause and pay boost of the "master" contract negotiated in February for the Port of New York was included in the West Gulf Coast pact, but the West Gulf dockworkers were committed to a grievance procedure

and not to strike over the container clause, and the guaranteed annual wage issue was relegated to further study by a joint panel of management and labor.

The striking longshoremen were members of the AFL-CIO International Longshoremen's Association.

Other settlements in the protracted dispute had been achieved for the ports of New Orleans, Miami, Hampton Roads, Va. and Baltimore Feb. 21, Philadelphia Feb. 23, Cambridge, Md. March 6, Baton Rouge, La. March 18 and Boston March 31.

The guaranteed wage pledge in Baltimore was for 1,800 hours of work a year; in New Orleans, there was agreement by both sides to begin studying the matter as well as the matter of a reduction of work crews.

Hard-Coal Pact. A three-year contract covering about 8,000 active miners in the anthracite mines of eastern Pennsylvania was approved March 16 by the policy committee of the United Mine Workers. The pact's medical provisions covered another 10,000 retired hard-coal miners.

Additional wage and fringe benefits provided by the new pact were estimated to total $2.85 a day. (Average hard-coal pay had been about $23 a day, or about $10 a day less than the soft-coal average.) The wage increases totaled $1.40 a day— 70¢ April 1 plus 35¢ April 1, 1970 and 35¢ April 1, 1971. The new benefits included three additional paid holidays (bringing the total to eight), higher vacation payments and, for the first time, paid Blue Cross and Blue Shield hospital/medical insurance.

Previously, health care benefits and pensions were covered by a 70¢-a-ton royalty paid into the anthracite health-and-welfare fund. But the dwindling hard-coal market and increasing production costs had strained the fund's ability to meet its payments.

National Rail Strike Averted. A threatened strike of the AFL-CIO Bro'hood of Railroad Signalmen against the nation's railroads was averted by an agreement reached April 13 after a 28-hour negotiating session in the office of Labor Secretary George P. Shultz. The union had announced April 8 that it would strike April

14 in a demand for a wage increment for skilled workers—a "skilled inequity adjustment."

A Presidential emergency board had recommended March 7 that the signalmen be granted a 20¢-an-hour skilled inequity adjustment, effective July 1, 1968, and that the union's demand for another one in 1969 be submitted to binding arbitration. The carriers accepted the proviso for binding arbitration, but the union did not.

The board also recommended a three-step 8½% general wage increase—3½% retroactive to July 1, 1968, 2% retroactive to Jan. 1, 1969 and 3% effective July 1. Signalmen eligible for the "skilled inequity adjustment," estimated at about 8,000 of the 10,000 union members, would receive a 14½% wage raise over the 18 months under the board's proposals.

Shultz told newsmen April 9, after the union's strike threat, that "the government simply isn't going to tolerate a national railroad strike" and would seek Congressional intervention if necessary. Shultz did not participate personally in the marathon negotiating session resolving the dispute; major credit for the accord was given to W. J. Usery, assistant labor secretary.

The final agreement, approved by the union's general chairmen and formally signed by the leadership April 18, provided a 22¢ hourly differential for skilled members and a 9¢ adjustment (both retroactive to July 1, 1968) for semiskilled members. Counting other increases under the three-step plan recommended by the Presidential panel, the contract raised the average base wage of skilled signalmen by 52½¢ (16%) an hour to about $3.80 and the pay of semiskilled men by 36¢ (12%) to about $3.37.

A Presidential emergency board Feb. 13 had proposed a 5%-a-year pay-raise pattern for conductors and engineers in settling their disputes with the nation's railroads. The board had been appointed by President Johnson Jan. 13 to hold off threatened strikes by the Bro'hood of Locomotive Engineers and the conductors' division of the new United Transportation Union. The board recommended pay raises of 5% in daily rates and 3½% in mileage rates, retroactive to July 1, 1968, plus another 2% in daily and mileage rates effective July 1, 1969.

The panel also advised (a) the unions to accept a no-strike moratorium until Jan. 1, 1970 and (b) the railroads to establish a fund to correct inequities among the wage categories. The fund would come from the equivalent of a 1% pay increase plus another 5¢ an hour for each employe.

The unions sought a 15% annual pay increase.

Airline Pay Accords. The Air Line Pilots Association (ALPA) and Pan American World Airways announced agreement June 4 on a new two-year contract that would make Pan Am pilots the highest paid of any airline—$59,000 annual salary (for captains) when the new Boeing 747 turbo jets were initiated into service later in the year. The pact provided salary increases totaling 17.5% over the two-year period. Maximum flight duty time was reduced from 85 hours a month to 80.

An ALPA pact with Northwest Airlines was settled June 13 after a six-hour strike by the carrier's 1,500 pilots, their first against the company. It was to provide a 12% pay rise for captains (currently averaging $28,000), 17% for copilots (currently $16,850) and 25% for second officers ($13,650). The monthly maximum duty time also was cut to 80 hours. The strikers also were to receive about 60%-70% of the pay hike retroactive to expiration of the last contract, April 30, 1968.

Ratification of a new three-year contract with Eastern Air Lines was announced May 2 by the International Association of Machinists. The pact, applying to 10,350 workers, called for a 32% pay rise—to $5.50 an hour for mechanics, $4.31 for ramp servicemen and $3.77 for cleaners and laborers.

Pan Am Strike. Virtually all flight service of Pan American World Airways was suspended during a strike by some 8,000 of the carrier's ticket sellers, clerical workers and cargo handlers Aug. 8–12. The striking employes were members of the International Brotherhood of Teamsters. Tentative agreement on a new three-year contract was reached after bargaining sessions at the Labor Department in Washington Aug. 8, but balloting by the membership was not completed until Aug. 12.

Average wages would be increased under the new pact from $3.30 an hour to $4.52. The figures included fringe benefits.

Breweries Struck. Strikes forced a nationwide shutdown of Anheuser-Busch breweries May 27–June 29 and closed down four major breweries in Milwaukee June 9–July 16.

The strike against Anheuser-Busch, the world's largest brewer and producer of Budweiser beer, was initiated by members of the International Brotherhood of Teamsters. Production was halted in the firm's breweries in St. Louis (5,000 employes), Tampa, Fla., Newark, N.J., Los Angeles, Columbus, Ohio, Jacksonville, Fla. and Houston, Tex.

The Milwaukee strike was called by production workers of United Brewery Workers Local 9 against the Jos. Schlitz Brewing Co.; Pabst Brewing Co., which also bottled Blatz beer; the Miller Brewing Co.; and Gettelman Brewing Co., a division of Miller's. The strikers returned to work July 16 after ratification of a new two-year contract providing wage increases of 75¢ an hour and additional benefits of 18¢ an hour over the contract's life.

Firemen Strike. Union firemen of Gary, Ind. went on strike in a wage dispute with the city Aug. 5–10. The firemen, members of Local 359 of the International Association of Fire Fighters, were seeking a $2,000 annual pay increase to raise their base pay to $9,400. The city had approved a $600 raise.

A county court injunction against the strike was issued three hours after it began, and Gary Mayor Richard G. Hatcher recommended Aug. 6 that absent firemen be suspended and demoted. Arrests warrants also were issued against four of the union's officials by the county court Aug. 6, but the officials made themselves unavailable. The suspensions were effective Aug. 7.

The fire fighters returned to work Aug. 10 after the Gary City Council agreed to establish a committee to discuss the firemen's 1970 wages and other issues.

Many members of Newark, N.J.'s 1,100-man fire department had engaged in a 14-hour strike July 11–12 in protest against a pay differential planned for their superiors. The strikers defied a temporary injunction but returned to work after Mayor Hugh J. Addonizio threatened absentees with dismissal. The strikers were members of the Fireman's Mutual Benevolent Association. The wage agreement in dispute called for a $2,500 annual pay increase for firemen and policemen and a 15% differential for officers. The proposed raise would bring the annual maximum for first-class firemen and policemen to $10,522.

American Motors Strike. A strike by the United Automobile Workers against the American Motors Corp. began Oct. 16 and ended Nov. 21. The company's plants in Milwaukee and Kenosha, Wis. and Brampton, Ont., involving about 11,000 workers, were idled throughout most of the strike. Agreement on the economic package of a new contract was reached late Oct. 16 after the strike had begun. The terms were accepted Nov. 4 by the Milwaukee employes but final settlement was balked by the 6,000-member Kenosha local, which objected mainly to a company proposal to eliminate a provision permitting the local to veto proposed overtime. The local approved the contract Nov. 21 after the veto right was abandoned by the union but retained for the individual worker. Production at Brampton (1,100 employes), which had been interrupted because of lack of parts, resumed Nov. 20.

The new pact, for one year, called for an increase of more than 40¢ an hour, or more than 8%.

147,000 Strike General Electric. More than 140,000 workers went on strike Oct. 27 against General Electric Co. (GE) plants across the country. The strike was backed by a coalition of 13 unions representing 147,000 GE workers, or more than 90% of the company's production and maintenance personnel. The firm employed 310,000 persons at 280 plants in 33 states.

A negotiating impasse led to the strike. GE's method of bargaining—known as "Boulwarism," under which the company made an original offer and then refused to alter it—was at issue.

The two largest unions in the bargaining and strike coalition—the AFL-CIO International Union of Electrical Workers (IUE) and the independent United Electrical Workers (UE)—filed charges Oct. 27 with the National Labor Relations Board (NLRB) of unfair labor practices against GE on the ground that it refused to bargain.

(The U.S. Court of Appeals in New York upheld by a 2-1 decision Oct. 28 a 1964 NLRB ruling that GE was guilty of unfair labor practices in its 1960 negotiations with the IUE. Judge Irving R. Kaufman, presenting the majority viewpoint, wrote: "We hold that an employer may not so combine 'take-it-or-leave-it' bargaining methods with a widely publicized stance of unbending firmness that he is himself unable to alter a position once taken." Castigating GE's "patronizing" attitude and "unbending patriarchal posture" in the 1960 negotiations, Kaufman said GE had negotiated to the greatest possible extent "by ignoring the legitimacy and relevance of the union's position as statutory representative of its members.")

IUE President Paul Jennings Oct. 26 called GE's refusal to revise its offer "arrogant." UE President Albert J. Fitzgerald, in issuing a strike order to his union Oct. 26, said GE, "convinced of its divine wisdom, has refused to change one penny, one period or one comma of the offer it delivered on Oct. 7."

That offer, GE's original wage offer, was for an immediate 20¢-an-hour wage increase plus an additional increase of 5¢ to 25¢ an hour for highly skilled workers (the average wage of the strikers was $3.25 an hour). GE included an offer to reopen wage talks in both the second and third years of the three-year contract.

The unions were seeking a 30-month contract with hourly wages raised 35¢ the first year, 30¢ the second and 25¢ the final six months; plus cost-of-living adjustments and an additional 50¢ for highly skilled workers.

Labor Secretary George P. Shultz Oct. 27 expressed the intention of the Nixon Administration not to intervene.

Shultz was criticized by Jennings for also expressing, on the same news broadcast, his opinion that GE was "putting up so much resistance" on the new-contract issues because "they are feeling the effects of the anti-inflation policies in the product market, so they can't just raise their prices so easily. That means that their profits will be squeezed by a large wage increase...."

President's Salary Doubled. A bill (HR10) doubling the President's annual salary—to $200,000—was passed by voice votes of the House Jan. 6 and Senate Jan. 15. President Johnson signed it Jan. 18 and thus made it effective for his successors. A provision of the Constitution prohibited a change in the President's salary during his term in office.

The Chief Executive's salary had been taxable since 1953 and amounted to $51,500 after taxes at the $100,000 level and to $78,000 at the $200,000 level. Additional annual allowances of $50,000 for official expenses and of $40,000 for travel expenses were tax-free. These latter amounts remained unchanged under the new legislation.

This was the fourth increase in the President's salary since it was first set at $25,000 a year for George Washington in 1789. The last raise (from $75,000) was in 1949.

Congress' Pay Raised. A 41% pay raise for Congress members and substantial raises for other top federal officials were assured by a 47-34 vote in the Senate Feb. 4 and a 12-3 vote of the House Rules Committee Feb. 5.

The pay increases took effect Feb. 14. Under a 1967 law, federal pay raises for top officials went into effect 30 days after their recommendation by the President unless vetoed by either the Senate or the House. The current increases had been recommended by ex-President Johnson in his budget message and endorsed by President Nixon.

The raise for Congress members was from $30,000 a year to $42,500, for Cabinet officers from $35,000 to $60,000, for the Chief Justice of the U.S. from $40,000 to $62,000 and for Supreme Court Justices from $39,500 to $60,000. Other new salary levels: $42,500 for circuit court judges and heads of major agencies, $40,000 for district court judges and chairmen of major boards and commissions, $38,000 for assistant departments secretaries and members of major boards and commissions, $36,000 for bureau chiefs and members of minor boards and commissions.

A special commission established under the 1967 law had recommended even higher salary levels (e.g., to $50,-000 for members of Congress), but Mr. Johnson had reduced all but the $60,000 recommended for Cabinet members. Congress' previous raise was from $22,-500 to $30,000 in 1964.

In the Senate Feb. 4, the 47–34 vote (26 D & 21 R vs. 18 D & 16 R) came after a three-hour debate climaxed by minority leader Everett McKinley Dirksen's announcement that Mr. Nixon supported the raises. The vote was on a resolution to veto the raises.

The Senate fight against the raises was led by Sen. John J. Williams (R, Del.), who insisted on a vote for the record. He asked: "If the members of Congress are to increase their own salaries by 40% and the salaries of the executive branch by 35% to 70%, . . . how can we, in good conscience, ask industry and organized labor to hold their price and wage increases down to approximately 5% so that we can combat the serious threat of inflation?" A similar point was raised in the House by Rep. H. R. Gross (R, Iowa). But his effort to force a record vote was defeated by the House Rules Committee, which refused Feb. 5, by 12–3 vote, to clear for floor action a resolution to veto the raises.

Vice President's Pay Raised. A bill (HR7206) increasing the vice president's annual salary from $43,000 to $62,500 was passed by voice votes of the Senate Aug. 7 and House Sept. 4 and was signed by President Nixon Sept. 16. The bill also raised the salary of the speaker of the House from $43,000 to $62,500 and the majority and minority leaders of the House and Senate and the president pro tempore of the Senate from $42,500 to $49,500.

The bill originally approved by the House March 18 would have raised the pay of the latter five leaders to $55,000, but the House Sept. 4 agreed to the Senate's amendment to reduce the figure to $49,500.

Price Developments

Steel Prices Increased. Bethlehem Steel Corp., the nation's second largest steel producer announced Feb. 3 that it had completed the cancelation of its recent (November 1968) $25-a-ton price cut by again raising prices for hot-rolled carbon steel. Major mills, including Bethlehem already had restored $17 of the reduction. Jones & Laughlin Steel Corp. followed Bethlehem's action later Feb. 3, National Steel Corp. and Armco Steel Corp. on Feb. 4 and on Feb. 6 the U.S. Steel Corp., Republic Steel, Inland Steel, Youngstown Sheet & Tube Co. and Wheeling Pittsburgh Steel Co.

The price increase brought the cost of steel sheets from $117 to $129 a ton and raised from $110 to $124 a ton the base price of hot-rolled bands. Both increases became effective Feb. 16. U.S. Steel, the nation's largest producer, had sought the higher price last December, but had retreated when Bethlehem and other producers went only to $117.

Aluminum Prices Increased. The Olin Mathieson Chemical Corp. March 26 raised prices 2¢ a pound, or 4%, on all its fabricated aluminum products, effective April 1. The company said, however, that it would not change its 27¢-a-pound price for primary aluminum ingot. (The Kaiser Aluminum & Chemical Corp. Jan. 13 had increased the price of aluminum ingots from 26¢ a pound to 27¢, the highest price since the 1920s. The increase, the first in the industry since June 1968, was attributed by Kaiser to general inflationary tendencies.) An Olin Mathieson spokesman said the increase had been taken ". . . to create a proper spread between the prices of primary metal and fabricated products which would recognize the true costs of fabrication and provide a reasonable return."

The Aluminum Co. of America (Alcoa) announced March 28 it would make selective price increases on fabricated aluminum products. Sheet products were raised 2¢ a pound effective April 1, common alloy coiled sheets 1¢ and common alloy flat sheets $\frac{1}{2}$¢ a pound. Other companies matched Alcoa's price increases March 31, and the other two of the Big

Three—Reynolds Metals Co. and Kaiser —did so April 1-2.

Olin Mathieson announced April 3 that it had rescinded part of its across-the-board increase of 2¢ a pound and that the new range would be between ½¢ and 2¢.

(The Kennecott Copper Corp., the largest U.S. copper producer, raised its price for copper 2¢ a pound Jan. 6 to 43¢ a pound in the U.S. Phelps Dodge Corp., the third largest producer, had made a similar increase a week previously.)

Oil Price Dispute. Texaco, Inc., the U.S.' third largest oil company and largest domestic seller of gasoline, announced Feb. 24 a .6¢-a-gallon raise in the wholesale price of gasoline for the continental U.S. (The N.Y. City price thus rose to 18.7¢ a gallon.) Texaco also announced a 20¢-a-barrel increase in the price it would pay for crude oil nationwide. This was the first nationwide crude oil price increase since the 1957 Suez Canal crisis. (The 1968 price for a barrel of crude oil averaged $2.94.) A Texaco statement said that the increase had been made "to partially offset cost increases and to encourage exploration for and development of new oil reserves."

Phillips Petroleum Co. and the American Oil Co., a subsidiary of Standard Oil Co. (Indiana), Feb. 26 raised wholesale gasoline prices .7¢ a gallon. They suggested that dealers raise their retail prices 1¢ a gallon. Both companies attributed the increase to rising labor costs. Standard Oil Co. of California raised the price it paid for crude oil by 15¢–20¢ a barrel March 1 and its wholesale price of gasoline by .6¢–.7¢ a gallon. The general rise in gasoline prices became nearly unanimous by March 3, when the Humble Oil & Refining Co., the chief domestic subsidiary of Standard Oil Co. (N.J.), raised wholesale prices .5¢–.7¢ a gallon (effective March 1). Most companies also had raised crude oil prices 14¢–21¢ a gallon.

Sen. Edward M. Kennedy (D, Mass.) urged in a letter to President Nixon March 5 that the Administration take action to force a reversal of the oil price increase. Kennedy April 1 made public a letter in which Bryce N. Harlow, assistant to the President for Congressional rela-

tions, indicated that the Nixon Administration would examine the possibility of raising foreign oil quotas to reduce domestic prices. (Since 1957, oil imports had been limited to about 12% of domestic production.) Harlow said in his letter, dated March 19, that the Office of Emergency Preparedness would consider the 1¢-a-gallon increase in its review of the oil import program. Kennedy asserted that domestic oil prices "are propped up to extraordinarily high artificial levels only because of governmental intervention and support, and thus the government has not only the right, but the obligation to prevent those prices from going even higher." The new increases were costing consumers $2 million a day, he declared.

Fourteen Senators—13 Democrats and one Republican—petitioned Attorney General John N. Mitchell to investigate the possibility of collusion among the 14 oil companies that had raised their gasoline prices. The petition, reported April 2, said: "Because of the stringent laws against price fixing, we think the fact that all these oil companies raised their prices by almost the same amount at the same time merits close consideration."

Sen. William Proxmire (D, Wisc.) had charged March 24 that a "secret" 1967 U.S.-Canadian agreement to limit Canadian oil imports had been designed to maintain high oil prices, not to protect U.S. national security. Proxmire said that the pipeline supply of Canadian crude oil "is more secure than any production from Alaska or from our offshore wells. If national security is really the underlying theme of the oil import program, the development of such oil should be encouraged." Proxmire claimed that the oil import restrictions were costing U.S. consumers $4 billion annually. (The Interior Department had said the cost was about half this figure.)

Testifying before the Senate Antitrust & Monopoly Subcommittee April 2, Walter Adams, an economics professor and acting president of Michigan State University, described the U.S. oil industry as "a government cartel" and "a honeycomb of artificial restraints, privilege and monopoly." Adams said that the expansion of oil import quotas would have the double effect of lowering consumer prices and, by conserving U.S. reserves, of promoting national security.

The Nixon Administration Feb. 27 had delayed a decision on Maine's application for a free trade zone. Commerce Secretary Maurice H. Stans said no decision would be made until the Administration completed its review of the oil import program (ordered by Mr. Nixon Feb. 20). Maine, supported by the other New England states, had sought the foreign trade zone at Portland and a subzone at Machiasport, where a refinery would be built to refine duty-free foreign oil. Sen. George D. Aiken (R, Vt.) charged that the Administration's delay represented a veto. He said : "It's the first rift in the honeymoon. The Republicans, like the Democrats, are working with the oil companies."

In testimony before the Senate Antitrust Subcommittee April 1, Professor Joel B. Dirlam of Rhode Island University said that federal oil policy, including restrictions, was costing New England residents $325 million annually. Dirlam estimated the "excess costs" at $167 million for gasoline and $158 million for heating oil. Dirlam claimed that the proposed refinery at Machiasport could save New England consumers $158 million a year.

Air Fare Boost Approved. The Civil Aeronautics Board (CAB) Sept. 12 authorized airlines to increase domestic air fares by an average of 6.35%. The board had approved a 3.8% rise Feb. 20, 1969. The new fare schedule, effective Oct. 1 and authorized through Jan. 31, 1970, provided for sharply higher short-haul fares.

All five CAB members agreed on the need for fare increases, but two members, Vice Chairman Robert T. Murphy and G. Joseph Minetti, held the increases to be too high. The airlines had argued that recent labor settlements and inflationary trends had depressed earnings.

The new rate structure, reflecting the fact that airlines' operating costs per mile were less on long-distance flights than on short trips, provided for a $9 basic "terminal" charge for all flights to cover airport expenses. Per-mile charges were set on a sliding scale ranging from 6¢-a-mile coach fares for trips of up to 500 miles and 4.8¢-a-mile fares for flights of over 2,000 miles.

The CAB also allowed airlines to trim discounts on promotional fares: "Discover America" discounts, for travelers flying at "non-peak" hours and away at least seven days, would decline from 25% to 20%; and youth-standby discounts would drop from 50% to 40%. The decision provided for first-class fares 25% higher than coach fares.

International Trade, Payments & Monetary Problems

U.S. Trade Surplus Drops, Gold Flows Out

Inflation in the U.S. was aggravated by a decline in the nation's exports as compared with imports. The shrinkage of the foreign trade surplus (there actually was a deficit if aid-financed exports were excluded) forced the U.S. to risk weakening the dollar's value by digging into its gold and foreign currency reserves in order to pay foreign creditors.

1968 U.S. Trade Surplus Low. The Commerce Department reported Jan. 29 that the U.S. surplus of exports over imports in 1968 had fallen to $726 million, the lowest level since 1937 and well below previous estimates. Calculated on a balance-of-payments basis, the overall trade surplus was only $100 million. The year's exports totaled $33.84 billion, up 9% from 1967, while imports rose 23% to $33.114 billion.

December 1968 figures, partly distorted because of a Longshoremen's strike, showed imports of $2.947 billion—$81 million above exports of $2.866 billion.

The department reported Feb. 28 that U.S. exports had exceeded imports by $115.6 million during January. On a seasonally adjusted basis, January's exports totaled $2.082 billion, imports $1.967 billion.

January's foreign trade had been hit hard by the East and Gulf Coast dock strikes, which had lasted from Dec. 20, 1968 to Feb. 15, when the New York port reopened. The department said that exports in January had declined 28% from December and imports had dropped by 34%.

The Commerce Department reported March 27 that in February the U.S. had suffered a $361.7 million trade deficit, the largest deficit for any month on record. On a seasonally adjusted basis, imports climbed 36% from January to $2,674,400, while exports advanced only 11% to $2,312,700. The continuation of the dock strike during the month was given as the reason for the large deficit.

The Commerce Department had reported Feb. 16 that the U.S. had achieved a small trade surplus for 1968—$90 million—as measured on a balance of payments basis. In 1967, the U.S. had a $3½ billion surplus.

Gold Holdings Drop. U.S. gold holdings increased about $137 million in 1968's fourth quarter, but during all of 1968, the U.S. lost $1.173 billion in gold holdings. This annual loss was about the same as in 1967. U.S. monetary reserves increased by $1.076 billion during 1968's fourth quarter and by $880 million during all of 1968. U.S. monetary reserves Jan. 1 totaled $15.7 billion, the highest level since the third quarter of 1965.

U.S. gold holdings declined $64 million in January. This gold outflow was the largest since May 1968. An additional $27 million decline in U.S. gold holdings was registered in February, and the U.S. gold stock at the end of February was $10.801 billion. Total U.S. monetary reserves dropped by $256 million during January to $15.-454 billion. But monetary reserves increased in February by $45 million because of a $61 million increase in foreign currency holdings and an $11 million increase in automatic drawing rights from the International Monetary Fund.

Kennedy: $35 Gold to Remain. Treasury Secretary David M. Kennedy Jan. 22 ruled out any change in the official U.S. price of gold. In a statement released shortly after he had been sworn in as a member of the Nixon Cabinet, he said: "We will not seek an answer to our problems by a change in the monetary price of gold. Calm study in cooperation with our friends—not unilateral actions or disruptive changes in the vital role of the dollar and gold—must remain the foundation of real reform and progress in the international financial system." Ron Ziegler, White House press secretary, said that President Nixon had endorsed the statement. The price of gold on European bullion markets fell sharply Jan. 23 following Kennedy's clarification of the U.S. position.

The gold markets had been shaken in December 1968 after Kennedy had intimated he would take a flexible position on the official price of gold. At that time Ziegler had denied that Nixon would act to change the official price, but the price of gold on the free market had increased steadily during the following five weeks. One major reason for the rise, however, was the fact that South Africa, the world's largest producer of gold, had not been selling on the free market and supply, therefore, was curtailed; fears over the unstable Middle East situation also had contributed to the price rise.

OECD Economic Meetings. A series of meetings of Organization for Economic Cooperation and Development (OECD) organs Feb. 10–14 offered high financial officials of the Nixon Administration their first opportunity to consult with their European counterparts. The meetings were centered on balance of payments problems and the world monetary situation.

Speaking at the conclusion of a meeting of the OECD Economic Policy Committee Feb. 11, Paul McCracken, chairman of the U.S. Council of Economic Advisers, expressed confidence that the U.S. would slow down its overheated economy and improve its balance of payments surplus in 1969. West Germany also voiced assurance that its economic policy was sound, though reports indicated widespread skepticism about Germany's ability to reduce its balance-of-payments surplus. France was guarded about the effects of its new controls and the path of its economy. (Both the French trade deficit and the German trade surplus had continued to increase through the end of 1968.)

At the annual OECD ministerial conference Feb. 13, U.S. Undersecretary of State Elliot Richardson confirmed the U.S. goal of restoring a sound balance of payments. Stressing the importance of a "sizable" trade surplus in achieving this, he called for a "more open system of world trade" and urged major nations to eliminate existing discriminations "as a matter of urgency." He attacked existing obstacles to freer trade, such as import quotas, agricultural protectionism and "the threat of new discriminatory arrangements in world trade"; he also condemned the imposition of border taxes as a method of adjusting payments problems.

On the question of monetary matters, Richardson said he was in favor of the existing international monetary system, and he urged early activation of the Special Drawing Rights (SDR) agreement within the International Monetary Fund. (Paul A. Volcker, U.S. Treasury undersecretary for monetary affairs, was reported to have stated Feb. 12 that the Nixon Administration was opposed to a change in the monetary system that would allow a wider fluctuation of currency values.)

France Curbs Currency. In a further effort to restore confidence in the franc, the Bank of France Jan. 20 ordered curbs on the outflow of valuable foreign currencies. Under the new regulation, foreign currencies deposited in French banks by French residents or companies established in France could be lent only to other French residents; if such currency were lent to a foreign institution, the lending bank was required to deposit with the Bank of France an equal amount of that currency. The regulation, effective in two stages Feb. 25 and March 25, affected all banks in France, including foreign banks and branches.

The new regulation was designed to halt the outflow from France of Eurodollars, dollars deposited in European banks or held by European governments and businesses or foreign branches of American banks or businesses. In recent weeks, as credit was tightened in the U.S., Eurodollar loans had increased substantially; U.S. banks wanted Eurodollars, on which there are no reserve requirements, in order to increase their lending ability in the domestic U.S. market where credit was tight. During the week ended Jan. 29, U.S. banks had borrowed a daily average of $6.17 billion in Eurodollars from European nations, including France. The French restriction, making Eurodollar loans less readily available, was expected to curb the inflow of funds into the U.S. and thus further tighten the domestic U.S. money market.

European Speculation Renewed. Monetary tensions rose again in Europe in February and early March as French labor unrest and rumors of an imminent devaluation of the franc fed speculation on the gold and foreign currency markets. The free market price of gold hit record highs, and an increasingly weak French franc led to a faltering British pound as well. However, fears of a major international financial crisis subsided when it became clear that a one-day general strike staged in France March 11 had not led to a renewal of the May 1968 unrest and that the franc would not soon be devalued.

The free-market price of gold, which had been steady at about $42 an ounce, began a climb to record highs late in February. By March 10 gold prices had reached a London peak of $43.82 and a Zurich peak of $43.75 to $44, the highest since the establishment of the two-tier

pricing system in March 1968. Many of the buyers were thought to be French; demand had pushed prices up in the insulated Paris market and francs were believed to have been smuggled out of France to buy cheaper gold in Zurich. (The French gold market, which had reached a peak of $48.26 an ounce March 10, had been consistently higher than the markets in Zurich and London.)

In an effort to curb the smuggling of francs out of France, the Bank of France March 7 ordered the Bank for International Settlements (BIS), acting as its agent, to reduce the price at which it would buy French banknotes from Swiss banks to about 9% below the official price in Swiss francs. The move penalized anyone attempting to convert French banknotes into Swiss francs or dollars to buy gold; Swiss banks would not exchange francs at a rate above that used by the BIS.

1968 Payments Surplus. The Commerce Department's Survey of Current Business reported in its March issue that the U.S. balance of international payments had achieved a $990 million surplus after seasonal adjustment in the fourth quarter of 1968 and a favorable balance of $160 million for the year. This was the first U.S. surplus since 1957. (In 1967 the U.S. had had a $3.57 billion deficit.) A Commerce Department report Feb. 16 said that the major item in the improvement during the fourth quarter had been the large repatriation of funds from abroad by U.S. corporations. "Some of these repatriations," the report said, "had to be made to bring net capital outflows for direct investments below the 1968 ceilings established under the program announced Jan. 1 [1968] to improve the balance of payments."

On a seasonally adjusted balance, official reserve transactions showed a favorable balance of $260 million during the fourth quarter; for 1968 there was a $1.62 billion favorable balance. (In 1967 the U.S. had a $3.4 billion deficit in reserve transactions.)

Foreign Investment Curbs Eased. President Nixon announced April 4 a relaxation of some restrictions imposed by Presidents Kennedy and Johnson on

American lending and investing abroad because of the balance-of-payments problem. Mr. Nixon said the problem would be attacked by dealing "with fundamentals" and not "patchwork" controls.

Among changes detailed by Mr. Nixon and other high Administration officials: (a) For direct investment abroad by American corporations, the minimum free from control would be increased from a $200,000 quota to a $1 million quota. (b) The allowed investment quota would be revised to permit either an amount based on the current 1965-66 base period or an amount equal to 30% of the 1968 foreign earnings; for banks, foreign loans could be made at the 1968 rate or up to 1½% of the bank's total assets, whichever was greater. (c) The effective rate of the interest-equalization tax would be reduced from 1¼% to ¾% (applied to purchases of foreign stocks and bonds by Americans).

The Administration also relaxed regulations for extractive industries, including oil, and for international airlines.

Interest Rates Worry Europeans. At their monthly meeting at BIS headquarters in Basel, Switzerland, April 12-13, central bankers expressed anxiety about spiraling interest rates in Europe, particularly within the Eurodollar market.

Some bankers at the Basel meeting reportedly felt that the U.S. should take some action to protect Europe from the effects of its anti-inflation campaign. However, the Americans at the meeting argued they could do little until U.S. inflation had been brought under control. Though no details of the discussions were released, the London Times reported April 15 that the bankers had decided to leave protective action up to the individual countries.

The spiraling interest rates in the Eurodollar market and throughout Europe were due in large part to tightened U.S. credit. Domestic restrictions intended to halt inflation had caused American banks to move into the relatively unrestricted Eurodollar market, causing interest rates to soar. (Since Jan. 1, U.S. banks had bought and repatriated almost $10 billion in Eurodollars [dollars owned by people or companies outside the U.S.].) Consequently, the Eurodollar interest rate for

three-month deposits had risen to more than 8½% and the situation was reflected in soaring interest rates throughout Western Europe. (The total Eurodollar market was reported to amount to about $20 billion.) Some banking circles were concerned that the trend had forced several countries to extend exchange controls to isolate their money markets from the Eurodollar market. Within the past six weeks, nine countries had increased their discount or bank rates, the rates at which commercial banks borrow from central banks (or, in the case of Switzerland, from large private banks). The nine nations were the U.S., Canada, Switzerland, Belgium, the Netherlands, Sweden, West Germany, Denmark and Great Britain. In addition, Italy, Belgium and the Netherlands had imposed restrictions on short-term capital movements.

Dollar Holdings Down. Foreign official holdings of U.S. dollars fell $1¾ billion in January to $10.789 billion, the lowest level since 1959, the U.S. Treasury disclosed April 25. European official dollar holdings fell $1½ billion to $5.434 billion. Total dollar liabilities to foreigners, however, rose $42 million in January to $33.897 billion, presumably because of a large increase in private holdings.

The January statistics reflected U.S. banks' heavy borrowings of Eurodollars to compensate for the credit squeeze in the U.S. U.S. officials said in Paris April 24, at a meeting of Working Party 3 of the Organization for Economic Cooperation & Development, that U.S. authorities had urged leading American borrowers in the Eurodollar market to moderate their borrowing activities, which had contributed to spiraling interest rates in Europe. (A U.S. Federal Reserve spokesman said April 25 that the Federal Reserve System had made no "effort to encourage banks to moderate their Eurodollar borrowings," but Paris sources insisted that Federal Reserve officials had asked leading Eurodollar borrowers to cut down on their borrowing.)

South Africa Draws from IMF. South Africa drew $66.2 million in foreign exchange from the International Monetary Fund April 15 and thus strengthened its ability to continue withholding gold from the free market. The transaction took place under the IMF's automatic drawing rights provision and did not involve the transfer of any gold; South Africa paid in its own currency (rands) for the foreign exchange—$46.2 million in U.S. dollars and $10 million each in Canadian dollars and Japanese yen.

The U.S. Treasury indicated April 15 that the U.S. had raised no objection to the South African action because it was in line with the fund's policy that drawings in the "gold tranche" (the first quarter of each member's quota) were "virtually automatic." However, the U.S. statement added that such action "by a country that has been in a basically strong balance of payments position with rising reserves may raise certain questions as to the consistency of the drawing . . . with the broader objectives of the IMF."

South Africa turned over $47.8 million in gold to the IMF in late July in payment for foreign exchange drawn in April. The drawing had raised speculation that South Africa might use it as a method of getting rid of some gold. (Repayments normally were made in the currencies originally drawn from the IMF.) The Wall Street Journal Aug. 4 cited U. S. Treasury officials who had denied that the South African repayment in gold would hurt the operations of the two-tier gold system, since under IMF rules South Africa couldn't repeat the transaction more than once a year.

Monetary Policies Studied

Germany Rejects Revaluation. The West German government May 9 decided against an upward revaluation of the mark and thus climaxed two weeks of massive currency speculation that had developed into the fourth major international monetary crisis in 18 months. West Germany planned alternative measures to check the speculation on the mark and to limit the country's growing export surplus.

The decision, described as "final, unequivocal and for eternity," was announced after several hours of intense debate in an emergency cabinet meeting.

Speculation in the foreign currency markets had reached a peak May 9 when more than $1 billion in foreign currencies poured into West Germany.

Almost every major currency, including the Japanese yen, was hit during the height of the crisis May 8–9. On a number of foreign currency markets the mark rose to points well above its official ceiling level (3.97 marks to $1 U.S.), while the British pound and French franc fell to their lower limits, forcing heavy intervention by the British and French central banks. The Dutch guilder and the Italian lira—both strong currencies—also fell almost to their official floors and were supported by the Netherlands and Italian central banks. U.S. Treasury and Federal Reserve officials pointed out May 9, however, that the speculation was basically a flow into marks, not a rush to escape other currencies.

More than 60 West German professors and lecturers May 11 issued a statement attacking the government's decision not to revalue the mark. "The decision of May 9 will lead to a further disruption of the international monetary system through economic intervention and thus strengthen the trends towards world economic disintegration," the statement declared. "It seems to us essential that urgent steps should be taken to create a monetary system in which the exchange rates are fixed independently of group interests and electoral campaign considerations." (West German parliamentary elections were to be held Sept. 28, French presidential elections June 1.) The signatories of the statement included Wilhelm Bauer and Herbert Giersch, two of the five "wise men" who annually report to the government on the state of the economy.

The French government May 7 and 9 had delivered two protests to the West German government against the decision not to revalue the mark. According to French Information Minister Joel le Theule, the messages expressed "surprise at the public and often contradictory statements of responsible authorities in the German Federal Republic, concerning an eventual revaluation of the Deutsche mark, since these statements had brought on a new wave of speculation, ending in the present crisis." The French had tightened credit restrictions May 8 in a

move that, they stressed, had been prepared 10 days earlier and had no direct
connection with the currency crisis. The
restrictive measures included regulations
to hold down expansion of bank and consumer credit.

Denmark, especially hard hit by the
speculation, raised its bank rate May 11
from 7% to a crisis level of 9%. This unprecedented action was in reaction to
heavy losses of foreign exchange during
the monetary crisis; it made the Danish
bank rate the highest in Europe. The
London Financial Times May 12 cited
estimates that Denmark's foreign exchange reserves had fallen to 600 million kroner ($79.8 million) by May 8,
from more than 3 billion kroner ($399
million) at the beginning of the year. It
was estimated that more than 700 million kroner ($93.1 million) were lost dur-
ing the first week of May; the heavy losses
forced a halt in Denmark's foreign exchange dealings May 9. To boost its
faltering position, Denmark May 9 obtained an emergency stand-by credit
of 235 million marks ($58.8 million) from
Germany and was believed to have made
considerable use of its Federal Reserve
swap facilities, borrowing up to 800 million kroner ($106 million).

As the markets opened May 12, funds
began to flow out of West Germany in
response to the decision against revaluation and to the recycling promise of
central bankers in Basel. The outflow,
however, was smaller than the inflow had
been during the previous two weeks, and
it slowed to a relative trickle May 13.
Bankers estimated that about $700–
$800 million had left Germany during
the two days ($600 million of it May 12),
while more than $4 billion had poured in
before the West German decision to
maintain the mark's parity. (Official
estimates indicated that the total influx
had included only about $150 million of
French reserves and $500 million of
British reserves. About 60% of the funds
had come from the Eurodollar market,
40% from national reserves.)

Bonn Plans Money Curbs. The West
German cabinet's economic committee
May 13 recommended "flanking measures" to support the decision against an
upward revaluation of the mark. The
recommendations, adopted by the

cabinet May 14, were aimed at curbing
liquidity and cutting the influence of
foreign trade and monetary pressures.
Reports indicated that the measures were
milder than had been expected, causing
some fear that they might not prevent
feared inflation.

The economic committee agreed on
five basic recommendations: (1) a
freeze on excess federal and state tax
revenues to shift up to $900 million into
a "business cycle fluctuation fund"; (2)
a budget cut of $500 million; (3) the pur-
chase of $1.1 billion of short-term Ger-
man Treasury notes in 1969 and $500
million in 1970; (4) continuation of tax
adjustments instituted during the November 1968 currency crisis (a 4% reduction of taxes on imports and a 4% added
tax on exports); (5) authorization for the
Bundesbank to demand 100% minimum
reserve requirements on foreign deposits.

The cabinet May 14 unanimously endorsed these recommendations to check
speculation and hold down prices, but
the conflict within the government over
revaluation of the mark continued.

Economy Minister Karl Schiller defended in the Bundestag (parliament)
his opinion that a "fundamental imbalance" between Germany and its
partners should have led to a mark
revaluation and that the government's
decision against a parity change could
result in an even larger export surplus.

Finance Minister Franz Josef Strauss
called Schiller "absolutely wrong" in
thinking that the mark had to be revalued
in order to maintain stable prices in
Germany. He attacked the 1961 revaluation of the mark for leading to price rises
that had persisted until 1966 and maintained that the mark was currently
undervalued only in relation to the currencies of "certain countries."

Schiller accused Strauss of setting off
the recent wave of speculation by making
vague comments about multilateral currency realignments and waiting too long
to clear up the resulting confusion about
his remarks.

Schiller also confirmed reports that
the outflow of funds from Germany was
slowing down. He reported that while
$645 million in speculative funds had
left the country May 12, only $148 mil-
lion left May 13. The reluctance of speculators to dissolve their mark positions

continued throughout the week, and by May 16 less than $1 billion of the estimated $4 billion in speculative foreign funds had left West Germany. West German bankers announced May 22 that about $1.3 billion, or slightly more than one-quarter of the speculative funds, had left Germany. (Otmar Emminger, a member of the Bundesbank Board of Governors, said June 17 that $2.5 billion of speculative funds had left the country and that most of the rest had been "neutralized" by the central bank.)

In a further effort to restrict monetary liquidity in West Germany, the Bundesbank (central bank) May 22 announced an increase in minimum reserve requirements for commercial banks, effective June 1. The action called for an increase by 15% in minimum reserve requirements on domestic deposits and by 50% on foreign deposits. Bundesbank president Karl Blessing told newsmen that the measure was expected to freeze about 2.5 billion marks ($625 million). He added that the Bundesbank had taken the action because "it is our legal duty to try to keep prices down and to prevent the boom from overheating."

Schweitzer on Exchange Rates. In a speech at Queens University in Kingston, Ontario June 2, Pierre-Paul Schweitzer, managing director of the International Monetary Fund (IMF), called for a "less defensive attitude" to changes in exchange rates. Citing the strains of "a notorious series of currency crises" and the "less spectacular but more ominous . . . introduction in some cases of restrictions on currency transactions, the tinkering with border taxes, the reimposition of tightening of capital controls and a sluggish growth of aid," Schweitzer asserted that IMF founders did not "envisage that a country would have to be so much concerned about the public's changing views on the strength of its currency." He added that the current troubles of the international monetary system stemmed from "a reluctance to dampen down excessive aggregate demand until the inflationary process has caused substantial damage; and also in an unwillingness to make necessary adjustments in exchange rates, not simply for reasons of national prestige, but also because this is no easy option in terms of its effect on the real income of particular sectors of the community."

U.S. Bank Rates Increased. Leading U.S. commercial banks June 9 increased their prime interest rate from 7½% to 8½%. The unusually large increase helped to boost interest rates on Eurodollar (dollars on deposit in banks in Europe) loans to record highs. At one point these reached 13% and were a factor in subsequent decisions to increase central bank interest rates in France, West Germany and Italy.

Bankers Trust Co. of New York City led U.S. banks in increasing the prime rate—the lowest interest rate commercial banks charge their largest and best customers. The action was attributed to the shortage of money available for lending, despite Federal Reserve restraints on the expansion of credit and money. The prime rate increase, the third in 1969, led to speculation that the discount rate (the interest the Federal Reserve Board charges on loans to member banks) would be increased from its current 6%. The gap between the two rates—at 2½ percentage points—was one of the largest ever recorded.

(U.S. Secretary of the Treasury David M. Kennedy met with representatives of leading banks July 7 and July 16. After each meeting he said that none of the bankers had indicated there would be another increase in the prime lending rate. During a Senate Finance Committee hearing July 8, some Democratic senators had charged that Kennedy had not done enough to prevent a July 9 prime rate increase by commercial banks. Kennedy had said he had no authority to prevent such increases. After Kennedy's July 7 meeting with the leading U.S. bankers, Rep. Wright Patman [D, Tex.], chairman of the House Banking Committee, charged: "The secretary had the 24 largest banks in the room for 2½ hours, and he could not bring himself to speak up for the American public and ask for a rollback in interest rates.")

The Bank of France June 13 increased its discount rate from 6% to 7% in response to rising international interest rates and domestic inflationary pressures. The new rate, highest in France since 1926, approached the record 7½% imposed during a monetary crisis that year. In addition to lifting the discount rate, the bank also increased rates for short-term export credits from 4% to 5% and for advances on securities from 7½% to 8½%. French commercial banks followed the Bank of France and lifted their prime rate from 6.2% to 7.2% June 17.

The West German Bundesbank (central bank) June 19 raised its discount rate from 4% to 5% in an effort to counter the dangers of "economic overheating." An earlier increase from 3% to 4% in April had failed to slow the economy.

The Bank of Italy increased its discount rate on certain transactions from 3.5% to 5% July 1. The first increase in 10 years, it was designed to stem the flow of capital from Italy.

The Belgian National Bank had increased its discount rate May 29 from 5½% to 6%. Brussels banking sources attributed the rise to an attempt to slow the nation's activity in the Eurodollar market and to draw back capital which had flowed out of the country during the crisis over speculation on the German mark.

Copenhagen Meeting Weighs Problem. The problems faced by the Eurodollar market were discussed at the 16th annual international monetary conference of the American Bankers Association, held in Copenhagen, Denmark June 16-20. Participants in the conference included the top executives of about 150 of the largest U.S. and foreign banks. William H. Moore, chairman of the Bankers Trust Co., June 19 rejected suggestions for external controls on the Eurodollar market, asserting the answer to the current increase in interest rates was not "to curb, limit or possibly seriously damage a market which is benefiting depositors and borrowers alike." According to the New York Times June 20, the meeting's overall assessment was that little relief could be expected in the Eurodollar market until the U.S. controlled its domestic inflation.

On the key question of U.S. inflation, Paul W. McCracken, chairman of the President's Council of Economic Advisers, speaking June 18, criticized bankers for being so slow in curtailing their lending. He suggested that U.S. banks might

have continued "for too long making commitments to lend funds that weren't readily going to be available." But he rejected the call for "more severe" tax and credit restraints in the U.S., emphasizing that the U.S. was not suffering "total inflation" and that it had "a high sensitivity to unemployment. . . . " The chairman of the Federal Reserve Board, William McChesney Martin Jr., warned June 20 that the danger of a financial "collapse" existed if measures were not taken to control inflation. In a pessimistic speech, he said that he would favor consideration of voluntary credit controls, "forced savings" and a higher surtax "if things get substantially worse."

U.S. to Curb Eurodollar Flow. The Federal Reserve Board June 26 moved to apply reserve requirements to Eurodollars borrowed by its member banks and to "moderate the flow of Eurodollars between U.S. banks and their foreign branches and also between U.S. and foreign banks."

Under the board's proposals, U.S. banks borrowing Eurodollars from foreign branches would be required to hold in reserve 10% of these borrowings exceeding the average amount outstanding during the four weeks ended May 28; this reserve requirement would also apply to assets acquired by a branch from its U.S. offices. To reduce "potential inequities," Eurodollar transactions up to a minimum base of 3% of a bank's total deposits were exempt from the reserve requirement.

Secondly, the plan imposed a 10% reserve requirement on foreign branch bank loans to U.S. residents when these loans exceeded the average amount outstanding in the four weeks ended May 28 or the actual amount outstanding June 25; member banks could chose which base period they preferred. Branches with less than $5 million in loans to U.S. residents "on any day of a relevant computation period" were exempt from the requirement.

Third, the Federal Reserve Board imposed a 10% reserve requirement on borrowings by member banks from foreign banks.

The proposals further stipulated that if a bank's Eurodollar borrowings fell below the May level, the "reserve-free base" would automatically be reduced to the level of the bank's current borrowings unless the board specifically waived the rule.

With the announcement of the proposed restrictions, interest rates on Eurodollar loans fell sharply June 27. However, dealers indicated that the immediate drop was probably psychological and that the long-range prospects for the Eurodollar market were not clear.

In announcing the proposals June 26, the board said they were "designed to remove a special advantage to member banks of using Eurodollars for adjustment to domestic credit restraint. The increasing magnitude of this practice has had a distorting influence on credit flows in the U.S. and abroad." Eurodollar borrowing had reached a record total of $13.38 billion in the week ended June 18, up $7 billion since the beginning of 1969 and averaging more than $1 billion a week in the first three weeks of June. The borrowing sent interest rates on three-month Eurodollar loans soaring to as high as 13% and caused upward pressure on foreign interest rates. Some foreign central bankers specifically had asked Federal Reserve officials to modify the impact abroad of U.S. domestic financial restraints.

U.S. Payments Balance Worsens. The U.S. balance of payments for the first two quarters of 1969 showed an increasing deficit when measured on the liquidity basis. Figures reported by the Commerce Department May 15 indicated a deficit of $1.78 billion, seasonally adjusted, for the first quarter of 1969 (compared with a $850 million surplus in the final quarter of 1968). And according to the department's figures released Aug. 15, the deficit for the second quarter on the liquidity basis grew to $3.792 billion after seasonal adjustment. (The largest liquidity deficit previously recorded in any quarter was the $1.78 billion deficit in the third quarter of 1950, the Wall Street Journal reported Aug. 15.)

When measured on the official reserve transactions basis, however, the balance of payments, seasonally adjusted, rose from a surplus of $300 million in the fourth quarter of 1968 to a surplus of $1.15 billion in the first quarter of 1969

and to a surplus of $1.249 billion in the second quarter.

(Explaining the difference in the two figures, the Commerce Department said Aug. 15: "Both balances reflect changes in U.S. official reserve assets. The liquidity balance also takes into consideration the changes in liquid liabilities to all foreigners, while the official reserve transactions balance includes both liquid and certain nonliquid liabilities, but only to foreign governments and central banks.")

SDR Plan Effected. The International Monetary Fund (IMF) announced July 28 the completion of ratification of the Special Drawing Rights (SDR) plan by the required 3/5 of the fund's members (67 countries) with 4/5 of the voting power.

The plan, an amendment to the IMF Articles of Agreement, provided for establishment of internationally managed reserves, called SDRs or "paper gold," to supplement existing gold and reserve currencies in settling international accounts.

A major obstacle in implementation of the SDR plan was overcome July 24 when the Group of Ten financial powers agreed on the amount of the reserve assets to be distributed.

The ten monetary officials also agreed to increase the present IMF quotas by one-third. Thus, while the SDR agreement would increase world liquidity by $9.5 billion over three years, an additional $6 billion to $7 billion in enlarged quotas would be available during the next five years.

(The Group of Ten consisted of Belgium, Britain, Canada, France, West Germany, Italy, Japan, Sweden, the Netherlands and the U.S. Switzerland was a partial participant.)

The decision on the amount of SDRs to be activated represented a major compromise between the U.S. and Europe. The U.S., supported by Canada and presumably Great Britain, had supported a massive infusion of paper gold—$4 billion to $5 billion annually for five years. European creditor nations, on the other hand, favored a much more cautious initial approach—$2 billion a year over three years. The monetary committee of the European Economic Community agreed July 23 to accept a $2.5 billion annual allocation for three years.

France Devalues Franc. The French government devalued the franc by 11.1% Aug. 8 in a move that caught other governments and the financial world completely by surprise.

The decision, which was announced following an unscheduled French cabinet meeting Friday evening, after most of the world's financial markets were closed for the weekend, reduced the value of the franc from .18 grams of gold to .16 grams of gold, or from 20.255 U.S. cents to 18.004 U.S. cents. (Depending on the method used to calculate the devaluation, the percentage change was 12.5% or 11.1%.) The new parity officially went into effect Aug. 10, following approval that day by the International Monetary Fund.

In a nationwide radio and television address Aug. 8, minutes after the announcement, French President Georges Pompidou expressed his conviction that the devaluation was "unavoidable." Noting that the franc had been "traded on foreign markets at a sizable discount," he said: "To pretend to overcome this handicap would be to choose a policy of brutal deflation that would impose on the country intolerable sacrifices and massive unemployment and which, moreover, would jeopardize our investments—hence, our future."

Pompidou stressed that the franc's devaluation was only a "starting point" toward restoring the French economy to health and that the government was preparing, "in the budgetary, financial and economic fields, a vigorous and rigorous overall action. . . ."

Finance Minister Valery Giscard d'Estaing, speaking after Pompidou, pointed out that the government's action was a "recognition of the franc's real value" as assessed by foreign currency buyers on the forward market, where the franc had been traded at a discount of 11% to 12%. "Had we not acted by the end of the year," he declared, "the real French reserves [reported central bank reserves minus short-term debts] . . . would have amounted to practically nothing. And at the end of the first half of 1970 . . . they would have had a nega-

tive balance." In addition, he explained, the weakness of "our monetary situation . . . exposed us to the threats of international speculation."

France's financial woes stemmed from national student-worker disruptions in May and June 1968. Reserves had fallen from more than $6 billion before May 1968 to $3.5 billion by the end of July 1969. Moreover, the reported reserves did not include reserve losses of more than $1 billion in short-term borrowings from foreign central banks. In addition, France's trade balance had worsened during 1969.

Price Freeze Ordered. In an effort to block a surge of price increases and inflation, the French government ordered a nationwide freeze on prices Aug. 10. The government decree, effective until Sept. 15, ordered virtually all industrial prices and wholesale and retail markups held at Aug. 8 levels. Although markups were frozen on 10 fruits and vegetables currently in season, the decree did not mention other farm prices, since action on these depended on the outcome of an emergency European Economic Community (EEC) meeting in Brussels Aug. 11–12.

The Finance Ministry warned that firms refusing to heed the price freeze would be subject to sanctions and future price control. A ministry source noted that exceptions to the order would be allowed only if a firm could prove that it had been forced to pay more for imports because of the devaluation.

14 African Nations Devalue. Representatives of the 14 former French colonies, currently independent members of the franc zone, met in Paris Aug. 10 and decided to realign their currencies with the devalued franc. The action was expected since the currencies of the 14 nations were pegged to the franc, their reserves were on deposit with the Bank of France and France was their chief market and source of imports and aid. The 14 countries: Mauritania, Senegal, Ivory Coast, Dahomey, Togo, Niger, Mali, Upper Volta, Congo (Brazzaville), the Central African Republic, Chad, Gabon, Cameroon and the Malagasy Republic.

Foreign Reaction. International reaction to the French devaluation was reserved but marked by surprise.

The U.S. Treasury Department issued a statement Aug. 8 describing the devaluation as "an adjustment to economic developments in France during the past year." The statement added: "This action will not affect the value of the United States dollar."

In Britain, treasury officials expressed confidence Aug. 8 that the French devaluation would not cause a devaluation of the pound. "There is no question of sterling following the franc," a spokesman said.

The British announced Aug. 13 that the trade deficit had widened in July to £37 million ($88.8 million), from June's deficit of £25 million ($60 million). The news hit the foreign exchange markets, where the pound was pressed under heavy selling and the Bank of England intervened repeatedly to support sterling.

The West German government welcomed the devaluation and reportedly viewed it as a vindication of its own refusal to revalue the mark upward.

Belgium confirmed Aug. 9 that the value of the Belgian franc would not be lowered, although Premier Gaston Eyskens conceded that the French action would hurt exports to France, one of Belgium's biggest customers.

The Italian Treasury Ministry asserted Aug. 9 that the "parity of the lira to the dollar and its value in gold will remain unchanged."

The U.S. dollar also came under pressure in Frankfurt, West Germany Aug. 14, as speculators bought German marks. The pressure lifted Aug. 18, however, and the value of the dollar increased in light trading, while the mark fell. The Belgian franc was also under considerable pressure, and the Belgian central bank tightened credit restrictions.

World Bank Raises Lending Rate. The International Bank for Reconstruction & Development (World Bank) disclosed Aug. 12 that it had increased its lending rate from 6½% to 7%. The decision, taken earlier by bank president Robert S. McNamara in consultation with the organization's executive directors, was revealed in a routine announcement of a $34 million loan to the Philippines that stipulated a 7% interest rate. World Bank officials said Aug. 12 that the rate increase was due to the rising cost of the organization's borrowings, which averaged 6.46% on bonds sold in fiscal 1969, compared with 6.17% in 1968. The new rate applied only to the bank's regular loans and did not affect the interest-free loans extended by the International Development Association (IDA), the bank's subsidiary for making soft loans.

Mark Allowed to 'Float.' Following a West German election Sept. 21 that was marked by sharp debate on proposals for revaluation of the mark, the coalition government Sept. 29 temporarily freed the German mark from its fixed exchange rate and allowed its value to fluctuate freely in foreign currency markets. The government took the action by ordering the Bundesbank (central bank) to disregard its IMF obligation to sell marks when buying sent the price more than 1% above its official parity (3.98 marks to the U.S. dollar). Foreign exchange markets in West Germany, closed since Sept. 25 in an effort to stave off speculative buying of the mark, were ordered to reopen Sept. 30.

In a supplementary action, the government also requested the Bundesbank to make "far-reaching" use of its powers to restrict the inflow of foreign funds by increasing the minimum reserve rate for foreign holdings in West German commercial banks.

Finance ministers and central bank officials, in Washington for the annual meeting of the IMF (International Monetary Fund), reportedly expressed approval of the West German action. Informing IMF delegates of the West German decision, IMF Managing Director Pierre Paul Schweitzer Sept. 29 said Bonn officials would "maintain close contact with the fund and resume the maintenance of the limits around par at the earliest opportunity." Noting that Bonn "technically" was not honoring its IMF obligations to support parity, he said he thought the action was the "wisest thing to do."

U.S. Treasury Secretary David M. Kennedy called the West German decision "understandable in the light of the present circumstances," and expressed the belief that it "will serve a constructive purpose in dampening potential speculative forces."

In foreign exchange markets Sept. 30, the mark increased in value by 4% to 5%. Trading was reported active, but orderly. The British pound improved, while the French franc remained under pressure and was supported by the Bank of France. The Belgian central bank suspended official trading of marks Sept. 30. The central banks of Italy, Sweden and Finland, which had already suspended official dealings in marks, continued their suspensions.

'Paper Gold,' Other Issues on Agenda. Top economic and financial officials from 112 nations gathered in Washington, D.C. Sept. 29–Oct. 3 for the annual, concurrent meetings of the International Monetary Fund and the three institutions of the World Bank Group—the International Bank for Reconstruction and Development (World Bank), the International Development Association (IDA) and the International Finance Corporation (IFC).

During the meetings, IMF delegates officially approved the allocation of Special Drawing Rights (SDRs)—also known as "paper gold"—and voted to increase the Fund's quotas. Proposals to increase the flexibility of currency values were among the most-discussed issues at the meetings, but no specific decisions were taken on the matter.

Reviewing the international monetary scene of the past year, IMF Managing Director Pierre-Paul Schweitzer warned in his opening address Sept. 29 that "the long delay in bringing inflation under control in the United States has had especially serious consequences" for the health of the world's economy. He expressed disappointment at the existence of inflation of "exceptional and surely unacceptable magnitude," but he praised U.S., British and French efforts to control it and stressed that these efforts "should be pressed to the point at which they show unequivocal results."

On the issue of currency stability, Schweitzer declared that foreign exchange markets had shown "strains and disturbances . . . too frequent for comfort" during the past year. He explained

that the Fund would "investigate whether a limited increase in flexibility of exchange rate variation would be desirable and attainable, with the necessary safeguards and through what means any such increased flexibility might be achieved."

In addresses Sept. 30, delegates from the U.S., Great Britain, France and Italy, speaking in the wake of the West German decision to "float" the mark in exchange dealings, cautiously supported the idea of investigating proposals for flexible exchange rates among currencies. U.S. Treasury Secretary David M. Kennedy concluded that proposals "to define and develop techniques of limited flexibility need not be looked upon as radical new departures from the mainstream of developments in the monetary areas." "Instead," he pointed out, "they seem . . . to fall within the framework of orderly and evolutionary change and of multilateral monetary cooperation." However, Kennedy stressed that the U.S. had "reached no conclusion on the desirability of any particular proposal."

Annual Reports Published. The international monetary meeting followed publications of the IMF and World Bank Group annual reports for fiscal 1969. The IMF report, released Sept. 21, revealed that members' purchases of currencies had reached a record high of more than $2.8 billion. "The high level of the fund's financial assistance during the period was largely a reflection of the continuing payments imbalance among industrial countries and recurring uncertainties in foreign exchange markets," the report stated. "At the same time," the document continued, "the fund's financial assistance continued to be important for a number of developing countries; the total amount of $527 million purchased by these countries was a slight reduction from that in 1967–68."

The World Bank-IDA report, issued Sept. 26, revealed that commitments by the bank, IDA and IFC during fiscal 1969 totaled $1.877 billion, almost double the level achieved in the previous year and 67% above the average of the previous five years. The World Bank extended 84 loans totaling $1.399 billion, compared with 44 loans totaling $847 million the previous year. IDA, the bank's soft-loan affiliate, extended 38 credits totaling $385 million, compared with 18 credits totaling $107 million in fiscal 1968.

U.S. Raises Swap Arrangements. The U.S. Federal Reserve System announced Oct. 9 that its swap arrangements with central banks of Austria, Denmark and Norway had been increased from $100 million to $200 million each. The Federal Reserve Aug. 29 had announced an increase of its swap credit line with Belgium from $300 million to $500 million. The increases brought the total swap network (a short-term facility under which a central bank pledges to exchange its currency for another nation's currency on demand for a limited amount of time) to $10.98 billion. The network included 14 central banks and the Bank for International Settlements and was administered by the New York Federal Reserve Bank during and following periods of heavy, short-term currency flows.

Bank Rate Increases. The Bank of France Oct. 8 announced an increase in its discount rate from 7% to 8%, the highest level in French history. The increase came in the wake of increasing pressure on the French franc in the foreign currency markets and was announced the same day the government approved the 1970 budget. French President Georges Pompidou told his cabinet Oct. 8: "All facts point up the formal and absolute determination of the government to insure balanced finances. The franc isn't threatened. The franc doesn't have to be defended. The measures that have been taken have been shaped so that the franc won't even be challenged."

(French commercial banks raised their prime rates Oct. 13 from 7.6% to 8.75% for short and medium-term loans.)

The West German Bundesbank (central bank) raised its discount rate from 5% to 6% Sept. 11. The new rate was the highest in 18 years. Karl Blessing, Bundesbank president, said the bank had felt "forced to act" since the "economy really needed strong measures to keep it from overheating." (The West German Lombard rate, which applies to rates charged commercial banks on Bundesbank loans, was raised from 6% to 7.5% Sept. 11 and to 9% Dec. 4.)

Commercial banks in Britain Sept. 17 raised their prime lending rate to 9%, effective Oct. 1. The action was taken "to reduce the current pressure on bank lending."

The Belgian central bank raised its discount rate to a record 7.5% from 7%, effective Sept. 18; it was the fifth increase in 1969. The action was explained as an effort to dampen inflation and to inhibit the outflow of funds from the country. The Belgian central bank had increased its discount rate from 6% to 7% July 30.

The central bank of Austria raised its discount rate on loans within Austria to 4¾% from 3¾%, effective Sept. 11. The move was an attempt to slow the outflow of gold from Austria to nations with higher interest rates. Other Austrian banks were required by law to follow suit and charge the new rate on loans.

The Italian Treasury Ministry announced Aug. 13 that the Bank of Italy had raised its bank rate from 3.5% to 4%, effective Aug. 14, for banks not covered by the June increase to 5%. The announcement said the measure was necessary to maintain stable prices and because of the international monetary situation. It added that excessive credit had threatened to increase prices and damage Italy's economic program.

Germany Makes Two IMF Drawings. West Germany gained $1.09 billion in foreign currencies from the International Monetary Fund (IMF) in separate transactions Nov. 25 and Dec. 10. The drawings were designed to replenish German reserves in response to the heavy outflow of funds following the revaluation of the mark.

The IMF announced Nov. 25 that Germany had purchased the equivalent of $540 million in seven currencies held by the Fund. The purchase was within Germany's gold tranche position in the IMF and restored the Fund's holdings of the West German mark to 75% of Germany's quota.

The IMF announced Dec. 10 that Germany had received a further $550 million from the organization. The second transaction represented repayment of Germany's past loans to the IMF under the 1962 General Arrangements to Borrow (GAB), an agreement under which the Group of 10 industrial nations pledged up to $6 billion in loans when needed to increase the IMF's supply of usable currencies.

Gold Prices Fall. The price of gold on the free market plunged sharply in November and early December, finally edging below the official price of $35 an ounce in trading on the London and Zurich bullion markets Dec. 8 and 9. (Prices on the Paris and Frankfurt markets also fell, but remained well above the London and Zurich lows.)

The official London closing price was set at $35.05 an ounce Dec. 8, but later unofficial dealings fell to a range of $34.90 to $35.10 an ounce. Zurich dealers quoted a closing price range of $34.95 to $35.15 an ounce Dec. 8. Prices continued to sag Dec. 9, closing at $35 an ounce in London and $34.90 an ounce in Zurich.

Dealers indicated that the price slump reflected a lack of buying interest rather than heavy speculative selling, since sales volume was small.

Gold prices on the free market rallied slightly Dec. 10–12, increasing to a final fixing of $35.10 an ounce in Zurich Dec. 11 and $35.30 an ounce in London Dec. 12.

IMF-South Africa Gold Accord. The International Monetary Fund (IMF) Dec. 30 announced approval of an agreement stipulating the conditions under which it would buy newly-mined gold from South Africa. The announcement followed a basic agreement reached by U.S. and South African officials in Rome Dec. 15 after more than a year of negotiations among the U.S., South Africa and major European countries.

Under the new arrangement, the IMF pledged to buy newly-mined South African gold at the official price of $35 an ounce when one of two conditions existed: if the free market price of gold fell to or below the official price, or if South Africa sustained a balance of payments deficit after selling all current new gold production on the free market over a six-month period.

Other provisions of the agreement stipulated that the IMF could buy up to $35 million quarterly from the South African gold stock held at the time the two-tier price system was instituted March 17, 1968. In addition, South Africa was authorized to continue using gold in its regular transactions with the IMF.

In return, South Africa pledged to sell most of its newly-mined gold "in an orderly manner in the private [free] market to the full extent of current payments needs." The IMF announcement added: "South Africa has also stated that when selling gold other than in the private market it intends in practice normally to offer such gold to the Fund. The Fund took the decision to purchase gold from South Africa with the understanding that members generally do not intend to initiate gold purchases directly from South Africa."

Wheat Price War

Surplus' Effect. Mounting surpluses caused major wheat-exporting nations to lower their prices and thus set off a major price war that undermined the price structure of the International Grains Arrangement (IGA). The main exporting signatories of the IGA—the U.S., Canada, Australia, the European Economic Community (mostly France) and Argentina—held several meetings but were unable to reach a workable solution to the price question. (Argentina, normally an exporting country but plagued with bad weather and poor crops, had recently supplied its traditional export markets with wheat imported from the Soviet Union, traditionally a wheat importing country.)

The price war had been building throughout the spring of 1969. The five IGA exporters had met in Washington in March but had found no solution. The U.S. called another meeting in Washington July 10–11 and, according to the London Economist July 19, indicated that if IGA members failed to observe the wheat price minimums stipulated in the agreement, the U.S. would consider withdrawing from it. A communique issued after the meeting stated that the five exporters had reviewed the price situation, had recognized "distortions" and had agreed that "corrective action" would be taken by some of the signatories to bring prices back into line. Following the meeting, Australia and the EEC, according to the Toronto Globe and Mail July 23, had announced that they would hold back some of their wheat exports temporarily, and a total collapse in the price structure was averted.

Price cuts on certain grades of wheat shipped from the eastern and gulf coasts were announced by the U.S. July 18, however. In order to maintain effective competition with the U.S., Canada announced price reductions July 21, but the Canadian cuts were not as large as those made by the U.S. The U.S. action was the first official announcement by an IGA signatory that it was selling below the minimum price level set in the arrangement, although other countries had been stretching the IGA regulations earlier to the extent that wheat prices had already fallen. (According to Business Week magazine Aug. 9, the French had begun the price war by cutting the price of wheat exported to Taiwan. The French, however, claimed that the action did not violate IGA terms, since the cut was based on their "internal price structure.")

The EEC announced an increase in subsidies for wheat exporters July 28; it thus allowed them to lower prices in retaliation for the U.S. and Canadian price cuts. (The increase in the subsidy, from 7% to 16%, went into effect July 31.) An EEC communique July 28 accused the U.S. and Canada of unilaterally undermining the IGA but stressed the Common Market's willingness to cooperate with IGA regulations; it indicated that the EEC measures would remain in effect only as long as the agreed minimum price levels were undercut by other countries.

Senior officials of IGA exporters called a special meeting in London Aug. 1–2. Though details of the session were not made public, Canadian Trade & Commerce Minister Jean-Luc Pepin indicated that the officials had discussed the "possibility of a rollback in prices" to the levels prevailing before the July 10 Washington meeting, the Globe and Mail reported Aug. 5. Pepin described both the U.S. and Canada as willing to return to the higher levels, but he said the EEC delegation had not accepted the proposal.

Unable to reach an agreement in London, the officials set up a standing technical committee to keep the international wheat situation under constant review. The committee, composed of technical experts from the five IGA exporters, met in London Aug. 11–12 and agreed on a new system for compiling world wheat statistics in order to provide exporting nations with better market data. However, it was unable to reach agreement on price levels.

Japan heightened the crisis July 30 by announcing that it refused to purchase U.S. and Australian wheat until the two countries reduced prices for wheat exports to Asia. (The U.S., Canada and Australia had lowered prices of wheat shipped to Europe but had retained the higher prices for wheat shipped to Asia; the U.S. and Canada had also retained higher prices for wheat exported to Latin America.) Japan announced Aug. 8 that it had decided to buy wheat from France, Belgium and Argentina but to maintain its boycott of purchases from the U.S., Canada and Australia, traditionally the three principal suppliers of wheat to Japan.

The controversy with Japan was eased Aug. 12 when the U.S. lowered wheat export prices for Asian and Latin American markets in an attempt "to help U.S. wheat regain its previously competitive position in a world market situation where current and projected supplies exceed demand by a large margin." Japan resumed purchases of U.S. wheat Aug. 12, following the U.S. announcement. Canada duplicated the U.S. action Aug. 13 and lowered prices for its wheat exports to Asia and Latin America, while Australia lowered prices for exports to Japan. Brazil, which had also halted wheat purchases, announced that it would end its boycott, the New York Times reported Aug. 14.

Canada again lowered wheat export prices Aug. 20. According to the New York Times Aug. 25, Canada had cut wheat export prices at least six times since the IGA went into effect July 1, 1968. In addition, the Australian Wheat Board was authorized to adjust prices for individual bids by importers without obtaining formal agreement of the government.

The U.S. announced another round of price cuts Aug. 26, but stressed that it was using "all possible restraint" in the reductions. The adjustments, which differed by grade of wheat and port of shipment, were intended "to maintain a competitive price for United States wheat in world markets," an announcement by Secretary of Agriculture Clifford M. Hardin stated. Hardin added: "We shall continue to use restraint because of our interest in preserving the International Grains Arrangement and urge other exporting countries to follow a similar practice. I hope today's action will bring price stability in world wheat markets."

(Hardin announced Aug. 11 that the U.S. had cut wheat acreage allotments for the 1970 crop to 45.5 million acres, from 51.6 million in 1969. Under the new order, the third annual reduction in acreage allotments, farmers were eligible for basic price support loans of $1.25 per bushel, plus additional payments for their share of wheat used domestically. In making the announcement, Hardin expressed optimism that after the "recent sessions of the major exporters, we are moving toward recognition of our determination to maintain the U.S. share of world wheat trade." He noted, however, that "it is likely there will be an additional buildup of wheat supplies by next July 1.")

Background—The wheat price war stemmed from a large world wheat surplus that, in turn, had developed from a steady upsurge in wheat production over a period of two years. In 1968 world wheat production reached a record 305 million tons, 10% above 1967 and 7% above 1966. By the beginning of 1969, the main IGA exporting nations had wheat surpluses totaling 3.2 billion bushels, or more than twice the amount of wheat exported in a single year. In addition, India and Pakistan, traditional importers, had achieved spectacular increases in wheat production through the use of improved fertilizers, better irrigation and high-yield strains of wheat; the two countries drastically reduced their imports of wheat in the past two years and were expected to become exporters by the mid-1970s. The Soviet Union (not an IGA signatory), which had been a large wheat importer, also had produced bumper crops in recent years and had become an exporter. (The U.S.S.R. and other smaller non-IGA signatories were reported to be exporting almost 20% of the wheat shipped in the world wheat trade.)

The International Grains Arrangement had been negotiated at the Kennedy Round tariff conference in 1967. Mainly an extension of the International Wheat Agreement of 1949, it went into force July 1, 1968.

1970

By early 1970 it was evident that the Nixon Administration was succeeding in slowing the rate of U.S. economic growth—but there was no clear evidence yet as to whether this controversial policy would halt the increasing inflation. Prices continued to climb during 1970, and so did wages. As the economy "cooled," the rate of unemployment soared, corporate profits declined, the auto industry was especially hard hit, and stock market prices plunged. Economists, government officials, legislators and businessmen argued with increasing concern as to whether the U.S. should institute wage and price controls. Congress passed legislation authorizing such curbs, but President Nixon said he would not use them. In the absence of wage-price controls, the Administration continued to rely partly on persuasion and partly on budgetary, monetary and other government tools in the attempt to keep prices and wages down. The President appointed a National Commission on Productivity to try to restore stability by averting excessive production costs, and he became embroiled in dispute with Congress over what he described as excessive Congressional spending. The drain in U.S. monetary reserves continued as a result of unfavorable balances of trade and international payments. International agencies, without much apparent success, attempted to combat an increasingly menacing worldwide inflationary tide.

Government Policy

Economy 'Cools,' Inflation Continues

By January 1970 there were indications
that the Nixon Administration was succeeding in at least one aspect of its anti-
inflation strategy. The economy, which
Administration spokesmen had considered
"overheated," was "cooling off." Industrial growth was leveling off, construction was declining, and unemployment was
growing. The increase in prices and wages
showed no sign of moderating, however,
and critics were already denouncing the
Nixon economic policy as a failure.

Economic growth halts. A slowing of
the U.S. economy—a major goal of the
Nixon Administration in its anti-inflation
efforts—was indicated by federal reports
released Jan. 15-16. But there was little
or no evidence that the inflation itself
was slackening. The Labor Department
reported Jan. 19 that consumer prices
had risen .6% in December 1969 and
said the rise in consumer prices during
the year 1969 had reached 6.1%, the
largest annual gain since 1951.

The slowdown was confirmed by reports Jan. 16 of December activity—
further declines in industrial production
and housing starts and the smallest gain
in personal income of any month in 1969.

Industrial production was reported by
the Federal Reserve Board Jan. 16 at a
level of 170.9 in December 1969, with

the 1957-59 period taken as 100. The
November 1969 index was (revised)
171.4. The decline went into its fifth consecutive month and amounted to a 3.7
point (2.1%) decline since July 1969. (The
December statistic reflected an 8% decline in auto assemblies to a seasonally
adjusted annual rate of 7.2 million units.
Other declines were registered in household appliances and television sets.)

The personal income data was reported Jan. 16 by the Commerce Department, which also reported that housing
starts reached a 1969 low in December
at an annual rate of 1,245,000, compared
with 1,297,000 in November and the
January 1968 peak of 1,878,000 housing
starts.

(The Commerce Department reported Jan. 9 that retail sales in 1969
rose 4%, from a total $339.32 billion in
1968 to $352.08 billion. However, govern-
ment economists noted that the figures
indicated that the volume of goods sold
in 1969 was somewhat less than 1968 because the increase in dollar sales fell
short of the year's overall rise in prices.

(The Commerce Department March 17
reported a decline in corporate profits
in the final quarter of 1969 at an estimated annual rate of $91.6 billion—about
$1 billion below the third quarter rate and
$4 billion below the $95.5 billion in the
first quarter. It was the steepest drop of
the year. On the basis of data from 900

57

companies, 1969 pre-tax profits were estimated at $93.8 billion—a $2.7 billion [3%] rise above the 1968 total. Total after-tax earnings fell about $600 million to a total $49.1 billion. Inventory profits [the value increase of goods between the time of purchase and the time taken from inventory] rose $2.5 billion from 1969's third to fourth quarters.)

1969 corporate financing. An SEC report Feb. 4 estimated that corporations raised a record $26.8 billion from the sale of securities in 1969. Sales of new corporate securities were 22% higher than 1968. The SEC said the sale of 1,836 new common stock issues brought gross proceeds totaling $7.7 billion, up from 1,130 issues at $3.9 billion in 1968. It was also reported that the number of companies registering stock with the SEC for the first time in 1969 reached 1,270—nearly double the 1968 figure. Debt financing totaled $18.4 billion and preferred stock financing registered a slight increase to $700 million. Financing by manufacturing firms declined $700 million to $6.3 billion.

Tight money policy criticized. The monetary policy of the Federal Reserve Board was criticized by Labor Secretary George P. Shultz Jan. 6 as "too tight right now." It could "precipitate an acceleration" of the current economic slowdown, he said. While a "policy of restraint" should be pursued, he said it should not be so drastic. Shultz stressed that his view was a personal one and not an expression of the Administration. He made the remarks at a news conference.

Similar criticism of the Administration's tight money policy was expressed by labor leader Walter P. Reuther and economist Walter W. Heller.

Reuther, president of the United Automobile Workers, said in Detroit Jan. 8 that "unless the government begins to do something about its overly restrictive economic policies and its obsession with fighting inflation, the economy will continue to worsen....." "We haven't got a recession yet," he said, "but if we keep moving the way we are, in three or four months we will." Reuther said the high cost of credit, sustained by Administra-

tion policy, was itself "the most inflationary" factor in the economy. He favored more selective monetary control —credit priorities with a fixed and lower interest rate for certain areas, such as housing, school and hospital construction, and with the remainder of available credit put "up for grabs at whatever costs" borrowers were willing to pay.

Heller, former chairman of the President's Council of Economic Advisers, warned Jan. 9 that "damaging economic and social consequences" might result unless the tight monetary policy were eased. "A modest relaxation" of the tight policy, which could contribute to the inflation, he said, seemed to be "the lesser risk" than too tight control which could lead to a recession.

His remarks were contained in an economic forecast released by the National City Bank of Minneapolis, of which Heller, chairman of the economics department at the University of Minnesota, was a director.

Home loan interest ceiling raised. An 8½% interest rate ceiling on federally-guaranteed home mortgages was effective Jan. 5. The increase (the rate since Jan. 24, 1969 had been 7½%) was announced Dec. 30, 1969 by George Romney, secretary of housing and urban development, and applied to all new loans, except for two special low-income programs, insured by the Federal Housing Administration and the Veterans Administration.

Romney said he took the action with "great reluctance" forced by "the realities of the marketplace." "Market yields on most types of investments," he said, "have risen by more than one percentage point" since January 1969.

Romney expected the new ceiling to "reduce to more reasonable size the discounts now prevailing." Although the increase would lead to higher interest rates on home mortgage loans, lenders were expected under the new rate to reduce the amount of "points," or discount, charged, currently running at a rate of 10 or more points.

The action was expected to increase the flow of funds in the mortgage market. In November 1969, savings associations closed 24% fewer mortgage loans than in November 1968, and commitments for future lending decreased to $876 million from a 1969 monthly high of $1.8 billion.

The increase to the 8½% rate was opposed by the National Association of Home Builders, which preferred formal credit controls, and backed by the Mortgage Bankers Association of America, which expected it to help ease the "intolerable" problems in the mortgage market.

Savings interest rates raised. The Federal Reserve Board and the Federal Deposit Insurance Corp. (FDIC) announced Jan. 20 increased interest rate ceilings that commercial and savings banks could pay their savings depositors.

The Federal Reserve raised maximum rates at commercial banks from: (1) 4% to 4.5% on regular passbook savings accounts; (2) 5% to 5.5% on a one-year savings certificate; (3) 5% to 5.75% on a two-year certificate; and (4) 6.25% to 7.5% on one-year certificates of deposit (CDs) —time deposits of $100,000 or more. CD rates would still remain below other short-term rates in the money market, minimizing possible large inflows of funds into banks. Rather, the rate increases were intended to help banks check a massive outflow of funds.

Although the regular passbook account rate of 5% was unchanged at savings banks, the FDIC raised the ceiling for 90-day deposits to 5.25%, to 5.75% for one-year deposits and 6% for deposits held for two years or longer.

Housing problem recognized. President Nixon Jan. 21 pledged his Administration would "take every possible step to solve this most serious housing problem consistent with the overriding need to contain inflation." The pledge was made in a statement affirming the "top national priority" of housing. The President had met Jan. 20 with George Romney, secretary of housing and urban development (HUD), and officials of the National Association of Home Builders, (NAHB). NAHB President Louis R. Barba said Jan. 21 that Presidential recognition "of our severe problems" was "of tremendous consequence."

In his statement, Nixon reaffirmed his intention to avoid unnecessary federal spending and urged "the private sector to follow this example by also postponing avoidable expenditures and increasing savings."

Paul W. McCracken, chairman of the Council of Economic Advisers, in briefing newsmen on Nixon's statement, conceded that the housing industry was "in a recession." Largely because of a severe shortage of mortgage funds, housing starts fell to an annual rate of 1.4 million in 1969—1.8 million at the start of the year and 1.2 million at the end. An "adequate" annual rate, Mc-Cracken said, would be from 1.5-1.7 million.

McCracken pointed out that he did not "see any evidence yet" that the economy as a whole was moving into a recession, and he expressed confidence that a federal budget surplus could ease the financing pinch for housing.

Romney, appearing before the NAHB convention in Houston, Tex. Jan. 19, said an end to inflation was "the absolutely indispensable foundation" for sound housing. He disclosed a new federal program to finance home purchases by low-income families and subsidize interest payments. The program, expected to initially provide financing for about 32,250 homes, involved sale of mortgages held by HUD's Government National Mortgage Association to the Federal National Mortgage Association. $500 million was to be allocated for subsidizing such sales as well as interest payments to the lender.

Labor Secretary George P. Shultz also addressed the homebuilders Jan. 19 and reiterated his view that a "moderate relaxation" of federal fiscal restraints "is in order." But he expected that "continued application of restraint" would ease the "inflationary pressure."

Both Shultz and Romney denounced labor contract settlements signed by the industry within the past year—some of which called for 50% increases over a three-year period—as inflationary. Romney, calling the wage settlements "outrageous," warned that "we cannot afford to neglect the wage-cost-price spiral." Shultz, renewing the Administration's stand against wage and price controls, indicated the government might direct its spending away from high-cost areas into low-cost areas.

President's Views & Actions

Nixon seeks Congress' aid. In his State-of-the-Union message, delivered Jan. 22, President Nixon called for Congressional aid in halting inflation, and he warned against dangers posed by unwise growth.

He urged Congress to join in "the battle to stop the rise in the cost of living." For his part, the President pledged to submit a balanced budget for 1971. As for crime, it was "one area" where he was requesting "an increase rather than a cut" in funds which would be directed toward law enforcement.

In his warning about growth, Nixon said "the critical question is not whether we will grow but how we will use that growth." While the 1960s had been a period of great economic growth, he said, there had also been great growth in crime, inflation and social unrest. "At heart," he said, "the issue is effectiveness of government" and the government had "proved unable" to fulfill the "large expectations" it had helped to generate.

"In the next 10 years we shall increase our wealth by 50%," he said, but "the profound question is: Does this mean we will be 50% richer in a real sense . . .?" Or would it mean that in the coming decade 70% of the population would live "in metropolitan areas choked by traffic, suffocated by smog, poisoned by water, deafened by noise and terrorized by crime?" "Shall we surrender to our surroundings," he asked, "or shall we make our peace with nature and begin to make reparations for the damage we have done to our air, to our land and to our water." It was an issue beyond partisanship, he asserted.

(In his continued persistent attention to the anti-inflation effort, President Nixon at a cabinet meeting Jan. 13 ordered further substantial cuts in the "final" figures submitted by the Budget Bureau for the fiscal 1971 federal budget. The "additional substantial cuts" were achieved, White House Press Secretary Ronald L. Ziegler said Jan. 19.)

Defense job cuts outlined. Defense Secretary Laird, at a news conference in Los Angeles Jan. 15, said about 1,250,000 jobs would be eliminated as a result of defense manpower and spending reductions already made or scheduled to be made before July 1, 1971. Laird said the layoffs would involve government civilian and military employes as well as defense industry workers.

At a speech later that day to the California Chamber of Commerce, Laird said military manpower strength would decrease by 300,000 men by June 30, 1970, representing a cut of about 35,000 men beyond previously announced reductions.

The Pentagon Jan. 9 had announced the elimination of 7,310 civilian jobs at 50 military installations around the U.S. at a reported saving of $57 million. The layoffs were a result of plans to reduce expenditures for fiscal 1970 (ending June 30).

School aid bill vetoed. President Nixon Jan. 26 vetoed the fiscal 1970 appropriations bill (HR13111) for the Labor and Health, Education and Welfare Departments as inflationary. The President signed his veto message and explained his action on a nationwide TV broadcast. He returned the bill without his signature, accompanied by his veto message, to Congress Jan. 27. The House had passed the bill Jan. 26 by voice vote. The Senate had approved the funds by a 74–17 vote Jan. 20. The veto was sustained by the House, and a smaller appropriation was ultimately enacted.

As originally adopted, the measure would have appropriated some $1.1 billion more than the President's requests and $1.26 billion more than requested in the fields of education and health. Noting that he had already ordered $7 billion cut from fiscal 1970 spending, Nixon said Jan. 26: "If I had approved the increased spending contained in this bill, I would win the approval of many fine people who are demanding more spending by the federal government for education and health. But I would be surrendering in the battle to stop the rise in the cost of living, a battle we must fight and win for the benefit of every family in this nation."

If his veto was upheld, he said, he would "immediately seek appropriations which will assure the funds necessary to provide for the needs of the nation in education and health" and would "work with the Congress in developing a law that will ease the transition of education reform and do so without inflation."

The bill he vetoed, he said, "simply provides more dollars for the same old programs without making the urgent new reforms that are needed" to improve the quality of education and health care. He said he would soon submit to Congress an education message proposing "a new and searching look at our American school system."

Nixon specifically cited the program for education aid to "impacted areas"—areas assisted because of the presence of federal installations and their personnel—as an example of the bill's "unfairness." $6 million was provided by the bill, he said, for one-half million people living in the richest county in the country, while only $3 million was provided for three million people living in the 100 poorest counties.

While the President repeated his objections to the "unfair" impacted-area program in his veto message Jan. 27, he suggested a compromise with Congress on the increased funds for the program, which benefitted 385 Congressional districts. Nixon said he would accept as a "temporary" expedient, higher funding for it than the $202 million he had requested. The bill would provide $600 million. (White House Press Secretary Ronald L. Ziegler later specified that the President was prepared to split the difference, i.e., accept about $400 million for the program).

A second compromise also was suggested in the veto message—Congress could retain the amount of the bill's appropriations for grant-in-aid programs but give the President discretionary authority to withhold funds if necessary to combat inflation. Current laws required full funding of such programs.

The President also disclosed in his message that the spending estimate for the fiscal 1970 budget had risen since April 1969 by $5.1 billion to a $198 billion total.

Nixon's action was criticized by Democratic leaders in Congress later Jan. 27. Senate majority leader Mike Mansfield (Mont.) spoke of neglect of "the nation's inner needs" and House Democratic leader Carl Albert (Okla.) called upon Nixon "to use the awesome power of his office, not against the children, the sick, the aged and the poor of this nation but rather against the giant monopolies which are the true culprits in causing inflation."

Democratic spokesmen deplored the veto. Gardner Ackley, former chairman of the Council of Economic Advisers under President Johnson, said Jan. 27 "there was no excuse" for the veto "on the basis of inflation." The difference of $1 billion or so in the funds bill, he said, was not "particularly relevant to the price level." Ackley, who was named Jan. 27 chairman of the Democratic Policy Council's Committee on Economic Affairs, objected to Nixon's insistence on a balanced budget as "a gross oversimplification for political purposes. You don't necessarily get a balanced and sound economy by having a balanced budget."

The veto of the appropriation was sustained by the House Jan. 28. A vote to override the veto was 226–191, or 52 votes less than the two-thirds majority required.

The victory was won in the face of a major lobbying effort organized by an Emergency Committee for Full Funding of Education Programs, a coalition of 80 groups with strong backing from the AFL-CIO, the National Education Association and the American Council on Education.

A trimmed-down version of the appropriation bill, which ultimately provided $19,381,920,200, was passed by 68–0 Senate vote Feb. 28, and the House March 3 accepted the Senate version by 228–152 vote. The House accepted a Senate clause providing that only 98% of the appropriations could be spent.

The second version also contained a spending limitation that would empower the President to withhold funds appropriated by the bill if he felt it necessary to hold down inflation.

Nixon signed the measure March 6.

Okun defends 'jawboning.' Arthur M. Okun, former chairman of the Council of Economic Advisers (CEA) in the Johnson Administration, blamed the Nixon Administration's rejection of wage-price guidelines for the estimated 4% rise in the wholesale price index in 1969. In a study due for limited distribution Jan. 22, Okun argued if the guidelines had not been abandoned, the index probably would have risen not more than 3.5%.

Basing his analysis partly on formerly confidential CEA-industry contacts, Okun said industries that had responded to private pressure from the CEA had increased their prices in 1968 at an average 1% rate, compared with the 6% price hike in 1969 after President Nixon had halted the policy of administration intervention in specific price decisions (popularly known as "jawboning"). Okun said industrial commodities not on the "responsive list" had increased their prices 2.9% in 1968. He conceded that the statistics were not conclusive proof that the end of "jawboning" had been the primary factor in the hurtling price increases of 1969. Okun suggested that "catch-up" action by industries such as steel, that had been subject to firm official pressure in the past, probably contributed to the 1969 price situation.

Among the commodities Okun listed as having been responsive to price restraint pressure from the government were gasoline, heating oil, crude oil, sulphur and sulphuric acid, steel, aluminum ingots, copper, automobiles, cigarettes, tires, paperboard, bottles, tin cans, newsprint, home laundry equipment and X-ray film. Although price restraints had not embraced all industrial commodities, Okun said the evident success of the restraints among the listed items probably helped to keep down prices in other industries.

As to CEA Chairman Paul W. McCracken's Sept. 23, 1969 argument that price and wage guidelines might divert inflationary pressures, making other wages and prices rise even more, Okun argued that lower prices on some items would bring them greater output and sales. He also said the diversion of purchasing power to other industries would not be inflationary, if they were not operating at capacity. With price restraints in effect in some sectors of the economy, Okun added, fiscal and monetary policies could aim at a lower level of overall dollar volume of economic activity "without any greater sacrifice of output and employment."

Executive's economic reports. In his first economic report to Congress, President Nixon Jan. 30 stressed the goal of achieving a slowdown in economic growth during the first half of 1970, but moving to a "moderately more rapid economic expansion" during the second half of the year. Nixon's economic report was accompanied by the annual report of the Council of Economic Advisers. The reports were formally submitted to Congress Feb. 2.

President's report—Citing 1969 as "a year of progress in the fight against inflation," the President's economic report explained that the government's "purpose has been to slow down the rapid expansion of demand firmly and persistently, but not to choke off demand so abruptly as to injure the economy." During 1969 a "sustained period of combined fiscal and monetary restraint" led to a decrease in the growth rates of federal expenditures, money supply, spending, production and profits, as well as a budget surplus. The increase in federal expenditures fell to $9 billion, compared with an average of $20 billion for the three previous years. Money supply increased at a 4.4% annual rate in the first two quarters and at a 0.7% annual rate in the two final quarters, compared with a 7% increase in 1968. The rise in total spending fell from 9.4% in 1968 to 6.8% in 1969, accompanied by declines in the growth of production.

Noting that "continuation of a low rate of growth of sales, production and employment" was probable for the first months of 1970, the report warned against a rekindling of the inflationary process through a too rapid increase in the demand for output. The report also cautioned against allowing the moderate slowdown to turn into a serious recession and warned against avoiding the first two dangers by imposing "such tight credit conditions as to paralyze the housing industry, preventing needed additions to the supply of homes and apartments."

To avoid all three dangers, President Nixon stressed the importance of retaining a balanced federal budget. "A prudent fiscal policy," the President asserted, "avoiding the risks of returning to budget deficits, and a prudent monetary policy, avoiding the risks of overly long and overly severe restraint, offer the best promise of relieving strains and distortions in financial markets, bringing interest rates down, and encouraging a sustainable and orderly forward movement of the economy. After some months of slow expansion of sales, output, and employment, which seems likely, a moderately quicker pace later in the year would be consistent with continued progress in reducing the rate of inflation." The report added that such a balanced budget and a "moderate degree of monetary restraint" would also "permit residential construction to revive and begin a rise toward the path of housebuilding. . . ."

(At his Jan. 30 news conference Nixon stressed the importance of the Federal Reserve System's independence. But, he added, "If monetary policy remains too restricted too long, we have a recession, and monetary policy will remain restricted unless the Federal Reserve, and those who are in charge of monetary policy, are convinced that fiscal policy is responsible." Pointing to his projections of a balanced budget, Mr. Nixon predicted that "the time is coming when monetary policy can be relaxed," and expressed optimism that "the present rate of inflation, which was less in the second half of 1969 than in the first half, will continue to decline, and that we will be able to control inflation without recession.")

Nixon's economic report projected a gross national product of about $985 billion during 1970, 5½% above 1969, as compared with the 1969 increase of 7.7% over 1968.

Nixon attributed the risk of some rise in unemployment during 1970 as "an unfortunate cost of having allowed the inflation to run for so long." However, he said that risk would be kept low through "the policy of firm and persistent disinflation on which we have embarked."

Advocating that government play a cautious role in the national economy, the report said: "Personal freedom will be increased when there is more economy in government and less government

in the economy. Economic domination, like any other government domination, is dangerous to a free society, no matter how benevolent its aims." Nixon stressed the importance of "strong and innovative financial institutions" and announced that he would appoint a commission "to study our financial structure and make recommendations to me for needed changes."

In reference to the world economy, the report stressed that inflation in the U.S. had "added to inflationary problems in other countries in recent years." The report added that inflation had also worsened the U.S. trade position, but said the deterioration of the trade balance had been arrested by the end of 1969.

In concluding his report, Nixon set forth the basic principles which he said "will continue to guide the management of economic policy" during his Administration:

"The integrity and purchasing power of the dollar must be assured"; "our economic policy must continue to emphasize a high utilization of the nation's productive resources"; "we must achieve a steadier and more evenhanded management of our economic policies"; "government must say what it means and mean what it says"; "we must preserve and sustain the free market economy in order to raise the standard of living of every American"; "we must involve the American people in setting goals and priorities by providing accurate, credible data on the long-range choices open to them, making possible much better informed public discussion about using the resources we will have in meeting the needs of the future"; and "the free economy of the future will rest squarely on the foundation of genuinely equal opportunity for all."

Economic advisers' report—The Council of Economic Advisers set a reduction in price increases and a revival of the growth of output as policy objectives for 1970. This could be done, the council stated, through "a path of moderate expansion of demand which will yield both a decline of the rate of inflation and a resumption of growth of output." Since the economic path for the first months of 1970 had already been set during 1969, the "policy problem for 1970 is to take actions in the first half of the year which will place the economy on the sustainable path of moderately rising output and significantly declining inflation in the second half."

The council's quarterly price projections, reported by the Wall Street

Journal Feb. 2, estimated a 4.7% annual rate of increase during the first quarter of 1970 (as in the final quarter of 1969), followed by 4% rate of increase in the second quarter, 3¾% in the third quarter and 3.5% or less in the final quarter. (In reference to the policy of jawboning—Administration attempts to get individual prices lowered—Nixon noted at his press conference that while it could be effective with regard to a single firm, "it is not effective with regard to the whole problem, and it's basically unfair.")

Concerning the projected GNP of $985 billion for 1970, the advisers explained that part of the smaller increase would be reflected in a smaller increase of real output, while part would be reflected in a decrease in inflation. They added that the GNP growth rate "has already been slowed to a rate which, although temporarily necessary, is lower than needs to be sustained for long in order to achieve significant disinflation. Therefore, we can tolerate a moderate rise in the rates of increase of GNP and of real output without reviving inflation and should have such a rise in order to avoid mounting unemployment."

Illustrating the economic report's contention that priorities in the national economy had to be carefully chosen, the advisers' report contained projections of U.S. output through 1975 and how that output would probably be divided among different sectors of the economy. The analysis showed that there would be no excess resources to handle new claims until 1973, when a small excess would become available. "The basic lesson of the estimates," the council noted, "is that the country is already at a point where, despite prospective growth of output, a decision to satisfy an existing claim will require giving up something on which people are already counting."

Although the council refused to recommend how the output should be divided, it stressed the importance of a modest budget surplus, combined with "moderate monetary restraint." "The long-run average size of the [budget] surplus or deficit should be determined by the amount of savings it is desired to make available for private business and housing investments," the advisers said.

On the international monetary scene, the council's report gave cautious support for "greater flexibility of exchange rates than has been evident in practice," but stressed that the U.S. could not "move its own parity with respect to other currencies." The council urged that members of the international monetary system "use the period of reduced tensions, which recent currency realignments and advances in providing needed liquidity have granted us, to consider how the international financial system might be made more capable of adjusting to possible future shifts in the world economy."

Nixon's anti-inflation buget. President Nixon submitted to Congress Feb. 2 a federal budget estimating outlays of $200.8 billion for fiscal 1971 (July 1, 1970–June 30, 1971) and receipts at $202.1 billion. The resultant surplus of $1.3 billion, he said, was "essential both to stem persistent inflationary pressures and to relieve hard-pressed financial markets."

"This anti-inflationary budget," he declared, "begins the necessary process of reordering our national priorities. For the first time in two full decades, the federal government will spend more money on human resource programs than on national defense."

Outlays for defense and space programs were reduced a total of more than $6 billion, while $3 billion was allotted for seven new initiatives in domestic programs—such as welfare reform, revenue sharing with the states and a clean water drive—that would cost $18 billion within four years. Reductions of $2.1 billion were scheduled, aside from the defense and space reductions, in 40 other budget items. One of these was a proposal to sell $750 million in strategic metals and other materials from the national stockpile (such sales were carried as an offset against expenditures, thus a cut in spending).

The proposed outlays were $2.9 billion higher than the estimated $197.9 billion of the fiscal 1970 budget. Since fiscal 1970 receipts were estimated at $199.4 billion, a $1½ billion surplus was anticipated. The increase in spendings from fiscal 1970 to fiscal 1971 was the smallest increase recorded since fiscal 1965.

(The fiscal 1969 budget showed a $3.2 billion surplus from receipts of $187.8 billion and outlays of $184.6 billion.)

The seven new initiatives (budget outlays in parentheses) were: a new family assistance plan ($500 million) to replace the current welfare program, the first quarterly payment ($275 million) for revenue-sharing, law enforcement ($310 million), environmental quality ($330 million), expanded food assistance to the poor ($764 million), mass transit and airways improvement ($468 million) and manpower training ($352 million).

Other smaller increases were budgeted for rural housing, vocational education, the Corporation for Public Broadcasting, alcoholism treatment, medical manpower and education for Vietnam veterans.

No new taxes were requested, but the revenue estimate was dependent in many areas upon Congressional action. These areas included: $700 million of "user charges," largely in the aviation field; $600 million from extension of automobile and telephone excise taxes; $675 million from an increase in postal rates; $1.2 billion from deferring federal pay increases for six months to Jan. 1, 1971; $500 million by modifying or repealing several politically sensitive programs, such as agricultural conservation, school milk and education aid for areas "impacted" with federal personnel; $215 million from revision of Medicaid; an

Budget Receipts
(In millions of dollars for the fiscal year)

	1969 actual	1970 estimate	1971 estimate
Individual income taxes	87,249	92,200	91,000
Corporation income taxes	36,678	37,000	35,000
Social insurance taxes and contributions (trust funds)	39,918	44,805	49,108
Excise taxes	15,222	15,940	17,520
Estate and gift taxes	3,491	3,500	3,600
Customs duties	2,319	2,260	2,260
Miscellaneous receipts	2,916	3,681	3,614
Total receipts	187,792	199,386	202,103

Budget Outlays and Authority
(In millions of dollars for the fiscal year)

	1969 actual	1970 estimate	1971 estimate	Recommended budget authority for 1971
National defense	81,240	79,432	73,583	73,153
International affairs and finance	3,785	4,113	3,589	4,723
Space research and technology	4,247	3,886	3,400	3,330
Agriculture and rural development	6,221	6,343	5,364	5,962
Natural resources	2,129	2,485	2,503	5,830
Commerce and transportation	7,873	9,436	8,785	13,714
Community development and housing	1,961	3,046	3,781	3,804
Education and manpower	6,825	7,538	8,129	7,830
Health	11,696	13,265	14,957	15,909
Income security	37,399	43,832	50,384	56,595
Veterans benefits and services	7,640	8,681	8,475	8,909
Interest	15,791	17,821	17,799	17,799
General government	2,866	3,620	4,084	4,236
Allowances:				
Revenue sharing	. . .	. . .	275	275
Civilian and military pay increases	. . .	175	1,400	1,400
Contingencies	. . .	300	900	1,200
Undistributed intragovernmental transactions:				
Employer share, employee retirement	−2,018	−2,307	−2,366	−2,366
Interest received by trust funds	−3,099	−3,781	−4,273	−4,273
Total outlays	184,556	197,885	200,771	218,030
Budget surplus	3,236	1,501	1,331	

increase in the wage base on which Social Security taxes were collected to $9,000 in 1971 instead of 1972. The proposed stockpile sale also was dependent upon action in Congress.

However, total receipts dependent upon Congressional action amounted to $1.6 billion, considerably less than in other recent budgets.

In addition, $1.2 billion was to be realized from a speedup in collection of existing taxes. The budget total also reflected plans to more than triple the sale of assets, mainly loans, from various federal-sponsored agencies. This activity, although outside the budget, chiefly Federal National Mortgage Association and federal home loan banks, was estimated to have reduced the budget spending total by $3.6 billion.

The "uncontrollable" items in the budget—Social Security, Medicare, public assistance grants to the states, interest on the national debt, etc.—rose $7.2 billion and comprised 69% (a record) of the budget.

Among other highlights of the 1971 budget: (a) there was no estimate of the cost of the war in Vietnam, reportedly because of the difficulty of a true accounting (the war cost was estimated at $28.8 billion for fiscal 1969, $23.2 billion for fiscal 1970); (b) defense and space programs for fiscal 1971 were budgeted at $10.8 billion less than in the last Johnson Administration budget presented early in 1969; this represented a $4.4 billion reduction by the Nixon Administration in fiscal 1970 and a new cut of $6.4 billion for fiscal 1971; (c) defense spending—$71.8 billion—amounted to 46% of the "federal funds" part of the budget if federal trust funds—which would have an $8.6 billion surplus of receipts over outlays—were not included; (d) this "federal funds" area of the budget, generally comparable to the old "administrative budget," would be in deficit by $7.3 billion; (e) the first budget to project revenues and outlays for four years, it revealed a possible revenue excess of about $22 billion in fiscal 1975 but "little, if any, margin" for fiscal 1972; (f) the President cited as "meritorious claims on our resources" for the future further budget surpluses and a further realignment of the tax burdens; (g) the federal debt held by the public would decline from $279.5 billion at the end of fiscal 1969 to $278.5 billion one year later and to an estimated $277.3 billion by the end of fiscal 1971; (h) federal civilian employment was scheduled to decline for the second consecutive year; (i) about 41% of estimated outlays were to be devoted to human resources—education and manpower, health, income security and veterans benefits and services.

SUMMARY OF PRESIDENT NIXON'S BUDGET
(Fiscal years ending June 30 unless otherwise indicated)

Defense—Defense Department outlays for 1971 of $71.8 billion, a $5.2 billion reduction from 1970, represented a figure that was 7% of the gross national product (smallest since 1951) and 34.6% of the total federal budget (smallest since 1950). Officials estimated that Pentagon procurement in 1971 would drop $7 billion and represent a job loss amounting to 1.6% of the total U.S. labor force—640,000 industrial jobs, 130,412 civilian employes of the Defense Department and a military personnel cut of 551,296.

The request for new obligational authority—authority for appropriations that would not all be spent in that fiscal year—totaled $71.3 billion, a reduction of $2.6 billion from the defense budget approved by Congress in December 1969 and a reduction of $11.9 billion from the Johnson Administration request in early 1969.

Space—The National Aeronautics and Space Administration (NASA) budget request for 1971 was $3.4 billion, or $500 million less than in 1970, $2.2 billion less than in 1966 and its lowest request since the early 1960s. Employment within NASA and on their contracts was expected to decline by a total of about 45,000 to about 144,000.

Crime—Anticrime and criminal justice programs were to get an infusion of $1.257 billion from the 1971 budget for intensified drives against narcotics traffic and organized crime and more aid to state and local law enforcement agencies. The total was almost $600 million more than the spending in 1969 for such programs and more than $300 million higher than the 1970 total.

The Justice Department budget was to rise to the billion dollar level for the first time.

A major increase in funds was requested for the Law Enforcement Assistance Administration to boost its aid to local and state law enforcement agencies. $480 million was requested, compared with $267 million in 1970 and an initial budget in 1969 of $67 million.

Other increases were recommended for the FBI (a $7.39 million increase to $257 million) and for the Bureau of Prisons ($9 million more to $88 million), the Civil Rights Division (to $5.1 million from $2.7 million), and the Community Relations Service ($1.6 million more to increase the number of urban centers from 35 to 50).

Foreign aid—Outlays for international programs were to decrease from the level of the two previous years to $3.6 billion. While U.S. contributions to international financial institutions were to be higher, less spending was planned for bilateral economic aid programs ($1.7 billion), the Export-Import Bank (reflecting higher sales of loans) and the Food for Peace program (reportedly because of the growing self-sufficiency of developing countries). The foreign aid total was proposed as an "interim level" pending a task force study of the program.

A smaller Peace Corps was projected by the budget, down 2,000 personnel to 10,000 trainees and volunteers, by the end of 1971, down $2 million in outlays to a request for $100 million.

A request of $622 million for military aid to other nations, only $3 million less than for 1970, was carried under the Defense Department budget.

Housing, urban development—The 1971 budget for the Housing and Urban Development Department (HUD) totaled $3.3 billion. It reflected plans to increase production of housing for low and moderate income families. Outlays for all federal housing programs were expected to rise from $2.8 billion in 1970 to $3.6 billion, with a $615 million

increase allotted for insured loans in rural areas for subsequent sale by the Farmers Home Administration, and a $294 million rise for payments supporting low income housing.

The urban renewal and Model Cities programs were to continue at their current levels—a $1 billion authorization for urban renewal and $575 million for Model Cities. Because of the addition in both programs of carry-over funds, actual spending was projected at $1.082 billion for urban renewal ($1.049 billion in 1970) and $530 million for Model Cities ($300 million in 1970).

In other programs, outlays were to increase from $475 million to $644 million in fiscal 1971 for low rent public housing, from $272.4 million to $313 million in 1971 for metropolitan development (planning grants, technical aid, new communities, etc.), from $15 million to $25 million in 1971 for urban technology and research (including $12 million for Operation Breakthrough for utilization of new technological methods for mass production of homes).

Outlays for rent supplements were budgeted at $41.4 million ($18.7 million in 1970), for the home ownership and rental housing programs at $102 million ($19.1 million in 1970).

HUD Secretary George Romney at a news conference Feb. 2 said his department's budget had been "cut to the bone" deliberately on the theory that an overall balanced budget would ease the troubled housing industry by making more capital available for private home building.

Transportation—Of the $7 billion in proposed outlays for transportation in fiscal 1971 (a $375 million rise over 1970), $4.6 billion (a $54 million decrease from 1970) were for highways. The highway trust fund would provide $4.4 billion for funding.

For mass transit, the Administration sought a $3.1 billion authorization over the first five years for its 12-year, $10 billion program. The first year's outlay for this was budgeted at $80 million.

Development funds for the supersonic transport (SST) plane were increased from $163 million in fiscal 1970 outlays to $275 million in 1971. Also increased —by $267 million to $1.3 billion—were outlays for operation of the air traffic control system and provision of grants for airport development.

Subsidies for construction of merchant ships were to rise $21.7 million to $112 million, and new budget authority, to authorize a new shipbuilding program, was increased $81.2 million to $199.5 million.

Education—Outlays for all education-related programs in fiscal 1971 were estimated at $10.7 billion. Of this, about $3.9 billion was for programs of the Office of Education (OE) and $1.2 billion for veterans education benefits. The OE budget represented a $130 million increase over the 1970 Administration request.

Elementary and secondary programs were to be allocated about $2.7 billion, about the same level as in 1970. The Head Start and Follow Through programs were to get slightly more funds to operate at a $408 million level.

$1.4 billion was budgeted for higher education outlays. Student aid programs were $50 million higher at $632 million, but no construction grant funds were requested and funds were to be reduced or eliminated for land-grant colleges, international studies and fellowships for college teachers.

Vocational education outlays were to rise $29 million to $290 million, funding of the National Science Foundation ($490 million) was maintained at the same level, while the Teacher Corps was to receive slightly less than in 1970—$30.8 million.

Poverty—Programs to aid the poor were expected to be increased by 10% over the fiscal 1970 level to a total of $32.9 billion in outlays. A $2 billion share ($140 million more than in 1970) was to go to the Office of Economic Opportunity—$381.1 million (about $2 million more) for community action programs, $24 million ($2 million more) for family planning, and $63.2 million ($6.3 million more) for legal services.

Outlays for food programs were hiked $623 million to a total of $1.6 billion, of which $1.2 billion was for the food stamp program (a $674 million increase), which was expected to reach about 7.5 million persons by the end of

the budget year. Child nutrition programs also were funded higher—by $12 million to a $314 million level accommodating 6.6 million children.

The Administration planned to reduce spending for the special milk program by $64 million.

Labor—A Labor Department budget of $2.9 billion, a $309.9 million increase over 1970, was largely directed into manpower training programs. Job Corps outlays were slightly higher, up $8 million to $180 million. Outlays for Job Opportunities in the Business Sector were more than doubled—from $129 million in 1970 to $296 million.

Welfare—Income security programs were expected to total $50.4 billion in 1971. The funds were necessary to cover an expected 13% growth in the numbers of beneficiaries for Social Security, railroad retirement, Civil Service retirement and unemployment compensation.

Outlays for Social Security were estimated at $33 billion in fiscal 1971 (covering an average of 26 million beneficiaries). (Unemployment compensation was expected to reach a weekly average of 1.3 million persons. One million beneficiaries each were expected to come under the railroad and Civil Service retirement programs.)

The federal share of public assistance payments was estimated at $4.8 billion. $500 million in outlays was requested for 1971 to initiate the proposed Family Assistance Program to replace the welfare system.

Health—Federal spending for health in 1971 was to rise $1.7 billion to a total of $15 billion. $1.5 billion of the rise was to cover increases in the Medicare and Medicaid programs. For Medicare, spending was expected to rise $1.3 billion to $8.8 billion. To finance the program a rise in the Social Security payroll tax financing the program was recommended, as was an increase from $4 to $5.30 in the monthly premium paid by individuals for insurance for physicians' fees.

For Medicaid, outlays of $2.9 billion ($244 million higher) were requested. Legislation was to be submitted to limit the federal share of Medicaid costs in an attempt to direct the program more into preventive and acute medical treatment programs.

Family planning services were to be funded at a $92 million level ($34 million more).

Also increased were outlays for medical research, manpower training and construction of health facilities—to a $2.2 billion level.

The hospital construction program under the Hill-Burton Act was put at a $305 million outlay level with focus on out-patient and ambulatory care rather than on general buildings.

Water, air pollution control—The budget incorporated the President's recent proposals to obligate the federal government to a $4 billion, 5-year commitment to aid local sewage treatment projects. For 1971, the obligation would be $650 million (compared with $800 million for 1970). An environmental financing authority would be established to purchase state and local obligations and help finance their share of the projects. The authority would also market its own securities to the public. Such bonds were to provide $6 billion, which, added to the $4 billion federal obligation, would fianance the President's $10 billion clean waters program.

For air pollution control, the budget included expenditures of $104.2 million by the Health, Education and Welfare Department (a rise of $24.5 million from the request for the 1970). The additional funds were to be directed toward research on power plant pollution. More research—on solid waste management—was to be funded at a $14,-336,000 level.

Interior Department—Interior's $1.7 billion budget included modest increases in many areas. In addition, parkland acquisition was to be emphasized, with $357.4 million made available from the Land and Water Conservation Fund

($157.4 million in a carryover from 1970, $200 million annual income from park fees, waterway fuel taxes, surplus property sales and outer continental shelf leases). The President requested an immediate use of $168.5 million in 1971 for parkland acquisition and grants to the states for park purposes. The remainder—$188.9 million, to be specifically requested later—was to be used to buy more parkland, especially in and near cities.

More funds also were to be made available from the department's budget for (proposed outlays in parentheses) the Bureau of Outdoor Recreation ($172.5 million), the National Park Service ($150 million), Bureau of Indian Affairs ($324.6 million), the Bureau of Reclamation ($295 million) and the Bureau of Mines ($101 million).

Agriculture—Agriculture Department outlays were to decline $454.7 million to $7,952,700,000. But the total reflected plans for increased Farmers Home Administration loan sales. Excluding the budgetary effect of such sales, which reduced outlays by the amount of the sales, the department's budget showed a spending increase over 1970 of $861 million, of which $674.3 million would go for the food stamp program.

Outlays for crop supports were estimated at $3.8 million, or $132.5 million more than in 1970. Spending rises of $157.9 million for cotton, $155.3 million for dairy and $32.1 million for rice supports were partially offset by expected decreases of $85.4 million for wheat, $50.7 million for tobacco, $36.7 million for soybeans and $40 million for all other crop supports.

A redoubled effort was to be made in loans for low and moderate income housing for rural families. Of the $2.2 billion ($1.6 billion in 1970) level anticipated for insured and direct loan commitments by the Farmers Home Administration, $1.5 billion was to go into housing loans.

Democrats question priorities. A Democratic Policy Council panel Feb. 22 attacked the Nixon Administration's budget program and called for further reductions in defense spending and more spending for domestic programs. The panel also

predicted that the budget's projected surplus would "likely vanish" since it was dependent upon some unlikely prospects, such as $2.1 billion in savings from ending programs generally supported by Congress, a postal rate increase and a delay in a scheduled pay rise for federal workers.

Further criticism was voiced at a public hearing Feb. 24 held by the Policy Council's committee on national priorities. Sen. Edmund S. Muskie (Me.) contrasted Administration proposals for spending $275 million for the supersonic transport plane against only $106 million for air pollution control, $3.4 billion for space against only $1.4 billion for housing. In a similar vein, Sen. Edward M. Kennedy (Mass.) said military housing was budgeted at $809 million against only $575 million for model cities, Pentagon public relations at $39 million against only $5 million for Justice Department civil rights enforcement.

(But the National Planning Association, an independent group based in Washington, endorsed the President's balanced-budget policy. In a report issued Feb. 8, the association said: "Rising investment will require higher savings out of current income somewhere in the economy. If consumers and businesses are unable or unwilling to save more, . . . the federal government must become a net 'saver' and supply funds to capital markets by running substantial budget surpluses.")

Foreign affairs message. President Nixon submitted to Congress Feb. 18 a foreign policy message outlining, and entitled, "United States Foreign Policy for the 1970's: A New Strategy for Peace." The President referred to it as the first "annual report" by an American president on the state of the world.

Nixon's message emphasized these twin themes: the U.S. would maintain its global treaty commitments but would also bring into its commitment appraisals a firm assessment of the U.S. interests involved. In his remarks on international economic policy, Nixon said: There was an urgent need for an adequate money supply—"it is clear that the relative role of gold must diminish." This in turn would require an improvement in "the mutual adjustment of national economies."

Anti-inflation moves pledged. Arthur F. Burns, who was sworn in Jan. 31 as the 10th chairman of the Federal Reserve Bank, told the House Banking Committee Feb. 7 that he would "do everything in my power to help this country prevent a recession." Burns said: "I welcome the cooling off in the economy that is now under way," but he added, "it is obviously not something I would like to see continued for very long."

Burns took the classic Federal Reserve position that the central bank's "major social responsibility" was to "protect the value of the dollar and preserve stable prosperity" rather than help housing or any other economic sector. (The House committee, headed by Rep. Wright Patman [D, Tex.], was investigating ways to improve the housing and mortgage situation.) Burns also said he would "not be surprised" if the jobless rate rose to more than 4.2%, but said he did not "anticipate any large increase in unemployment."

Economic Decline Gains Impetus

Economic indicators decline. According to preliminary figures released Feb. 26, the Commerce Department's composite index of leading economic indicators fell 1.8% in January. It was the sharpest drop since the 1957 recession. Since early 1969, the index had been fairly stable, indicating a leveling off of the economy.

The preliminary figures, which included only seven of the 12 indicators showed a decline to a seasonally adjusted 149.3% of the 1963 average from 152.1% in December 1969. The following four indicators declined: the average workweek for production workers, new durable goods orders, new building permits and the average weekly initial claims for state unemployment insurance (job-benefit claims rose in January, but the indicator was treated inversely in the index). Indicators recording gains were plant and equipment orders, industrial-materials prices and the ratio of price to unit labor costs in manufacturing.

Prices up in January. The Labor Department reported Feb. 19 that the Consumer Price Index in January, adjusted to reflect normal seasonal changes, indicated an inflationary rise of .6%; the unadjusted rise was .4%. The unadjusted index rose to 131.8 against a base period of 100 in 1957–59. Thus a typical city family paid $31.80 more for products and services than in 1957–59.

On a city basis, the index rose .7% in New York (largely because of a subway fare hike from 20¢ to 30¢), .6% in Chicago, .5% in Philadelphia, .2% in Detroit and .1% in Los Angeles. Contributing mostly to the rise were food and transportation costs; higher prices for insuring, registering and repairing automobiles; and a sharp food price rise of .6%.

The January decline in consumer purchasing power meant 13¢ less a week in the real spendable earnings of a worker with three dependents. However, a worker's take-home pay increased 22¢ a week, primarily because of the reduction in the income surtax from 10% to 5% Jan. 1. Wage increases were scheduled for workers whose union contracts included automatic increases tied to the Consumer Price Index.

The department revised the January Wholesale Price Index to show a 9.6% annual rate of increase, instead of the 8.4% rate reported Jan. 28. The index was placed at 116% of the 1957–59 average.

According to preliminary figures released Feb. 26, the overall index rose only .3% (to 116.3% of the 1957–59 average) in February. The index was 4.7% ahead of the February 1969 figure. A full 1% rise in farm produce prices accounted for most of the index increase; cattle and hog prices rose "substantially," as did fresh fruit prices. However, processed foods and feeds declined .2%; other declines included cocoa beans, eggs, chickens, fresh and dried vegetables. Industrial wholesale prices increased less in February than in other recent months.

Sharp rise in jobless rate. The nation's unemployment rate for January showed the sharpest monthly increase in more than nine years, according to a report Feb. 6 by the Labor Department's Bureau of Labor Statistics. The report set January's seasonally adjusted jobless rate at 3.9%, the highest level since November 1967. The jobless rate for December 1969 was 3.5%, revised upward from an original report of 3.4%. The September and October 1969 rates had been revised downward to 3.8%.

According to the report, the increase in unemployment hit blue-collar workers harder than men with white-collar jobs and affected whites more than Negroes. However, the 6.3% jobless rate for black workers was still far above the 3.6% rate for whites.

In a San Francisco speech Feb. 6, Treasury Secretary David M. Kennedy said the January rise in unemployment "along with other evidence may indicate a definite easing of labor markets. . . . Easier labor markets, declining corporate profits and the expected slowdown in the rate of price increases hopefully will reduce inflationary pressures of wage settlements."

Reflecting nationwide layoffs in the auto industry, unemployment rose .3% in February to a seasonally adjusted 4.2% of the national labor force, the Labor Department reported March 6. The jobless rate thus surged beyond the 1968–69 average level of 3.5%, reaching its highest level since October 1965.

The January (3.9%) and February levels marked the largest two-month increase since the business slump of 1957–58. Michigan, capital of the auto industry, experienced rising unemployment during January, according to the Michigan Employment Security Commission Feb. 16. Unemployment in that state climbed to 5.2% from November 1969's 3.5% level.

Auto cutbacks, layoffs. In the wake of dipping car sales and a resultant pileup in car dealers' inventories, the Big Three auto firms (General Motors, Chrysler and Ford) were compelled to cut production in the first three months of 1970 through week-long layoffs, short workweeks and plant slowdowns in production line speed. From the beginning of January through mid-February about 19,000 workers were laid off. At the end of February total industry layoffs approached 30,000.

From January through mid-February General Motors Corp. (GM) reduced assembly plant schedules, with three- and four-day work weeks plus week-long closings, at 33 plants in seven states. Indefinite layoffs affected about 7,500 workers. New GM furloughs at the end of February raised the total to 7,775.

"Indefinite manpower reductions" at 18 Ford Motor Co. plants from mid-December to Jan. 20 affected 3,545 workers.

Big Three production had slackened in 1969 although 1969 was the industry's fourth best year (1965 was the record year). Although truck output reached a record 1,965,487 units in 1969, new car production fell 7% to 8,218,920 units from the 8,843,007 cars assembled in 1968: GM built 4,420,430 cars (4,482,-302 in 1968); Chrysler, 1,392,454 (1,559,-975 in 1968); Ford, 2,163,138 (2,396,925 in 1968); and AMC, 242,898 (269,334 in 1968).

Car sales in the U.S. in 1969, including imports, fell .7% short of the 1968 record of 9,624,819 sales. 1969 figures totaled 9,564,375. U.S.-produced car sales figures began a decline in July which continued through early 1970: compared with similar periods in 1968, auto sales fell 5% in the second half of 1969 and dipped 8% in the last three months of the year.

GM, Chrysler and Ford all reported lower profits for 1969. Chrysler's earnings, the lowest since 1963, unexpectedly had dropped 69% to a net income of $88.8 million ($1.87 a share). GM profits declined 1.2% from 1968's $1.73 billion ($6.02 a share) to $1.71 billion ($5.95 a share). Ford's net income fell 12.8% from net earnings of $626.6 million ($5.73 a share) in 1968 to $546.5 million ($5.03 a share). Fourth quarter figures had disclosed a 12.2% drop in earnings for Ford, a loss of $4.4 million (10¢ a share) for Chrysler (its first final quarter loss since 1959 and its first loss in any quarter since the third quarter of 1961), and a 14% drop for GM in that company's lowest final quarter earnings since 1964.

As 1970 began, the industry encountered its worst January since 1960: sales plunged 16.5% to 538,998 units compared with 645,400 cars a year earlier. GM was the hardest hit as its sales slipped 23% below 1969 figures and its share of the market dipped from 54.1% the previous January to 49.9%. Only AMC survived the downward trend with its report of a 13.4% gain.

Although the steep sales slump continued through mid-February with an 18% drop in sales, late February figures, recording an estimated 1.4% drop, gave the industry its best showing since early November 1969.

Because of financial troubles growing out of lagging car sales, Chrysler March 3 was forced to cancel a $13.8 million contract with the federal Job Opportunities in the Business Sector (JOBS) program. The contract, signed in May 1969, was the largest of any federal manpower program; Chrysler had agreed to train 4,450 hard-core unemployed during a two-year period at a cost of $13.8 million to the Labor Department. However, layoffs and production cutbacks at Chrysler had resulted in the furlough of about 1,200 former hard-core jobless trainees.

Chrysler's proxy statement March 12 reported a cut of 2,500 to 3,000 salaried (white collar) jobs during the past six months as part of a cost-cutting drive begun during the summer of 1969. It was also disclosed that executive bonuses had been dropped during 1969.

■Faced with a general slump in big car sales, GM announced April 16 it had stopped production on its full-sized Oldsmobile at two assembly plants, in Doraville, Ga., and South Gate, Calif. Sales of the model, which would continue to be produced at three other plants, dropped 22.3% to 148,028 units, between Oct. 1, 1969 and March 31, from 190,-591 units 12 months earlier. The company said the cutback would not involve worker layoffs.

■In a renewed effort to keep dealer inventories and lagging car sales on an even keel, GM had announced April 2 the closing of seven (of 23) U.S. assembly plants for 1-5 days in April. The action would affect about 33,000 workers.

Truck sales. In March, truck sales of the Big Three fell 12.1% to 126,571 units, down from 143,950 in March 1969. Sales fell again in April 6.3% in the fourth consecutive monthly decline; in April, 139,799 units had been sold, compared with 149,192 sold during the same month in 1969.

Foreign car sales. In January, imported cars shared 13.5% of the U.S. market, compared with 11.4% a year earlier, it was reported Feb. 5. Although import sales had increased only 1.2% that month (84,000 units sold, up from 83,000 12 months earlier), their percentage in the market was comparatively larger because of plunging sales in Detroit.

As domestic car sales continued to slide, foreign car makers cut into the market with a 15% increase in sales in the first quarter, the Wall Street Journal reported April 6. The number of units sold in the first quarter totaled 84,000 units, up from 83,000 12 months earlier.

According to the Wall Street Journal May 6, the imports' share of the market declined slightly to 13.3% in April. For the first four months of 1970 foreign car sales totaled nearly 375,000 units, a 13% share of the total market, compared with a 10.6% (330,000 units) a year earlier.

Pentagon announces base cuts. Defense Secretary Melvin R. Laird announced March 4 that 371 military bases in the U.S. and abroad would be closed or cut back in an economy move expected to save $914 million in defense spending. Laird said the cuts were a result of Congressional budget reductions of more than $4 billion for fiscal 1970, ending June 30, and expected reductions in the fiscal 1971 budget. The Pentagon had announced smaller cuts in base activities in October 1969.

Laird said the reductions would remove 93,900 persons from Defense Department payrolls, affecting the jobs of 58,600 civilians and 35,300 military personnel. The Pentagon said additional cuts could be expected in order to meet the department's "budgetary limitations." Department spokesmen, who announced details of the reductions March 6, said that about 75% of the civilian employes who would lose their jobs or be reassigned due to the cuts were blue collar workers.

More Money Made Available

Construction funds freeze ended. President Nixon March 17 ended a freeze imposed Sept. 4, 1969 on $1.5 billion of construction funds used for federal-state projects, mostly highways. About $300 million of the amount represented the state and local share of financing such projects.

The action, the first official move in more than a year toward an expansionary fiscal policy, could result in a $600 million increase over the January estimates in the fiscal 1971 budget spending. Nixon said the move was "no signal that our effort to sustain a strong budget has relaxed" but added it was action to help the economy "achieve a stable growth."

Paul W. McCracken, chairman of the Council of Economic Advisers, commenting on the move, said the economy was "still strong," predicted that the rate of inflation would decline and favored action, like this, to move the economy toward "more sustainable expansion."

House Republican Leader Gerald R. Ford (Mich.), who met with Nixon and McCracken, said "the problems of inflation have been defeated" and "the danger of any recession is nil."

Reserve Board eases money. Testifying before the Senate Banking and Currency Committee March 18, Federal Reserve Board Chairman Arthur F. Burns disclosed that the Federal Reserve was relaxing its restrictive monetary policy and easing credit to encourage at least a 2% growth in the nation's money supply (currency and demand deposits). Growth in the money supply had been cut off since June 1969. Although Burns did not specifically say the board had reversed its policy, he called attention to the rising weekly figures in the "monetary aggregates" (money supply, total bank deposits and bank credit).

In prepared testimony, Burns noted a "marked decline" in interest rates which, he acknowledged, had recently been reversed (apparently temporarily) for longer-term bonds. Under later questioning, Burns forecast that mortgage interest rates would be "a little lower" by the end of 1970 and "appreciably lower" by 1972.

Concerning the current economic situation, Burns said, "we must be prepared for some relatively unfavorable news in the weeks ahead," but said present cumulative indicators did not mark a "business recession." Among his other points:

■The downturn in consumer durable goods, mainly automobiles, "may already be in large part behind us." Citing favorable prospects for "an early pickup in buying," Burns said the sector could become a "stimulus" for the economy.

■Housing construction might continue to decline, but there were indications of an improved situation at the start of the summer.

■Defense spending would continue to decline, but other federal spending was scheduled to rise.

■State and local government spending was growing less rapidly than usual.

■Business investment in plant and equipment would remain at a "very high level throughout this year." However, it would probably not be as strong as indicated by the survey, conducted by the Commerce Department and the Securities and Exchange Commission, that had been made public March 11. The survey had projected a 10.6% ($8 billion) increase in investment to $83.6 billion. The Administration had cited the survey as evidence against likelihood of a recession in 1970.

Federal Reserve eases credit. The Federal Reserve Board's Open Market Committee confirmed May 11 that it had voted 9–3 to ease credit at its meeting Feb. 10. The majority directive adopted in February had said open market operations should be "conducted with a view to moving gradually towards somewhat less firm conditions in the money market." However, it was made clear that should money and bank credit indicate a trend to deviate from a moderate growth pattern, the committee's directive would be promptly modified.

The three board members dissenting on grounds that the action was premature and "could strengthen market expectations of substantial easing," were FRB member Andrew F. Brimmer, Alfred Hayes, president of the New York Federal Reserve Bank, and Philip P. Coldwell, president of the Dallas Reserve Bank.

In other developments:

■The Federal Reserve Bank of New York confirmed May 11 that there had been a shift in Federal Reserve policy in April when it tightened credit to counteract an "unexpected" increase in the money supply. Since mid-January, the Federal Reserve reportedly had implemented a basic operational change by switching from an emphasis on money market conditions as the primary target of its credit policy to a concentration on the rate of growth of money aggregates, especially bank credit and the money supply. According to the bank, those aggregates had "expanded strongly" in April, causing the Federal Reserve to "interpose some resistance to the acceleration that developed."

■Banking data released by the St. Louis Federal Reserve Bank June 4 revealed that the Federal Reserve had extended its policy of gradual credit expansion in the last two weeks of May. Although the money supply had declined by $1.3 billion to $203.9 billion, the seasonally adjusted annual rate of increase in money during the March–May period was computed at 9.8%, up from 9.2% a week earlier.

Banks lower prime rate. Major commercial banks March 25–26 followed the lead of two small banks that reduced their prime (or minimum) lending rate from 8.5% to 8%. The prime rate, the banks' basic interest fee on business loans to their most credit-worthy clients, had been set at 8.5% June 9, 1969.

The first bank to take action was the Lincoln National Bank in Philadelphia, which lowered its interest rate Feb. 25. Although several small banks followed suit, most large banks dismissed Lincoln's move as insignificant. Disclaiming any intention to lower their rate, the big banks cited heavy loan demands and an insufficient decline in high money-market rates.

The Irving Trust Co. in New York, the 12th largest bank in the U.S., spurred the country's other banks to action when it announced March 25 it would reduce its prime rate to 8%. First National City Bank, Chase Manhattan Bank and Morgan Guaranty Trust—the nation's second, third and fourth largest banks, said they would lower their prime rate.

Several major banks at first resisted a rate reduction but all finally conformed March 26.

In announcing their acquiescence to the 8% rate March 26, several holdout banks warned that a tight credit situation would continue and said they expected other interest charges, usually tied to the prime rate, to come down slowly. They said they would scrutinize all loan applications closely, noting that short-term investment funds were still depleted.

Irving Trust Chairman George A. Murphy justified his bank's action as a step to "assist the Federal Reserve in cushioning recessionary trends now that the program to slow down inflationary pressures is beginning to take hold." Conceding that a high loan demand did persist, Murphy indicated it had been offset by "recent declines in short-term money-market rates [which] reflect the less restrictive monetary policy currently imposed by the Federal Reserve." Bank of America President A. W. Clausen said the reduction was in the public interest and could have a "favorable public policy impact."

White House Press Secretary Ronald L. Ziegler said the Administration was pleased with the reduction and said it would be an "important factor in improving access to credit at a more reasonable cost for the housing industry, state and local borrowers and small business."

The prime rate cut and an accompanying two-day rally on Wall Street (March 25–26) was reflected in London and other European stock markets by a surge in stock prices. European market traders and financial analysts said the U.S. prime rate reduction would help relieve tension in international money markets and ease international interest rates.

Home Loan Bank sets new rates. The Federal Home Loan Bank Board announced changes in interest rate ceilings Jan. 21 and April 16.

The board Jan. 21 increased to 7.5% the amount of interest that savings and loan associations would be permitted to pay on certificates of deposit of $100,000 or more, held for a year or longer. The change was instituted to make savings and loan rates competitive with new rate ceilings for commercial bank deposits that had been established Jan. 20 by the Federal Reserve Board and the Federal Deposit Insurance Corp.

In order to sustain the volume of mortgage lending, the board said April 16 it would make annual advances to savings and loan associations to permit them to convert all outstanding borrowings at a subsidized 7.25% interest rate; the previous rate had been 7.75%.

The program excluded savings and loan associations with borrowings from regional Home Loan Banks in excess of 25% of all savings. The program was described as a temporary measure until Congress enacted a $250 million subsidy program for the advances. It was designed primarily to discourage repayment of nearly $10 billion in outstanding advances as rising savings flows swelled the total supply of savings funds.

In related developments:

■New Jersey Banking Commissioner James C. Brady Jr. announced April 15 an increase in the state ceiling on interest rates on conventional home mortgage loans from 7.5% to 8%. The purpose of the higher rate was to offset drastically reduced housing construction in New Jersey by attracting investment funds from outside the state.

■Leading housing economist Saul B. Klaman, vice president of the National Association of Mutual Savings Banks, said April 20 that "premature credit ease" could have a reverse effect by producing less money for housing. Klaman warned against a recurrence of the "over-kill syndrome," which in 1968 had resulted in a pattern of premature easing of credit, resurgent inflationary pressures and then excessively severe credit restraint. He said he was disturbed about "massive" federal funding in the housing sector because of possible damage to private mortgage financing institutions. Taking particular note of savings and loan associations, Klaman said they were becoming mere "conduits for the channeling of Federal Home Loan Bank Board advances to mortgage borrowers."

Nixon denies recession. At an impromptu news conference March 21, President Nixon said his administration's economic policies had "taken the fire out of inflation" and would avert any recession.

Nixon said that his regime's relaxation of monetary restrictions and its release of frozen federal construction funds had anticipated the need for renewed economic growth later in the year. By the time the new measures had taken effect, he said, the steps taken in 1969 to cool the economy would be in operation. Nixon said he expected consumer prices to level off before the end of the year.

Taking issue with those who charged that the 4.2% rise in unemployment was recessionary, Nixon noted that the 1960–65 unemployment rate had fluctuated between 5.2% and 6.7%; he said no "fair-minded appraiser" of the economy would have described those years as a recession.

In a related development, chief presidential economic adviser Paul W. McCracken, chairman of the Council of Economic Advisers, disclosed Feb. 16 that the Administration expected an average unemployment rate of 4.3% in 1970. At that rate, an average of 700,000 to 800,000 workers would be out of work in any given month. Testifying before the Joint Economic Committee, McCracken pointed out that much of the rise would reflect "an increase of roughly one week in the median duration of unemployment," rather than a large increase "in the number experiencing some employment during the year." (The same estimate had been disclosed by Federal Reserve Board Chairman Arthur F. Burns before the House Banking and Currency Committee Feb. 7.)

In response to tough questioning by Sen. William Proxmire (D, Wis.) on how the Administration would respond to a higher jobless rate than its projection, McCracken would only say that its strategy to "quicken" the economy in the last half of the year would tend to check the rise in unemployment.

Nevertheless, two of Nixon's 1968 campaign advisers, currently private New York economic consultants, offered gloomier predictions to a Senate banking subcommittee March 12. Pierre A. Rinfret said that the "direct cost" of curbing inflation would be increasing unemployment—possibly as high as 5.5% at the end of 1970. Alan Greenspan predicted that the jobless rate would average 5.2% in the final quarter of 1970 and would continue to rise to an average 5.6% in 1971's June quarter. His analysis was based on estimates that output for each man-hour would advance steadily, while total real output would continue to grow "subnormally." Furthermore, a major cutback of about .5 million workers in the

armed forces would swell the ranks of civilian employes.

Jobless rate up .2% in March. Contrary to Administration expectations, the seasonally adjusted unemployment rate for March unexpectedly climbed from February's 4.2% rate to 4.4% in its third consecutive monthly increase and steepest quarterly gain since the recession year of 1960. The adjusted percentage figure represented 3,657,000 unemployed workers, up 230,000 from the February figure. The number of workers without jobs for 15 weeks or longer rose to an adjusted figure of 545,000 in March, compared with 465,000 in February. The increase was mostly concentrated among adult full-time workers who were affected by a 4% rate (up from February's 3.7%) due to layoffs in the manufacturing and construction sectors of the economy. White collar workers were hit by a 2.7% jobless rate (up from 2.3% in February) because of cutbacks in the defense and space industries.

In related developments:

■Leading manpower economist Dr. Charles C. Killingsworth, in a statement prepared for a public hearing in Detroit held by the House Select Subcommittee on Labor March 30, forecast an unemployment rate of 8% by mid-1971. He also said that unemployment would very likely reach 5% by the end of 1970. He warned that the Nixon Administration had underestimated the seriousness of the progressively rising jobless rate by viewing it as merely a transitional problem. Criticizing the Administration's plans to shift its manpower program from federal to state control, Killingsworth suggested that public service employment should be the next step in manpower development.

■Zenith Radio Corp. disclosed in a letter to Commerce Secretary Maurice H. Stans plans to lay off about 3,000 workers, 38% of them Negroes, during 1970, the Wall Street Journal reported March 10. Zenith Chairman Joseph S. Wright blamed the layoffs on the government's lack of support in the electronics industry's struggle against Japanese competition.

Postal strike, wages & rates up. Following the first strike by postal workers in the 195-year postal system's history, an agreement on wage increases was reached April 2 between the Administration and seven national postal unions. President Nixon asked Congress April 3 for postal rate increases to offset the costs of the agreement.

The agreement called for a two-step pay rise—(1) 6% retroactive to Dec. 27, 1969 to cover all federal employes, including military personnel, except some 750,000 blue-collar workers covered by independent wage boards across the country; and (2) an additional 8% pay boost for postal employes upon enactment of the postal reorganizational plan.

The agreement also called for reaching the top of the postal pay scale after eight years, instead of 21, the provision to be approved in collective bargaining negotiations to be initiated immediately upon enactment of postal reform.

The President's message to Congress April 3 stated the Administration's commitment to "a policy of pay-as-you-go." He proposed that Congress increase the postal rates—the first-class regular mail rate to 10¢, the second-class rate by 12%, the single piece third-class rate by 67%, and the third-class bulk rate by 5%. A 15% rate rise for parcel post also was to be requested of the Interstate Commerce Commission.

In addition, Nixon proposed to accelerate the fiscal 1971 collection of estate and gift taxes and urged Congress to consider and adopt permanent revenue measures for fiscal 1972 to meet the additional wage outlays.

In repeating his request to Congress for reform of the postal service, he said if the action had been taken earlier "the postal work stoppage would have been averted."

(The seven postal unions involved in the national agreement: National Association of Letter Carriers; National Association of Post Office and General Services Maintenance Employes; National Association of Post Office Mail Handlers, Watchmen, Messengers and Group Leaders; National Association of Special Delivery Messengers; National Federation of Post Office Motor Vehicle Employes; National Rural Letter Carriers Association; and United Federation of Postal Clerks.)

The wage-protest strike began in New York March 18 and spread rapidly across the country, defying the Federal Code forbidding strikes against the government, court injunctions, appeals from union leaders to return to work, a pledge by the Administration to begin immediate discussions on all issues, and a Presidential declaration that the issue involved survival of the government.

The major strike issue was wages. Members of the National Association of Letter Carriers, who initiated the strike, were paid a $6,176 starting salary, reaching a maximum of $8,442 after 21 years. Their salary, as well as that for the 700,-000 employes in the postal department, was set by Congress. And, although President Nixon had provided for $175 million in postal pay increases in his budget, postal pay legislation including a 5.4% increase that was to have taken effect in October 1969—was bogged down in Congress.

The 5.4% increase had been approved by the House in October 1969, but, in the face of a threatened Presidential veto on anti-inflationary grounds, the Senate in December 1969 scaled down the increase to 4%, effective in 1970. But Sen. Gale W. McGee (D, Wyo.), chairman of the Senate Post Office Committee, said the President had threatened subsequently to veto even this.

The measure was further complicated by being linked to the Administration plan for reform of the Post Office Department by transformation into a public corporation.

The dispute moved from the strike stage into negotiations March 25. Postal workers in New York, the last remaining stronghold of strike action, began returning to work March 25, and federal troops that had been moved into the city to help move the mail were withdrawn from the post offices. The troops had been used to sort the mail and had begun deliveries earlier that day.

Federal pay raise enacted. Legislation to provide a 6% pay raise, retroactive to Dec. 27, 1969, to postal and civil service employes and military personnel was passed by Congress April 8–14 and signed by President Nixon April 15.

Quick enactment of the legislation came in the wake of the postal strike.

The $2.6 billion package would go to the 700,000 postal employes, 1.4 million other federal civilian employes and 3.5 million servicemen.

The measure was approved by the Senate April 8 by an 84–1 vote and by the House April 9 by a 370–7 vote. But minor Senate changes requiring House approval, and some objection to including Congressional staffers in the pay raise, delayed final passage until April 14, when the House by voice vote sent the measure to the President.

A $2.2 billion bill to increase pay for federal employes by an average of 6.2% was approved by the Senate Dec. 30 and House Dec. 31.

Nixon raises GI benefits. White House Press Secretary Ronald L. Ziegler announced March 28 that President Nixon had accepted as "reasonable" and signed March 26 a compromise bill that would increase by 34.6% the monthly educational allowances to GI veterans, retroactive to Feb. 1, 1970.

The compromise bill emerged from a Senate-House conference committee after the President had threatened to veto the Senate's proposal for a 46% boost in GI benefits as inflationary. Nixon had originally proposed that the allowances be increased by 13%. The new benefits would affect about 736,000 veterans now receiving educational training and all future Vietnam war veterans who entered the program.

Among the major provisions of the new legislation:

■An increase from $130 to $175 a month paid to full-time students by the Veterans Administration for academic training in institutions of higher learning, apprenticeship schools, correspondence courses and other programs for which veterans were eligible for GI benefits.

■An increase for part-time students, and for veterans with dependents.

■Vocational rehabilitation payments would also be increased from $100 to $135 a month for a single, full-time student.

■Several provisions designed at aiding the veteran with a limited education to go back to school. Those veterans would be permitted to enroll in a limited number of noncredit college courses and still receive the stipend for attending school.

■Extra payments of $50 a month would be made available to veterans who need special educational tutoring.

Nixon asked Congress April 2 for an additional $65 million for medical care of veterans. The request reflected inflationary pressures, budgetary restrictions and the need for improved facilities for returning Vietnam war casualties.

Rail settlement imposed. Legislation (SJ Res 190) to avert a threatened railroad strike by imposing a settlement was approved by Congress April 8 and signed by President Nixon April 9. The settlement imposed on the nation's railroads and four shopcraft unions a contract negotiated in December 1969 and approved by three of the unions, representing machinists, boilermakers and electrical workers, but rejected by the fourth, representing sheet metal workers. It called for a 68¢-an-hour increase in the $3.60 hourly rate for the 48,000 workers involved. The imposed pact also contained a new work rule permitting members of all four unions to do "incidental work" in job jurisdictions of all four unions. The rejection of the contract by the sheet metal workers had been based on opposition to this provision, which they considered a threat to their job security and union.

The imposed settlement had been recommended in March by President Nixon, but Congress had imposed instead a 37-day strike ban, which expired April 10. No progress in negotiations was made during the interval.

The Louisville & Nashville Railroad was hampered in the Louisville, Ky. area by a wildcat strike April 8 by 1,600 members of the four shopcraft unions protesting the emergency legislation. But the work stoppage, which idled about 4,000 of the carrier's 5,100 Louisville-area employes when picket lines were honored by members of other unions, was enjoined April 9 by a temporary restraining order from U.S. Judge James E. Gordon.

Education aid authorized. A $24.6 billion education bill (HR514) was approved by a 74–4 Senate vote April 1 and 312–58 House vote April 7. It was signed by President Nixon April 13 with "considerable reluctance" because, he said, while the spending authorized was for "important education programs" for fiscal 1971, it also was "excessive and misdirected."

The $24.6 billion authorized—the most costly education aid bill ever approved by Congress—would extend for three years basic aid programs for elementary, high and vocational schools. About $15.2 billion of the total was authorized for school districts with large numbers of poor children; more than $1 billion a year was authorized for "impacted area" schools where enrollments were swollen by children of federal workers. Such funds also were extended for the first time to districts containing federally financed public housing projects, Cuban refugee families and migrant farm workers.

The bill also authorized use of funds in poor neighborhoods for special teacher bonuses, sometimes referred to as "combat pay."

Nixon specified his objections to the bill: spending was authorized "at a far higher level than that which can be accommodated in any fiscally responsible budget"; the impacted-area authorization was increased, although he had voiced objection to the program previously; students receiving loans under the national student defense loan program would have these loan payments canceled if they entered teaching or the military service, although "there is no evidence" that more students had entered teaching within the past 12 years as a result of the provision and no clear reason to think that military enlistments would be increased because of it.

Prices Soar, Profits & Securities Slump

Price indexes up in March. According to the Labor Department's revised wholesale price index for March, published April 6, wholesale prices increased twice the amount quoted in the department's preliminary report March 25. The actual index increase was .2% (a 2.4% annual rate), raising the index to 116.6% of the 1957–59 average. This was the smallest advance since the 2.4% annual rate of September 1969. The March index was 4.4% over the March 1969 figure.

The Labor Department reported April 22 that the consumer price index (CPI) for March, seasonally adjusted, rose .4% (a 4.8% annual rate). On an unadjusted basis,

the CPI climbed .5% to 133.2 (compared with 1957–59 prices) from 132.5 in February, and 6.1% over the past 12 months. The CPI for February had risen .5% on both an adjusted and unadjusted basis.

Assistant Commissioner of Labor Statistics Joel Popkin said the March increase was "still significant" in terms of the rate of inflation, but added that seasonally adjusted figures had shown "some easing" from the rate of increase during the late fall and early winter of 1969–70.

Higher prices for consumer services, especially mortgage interest rates and medical care, accounted for 70% of the March increment: rising mortgage interest rates, caused by the January rate hike in the Federal Housing Administration's mortgage ceiling, made up 28% of the overall increase; medical care contributed about 10%. A slackened .1% rise in food prices was assisted by a drop in egg prices. New car prices fell for the first time since September 1969, but total consumer durable goods rose .4%. Transportation prices declined .2% and gasoline prices fell 1.2%.

(Secretary of Labor George P. Shultz said in New York April 20 that the CPI increase was not slowing to a satisfactory pace, but voiced optimism that consumer prices would drop by the end of the year. Along with a parallel increase in labor output per man-hour, Shultz predicted that the consumer price situation would bring "a real growth of the economy on an orderly basis." He said present measures to slow the economy would not prevent "sustained high employment." He added that the moderate increases in the wholesale price index demonstrated the positive effects of the Administration's tight-money policy.)

A revised wholesale price index for April, issued May 11, showed that wholesale prices had remained stationary at the March level of 116.6% of the 1957–59 average, rather than declining .1% as reported April 29. The revised index was 4.2% higher than the April 1969 index. Prices of key industrial commodities rose by .3% to 116.2% from March's 115.8%.

In their sixth consecutive monthly decline, the prices farmers received for their products fell 3% in April, the Agriculture Department reported April 30. However, they remained 4% above the April 1969 level.

Incomes & output. The profit squeeze hit manufacturers harder in 1969 than any year since 1963, the Federal Trade Commission and Securities & Exchange Commission reported April 8. After-tax factory profits amounted to 4.8¢ of each sales dollar, a decrease from 5.1¢ in 1968; the 1963 level was 4.7¢.

U.S. companies reported large gains in profits of overseas subsidiaries. These gains helped to offset dipping corporate sales and profits at home, the Journal of Commerce reported April 1. Among companies reporting increased earnings abroad in 1969:

■International Business Machines Corp. (IBM) would have recorded a decrease in total net earnings in 1969 without its sharp increase in overseas profits.

■The food company CPC International, Inc. reported that its overseas earnings were rapidly overtaking its domestic profits (foreign business equaled $1.20 a share compared with $1.22 a share on the domestic market) and would probably exceed them in 1970.

■Overseas subsidiaries of Ford Motor Co. earned 29% of the company's net profits, compared with 19% in 1968.

■General Motors Corp. profits abroad surged to $160 million after taxes.

The First National City Bank in New York reported April 23 that its survey of 692 non-financial corporations and their profit margins in the first quarter of 1970 indicated one of the steepest declines in corporate earnings in the past several years. The survey said that despite the reduced tax surcharge, after-tax corporate profits had fallen 7% to $3.65 billion from the first quarter level of 1969, which was $3.93 billion. The figures represented a 10% decline from the $4.05 billion earned by the same firms in the fourth quarter of 1969. The survey attributed the drop in profits to cost-price pressures, slow sales and labor difficulties amid spiralling inflation.

The bank's Monthly Economic Letter, published April 5, said a survey of more than 3,500 corporations showed that 1969 profit margins had been among the lowest in 25 years.

Total first quarter earnings of 665 companies surveyed by the Wall Street Journal plunged 8.9% from a year earlier, it was reported May 4. This was the most striking first quarter decline since 1967 (when profits fell 9%).

Especially hard hit were electrical equipment and electronics concerns which suffered a 56.7% loss. The auto industry experienced its worst first quarter earnings since the 1958 recession. The airlines also announced deficits: United Air Lines, the U.S.' biggest carrier, announced April 30 a $15.1 million quarterly deficit—compared with its $1.2 million loss in the first quarter of 1969; Pan American World Airways sustained a $20.1 million loss, compared with $10.8 million a year earlier.

Although profit deficits were widespread, some companies posted gains; among them: nonferrous metals companies (with a 27.3% increase), finance companies, farm equipment producers, tobacco companies, distillers and drug manufacturers.

Citing a continuing "sluggish growth" in individual incomes since August 1969, the Commerce Department reported March 18 that personal income (seasonally adjusted) rose $3.3 billion in February to an annual rate of $777.6 billion. The increase was almost $500 million less than the revised January gain. The $1.7 billion rise in February of wages and salaries was the smallest in two years. In March, personal income rose $4.1 billion to an annual rate of $782.6 billion—a rate increase similar to January and February figures but higher than gains registered in late 1969. The increase in wages and salaries was $2.4 billion in March.

Reports issued April 16 showed that the nation's total output declined during the first quarter of 1970, although March economic indicators appeared to foreshadow an end to the slowdown in the economy. Preliminary March figures for several major indicators, published April 16, disclosed:

■The gross national product (GNP), measured in constant 1958 prices, fell $2.9 billion to $726.9 billion in the first quarter, compared with the small $800 million decline in 1969's fourth quarter. Measured in current prices, the GNP increased $8.2 billion to an annual rate of $960.4 billion by March 31. Sliding at a 1.5% annual rate, the real GNP experienced its sharpest slump for a quarter since the 1960–61 recession.

The Labor Department reported May 1 that productivity, or output per manhour, in the private sector of the economy had declined in the first quarter at a yearly rate of .6%, after the fourth quarter in 1969 had registered a 1.6% rise in the annual rate. As hourly worker compensation continued to climb in the first quarter, unit labor costs had increased at an annual rate of 8.4%.

■Following a consecutive seven-month decline, the Federal Reserve Board's index of industrial production gained slightly to reach 170.2 (of the 1957–59 average), compared with 169.8 in February. The board also reported a 9% increase in auto production after auto assemblies had fallen to an annual rate of 6.5 million units in February. Manufacturing slipped to 169 from 170 in January and 171.8 a year earlier.

■Although government and private analysts had predicted a decline, housing starts rose for the second consecutive month after a steep slide in late 1969 and early 1970. Climbing at an annual rate of 1,383,000, housing starts in March were up from a seasonally adjusted annual rate of 1,321,000 in February and 1,197,000 in January. Nevertheless, housing economist Saul B. Klaman remained pessimistic about an end to the housing slump, saying that optimism would be "entirely premature."

The Commerce Department said May 1 that new construction in March was at an annual rate of $90.2 billion, down from February's revised rate of $90.7 billion and far below the $91.7 billion rate of 12 months before.

Following a rise in construction spending in January and February, building outlays for March dropped .6% to a seasonally adjusted $90.2 billion rate, the Commerce Department reported May 3. The decline was principally in the public construction category, which fell to a $28 billion rate from $28.6 billion

in February. In February, building outlays had risen .9% to a seasonally adjusted $90.7 billion. Construction outlays for the first quarter rose to a $90.3 billion annual rate, up from the $89.7 rate in the fourth quarter of 1969.

The Federal Reserve Board reported May 4 that outstanding consumer installment credit rose in March by a seasonally adjusted $198 million—the smallest monthly increase since a $190 million rise in May 1967. The March increase was down from a $418 million rise in February (after four consecutive months of diminishing increases). The March figure placed the average monthly rise during the first quarter at $332 million, well below the $568 million average monthly increase in the fourth quarter of 1969 and the $695 million monthly average in 1969's first quarter.

Mortgage funds bolstered. The White House announced April 24 that commercial banks, life insurance companies and pension fund trustees had pledged a $2 billion increase in investment loans for residential mortgages in 1970. The announcement climaxed a campaign by the Administration since February to engage private funds to alleviate a home mortgage credit shortage. A Treasury official said the increase, which brought to $7 billion the amount of credit available to the housing industry from private sources, could stimulate financing for about 150,000 new homes. The announcement said that commercial banks would raise their direct residential mortgage investments from $3 billion in 1969 to $4 billion in 1970, insurance companies would increase their commitments to $2.55 billion, or $550 million more than planned for 1970, and pension fund trustees would invest $500 million in home mortgages in 1970.

Car industry profits dip. The three largest manufacturers of the auto industry—General Motors Corp., Ford Motor Co. and Chrysler Corp.—announced significant declines in earnings for the first quarter of 1970. Chrysler April 20 reported a $29.4 million loss—its second consecutive quarterly deficit and the worst quarter in its history (it had lost $34.2 million in the third quarter of

1959). The two largest manufacturers, GM and Ford, announced April 27 that they also had suffered dipping profits.

Citing increased material, labor and interest costs, Chrysler blamed its first quarter loss on the general economic situation in the nation: "Public concern over inflation and general economic conditions, including some pressure upon real disposable personal income, has meant that people not only bought fewer passenger cars in the first quarter, but also tended to buy lower-priced models with fewer options." The company also said that besides a 35% production cutback in the first quarter, shipments to North American dealers had been reduced about 90,000 units by March 31.

GM's net income dipped 33.4% to $348.3 million ($1.21 a common share) from $522.7 million ($1.82 a share) in the first quarter of 1969; it was the lowest first quarter figure since 1961. Dollar sales declined 14%. The company also said its hourly work force had fallen off 9% from an average 462,754 workers a year ago to 423,329.

At Ford, profits slumped 25.8%, producing a net income of $124.4 million ($1.51 a share) down from $167.7 million in 1969's first quarter, making the quarter the lowest for the company since 1967. Sales declined to $3.4 billion, compared to $3.6 billion a year earlier.

McCracken, Friedman statments. Paul W. McCracken, chairman of the President's Council of Economic Advisers, said in Dallas April 28 that the economy was showing signs of new strength. After two quarters of zero growth or decline, McCracken said, "evidence suggests that the pace of the economy is now beginning to quicken, and it is reasonable to hope that statistics of incomes, output, productivity and profits will make better reading as we move through the year." He predicted that rising inflation would begin to level off if, as he expected, the economy continued to grow "for the remainder of the year." His views were contained in a speech to the Financial Analysts Federation.

McCracken said there had been a large reduction in the rate of non-food commodity price increases. Commodity prices rose at an annual rate of 1.7% in the first quarter, compared with 3.9% in the last half of 1969 and 4.9 % in the first half of 1969, he reported. McCracken said his optimism at the state of the economy was based on the commodity price index, which, he said, would be the first likely indicator of cooling of the over-heated economy.

Milton Friedman, professor of economics at the University of Chicago and a presidential adviser, told a business economists' conference in Chicago May 1 that the economy was nearly halfway through a mild recession that had begun in third quarter of 1969. He said he expected the recession to end in the third or fourth quarter of 1970. He also said that the Cambodian involvement was not likely to materially change the percentage of GNP being spent on the war; he estimated the annual overall cost of the Vietnam War to be in the neighborhood of $20 billion.

Friedman said that one key to the economy's health lay in whether the Administration and the Federal Reserve Board would continue their present monetary and fiscal policies or would adopt a less restrictive policy toward expansion. Friedman said he believed the Administration would resist the "hysteria from Wall Street" and growing pressures from politicians to stimulate the economy. He warned that any measures that would affect the chances of halting inflation could lead to prices rising at an annual rate of 8% to 12% and "almost certain recourse to wage and price controls." Under the present policies, he said, "I think if we are lucky the rate of price increases will fall to about 3% by the end of this year, and continue to fall to 1.5%–2%."

Friedman said the jobless rate would probably rise to 5% or 6% by the end of 1970, followed by a decline in the first or second quarter of 1971, when real output could reach a growth rate of 4% or 4.5%.

Stock market plunges. Inflation, declining first quarter corporate profits and economic uncertainty, coupled with anxiety over U.S. involvement in Cambodia, created conditions that drove securities markets to their lowest levels since 1963 during April and the first part of May. The plunging stock averages came on top of a market decline of 250 points since November 1968.

On April 27 the Dow-Jones (D-J) industrial stock average plummeted 12.14 points to 735.5, the lowest level since the 711.49 recorded the day of President John F. Kennedy's assassination Nov. 22, 1963. Trading volume on the New York Stock Exchange (NYSE) was moderate, with 1,208 out of 1,587 stocks traded for the day. The New York Times combined stock average fell 5.94 points to 425.09 April 27, and the NYSE's composite index fell to 44.74, its lowest point since January 1967.

The D-J industrial average lost another 10.82 points April 28, sliding to 724.33.

In response to the severe market drop, President Nixon April 28 authorized Houston businessman John L. Spafford to quote his views, described as optimistic, on the current economic situation. According to Spafford, the President said: "I'm going to urge the people not to let such factors as employment being down, business being off and the stock market being down cause you to become deeply concerned to the point where you lose faith in the economy." The President reportedly predicted signs of an upturn in the economy during the fourth quarter of 1970. Spafford also quoted Nixon as saying: "Frankly, if I had any money I'd be buying stocks right now."

The market rallied April 29, pushing the D-J industrial average up 13.06 points to 737.39—its strongest increase in five weeks. It was the first time in 20 sessions that gaining stocks outnumbered losers on the NYSE. American Stock Exchange (Amex) prices also climbed, advancing the Amex index .28 to 22.03.

Brokers described the rally as a technical rebound caused by internal market factors. The rise was also linked by observers to a meeting that morning between Paul W. McCracken of the Council of Economic Advisers, and six representatives of the securities industry, at which assurances were traded that major brokerage houses were not on the brink of bankruptcy and that the government would continue to fight inflation. The market's downward trend resumed April 30.

Prices on the London and European stock markets reacted sharply to Wall Street's slipping market. Events in New York also sparked heavy speculation on gold and exerted some pressure on the British pound and Eurobonds. In London, the Financial Times index of industrial shares closed April 28 at 366.0, down 10.1 points and the Reuters industrial index fell 16.4 points to 565.2. The Tokyo exchange's index fell 4.32 points to 172.19 April 29. The Eurosyndicat index, comprising the 100 top grade stocks traded on the major European exchanges, was down to 148.27 April 29 from 154.12 the previous week.

President Nixon's announcement of U.S. intervention in Cambodia and the news of the bombing of North Vietnam sent stock and bond prices tumbling May 4. The D-J industrial average dropped 19.07 points to close at 714.56, a 27.52% decline from the Dow indicator's high of 985.21 Dec. 3, 1968.

The market dropped again May 5, with the Dow indicator losing 4.82 points to close at 709.74—its lowest figure since Aug. 9, 1963's 708.39.

In an effort to stem the market decline and stimulate stock purchases the Federal Reserve Board May 5 reduced margin requirements for stock purchases from 80% (in effect since June 1968) to 65%, effective the next day. The reduction cut the margin requirement to its lowest level in nearly seven years. But after some initial advances, stock prices resumed their plunge and did not rebound until the end of the month. Among developments that followed:

May 13—The D-J stock average plunged 10.75 points to close at 693.84—its lowest level since the market closed at 690.71 on July 29, 1963. It was the sixth time during May that the average had sunk more than 10 points in one trading session. Analysts had no specific explanation for the day's selloff. Trading was moderately active; declines on the NYSE outpaced advances by 1,141–226. The American Stock Exchange (Amex) also suffered a significant decline as its index dipped .23 points to 21.22.

May 14—Another market record low was set as the D-J average toppled 16.70 points during the day and then rallied to close at 684.79 (off 9.05 points), its lowest average since the 684.27 level reached April 2, 1963. The New York Times combined average also reached a new low since 1963 as it fell 5.70 points to 393.90.

May 15—The rally of the previous session held its own, pushing the D-J average soaring upward 17.43 points to close at 702.22 in the largest single-day advance since the 18.61 leap recorded April 8, 1968. The rebound was attributed to technical factors related to an "oversold" market.

May 18—For the first time in 11 Monday sessions, advancing stocks outnumbered declining issues 735–588. The D-J average clung to the market rally of May 15 with a slim .59-point gain, closing at 702.81.

May 19—The slight advance of the previous session's D-J average was counteracted with a loss of 11.41 points to finish at 691.40, erasing more than one-half the gains of May 15's 17.43 rebound.

Businessmen blame Nixon policies. A Louis Harris poll of executives of 500 of the nation's largest corporations revealed that 78% of the 537 businessmen questioned thought that President Nixon's policies had contributed to the stock market's decline, it was reported May 11. The poll, commissioned by Time magazine and taken after the announcement of Cambodia's invasion, reported that 80% believed the U.S. would have inflation and rising but controllable unemployment for the rest of 1970. Nixon's anti-inflation policies were supported by 40%; 55% said they thought the economy was now in a recession.

President optimistic. President Nixon predicted May 8 that 1970 would be "a good year" economically. The President's assessment was given in response to a question at his Washington press conference devoted primarily to the domestic reaction to U.S. intervention in Cambodia.

Nixon conceded that the nation's unemployment rate, which had risen to 4.8% in April, was "too high." However, he pointed out that during the 1961–65 period the jobless rate had averaged 5.7%; he said he hoped unemployment in 1970 could be kept below that figure. (The administration had been projecting a 4.3% jobless rate for 1970.) The President said that the April figure was a sign that the economy was cooling in response to "our fight against inflation."

Nixon said he believed there would be an upward movement in the gross national product (GNP) "in the last of the second quarter and throughout the third and fourth quarters"; he said he expected the GNP figure to pass the trillion-dollar mark by the end of the year.

The 4.8% unemployment figure, leaked to the Washington press May 7, had been confirmed by a Labor Department report the next day. The report said the actual number of jobless had dropped by 181,000 in April, but that in seasonally adjusted terms unemployment had increased by 291,000 to a total of 3,948,000 workers. Employment dropped to 78.9 million, while the number of part-time workers rose to 2.1 million, a figure that analysts said indicated a slack-work situation.

The report said unemployment for full-time male workers rose from 2.9% to 3.2% in April. There also was a significantly sharp rise in the jobless rate for Negroes—from 7.1% to 8.7%, compared with the increase from 4.1% to 4.3% for whites.

Labor Department job analyst Howard Stambler noted that employment gains "have come to a virtual standstill" since December 1969, while the total number of unemployed had risen 1.1 million in the same period.

Budget deficits expected. The Administration May 19 revised its budget forecasts and predicted deficits of $1.8 billion in fiscal 1970 and $1.3 billion in fiscal 1971. Surpluses of $1.5 billion and $1.3 billion for those fiscal years, respectively, had been forecast in February.

In addition, President Nixon asked Congress for a new tax on leaded gasoline—$4.25 per pound of lead, or an average of 2.3¢ a gallon, to be collected from manufacturers or importers of lead additives sold to oil refiners. The tax was to be an incentive for development of lead-free fuel, a clean-air proposal, in addition to a way to raise $1.6 billion in revenue in fiscal 1971.

The change from surplus to deficit in fiscal 1970 was attributed largely to a $3 billion shortfall in receipts, mostly from the corporate profits tax. The spending estimate for fiscal 1970 rose slightly from $197.9 billion in February to $198.2 billion. Although some items, including federal pay, rose $3 billion, the increases were offset by lower spending in other programs. notably space and Model Cities.

As for fiscal 1971, the budget remained "tight" and "fiscally responsible," according to the Budget Bureau. Outlays were estimated at $205.6 billion, a $4.8 billion rise from February, $2.3 billion of which came from "uncontrollable" items, such as interest on the debt. Estimated revenues also rose by $2.2 billion, although they depended upon Congressional action in many areas, such as the new tax and acceleration of the collection of gift and estate taxes. The spending increases covered federal pay ($1.4 billion), federally aided construction, housing and construction incentives, education, veterans benefits and school desegregation. Reductions were estimated for welfare aid and revenue sharing, largely because of legislative delay.

In his statement, Nixon said Congress "must cooperate if spending is to be controlled." He warned that if federal spending "were to exceed the potential yield of the tax system, I would not hesitate to ask Congress for further increases in taxes when I present my budget."

Stocks dive to 7-year low. Prices on the New York Stock Exchange May 25 recorded their largest single-day decline since the assassination of President John F. Kennedy Nov. 22, 1963. The Dow Jones (D-J) industrial stock average dropped 20.81 points to 641.36, a decline of 34.5% from the index's high of 985.21, registered Dec. 2, 1968. The New York Stock Exchange's composite index fell 1.24 points to close at 38.20, and the Standard & Poor's composite index fell two points to 70.25. The next day, May 26, the D-J indicator sank another 10.20 points to finish at 631.16, its lowest level since closing at 626.21 on Nov. 19, 1962.

The market's heavy two-day loss climaxed declines that had brought the D-J averages down 134 points in the previous five weeks. Similar declines were registered in American Stock Exchange prices; the Amex index dropped .49 to close at 19.57 on May 25 and .21 to close at 19.36 on May 26.

The Dow index's decline was registered as follows during the week prior to May 25: 11.41 points to close at 691.40 May 19; 14.85 points May 20; 11.30 on May 21; 3.08 on May 22.

Not one issue on the New York or the American exchanges posted a 1970 high May 25. Of the 1,808 stocks listed on the NYSE, more than half (911 issues) set new lows for 1970 and declines outnumbered advancing issues by 1,370 to 130. On May 26, volume on the NYSE mounted to 17.03 million shares, the heaviest trading in two months; 943 of the 1,027 declining issues were traded at new 1970 lows, while advancing issues totaled 388.

Administration reaction. Faced with what many market observers termed a "crisis in confidence" in his Administration's policies, President Nixon held a 40-minute conference May 21 with Bernard Lasker, an old friend and chairman of the New York Stock Exchange. During the meeting, the President reportedly reiterated his prediction that an economic upturn would occur later in the year and "present adjustments in the economy will give way to renewed expansion." White House Press Secretary Ronald L. Ziegler quoted the President as saying that the Administration's tight federal budget would permit "a continuing expansionist monetary policy by the Federal Reserve."

Lasker, who had requested the meeting during a White House visit in April, reported to the NYSE board of governors later that afternoon that he had tried to convey to the President his feeling that investor confidence had been shaken and was at the root of the bear market situation. He reportedly suggested that the two major factors affecting the market had been concern over the Vietnam war and the disclosure that the new federal budget would have a deficit rather than a slight surplus.

The President's economic aides continued to reflect Administration confidence at the market's future. Budget Director Robert Mayo commented May 25 that he thought "the stock market will find a new level and make its own adjustments" in line with the economy's own realignment. Speaking to the Pennsylvania Bankers Association in Atlantic City the next day, Secretary of Labor George P. Shultz termed the stock market decline "a kind of neurosis."

Stock market in record rally. Prices on the New York Stock Exchange dramatically reversed their recent declines May 27 in the largest single-day gain ever recorded by modern market indicators. The Dow Jones industrial stock index of 30 blue-chip shares shot up 32.04 points to close at 663.20. The gain topped by .01 point the previous one-day record, recorded on Nov. 26, 1963, the Tuesday following the funeral of President John F. Kennedy. The May 27 rally came unexpectedly and on the heels of a series of losses that had driven the D-J index down by 71.65 points in the previous six trading sessions. The rally continued May 28 and 29, and brought the Dow index to 700.44, recouping about two-thirds of the total losses registered in the past month.

The American Stock Exchange (Amex) index climbed .60 points to 19.96 May 27, the largest one-day advance since the index's inception in October 1962. The Amex turnover of 5,887,105 shares was the highest for the year.

Other market indicators also recorded unusually strong advances during the three-day upsurge. Among the highlights: the D-J average surged 20.95 points to close at 684.15 May 28 and 16.29 points May 29 to reach 700.44. The New York Times combined average of 50 stocks jumped 19.15 points to 376.69 May 27 and ended the week at 397.42. Standard & Poor's 500-stock index moved up 3.48 points to 72.77 on May 27.

During the three-day period, more than 1,000 issues on the New York Stock Exchange (NYSE) posted price advances. On May 27, gains outpaced declines by 1,312 to 191, while volume registered 17.46 million shares, the second highest total of the year. The following day, volume reached 18.91 million shares, the highest level of the year; 1,211 issues gained and 271 declined.

The bond market, which had been in a steady decline since late March, also experienced a wide recovery May 27; government bonds rallied almost two points and corporate bonds made substantial advances.

Analysts differed in their explanations of the stock market's rebound and cited both technical and external factors. Some said President Nixon's pending White House dinner May 27 with business and financial leaders [see below] had a reassuring effect on investor confidence. The market's advance May 28 was mostly attributed to technical factors. The spurt May 29 was reportedly touched off by a wire-service report which quoted "an authoritative Administration official" as saying that the President did not intend to propose higher taxes even if the federal budget reached $5 billion.

Spurred by the Wall Street rebound May 27, stock prices in London closed markedly higher May 28. The Financial Times index jumped 11.4 points to 332.4 and the Reuters industrial index rose 23.5 points to 520.6. The Tokyo Stock Exchange's 225-share index made the largest gain in its history, 79.46 points, to close at 2,009.10.

Economic Controls Debated

Burns, Romney for wage-price guidelines. In two speeches the same day, May 18, Federal Reserve Board Chairman Arthur F. Burns and Secretary of Housing and Urban Development George Romney called for new Administration intercession to restrain the current wage-price spiral. The speeches placed both men in opposition to the President's Council of Economic Advisers (CEA) which officially opposed any guidelines or other government intervention in private wage-price decision-making.

In a major policy speech to the American Bankers Association Mone-

GOVERNMENT POLICY

tary Conference in Hot Springs, Va., Burns warned that the Administration's exclusive reliance on monetary and fiscal measures to combat inflation could cause "a very serious business recession." He then voiced a surprise recommendation for a "useful—albeit a very modest" incomes policy (a wage-price program under which government presumably would pressure management and labor to hold down increases) to "speed us through this transitional period of cost-push inflation." Although Burns avoided detail and stressed that primary reliance must remain on monetary and fiscal measures, he referred to Canada's current six-month price pause as "fascinating." He was explicit, however, that he was thinking in terms of a temporary program that would "stop well short of direct wage and price controls."

Speaking after Burns at the same meeting, CEA Chairman Paul W. McCracken repeated his objections to a direct wage-price policy, saying it would not work when price increases were "rampant." However, he admitted that economic conditions were more conducive to voluntary control now than in 1969.

Addressing a New York meeting of the Institute of Collective Bargaining and Group Relations, Romney expressed dissatisfaction with the Administration's present anti-inflation program of tight spending and credit policies; he said his disenchantment was shared by others in the Administration who had not spoken out publicly. Romney said: "Without question, vigorous fiscal and monetary restraint can eventually bring inflation under control. But if the only actions taken are of a fiscal and monetary nature, this control over inflation comes at some risk of unacceptably high unemployment and unacceptably low rates of housing production and community development." To further assist the government's anti-inflation battle, Romney advocated the establishment of a Presidential commission to apply pressure against excessive wage or price increases by calling public attention to them.

The two proposals, especially the Burns recommendation, stirred reaction both within the U.S. and abroad. Among developments:

Senate Majority Leader Mike Mansfield (D, Mont.) May 21 called for "serious consideration" of standby wage, price and profit controls, as well as larger down payments on installment sales, to offset the current "recessionary" business slow-down.

A House Government Operations subcommittee May 26 approved, 5 to 1, a bill requiring the CEA to set anti-inflation wage-price guidelines for business and labor to follow at the request of the President. The measure, introduced by Rep. Henry S. Reuss (D, Wis.), evoked immediate opposition from the Administration. At a news conference in Los Angeles the same day, CEA Chairman McCracken said the Administration was "emphatically" opposed to mandatory wage-price controls; he said he saw little value in voluntary controls. Treasury Secretary David Kennedy said he saw "no need for [standby wage-price powers] at the present time."

David Rockefeller, chairman of the Chase Manhattan Bank, said at a New York news conference May 25 that he was "strongly opposed" to any federal action "carried to the point of all-out wage and price controls." However, he urged both business and labor to take "a more responsible attitude" toward wage and price increases; he added he would favor "exploring the possibilities" of less drastic measures to maintain the "balance between productivity gains and wage and price increases."

Pierre-Paul Schweitzer, director-general of the International Monetary Fund, said in Geneva May 19 that the U.S. was "imparting a serious inflationary bias to the world," declaring that no country should shun an incomes policy when it was needed. In Paris, the Organization for Economic Cooperation and Development (OECD), a body representing 22 nations, suggested that formal wage-price guidelines would help align high employment in the U.S. with price stability. The OECD recommendation, reported May 26, was made in a 46-page review of the U.S. economy.

Wage, price controls urged. Calls for some form of "incomes policy," or restraint on wages and prices, to check the continuing inflation came from various sources May 27–June 16.

Assistant Treasury Secretary Murray L. Weidenbaum told the Joint Economic Committee of Congress June 2 it was his personal opinion it was time "to give some serious consideration to an incomes policy."

In somewhat similar language the same day, Thomas J. Watson Jr., chairman of the International Business Machines Corp., testifying before the Senate Foreign Relations Committee, urged that "the Administration give serious consideration to resorting at once to the guidelines approach to wages and prices." Watson identified the war in Indochina as "a major obstacle" to the nation's economic health and said "we must end this tragedy before it overwhelms us."

Economist John Kenneth Galbraith also coupled a call for an end to the war with economic testimony June 16 before the House Banking Committee. He advocated an emergency freeze of all prices and wages for about six months and a permanent system of statutory controls over the prices and wages of large corporations and unions. He said "all of this action needs to be combined with a speedy liquidation of our adventure in Indochina." It was the committee's opening hearing on a measure to give the President temporary authority to freeze prices and wages at May 25 levels.

There were also moves in Congress to revive the voluntary wage-price guideposts and to have the Administration publish a monthly analysis of inflationary developments in the wage-price field.

The Senate Democratic Policy Committee unanimously adopted a resolution June 16 calling for revival of the guideposts, a national conference on inflation and unemployment, Presidential use of his standby authority to ration credit and Administration cooperation with Congress for action "as may be required to check the decline in the economy."

Nixon dinner for business leaders. President Nixon held a "private" dinner at the White House May 27 for 45 of the nation's top business executives and financiers to discuss foreign policy and economy. The dinner was interpreted as an effort to bolster confidence in the financial and corporate communities which had been shaken by sagging company profits and steady losses on Wall Street.

During the wide-ranging discussion which took place, Nixon reportedly expressed strong opposition to mandatory wage and price controls, but left the impression that he was open to some form of voluntary wage-price restraints. The President was quoted as saying the economy was healthy and would begin to recover in the third quarter of 1970. He also said the gross national product would near $1 trillion by the end of the year.

According to press accounts, Federal Reserve Board Chairman Arthur F. Burns prefaced a three-minute talk by acknowledging the financial community's concern over the state of "liquidity" (ready cash) in the economy. He said the Federal Reserve, in its capacity as a lender of last resort, would readily furnish necessary credit in the event of any liquidity crisis. Burns reportedly said there had been no expansion of the money supply during the last five months of 1969, but that the Federal Reserve had begun increasing the money supply during the first three months of 1970 at a 4% annual rate and then at a 10% annual rate in April. (In its publication Quarterly Economic Trends, May 28 issue, the St. Louis Federal Reserve Bank released data showing a rapid acceleration at a 6% annual rate in the nation's money supply in the quarter ended May 20.)

(Again reflecting Administration efforts to soothe anxieties about the economy with predictions of a forthcoming upturn in the economy in the latter half of the year, Vice President Spiro T. Agnew, in a May 28 speech in a Republican fund-raising luncheon in Huntington, N.Y. said, "1970 is going to be a good year for business, with an upturn in the second half." Agnew said it was important to keep the recent stock market decline in perspective and suggested that "Wall Street is capable of overreacting in both directions.")

Public debt ceiling raised. The Treasury Department asked Congress May 25 for an additional $18 billion in borrowing authority that would raise the nation's "permanent" debt ceiling to $395 billion. Administration spokesmen said lagging corporate profits and other economic factors had reduced government tax revenues, thus necessitating the request. Without congressional action before June 30, the debt ceiling would fall to $365 billion on July 1.

The Treasury's request touched off a round of criticism from Democratic leaders in Congress. At a news conference May 26, Senate Majority Leader Mike Mansfield (Mont.), House Majority Leader Carl Albert (Okla.) and Speaker of the House John McCormack (Mass.), declared that rising unemployment and continued inflation had plunged the economy into a crisis situation. They urged the President to summon a national conference of business and labor leaders and professional economists to assist Congress in the formation of national economic policies. Mansfield also said the President should consider wage and price controls; he called for firm action to reduce interest rates.

A bill raising the temporary public debt limit to $395 billion for fiscal 1971 and the permanent debt ceiling to $380 billion was passed by 236–127 House vote June 3 and 64–19 Senate vote June 29. President Nixon signed HR 17802 June 30.

Prices continue to climb. The price increases continued:

■The Labor Department reported May 20 that consumer retail prices experienced their biggest jump since December 1969. Rising an inflationary .6% (.5% on a seasonally adjusted basis) to 134% from 133.2% of the 1957–59 average, the consumer price index (CPI) indicated that the dollar was now worth less than 75¢ in terms of 1957–59 purchasing power. Up a sharp annual rate of 7.2%, the CPI was 6% higher than a year earlier. The increase would have been more severe except that grocery prices, which had advanced every month since October 1969, maintained a steady 4.9% annual rate. A rise in service prices at a 10.6% annual rate accounted for about four-tenths of the overall increase in the index.

The Labor Department's report was issued one day after President Nixon

had declared that price increases were "beginning to slow down." Assistant White House Press Secretary Gerald Warren said the White House was "disappointed" by the reversal of a slower trend in the index during the two quarters preceding April, but expected it to be only "temporary."

The Labor Department reported June 18 that in May the consumer price index rose .4% to 134.6.

The Labor Department said, however, that after adjustment of the statistics to account for normal seasonal changes in some consumer prices, the increases for both April and May amounted to .5%. The May index improvement over the April rise (.6%) was called a significant improvement over the turn of the year by Joel Popkin, assistant commissioner of labor statistics. The chief reason for the improved May mark was the smallest rise in price of services since 1969.

The CPI showed that food prices resumed their rise in May after being essentially stable during April. Meat prices were down, but the price of vegetables, fruits and dairy products rose. Among other important items in increasing the overall price level for May were used cars, the cost of buying a new home, housekeeping supplies, apparel, rent and public transportation. Of the items that declined, the price of gasoline was considered the most important.

■According to preliminary statistics released by the Labor Department May 26, wholesale prices in May rose .2% (a 2.4% annual rate) to 116.8% of the 1957–59 average. (The .2% figure was confirmed by the department June 5.) The increase reversed a downward trend in the index that had characterized March and April figures. A consecutive .3% rise in prices of key industrial commodities offset a .5% decline in prices of farm products and processed foods.

■The Agriculture Department reported May 28 that prices paid to farmers for their products advanced one-third of 1% in May, ending a two-month decline. Higher prices for vegetables and fruits were mostly responsible for the increase.

Leading indicators dip in April. A .1% decline in the Commerce Department's composite index of "leading" economic indicators for April, published May 14, illustrated the continuing sluggishness of the economy. The index, at its lowest point since November 1968, dropped to 147.8% of the 1963 average. It was also reported that the March index had been revised to show a steep 1.7% decline.

Four indicators fell—the average work week for production workers, industrial materials prices, prices of 500 stocks and the average weekly initial claims for state unemployment insurance (inversely treated). The four rising indicators were new durable goods orders, plant and equipment orders, new building permits and the ratio of price to labor unit cost in manufacturing.

Among other statistics released May 14:

■The price index for the gross national product (GNP) was revised upward to a 6.2% annual rate increase for the first quarter, its fastest pace since 1951. The new figure was much larger than had been anticipated on the basis of preliminary estimates. In 1958 dollar terms used to remove inflationary effects, the real GNP (physical output of private and governmental goods and services) slumped at a 3% annual rate to $959.6 billion, the Commerce Department said.

■Industrial production resumed its steady decline, according to the Federal Reserve index which fell .4% from 171.1% to 170.4% of the 1957–59 average. It was the eighth drop in a nine-month period and carried the index back to its January–February level. In a slow overall 2.5% descent, output declined seven months in a nine-month period.

■Total personal income rose at an annual rate of $17.8 billion to a record $801.1 billion seasonally adjusted annual rate, the Commerce Department said. Income would have fallen for the first time in five years by $1 billion, but was rescued by a 15% increase in Social Security benefits and a 6% federal pay increase.

■Pre-tax corporate profits dropped sharply to an $85.1 billion seasonally adjusted annual rate in the first quarter, their lowest level since 1967. They declined nearly 7% from 1969's fourth quarter and 11% from that year's first quarter on an annual rate basis.

Other statistics. The following additional economic data was released by various government agencies:

■Total business inventories demonstrated an unusually slight increase of $150 million in March, the Commerce Department said May 12. An increase of $830 million for the full first quarter was the smallest since 1967. Business sales dropped $1 billion, making the ratio of inventories to sales 1.59 against 1.57 in February.

■After two consecutive monthly advances, housing starts took a steep fall in April to a seasonally adjusted annual pace of 1,181,000. According to the Commerce Department report May 17, April starts were down 14.7% from March's upward-revised 1,384,000.

■The Commerce Department said June 1 that construction spending in April slowed for the second straight month, as outlays for commercial buildings fell off sharply. At a seasonally adjusted rate, outlays declined 1.3% from the upward revised $90.3 billion in March. The entire April decline was in private construction, which dropped to a $60.7 billion rate from $62.3 billion in March.

■The Federal Home Loan Bank reported May 25 that average interest rates on conventional mortgages declined in April for the first time in 16 months. The monthly average was 8.40%, down from 8.47% in March. However, the average was well above the 7.62% a year earlier. Preston Martin, chairman of the Bank board, commented that, while the decline was "highly encouraging, it was too early to indicate a trend or turning point"; improved mortgage rates that usually followed market rates could be reversed if market rates took an upturn.

Outside the government, findings of the following two reports were announced May 27:

■Dun & Bradstreet Inc. reported that the total number of business failures fell to a 16-year low in 1969, but average liabilities of failing companies reached a new high. In the fourth straight year that business collapses had declined, 9,154 commercial and industrial companies reported failures for 1969, compared with 9,636 in 1968. The average liability for each failing company in 1969 surged to $124,767 from $97,654 in 1968; total liabilities advanced to $1.14 billion from about $941 million.

■A survey by the National Industrial Conference Board disclosed that consumers were growing more pessimistic about the economy and were beginning to moderate their spending plans. The study of 10,000 families, conducted during March and April, disclosed that 19% of the interviewees thought business conditions were bad, an increase from 16% registered by a similar survey taken in January and February; 36% intended to buy major appliances in the next six months, down from 39% in the January-February sample.

Unemployment reaches 5%. Unemployment rose for the fifth straight month in May and reached 5% of the labor force, the Labor Department said June 5. It was the largest five-month increase (from 3.5% in January) since the 1960 recession and the highest rate since February 1965; the May figure represented an increase of 1.3 million in the number of jobless since January. It was estimated that 3,384,000 workers were jobless for the month; on a seasonally adjusted basis, the figure was raised to 4.1 million.

Most of the increase in unemployment affected white, adult, full-time workers in the manufacturing and construction industries. Only an estimated one in five workers had been jobless for 15 weeks or longer, but their number, 612,000, had increased by 200,000 since the beginning of the year.

Negro unemployment declined from 8.7% to 8% in May, but was still higher than the 7.1% figure of March. The rate for whites rose from 4.3% to 4.6% in May.

Harold Goldstein, assistant commissioner of labor statistics, said that on the basis of total joblessness and insured unemployment, the current job situation was much milder than during either of the major postwar recessions.

The Labor Department reported June 14 that the rise in the nation's unemployment in 1970 had victimized skilled white workers in the aircraft, aerospace, automobile and weapons industries more than any other group in the U.S. civilian labor force. That unemployment, the department said, was centered among skilled whites in the Midwest and on the West Coast.

The rise in unemployment among skilled whites, the department said, "suggests that cutbacks in the defense and aerospace fields, the impacts of which are also being felt in many other industries, have been primary factors in halting the growth of factory employment since mid-1969." The report also said that the housing slump and the slower pace of automobile sales added to the rise in unemployment.

The report said the unemployment had less of an impact on Negroes, primarily because they had never been largely represented in the industries showing substantial job losses since mid-1969. The report warned, however, that even though joblessness had been less severe in other industries, there were indications that it was spreading. The report noted that in other "goods-producing sectors of the economy—mining, construction and agriculture—employment has remained at a virtual standstill since last fall."

The 1970 trend showing a rise in unemployment in the defense and automobile industries continued to creep upward. The report said employment in the last 10 months had dropped 21.1% in ordnance and related defense hardware, 9.1% in aircraft and aircraft parts production, and 13.2% in automobiles and automotive equipment.

The department said that the Pacific Coast area, "which contains only one-eighth of the nation's labor force, has accounted for about one-fifth of the national increase in state-insured unemployment" from April 1969-April 1970. The department attributed the rise in cutbacks in aerospace and defense related industries.

The climb in unemployment in the Midwest was attributable, the department said, to cutbacks in automobile productions.

1970 jobless rate projected—Herbert Stein, a member of President Nixon's Council of Economic Advisors, told a

Congressional subcommittee June 15 that the U.S. unemployment rate would probably remain near the 5% mark for the remainder of 1970.

Stein told members of the Joint Economic Committee on the subject of changing national priorities that "we are running below the path (in the economy) that we would have chosen."

The Washington Post reported that Stein's testimony represented the first time a high level administration official had conceded that the job outlook was less optimistic than predicted at the start of 1970. Stein rejected the idea, however, that the time had come to "pump up the economy," and instead predicted that to cure inflation the economy must "go through a period of slack."

Stein told the Congressional panel that full employment for the nation's civilian labor force was not the "optimum feasible path" in view of the state of the nation's economy. Stein said that because of the need to hold down inflation, the economy still had to perform below its potential.

ICC grants interim freight-rate rise. The Interstate Commerce Commission (ICC) May 27 authorized the nation's railroads to put into effect upon 10 days notice temporary freight-rate increases of up to 5%. The commission thus suspended proposed 6% increases pending a full investigation. Six ICC members approved the increase. Two commissioners did not vote.

The ICC authorization said that the interim 5% rise would be subject to later refund if the investigation of the railroads' request for a 6% rise showed the increase unjustified. The commission also imposed restrictions on rate rises for shipping certain commodities—including coal and coke, iron ore, pig iron and iron and steel scrap, grains and fresh fruits and vegetables. Most of the nation's railroads had requested the increase in March, claiming that a 6% freight-rate rise that went into effect in November 1969 and rises in 1968 and 1967 still did not offset the increased cost of wages and materials.

Government Action, Nixon Bars Curbs

Nixon appeals for restraint. President Nixon delivered an economic address to the nation June 17 appealing for restraint in wage and price decisions, but he ruled out mandatory controls in the fight against inflation and recession. While reaffirming his basic economic policy to cut federal spending and apply firm and steady restraint to the economy, Nixon announced several specific supplementary actions "to speed up the fight against inflation."

Among them were designation of two new federal bodies and establishment of "a periodic inflation alert" system, prepared by the Council of Economic Advisers, to "spotlight the significant areas of wage and price increases and objectively analyze their impact on the price level." This, he said, would "call attention to outstanding cases of price or wage increases."

One of the new bodies to be appointed was a National Committee on Productivity which would include representatives from business, labor, the public and government. Its duty would be "to point the way toward" growth of productivity. "We must achieve a balance between costs and productivity that will lead to more stable prices," he said. The commission was to convene within the next few months a special President's Conference on Productivity with leaders of business, labor, government and the public participating.

The second body to be established was a Regulations and Purchasing Review Board which would review all government actions "to determine where federal purchasing and regulations drive up costs and prices." Import policy would be reviewed "to see how supplies can be increased to meet rising demand without losing jobs here at home."

The President also presented a list of legislative demands. Congress should not "play politics with inflation," he said, "by passing legislation granting the president standby powers to impose wage and price controls. The Congress knows I will not impose controls because they would do more harm than good."

Instead, Congress should "cooperate," he said, and pass legislation to: (a) expand and strengthen the unemployment insurance system; (b) provide an automatic increase in manpower training funds in times of high unemployment, as embodied in the Manpower Training Act; (c) provide a full appropriation for the Office of Economic Opportunity and an immediate supplemental budget of $50 million for a training and support program for young people in the summer; (d) protect the small investor by establishing an insurance corporation with a federal guarantee against losses caused by financial difficulties of brokerage houses; (e) tie Social Security benefits to the cost of living; (f) inject as much as $6 billion into the housing market by enactment of the Emergency Home Finance Act of 1970; (g) give the Small Business Administration greater authority to stimulate loans to small businesses at lower interest rates; and (h) provide emergency assistance to railroads in financial difficulties.

The President also urged Congress "to join me in holding down government spending to avoid a large budget deficit." If a bill were introduced calling for more spending, he said, it should be coupled with one to raise the taxes to pay for the new program.

In his appeal for wage and price restraint, Nixon said: "If businessmen and workingmen are willing to raise their sights by lowering their demands, they will help themselves by helping to hold down everybody's cost of living. I believe there is a new social responsibility growing up in our economic system on the part of unions and corporations. Now is the time for that social concern to take the form of specific action on the wage-price front."

He would not, he declared, "take this nation down the road of wage and price controls," which "only postpone a day of reckoning" and "rob every American of a very important part of his freedom."

Nixon said he was "convinced that the basic economic road we have taken is the right road, the responsible road, the road that will curb the cost of living and lead us to orderly expansion." But he conceded some problems: "The mo-

mentum of four years of inflation was stronger than had been anticipated. The effect on unemployment is greater than we foresaw. The pace of our progress toward price stability and high employment has not been quick enough."

"Unemployment has increased," he said, "the price index continues to rise, profits have gone down, the stock market has declined. Interest rates are too high."

He indicated that a large measure of blame for the difficulties lay upon the preceding Democratic Administrations. In the decade of the sixties, he said, "federal deficits totaled $57 billion." In the three years before the Nixon Administration took office, federal spending rose an average of 15% a year while his Administration had "slashed" this to 7% in the current fiscal year and intended to again halve the increase in the next fiscal year.

Basically, the President said, the nation was confronted with two difficult problems—dealing with the "transition from a wartime economy to a peacetime economy," and avoiding a recession while ending a major inflation. The economy, he said, would have to adjust to reduced defense spending, to the degree of "a historic reordering of our national priorities." The President added that "there is no more important goal than to curb inflation without permitting severe disruption."

"This is an activist Administration," he said, "and should new developments call for new action in the future, I shall take the action needed to attain that goal."

Productivity commission. President Nixon named 23 members to his new National Commission on Productivity July 10. He asked the newly appointed commission to seek a balance between costs and productivity that would help stabilize prices. Noting that productivity in the past two years had grown at a "much slower rate than usual," the President instructed the commission to seek ways to increase the nation's output.

In addition to five officials from the Administration, the newly composed body included groups of six members representing business, labor and the general public. A chairman was not designated. The commission's members were:

Representing business—Harlee Branch Jr., chairman of the Southern Co.; Edward W. Carter, president of Broadway-Hale Stores, Inc.; George E. Keck, president of United Air Lines; R. Heath Larry, vice chairman of the U.S. Steel Corp.; James Roche, chairman of the General Motors Corp.; and Walter Wriston, chairman of the First National City Bank (N.Y.) From labor—I. W. Abel president of the United Steelworkers of America; Joseph A. Beirne, president of the Communications Workers of America; John H. Lyons, president of the International Association of Bridge, Structural and Ornamental Iron Workers; George Meany, president of the AFL-CIO; Floyd E. Smith, president of the International Association of Machinists and Aerospace Workers; Leonard Woodcock, president of the United Auto Workers of America. From the public—William T. Coleman Jr., partner, Dilworth, Paxson, Kalish, Levy and Coleman, law firm in Philadelphia; John T. Dunlop, dean of arts and sciences at Harvard University; Howard W. Johnson, president of Massachusetts Institute of Technology; Edward H. Levi, president of the University of Chicago; Arjay Miller, dean of the Graduate School of Business, Stanford University; W. Allen Wallis, President of the University of Rochester. From the Administration—David M. Kennedy, secretary of the treasury; Maurice H. Stans, secretary of commerce; James D. Hodgson, secretary of labor; Paul W. McCracken, chairman of the Council of Economic Advisers, and George P. Shultz, director of the Office of Management and Budget.

Mansfield rebuts Nixon on economy. Senate Democratic leader Mike Mansfield (Mont.) delivered a broadcast rebuttal June 24 to President Nixon's June 17 economic address.

Mansfield said it was "an economic fact" that the country was in a recession and that the root cause was a "distorted use of the nation's resources," particularly in supporting the war in Southeast Asia and in neglecting domestic problems. "We are using our resources at a reckless rate and with dubious wisdom in other places and in other ways," Mansfield declared. And inflation, unemployment and war "spell recession," he said. "References to the mistakes of the past cannot paper over it. The rhetoric of a radiant tomorrow does not alter it."

The rebuttal was broadcast free by the National Broadcasting Co. June 24 and by the American Broadcasting Co. June 25 in response to Democratic efforts to attain equal access to the air waves to counter appearances by the Republican president. The Columbia Broadcasting System also had pledged free time for such use on a regular basis.

Mansfield said government spending was "seriously out of date" with priori-

ties "determined largely by yesterday's fears and fallacies." "For too long we have pursued the nation's security all over the globe," he said, and "forgotten that the nation's security begins at home."

Mansfield said the Congressional Democrats did not believe that the nation's economic problems would disappear "if only they are let alone by government." But they would, he said, "give the most respectful consideration to whatever the President may propose to halt the inflation and high unemployment and to terminate our involvement in Vietnam."

Defending Congress' record on economic matters, Mansfield said it had cut the President's budget $6.4 billion in 1969, closed $6.6 billion of tax loopholes and passed a selective credit control law unused by the Administration. This year, he said, it was proceeding with its own housing measure, would probably reduce the President's budget again and would adopt Administration programs on manpower and unemployment compensation.

He praised the President's plans for a productivity commission and indicated further measures were needed. Although it could not very well do it itself, he said, Congress would support Administration efforts to fasten the attention of business and labor on "the consequences of excessive wage and price increases" or to establish wage and price guidelines.

Economic index down for May. The Commerce Department reported June 26 that the government's composite index of "leading indicators" of the economy had declined by .8% in May. The index in May was 147.3 with 1963 taken as 100. The report indicated that although the dip remained modest, the index did not point to any significant early change in the state of the economy.

The index had been steady at about 152 in the third and fourth quarters of 1969, dropped to 149.6 in the first quarter of 1970, was 148.5 in April and then fell to the May level of 147.3.

In a second part of the report, the Commerce Department said that labor costs per unit of output in manufacturing resumed a rise in May after an April decline. The report noted that this rise probably reflected the sharp decline in industrial production in May. The index, with 1957–58 as 100, was at 118.1 in May, up from 117.6 in April. The index had fallen in April from 117.8 in March.

Drop in May industrial output. The Federal Reserve Board (FRB) reported June 12 that the industrial output of the nation's factories, mines and utilities, a key indicator of the buoyancy of the U.S. economy, had sagged in May to its lowest level in 18 months. The FRB noted that some of the May slippage may have been attributable to shortages of supplies in some industries that were affected by work stoppages in the rubber industries and protracted trucking strikes.

The index of industrial production, which was based on the production of the years 1957–59, taken as 100, dropped .8% to 169. It was the lowest level since December 1968, when the index dipped to 168.7.

The May drop paralleled the uncertain signs marked by the index in 1970. The index rose in March and then declined in April. But the April sag merely eliminated the March gain, bringing the index back to its February level.

The FRB's industrial production index dropped again in June, the board reported July 15. The decline of .5 to 168.6 amounted to a .3% drop. Since its 174.6 peak in July 1969, the index had fallen a total of 3.4%.

A six-month decline in the Gross National Product (GNP) appeared to have ended in the second quarter, according to preliminary data released by the Commerce Department July 16. The seasonally adjusted annual rate of nation's total output of goods and services increased by $10.6 billion to $970.1 billion, up from $959.5 billion in the first quarter. Almost the entire gain, however, was attributed to higher prices, and there was only a marginal gain— about 3/10 of 1% at an annual rate—in the real GNP.

Personal income rate falls. The Commerce Department reported June 17 that for the first time in almost five years the total personal income of Americans declined during the month of May to a seasonally adjusted rate of $793.5 billion. The mark was $7.8 billion below the

April level of $801.3 billion, the sharpest monthly drop on record.

The department said, however, that the drop was attributed to special factors. The discrepancies between the April and May figures, the Commerce Department reported, resulted from the retroactive increases in Social Security benefits and federal salaries that were paid during April. The department said that slightly more than $8 billion of the sharp $18 billion rise in April personal income was due to a lump sum retroactive payment in Social Security payments which did not appear in the May figures. Commerce also said personal income in the first five months of 1970 averaged $786 billion, $56.5 billion (7¾%) above the same period for 1969.

The Commerce Department reported July 18 that personal income had dropped in June to a seasonally adjusted annual rate of $798.8 billion from $799.8 billion in May. The department noted, however, that there would have been a month-to-month increase in June if about $3.75 billion of retroactive federal pay raises had not been added to the May figure. Excluding this factor, personal income would have gained about $2.75 billion.

Unemployment rise seen. Secretary of Labor George P. Shultz said June 16 that unemployment among the nation's civilian working force would probably climb above the 5% rate recorded in May, the highest monthly figure since 1965. Shultz said the government's weekly tally of unemployment compensation claims was still rising through June, indicating, he said, that the number of jobless persons would rise in some of the coming months.

Shultz's predictions came in his first interview since he was named by President Nixon to head a new White House superagency, the Office of Management and Budget.

Shultz criticized Congress for not acting on the measures he said the President had sought to ease the impact on unemployment resulting from cutbacks in aerospace and defense spending and the Administration's anti-inflation drive. Shultz also projected that inflation would slow toward the end of 1970 and said the President's economic policies would result in a nearly balanced budget by the end of Nixon's term.

In a related development, Paul W. McCracken, President Nixon's principal economic advisor, projected June 21 that the nation's unemployment figures could get worse. McCracken, the chairman of the President's Council of Economic Advisors, said he expected another half-point rise in the 5% unemployment rate. He predicted, however, that the U.S. was "not very far" from the peak in unemployment. He added that some evidence indicated inflation was being slowed and that a significant change could be expected in 1971.

Jobless rate falls. A drop in the nation's seasonally adjusted unemployment rate from 5% in May to 4.7% in June carried the closely watched jobless figure downward for the first time since November 1969. However, officials of the Labor Department, which released the unemployment figures July 2, said the "underlying employment situation" was essentially unaltered from previous months.

A decline in the jobless rate among adult women from 5.1% in May to 4.5% accounted for most of the overall decline in the June rate. Seasonally adjusted rates for adult men (3.5%), married men (2.6% in May to 2.5%) and teenagers (14.3% to 14.6%) remained relatively steady. The real number of unemployed persons increased 1.3 million to 4.7 million, but declined to 3.9 million from 4.1 million on a seasonally adjusted basis. With unemployment ordinarily rising sharply at the beginning of the summer, the month of June experienced an unusually small 2.3 million increase in the civilian labor force to 84.1 million, showing a 430,000 decline on a seasonally adjusted basis; a smaller than usual influx of youth into the summer job market was responsible for holding down the increase.

The June decline occurred only among white workers whose jobless rate, which had been rising since December, slipped to 4.2% from 4.6% in May. Meanwhile, the Negro jobless rate returned to its April level of 8.7%, after having slipped to 8% in May.

In June, the total figure for workers jobless for 15 weeks or more reached 685,000, compared with 385,000 a year earlier. The average period of unemployment registered 9.5 weeks in June, up from 9 weeks in May.

During the April-June quarter, the labor force grew only 100,000 and unemployment averaged 4.8%, with 1.1 million more workers out of work than in the October-December quarter of 1969. Jobless rates averaged 8.4% for Negroes and 4.4% for whites.

Reserve removes interest ceilings. The Federal Reserve Board June 23 suspended indefinitely statutory interest rate ceilings on certificates of deposit of $100,000 or more with maturities of one to three months. The ceilings had been 6.25% for maturities of 30 to 59 days, and 6.5% for maturities of 60 to 89 days.

The Reserve justified the surprise move on the basis of "current uncertainties in financial markets" and indicated that the action was intended to give banks sufficient funds to meet requests for capital from corporate borrowers. The action was apparently sparked by bankruptcy proceedings by the Penn Central Railroad, which had not been able to raise enough capital to meet its credit obligations.

The Federal Deposit Insurance Corporation took parallel action for state-chartered banks under its regulation.

The Reserve said the suspension would not interfere with Administration anti-inflation policies, because any increase in bank loans would not raise total credit flows "to the extent that they simply represented a transfer of borrowings from other financial avenues, as for example the commercial paper market."

Congressional spending scored. A top Nixon aide charged July 3 that Congress was "fiscally irresponsible" and said Congressional spending would be a major Republican campaign issue in the fall. John Ehrlichman, executive director of the President's new Domestic Council, said that "hopefully" the elections would result in a Congress more sympathetic to the Administration's policies.

Speaking at a news briefing on the newly created Domestic Council and Office of Management and Budget that went into operation July 1, Ehrlichman suggested that the President would not hesitate to veto actions by the Democratically-controlled Congress if he considered them fiscally dangerous. Of Nixon's recent veto of hospital funds, overridden by Congress June 30, Ehrlichman said the President was not against health care but did not want his hands tied by compulsory spending measures included in the bill.

Ehrlichman said that in the Economy Act of 1970, Nixon had asked Congress to eliminate 14 wasteful and inefficient programs but that Congress "perpetuated all 14 and increased the authorizations for some of them."

In a related development, Republican Congressional leaders charged July 7 that Congressional Democrats were jeopardizing the Administration's anti-inflation program with their "spendthrift ways." House Minority Leader Gerald Ford (R, Mich.), emerging from the President's weekly meeting with Republican Congressional leaders, said "if this spendthrift Congress" continued to appropriate more money than the Administration requested, it would hamper the battle to control inflation and "will be a very legitimate campaign issue in 1970."

Senate GOP Leader Hugh Scott (R, Pa.) pointed out that the wholesale price index rose only 1.4% in the second quarter of 1970 compared with 5.3% in the first quarter and 5.4% in the fall of 1969. He said the Administration's policies "are beginning to work" and that consumers should notice the change later in the year. The two leaders also said the President was concerned over Congress' failure to act on several measures he considered "absolutely essential" to convert to a peacetime economy.

Nixon warns Congress on spending. President Nixon, in a strong White House statement issued July 18, asked Congress to impose a ceiling on its spending. He said Congressional overspending threatened to exceed the Administration's 1971 and 1972 budget limits and produce a "massive deficit." The President warned that such a deficit would lead to a degree of inflation that eventually would require "difficult and painful measures"--higher taxes, spending cuts or vetoes of appropriations bills.

Nixon, asserting that he did not insist on a strictly balanced budget each year, conceded that sometimes the economy called for a deficit situation. He said, however, that one guideline should not be violated: "Except in emergency conditions, expenditures must never be allowed to outrun the revenues that the tax system would produce at reasonably full employment"; the government must never allow its long-run spending to push outlays high enough to cause increased tax rates or inflation.

Noting that Congressional action on the 1969 tax bill had reduced needed revenue by $3 billion for fiscal 1971 and by $5 billion for fiscal 1972, Nixon urged Congress to act on his proposals to tax leaded gasoline, speed the collection of estate and gift taxes and raise postal rates.

In anticipation of arguments that cuts in space and defense spending, in addition to a change in national priorities, would solve the budget problem, the President asserted that his budget for 1971 had made good headway. He said that his Administration had cut military and space outlays by some $6 billion and thus permitted expenditures for human resources to exceed defense spending for the first time in 20 years.

The President advised Congress, in making its appropriations, not to act on each expenditure as an isolated item but to study it within the context of overall spending as a potential source of higher taxes or prices.

Nixon reminded Congress that on July 6 he had signed the fiscal 1970 supplemental appropriations bill (HR-17399), which set a ceiling on government spending in fiscal 1971 (at about $200.8 billion plus a $4.5 billion "cushion" for uncontrollable cost rises). He charged that Congress had made a "travesty" of the bill by making exceptions and approving measures with mandatory spending provisions. He therefore asked Congress to impose on its own total spending a "firm" ceiling from which uncontrollables such as interest on the public debt would be exempt and to which both

Congress and the Executive would be responsible.

Senate Majority Leader Mike Mansfield (D, Mont.) July 18 expressed doubt that Congress would comply with the Administration request for a Congressional ceiling on spending without exemptions for popular programs. He agreed there had been a trend to increase spending without raising revenues, but he said Congress had made an effort to reduce spending. He said the President should cut defense, foreign aid and space expenditures. House Majority Leader Carl Albert (D, Okla.) termed the Nixon statement an "ill-advised attack on Congress" and merely "another effort to camouflage the disastrous economic policies" of his administration.

Press conference comments—President Nixon July 21 again assailed overspending by Congress. At an impromptu press conference, he predicted that Americans would turn on the "big spenders in Congress" when it was learned they were "primarily responsible for higher prices and eventually even higher taxes." He said Congressional restraint in spending would be one of the factors governing a balanced budget for fiscal 1972. The other factor would be the economy, which, Nixon said, he expected would move upward in the last half of fiscal 1971 and would continue upward in fiscal 1972. He said his economic advisers had assured him that the economy's "downturn has bottomed out" and that the last half of the year would see an increase in productivity.

Nixon asserted that a cooling in the economy was indicated by the wholesale price index and other inflator indicators. He said his advisers had told him he could forecast that "leveling of the rise in wholesale prices will be reflected as the year goes on in a downturn of the rate of increase in the consumer price index."

Nixon acknowledged that a cooling in the economy had caused "some upturn in unemployment," which, he said, had been aggravated by the dismissal of 700,000 men from the armed forces and defense plants as part of the nation's switch from a wartime to a peacetime economy. In answer to a question on further cuts in the fiscal 1972 defense budget, Nixon reiterated his July 18 observations that the budget had already been cut. He said: "To suggest that the money for big, new domestic spending programs can come out of substantial cuts in defense, I think, is not realistic."

Nixon called it unfair to the American people to suggest the possibility of tax-cuts for 1971 and 1972.

Nixon declared July 30: A tax increase could be avoided and inflationary budget avoided in 1972 but "only if we get the cooperation of the Congress in these next two to three months. . . . If the Congress does not cooperate in holding down spending, it will be necessary then, to look hard about where we're going to find the money, and that means more taxes."

(Senate Majority Leader Mike Mansfield [D, Mont.] told reporters the day after the news conference that Congress would trim appropriations by a net of $5 billion during the current session. He said the defense appropriations bill would be the chief vehicle for future cuts in spending.)

Nixon sees successes. President Nixon, responding to questions at his press conference in Los Angeles July 30, again asserted that his anti-inflation policies had produced "some cooling of the inflationary forces" at the cost of an economic slowdown.

Asked whether he would continue his anti-inflation program in view of a possible rebellion over unemployment, Nixon reiterated his point that the economic slowdown had been caused in part by the transition from a wartime to a peacetime economy in which 800,000 persons were released from the military sector, thus augmenting the unemployment problem. Nixon said the transition was difficult and was one of the reasons the Administration had pleaded with Congress to act more swiftly on extending unemployment insurance and other cushioning measures. Nixon predicted that on a long-term basis the economy would move upward and unemployment would decrease.

Concerning the wholesale price index which in July had recorded its largest increase in six months, the President said he was less interested in what happened during a one-month period than in the index's trend over six months. He added that on the basis of other economic indicators, inflation showed signs of cooling and would continue to cool as long as budget problems were handled responsibly.

Meany disputes Nixon on economy—AFL-CIO President George Meany, at a news conference in Chicago Aug. 3, disputed as "absolute and complete nonsense" the President's contention that present unemployment partly resulted from a wartime to peacetime shift in the economy. He asserted that the Administration's "game plan" against inflation was not working and warned that unemployment would probably increase. He said he saw no signs of an economic upturn in the second half of the year. Meany said he was not prepared to recommend wage and price controls, although according to the record, he said, they were perhaps necessary.

Meany made his remarks following a summer meeting of the AFL-CIO's executive council. He said the council had adopted a statement on the national economy, urging various measures to fight the present critical economic situation; among them were proposals calling on Congress to (1) direct the Federal Reserve System to set selective credit controls and maximum interest rates on certain types of loans, (2) enact laws requiring investment of tax-exempt funds and bank reserves in government-guaranteed mortgages to help meet the goal of 26 million housing units in ten years, and (3) take steps to curb dominant corporations from increasing prices at will and to check what it called an increasing concentration of economic power in a narrowing group of gigantic corporations and banks.

U.S. deficit for '70 up. The Western White House in San Clemente July 28 announced a deficit of $2.91 billion for fiscal year 1970, ended June 30. The figure was somewhat larger than originally estimated. The deficit increase was largely attributed to a decrease in revenues caused by the decline in corporate profits. Federal expenditures totaled $196.75 billion, up from $184.56 billion in fiscal 1969; total revenues were $193.84 billion,

exceeding the $187.79 billion of fiscal 1969.

George P. Shultz, director of the Office of Management and Budget, made the announcement following a meeting with President Nixon and other top Administration officials to discuss the fiscal 1972 budget. Shultz called the results of the fiscal 1970 budget "a strong and satisfactory performance."

In Washington, Paul A. Volcker, undersecretary of the treasury for monetary affairs, commented that a "modest" deficit in a sluggish economy which cut into revenues was "not disturbing in any sense."

Neither Shultz nor Volcker would discuss the specific budget outlook for fiscal 1971, which began July 1, except to deny reported estimates of a $10-$15 billion deficit. However, Shultz said the President's rule-of-thumb for the fiscal 1971 and 1972 budgets would be spending within the amount of revenues stimulated by full employment. He said the Administration would work for a balanced budget in 1972 with full employment without inflationary price increases.

For the first time since the U.S. expanded its involvement in the Vietnam war in 1965, military spending ($78.31 billion) ran slightly below previous fiscal year totals ($79.15 billion in 1969). Shultz appraised the present cost of the war at an annual rate of $29 billion, but said the total would drop to $14.5 billion by the spring of 1971 when a reduction of 150,000 troops was scheduled.

In a joint prepared statement, Shultz and Treasury Secretary David Kennedy enumerated the various reasons for the deficit results, among which were (1) $457 million more in interest payments on the public debt, (2) $267 million over the budget estimate for the Post Office Department because of the postal pay raise and (3) income tax receipt shortfalls (individual income tax collections ran $1.8 billion, and corporate profits taxes $4.2 billion, below government estimates in January.)

In a related development, a tally taken by the Congressional Joint Committee on Reduction of Federal Expenditures, released June 30, forecast a budget deficit for fiscal 1971 reaching between

$5 billion and $10 billion. The calculation was based on a study of collective actions and inactions of Congress and its committees.

Congressional hearings. A generally optimistic—if cautionary—view of the nation's economic outlook was expressed in testimony at hearings of the Congressional Joint Economic Committee on the state of the economy at midyear. Among views heard:

■Warnings against a possible massive budget deficit were delivered July 9 by Donald T. Regan, president of the Merrill Lynch, Pierce, Fenner & Smith stock brokerage firm; Henry Kaufman, partner and economist of Salomon Brothers & Hutzler; and A. W. Clausen, president of the Bank of America. Discussing fears of a "liquidity crisis" (a shortage of funds to pay business bills and debts), Regan said there was no need "to push the panic button." Kaufman said the term "liquidity crisis" had been too glibly used and that the crisis affected only "borrowers who cannot redress their liquidity because of the deterioration of their credit standing and, to some extent, a few institutions having marginal and non-marketable assets." Otherwise, he said, there was no evidence of a malfunction in the money market or the market for high-grade bonds. Regan and Kaufman predicted lower interest rates as the year progressed. Clausen, who warned of the danger of a longer-term tightening of capital and liquidity, said reassuringly that "most of the immediate problems have been identified and are being treated properly by the policy tools which exist."

■Daniel H. Brill, former director of research at the Federal Reserve Board (FRB) and currently senior vice president of the Commercial Credit Co., and Harvard Prof. Otto Eckstein, a former member of the President's Council of Economic Advisers (CEA), urged July 13 that the FRB permit greater expansion in the money supply than in the first half of the year. They said this action would help restore "liquidity." Both strongly advised a federal incomes policy to induce more voluntary wage and price restraint. Cyrus S. Eaton, 86, Chesapeake & Ohio Railroad chairman, told the committee the same day that he expected "a devastating depression unless the war in Southeast Asia is brought to a quick and complete conclusion."

■Two former presidential economic advisers offered conflicting views July 16. Walter W. Heller, adviser to Presidents Kennedy and Johnson, said inflation was on the wane. He urged the Administration to stimulate the economy in an effort to avoid increasing idleness and stagnation. Raymond J. Saulnier, who had served in the Eisenhower Administration, advised an opposite course of continued anti-inflation measures to prevent a "wage explosion" from turning into a "price inflation far beyond anything we have seen." Although both opposed mandatory wage-price controls, they differed widely on steps just short of controls. Heller urged a return to the guideposts he had helped implement as chairman of the President's Council of Economic Advisers; Saulnier, who had also been a CEA chairman, warned that it would be a "serious mistake" to adopt an incomes policy intended as "a shield behind which we could safely resume expansionist monetary and fiscal policies."

■Two of President Nixon's economic advisers testified July 20. CEA Chairman Paul W. McCracken said that the economic slump was "about over," as the rate of inflation exhibited stronger signs of diminishing. He said that the adjustment of the economy had produced "no cumulative decline in business activity" and that the "existence of slack in the economy means that increase in demand can be translated primarily into output increases, rather than price increases." McCracken said he expected a "further moderate rise in unemployment rates over the average level that prevailed in the second quarter [just over 4.8%]." He called a reported Federal Reserve Board estimate of a 6% jobless rate "too high" and declared that it "certainly ought not to be the basis for policy." On the current task of government policy, McCracken indicated he would seek a more rapid growth of money and credit than in the first half of the year in order to encourage economic expansion to help overcome "the low average of liquidity" in the economy.

In his first appearance before Congress as director of the Office of Management and Budget, George P. Shultz testified July 20 that defense cutbacks would have a "direct impact" on 1.3 million workers by mid-1971, over and above the 700,000 persons already affected since early 1969. He clarified his statement by saying that not all those affected would necessarily lose their jobs.

Both Shultz and McCracken backed the President's call for a Congressional ceiling on spending. They said they expected an increase in productivity (output per man-hour) as the economy expanded to help deflect the impact of higher wages on business costs.

■ Two top Democratic economists July 22 advised the government to use fiscal and monetary policy to expand the economy and fight "the economic retardation that is increasing unemployment and harming living standards" (in the words of Paul A. Samuelson of the Massachusetts Institute of Technology, a former president of the American Economic Association). Samuelson and Gardner Ackley, chairman of the Council of Economic Advisers under President Johnson, said the economy could be expanded without danger of increasing inflation. Ackley said he would not be concerned if the budget deficit reached $10 billion in the economy's current situation. Both men agreed that a vigorous upturn in the economy was unlikely. Samuelson added that near future policy should not be based on the assumption that the recession had passed.

With the support of Yale University Prof. Henry C. Wallich, who also testified July 22, Ackley and Samuelson opposed the use of wage and price controls, except in "emergency situations." Wallich, however, proposed new uses of the tax law to reinforce wage-price guidelines in a suggestion that a study be made to determine whether an income tax penalty or concession could be attached to the degree of compliance with the guidelines by individual companies.

■ Following a stream of witnesses who had suggested that the economy was ripe for a more stimulative monetary policy, Federal Reserve Board Chairman Arthur F. Burns told the committee July 23 that the money supply's current rate of ex-

pansion—above 4%—was "about right" and "what it should be for the present."

Burns firmly opposed "strong pressures to increase government spending and rapidly expand the money supply." He warned that a more expansionary policy might rekindle inflation at home and also weaken the dollar in international markets.

In answer to money theorists who argued that the Federal Reserve should set a fixed, long-term target for money supply growth, Burns replied: "Our obligation as a central bank is . . . to promote monetary conditions conducive to full employment, rapid improvement in productivity, reasonable price stability and equilibrium in the balance of payments. We do not propose to let adherence to any fixed growth rate of the money supply stand in the way of achieving these objectives."

In more than two hours of generally optimistic testimony, Burns said the economy's performance had "left much to be desired," but he predicted that the economy's downturn was near the bottom, full employment (generally defined as an unemployment rate of about 4%) would be restored in 1971, productivity would increase, and rising unit labor costs and industrial commodity prices would begin to wane in the latter half of 1970. He denied that the FRB had forecast a 6% jobless rate by early 1971 and emphasized that further declines in employment and industrial output would have to be stopped to avoid a deterioration in business and consumer attitudes.

Burns stressed that the FRB was able to shift policy quickly in response to changes in the economy in its capacity as "a lender of last resort." However, pointing out the limited emergency powers of the FRB, Burns proposed the establishment of a new federal lending corporation to guarantee loans to creditworthy business firms unable to borrow money through normal channels. He proposed that the new agency take the form of a three-man board, composed of the treasury secretary, the FRB chairman and a director appointed by the President, that would act in consultation with the House and Senate banking committees.

First 'inflation alert' posted. The first "inflation alert" report of the President's Council of Economic Advisers (CEA) was issued Aug. 8. CEA Chairman Paul W. McCracken, who submitted the report to the new National Commission on Productivity, said the report's purpose was to "lift the visibility" of inflationary developments in order to encourage improved public policies.

The report was devoted heavily to an historical and academic analysis of inflationary developments since the Eisenhower Administration. Its basic conclusion was that inflation would eventually respond to tight fiscal and monetary policies, such as those currently being pushed by the Nixon Administration.

However, the report conceded that the longer inflation persisted, the slower would be inflation's reaction to those policies. It also said fiscal and monetary measures would have to reach wholesale, retail and service prices, and wages, before they could effectively reduce the overall pattern of inflation.

Although the report said that inflationary pressures could not be explained in terms of price behavior, it indirectly attributed the year's rise in the wholesale price index to sharp wage increases, exceeding productivity, in the trucking and construction industries; it also cited price increases outpacing costs in the tobacco and tire industries.

Among other highlights, the report said:

■The construction industry's average annual 15% wage spiral exceeded "even a generous estimate of gains in output per man-hour" and could not fail to raise costs connected with the industry.

■Metals and metal products were the largest contributor in increases in the wholesale price index for 1970, while basic iron and steel and nonferrous metals were responsible for more than half the group's contribution.

■Machinery and equipment, reflecting metals price increases, added about 13% of the overall wholesale price index increase during the first half of the year.

■Bituminous coal registered the most striking single price increase (up at a 56% annual rate in the first half of 1970), which the report attributed to a swift increase in demand rather than higher wage settlements.

■Electric power rates for consumers increased slowly during 1970, despite the coal price hikes and higher interest rates, but would probably quicken their pace in the near future.

The Journal of Commerce reported Aug. 11 that the report had received mixed reactions from industries and unions it cited. Most claimed they had been singled out unfairly. One exception was the trucking industry which agreed its new labor contract was inflationary.

Nixon vetoes fund bills. President Nixon vetoed two fund bills as inflationary Aug. 11. Together, the bills provided $1 billion more than his budget requests. The vetoed bills would have provided $4.4 billion for the Office of Education ($543 million more than requested) and $18.1 billion for the Housing and Urban Development Department (HUD), the National Aeronautics and Space Administration (NASA) and other agencies ($541 million more than Administration proposals).

The veto of the education bill was overridden by Congress, and the measure became law Aug. 18. But the veto of the HUD and agencies bill was sustained, and that version of the legislation died when a House vote Aug. 13 fell 63 votes short of the two-thirds needed for repassage.

The vetoes were the third and fourth of Nixon's presidency. His first—of a $19.7 billion labor-welfare appropriation bill Jan. 26, was sustained by Congress and resulted in a $600 million reduction in appropriations. His second—of a three-year $2.79 billion authorization for the Hill-Burton hospital construction program June 22—was overridden by both the House and the Senate.

Nixon explained Aug. 11 that "if I were to sign these bills that spend nearly $1 billion more than we can now afford, I would be saying 'yes' to higher prices, 'yes' to higher interest rates, 'yes' to higher taxes."

In a letter to the House, to which he returned the vetoed bills, Nixon said: "I flatly refuse to go along with the kind of big spending that is wrong for all the American people."

The HUD-NASA appropriations bill (HR17548), also carrying funds for 22 other agencies and offices, had been passed by House voice vote July 29 and 70-8 Senate vote Aug. 4.

The bill would have provided $105 million more than the Administration requested for veterans' medical care, $350 million more than the Administration requested for water and sewer grants and $350 million more than requested for urban renewal. The HUD appropriation of $3,643,081,000 was $650,060,000 more than Administration requests. The Veterans Administration total appropriation of $9,065,528,000 was $105 million higher than requested. The total for NASA—$3,268,675,000—represented a $64,325,-000 cut in the Administration request.

The education appropriations bill (HR16916) had been cleared by Congress July 28.

The House, considering both vetoed bills Aug. 13, passed the $4.4 billion Office of Education bill with 20 votes more than the two-thirds needed. The vote was 289-114 (212 D & 77 R vs. 101 R & 13D).

The vote consigning the $18.1 billion HUD-agency bill to revision was 203-195 (181 D & 22 R vs. 155 R & 40 D).

In the Senate Aug. 18, only three Republicans made floor speeches in support of the President's position on the education bill. Sen Robert P. Griffin (Mich.), assistant minority leader, warned that a vote to override would impair "the credibility of Congress" as to its determination to fight against inflation.

The argument to override was presented by Senate Democratic leader Mike Mansfield (Mont.), who cited figures: that of the $670 Congress would appropriate that year for every American citizen, $375 would go for defense and only $22 for education, and that if Congress had not hiked the Nixon education budget by $453 million the per capita educational investment would be $19.97. "It is so easy to vote millions for ABMs and SSTs and then to reject money for the ABCs," he said. "The issue here is not government spending, but national priorities, not priorities by rhetoric but priorities by action."

Both Senate Republican leader Hugh Scott (Pa). and Chairman Gordon Allott (Colo.) of the Republican Policy Committee joined in the vote to override.

The Senate's vote to override the education bill veto was 77-16, with all the 54 Democrats present voting to do so in an unusual display of party unity.

Wage control authority enacted. President Nixon signed a bill Aug. 17 authorizing him to impose controls on wages, prices and other items but he reiterated his intention not to use such authority. He also objected to other features of the bill, which was approved by the Senate Aug. 12 and House Aug. 13. The basic bill extended the Defense Production Act providing federal controls for defense materials and facilities. Were it not for the need to extend the basic law, Nixon said, he would veto the bill.

In addition to the wage-price power, he objected to the bill's provision to establish a cost accounting board to monitor defense procurement contracts and requested Congress to revise the provision to place the board in the executive branch. He also criticized a $20 million limit set under the bill for permissible guarantees of defense production loans as "arbitrary" and a barrier to effective management of defense production.

Democrats score Nixon record. The Committee on Economic Affairs of the Democratic Policy Council, in an Aug. 15 statement, assailed the Nixon Administration for imposing economic policies that permitted the nation's productivity to stagnate and inflation to continue.

The statement, written by Gardner Ackley (chairman of the Council of Economic Advisers [CEA] under President Johnson) and approved by the committee, took issue with President Nixon's veto of the education and housing spending bills as having "no economic justification." It also criticized the Administration's refusal to institute voluntary wage and price guidelines and said the purpose of the Administration's "inflation alert" was unclear. The policy statement concluded that "the weakening of the economy has been allowed to proceed too far" and that a "redirection of policy toward expansion" was needed.

Democrats scored on spending. President Nixon chastised the Democratic Congress Aug. 17 for failure to enact his proposals on federal spending reductions. Recalling his proposals in February for $2.1 billion in savings—$1.1 billion by Executive action and $982 million by Congressional action—Nixon said his actions had resulted in savings of $983 million, representing 100% of the options available to him while Congress had approved reductions amounting to only 46% of the goal he had set.

House Speaker John W. McCormack (D, Mass.) replied later Aug. 17 that the President should "devote his attention to the real problems and quit playing his partisan political games." The downturn in the economy resulting from "failures" in the Administration's economic policy, he said, cost the Treasury $4 billion in fiscal 1970 revenues and "probably" would cost it $15 billion in 1971.

Another attack on the Democrats on the spending issue was made Aug. 20 by Vice President Agnew in a campaign fund-raising speech in Los Angeles for Sen. George Murphy (whom Agnew called "a Republican in the best sense of the word").

Agnew said if the spending programs proposed by the Democrats on the Senate Labor and Public Welfare Committee were adopted, the "American private enterprise system would be taxed beyond its capability and collapse." He added: "We'd no longer have a free economy. We'd have socialism."

Agnew also directed a personal attack against Democratic National Chairman Lawrence F. O'Brien, charging that a Wall Street brokerage firm had collapsed "under his adroit management" and it was "small wonder" that the Democratic party was "not faring too well either" since "it cannot find men more qualified than Larry O'Brien to lead it."

O'Brien said later Aug. 20 that his former firm, McDonnell & Co., was "one of many firms that was victim of the Nixon Administration's disastrous economic policies—policies that have left Wall Street in a deep recession." He noted that the firm's chairman was the brother-in-law of White House aide Peter Flanigan.

Federal Reserve acts. The Federal Reserve Board (FRB), by a unanimous decision Aug. 17, imposed for the first time a reserve requirement on funds banks receive through affiliates' commercial paper. It also reduced time-deposit reserve requirements for member banks from 6% to 5% on total deposits of more than $5 million.

The two-fold action, both technical and expansionary in effect, would be applied Sept. 17 to coincide with the fall period's seasonal expansion of deposits and required reserves; it would have a net effect of freeing about $350 million, hitherto kept idle in bank reserves, that was expected to be used in financing housing and state and local governments.

An FRB spokesman Aug. 23 clarified the new reserve rules. He said commercial paper would be subject to demand-deposit reserve requirements of up to 17.5%, and not 5% as implied by the Aug. 17 FRB statement. He explained that the new 5% reserve requirement would apply only to commercial paper of 30 days or more maturity. The effect of the 17.5% reserve rule would be to compel major banks to refund some $2 billion of under 30-day paper sold by their holding companies, either with longer-term obligations or in unregulated markets, such as federal funds or Eurodollars.

Among earlier developments:

■The Federal Reserve's Open Market Committee voted 11-1 May 5 to expand the nation's money supply by increasing the seasonally adjusted measure of currency and private demand deposits in banks from the favored annual rate of 3% to 4%. St. Louis district bank president Darryl R. Francis dissented on the ground that the increased rate would imply an "excessive" 6% annual rate of increase in the February-June period. The actual increase in the second quarter money supply had been at a 4.25% annual rate. In another action, the committee suspended the customary limit on the Reserve's account manager to increase the system's holding of U.S. government securities by no more than $2 billion.

The Open Market Committee, at its meeting May 26, decided to concentrate on "moderating pressures on financial markets," rather than achieving a "target" growth of the money supply. A summary of the meeting's proceedings said the members had voted unanimously to maintain bank reserve and money market conditions "consistent with the committee's longer-run objectives of moderate growth in money and bank credit."

It was confirmed Sept. 21 that the committee, at its meeting June 23, had voted unanimously for a more rapid growth rate in the third quarter at about a 5% annual rate. It was reported that the second quarter money supply growth rose at a 4.2% rate, instead of the prior estimate of 4.5%. At the June meeting, which immediately followed disclosure of the Penn Central's liquidity crisis, the committee said its policies would again be aimed at moderating pressures on financial markets.

■The New York Federal Reserve Bank's monthly review, issued Aug. 6, said that recent fears of a liquidity crisis in the nation's short-term money market, which had been sparked by the Penn Central's petition in June to reorganize, were "exaggerated." The bank said the number of "acute liquidity problems" had been "relatively few," and in some cases were "symptomatic of deeper difficulties" that had little relation to recent business activities or economic policies.

■Statistics released Aug. 13 by the New York Federal Reserve Bank indicated that the Federal Reserve was continuing a policy of modest credit expansion. Besides recent growth in monetary aggregates, net borrowed reserves of commercial banks rose an average $945 million in the week ended Aug. 12 from $854 million in the previous week.

McCracken sees expansion. Paul W. McCracken, chairman of the President's Council of Economic Advisers, said Aug. 17 that there was "some evidence" that the economy was embarking on a "moderate pace of expansion" for the rest of 1970.

In a speech at the University of Wisconsin, the President's chief economic adviser said, however, that recent economic statistics "suggest no surging rebound for the economy." He rejected the idea that the economy should operate at below capacity for a long period as a cure for the nation's economic ills. McCracken said a strong increase in demand would be required to stave off "an unduly protracted period of excessive slack and unemployment."

McCracken stressed that three recent economic developments had not received proper attention: (1) the decline in defense spending over the past two years (McCracken said defense spending, corrected for inflation, had declined $12 billion between fiscal 1968 and fiscal 1970 and would decline by $20 billion from fiscal 1968 to the end of current fiscal year 1971); (2) the sharp increase in output per man-hour (productivity), and (3) a notable improvement in the world trade position of the U.S.

Prices continue up. Government statistics showed continued price increases as the second half of 1970 began. Wages also rose:

■ The Labor Department reported Aug. 9 that in July wholesale prices had made their sharpest increase since January. The wholesale price index passed the agency's original estimate of a 6% annual rate as it climbed to 117.7% of the 1957–59 average and to an annual rate of 7.2%. Most of the upward revision appeared in the erratic food prices category, while the key industrial commodities index increased .2%.

■ The Labor Department's consumer price index (CPI) in July rose a seasonally adjusted .3% (an unadjusted .4%), which was the same percentage increase recorded for June. It was the index's smallest two-month advance in two years.

■ Average farm prices took their biggest drop since 1948 as the Agriculture Department Aug. 31 reported a 3% decline for the month ending Aug. 15. Such prices were a fraction of 1% below year-earlier figures and about 4.8% below February levels. Analysts pointed out that the report's data did not reflect price increases that hit grain markets because of the corn blight.

■ According to the Labor Department July 22, collective bargaining settlements in the first half of 1970, covering 1.9 million workers, averaged a 14.6% first-year wage and benefit increase, up from 10.9% for all of 1969.

Unemployment at record 5.1%. Unemployment reached its highest level since October 1964 when the August jobless rate edged up from 5% in July to 5.1% of the seasonally adjusted labor force.

In July, unemployment had rebounded to May's record five-year high of 5% of the seasonally adjusted labor force, after slipping to 4.7% in June.

According to a Labor Department report Sept. 4, total unemployment in August was 4.2 million, down 300,000 from July, at a somewhat less than normal decline for the season. Most of the rate increase was centered among teenagers, particularly white girls.

Total payroll jobs and the average work week in manufacturing continued to drop. Manufacturing and construction jobs declined by 75,000 and 40,000 respectively, after seasonal adjustment; the jobless rate for construction workers rose from 11% to 12.2%, and for blue-collar workers from 6.6% to 7%.

Economic indicators up. A strong advance in the Commerce Department's key composite index of leading economic indicators, shown in figures released Aug. 27 for the month of July, lent statistical support to the Administration's view that the economy was on the verge of an upturn. (President Nixon's four chief economic advisers had advised him in San Clemente Aug. 24 that the rate of inflation had slowed and business had begun to expand without incurring a recession. Meeting with the President were Paul W. McCracken, chairman of the CEA; Arthur F. Burns, Federal Reserve chairman; George P. Shultz, head of the office of Budget and Management; and Treasury Secretary David M. Kennedy.)

The 1.6% gain of the July index, based on eight of the 12 indicators, was the strongest since April 1969. It also marked the first time in more than a year that the index had advanced two months in a row which included a .3% advance in the June index. Six of the eight indicators showed improvement, including an increase in the manufacturing work week, a decline in

initial claims for unemployment insurance, a rise in new orders for durable goods, increasing orders for new plant and equipment, higher stock market prices and a rise in the ratio of prices to unit labor costs in manufacturing. Unfavorable changes were a decline in building permits for new houses and a drop in industrial materials prices.

Housing starts rose sharply in July to an annually adjusted 1,585,000-unit annual rate, which the Commerce Department said Aug. 17 was the highest level in 17 months. An increase of more than 15% from June's upward-revised 1,375,000-unit pace and a gain of almost 11% from a year earlier, bolstered forecasts of an upturn for the category. The largest gain was recorded for apartment buildings of five or more units.

Construction spending in June nosed up .5% to a seasonally adjusted annual rate of $88.8 billion after three monthly declines, the Commerce Department said. A steep increase in nonresidential construction offset a downturn in the residential sector. Second quarter outlays, at an annual .rate of $89 billion, trailed levels of a year earlier and this year's first quarter.

Among other economic data:
■Revised figures for the second quarter "real" Gross National Product (GNP), adjusted for inflation, advanced at a .6% rate. This indicated revived growth in the nation's output of goods and services. The seasonally adjusted annual rate was $971.1 billion, or $11.6 billion above the first quarter's $959.5 billion and $47.4 billion over the figure for a year earlier. The upward revision was largely the result of an accumulation of business inventories at a $2.9 billion annual rate in the second quarter.

The rate of inflation, as measured by the GNP price index, was revised upward .to a 4.3% annual rate (from 4.2%), still the lowest pace since a 4.2% annual rate of increase in the third quarter of 1968.
■Well below the year-earlier level of 174.3, industrial output in August eased to a seasonally adjusted 169.0 of the 1957–59 average from July's 169.2. The Federal Reserve Board index of industrial production for August, published Sept. 14, dimmed Administration hopes of an

economic upturn raised by the .2% July increase, which had appeared to halt the index's slow but steady decline since its peak at 174.6 in July 1969.

■The impact of defense spending on the nation's economy fell in the second quarter to its lowest point since 1966, the Commerce Department said Aug. 31. Spending for military equipment dropped $5.7 billion to $33.6 billion in the fiscal year ended June 30. In the second quarter, Pentagon purchases of goods and services made up 7.9% of the gross national product (GNP), down from 8.3% in the first quarter. Manufacturers' new orders for defense products dropped 3.3%, but soared 76.6% in July, the first month of the third quarter.

■ Following an unusual $1½ billion decline in June, personal incomes climbed $3.6 billion in July to a seasonally adjusted annual rate of $801.8 billion.

■Pre-tax corporate profits, which had been falling rapidly, dropped only slightly in the second quarter to an $82.3 billion annual rate from the first quarter's downward revised $82.6 billion pace and $93.4 billion a year earlier. It was the fourth straight quarterly decline in pre-tax profits, and the rate was the lowest since the $78.8 billion pace in the third quarter of 1967.

The second quarter profits of 560 early-reporting companies, polled by the Wall Street Journal for a survey published July 30, trailed by 7.3% figures reported a year earlier. However, the year-to-year decline was smaller than that of the first quarter which had showed an 8.9% drop from a year earlier.

The First National City Bank's New York monthly economic letter, published Aug. 7, said its analysis of 1,404 nonfinancial corporations indicated that the 18-month falling trend in corporate profits might be ending. The survey showed an average decline of 6% in second quarter profits, compared with an 8% first quarter decline a year earlier.

Government economic statistics. U.S. savings bond sales outpaced redemptions (cash-ins) by $7 million in August, the Treasury Department reported Sept. 3. The figures marked the end of a 20-month run on bond holdings, which began in December 1968, during which sales were topped by redemptions reaching a net of almost $3 billion. The $7 million margin represented a significant advance over July's $56 million net drain and $94 million outflow of August 1969.

Sales of Series E and H bonds declined to $388 million in August from $402 million in July, but were up from $348 million a year before. Redemptions dropped to $381 million from $458 million in July and $442 million in August 1969.

The Commerce Department reported that the federal budget, measured on the national income accounts basis, operated at a vast $14.3 billion annual rate deficit in the second quarter, the largest quarterly deficit since World War II. The first quarter had seen a $1.7 billion rate of deficit. Federal spending in the second quarter soared to a $210.9 billion annual rate from the $197.7 billion pace of the first quarter. The department report said that most of the increase reflected a 15% boost in Social Security benefits and a 6% federal pay raise.

Stock market gains. The Dow-Jones industrial average of stock prices Aug. 21 burst upward 15.81 points in its best advance since mid-June, as the stock tape closed two minutes late at 745.41, the indicator's highest level since late April. Volume on the New York Stock Exchange (NYSE) reached its highest turnover in more than a month at 13.42 million shares. The following Monday session, Aug. 24, recorded another record gain as the Dow barometer soared 14.17 points to close at 759.58 and widen its gains of the past five sessions to more than 50 points. Volume boomed to 18.91 million shares, marking the NYSE's heaviest trading day since May 28. The market's vigorous gains were ascribed to evidence of easier credit, a healthier economy and technical factors.

Pessimism Spreads

Reports from business and government sources in the early fall of 1970 were widely interpreted as indicating growing uneasiness over the economy's prospects.

Inflation and the general state of the economy increasingly became a dominating issue in the midterm Congressional elections.

Spending plans cut. The business community continued to trim its 1970 capital spending plans, according to joint projections issued by the Commerce Department and the Securities and Exchange Commission (SEC) Sept. 2.

According to their figures, spending outlays totaled $80.52 billion at a downward-revised increase of 6.6% from 1969. The lower estimate was interpreted as another positive sign in efforts to attain moderate economic growth with less inflation, as previous surveys had indicated increases as high as 9.8% against an 11.5% hike in 1969. However, some analysts predicted an even greater lag in capital outlays.

At annual rates the new quarterly figures were: first quarter (actual)—$78.22 billion; second quarter (actual)—$80.22 billion; third quarter (planned)—$81.05 billion; and fourth quarter (planned)—$82.24 billion.

Personal income, housing starts. Doubts about a solid economic upturn in 1970 were strengthened by Commerce Department reports Sept. 17 that (1) housing starts fell 10% in August after three monthly gains, and (2) the increase in personal income narrowed to $4.1 billion from July's $5.1 billion gain.

August housing starts, at a seasonally adjusted annual rate of 1,431,000 units, were down from July's upward-revised 1,591,000 rate, but were 3% above the year-earlier rate of 1,384,000. The August decline was ascribed to "statistical aberrations" and affected larger apartments rather than one-family homes.

Harold C. Passer, assistant commerce secretary for economic affairs, said Sept. 17 that a substantially higher permit issuance and the high level of starts relative to recent figures indicated continued strength in residential construction.

Personal income rose to a seasonally adjusted annual rate of $807.4 billion, about $800 million more than the average pace for the first eight months of the year. Wages and salaries advanced $2.5 billion, comprising more than half the increase. The month's slack in personal income mostly reflected weakness in the manufacturing sector where payrolls rose only $100 million to $160.2 billion annual rate after climbing $600 million in July.

Nixon policies under fire. AFL-CIO President George Meany, in his annual Labor Day message, blamed the Nixon Administration's "ill-conceived" policies and actions for the current inflation and strain on the average worker's family budget. Declaring that the Administration had applied its policies unequally, Meany added: "We can see no justification, no economic reason, and no human reason why workers should be asked to bear the major burden of recession and inflation in order to maintain astronomical profits for banks and corporations . . ."

(Meany, interviewed on the CBS "Face the Nation" program Sept. 6, said that the state of the economy and inflation would be the key issue in the fall Congressional elections and "the determining factor in who we support and who we don't support is going to be the position of congressmen and senators on domestic issues.")

Three former Democratic chairmen of the President's Council of Economic Advisers Sept. 23 criticized the Administration's economic strategy. In a white paper for the Senate Democratic Policy Committee, Walter W. Heller, Gardner Ackley and Arthur M. Okun called for a "significantly more expansionary policy" to check a long period of "chronic and creeping paralysis" and high unemployment in the economy. Without a change, they said, the economy would sustain up to $150 billion in losses of output and income. The three economists added that "there is no basis of confidence that price increases in the closing months of 1970 will be less rapid" than at the start of the Nixon Administration.

(Writing in the quarterly letter of the National City Bank of Minneapolis Sept. 28, Heller again urged the Administration to adopt a more expansionary policy to offset the continued slack in the economy. He agreed with the Administration view that the economy was in the process of an upturn upon the passage of low points in output, profits and stock prices, and high points in inflation and interest rates. However, he said he saw little chance of a "quick snapback" from the year's business slump.)

Banks cut prime rate. Morgan Guaranty Trust Co., New York's fifth largest bank, led several major banks Sept. 21 in trimming the prime, or minimum, interest rate for creditworthy corporate borrowers from 8% to 7.5%. The First Pennsylvania Banking and Trust Co., Philadelphia's largest bank, had initiated the cut Sept. 14 in the wake of similar moves by two small banks in Maine and Wisconsin. The reduction, which became general Sept. 22, was the first change in the prime rate since March 25.

Also reducing their prime rates were the Bank of America in San Francisco, the nation's largest bank; Chase Manhattan Bank and Chemical Bank, the nation's third and sixth largest banks.

A Morgan Guaranty spokesman said the reduction was "a response to market conditions and monetary policies as we see them."

In Washington, the White House did not comment on the cut, although the Administration had indicated its approval after the Philadelphia bank took the initial step.

Nixon vs. spending bills. A bill authorizing an additional $1 billion in fiscal 1971 for construction of sewer and water facilities became law Oct. 6 without the President's signature. The President announced his action that day in a statement criticizing Congress for authorizing "excessive spending when there is little hope of appropriating a like sum without an increase in revenues." He said the authorization exceeded the Administration's request by $850 million. He withheld veto action on the grounds that it was only an authorization, not an actual appropriation.

A previous bill vetoed by the President, the fiscal 1971 appropriation bill for the Housing and Urban Development Department and independent offices, carried $500 million for the sewer and water program. The additional $1 billion had been approved by 282–32 House vote Sept. 10 and Senate voice vote Sept. 21.

Nixon signed a $5.2 billion appropriation bill for public works Oct. 7 but criticized Congress for putting "too much pork in this barrel." He directed his criticism at the public works appropriations, saying he had requested funds to initiate 37 new projects that would ultimately cost $1.3 billion, while Congress approved 102 costing $4.5 billion. Nixon said he would "consider all means possible to minimize the impact of these inflationary and unnecessary appropriations."

Higher federal budget deficit. House Ways and Means Committee Chairman Wilbur D. Mills (D, Ark.) Oct. 12 forecast a federal budget deficit ranging between $12 billion and $20 billion for current fiscal year 1971. The estimate, based on his committee's staff findings, was double the estimate of late spring but coincided with recent unofficial projections by the Administration of a $10 billion–$15 billion deficit.

Speaking in Miami Beach to the American Bankers Association convention, Mills said the deficit would reach his projection figures even "if Congress did everything that the budget requested us to do." He said revenue estimates, made when the budget was prepared in 1969, had not attained their expected levels. At a follow-up press conference, Mills specified that his figures pertained to the overall "unified" budget, which included receipts and outlays of large federal trust funds, such as Social Security; the previously used "administrative" budget had excluded these items.

In other remarks to the convention, Mills indicated that Congress would approve all the Administration's revenue-raising measures with the possible exception of the tax on leaded gasoline. He said the committee would cooperate with the Treasury Department in finding ways to raise about $1.6 billion annually. Mills expressed willingness to adopt the Administration's proposal for an accelerated collection of estate and gift taxes.

Both Mills and Senate Majority Leader Mike Mansfield (D, Mont.), who also addressed the convention, presented pessimistic views concerning the current state of the economy.

Mills warned of mounting inflationary pressures caused by the budget deficit and prolonged heavy spending at all levels of government. He said he foresaw no immediate end to inflation, which he predicted would cause a "serious recession" unless checked. He blamed the Federal Reserve System's easy credit policies in the second half of 1968 for blunting the anti-inflation impact of the 10% federal income tax surcharge. Mills said he felt present monetary policies were "probably just about right," but might need to be eased to help surmount the unemployment rate.

The Treasury reported Oct. 28 that the federal budget deficit had deepened to $7.76 billion in the first quarter of the current fiscal year, beginning July 1. The deficit was more than three times the year-earlier total of $2.47 billion. September receipts were $18.7 billion, outlays $17.4 billion. The annual spending rate ran near $217 billion, an increase over the $202 billion rate a year earlier.

Nixon orders '72 spending limit. Administration sources disclosed Oct. 24 that President Nixon had imposed a spending ceiling of $225 billion for the fiscal 1972 federal budget being prepared for presentation to Congress in January 1971. Analysts said the ceiling indicated that spending might rise $15 billion–$20 billion from current levels.

The new budget was being prepared according to a new budget deficit gauge called the "full employment" budget. Under the new concept, the upper limit of federal spending should be equal to the total tax receipts received by the government if the economy were operating at "full employment" (no more than 3.8% unemployment). According to budget information sent to federal agency heads by the Office of Management and Budget, the President had ordered a "full employment" surplus of about $5 billion for the new budget.

Business Council on wages. In a panel discussion held by the Business Council in Hot Springs, Va. Oct. 17 and attended by top White House economic advisers, leading corporation executives aired their views that Administration economic policies were correct, but were inadequate in controlling inflation. The businessmen expressed particular concern over the Administration's handling of union pressures for wage increases.

Indicating little enthusiasm for a revival of government wage-price guidelines and none at all for controls, the executives proposed that the government develop new policies to restrain spiraling wage increases, particularly in the construction industry, and to increase the output of certain groups of workers, such as those in the service industries.

The problem, as articulated by Donald C. Burnham, board chairman of Westinghouse Electric Corp., was that "wages are going up so much more than productivity" of workers, causing per-unit costs of production and prices to rise. He said the problem was affecting various sectors of the economy; for example, the inflationary pattern of wage increases in the construction industry was "spilling over" into the services and industrial sectors of the economy. Ellison L. Hazard, chairman and president of Continental Can Co., reported that construction union members were earning $2.70-$4 an hour more than regular workers at industrial plants.

To meet the problem of excessive wage increases in the construction industry, S.D. Bechtel, senior director of the Bechtel Corp. in San Francisco, suggested "opening up hiring" to minorities and non-union workers, elimination of restrictions on types of construction jobs open to different craft unions and ending restrictions on prefabrication and off-site construction.

Fred J. Borch, board chairman of the General Electric Co. and chairman of the Business Council, conceded that the council had not devised any solutions to the construction wage problem: rather, he said, the council's purpose was to awaken the Administration to the problem. Borch said that once the government had recognized the problem, it would have the "ingenuity" to solve it.

Paul W. McCracken, chairman of the President's Council of Economic Advisers, said after the meeting that the Administration acknowledged the problem did exist, but not to the extent suggested by the council. He pointed out that 75% of the labor force was not unionized and that taking the labor market as a whole, compensation per man hour had slackened and gains in output had been "coming along better."

Jobless rate, wholesale prices up. Administration hopes for a better outlook in the economy before the November elections were dashed by preliminary statistics for September. The unemployment rate was at its highest level since January 1964 and an increase in the wholesale price index canceled out a much heralded decline in August.

The jobless rate in September mounted steadily to a seasonally adjusted 5.5%, up from 5.1% in August, and just below the 5.6% figure of January 1964, the Labor Department said Oct. 2.

Total unemployment in September rose to a seasonally adjusted 4,607,000 persons from 4,231,000 (before adjustment, to 4,292,000 from 4,220,000).

Jobless rates increased for: those who had lost their jobs—by 100,000 to about 2.1 million persons; adult women (25 years old and over)—to an unadjusted 4.4% from 4.1% in August (but the rate for adult men stood at the August level of 3%); women from the age of 20—to an adjusted 5.1% from 4.8%; whites—to an adjusted 5.1% from 4.8%, and for blacks to 9% from 8.4%, maintaining the ratio of black to white unemployment below a 2-1 pattern; blue collar workers—to 7.5% from August's 7%; construction workers—from 12.2% to 13.8%.

Two leading labor force indicators, the seasonally adjusted average workweek and weekly overtime of rank-and-file workers, fell sharply in September. The only positive sign in the report was that employment was "essentially unchanged."

Democrats and the AFL-CIO said Oct. 2 that the report was evidence that the Nixon Administration's economic "game plan" for fighting inflation was failing. AFL-CIO President George Meany said the Administration could not duck responsibility for policies "that have caused widespread suffering among families of the unemployed, up nearly two million since the Administration took over."

In an unusual White House briefing Oct. 2, Paul W. McCracken, chairman of the President's Council of Economic Advisers, gave reassurances that the statistics did not represent any "major deterioration in the economy." He focused his attention mainly on the large seasonally adjusted decline in the private, nonfarm average workweek, which he called a "statistical aberration" because of the Labor Day holiday which fell during the survey week.

Unemployment edged up to a seasonally adjusted 5.6% in October. Nonfarm payrolls dropped 481,000 on a seasonally adjusted basis, mostly because of a strike at General Motors Corp. Although the jobless rate was below the Democrats' pre-election 6% projection, the indicator was at its highest level since November 1963 and matched the 5.6% of January 1964. Bureau analysts discounted October's .1% increase as having little statistical value. But a government economist noted that if the Administration's explanation for September's 5.5% rate were valid, there would have been, apart from the General Motors strike, a decline in the jobless rate and an increase in the average factory workweek.

Wholesale prices, an indicator of retail trends, rose sharply in September to 117.8% of the 1957–59 average on both an adjusted and unadjusted basis. It was the third largest monthly gain in 1970 for the index, exceeded only by .6% and .8% gains in July and January.

The September rise was largely influenced by high increases in prices of farm products, which rose 3.9%. The industrial commodities index, regarded as a key indicator because prices in that category were not as subject to volatile changes, rose .3% (adjusted and unadjusted) instead of the .2% estimate.

The wholesale price index remained at 117.8 in October although individual elements rose or fell. The farm product and food categories fell 2.1% and 2.7%, respectively for the quarter. Unadjusted industrial wholesale prices, however, soared .8% to their highest level in 14 years. The industrial index, seasonally adjusted, rose .5% to 118.2. More than 60% of the increase was ascribed to higher prices of 1971-model cars.

Jobless areas—The Labor Department announced Oct. 27 that the Bureau of Labor Statistics was adding five major urban areas, including Los Angeles, to the list of "substantial unemployment areas." Although two other areas were dropped from the classification—given to any major labor market anticipating a 6% or more jobless rate for at least two months—the number of those listed mounted to a total of 38 areas (out of 150 major labor markets in the U.S.). The list was at its highest level since June 1964; only five areas had been listed in October 1969.

The five areas added to the list were Los Angeles-Long Beach, San Diego and San Bernardino-Riverside-Ontario in California; Lawrence-Haverhill, Mass.; and New Brunswick-Perth Amboy, N.J. Removed from the list were Utica-Rome, N.Y. and Kenosha, Wis. Thirteen smaller areas were also added to the category.

News of the additions to the list first came from House Speaker John W. McCormack (D, Mass.), who cited the changes as evidence of "accelerating" unemployment. He said there were signs that the national unemployment figure was near 6% and suggested that the Administration was purposely withholding the October figures until after the election. (Labor Department officials later said the release of the figures had long been scheduled, according to departmental procedure, for Nov. 6.) Referring to the GOP's tactics in the current campaign, McCormack asserted that President Nixon and members of the Administration were ignoring the "major issue—the economy" and a situation where "almost three million more Americans are out of work than when [Nixon] assumed office, millions more have seen paychecks shrink, and all Americans have watched helplessly as the purchasing power of their dollar has shrunk and the value of their savings has diminished."

(The Labor Department reported Oct. 20 that swelling unemployment in the third quarter of 1970 had hurt most severely black teen-agers in urban slums whose jobless rate grew to 34.9% from 29.3% a year earlier. Total national unemployment reached 4.34 million [5.2% of the civilian labor force], compared with three million [3.7%] in 1969's third quarter. In poverty neighborhoods, joblessness climbed to 8.3%, compared with 6.8% a year ago.)

Consumer prices rise. The consumer price index (CPI) rose .2% (a 2.4% annual rate) in August to 136% of the 1957-59 average, the Labor Department said Sept. 23. On a seasonally adjusted basis, the increase was the slimmest since December 1968, and on an adjusted basis, the smallest since September 1967.

Herbert Stein, a member of the President's Council of Economic Advisers (CEA), hailed the report as "the most solid evidence" that the Administration's anti-inflation policies were working. The CPI increase for August was ascribed to higher prices for consumer services.

But consumer prices rose .4% (a 4.8% annual rate) in September, double the August increase, the Labor Department reported Oct. 21. On a seasonally adjusted basis, the CPI climbed .5% (a 6% annual rate) to 136.6% of the 1957-59 average—the sharpest monthly increase since May.

In an unusual White House statement to explain the unfavorable figures, chief economic adviser Paul W. McCracken pointed out that "inevitable wobbles" occurred in monthly statistics, while quarterly statistics were steadily improving. The annual rate of increase for July-September after seasonal adjustment was 4.2%, compared with 5.8% in the second quarter and 6.3% in the first quarter.

Nevertheless, labor reacted strongly to the figures. AFL-CIO President George Meany charged that since the Nixon Administration took office, the cost of living (COL) had risen "more than 10% at the same time unemployment among American workers had jumped nearly two million." Labor leaders' criticism focused on a companion report issued by the Bureau of Labor Statistics which indicated that workers' purchasing power was diminishing in face of the COL increase and shorter working hours.

Despite a 3¢ an hour wage increase, "real" (spendable) earnings of a worker with three dependents fell to $77.68 (in terms of 1957-59 dollars) a week from $78.51 in August; they were down 2% from $79.27 in September 1969.

Leading indicators down. The Commerce Department's composite index of "leading" economic indicators fell .3%

in August to 115.4% of the 1967 average, following a 1.6% gain in July. The new statistics, released Sept. 28, clouded Administration expectations of an economic rebound.

Underscoring the uncertainty of an economic upturn, Assistant Treasury Secretary Murray L. Weidenbaum warned that the expected recovery was apt to be moderate and steady. The central question, he said, was whether the economy would expand quickly enough to absorb a growing labor force.

The composite index of indicators for September registered a 1% drop, sending the index to its lowest level since September 1968. Assistant Commerce Secretary Harold C. Passer noted Oct. 28 that the index reflected the distorting influences of the General Motors strike and the Labor Day week. But the two straight monthly declines in the index since a 1.6% rise in July appeared to support the view that the economy was sluggish. The September index fell to 113.4% of the 1967 average; the third quarter indicators showed a .4% rise after declining 1.2% in the second quarter.

Of the eight available indicators, five declined and three gained. Those falling were the average workweek of production workers, new durable goods orders, industrial materials prices, the ratio of price to unit labor costs of manufacturers, and the average weekly initial claims for state unemployment insurance (treated inversely). The rising indicators were building permits, stock prices and new orders for plant and equipment.

Other economic data. Capital spending plans of U.S. businesses for new plant and equipment projected a modest 2% increase to $82.5 billion in 1971, according to a McGraw-Hill Publications survey released Nov. 5. The projected increase, the smallest in 10 years, contrasted with the 6% estimated increase to $80.5 billion in 1970. Manufacturing industries planned a 2% drop to $31.45 billion in 1971.

Companies reported that soaring construction costs were the major block to new investment. However, declining profits, high interest rates and liquidity shortages were also cited as factors.

Preliminary spending plans for 1972 totaled $86.25 billion.

■ Personal income rose $5.4 billion in September to an $811.8 billion seasonally adjusted annual rate, topping August's downward-revised $3.1 billion increase and indicating a sluggish economy. The Commerce Department Oct. 14 ascribed September's acceleration chiefly to an 8% retroactive postal pay boost. Discounting the unique factor of the retroactive payments, the September increase was at an annual rate of $3.4 billion, slightly higher than August figures. Personal income for the first nine months of 1970 was at a seasonally adjusted $796.9 billion annual rate, about $55.2 billion (or 7.5%) higher than the corresponding period in 1969.

Personal income declined in October to an annual rate of $809.5 billion, a decrease of $2.4 billion from September. The decrease was attributed largely to the General Motors strike, with manufacturing payrolls showing a decrease of $5.2 billion. In addition, government payrolls declined by $1.3 billion due to retroactive payments to postal workers.

■ The rate of the nation's Gross National Product during the third quarter was $985.5 billion annually. The GNP price index increased 4.6% during the third quarter.

■ Industrial output in September dipped sharply 1.7% to a two-year low, according to figures released by the Federal Reserve Board Oct. 15. The board's index of factory, mine and utility physical output fell to 166.1 (base: 1957–59 = 100), the lowest level for the seasonally adjusted indicator since the 165.9% recorded in September 1968. Almost two-thirds of the decline from August's downward revised 168.9% was ascribed to the General Motors strike, which began Sept. 14. The September index was 4.9% below its peak of July 1969.

In October the nation's industrial production took the sharpest plunge in 11 years, with only half the drop attributable to the General Motors Corp. strike. The FRB's industrial output index dropped to 162.4% of the base. The third consecutive monthly decrease, the 2.3% October plunge was the largest since the 3.2% drop in August 1959 during a steel strike. The production index in October was 7% below the peak 1969 figure reached in July of that year and was at its lowest level since January 1968 when it was 161.5% of the 1957–59 average. The report said the GM strike accounted for about half of the decline and that the other half reflected "further curtailments in output of consumer durable goods other than autos, business and defense equipment, and industrial materials."

■ Housing starts exhibited new strength in September by advancing 6% to a 1,504,-000-unit seasonally adjusted rate. Commerce Department figures Oct. 18 revealed that third quarter housing starts rose a sharp 17.1% from the June quarter to 1,506,000 units.

■ The Commerce Department's Census Bureau said Nov. 14 that its quarterly survey of intentions to buy new cars and new homes showed that third quarter spending plans were at a low ebb. The October survey produced only slight changes from the results of the July survey. The index of expected new car purchases in October was 103.8% of a 1967 base period; the index of expected house purchases was 95.6%. The report said 13% of the households canvassed reported their income had fallen in the last 12 months and 7.3% expected their incomes to decline "substantially."

■ The Federal Reserve Board said Nov. 4 that consumers' outstanding installment debt in September outpaced August's $232 million growth at a seasonally adjusted $359 million rate. The increase was smaller than most of the gains in 1969 as consumers exhibited caution in their spending plans. The third quarter average of $345 million was slightly down from the second quarter's $384 million and well below 1969's third quarter average of $640 million.

3d-quarter profits. Reports on corporate profits during 1970's third quarter were conflicting. The Commerce Department reported Nov. 13 that corporate profits had risen in the third quarter to an $85 billion annual rate before taxes. The first increase in four quarters, the profits were up $3 billion from the second quarter in 1970 but still $5 billion below the third quarter of 1969. Corporate earnings after taxes rose $1.5 billion to a $45.4 billion annual rate in the third quarter.

According to other data, however, profits continued to lag into the third

quarter as company executives expressed pessimism about the fourth quarter's showing because of the strike at General Motors Corp. (GM). A survey of 572 early-reporting firms by the Wall Street Journal disclosed Oct. 29 that net earnings for the third period trailed 1969 figures by 9.8%, compared with the second quarter's 7.3% decline from the 1969 period.

A moderate improvement in the overall corporate picture over the Journal's second quarter tally was knocked out by a poor showing at the nation's largest corporation. General Motors reported Oct. 28 a $77.1 million net loss for the third quarter, which included two weeks of the strike that began Sept. 14. Compared with $230 million in third quarter earnings for 1969, the 1970 quarterly figure marked the deepest deficit in the corporation's history and the first quarterly loss since early 1946 when the company was closed by a strike. GM blamed its loss on the United Auto Workers walkout and "a longer shutdown in the U.S. and Canada for model changeovers."

Reflecting a profit pinch in the steel industry, Bethlehem Steel Corp. turned in the poorest showing among the major producers with a 59.3% decline in third quarter profits, despite substantial benefits from an accounting change.

Although net income at the No. 2 steelmaker was only 33¢ a share, the usual 45¢ quarterly dividend was declared. Jones and Laughlin Steel Corp. posted a $333,000 net loss for the quarter Oct. 29. Lykes-Youngstown Corp., a diversified steel producer, omitted its 15¢ dividend on its common stock and deferred dividends on its preferred stock.

Other companies which also posted profit losses:

The Penn Central Co., whose railroad subsidiary was in bankruptcy reorganization, reported Nov. 4 a third quarter loss of $70.3 million, forcing its nine-month deficit to $194.5 million against a $17.6 million profit in 1969's nine-month period.

Lockheed Aircraft Corp.'s net earnings for the third quarter ended Sept. 27 plunged to $2 million (18¢ a share), compared with the $6.2 million (55¢ a share) posted for the corresponding 1969 period. Despite the profit loss, sales showed a marked increase to $565 million from $422 million, it was reported Nov. 3. The loss was ascribed to larger aircraft costs, rising interest expenses and general and administrative expenses.

Ling-Temco-Vought Inc. in Dallas posted a $5.1 million net loss for the third quarter Nov. 3, compared with the $2.4 million operating income reported by the conglomerate a year earlier. High interest costs and debt charges were blamed for the loss.

Auto sales plunge. Car manufacturers in Detroit reported Nov. 4 a 30% dip in sales during late October from the corresponding period of 1969, threatening the industry with its slowest sales year since 1962. General Motors, the nation's leading auto manufacturer, posted a 69.7% drop in sales, which was ascribed to the United Auto Workers strike at the company. The steep decline in sales at GM was responsible for the poor showing of the industry as a whole, for the three other major auto makers posted increases for the same period. At Chrysler, sales totaling 61,354 units marked a record 10% increase for the final third of the month, compared with year-earlier figures. Ford Motor Co. and American Motors Corp. recorded gains both for October and the final third of the month. Industry volume for October dropped 23% from 1969 levels, as an estimated 626,200 cars were reported sold.

Walker blames Democrats. Treasury Under Secretary Charles E. Walker Oct. 31 delivered the Administration's main pre-election rebuttal to what he termed "vicious" Democratic attacks on President Nixon's economic policies. In a speech to bankers attending a Georgetown University forum, Walker contended that the Administration was just beginning to cure the "legacy" of preceding Democratic administrations by bringing inflation and a "badly overheated economy" under control. Asserting that a housing boom was on the horizon and the path to full employment was "clearly charted," Walker added: "It is a record on which we are proud to run."

Walker said that the "legacy" of Democratic policy makers-turned-critics included a war costing up to $30 billion annually imposed on an economy with full employment, delayed enactment of tax increases to pay for the war and programs that added some $35 billion to domestic spending in the four years ended in mid-1969. Walker said the Democrats' aim "to have guns, butter, fat and a Great Society, all within a few years, assured that the economy would fall prey to the ravages of deep and accelerating inflation."

In subsequent remarks to reporters, Walker pointed out that the economy, in terms of gross national product, was on the upturn in the July-September quarter. He said that any current signs of deterioration in the economy would be the result of the General Motors strike, not Nixon economic policies.

Arthur M. Okun, one of President Johnson's chief economic advisers, issued a statement later Oct. 31 in reply to the Walker speech. Okun expressed "shock" that the Administration was prepared to run on a record that was "not the record the American people were promised." He said the record showed a higher degree of inflation than existed when President Nixon took office, in addition to "surging unemployment, higher interest rates, lower profits and a one-quarter drop in stock market values."

Among related developments:

■ Herbert Stein, a member of the President's Council of Economic Advisers, said in London Oct. 28 that the Administration's fight against inflation had gone beyond fiscal and monetary measures; he cited such initiatives as manpower programs, efforts to improve collective bargaining in the construction industry, formation of the Productivity Commission, establishment of "inflation alerts," and a review of government procurement and regulation policies.

Stein offered several projections for the economy in the coming two years. He said the Administration's goal of reducing unemployment to a rate of 4% or less by mid-1972 would require an increase in real (or physical) output of more than 6% in the next two years (real output in the 1970 third quarter advanced at a 1.4% annual rate). Stein's projections included an annual price inflation rate of about 3% (recent prices had been rising at a 5% annual rate).

■ George Meany, president of the AFL-CIO, said in an interview Oct. 27 that the Administration had misled the country with optimistic statements about the economy. He said the economy had not improved and showed no signs of improving.

■ Sen. Edward M. Kennedy (D, Mass.), speaking at a campaign rally in Taunton, Mass. Oct. 30, accused the Administration of a "pie-in-the-sky" approach in its economic policies, particularly on unemployment. Kennedy said: "The crisis of present unemployment in 1970 has become lost in the promise of full employment in 1972..."

■ Democratic National Chairman Lawrence F. O'Brien replied in a radio interview Oct. 31 to charges that the Nixon Administration had inherited current economic ills from the Democrats. O'Brien, declaring that President Nixon had brought about a deterioration in the economy that was "almost beyond comprehension," noted that Nixon took office with a $3.3 billion budget surplus, the lowest unemployment rate in decades and 95 consecutive months of economic growth.

Wage-Price Debate Follows Election

Following the inconclusive Congressional and gubernatorial elections of 1970, fresh debate flared on the issue of wages, prices and economic policy.

Election results mixed. The Nov. 3 elections for Congress and governorships, after a bitter campaign, produced victory claims from leaders of both parties in the Senate.

President Nixon, who campaigned more vigorously than any recent president, said Nov. 4 that the voters had given him an 'ideological' majority in the Senate.

Democratic leaders claimed success in the House and in state houses across the U.S.

These were the major results:

The Republicans gained a net two seats in the Senate.

The Democrats gained a net 11 governorships, reversing the Republican margin of 32-18 in governorships to 29-21 in favor of the Democrats. The Democrats also gained a net nine House seats to increase their margin of control to 255-180 when the 92nd Congress convened in January 1971.

The Republicans claimed success in the House elections because the Democratic gain was far below the 38-seat average improvement for the non-presidential party in off-year elections. Democrats discounted the claim because Nixon was the first president since Zachary Taylor failing to carry his party into power in Congress upon assuming office. Hence, there were not the usual number of vulnerable Republican seats— marginal winners carried the first time on the president's coattails—to regain.

Pollster George Gallup Sr. said Nov. 5 the results indicated that the working man voted in the Democratic column and the Republicans "went after the wrong group" in the campaign.

White House Press Secretary Ronald L. Ziegler, although conceding that the nation's economic problems had been a "drag" on GOP candidates, reiterated Nov. 5 that GOP Senate gains were a "tremendous success" and the Administration's campaign effort had been "very much worthwhile" since it had succeeded in "changing the ideological makeup of the Senate."

Election aftermath. The Washington Post reported Nov. 6 that President Nixon's economic advisers believed the election results "cannot be ignored," indicating that the Administration was not happy with the returns as a clear mandate for the Administration's economic "game plan."

The Post reported that Paul W. McCracken, chairman of the President's Council of Economic Advisers, said he thought the electorate had been less concerned about inflation than specific problems, such as regional unemployment, health, pollution and housing. He conceded that national economic policy must "be responsive to the national will."

The advisers were said to believe that there was room for economic expansion in order to reach full employment by 1972 without more inflation.

In a related development, the Wall Street Journal said Nov. 9 that President Nixon had told a cabinet meeting that he did not view the elections as any reason to change the "game plan" for restoring optimum economic growth and "full employment" by mid-1972. White House sources indicated the President was counting on easier monetary policies by the independent Federal Reserve Board, rather than budget increases, to stimulate the economy.

Martin urges incomes policy. William McChesney Martin Jr., former chairman of the Federal Reserve Board, strongly recommended Nov. 5 the use of wage and price guidelines in some form of incomes policy. In a speech to the Washington, D.C. Board of Trade, Martin said fiscal and monetary policies were not adequate measures to control inflation "under present circumstances."

Concerning the Administration's goal of returning the nation to "full employment" (usually considered a 4% or lower jobless rate), Martin warned that it "can't be achieved by going the easy route of forced growth, having the Federal Reserve print money to augment savings, running [budget] deficits three or four times" the level normal in more prosperous periods "without having gyrations and dislocations that make a field day for the tactician, manipulator and wheeler-dealer."

Martin criticized as "self-defeating" the Administration's refusal to use the Johnson Administration's practice of "jawboning," or Presidential persuasion, on wage-price decisions. While opposing legislated wage and price controls, Martin counseled that an incomes policy would be "advantageous to labor, management and everyone else." He stressed that the economy required more "self-discipline" and the "responsibility that a free society places on all of us."

Economy assessed. Opposing views on Administration policies and the economy were presented by two of New York City's largest banks, First National City Bank (Citibank) and Chase Manhattan Bank.

Citibank's Monthly Economic Letter, published Nov. 6, reassured its readers that inflationary pressures "have been lessening and will continue to do so." The bank asserted that the economy was "poised for a vigorous upturn," although it said that the degree of slack in the economy (defined as the margin of under-utilized manpower and equipment) would not narrow nor would the unemployment rate fall until the economy's real rate of growth exceeded a 4% annual rate.

Chase Manhattan's chief economist, William Butler, had told a press luncheon in New York Nov. 5 that he believed the Administration was studying changes in its "game plan" in order to stimulate the economy further. Without more vigorous stimulation, Butler said he foresaw continuing high levels of unemployment and a weak economy.

Butler said the economy's response to increases in the money supply at a near 5% annual rate had been sluggish. The Chase Manhattan model for 1971 called for 3.5% "real growth" (minus inflation) and a 6% growth rate to restore the economy to "full employment" (about a 3.8% jobless rate).

The two banks' economists differed most widely on the question of wage-price action by the Administration. Citibank inferred that the government had no need to involve itself directly in wage-price matters because fiscal and monetary policies had been satisfactory weapons in the fight against inflation. The bank's publication said: "Because monetary policy has reduced overall demand in the economy, businessmen are finding it increasingly difficult to offset excessive wage demands by raising prices. This helps to explain why more businessmen are presently in favor of some kind of wage-price guidelines or controls. Their very espousal of controls, therefore, suggests that they expect monetary and fiscal policies will continue to dampen demand in the economy. For if inflation were expected to accelerate, they would not be so apprehensive about their ability to protect profits by increasing prices."

Chase's Butler said wage-price guidelines were needed as a secondary tool to combat inflation; he was quite clear that he did not think they were a substitute for fiscal and economic curbs. As a guideline for wage negotiations, Butler proposed that normal gains in productivity of 3.2% plus the annual increase in the cost of living be applied as a moving adjustment.

Wage-price debate continues. The significance of wage increases appeared as a new Administration theme in a speech delivered by Herbert Stein to the California Bankers Association at Newport Beach, Calif. Nov. 7. It was the Administration's first economic policy statement since the election in which economic issues were the main target of the Democrats.

Stein, a member of the Council of Economic Advisers (CEA), said the Administration's goals of "full employment" by mid-1972 and further progress in halting inflation could be achieved only if the recent wage increases began to moderate. Stein said the CEA expected the wage increase rate to wane as a result of "slower consumer price increases, continuing unemployment, the resistance of employers suffering from lower profits, and the recognition that rapid wage increases run on a collision course with full employment." The main point of Stein's speech was that a substantial reduction in the rate of inflation could occur only if compensation per man-hour rose "at less than the rate of about 8% a year."

Stein reiterated the Administration's hesitation to adopt wage guidelines because of the risks of interfering with the free market system of setting prices and wages. However, he conceded, "It would be unfortunate to allow ideological purity to stand in the way of our real objectives."

Stein reaffirmed the Administration's plan to use budget and monetary policies to expand demand for purposes of achieving "full employment" by mid-1972. However, he said, "If, contrary to our expectations, it should become clear that we are not continuing to progress toward less inflation as we move on the path to full employment, then the path will have to be reconsidered. No government can sensibly commit itself irrevocably to the achievement of a certain unemployment rate by a certain date without regard to the consequences that may emerge, including the consequences for inflation."

On an optimistic note, Stein cited three reasons for belief that a lower unemployment rate was compatible with a slower rate of inflation: (1) the inflation rate responds to the jobless rate with some lag; (2) the unemployment rate would continue at an unusually high level, retarding wage and price increases; and (3) a period was approaching in which productivity (output per man-hour of work) would accelerate at an exceptionally fast rate.

In a related development, the New York Federal Reserve Bank's monthly review said Nov. 8 that "rocketing wage settlements" were an indication that inflation persisted, despite signs of moderating prices in the third quarter. The bank said that in the first three quarters of 1970, "the mean first-year wage-and-benefit settlement for collective-bargaining agreements covering 5,000 or more workers was 14.7%," compared with a 10.9% increase for all of 1969.

CED urges wage-price guidelines. The Committee for Economic Development issued a policy statement Nov. 23 calling for creation of a new government body to set voluntary wage and price standards. The committee, a group of 200 corporate executives and educators, stressed, however, that no "arm twisting" should be applied.

The CED report recommended the creation of a three-man Board on Prices and Incomes to develop "broad norms of appropriate noninflationary wage and price behavior that would give some guidance to business and labor" and publish public reports on those cases in which policy "deviates substantially from such broad norms." "Our own observations suggest that major firms wouldn't be insensitive to official requests that they take the public interest in price stability into specific account when they make price and wage decisions," the group said.

"The evidence from past U.S. and foreign experience regarding the effectiveness of these policies is mixed," the report continued, but added that "on balance, it seems to indicate that wage-price policies cannot prevent the inflation generated by a badly overheated economy, but can help lessen upward price pressures that may be present even when aggregate demand is not excessive." The group concluded that while voluntary wage-price policies were "not a panacea," they could be a "possibly useful adjunct" to other monetary and fiscal policies and should be included among the U.S. "tools for reconciling price stability and high employment."

The 90-page report, approved 51–6 by the CED Research and Policy Committee, also recommended a restructuring of labor laws to "bring about a better balance in the relative powers of unions and management" and to reduce the union's power to restrict the labor supply or put "undue restrictions on productivity improvements." In addition, the report called for selective credit controls; "basic structural and institutional changes which would increase competition in markets for labor and products"; use of the current "inflation alert" system to "highlight important prospective developments rather than being solely directed at decisions that have already been taken"; more federal government effort in providing jobs, training and welfare; and repeal of the Davis-Bacon Act which required the government to pay the prevailing wage rates in construction work.

In a related development, a group of 58 House Democrats called on President Nixon Nov. 23 to work out "long-term guideposts for noninflationary wage-price behavior." The congressmen, all members of the liberal-oriented Democratic Study Group, also urged Nixon to "stand ready" to use a law signed in August which authorized the President to impose temporary wage, price, interest rate and rent freezes.

"Such a freeze is necessary if labor is going to be asked to use restraint," the group said.

Federal Reserve cuts discount rate. The Federal Reserve Board cut its discount rate from 6% to 5.75% Nov. 10, auguring a reduction in the 7.5% prime lending rate at commercial banks. The board said the purpose of the small reduction was to put the fee it charged member banks for loans "into better alignment with short-term rates generally."

The reduced discount rate went into effect Nov. 11 at six of the 12 district Reserve banks—Boston, Richmond, Atlanta, St. Louis, Minneapolis and San Francisco. The discount rate was lowered by five more district banks Nov. 12, leaving only the Philadelphia bank at 6%. The five banks were New York, Cleveland, Chicago, Kansas City and Dallas.

The FRB Nov. 30 again cut its discount rate—from 5.75% to 5.5%. The reduction, which went into effect Dec. 1, was described as a technical move in keeping with the continued downward momentum of short-term interest rates.

While the reduction was not a surprise to money market analysts, three unrelated companion actions concerning Eurodollars were unexpected. In an effort to re-enforce the U.S. balance of payments position, the FRB altered its rules for reserve requirements against Eurodollar borrowings of U.S. banks. The purpose was to induce U.S. banks to avoid early or sudden repayments on their Eurodollar borrowings from overseas branches. The repayments, which had been increasing, had the effect of augmenting the dollar holdings of foreign central banks, which in turn became a potential claim against the U.S. gold stock.

Prime bank rate cut. Commercial banks Nov. 12 cut their prime rate, the fee charged by banks for loans to their most creditworthy corporate borrowers (reported to be a total 650–700 corporations), from 7.5% to 7.25% in the third reduction for 1970.

New York's Chase Manhattan Bank took the initial step, which was quickly followed by the nation's 10 major banks and was expected to become general.

Chase said it was acting "in view of changing conditions in the money market, the easing of loan demand on banks, and the action of the Federal Reserve banks in lowering the discount rate."

The reduction, part of a general trend toward lower money costs, was smaller than money market specialists had forecast. Among reasons cited for the quarter-point reduction instead of the expected half-point: settlement of the General Motors strike that was expected to spur corporate loan demand at a time when bankers looked to a major seasonal increase; the banks' desire to make the prime rate more flexible through smaller and more frequent adjustments; and the Federal Reserve Board's quarter-point reduction in its discount rate.

The Chase Manhattan Bank late Nov. 20 again reduced its prime rate—from 7¼% to 7%, effective Nov. 23.

In a statement announcing the Chase action, Chairman of the Board David Rockefeller explained that "we feel this reduction should be undertaken in light of the substantial further decline in interest rates generally which has occurred over the past 10 days."

The Bank of America in San Francisco followed suit Nov. 20, lowering its prime rate to 7% in "response to further softening in short-term money rates." The Citizens & Southern National Bank in Atlanta, and the North Carolina National Bank in Charlotte also reduced their rate to 7% Nov. 20.

Leading New York banks followed Chase Nov. 23 in reducing their prime rate to 7%.

Banks across the nation again pared their prime rates Dec. 22. The latest cut was to 6.75%. The reduction was the fifth of the year and trimmed the key rate to its lowest level since Jan. 7, 1969. Chase Manhattan again took the initial step, which was quickly followed by the rest of the banking community.

White House Press Secretary Ronald L. Ziegler said President Nixon was "pleased" by the cut, which the Administration regarded as "further evidence that the credit market is becoming easier and more conducive to economic expansion."

Chase described its decision to again lower the lending rate as part of its policy to maintain "a flexible prime rate that is fully responsive to money market rates" which had continued to decline.

Mortgage ceiling cut. The maximum interest rate on home mortgages backed by the Federal Housing Administration and the Veterans Administration was lowered Dec. 1 from 8.5% to 8%.

George W. Romney, secretary of housing and urban development, ascribed the cut to the general decline in interest rates. He said the lower ceiling should assist lagging housing construction and enable more middle-income families to move into the market by stretching subsidy funds to cover about 12,000 more units than planned under the fiscal year's budget.

Federal budget deficit. The Commerce Department reported Nov. 13 that the federal budget, as measured on a "national income accounts" basis, showed a deficit of $11.2 billion in the third quarter, compared with $14.2 billion in the second quarter. The second quarter deficit was the largest quarterly deficit recorded in 25 years. Third quarter spending decreased to a $206.7 billion annual rate, compared with second quarter spending which was at a $210.9 billion annual rate. Receipts in the third quarter fell to a $195.5 billion annual rate from $196.7 billion in the second quarter.

The Treasury reported Nov. 24 that the deficit for the fiscal year ended June 30 (fiscal year 1970) was $2.845 billion, $63 million less than a government forecast of $2.908 billion. Outlays totaled $196.587 billion and receipts $193.743 billion.

Consumer prices up. The Labor Department reported Nov. 24 that consumer prices had risen in October for the second consecutive month. The Consumer Price Index showed an adjusted .5% and an unadjusted .6% increase in October, compared with a .5% adjusted and a .4% unadjusted increase in September. The October unadjusted .6% increase, representing a 7.2% annual rate, was the sharpest advance since April.

White House Press Secretary Ronald L. Ziegler noted that the Administration looked on the CPI figures for October with "some concern," but added that the increases were still less than those recorded earlier in 1970. AFL-CIO President George Meany, however, criticized the Administration's economic policies as "an abysmal failure," and added that "the workers that still have jobs, the consumers and the jobless are paying a high price for that failure."

The consumer price rise abated somewhat in November. Prices advanced a seasonally adjusted .3% to 137.8% of the 1957–59 average in their slimmest increase since August's .2%.

The Labor Department said Dec. 24 that the increase had put the consumer price index, which rose at a 3.7% annual rate, 5.6% above a year earlier. The index also rose .3% on an unadjusted basis, a sharp decline from the .6% unadjusted increase in October.

The rising pace of the index was curbed by a continuing slack in food prices which fell an adjusted .1%, following a .1% increase in October. Another important price decline was recorded for (conventional) mortgage interest which fell .3%, the steepest decline in over three years.

Among rising prices, services advanced a strong .6%–8.4% higher than a year earlier.

Workers' purchasing power continued to diminish as shorter work weeks cut into weekly earnings. "Real" (spendable) earnings for a worker with three dependents fell to $76.84, down .8% from $77.44 in October and 1.8% from $78.25 a year earlier.

Paul W. McCracken, chairman of the Council of Economic Advisers, welcomed the November price report as "good news." Although he warned against the erratic nature of monthly figures, McCracken said the figures were evidence that Administration economic policies were "slowly making progress."

In December consumer prices rose .5% (at a 6.6% annual rate), on both a seasonally adjusted and unadjusted basis, to 138.5% of the 1957–59 average.

The rise in the consumer price index for all of 1970 amounted to 5.5%. This was the second steepest rise in the cost of living since the Korean war year of 1951 (the costliest inflationary year was 1969).

Monthly indexes in 1970 averaged 6% higher than during 1969, when the average rise was 5.4%.

Consumer prices climbed at an annual rate of 6% in the first half of 1970, 4.9% in the second half. On a quarterly basis, the CPI rose at an annual rate of 6.3% in the first quarter, 5.8% in the second quarter, 4.2% in the third quarter and 5.7% in the fourth quarter.

Jobless rate continues climb. The unemployment rate continued its steady climb in November, reaching a 7½-year high of 5.8% of the seasonally adjusted labor force, the Labor Department said Dec. 4. The rate had been 5.6% in October.

White House Press Secretary Ronald L. Ziegler said the President's Council

1970 Consumer Price Index			
From the Department of Labor			
(1957–59 = 100)			
	Index for Dec. 1970	Percentage Change From Nov. 1970	From Dec. 1969	Point Chg. From Nov. 1970
All items	138.5	+0.5	+5.5	+0.7
*Food	132.8	+0.3	+2.2	+0.4
†Housing.........	140.1	+0.6	+7.4	+0.7
‡Apparel & upkeep .	135.9	+0.1	+3.9	+0.2
Transportation....	135.5	+0.8	+7.2	+1.1
Health & Recreat'n.	147.4	+0.3	+5.6	+0.5
Medical care	169.8	+0.7	+7.4	+1.1
Personal care ...	132.8	+0.4	+3.7	+0.5
Reading & recreation	139.6	+0.2	+5.2	+0.3
Other goods, services	140.1	+0.2	+4.9	+0.3

*Includes restaurant meals. †Includes hotel and motel rates, home purchase and other home-owner costs not shown separately. ‡Includes infants' wear, sewing materials, jewelry and apparel upkeep not shown separately.

of Economic Advisers had calculated that the jobless rate would have ranged between 5.3% and 5.5% had not the General Motors strike indirectly caused a 400,000 rise in jobless figures. However, some government economists, traditionally nonpolitical, noted that reduced employment in defense-related industries was an equally significant factor in the November showing. One economist observed that the jobless increase attributable to the strike was "more like" 100,000 than 400,000 and that the effects of the strike had not deepened since October.

The number of unemployed persons rose to 4,858,000 on an adjusted basis from 4,667,000 in October. The November figures largely reflected a sharp increase in the unemployment rate for women aged 20–24 to 9.5% from 7.5% in October.

In December the unemployment rate reached 6.8%, the highest level since the 6½% of October 1961. The 1970 average unemployment rate, without seasonal adjustment, was 4.9%. The number of jobless workers in December on a seasonally adjusted basis was 5,146,000 (4,634,000 unadjusted).

The December figure disproved predictions by the Nixon Administration that the jobless rate would drop after the General Motors strike ended and workers in auto-related industries returned to work. The expected pace of job recalls apparently had not materialized because of the weak economic situation in those industries. The Administration forecast of an average annual rate of less than 5% was realized by a year-end total of 4.9%, which was, however, up from 1969's 16-year low of 3.5%. The BLS said average total employment for 1970 rose 730,000 to 78.6 million.

White House Press Secretary Ziegler conceded that the December jobless rate was "not expected" but said it reinforced the Administration's decision to move from an anti-inflationary to a more "expansionist" policy. Ziegler said the economy's current transition from a wartime to a peacetime economy, to which he ascribed the high level of unemployment and current business downturn, would produce the "least severe dislocation in this century."

Among the highlights of the December increase, which affected almost every major category of workers:

■ The jobless rate for the general category of white-collar workers (including professional, technical, managerial, sales and clerical personnel) peaked at 3.7% (up from November's 3.5%), the highest level since 1958 when the government first began collecting data on it.

■ White workers' unemployment remained at the 5.5% November rates although the rate for black workers increased to 9.3%, up from 8.8% in November. The October rate for blacks had been 9.3%.

■ Long-term unemployment (15 weeks or more) crossed the million mark for the first time since 1964, as the average term of joblessness stretched to 9.8 weeks from 9.4 weeks in November and 8.1 a year earlier.

No major jobless areas added. The Labor Department reported Nov. 26 that no new major metropolitan areas were added in November to the Bureau of Labor Statistics' list of "substantial unemployment areas." It was the first time in 10 months that no new areas had been added. Two cities, Saginaw, Mich. and Corpus Christi, Tex., were deleted from the list, which dropped to 36 areas. In the category of smaller areas, 23 areas were added, bringing that category to a total of 611.

1970 jobless data. The Bureau of Labor Statistics issued a year-end report on 1970 unemployment. Unemployment in poor urban areas rose sharply in 1970, after declining in 1969:

	1969	1970
Teen-aged residents	19.9%	24 %
black youths	27.9%	35.8%
white youths	13.8%	16.3%
Adult men	3.6%	6.2%
whites	3.1%	5.7%
blacks	4.3%	7.1%
Adult women	5.1%	5.7%

In non-poor urban areas, the jobless rate grew from 1.9% to 3.3%. Other figures for these areas:

	1969	1970
Blacks	3.1%	4.5%
Whites	1.8%	3.2%
Women	3.3%	4.5%
Teen-agers	11.4%	14.5%

Of 3.4 million workers in poor neighborhoods, 3.2 million were employed and 213,000 were unemployed; of 23.2 million non-poor workers in urban areas, 22.4 million were employed and 767,000 were jobless.

Economic indicators up. The Commerce Department's composite index of leading economic indicators rose 1.4% in December 1970, following a .6% increase in November. The increase in the index to 116.4% of the 1967 base brought the index, an indicator of future economic trends, to its highest level since February 1970.

Of eight (of 12) leading indicators available, five rose—the average workweek in manufacturing, new durable goods orders, new building permits, the average price of 500 common stocks and the average weekly initial claims for state unemployment insurance (inversely treated). The three indicators reporting declines were plant and equipment contracts and orders, industrial material prices and the ratio of price to unit labor cost on manufacturers.

Industrial output slides again. Industrial output declined .6% in November to 161.4% of the 1957–59 average, the FRB reported Dec. 15. It was the fourth straight month that the index of factory, mine and utility output had declined, standing at 7.6% below the peak of July 1969 reached before the economic slowdown began. The month's decline was concentrated in the output of business and defense equipment and industrial goods. With the automotive component showing a slight rise, the 10-week General Motors strike was no longer a factor in the index's decline.

Before the board issued its report, a "clock" intended to constantly measure the nation's gross national product (GNP) was unveiled at the Commerce Department with President Nixon attending the celebration. The unveiling marked the first time that the nation's total output achieved a $1 trillion annual rate on a daily basis (neither the full-year GNP nor the fourth quarter annual rate was expected to reach the $1 trillion level). Department officials pointed out that the clock assumed a 6% annual rate of growth in GNP and thus might not be an accurate forecasting device or mirror of particular periods.

Without mentioning the factor of inflation, compensated for in the "real" GNP, President Nixon hailed "the first trillion dollar economy for any nation in the history of the world."

Housing starts, personal income. Housing starts in November burst upward 7.8% to a seasonally adjusted annual rate of 1,692,000 units, the Commerce Department reported Dec. 17. In a separate report, the department said personal income in November rose $2.4 billion to an adjusted annual rate of $812.4 billion after having declined in October $1.9 billion (revised) [see p. 773B1], but was well below the average monthly gains for 1969.

The strong gain by housing starts from the 1,570,000-unit rate of October put November starts at their highest level since January 1969. Harold C. Passer, assistant secretary of commerce for economic affairs, said housing starts were headed "for their highest level in two decades."

Personal income for the first 11 months of 1970 achieved a $799.5 billion rate which was $52.9 billion (about 7%) above the year-earlier figure. However, the gain lagged behind the $60.5 billion (an 8.75% rise) in the first 11 months of 1969.

Machine tool orders at 12-year low. The National Machine Tool Builders Association reported Dec. 27 that machine tool orders dipped in November to their lowest level since the $32.2 million figure in November 1958. The figure reversed an upward trend since summer.

Second inflation alert. The Nixon Administration's second inflation alert, issued by the President's Council of Economic Advisers Dec. 1, specifically criticized wage or price actions in the auto, oil, rail and construction industries. The report was the nearest the Administration had come to "jawboning," or attempting to influence private wage and price decisions; however, no specific action, or threat of action, was indicated.

The main thrust of the report appeared to be aimed at the persistent upward rate of average wage increases. Although the report conceded that a possible rise in business profit margins was also disturbing against the backdrop of inflation, the council noted that profits for each unit of output were nearly 20% below their peak in 1966. The council warned that unless the wage-price "spiral" indicated some moderation, the government could not implement its policies to expand the economy and reduce unemployment.

Criticizing the General Motors wage pact and proposed rail pay increases as inflationary, the council said inflation would never end if everyone expected a wage or price increase equal to earlier increases. The report conceded that the fight against inflation would involve some unfairness: "Slowing down inflation means that those who come later will get smaller wage or price increases than those who came earlier." On the practice of allowing for future inflation in labor contracts, the report warned that general application of the principle would be "a recipe for permanent rapid inflation—and also for persistent unemployment, because the government would be bound to try to check the inflation by generally restrictive policies."

Another theme of the report was that companies and workers were pricing themselves out of markets and jobs on the principle that costs out of line with general trends would lead to the economic system's own imposition of sanctions. The council pointed out that the construction industry's 17.5% average wage increase during the first nine months of 1970 had benefited some 504,000 workers but had also put 324,000 workers on the unemployment rolls.

Citing the 6%–7% increase in 1971 model auto prices, increasing consumers' costs by nearly $2.5 billion, the report said the increases left the domestic industry wide open for heavier competition from foreign cars. (Chrysler raised its 1971 prices Dec. 1 by an average .5% [about $15 a car]. The Ford Motor Co. raised prices Dec. 8 an average of $15 a car.)

Among the report's comments concerning various industries:

■ In the car industry, the report warned that if the United Auto Workers wage settlement (about 7% a year) with General Motors Corp. were generalized throughout the economy, it "would crowd further upward costs per unit of output and, therefore, the price level."

■ The report admonished the Texas state oil authorities for permitting a rollback in the oil production rate for December, thereby reducing the output of crude oil supply, merely on the request of one major oil company that complained of excessive oil inventories.

■ The report sharply rebuked a special Presidential emergency board for its recommendation Nov. 9 that railroad workers receive pay increases exceeding an annual average of 9%. The report said the board's allowance for an annual 6% increase in consumer prices "would saddle the industry with rising costs," and retard stability in the price-cost level.

Rail strike despite 37% raise plan. A Presidential emergency rail panel recommended Nov. 9 a 37% increase in wages over three years for 600,000 railroad workers. The board also recommended formation of a permanent unit to negotiate rail wage and work-rule issues. The rail workers, however, found the proposed raise too little and walked out Dec. 10 in a brief strike that was halted only by Congressional action.

The proposals were presented in the railroads' dispute with four AFL-CIO unions that had threatened a nationwide strike for a 40% increase. The board was appointed by the President under the Railway Labor Act, which also carried a 60-day ban against a strike and lockout.

The wage increase proposal would boost wages by $1.32 an hour over the current average wage of $3.60 an hour.

Administration spokesmen expressed support Nov. 9 for the panel's report, especially the prospect for a multiyear wage agreement, new bargaining apparatus and the possibility, according to Assistant Labor Secretary W. J. Usery, that the recommendations might help "resolve the fireman-manning issue" as well as the wage dispute with the four unions.

The proposed $1.32-an-hour wage increase was not acceptable to the unions. C. L. Dennis, president of the Brotherhood of Railway, Airlines and Steamship Clerks, rhetorically asked Nov. 9 if he could be expected "to live with that in the transportation industry when the government okays $1.65 an hour [more] for the teamsters?"

Dennis said Nov. 10 his union would strike Dec. 11 unless a prior accord were reached. The other three unions—the Brotherhood of Maintenance of Way Employes, the United Transportation Union and the Hotel and Restaurant Employes Union—rejected the Presidential panel's recommendations Nov. 11 but withheld a strike date in favor of further negotiating on the basis of the panel's report.

The carriers announced Nov. 24 that they would accept the wage settlement—even though the cost to the carriers by 1974 was estimated at five times their pre-tax profits—if the unions would agree to the board's recommendations for elimination of certain work rules. However, the unions reaffirmed their opposition to the board's proposals.

President Nixon asked Congress Dec. 7 for legislation ordering a 45-day delay in the strike deadline to permit continued bargaining. Congress approved a bill to provide an immediate 13½% increase in retroactive pay—recommended by the presidential panel for the contract's first year—and to defer the strike deadline until March 1, 1971.

But enactment came past the strike deadline. President Nixon signed the legislation at 2:10 a.m., and the strike had begun at 12:01 a.m. Dec. 10.

The carriers then sought and obtained at 3:17 a.m. from U.S. District Judge John H. Pratt in Washington a temporary restraining order forbidding the strike. Three of the unions—the Brotherhood of Maintenance of Way Employes, the United Transportation Union and the Hotel and Restaurant Employes—canceled their strikes.

But there was no general return to work because the BRAC picket lines remained intact and Dennis avoided marshals seeking to serve the court order. About 6 p.m., Pratt found BRAC guilty of contempt of his earlier order and set the $200,000-a-day fine for every day the union remained on strike after midnight. Dennis ordered a return to work minutes later.

Nixon steps up economic moves. President Nixon, in a speech to the National Association of Manufacturers in New York Dec. 4, asserted that his "game plan" was working against inflation. At the same time, he pledged various steps to expand the economy "to its full potential for growth," to reduce prices and to curb rampant wage settlements in the construction industry.

Admitting that the nation had paid the price of added unemployment and a corporate profit squeeze during the nation's transition "from war to peace, from inflation to stability," Nixon said the workingman and the businessman had earned the right "to reasonable stability and a new steadiness of growth in our economic life." Nixon outlined three areas as the next phase of the Administration's economic "game plan" to stimulate the economy toward its full growth potential and employment, while continuing to reduce inflation: a "full employment" balanced budget for the next fiscal year, an expansionary money and credit supply, and a strong revival in housing construction. Nixon disclosed that Arthur F. Burns, chairman of the Federal Reserve Board, had made a "commitment" to him that the Federal Reserve System would "provide fully for the increasing monetary needs of the economy."

In another effort to resist inflation, the President said steps had been taken to change some government regulations that contributed to higher prices. As an example, Nixon said he had ordered the Interior Department to take over the states' responsibilities for oil and gas production on all federal offshore lands. State restrictions had held down the supply of crude oil, tending to raise prices. In a related move, the President authorized an increase in imports of Canadian oil, which would help augment the oil supply and lower prices.

In some mild "jawboning" action, Nixon said he would propose legislation to change the collective bargaining structure of the construction industry if the industry's collective bargaining commission so recommended. The President warned that unless labor and management in the industry, where wage settlements doubled the national average, instituted their own reforms, the government would intervene in wage negotiations on federally sponsored construction projects.

On a more general note, the President exhorted business and labor to use restraint on wages and prices in return for the government's efforts to stimulate the economy: "If business and labor expect public policy to help stimulate real expansion, then business and labor should be prepared to offer the public some real help in curbing inflation." He added: "This is the moment for labor and management to stop freezing into wage settlement and price actions any expectation that inflation will continue in the future at its peak rate of the past. Any wage or price decision that makes the flat and irreversible assumption of a high rate of inflation ahead is against the public interest and against the real interest of the workingman."

The President also noted that productivity of output per manhour was rising, making it an appropriate time for business to reshape its pricing policies and pass to the consumer its savings in production costs.

Burns proposes wage-price board. Arthur F. Burns, chairman of the Federal Reserve Board, Dec. 7 proposed an 11-point anti-inflation plan, including creation of a wage-price review board. Declaring that the U.S. faced nagging inflation and substantial unemployment, Burns called for a review board, with wide authority but lacking enforcement power, to investigate and advise on prices and wages.

Without much elaboration, Burns outlined the other 10 points to the review board:

Lower import quotas on oil and other commodities; more vigorous enforcement of the antitrust laws; expansion of federal training programs to increase the supply of skilled workers where wages are rising with exceptional rapidity; creation on a nationwide scale of local productivity councils to seek ways of increasing efficiency; a more aggressive pace in establishing computerized job banks; liberalization of depreciation allowances to stimulate plan modernization; suspension of the Davis-Bacon Act (fixing wages on federal construction projects) to help restore order in the construction trades; modification of the minimum wage laws in the interest of improving job opportunities for teen-agers; establishment of national building codes to break down the barriers to the adoption of modern production techniques in the construction industry; and compulsory arbitration of "public interest" labor disputes.

Burns warned against "excessive" monetary expansion or "unduly stimulative fiscal policies" in an effort to regain "our full output potential overnight."

Nixon defends policy. President Nixon, at his Washington news conference Dec. 10, said he believed his economic policies were working.

"First, we've cooled off the inflation," he said. "It is beginning to recede—the rate of inflation. Second, we are now moving into the second half of our plan of expanding our fiscal policy and that, together with an expanded monetary supply, we believe will move the economy up."

Nixon also took up the issue of unemployment, which, he argued, had been lower during his Administration than "any peacetime year in the sixties." He noted that in 1960–1964 unemployment was "always over 5%." In contrast, Nixon said unemployment during 1970 would average 4.9% (the November rate was 5.8%). Nixon said the Adminis-

tration's goal was a jobless rate under 5% "without war."

Asked whether he thought his original opposition to wage-price guidelines had been a mistake, Nixon said it would have been improper for him to pressure labor and management "at a time that the government was the major culprit in contributing to inflation." Explaining his former resistance as a matter of "timeliness," Nixon said that since the Administration had done its part in the fiscal and monetary areas, the time had come for labor and management "to quit betting on inflation and to start help fighting inflation."

Farm bill cleared. The farm bill extending basic support programs for three years was approved by the Senate Nov. 19 by a 48–35 vote. The bill, which President Nixon signed Nov. 30, imposed a limit for the first time on the amount of subsidies an individual farmer could receive—a limit of $55,000 a year on each of three basic crops: cotton, wheat and feed grains.

In addition to extending the price support programs for three years for cotton, wheat and feed grains, the legislation included a new "set aside" plan designed by the Nixon Administration to permit a certain percentage of a farmer's land to lie idle to qualify for federal payments and price supports. The set-aside land would be in addition to acreage idled for a farmer's conservation base.

Opposition to the legislation came largely from the Midwest and South on the grounds it would lower farm incomes and prove to be "disastrous to the cotton South." The latter phrase came from Sen. Allen J. Ellender (D, La.), chairman of the Agriculture Committee. Others denouncing the bill were Sens. George S. McGovern (D, S.D.), Stuart Symington (D, Mo.) and Walter F. Mondale (D, Minn.). Joining in the vote against the bill were Sens. Edward M. Kennedy (D, Mass.), Edmund S. Muskie (D, Me.) and Harold E. Hughes (D, Iowa).

The cost of the farm subsidies was expected to remain at the $3.8 billion annual level.

Tony Dechant, president of the 250,-000-member National Farmers Union, called Nov. 7 for defeat of the bill, warning that "in every district where it was an issue [in the recent elections], the Nixon proposal was rejected by the defeat of a Republican."

Agriculture Department funds. Congress approved and sent to the White House by voice votes of both houses Dec. 8 a bill appropriating $8,090,856,-550 for the Agriculture Department in fiscal 1971. The total was $342,502,050 more than the Administration's request and $7,260,400 more than the fiscal 1970 appropriation. President Nixon signed the bill Dec. 22.

The increases over the budget request largely reflected Congress' continuation of the agricultural conservation program, for which $195.5 million was allotted in advance program authorization, and continuation of the special milk program, for which $104 million was provided. The Administration favored an end to both programs.

Of the total appropriation, $4,077,-680,000 was for the department's corporations, $670,422,000 for credit agencies and $3,342,754,550 for general activities.

In the corporation area, the Federal Crop Insurance Corporation received $12 million, the Commodity Credit Corporation $3,363,155,000, Public Law 480 (export of surplus) $702,500,000.

Of the credit agencies, the Rural Electrification Administration received $480,413,000, of which $128,800,000 was for telephone loans, and the Farmers Home Administration received $190,-009,000.

Major items under general activities included $270,784,000 for the Soil Conservation Service, $150,922,000 for the Consumer and Marketing Service, $512-150,000 for the Stabilization and Conservation Service, and $1,825,974,000 for the Food and Nutrition Service (special milk program $104 million; child nutrition programs $301,974,000, food stamp program $1.42 billion).

Vetoed fund bill revised. Congress cleared for the President's signature Dec. 7 a bill appropriating $17,709,525,-300 for fiscal 1971 operation of the Department of Housing and Urban Development (HUD), executive offices and independent agencies. A previous version of this appropriations bill providing $18 billion had been vetoed by President Nixon, and the veto was upheld by the House. President Nixon signed the revised bill Dec. 18.

The revised bill (HR19830), passed by 375-10 House vote Nov. 24 and 74-1 Senate vote Dec. 7, was $300 million less than the first version but still $241.3 million more than the Administration's request. The revision consisted of cutting $150 million from the urban renewal program and the same amount from grants to rural communities for water and sewer facilities.

In the Senate Dec. 7, proposals were defeated to restore $150 million for the water and sewer grants and to eliminate $110 million for a space shuttle program.

Among the items included in HR19830 were (figures in parentheses Administration request): HUD $3,343,081,000 ($2,993,021,000); National Aeronautics & Space Administration $3,268,675,000 ($3,333,000,000); Veterans Administration $9,065,528,000 ($8,960,528,000); National Science Foundation $513 million ($513 million); Appalachian regional development program $293,500,000 ($295,-500,000); civil defense (Defense Department) $72,100,000 ($73,800,000); urban renewal $1,200,000,000 ($1 billion); and water and sewer facilities grants $350 million ($150 million).

Last of nation's silver sold. The U.S. Treasury sold the last of its marketable silver Nov. 10, ending the government's 194 years as a silver trader. The government's remaining 1.5 million ounces of silver were auctioned off at about $1.84 an ounce to the Franklin Mint in Franklin Center, Pa., the world's largest private mint. The sale also marked the end of bimetalism (gold and silver) as the nation's monetary standard.

The Treasury had been selling from 300,000 ounces-3.3 million ounces of silver every week since Aug. 4, 1967. The government's only remaining stocks of silver were about 35 million ounces of mostly raw metal to be used for Eisenhower silver dollars and about 165 million ounces in the Defense Department's strategic stockpile.

Prices & Wages

Price Action

Steel price guarantees. Bethlehem Steel Corp., the nation's second largest steel producer, initiated a policy of price stability guarantees Feb. 5. It was soon followed by the rest of the industry. The industry pledged not to raise prices of basic big-volume steel products more than once annually. However, Bethlehem Steel stipulated that the policy would be flexible in the face of competitive situations requiring a price change. The company said the price policy was intended to assist its clients in their business planning.

Bethlehem announced the stability guarantee less than a month after leading the industry Jan. 16 in raising prices of some construction steel categories by 5%. Following Bethlehem, the steel industry had increased the prices of structural shapes (beams, girders, columns) and steel plate by $7 a ton (effective March 1) and of sheet piling by $10 a ton (effective Feb. 15). Bethlehem had blamed the increase on higher costs, including rising prices of raw materials and transportation, a 10% increase in local and Pennsylvania state taxes, repeal of the 7% federal investment tax credit, and air and water pollution control measures expected to cost $200 million (or 11% of all industry spending in the next five years).

National Steel Corp., the fourth largest steel mill, announced Feb. 8 its support of the price guarantee policy. It said the policy would go into effect immediately in categories of construction steel that had received the recent 5% price boost.

Announcements standardizing the price guarantee among the eight largest steel mills in the nation were made by Armco Steel Corp., Youngstown Steel & Tube Co. (Feb. 9); Republic Steel Corp., Wheeling-Pittsburgh Steel Corp. (Feb. 11); U.S. Steel Corp., Jones & Laughlin Steel Corp. (Feb. 12). However, some companies included a provision in their announcement. Republic said that volatile prices of raw materials might force the company to exempt certain steel products from the price policy. Wheeling-Pittsburgh said it would exclude nickel-coated strip. U.S. Steel, the nation's No. 1 producer, said it would maintain for one year "its published prices made effective at any time during the balance of 1970," thereby providing an apparent safety valve in anticipation of forthcoming labor negotiations in the summer of 1971.

The industry's first major price increase since the new policy was announced by Republic in Cleveland March 30. The company said it would raise prices, effective April 15, about 4.5% (from $7 to $11 a ton) on most types of steel-bar products (comprising nearly

129

15% of total steel shipments). Recognizing current inflationary trends in the economy, the company said it was making the move reluctantly, but out of necessity because of higher costs in labor, materials, services and freight, plus heavier state and local taxes.

As other steel companies followed Republic's lead April 1 on steel-bar price boosts, U.S. Steel broadened its price increases to include semifinished steels in the rod and wire categories. It again widened its increases April 3 to include "oil country goods" (pipe products used in oil production) and said prices on certain sizes of standard pipe and miscellaneous line pipe would be increased 4.9%, effective May 1. The oil country goods increases, initiated by CF&I Steel Corp. March 30, were to become effective April 11 and ranged from $12–$16 a ton (the CF&I hikes ranged from $16–$20 a ton).

Bethlehem Steel announced April 30 that it was raising prices of steel sheets, the industry's biggest volume product (accounting for 35% of its shipments), by an average 4.7%, effective June 1. U.S. Steel May 12 announced a similar raise, as did Jones & Laughlin, Youngstown Sheet & Tube and Wheeling-Pittsburgh Steel May 15. Base prices of hot-rolled, cold-rolled and hot-dipped galvanized sheet had been increased by more than 3% Feb. 1, making the June 1 increase the second 1970 hike on those products.

At a May 4 press conference preceding the annual meeting of the U.S. Steel Corp., President Edwin H. Gott said higher steel prices were needed to offset rising costs. Among the cost increases was a scheduled boost in wages Aug. 1.

In a related development, two members of the industry also raised prices on concrete reinforcing bars, a key item in construction and road building. It was the third increase of its kind in an 11-month period. Armco Steel Corp. confirmed May 20 it had lifted rebar prices by $10 a ton, effective May 15. U.S. Steel announced May 20 it was raising the base price $10 per ton to $118 per ton, effective June 1.

U.S. Steel announced Aug. 4 that it was increasing prices of tin mill products by as much as 11.8% on shipments beginning Oct. 1. This nearly expended possible steel price increases for the year

under the industry's price guidelines policy.

Bethlehem Steel announced Sept. 11 that it had eliminated extra charges on certain galvanized steels, effective Sept. 1. This amounted to a price reduction of about $5 a ton, but it affected less than 1% of the industry's volume.

The Wall Street Journal observed Sept. 14 that Bethlehem, by publicly cutting prices of smooth-finished galvanized steels, was apparently seeking to curb a trend in the industry toward negotiated pricing manifest in the quiet price reductions by other producers. The Journal said a public price cut would have the effect of forcing the rest of the industry to offer the reduced quote to all customers, thus discouraging any further shading.

Steel price revisions initiated by Armco Steel Sept. 25 on cold-rolled sheet were followed Sept. 29 by Bethlehem Steel. The price reductions, establishing a sub-prime grade at a 4% lower price, were seen as an attempt to combat under-the-table action in the industry.

U.S. Steel Corp. reacted strongly Oct. 2 to Armco's pricing action by setting its quote at $9 a ton less for cut sheets and $12 less for coil. The company said it would not sell "secondary" (low-grade) coils, priced at $30–$35 a ton below prime, after Oct. 31.

U.S. Steel's move to split cold-rolled sheet steel into two price categories and to discontinue the sale of most "secondary" sheet steels was regarded as a significant change in steel pricing policy. The Wall Street Journal reported Oct. 14 the view of some analysts that dropping secondary sales was based on a gamble that steelmakers could improve mill operations and reduce the amount of rejected steel that had to be reprocessed.

Copper price up & down. In a surprise move, the nation's biggest domestic copper producers, Kennecott Copper Corp. and the Phelps Dodge Corp., boosted their prices by 7%, from 56¢ to 60¢ a pound. Phelps Dodge took the lead March 30, making its increase effective the next day; Kennecott followed suit April 6.

The price increase was unexpected in view of an on-going study by the Nixon

Administration of copper prices. Further information about the study was disclosed at a White House news briefing May 24. Hendrik Houthakker, a member of the President's Council of Economic Advisers, said the study was leaning towards anti-trust action. Consequently, the Justice Department, he said, was undertaking its own study on the legality of the industry's two-price system.

In a related development, the Anaconda American Brass Co., a subsidiary of the Anaconda Co., announced May 26 it was canceling a price increase on copper water tube. Increases on other copper-bearing products, however, remained in effect.

Prices of copper made from foreign ores and scrap fell below domestic copper prices for the first time in seven years Aug. 7.

Phelps Dodge, the nation's No. 2 copper producer, cut prices Oct. 21, effective immediately, to 56¢ a pound from 60¢. It was the first domestic price reduction since Jan. 11, 1961. The company indicated that the price action was a result of competition from foreign producers and the sliding "world price" of copper posted on the London Metal Exchange.

Anaconda Co., the third-ranking producer, and Inspiration Consolidated Copper Co. fell into step with the price rollback Oct. 22. The slash was also matched in Canada by International Nickel Co.

In another comparable and related price action, Phelps Dodge announced Oct. 22 it was lowering base prices for most brass mill products by 4¢ a pound.

Phelps Dodge Nov. 11 again cut the basic price of domestic primary copper. The price was lowered to 53¢ a pound for copper wire bar from 56¢, effective Dec. 1. The company's announcement did not explain the reason for the cut, but it was noted that copper scrap and spot quotations on the London Metal Exchange had fallen below the U.S. market level.

Lead prices cut. An industry-wide reduction in lead prices was started by American Smelting & Refining Co. (Asarco) July 8 when it cut its prices from 16.5¢ a pound to 15.5¢. St. Joe Minerals Corp., Anaconda Co. and U.S. Smelting Refining & Mining Co. made similar reductions the same day. Asarco spokesmen

attributed the reduction to excessive lead inventories. Amax Lead & Zinc Inc. and Cominco Ltd. of Canada July 9 also announced price cuts—Amax to 15.5¢ and Cominco to 16¢—to remain competitive.

Led by Asarco, U.S. lead producers Aug. 7 lowered prices by one-half cent. Then, in the industry's third reduction in less than 60 days, lead prices were lowered by Asarco Sept. 1 to 14.5¢ a pound from 15¢. The company said the abnormally high inventories and prevalent discounting from published prices made the reduction necessary. Other major producers, who had conformed to Asarco's cuts Aug. 7 and July 8, said the reduction was unwarranted and refused to follow suit.

Aluminum prices up. Kaiser Aluminum & Chemical Corp. touched off another round of price increases on basic aluminum April 8 by raising its prices by 1¢ to 29¢ a pound, effective April 14. This was the third time in 15 months that the company had taken the lead in boosting U.S. aluminum prices. Four other major producers announced comparable price increases April 9; they were Aluminum Co. of America (Alcoa), Reynolds Metals Co., Revere Copper & Brass, Inc. and Alcan Aluminum, Ltd.'s U.S. subsidiary.

Auto makers raise prices. In the first new-model pricing action by a leading car maker for this year, Chrysler Corp. Aug. 3 announced a 3.8% increase for its 1970 models. The company also indicated it might raise prices of its 1971 truck models by more than 5% and confirmed it would trim its truck-warranty coverage. It said it would drop its five-year (50,000 miles) power-train warranty on light trucks and liberalize the basic warranty to 12 months with no milage limit for one year (12,000 miles); the company said it might take similar action on heavy trucks.

On the heels of the Chrysler announcement, the Ford Motor Co. said in a letter to car dealers Aug. 5 concerning advanced billing prices that 1971 car and truck prices would be raised by 5%-6% and the company would discontinue its optional five-year warranty on engine and related parts. The one-year warranty covering most Ford car parts would apparently remain in effect for 1971 models.

General Motors Corp. Aug. 24 joined the other "Big 3" car makers in raising prices on 1971 truck models. GM said it would tentatively boost prices between 4.9% and 6.3%.

Ford Sept. 16 raised prices on 1971 models by an average $156 a car, or 4.8%, and on cars with optional equipment by $153 a car, or 5%. Ford indicated that its car prices, which reached their highest level in 14 years, might be increased even further pending a new labor contract settlement and the announcement of GM's price plans.

The expected GM announcement was made Sept. 24, raising prices to their highest level on record for the industry. GM prices were raised an average $208 (or 6.2%) per 1971 model car. The company said that tentative average prices were up $136, or 4%, from 1969. The effect of standardizing formerly optional equipment and a 5% price increase on optional equipment actually hiked prices about $245, or 6%, above 1969 prices. GM said the price increases were tentative and hinted that they might go up even higher after settlement of the GM strike.

Chrysler Corp. undercut the Ford and GM boosts with an announcement Sept. 29 that it was raising its suggested retail prices for 1971 models by close to $200 a car, or an average 3.7%. The company also cut dealer markups on some cars.

Ford Oct. 9 increased prices again on 1971 models. The company said the average rise would be $14, or .3%, per car. It said the new increases reflected changes "in competitive market conditions"—an apparent reference to the GM increases, which had topped Ford's original price hikes.

FTC plans curbs on car list prices. The Federal Trade Commission announced Oct. 9 proposed rules to end the practice of listing new car prices that inaccurately reflected the real cost to the consumer. The draft regulations would prohibit the listing of inflated "sticker" prices; publication of list prices excluding federal taxes, dealer handling and other hidden charges; and issuance of sales invoices to dealers without conspicuously disclosing in prominent type the possi-

bility of future rebates, allowances, discounts and other incentive awards from the manufacturer to the dealer.

At public hearings held in 1969, it was revealed that retail prices (sticker prices) of passenger cars ranged between 10%-20% above the actual prices charged by dealers.

U.S. inquiry on oil price hikes. The government announced Nov. 12 a major investigation into the price increase of crude oil posted Nov. 11 by the Gulf Oil Corp. and Nov. 12 by the Atlantic Richfield Co. The 25¢-a-barrel increase for crude oil raised prices from $3.10 to $3.35 and was the first increase since early 1969. The action included a companion boost of .7¢ a gallon on wholesale gasoline.

The Nixon Administration expressed its concern in the investigation by assigning Paul W. McCracken, chairman of the Council of Economic Advisers (CEA), a "major role" in the inquiry. However, oil officials stressed that the inquiry did not represent change of policy concerning "jaw-boning" in that oil, partly regulated by the government because of import controls, was a special case.

George A. Lincoln, director of the Office of Emergency Preparedness (OEP) and chairman of the Oil Import Policy Committee, said the inquiry into "the reasons for and consequences of the increase" was mandated under the 1959 oil import proclamation requiring him as chairman to keep a constant surveillance of oil imports "in respect to national security." The announcement by Lincoln did not specify what recommendation would be made to the President if the price boost was found to be unwarranted.

CEA spokesmen conceded that McCracken's participation in the inquiry represented government "activism" in a specific price situation and reflected the council's "growing concern" with wage and price levels since general excess demand in the economy had subsided. They said the council was chiefly concerned with "cost-push" inflation (when costs [mainly wages] outpaced productivity, pushing prices upward as manufacturers sought to maintain profit margins).

Gulf Oil said Nov. 15 that it would "cooperate fully" in the investigation, although it had not yet heard directly from OEP which was conducting the inquiry.

The company said it believed that the facts would prove the increase "fully justified and long overdue" in view of "the industry's ability to supply the energy necessary" to meet the public's need without compromising national security. Concern was expressed over the decline in domestic oil reserves which the industry had been unable to augment fast enough nor generate adequate return to "justify the exploration needed to increase the reserves."

Wage Developments & Labor Costs

Workers' pay rates continued to climb during 1970. Long negotiations and costly strikes frequently preceded the agreements on wage increases.

The Labor Department reported April 30 that during the first quarter of 1970, labor settlement increases over the life of the contracts signed averaged 8%, a slight decrease from the 8.2% average for the whole of 1969. In wages alone, the average per year increase over the life of the contract was 8%, up from 7.6% in 1969. The average first-year wage increase was 10.8%, up from 9.2% in 1969.

GE strike accord reached. Bargaining committees of the International Union of Electrical Workers (IUE) and the United Electrical Workers (UE) approved an agreement Jan. 30 to end a three-month strike by 33,000 workers against the General Electric Co. (GE). The 40-month contract, ratified by the IUE and UE memberships in votes announced Feb. 3, would give the company's electrical workers an additional $1.05 an hour in wages and benefits at an estimated cost to GE of nearly $1 billion.

The IUE and UE conference boards, composed of representatives of union locals, voted Feb. 1 to recommend ratification of the agreement. The accord was expected to provide a basis for settlements between GE and 10 smaller striking unions. One of the 10, the American Flint Glass Workers Union in Logan, Ohio, ratified the contract Feb. 3.

J. Curtis Counts, chief federal mediator, in announcing the basis for the agreement reportedly reached during negotiations Jan. 26, hailed the accord Jan. 29 as "showing that collective bargaining can work." Although Labor Secretary George P. Shultz had resisted pressures to intervene in the strike, federal mediators had entered the negotiations Dec. 14, 1969 when there appeared to be no progress towards a settlement. Counts had personally directed mediation efforts since Jan. 7.

At a news conference Jan. 30, UE president Albert J. Fitzgerald said the accord was the "first negotiated settlement" with GE in 20 years, a reference to what it called the company's "Boulwarism" method of bargaining.

Chief GE negotiator John R. Baldwin described the settlement Jan. 30 as "obviously inflationary" but "not superinflationary," and said it was in line with other recent labor settlements.

The $1.05 an hour package included wage gains and cost-of-living adjustments expected to total 81 cents an hour over the period of the contract. The additional 24 cents an hour included the estimated cost of benefits such as sick leave and improvements in vacation, pension, and health and welfare programs. Union spokesmen said the package would provide an average wage and benefit increase of 7.5% annually.

The wage provisions of the settlement provided an immediate increase of 20 cents an hour, an hourly increase the second year of 15 cents, effective 15 months after the first increase, and a third-year increase of 15 cents effective after another 14 months. Pre-strike wages for GE workers had averaged $3.25 an hour. A three-cent-an-hour cost-of-living adjustment, reflecting rises in living costs since the previous contract expired, was to be granted along with the first wage increase. Further adjustments were to be made in October of 1970, 1971 and 1972 at the rate of one cent an hour for each .3% increase shown in the Consumers Price Index for the preceding year.

Cincinnati city workers strike. A 31-day strike in Cincinnati by 2,400 city employes ended Feb. 5 with agreement on a 13-month contract calling for pay raises of from 22¢ to 54¢ an hour. About 1,400 workers received a 30¢ hourly wage boost.

The workers were members of the State, County & Municipal Employes (SCME) union. The work stoppage resulted in a massive garbage pileup and a lack of street maintenance and waterworks service. Police and firemen were not involved.

During the strike, a sewage treatment plant had to be closed for repairs and 260 million gallons of raw sewage poured into the Ohio River in violation of an interstate agreement. Three strike leaders were jailed for nine days for violating a picketing ban. Two had been sentenced to 20 days each, the third for 10 days, plus fines, but the union refused to negotiate until a court-ordered release was obtained. The new pact called for joint action by the city and union to seek court dismissal of charges and penalties.

The pact also provided for reinstatement of striking employes, who had been informed by the city midway in the strike that they faced dismissal if absent after three days.

An outside agency was to be hired under the pact for evaluation of job rates, classifications and duties.

Detroit construction pact. Agreement on a two-year contract barring strikes during negotiations over working condition was reached in Detroit Feb. 19 in coalition bargaining by 24 unions and 18 employer organizations in the construction industry. The settlement, covering 40,000 of the 60,000 building trades union members in the Detroit area and attained prior to expiration of any of the current contracts, called for wage and benefit increases worth $2 an hour, or approximately 12% in the first year and 11% in the second. It also provided for negotiation of specific working conditions in each trade and established a ceiling on employers' costs.

Westinghouse pact. Final settlement on terms of a new 40-month contract was reached in Pittsburgh March 1 between the Westinghouse Electric Corp. and four unions. The settlement averted a major nationwide strike set for that day.

The new pacts, covering about 80,000 workers, called for a 15% wage boost, excluding cost-of-living adjustments (which were based on future consumer price index levels). A 20¢-an-hour wage rise was retroactive to Jan. 5. Skilled employes would get additional raises of from 5¢ to 25¢ an hour. Additional hourly wage boosts of 15¢ were set for March 15, 1971 and May 15, 1972. The average pay under the old contract was $3.25 an hour.

The contract also provided for increases in pensions (from $65 a month to $120 a month for a worker retiring with 20 years of service), a new fifth week of vacation after 30 years' service and four weeks after 15 years, plus increases in sick pay, hospitalization and maternity leave.

Negotiations had opened in September 1969 and continued since Nov. 9, 1969, when the old contracts expired, on a day-to-day, contract-extension basis. The International Union of Electrical Workers, representing 40,000 Westinghouse workers at 39 plants across the country, and the United Electrical Workers, representing 8,000 workers, and the International Brotherhood of Electrical Workers, representing 18,000 workers, agreed to the new pact Feb. 28. The fourth union, the Federation of Westinghouse Independent Salaried Unions (representing 16,000 white-collar workers), went on strike for three hours at 53 plants before settling March 1.

N.Y. gravedigger strike & raise. Gravediggers in the New York metropolitan area went on an eight-week strike before accepting a new contract March 9 that would provide $23.50 more a week in wages by July 1 ($13 retroactive to Jan. 1, $10.50 more July 1). The pre-strike offer was $22 a week over three years. The weekly wage under the old pact was $126.50.

Las Vegas casinos struck. Most of the gambling casinos along the Las Vegas Strip were closed by a strike and lockout March 11-15. The strike by 14,000 bartenders, cooks, waitresses and maids began March 11 at three hotel-casinos. Another 13 locked out the union members. Three other hotels, which bargained separately and had agreed to accept terms set by the others, remained open. It was the union's first strike in Las Vegas.

A settlement was achieved March 15 after negotiations prompted by Nevada Gov. Paul Laxalt. It called for a three-year contract to provide for a 31.5% increase in wage and fringe benefits.

The estimate of the total loss in revenue for the struck casinos was $600,000 daily.

Baltimore press strike ended. A 10-week strike halting publication of Baltimore's three daily newspapers ended with approval of a new contract March 15 to provide a $48 weekly pay boost over three years for pressmen. The strike began Jan. 1 and picket lines were honored by other newspaper unions. The newspapers were The Sun, the Evening Sun and the News American. It was the city's second newspaper blackout in five years.

San Francisco employes strike. A strike by San Francisco municipal workers closed down the city's schools and transit system and curtailed health services March 13-16. About 14,000 of the city's 22,000 employes were involved. The strike was called by four unions in a dispute with the Board of Supervisors over the size of a proposed wage increase package. The strike ended with agreement on a $6 million package, a $1,250,000 increase over the board's pre-strike offer.

Seattle garbage settlement. Seattle garbage workers, members of the International Brotherhood of Teamsters, ended a six-day walkout April 8 and accepted a three-year pact with a total pay raise of $1.22 more an hour.

Atlanta strikers win 4.3% raise. Atlanta, Ga. city employes went on strike 37 days in a wage dispute with the city administration. The strike, which began March 17, ended April 22 with agreement on a one-step 4.3% pay increase for most of the 2,314 employes involved. The workers, whose pre-pact wages were $355 a month to start and $438 after five years, had sought a 4.5% raise. They were members of the AFL-CIO American Federation of State, County and Municipal Employes union.

Teamsters' raise raised. A tentative agreement on a new trucking contract covering some 450,000 members of the International Brotherhood of Teamsters was reached in national negotiations in Washington April 2. But it was rejected April 3 by leaders of 50,000 truck drivers in Chicago who were conducting separate negotiations. The Chicago drivers, after a 12-week strike and lockout, finally won better terms July 3, and the Chicago settlement was extended to the rest of the industry.

The national bargaining, joined March 30 by J. Curtis Counts, director of the Federal Mediation Conciliation Service, had continued past the expiration date of the old three-year contract March 31, but thousands of drivers walked off their jobs, shutting down 72 trucking companies in 37 cities by the end of the day. There was a general return to work after announcement of the tentative accord, but wildcat strike activity increased after the Chicago rebuff. The industry bargaining group, Trucking Employers, Inc., representing some 1,100 large truckers and, indirectly, the regional associations of some 12,000 trucking firms, said there were significant driver walkouts in 16 cities, including Chicago, San Francisco, Los Angeles, St. Louis, Cleveland and Atlanta by April 7.

The tentative agreement, reached April 2 after three months of bargaining, would provide a $1.10-an-hour raise for hourly-rate drivers (averaging $4 an hour) and a 2¼¢-a-mile raise for long-haul drivers (getting 12½¢ a mile). It also called for an additional $4 a week per worker for the union's health and pension funds and cost-of-living hikes of up to 8¢ an hour in the second and third years of the contract, which would extend to June 1, 1973. The raise totaled 27%.

Frank E. Fitzsimmons, acting president of the Teamsters, appealed for a return to work by the strikers and flew to Chicago to gain concurrence from the nine Teamsters locals and the independent Chicago Truck Drivers Union bargaining separately. But, claiming a different cost-of-living climate, the Chicago group rebuffed the national agreement and held out for a three-year wage hike of $1.70 an hour and higher fringe benefits, amounting to about a $2.50 hourly package increase.

The Chicago dissidents April 9 signed a new three-year contract covering about 8,000 drivers and 500 relatively small firms (among 1,200 trucking firms in the area). The Chicago pact, priced at a $2.10 package increase per hour per worker contrasted with the $1.20 cost of the national pact, would provide a $1.65 total wage increase, $10 more a week for pension and health funds, an extra holiday, additional vacation pay and a larger bonus for night work.

Some 800 Chicago area trucking companies April 10 locked out 32,000 drivers (and 9,000 warehouse workers) to bolster the national pact. In return, some 32,000 Chicago drivers went on strike April 13 to gain the Midwest provisions.

The Chicago area trucking companies agreed July 3 to a contract providing wage increases of $1.65 an hour over 36 months. Immediately after the Chicago settlement was made public, a separate announcement was made that the increase provided by the national pact would be $1.85 an hour over 39 months. The additional 20¢ an hour more was due to the national pact's extra three months' duration.

The Chicago agreement also called for increases totaling $10 a week in health, welfare and pension fund payments, and the national pact was revised in this area from an increase of $4 a week over the 39-month period to $8.

N.Y. tugboat strike ends. A 60-day tugboat strike in New York harbor—the longest in the port's history—ended April 1 with agreement on a new contract to provide a 41% wage increase over three years. With fringe benefits, the cost of the settlement—considered one of the highest ever attained in an industrial dispute—was estimated at a 53.5% rise for half the workers and a 58.5% rise for the others (oil barge workers).

The pact called for annual wage increases of 20% the first year and 10% in each of the second and third years. The fringe benefits included a $10-a-month pension for each year of service starting after 20 years at age 55 and overtime compensation for oil barge workers. The hourly wage scale would rise from $5.39 currently to $7.83 in the third year for captains and from $3.95 to $5.73 for deckhands.

Grape workers' pact. The first labor contract covering table-grape pickers in the U.S. was signed April 1 in Los Angeles. The settlement was reached between the United Farmworkers Organizing Committee and two Coachella Valley growers—David Freedman & Co. and Wonder Palms Ranch. The signing of a third table-grape producer, Travertine Ranch, was delayed because of illness. The three growers accounted for about one-eighth of the valley's table-grape production, which totaled 10% of California production. About 750 workers were covered by the pact, which called for a $1.75 an hour minimum wage, a picking bonus of 25¢ a box, a company contribution of 10¢ an hour per worker for the union's health and welfare fund and two cents a box for a union economic development fund for displaced, sick or elderly workers.

The union's agreement on a similar contract with the Bianco Fruit Corp. and the Dispoto Co. was announced in Fresno, Calif. May 21. The two-year pacts covered about 2,000 workers and were the first attained with major table-grape growers in San Joaquin Valley. Base pay under the pacts would rise to $1.90 an hour in the second contract year.

Chavez calls 'salad bowl' strike. Cesar Chavez' AFL-CIO United Farm Workers Organizing Committee (UFWOC) Aug. 24 struck 35 vegetable growers in California's Salinas Valley, known as the "salad bowl of the nation." The strike, which involved a dispute with the Western Conference of Teamsters, was called after growers demanded that contracts signed with the Teamsters be honored despite a UFWOC-Teamsters Aug. 12 "peace pact" giving Chavez's union jurisdiction to organize field workers.

About 10,000 workers were involved in the strike, which affected smaller growers in Santa Maria Valley as well as the large Salinas Valley ranches. The area produced 70% of the nation's iceburg lettuce and about half the carrots, celery and strawberries grown in the U.S.

Chavez announced the first victory of the strike Aug. 30 when he ordered 900 workers back to work under a contract signed with Inter Harvest Inc., a subsidiary of United Fruit Co. and the largest lettuce grower in the valley. UFWOC spokesmen said the contract terms raised the per-hour salary of field hands operating machine lettuce pickers to $2.10 and the per-carton pay of hand pickers to 40.5¢. Machine pickers had been getting $1.75 and were to get $1.85 under the Teamsters pact. Hand pickers had received 31.5¢ and were to get 36¢.

N.Y. papers, printers agree on pact. The New York Times and negotiators for the Typographical Union No. 6 agreed on a new contract May 24 after protracted bargaining and only hours before a threatened closedown of the Times.

The new three-year pact called for wage increases of 15% the first year, 11% the second and 11% the third, for a compounded total of 41.7% (or $76.89 a week for day work). Under the old contract, printers were earning $184.27 for 35 hours of day work (the day shift also was reduced to 34½ hours under the new pact).

Other provisions included corresponding wage hikes whenever the cost-of-living index rose more than 6% a year; company payment into the union welfare and pension funds of $7.82 a man per week; increased payments for use of perforated paper tapes to set stock market tables; continued union jurisdiction if composing room operations were moved outside the city but within a 75-mile radius.

The contract was only one of many to be settled among four New York area newspapers—the Daily News, The Post and Long Island Press in addition to the Times. A tentative settlement between the printers and the News on the Times' pattern was announced May 26. Similar settlements were negotiated with the Post May 29 and Press June 8.

The old contracts had expired March 30 but negotiators, assisted by mediator Theodore W. Kheel, agreed to continue contract talks. Three of ten unions involved had authorized strikes, but no call was issued. The craft unions represented printers, pressmen, photoengravers, mailers, stereotypers, paper handlers, drivers, machinists and electricians.

Kheel told an interviewer May 25 that the bargaining had been "severely handicapped by the economic schizophrenia that served as a backdrop. . . . With living costs continuing to soar upward while the plunge in the stock market seemed to foretell a business decline, there were opposite pressures on each side forcefully pulling them apart."

The Times raised the newstand price of its daily edition from 10¢ to 15¢ June 1 and announced a 14¢-a-line increase in most advertising rates, effective Aug. 1. The Post had raised its newstand price from 10¢ to 15¢ May 18.

Rubber workers strike. A seven-week strike by the AFL-CIO United Rubber Workers (URW) union against the Goodyear Tire and Rubber Co. ended June 10 upon ratification of a new three-year contract. The strike, involving about 23,000 employes at 15 Goodyear plants, had started when the old contract expired April 20.

The strike spread May 6-7 to nine plants of the B. F. Goodrich Co., where URW contracts also expired April 20. A tentative settlement, covering some 11,000 workers and patterned on the Goodyear pact, was reached June 12.

The Goodyear pact called for wage increases totaling 82¢ an hour over the three-year period (30¢ immediately, 26¢ more effective in 1971 and another 26¢ in 1972). Skilled tradesmen would receive additional hourly rate hikes of 15¢ immediately and 10¢ more in 1971. Prepact hourly wages averaged $3.87.

Fringe benefits included an additional annual holiday (10 in all), five-week vacations after 20 (instead of 22) years' service, a drug plan—the company would pay for prescription drugs exceeding $1—and an occupational health program to be developed after a university study. The package settlement was estimated by the company to equal about $1.30 an hour per employe in wages and fringes, or an 8% increase over the previous package. The Goodrich package was estimated by unionists at $1.39 an hour because of higher pension costs.

The union dropped one key demand for a cost-of-living escalator provision.

TV technicians approve pact. The National Association of Broadcast Employes and Technicians approved a new contract with the National Broadcasting Co. June 12. It called for a $55-a-week average wage rise over a three-year period (7% annual increase) for 1,300 engineers, technicians and maintenance personnel in New York, Chicago, Washington, Cleveland, San Francisco and Burbank, Calif. The average wage had been $260 a week.

GM negotiators agree on pact. Negotiators for the United Automobile Workers and General Motors Corp. (GM) reached agreement Nov. 11 on the major terms of a new national pact that would end the union's eight-week strike idling GM's 400,000 employes.

UAW membership ratification of the agreement was announced Nov. 20, and workers began returning to the job Nov. 23, the date the new contract became effective.

The ratified agreement constituted a three-year pact to provide 79¢ more an hour in average pay by the end of the third year, a cost-of-living (COL) escalator clause without a ceiling, an early retirement program and a fourth week of vacation for workers with 20 years of service.

The pay raise included 51¢ an hour, or 13% more, in the first year, plus raises of 14¢ an hour, or 3%, in each of the next two contract years. The wage rise would represent a 20% increase over the three years. Pay adjustments flowing from the cost-of-living clause would be added to this. It was anticipated that hourly labor costs under the new pact would rise from $5.78 to $7.50, a 30% increase, or an average increase of 10% a year.

The COL or inflation increment would be paid annually until March 1972, when quarterly installments would be initiated.

The retirement program would provide $500 a month pension to workers with 30 years of service at age 58 at the beginning of the new pact and at age 56 by the end of the pact. There was a move-

ment within the rank-and-file union membership for a "30-and-out" retirement program—the $500 monthly pension after 30 years of service without any age minimum.

Ford-UAW settlement. Negotiations for Ford Motor Co. and the United Automobile Workers reached agreement on a new three-year contract Dec. 7. The terms were similar to those set between the union and the General Motors Corp. The first-year pay increase of 50¢ an hour was to be distributed at Ford in two hikes—26¢ retroactive to Sept. 15 and the remainder retroactive to Nov. 1. Ford workers also received an unbroken paid vacation period from the day before Christmas through New Year's Day.

The Ford pact, covering 166,000 workers, was approved Dec. 8 by the UAW's Ford Council. Ratification by the union membership was announced Dec. 15.

At its convention in Atlantic City, N.J. April 20–24, the UAW had adopted its demands for the year's bargaining with the automakers. It had simultaneously rejected the government's plea for wage-demand restraint. Leaders of the union's 225,000-member Skilled Trades Department had been addressed March 11 by Sen. Edmund S. Muskie (D, Me.), who attacked the Administration's anti-inflation policies. "We appear to be headed straight toward a recession," he said, "and, what is worse, an inflationary recession."

Northwest Airlines strike ends. An agreement on a new pact ending a five-month strike was reached Dec. 11 by negotiators for Northwest Airlines and the AFL-CIO Brotherhood of Railway and Airline Clerks (BRAC). The terms of the 39-month pact, ratified by the union membership by a 6–1 margin, called for average wage increases of 37.6% and improvements in job classifications and work rules. The raises were retroactive to Oct. 1, 1969. The old contract had expired Sept. 30, 1969.

Other wage settlements. 2,200 cement masons ended a 48-day strike in Chicago July 20 with ratification of a two-year contract providing a $3.25 an hour increase in wages and benefits (prepact wage: $5.90 an hour).

■The 13,000-member International Brotherhood of Firemen and Oilers and the nation's railroads agreed June 14 on a two-year pact providing wage increases ranging from 46¢ to 81¢ an hour and a "letter of intent" to correct job classification inequities. The union was the last of the shopcraft unions to settle on wage negotiations begun in 1968.

■A 17-day wildcat transit strike in Cleveland ended July 17 with agreement offering the 1,900 workers involved a 75¢-an-hour increase over two years.

■ A two-week Indiana teachers' strike ended Sept. 21 when members of the Hammond Teachers Association agreed to a settlement providing a salary increase.

■ A Toledo, Ohio strike ended Oct. 2 when teachers ratified a new pay schedule providing from $100 to $1,000 in pay increases.

■ The 11,500-member Philadelphia Federation of Teachers struck Oct. 16 after a 30-day truce, negotiated after a two-day delay in opening the term in September, expired without a contract settlement. The city's 275 schools, serving 295,000 students, resumed full operations Oct. 21 after preliminary agreement on a two-year contract package valued at $57.3 million.

Full agreement on the contract was reached Nov. 6 and ratified by the teachers Nov. 11. The contract provided an average annual pay increase of $1,050.

International Trade, Payments & Monetary Problems

U.S. Trade Imbalance, Decline in Monetary Reserves

Inflation in the U.S. received additional impetus during 1970 from the continuing unfavorable trade balance. Although the U.S. had a $2.7 billion surplus of merchandise exports over imports for the year, the exclusion of aid-financed exports transformed the balance into a $3.2 billion deficit—which actually was an improvement over the $4.4 billion deficit of 1969 and the $5.1 billion deficit of 1968. The continued trade deficit meant an extension of the deficits in the U.S.' balance of international payments and a continuation of the drain in monetary reserves. Ultimately, there was an increase in gold prices and a continuation of the decline in the value of the dollar.

Exports in 1970 totaled $42.66 billion, a 14% increase over 1969's $37.33 billion that centered in civilian aircraft, steel and steel scrap, coal, chemicals, machinery and agricultural products. An 11% increase in 1970 imports from $36.04 billion in 1969 to $39.6 billion was ascribed mainly to rising imports of consumer goods.

On an annual basis, from the end of 1969 to the end of 1970, monetary reserves fell $2.5 billion. The decline was centered mostly in foreign currency holdings, reflecting repayment of various "swap" transactions with other countries. Gold stocks dropped $787 million, mostly gold payments to the International Monetary Fund (IMF). By the end of 1970 the U.S.' monetary reserves totaled $14.487 billion, comprising $11.072 billion in gold, $851 million in Special Drawing Rights (SDRs, or "paper gold"), $625 million in foreign currencies and $1.935 billion in automatic drawing rights in the International Monetary Fund.

Gold price slump continues. The price of gold on the free market fell below the official level of $35 an ounce Jan. 8 and remained at record lows for a week. (Although free market gold had traded below $35 an ounce several times in recent weeks, the official fixing price in the London and Zurich markets had not been lower than the formal price since the institution of the two-tier gold system in 1968.)

Final fixing prices in the London free market fell from $34.95 an ounce Jan. 8 to $34.85 an ounce Jan. 14, with unofficial trading reportedly even lower than that figure. Zurich free market prices also fell below $35 an ounce, and prices in Frankfurt and Paris markets weakened.

Central bankers discussed the continuing downtrend in free market prices at their regular monthly meeting at the Bank for International Settlements in Basel, Switzerland Jan. 11. Responding to speculation that some European bankers favored revival of a central bank-operated gold pool, Swiss National Bank President Edwin Stopper denied that any

U.S. BALANCE OF TRADE FACT SHEET

[In billions of dollars]

	F.o.b. basis	C.i.f. basis, excluding aid financed exports
1970	+2.7	−3.2
1969	+1.4	−4.4
1968	+1.0	−5.1
1967	+4.1	−1.4
1966	+3.8	−1.5
1965	+5.3	+.6
1964	+7.0	+2.3
1963	+5.3	+1.2
1962	+4.6	+.9
1961	+5.7	+2.5
1960	+4.9	+1.8

Source: U.S. Department of Commerce.

such proposals had been brought up at the meeting. U.S. Federal Reserve Board Chairman William McChesney Martin added: "The U.S. is opposed to the reforming of the gold pool. The gold pool has been terminated." (A gold pool, supported by central banks, had been abolished when the two-tier system was instituted.)

Germany sells gold to U.S. The U.S. Treasury announced Jan. 9 that it had purchased $500 million in gold from West Germany in December. The transaction, by far the largest single U.S. acquisition of gold in recent years, increased U.S. gold reserves to about $11.7 billion. (The U.S. gold stock had declined from $22.86 billion in 1957 to $11.17 billion at the end of November 1969.) West Germany sold the gold to replenish its dollar reserves, which had been depleted following the upward revaluation of the mark in October 1969. Total reserves of the West German Bundesbank (central bank) had fallen from $11.7 billion Sept. 29, 1969 to $6.1 billion Dec. 23, 1969.

West German sources disclosed Jan. 21 and 22 that the Bundesbank had cashed in before their due date U.S. Treasury notes valued at two billion marks. These actions were taken to boost West German reserves. (The 4½-year notes had been purchased in the U.S. fiscal years 1968 and 1969 as part of an agreement to offset the foreign exchange costs incurred in retaining U.S. armed forces in Germany.)

A Bundesbank source, cited by the Wall Street Journal Jan. 22, said that the

second billion marks worth of notes had been exchanged at the mark's old 25¢ (U.S.) exchange rate for $250 million worth of marketable U.S. securities. He added that an exchange rate for the first billion had been agreed on, but he disclosed only that the rate was "probably different" from the one governing the second transaction.

South African & Austrian gold sales to IMF. The IMF announced Feb. 2 that it had purchased $98.3 million worth of gold from South Africa in January. The sale included $63.5 million worth of gold under the free-market-price clause in the December 1969 agreement on the sale of newly-mined South African gold to the IMF. South Africa also sold $34.8 million worth of gold to the IMF for sterling in accordance with the December agreement.

The IMF statement also reported a $4.4 million gold purchase from Austria. The Austrian and South African purchases increased the Fund's gold stocks by $102.7 million to $2.671 billion.

Criticizing the 1969 agreement authorizing the South African sales to the IMF, U.S. Rep. Henry S. Reuss had complained Jan. 16 that "the United States has gained nothing from this agreement, since under any circumstances South Africa would have been forced to sell the preponderance of its gold output in the free market." Reuss claimed that the agreement "institutionalizes South Africa as a supplier of additional monetary gold—gold that only the U.S. is ultimately obliged to accept at a fixed price. Should gold lose its mystique as a reserve asset, or if the free market can-

BALANCE OF PAYMENTS FACT SHEET

[In billions of dollars]

Balance of payments	Official settlements basis	Liquidity basis
1970	−9.8	−3.8
1969	+2.7	−7.0
1968	+1.6	+.2
1967	−3.4	−3.5
1966	+.3	−1.4
1965	−1.3	−1.3
1964	−1.5	−2.8
1963	−2.0	−2.7
1962	−2.7	−2.2
1961	−1.3	−2.4
1960	−3.4	−3.9

Source: U.S. Department of Commerce.

not absorb most of South Africa's output, the U.S. could be called on to make excessive gold purchases."

In a letter countering Reuss' position, Treasury Undersecretary Paul A. Volcker defended the pact as "fully consistent with the continued effective functioning of the two-tier [gold] system." He added that it "represents a formal recognition of the two-tier system and its essential operational characteristics by the IMF membership itself."

(South African gold production reached a record 31,275,874 ounces in 1969. This topped the 1968 record by 107,000 ounces. The 1969 production, the Journal of Commerce reported Jan. 27, was valued at $1.1 billion, $4 million above the 1968 production. The Wall Street Journal Feb. 16 quoted Samuel Montagu & Co., a London merchant banker and bullion dealer, as reporting that world production of gold in 1969 had reached about 40.66 million ounces excluding Soviet output. The 1968 world output had totaled 40.7 million ounces.)

IMF allocates 'paper gold.' The International Monetary Fund (IMF) announced Jan. 2 that it had completed allocation of $3.414 billion in special drawing rights (SDRs or 'paper gold') to 104 members participating in the program. The allocation, completed Jan. 1, was in accord with a resolution adopted by the IMF Oct. 3, 1969 authorizing distribution of $9.5 billion in SDRs over a three-year period. Allocation of the first year's reserve assets was based on calculation of 16.8% of each participant's quota in the IMF as of Dec. 31, 1969. Under the plan, participants were required to accept SDRs in place of real gold and convertible currencies from other participants with balance-of-payments deficits.

Allocations ranged from $504,000 for both Botswana and Lesotho to $866.88 million for the U.S. (France and South Africa received allocations, although they had not completed requirements for participation until December 1969. South Africa had abstained from voting on the SDR proposal in October 1969.) Other major allocations: Great Britain, $409.22 million; West Germany, $201.6 million; India, $126 million; Ja-

pan, $121.8 million; Canada, $124.32 million; France, $165.48 million; and Italy, $105 million.

In its first report on use of the SDRs, the IMF disclosed March 2 that SDR holdings by industrial nations had risen in January by $66.8 million to $2.343 billion, while holdings by less developed nations had decreased by $78.7 million during the month to $774.3 million. IMF holdings of SDRs had increased from zero to $12.3 million at the end of January.

(The U.S. Treasury revealed May 15 that the U.S. had used its SDRs for the first time. In a normal IMF transaction, the U.S. used about $20 million of SDRs as partial repayment of short-term "swap" credits from Belgium and the Netherlands drawn by the Federal Reserve System in 1969 and 1970.)

France draws IMF currency. The IMF announced Feb. 2 that it had called on four participants in its General Arrangements to Borrow (GAB) to help finance a $485 million purchase of foreign exchange by France. This was France's second and final drawing under the $985 million standby arrangement approved by the IMF in September 1969.

The four GAB participants—Canada, Italy, Japan and the Netherlands—put up $93.5 million in their respective currencies to replenish the Fund's holdings of currencies to be used for the French purchase. (West Germany was originally to have supplied about $90 million worth of the currencies for the second French drawing, but since its reserves had decreased so strongly following the upward revaluation of the mark in October 1969, the IMF substituted other currencies for Germany's portion.) In addition to the $93.5 million from GAB nations, the Fund also sold $98.5 million worth of gold to 12 countries and used the equivalent of $293 million from its regular holdings of members' currencies in order to finance the French transaction.

European bank rate changes. The Austrian National Bank announced Jan. 21 that it had raised its discount rate from 4.75% to 5%, effective Jan. 22. Officials explained that the move was designed to adapt the Austrian rate to international interest levels as well as to influence a domestic economic boom that had threatened to overtax Austrian production potential. The bank rate had been raised to 4.75% in September 1969.

The Bank of England announced March 5 that it had reduced its bank rate to 7½% from 8%, the crisis level which had been maintained since February 1969. A bank spokesman explained the action: "In view of the strength of the pound sterling in international exchange markets and the inflow of funds to London, which continue to be substantial, the lower level of bank rate is consistent with the British government's present policy of monetary restraint."

The West German Bundesbank (central bank) raised its discount rate March 6 from 6% to an unexpectedly high 7½%, the highest level since World War II. The rate had been increased to 6% in September 1969. The bank also raised the Lombard rate, the cost of short-term credit on securities, from 9% to a record 9½% and announced that, effective April 1, minimum reserve requirements on foreign deposits would be increased by 30%. Economy Minister Karl Schiller explained that the new discount rate was in line with international interest rates and noted that it had joined the British level "in a rendezvous maneuver."

Italy's discount rate was increased from 4% to 5½% March 6 in an effort to lessen a strong outflow of the lira. The rate had been raised to 4% in August 1969.

In a further development, the U.S. Federal Reserve Board announced March 11 that it had increased its currency "swap" arrangement with Italy by $250 million to $1.25 billion, bringing the total credit arrangements with 14 nations and the Bank for International Settlements to $11.23 billion. In addition, the U.S. Treasury March 11 initiated a separate $250 million credit facility for Italy.

(For the first time in more than a year, interest rates on three-month Eurodollar loans fell below 9% March 11, with a drop to 8⅞%. A reduction in borrowings by American banks was cited as the main factor in the drop.)

EEC credit plan set. Meeting at Brussels headquarters Jan. 26, the Council of Ministers of the European Economic Community approved a $2 billion plan for short-term monetary assistance to members with balance of payments problems. Under the scheme (part of the Barre monetary cooperation plan proposed by Raymond Barre, a vice president of the EEC Executive Commission), any EEC member with balance of payments difficulties could automatically withdraw for a period of three months its contribution to the first $1 billion of the plan and would have the option of withdrawing all or part of the second $1 billion if the members' central bankers approved. (Contributions to the first $1 billion were set as follows: West Germany and France, $300 million each; Italy, $200 million; Holland and Belgium-Luxembourg, $100 million each.)

(The Barre plan had been presented to the council by the commission in February 1969 and had been approved in principle in July 1969.)

Europe & the U.S.

The growing inflation in the U.S., exacerbated by a decrease in U.S. farm exports caused by European Economic Community policies, resulted in a growth of anger in the U.S. at what was deemed selfishness on the part of the EEC nations. EEC spokesmen, in return, expressed unhappiness at U.S. policies. At least some of the European distress, in which Japan joined, was occasioned by prospective trade legislation calling for quotas on the U.S. importation of textiles and shoes. The measure was passed by the U.S. House of Representatives, but it died in the Senate at the end of the year.

EEC-U.S. tensions. Tensions between the EEC and the U.S. were heightened with direct attacks by U.S. officials on EEC trade policies and published rebuttals by the Common Market.

In a speech to the West German Foreign Policy Association in Bonn Feb. 12, U.S. envoy to the EEC J. Robert Schaetzel said that U.S. public support for the EEC had "largely evaporated and been replaced by irritation, frustration and a brooding sense of apprehension as to what the future will hold." "There is a strong feeling in the U.S. that Europe is insensitive to the economic problems and the political and military burdens we must carry," he added, warning that U.S. troop commitments in Europe were "bound to be affected" by the Common Market's economic policies. Schaetzel complained that EEC agricultural tariffs had caused a decline in U.S. farm exports to the community and added that "as surpluses built up in Europe due to the high price levels of the common agricultural policy, the community began dumping agricultural goods in certain of our traditional markets." In addition, Schaetzel charged that EEC preferential trade arrangements ran the "risk of fatally undermining" the General Agreement on Trade and Tariffs.

In a paper released Feb. 26, the commission defended its agricultural policies and charged "that various events and tendencies in the United States have caused disappointment and concern in the community." Admitting that there was a drop in U.S. agricultural exports to the EEC between 1966 and 1968, the paper stressed that "the community is still the most important market by far for U.S. agricultural exports." The statement added that the decline which took place was not confined to U.S. exports to the EEC, but affected U.S. farm exports throughout the world. "It would therefore be unreasonable to attribute the recent drop in U.S. agricultural exports to the community solely to the effects of community protection," the statement concluded.

The commission's statement also attacked U.S. measures that affected the Common Market such as the failure to repeal the American Selling Price system of calculating import duties, the increase of duties on certain woolen products in 1968 without following regular GATT procedures and without compensation offers, and the 1968 introduction of import restrictions on some mechanical industry products. The commission expressed particular concern over what it held was a danger that the U.S. would abandon the "broadly liberal policy" of trade it had practiced since World War II. Such a development, the statement said, "would inevitably start a chain reaction detrimental to the expansion of world trade." The commission concluded that it was "more necessary than ever for the two leading partners in world trade, the United States and the community, to agree that the problems affecting individual sectors or causing temporary difficulties between them must be overcome."

The commission's policy statement preceded a visit of high-level EEC officials to Washington, D.C. March 2 and 3. The talks were to have centered on "a wide range of issues outstanding between the community and the U.S., including agricultural and industrial trade problems, preference policy toward developing countries, and the current meetings in Geneva under the GATT." The Common Market team, led by commission member Jean Francois Deniau, met with Secretary of Commerce Maurice H. Stans, Undersecretary of State Elliot L. Richardson, Chairman of the Council of Economic Advisers Paul W. McCracken and other U.S. trade and economic officials.

Commenting on the Washington talks, U.S. Assistant Commerce Secretary Kenneth N. Davis said March 10 that the U.S. and the Common Market were "far apart" in their thinking on trade policies and that U.S. officials considered the European value added tax system (TVA) as "a major non-tariff barrier."

Noting that certain of Davis' statements called for "clarification," the EEC Commission claimed March 11 that the TVA, "which is imposed equally on domestic and foreign products consumed in a country," could not be considered a "border tax" and thus a non-tariff barrier. In reply to Davis' assertion that U.S. Congressional abolition of the American Selling Price (ASP) system of duties on chemical imports might be contingent upon EEC dismantling of non-tariff barriers, the commission statement pointed out that "elimination of the ASP by the U.S. was negotiated in the Kennedy Round in return for tariff and non-tariff concessions offered by the Community and other European countries. It would therefore be very surprising if its abolition were to be linked to new conditions."

EEC commission's annual report. The annual report of the Common Market Executive Commission stressed the need for greater collaboration with the U.S. "to overcome unduly numerous difficulties and conflicts of interest . . . since . . . both have extensive responsibility for development of the world economy." Released Feb. 16 in Brussels, the report reviewed EEC activities during 1969 and outlined goals for 1970.

According to the commission, the most significant events of 1969 included the decision to complete the EEC's 12-year transitional period and enter into the "final stage" by Jan. 1, 1970; the summit meeting held at The Hague, where the Six set the stage for enlargement of the organization; adoption of the principles of the Barre plan on economic and monetary coordination; signing of association and trade agreements with third countries; agreement on provisions for a new financial regulation for the common agricultural policy; and the decision to create the Common Market's own financial resources to replace the current system of financing the organization and its activities through contributions from national budgets.

The commission cited the growth of protectionist tendencies in the U.S. and the U.S. concern over the EEC's agricultural policy as particular problems in U.S.-EEC relations. Pointing out that numerous protectionist bills were currently before the U.S. Congress, the report also expressed concern at attempts by the U.S. to obtain "voluntary" quotas from countries exporting certain products to the U.S. Concerning the EEC's common agricultural policy, the report explained that the Common Market was still the most important outlet for U.S. farm exports, even though they had shown a decline since 1965.

Economic, monetary goals set. Common Market finance ministers, meeting in Venice May 31, took a first step toward creation of a common currency in deciding to hold for the present the fluctuation rates of their national currencies to the present .75% above and below official parity, regardless of what other countries or the International Monetary Fund decided. The six ministers also agreed in principle to establish a full economic and monetary union within nine years in which all EEC na-

tions would have common tax and budget policies, a common exchange rate between their currencies and freer capital movements. The May 31 decision was reaffirmed in a meeting of foreign and finance ministers in Luxembourg June 9.

ECE report on 1969 European trade. The United Nations Economic Commission for Europe (ECE) reported March 18 that all but five west European countries showed considerable economic growth in 1969.

The combined gross national product of industrialized countries in western Europe increased by 6% in volume, compared with 5% in 1968, while industrial production increased by 8.5% in 1969, compared with 7.5% in 1968. Only Ireland, Italy, the Netherlands, Norway and Great Britain failed to show substantive economic growth in 1969. Among the less industrialized nations of southern Europe, all but Portugal enjoyed growth rates of 7%–9% during 1969. According to the ECE, the increases were the result of two main factors—a general upsurge in industrial investment and an increase in trade.

Total trade between western European nations in 1969 increased by more than 20% in 1969, compared with 12% in 1968; trade between Common Market countries increased by almost 30%. Although west European exports to the U.S. increased by only 5% (compared with a 25% rise in 1968) exports to eastern Europe increased by 12% (8% in 1968) and to all other countries by 14% (9% in 1968).

(The 22-nation Ministerial council of the Organization for Economic Cooperation and Development [OECD] warned May 24 that inflationary price increases in 1969 were twice as high as the average of the past 10 years and pledged to give priority to the fight against inflation.)

GATT studies world trade. The General Agreement on Tariffs and Trade, in its annual report released Sept. 14, reported that the volume of world exports had risen by 10% during 1969, while the value of world exports had increased by 14% to $272 billion. The difference, the report said, was due to "strong inflationary pressures in a large number of trading countries. . . ."

In its forecast for 1970 trade, GATT predicted an increase in the volume of world exports by 5%–6% and in the value of world exports by 8%–10%, increasing their earlier estimate that the value of trade would rise from 4% to 8% during 1970. The revised estimate was based on economic developments in the industrialized nations along with a continuation of the "sharp upturn" in prices.

In analyzing regional trade patterns, GATT reported that during 1969: trade among European Economic Community members had risen by 26%, between European Free Trade Association members by 17%, between the U.S. and Canada by 14%, and between the U.S. and Japan by 20%.

Trade debate. Hendrik S. Houthakker, a member of the Council of Economic Advisers and regarded as the top spokesman for the Nixon administration on trade matters, Aug. 24 reaffirmed the Administration's commitment to freer trade and rejected any new import quotas.

His attack on quotas, made in a speech to a trade group in San Francisco, included remarks that the Administration had "reluctantly" supported quotas on textiles in a trade bill pending before the House only to enhance the U.S. position in negotiating voluntary agreements with Far Eastern countries to limit their textile exports to the U.S.

In related developments involving the trade bill, which had been approved by the House Ways and Means Committee in July, Rep. Hale Boggs (D, La.) said in Paris Aug. 21 that a possible trade war could erupt if Europe or Japan decided to retaliate against the bill. Boggs, chairman of the Joint Economic Committee's subcommittee on trade, said officials in Great Britain, France and the General Agreement on Tariffs and Trade (GATT) based in Geneva had expressed concern over the bill. Boggs criticized the U.S. for not elucidating its trade policies and making it clear that the bill's provisions would not impose quotas but would authorize the President to negotiate them.

Secretary of Commerce Maurice H. Stans said Aug. 31 that the possibility of trade war was "a lot of nonsense." He pointed out that any foreign reprisal against U.S. exports, subject to the rules of GATT, would be limited in dollar value to the extent of the losses suffered by the exporting nation in the U.S. market.

EEC Executive Commissioner Ralf Dahrendorf warned the U.S. Oct. 16 that the Common Market would consider retaliation if the trade bill were adopted.

Speaking at a press conference following two days of talks in Washington, Dahrendorf said that the legislation, as approved by the House Ways and Means Committee, could "change the entire complexion of world trade." He added that the bill had had "a curious and unexpected side effect in Europe—it has brought member countries together and made common action possible when many thought common action was not possible." He stressed hopes that a trade war could be averted.

Addressing the same press conference, Nathaniel Samuels, U.S. deputy undersecretary of state for economic affairs, agreed with Dahrendorf's hopes. Samuels stressed that the U.S. and the Common Market had agreed to continue discussing their differences, particularly those concerning the EEC's agricultural policies and the organization's preferential trade arrangements with Africa and other areas. "Rising trade protection sentiment [in the U.S.] . . . is fed and stimulated by protectionist policies pursued in the rest of the world," Samuels asserted.

House passes trade bill. The controversial trade bill, which would revise current U.S. policy and, among other things, impose quotas on imports of textiles and shoes, was passed by the House Nov. 19 by a 215–165 vote.

The bill was flexible enough, however, for the President to exempt countries and categories from the imposition of quotas and to negotiate agreements with countries for more imports than formulated under the bill.

Other major features of the legislation: (a) Current provisions for relief to industries or workers adversely affected by imports were liberalized; (b) the President would have authority to eliminate the American Selling Price (ASP) system of evaluating imports for calculation of duties; (c) the President also would have authority to reduce tariffs by up to 20% (a provision intended for relief of countries harmed by import curbs stemming from the bill); (d) as long as import restrictions were maintained for oil, they must be in the form of quotas; (e) a new tax incentive for exports—deferral of tax on profits earned from export—was to be established; (f) Presidential power to retaliate against countries unfairly treating U.S. exports was to be strengthened; and (g) new import curbs would be imposed on mink and glycine.

A group of 4,390 economists urged President Nixon Sept. 18 to veto the import-limiting bill if it came to him in the form prepared by the House Ways and Means Committee. Former Sen. Paul H. Douglas, who initiated the appeal to Congress and the White House, said the import quotas contained in it made the bill worse than the Smoot-Hawley Tariff Act of 1930, which set high tariffs on many imported products.

Passage of the bill was marked by intensive lobbying activity on behalf of the bill's protectionist provisions.

Europeans decry U.S. trade bill. The industry federations of the European Economic Community and European Free Trade Association nations issued a joint statement Nov. 26 expressing "their serious concern at the content of foreign trade legislation now under consideration by the United States Congress."

The statement warned: "If access to the United States market should be blocked for an increasingly wide range of our goods, balance of payments considerations, among others, will eventually force our governments to react to restrictive policies." The statement was given to U.S. ambassadors in the 14 West European countries with a request that it be forwarded to President Nixon, Rep. Wilbur D. Mills (D, Ark.), chairman of the House Ways and Means Committee, and Sen. Russell Long (D, La.), chairman of the Senate Finance Committee.

Nixon for changes in bill. President Nixon said at his press conference Dec. 10 that the House-passed trade bill should be limited to textile quotas and limited in other curbs because "the key question is

jobs." While it was good to apply a quota to save jobs in the U.S., it "doesn't make sense if it's going to cost us more jobs in America because of cutting down the exports that we make abroad."

Ultimately, the Senate refused to act on the bill, and it died at the end of the year.

Inflation Seen as Endangering World Economy

BIS warns of world recession. The Bank for International Settlements (BIS) warned June 8 that the world would face an "inescapable" recession if international inflation was not controlled. In its annual report and presidential address presented in Basel, Switzerland, the BIS criticized U.S. economic policy as inadequate to control U.S. inflation and advocated adoption of wage and price controls.

Speaking to central bankers from nearly 50 countries, BIS President Jelle Zijlstra of the Netherlands warned that U.S. balance of payments deficits formed the "breeding ground for a continuing international inflationary process." He reported that most countries averaged 8% wage increases in 1969, with cost of living increases reaching 5%, and warned of the tendency for wage increases to exceed productivity. He added that efforts to bar an expansive monetary policy were "ultimately bound to encroach on profit margins and to make recession inescapable."

The report, signed by BIS General Manager Gabriel Ferras and written under the direction of U.S. economist Milton Gilbert, rejected U.S. proposals for greater foreign exchange flexibility as a method to provide more international currency revaluations and thus indirectly help correct the American payments balance deficits. "It may be doubted whether the countries prepared to revalue would be sufficient in number or in economic strength to produce the desired result," the report asserted. "Furthermore," it continued, "serious tensions could well arise if partner countries of the United States were to be faced repeatedly with the dilemma of whether to accumulate unwanted dollars in their reserves or to revalue."

Criticizing U.S. efforts to check inflation, the report said: "The fear of overkill and the leaning toward gradualism blunted the priority on monetary stability. It may be, in fact, that the adjustment turned out more gradual than intended and slowed down the impact on the price-wage spiral." The report added that the Nixon Administration's aim of holding inflation to an annual rate of 3.5% by the end of 1970 depended on the realism of the budget surplus, which it called "optimistic," particularly in light of the Administration's announcement in May that there would be federal budget deficits for 1970 and 1971.

Acknowledging that excess demand in the U.S. had been supressed recently, the BIS report nevertheless warned that "the lag in checking price and wage rises has been all too evident. Thus the situation has become one in which more direct wage-price policy, formal or informal, might well be contemplated."

The report noted that wage-price guidelines in several countries during 1969 had demonstrated that "delays in tackling inflation are not only costly but serve to make corrections later more difficult," and that "where demand inflation is the problem, restrictive monetary policies are no substitute for adequate fiscal measures." In addition, the report said, "it has become increasingly evident that incomes policy broadly conceived may be a prerequisite of orderly economic development. Few central banks or ministries of finance would dissent from the view that incomes policy cannot make up for the inadequacies of other measures. At the same time, few would profess faith that wage push can be dealt with by monetary and fiscal actions alone."

(BIS bankers agreed at a meeting June 7 that a Canadian decision to float the dollar was no threat to the international monetary system.)

IMF cites inflationary pressures. Analyzing the performance of the world economy during 1969 and early 1970, the executive directors of the International Monetary Fund (IMF) Sept. 7 called for "restoration of financial stability in the major industrial economies, and particularly in the United States."

In their annual report for the fiscal year ending April 30, the directors cited the existence during 1969 of "severe inflationary pressures" along with "a series of developments serving to improve the adjustment of payments imbalances in several major countries. . . ."

Citing inflation as a "widespread problem among industrial countries," especially the U.S., the report warned that its continuation "would inevitably handicap or frustrate domestic stabilization programs among developed and developing countries alike." The directors admitted that inflation control had been rendered "particularly difficult by strong cost-push forces, with wage settlements substantially in excess of normal productivity growth having become commonplace." The report noted that the domestic stabilization plan developed by the U.S. in 1969 was "clearly behind schedule in slowing the pace of price and cost increases," and that it had had "a more severe impact on the real economy than was expected or hoped for."

In response to the worldwide inflationary problems, the IMF called for a "greater adaptability of policy to changing circumstances." The report urged a "strengthening of fiscal policy, so that monetary policy could be geared relatively more to the external position than has proved feasible in the past."

In addition, the report focused attention on "incomes policy," defined as a "wide variety of possible measures—ranging from moral suasion to direct controls—to affect the movement of wages and prices in the public interest." The directors suggested that incomes policy "could prove very useful as an adjunct to basic fiscal and monetary policies."

In the area of balance of payments, the IMF reported that 1969 had brought some progress "as the external positions and prospects of several European countries improved markedly." The report cited continuing U.S. payments problems but noted "remarkable improvements" in the British and French positions and a continuation of a strong position in Japan.

While the first three quarters of 1969 were marked by uncertainty and crisis in the foreign exchange markets, the final quarter recorded a major change due to developments such as the devaluation of the French franc, revaluation of the German mark and a surplus in the British balance of payments. Also contributing to the improvement was the establishment of the Special Drawing Rights (SDRs) within the IMF, an increase in the fund's quotas and an agreement on the sale of newly mined South African gold.

The flow of international trade reflected strong levels of demand and production during 1969, with the value of world exports expanding by 14% from 1968 and the volume of world exports increasing by 10% from 1968. Total world output during 1969 increased by about 5.5% over 1968, despite a decrease in the U.S. economy's growth rate to less than 3%. The other industrial nations, however, as well as the less developed countries as a group, expanded their real GNP by about 7% in 1969.

In a final recommendation, the directors expressed their hope that the 1970s would "witness a major improvement in the volume, quality, and effectiveness of development assistance." Noting that during the 1960s, "the flow of capital and official aid to the developing countries failed by a substantial margin to keep pace with the relative growth of GNP in the industrial countries," the directors urged industrial nations to "endeavor to give a higher priority to their economic assistance to the developing nations not only because of the sheer immensity of the problems and needs of those nations, but also because of the broad interests of the industrial countries themselves."

IMF's proposals on exchange rates. In a comprehensive analysis of the mechanism of exchange rate adjustment, the executive directors of the International Monetary Fund concluded that the existing par value system of exchange rates "remains the most appropriate general regime to govern exchange rates in a world of managed national economies."

However, the directors, in a report entitled "The Role of Exchange Rates in the Adjustment of International Payments," stressed that "stability" in exchange rates did not mean "rigidity" and recommended that members study possibility of adopting slightly wider

margins around parity. The report, released Sept. 13, was later presented to the board of governors at its annual meeting Sept. 21–25 in Copenhagen.

Stressing the importance of retaining the current par value system, the directors rejected three alternative systems that had been suggested and discussed: (1) an overall system of fluctuating exchange rates; (2) a system of parities with substantially wider margins; and (3) a system "under which parities would be adjusted at fixed intervals on the basis of some predetermined formula which would be applied automatically."

Instead, the report urged an adaptation of the existing par value system to meet the needs of the economic situation. Thus the IMF was obligated to review and change its policies when necessary, while IMF members were required to pursue "internal policies that will keep the growth in aggregate demand in line with the development of available resources," and to show a willingness to make changes in their exchange rates when they are "appropriate to restore equilibrium."

"The latter consideration," the report continued, "is of particular importance because in present conditions of international mobility of capital, expectations that parities may be changed can lead to large disruptive movements of funds."

The report made three specific points:

(1) The directors stressed that adjustment of parities when necessary should be made promptly since "delay in effecting such adjustment will clearly aggravate the underlying disequilibrium."

(2) The report stated that although a "substantial widening of the permitted margins for market rates would risk the erosion of the safeguard that internationally agreed parities provide against changes in a country's competitive position as a result of actions by other countries," the possibility of adopting slightly wider margins than the existing 1% would still confine fluctuations in market rates to "magnitudes that could be expected to have only a minor effect on countries' competitive positions." (The directors discussed margins of 2%–3%, but declined to recommend any specific margin.)

(3) Recalling that "occasions have arisen in the past in which exceptional

pressures induced individual countries to suspend the observance of their par value obligations and to move to a fluctuating rate," the directors agreed that "any departure by a member country from its par value obligations would necessitate, from the standpoint of the international community, the institution of adequate safeguards to take the place of the safeguards of the par value system which the member was no longer observing." The report stressed, however, that on the issue of temporary deviations from the par value regime, the directors had not yet "come to a final view" and intended to give the issue "further consideration."

World Bank/IMF meeting. Members of the World Bank Group and the International Monetary Fund gathered in Copenhagen, Denmark Sept. 21 - 25 for their annual meeting and agreed that the essentials of the present international monetary system should be retained as recommended in the IMF report of Sept. 13.

The delegates also agreed that the major international problem plaguing the system at present was inflation, particularly in the U.S. Speeches focused on ways to introduce more flexibility into the foreign exchange system without changing the basic principles of the IMF and on measures to control world inflation.

In his opening address to the conference Sept. 21, IMF Managing Director Pierre-Paul Schweitzer suggested that the U.S. finance its continuing balance of payments deficit through use of reserve assets rather than dollars in order to avoid an "excessive" buildup of dollars in other countries. "Until the payments position of the United States is brought into balance, it is important that the deficit should be financed by the use of United States reserve assets to the extent necessary to avoid an excessive expansion of official holdings of dollars by other countries," he said. "A policy of this kind is indeed necessary if control over the issuance of Special Drawing Rights (SDRs) is also to provide the means of regulating the aggregate volume of world reserves."

Stressing that "arrest of the generalized inflationary trend in the industrial countries is imperative for the longer-run health of the world economy," Schweitzer urged, with specific reference to the U.S. and Canada, "care, in the current situation of economic slack, to avoid excessively expansionary policies that might nullify the progress already made against inflation."

Schweitzer reiterated the IMF position that monetary and fiscal policies alone might not be adequate to halt inflationary trends, and called for supplementary use of "incomes policies" in this effort. He added: "With pursuit of policies giving emphasis to the elimination of inflation and regaining of price and cost stability, the United States will have an excellent opportunity to recoup losses of recent years in its external trade account thus to effect a fundamental strengthening of its balance of payments position."

In a news conference Sept. 24, Schweitzer qualified his statement urging the U.S. to use its reserve assets rather than its dollars. He explained that he did not intend to suggest that other countries immediately embark on a program to "cash in" their dollar holdings as several press reports had speculated. Schweitzer said he was only advocating the necessity for an "orderly and rational" growth of world reserves.

U.S. Treasury Secretary David Kennedy Sept. 24 reasserted the U.S. policy of exchanging foreign-held dollars for reserve assets such as gold.

Robert McNamara, president of the World Bank Group (consisting of the International Bank for Reconstruction and Development, International Development Association and International Finance Corporation), told the meeting Sept. 21 that the developing world was facing a growing social and political crisis that threatened "to round off this century with years of unrest and turbulence: a time of troubles during which the forces of historical change threaten to disintegrate our frail 20th century society."

McNamara cited the U.S. as the "single exception" to the developed nations' general decision to increase foreign assistance to .7% of their GNP. "It is inconceivable to me," he said, "that the American people will accept for long a situation in which they—forming 6% of the world's population but consuming almost 40% of the world's resources—contribute less than their fair share to the development of the emerging nations."

McNamara also criticized almost all of the industrial nations for the "folly" of spending 20 times more on military activities than on foreign aid.

In his closing remarks Sept. 25, McNamara proposed that the bank proceed "promptly with an international investment insurance plan to help accelerate the flow of private capital into the developing countries by protecting investors from political risks beyond their control." He announced that the bank planned "a major study of the debt problems that face our member countries." In addition, he gave limited support to a plan linking SDRs with foreign aid by stressing that the bank was prepared to assist the IMF in any study of the matter.

U.S. Treasury Secretary Kennedy assured foreign officials Sept. 22 that the U.S. was "as fully aware of the danger of too-fast expansion and renewed over-heating as we were of deep recession," and that the Administration did not intend to let inflation and the dollar outflow mount again. Kennedy skirted the issue of foreign exchange flexibility, stating only that the recent IMF report on the issue indicated "a desire to test the possible need for formal amendments against the evolving situation."

European Economic Community members, although differing among themselves on the overall issue of increased currency flexibility, stressed that no outside decision should be forced on them, since they had agreed to reduce and in 10 years to eliminate all currency fluctuations within the community. Italian Treasury Minister Mario Ferrari-Aggradi explained Sept. 22 that by 1980 the Common Market could "examine the possibility that the European currencies fluctuate together vis-a-vis the dollar within a wider band."

Japanese Finance Minister Takeo Fukuda spoke out against currency fluctuations Sept. 22, claiming that even talk of more flexibility risked speculative movements in the foreign exchange markets.

Canadian Finance Minister Edgar J. Benson Sept. 22 expressed favor for wider parity bands in order to allow "more elbow room" to cope with currency surges. He added that Canada would end its floating dollar as "Canadian economic growth responds to more expansionary policies and as other countries stem their inflation," but he refused to mention any specific date.

In speeches Sept. 23, officials of developing countries advocated an end to the decline in foreign assistance and expressed hope that SDRs would be directly linked to the extension of foreign aid. Israeli Central Bank Governor David Horowitz suggested that donation of SDRs to "countries with underutilized manpower" would be an anti-inflationary move.

OECD warns on inflation. The economic policy committee of the Organization for Economic Cooperation and Development Nov. 17 warned members against the "widespread and serious" problem of inflation and agreed that "it was necessary to bring about a significant reduction in inflationary expectations in the near future."

In a communique published following a two-day meeting, the committee urged each member country to "pursue a range of measures appropriate to its situation and institutions." However, the committee refused to take positions on specific recommendations made in a controversial and unpublished report on inflation prepared by OECD experts and submitted to them Nov. 16 by the organization's secretary general, Emile Van Lennep. Informed sources said the original version of the report had hypothesized that it might be necessary to accept higher unemployment rates to control inflation. Van Lennep told a press conference Nov. 17 that this recommendation would not be included in the final document. Reports indicated that the committee had rejected any mention of increased unemployment.

U.S. debtor status. The Federal Reserve System reported Sept. 15 that the U.S. had moved from a creditor to a debtor status with foreign central banks in the past six months. Charles A. Coombs, senior vice president of the Federal Reserve Bank in New York and manager of the government's transactions in international monetary markets, said that foreign governments had fully repaid their borrowings under reciprocal credit arrangements, also known as "swap lines." However, as of Sept. 10, the Federal Reserve owed $220 million to the Netherlands Bank and $95 million to the National Bank of Belgium.

Gold price at 1970 high. The price of free market gold reached an 11-month high in October. Moderate speculative buying increased the price to $39.19 in London Oct. 27. Gold prices fell Oct. 28, dropping to close at $38.675 in London and $38.75 in Zurich.

The increases had little influence on foreign exchange markets.

U.S. money supply's growth. The Federal Reserve Board Nov. 27 issued revised figures on the nation's money supply. Figures for 1969 (December 1968–December 1969) showed that the money supply had risen 3.1% during the year but confirmed an absence of growth during the last half of 1969. Over the first 10 months of 1970, the money supply expanded at a 5.5% annual rate.

1971

1971 was the year in which President Nixon imposed
wage-price controls and devalued the dollar—after long
opposing both measures. The year started with the
President and Congress blaming each other for failing
to halt inflation. Prices and wages continued upward,
the U.S.' foreign trade and payments position
worsened, and waves of speculation attacked the dollar.
Nixon applied pressure early in 1971 to force steel
producers to revoke a large part of a prospective price
increase, but steel wages and prices went up anyway by
the middle of the year. Late in March Nixon created
machinery to stabilize wages and prices in the construction industry. By early August Nixon's opposition to
price-wage boards had crumbled, and he pronounced his
mind "open" on the subject. In mid-August he imposed
a 90-day wage-price freeze—Phase One of a new policy
that was a complete reversal of his former staunch rejection of economic control. In an additional policy
turn-around, Nixon ended the dollar's convertibility
into gold and imposed a 10% surtax on imports. Wage,
price and other economic control bodies were formed,
and Nixon's Phase Two, which followed the 90-day
freeze, continued and expanded the policy of controls.
And after long, international negotiations, the Nixon
Administration formally agreed to devalue the dollar.

Government Policy

Inflation Continues, President & Congress Dispute Blame

Richard M. Nixon began his third year as president with only minor indications of even partial success in his "game plan" for stemming the inflation that was sapping the nation's economic strength. The 91st Congress adjourned Jan. 2 after a second session that was the longest since 1950, but Nixon assailed it as having accomplished little. The Democratic leadership rejected Nixon's charge of inaction and retorted that Nixon was at fault for any failures of the session.

Nixon cites Congress' failures. President Nixon predicted Jan. 5 that the 91st Congress would be remembered "not for what it did but for what it failed to do." In a critical statement issued by the White House, Nixon said "the 91st Congress had the opportunity to write one of the most productive and memorable chapters in the history of the American government. That opportunity was lost. The nation was the loser."

The President directed much of his criticism against the Senate which, in the final month of the session, he said, had presented the nation "with the spectacle of a legislative body that had seemingly lost the capacity to decide and the will to act." This resulted in "major failures," he said.

"In probably no month in recent memory did the reputation of the whole Congress suffer more in the eyes of the American people," he continued, "than in the month of December 1970. In these times when the need to build confidence in government is so apparent, that was good neither for the Congress nor for the country. Let us hope that it never takes place again."

Nixon urged the 92nd Congress to "open the new year in a new spirit." He added that it "may wish to consider revision of the turn-of-the-century work schedules and procedures that now obtain on Capitol Hill." While there were many "excuses" for Congressional inaction, he said, "there are no good reasons."

Administration record assailed—In rebuttal to President Nixon's attack, Rep. Carl Albert (D, Okla.) said later Jan. 5 that "not Congress but the Administration will surely be remembered for what it failed to do—for its failure to halt inflation, for its failure to stop rising unemployment and for its failure to gain and hold the confidence of the country."

AFL-CIO President George Meany Jan. 3 assessed the domestic record of the Nixon Administration in its second year as "even worse than the first." Meany had given the Nixon Administration a zero rating for its first year. For its 1970 record, he told a UPI interviewer, the

157

Administration deserved a "second goose egg, only bigger."

Pointing out the persistence of high prices and high interest rates and the problem of rising unemployment, Meany said the Administration "has failed completely in what has been referred to as its economic game plan."

As for Congress, Meany said the 1970 session had achieved "some constructive things" but the overall image of the legislative branch, he said, was one of "almost chaos" because of "outdated" procedures.

Meany said the federation's top legislative objective in the 1971 session of Congress would be to gain enactment of a national health plan.

"Now . . . in terms of the unemployment front, here we find that the rate of

unemployment for this year will be approximately 4.9%. That is too high even though we could perhaps point to the fact that over the past 20 years there'd been only three peace-time years in which unemployment was less than 5%—the years were '55, '56, '57."

"What we're going to do first is to have an expansionary budget. It will be a budget in deficit as will be the budget in 1971. It will not be an inflationary budget because it will not exceed the full employment revenues."

"We also, according to Dr. Arthur Burns, will have an expansionary monetary policy, and that will, of course, be a monetary policy adequate to meet the needs of an expanding economy."

". . . I do not plan to ask for wage controls or price controls. . . . I have con-

Appropriations
91st Congress, 2nd Session (1970)

Designation	Administration Request	Appropriation
Labor-HEW, fiscal 1970	$16,495,237,700	$19,381,920,200 (March 5)
Treasury, Post Office, Executive Office	9,567,693,000	9,525,711,000 (Sept. 26)
Legislative Branch	421,464,899	413,104,220 (Aug. 18)
Office of Education	3,966,824,000	4,420,145,000 (Aug. 18)
Supplemental, 2d, fiscal 1970	6,580,171,902	6,021,535,005 (July 6)
Independent Offices-HUD	17,468,223,500	18,009,525,300 (vetoed Aug. 11)
State-Justice-Commerce	3,445,548,000	3,302,422,500 (Oct. 21)
Interior-Related Agencies	2,034,871,600	2,028,524,700 (July 31)
Transportation-Related Agencies	7,164,963,000	*
Foreign Aid	2,876,539,000	2,534,310,000 (Dec. 31)
District of Columbia	825,158,000	636,118,200 (July 16)
Agriculture-Related Agencies	7,531,775,500	8,070,856,550 (Dec. 8)
Military Construction	2,134,800,000	2,037,814,000 (Nov. 25)
Public Works	5,269,181,000	5,244,265,000 (Oct. 7)
Defense Department	68,745,666,000	66,595,937,000 (Dec. 29)
Labor-HEW	18,759,377,000	18,969,392,500 (Dec. 30)
Independent Offices-HUD	17,468,223,500	17,709,525,300 (Dec. 7)
Supplemental, 1st, fiscal 1971	1,928,985,264	1,853,372,792 (Dec. 28)

*Continuing resolution authorized spending at 1970 level until March 30, 1971.

sidered all those options. I have decided that none of them at this time would work."

". . . I do not plan to ask for new taxes. I had considered the possibility of a value-added tax as a substitution for some of our other taxes, and looking to the future, we may very well move into that direction. But this year I do not think it is realistic to propose a new tax—either new taxes or tax reform."

Blue-collar pay hike vetoed. President Nixon vetoed a bill Jan. 1 that would have provided a 4% pay increase for federal "blue-collar" workers. The bill, which called for about $130 million in pay hikes for federal truck drivers, laborers and others under the wage board pay system, was criticized by the President as "too costly and . . . unwarranted." The workers involved, he said, already received 4% more than workers in private industry doing comparable work and the measure would put them 8% ahead.

Nixon's TV interview. President Nixon claimed Jan. 4 that the primary achievement of the first two years of his Administration was that "we can now see the end of Americans' combat role in Vietnam in sight." In an hour-long, televised conversation with four network correspondents, Nixon discussed various topics. Among his remarks on the economy:

". . . We find that insofar as our efforts to control inflation are concerned, that while the progress has not been as fast as we would have liked, that the Wholesale Price Index is half of what it was a year ago, the retail Consumer Price Index is turning down, not as much as we would like, but turning down. We are beginning to make real progress in fighting inflation."

Poll indicates pessimism—The results of a seven-nation Gallup Poll, reported Jan. 2, showed that Americans were more pessimistic in 1971 than 1970 about the nation's general economic situation. The poll, which canvassed 1,517 adults in more than 300 U.S. localities during the last weeks of 1970, found that 74% (compared with 57% polled during a similar survey in 1970) forecast rising unemployment, 64% (against 66% in the

previous year) predicted strikes and industrial disputes, while 73% (against 61% in 1970) foresaw economic difficulty. Among the other nations polled (Great Britain, Greece, the Netherlands, Sweden, Uruguay and West Germany), Americans were the least confident of the employment outlook for 1971.

Unemployment at 6%. The December 1970 unemployment rate, the Bureau of Labor Statistics (BLS) reported Jan. 8, reached 6%, the highest level since December 1961.

The December figure disproved predictions by the Nixon Administration that the jobless rate would drop after the General Motors strike had ended and workers in auto-related industries returned to work. The expected job recalls apparently had not materialized because of the weak economic situation in those industries. The Administration forecast of an average annual rate of less than 5% was realized by a year-end total of 4.9%, which was, however, up from 1969's 16-year low of 3.5%. The BLS said average total employment for 1970 rose 730,000 to 78.6 million.

White House Press Secretary Ronald L. Ziegler conceded that the December jobless rate was "not expected," but said it reinforced the Administration's decision to move from an anti-inflationary to a more "expansionist" policy. Ziegler said the economy's current transition from a wartime to a peacetime situation, to which he ascribed the high level of unemployment and current business downturn, would produce the "least severe dislocation in this century."

Presidential Action

Business tax cut. President Nixon Jan. 11 set forth new liberalized rules for depreciation write-offs on business equipment, creating a $2.6 billion tax reduction for business in 1971. In a statement issued from the Western White House in San Clemente, Calif., the President said the new rules would spur employment, promote economic growth, increase competitiveness of U.S. goods abroad and clarify an important section of the Internal Revenue Code.

The rules, designed to act as a long-range stimulus to capital spending by business, would: (1) set up an "asset depreciation range system" to permit a 20% margin period (shortened or extended) over which business could write off the cost of equipment; (2) introduce various technical changes in permissible methods of figuring depreciation, retroactive to Jan. 1; and (3) drop the "reserve ratio test" standard limiting by means of a time schedule the amount of depreciation write-offs. The new regulations would not apply to equipment purchased by electric, gas and telephone companies.

The Treasury Department estimated that the business tax cut would result in an $800 million loss in federal revenue for fiscal year 1971 (ending June 30), rising to $4.1 billion in fiscal 1976 and declining to $2.8 billion in fiscal 1980.

Two lawyers from the Public Interest Research Group, a Washington law firm founded by consumer advocate Ralph Nader, filed suit in Washington's U.S. district court Jan. 11 to prohibit the Treasury from implementing the new rules. The lawyers sought the injunction on grounds that the changes were illegal because the public had not been notified in advance and public hearings had not been held. The Treasury said the new rules fell under a legal standard for "reasonable deductions" that did not require Congressional action. Treasury Secretary David M. Kennedy said House Ways and Means Committee Chairman Wilbur D. Mills (D, Ark.) had agreed that legislation was not necessary for the changes to go into effect.

The Treasury Jan. 12 implied that the President's statement on the depreciation rules changes merely indicated "approval" and not a final decision. Department officials said the regulations could be altered after public hearings were held.

Nixon wins steel roll-back. Early in January President Nixon won a major reduction in what appeared to be a large price increase planned by the steel industry.

Nixon, in a tough statement issued through White House Press Secretary Ronald L. Ziegler Jan. 12, denounced the Jan. 11 decision by Bethlehem Steel Corp. to increase its prices up to 12.5%

on construction industry products. The President warned the steel industry that the government might permit an increase in steel imports to dissuade the rest of the industry from making corresponding price hikes. The statement was considered Nixon's most dramatic public censure of a company since he took office.

Bethlehem's increases, representing boosts of about 12% in most cases, on products affecting 16% of industry shipments, were reported the sharpest in the industry's history. Structural shapes and sheet piling were increased $16 a ton and carbon steel plates $17 a ton. Before the Nixon statement, Lukens Steel Co., a major plates producer, matched the Bethlehem increase on carbon steel plates; Alan Wood Steel Co., a few hours after the announcement from the Western White House in San Clemente, Calif., followed with a similar boost and a $20-a-ton price increase on floor plate, a product not produced by Bethlehem.

Nixon termed the Bethlehem price increases "enormous" and expressed concern over their effect on the construction industry, "where costs have already been virtually out of control." Ziegler said the President had ordered his Cabinet Committee on Economic Policy to review the increases and make prompt suggestions for action; the matter of foreign steel imports was to be a part of the review, including the relationship of domestic steel prices to world market prices.

Following Nixon's denunciation of the Bethlehem price increase, United States Steel Corp., the nation's largest steel producer, announced price increases Jan. 17 averaging 6.8% on construction industry products. Bethlehem responded the next day by rolling back its prices to correspond more closely with U.S. Steel's price levels.

U.S. Steel raised prices on H-piles and wide-flange beams by $11 a ton, on standard structural shapes by $10 a ton, on carbon-steel plates and floor plates by $12 a ton, and on sheet piling by $9 a ton. The company stressed that it was not changing the extra fees added to base prices for processing and handling to customer specification, making the ultimate cost to the customer somewhat less than the average 6.8% boost on base prices.

The increases, effective March 1, would augment the company's overall revenue by 1.2%. However, U.S. Steel said the price increases alone "will do very little to cover the inflationary costs incurred during the past year."

Among the cost increases, which the company said added up to 22%, were labor costs that "escalated many times more than output per man-hour" and $225 million spent for pollution control during the past five years. Indicating that future price boosts would be necessary to meet future costs (an apparent allusion to the expiration of the steel industry labor contract July 31). U.S. Steel concurred with Bethlehem's abrogation of the industry's agreement not to raise prices more than once a year in any product line.

Late Jan. 17, Kaiser Steel Corp. in Oakland, Calif. posted price increases similar to those of U.S. Steel.

Apparently referring to President Nixon's threat to relax steel import controls, the statement by U.S. Steel noted that foreign producers, who were also raising their prices, were engaging in unfair competition by selling their products in the U.S. at prices lower than those prevailing in their home markets. The company also observed that foreign steelmakers had the advantages of lower labor costs and government subsidies.

A U.S. Steel spokesman disclosed that Edwin H. Gott, the company's chairman and chief executive officer, had traveled to Washington before the announcement to explain the company's position. It was later reported that he had met with Paul W. McCracken, chairman of the President's Council of Economic Advisers, and White House aide Peter Flanigan.

Bethlehem said Jan. 18 it was revising its prices effective March 1, in order "to be competitive with other producers." The company said its adjusted increases would be $9 a ton on sheet piling, $10 a ton on standard structural shapes, $11 a ton on H-piling and wide-flange beams and $12 a ton on carbon plates. Bethlehem did not change its extra charges for delivery and handling. Lukens Steel Co. (Coatesville, Pa.) and Alan Wood Steel Co. (Conshohocken, Pa.) also reduced their previous increases of $17 a ton on plates to $12 a ton. Several other steel producers raised their prices for the first time to conform to the U.S. Steel pattern.

Prior to revising its prices, Bethlehem had been firm on its 12.5% boost, despite repercussions from the White House. Stewart S. Cort, chairman and chief executive officer of Bethlehem, said Jan. 13 that he had notified CEA Chairman McCracken before the company's announcement. Cort said McCracken had not been "enthusiastic" about the changes, but that he had given no indication of the President's sharp reaction. Cort said the company would not back down on its "best business judgment." In an effort to bolster the company's action, a preliminary earnings report for 1970 was released Jan. 14 showing the company's profits dropped 43% to $2 a share and its fourth quarter profits plunged 59% from the third quarter.

White House Press Secretary Ronald L. Ziegler said Jan. 18 that the Administration was "pleased" with the Bethlehem revisions but tempered his statement with the comment that the White House was not "sanguine" about the new price level any more than the original boost. He added that the Cabinet Committee on Economic Policy would continue studying the effects of the price increases on the market.

U.S. Steel announced price increases May 5 averaging 6.25% on steel items used to make consumer products. President Nixon made known his "disappointment" at the price action, although the size of the increases fell within the range indicated as acceptable by the White House.

Prices were raised on hot-rolled sheet and strip $9 a ton, on hot-rolled bands $8.50 a ton, on cold-rolled sheets $12 a ton, and on galvanized sheets, aluminum coated and long ternes $13 a ton. The increases were effective June 16 and July 1. June 16 was the expiration date of the one-year price freeze initiated in 1970 by Bethlehem Steel Corp.

In announcing the price increases, which affected one-third of total industry volume, U.S. Steel noted that prices had remained stationary while rising costs, specifically wage increases, made the price action necessary.

Major steelmakers adopted the average 6.25% price increase May 6, assuring that the increases would become industry-wide.

Copper changes. Phelps Dodge Corp., the second largest U.S. producer of primary copper, cut its prices Jan. 12 for electrolytic copper cathodes (a form of pure copper) from 53¢ to 50⅜¢. It was the third reduction in basic market prices in less than three months. The reduction reflected a continued slump in open market trends abroad, where prices had been running about 5¢ a pound lower than U.S. prices, as well as inadequate demand to absorb apparent oversupply.

Phelps Dodge boosted its basic price on copper by about 4.7% to 52.375¢ a pound March 29. The boost corresponded to an upward world market trend; current copper quotations on the London Metal Exchange ranged between 53¢ and 55¢ a pound.

AT&T accepts FCC rate plan. American Telephone and Telegraph Co. (AT & T) announced Jan. 13 it had agreed to postpone its original application for rate increases averaging 6% for interstate telephone calls. The company said it would file instead for lower interim increases according to a rate structure proposed by the Federal Communications Commission (FCC) Jan. 12. AT & T said it would accept the FCC plan which would give it an additional income of $250 million, compared with the $545 million a year under its own plan, but the company reserved the right to file for higher rates after full hearings on the increases were held.

ICC delays rate hikes—The Interstate Commerce Commission (ICC) Jan. 25 postponed an 11%–58% increase in freight rates on mobile homes at the request of the Administration which called the rates "highly inflationary and unjustified."

The request was made in an unpublished letter to ICC Chairman George M. Stafford from Caspar W. Weinberger, acting as head of the new Regulations and Purchasing Review Board. The letter asked for a public hearing on the increase which was to be effective Feb. 1.

The review board had been set up in 1970 as part of the Administration's effort to intervene in government regulatory agency decisions it regarded as inflationary. In addition to Weinberger, the board included White House aide Peter Flanigan; Paul W. McCracken, chairman of the Council of Economic Advisers; Commerce Secretary Maurice Stans; and Assistant Attorney General Richard McLaren.

Chrysler, UAW agree on pact. Chrysler Corp. and the United Automobile Workers (UAW) reached agreement Jan. 19 on a new three-year contract following the pattern of pacts signed with General Motors Corp. and Ford Motor Co. The pact, covering 110,000 Chrysler workers, called for a 51¢-an-hour average pay hike in the first year and 14¢ an hour more in each of the next two contract years plus a cost-of-living increase figured annually the first two years and quarterly in the third year. The wage increases were retroactive to Nov. 2, 1970. Prepact wages averaged $4.02 an hour.

The pension provision would permit retirement on a $500-a-month pension after 30 years of service at age 58.

Chrysler and the union also agreed to establish a joint committee to study establishment of a pilot program for a four-day week for assembly line workers.

Ratification of the pact by the rank and file membership was announced by the union Feb. 3.

Some 10,000 salaried workers represented by the UAW went on strike against Chrysler for about three hours Feb. 2 before agreement was reached, and the pickets withdrawn, to include in their contract provisions for a 13% pay hike retroactive to Nov. 2, 1970.

(A UAW strike against the International Harvester Co., affecting about 40,-000 workers, began Jan. 13 and lasted until negotiators reached agreement Jan. 22 on a new pact also generally following the automotive industry pattern. Production was not resumed until Feb. 1, however, because of a delay in ratification of the contract by six holdout locals.)

Car sales down in 1970—Sales of the four major U.S. car producers (General Motors Corp., Chrysler Corp., Ford Motor Co. and American Motors Corp.)

dropped 15.9% in 1970 to their lowest total since 1962 when they sold 6,752,000 cars. The overall 1970 total of new cars sold was 7,115,537 units, down from 8,-464,375 in 1969.

The only company posting a sales gain for 1970 was American Motors with 258,372 cars sold, up 7.85% from 239,548 units in 1969. Declining sales were registered by: General Motors—3,294,174 units, down 25.8% from 4,439,-475 in 1969; Ford—2,209,687, off 5.24% from 2,332,104; and Chrysler—1,353,-304, down 6.8% from 1,453,248.

'State of the Union.' President Nixon delivered before a joint session of Congress Jan. 22 his second State of the Union Message. In his message he outlined proposals for a $16 billion annual sharing of federal revenue with state and local governments and for a sweeping revision of the cabinet departments—a reduction from 12 to eight.

Major emphasis also was put on welfare reform, environmental cleanup, expansion of park lands and open spaces and a health program, including a $100 million campaign to find a cure for cancer.

The address dealt only with domestic issues. The President announced he would submit a separate report later to Congress and the nation on foreign policy.

In his address, broadcast by the major television networks, the President said "America has been going through a long nightmare of war and division, of crime and inflation" and was now "ready for the lift of a driving dream." He urged Congress to adopt his program and open "the way to a new American Revolution—a peaceful revolution in which power was turned back to the people—in which government at all levels was refreshed and renewed, and made truly responsive."

Nixon said his program would be presented within the context of an expansionary budget, a "full-employment" (no more than 3.8% unemployment) budget "designed to be in balance if the economy were operating at its peak potential." "By spending as if we were at full employment," he said, "we will help to bring about full employment."

He asked Congress to cooperate within this context and resist "expenditures that go beyond the limits of the full-employment budget." And he urged labor and management to make "a much greater effort" to "make their wage and price decisions in the light of the national interest and their own self-interest."

Nixon resubmits 40 proposals. President Nixon Jan. 26 resubmitted to Congress as his first legislative message about 40 legislative proposals requested but not acted upon by the 91st Congress. While they were not among the "major" legislative goals of the Administration, Nixon said, they were "in the national interest" and "necessary."

Among the 40 proposals resubmitted Jan. 26: (a) $1.5 billion to help in desegregation of school districts; (b) tax increases of .5% on the 8% federal tax on airline passenger tickets, of $2 on the $3 departure tax on international flights, of 2¢ on the 4¢-a-gallon tax on diesel fuel plus higher truck taxes based on vehicle weight; (c) a $100 million contribution to the special fund of the Asian Development Bank and $900 million to the special fund of the Inter-American Development Bank; (d) a drug code; (e) "seed capital" for minority businesses.

Budget 'expansionary but non-inflationary.' President Nixon submitted to Congress Jan. 29 to $229.2 billion budget for fiscal 1972 with an estimated deficit of $11.6 billion.

The revenue estimate of $217.6 billion was based on an optimistic economic forecast of an $88 billion increase in the gross national product (GNP), or total private and government output, to a $1.065 trillion level in 1971. The GNP rose $45 billion to $977 billion in 1970.

The government projection—representing a 12% GNP increase in the 12-month period ending in the fourth quarter—conflicted with the consensus of private forecasts that the GNP increase in that 12-month period would be more in the 7% range from $1.045 trillion to $1.05 trillion.

The federal estimate of the fiscal 1971 deficit was revealed Jan. 29 to be $18.6 billion, a drastic revision from the original estimate of a $1.3 billion surplus, later revised (May 19, 1970) to a forecast of a $1.3 billion deficit.

But the fiscal 1971 and 1972 budgets, put in the context of the "full employment" concept, were estimated to be in surplus for 1971 and approximately in balance for 1972. The Jan. 29 budget was the first U.S. budget formally committed to the "full employment" surplus concept—a theory holding projected spending to the amount of revenues the economy could generate under its existing tax structure operating at full capacity, as indicated by an acceptable unemployment rate of 4%.

President Nixon stressed the concept in his budget message, saying it was "in the nature of a self-fulfilling prophecy: By operating as if we were at full employment, we will help bring about that full employment." His full employment budget—"expansionary but not inflationary"—was designed, he said, to bring about "a prosperity without war and without runaway inflation."

The budget contained no new tax proposals and incorporated the President's goal to forward "a peaceful revolution in which power will be turned back to the people." Basic to this goal were his plans for government reorganization—initiation of a revenue sharing program with states and localities, a realignment of cabinet departments and enactment of welfare reform.

As for spending priorities, defense spending would increase $1.5 billion although it would decrease to 32% of total budget outlays and 6.8% of the GNP, the lowest proportions since 1950 and 1951, respectively (these figures did not include defense-related programs of the Atomic Energy Commission and the Selective Service System, which would increase the proportion to 34% of the budget).

President Nixon contrasted this with the projected increase in total spending for human resources—from 41% of the total budget to 42%.

Increased spending also was projected for environment, parks and natural resources, poverty, welfare and Social Security, science, health, civil rights, education, law enforcement, housing, veterans and the supersonic transport (SST) project.

Farm subsidy outlays would decrease from the previous fiscal year. Less spending was also projected for transportation, space and the Vietnam war. (Reports from Pentagon sources put the cost of the war at about $14.4 billion for fiscal 1971 and approximately $12 billion for fiscal 1972.)

The fiscal 1972 spending total represented an increase of $16.4 billion, or 8%, over fiscal 1971.

The spending increase for fiscal 1971 was $16.2 billion (a total of $212.8 billion), but the original estimate was $2.9 billion. However, unemployment benefits alone nearly doubled—$5.9 billion—from the estimate of $3.2 billion. The budget estimate for fiscal 1972 was based on the assumption that unemployment—currently at 6% —would average 4.8% between mid-1971 and mid-1972, with jobless benefits running about $5.06 billion for the year.

The outlays total of $229.2 billion was within $100 million of the hypothetical figure for total revenues based on a "full-employment" budget—$229.3 billion. Holding to this ceiling and maintaining the budget's balance on this basis, the President said, would promote orderly economic expansion without "losing ground in the battle against inflation."

The revenue area of the budget was predicated on the nation's economic upsurge—that revenues would rise by $23.4 billion to $217.6 billion in fiscal 1972 compared with a $500 million rise to $194.2 billion in fiscal 1971.

Nixon reiterated requests for increasing the Social Security taxable income base to $9,000 a year, retroactive to Jan. 1, and for raising truck and diesel fuel taxes and imposing a tax on lead used in gasoline, although the latter was basically an environmental proposal.

The President also requested reform of the budget process itself, particularly in federal credit programs that, he said, "escape regular review by either the executive or the legislative branch" and were not "coordinated well" with overall debt management. The Federal National Mortgage Association and five other housing and farm credit agencies were expected to borrow a net $7.5 billion in fiscal 1971 and $9.2 billion in fiscal 1972, which would increase their debt outstanding to $52.5 billion in mid-1972.

Some highlights of the fiscal 1972 budget:

Defense—Defense outlays for fiscal 1972 were projected at $76 billion, a $1.5 billion increase over fiscal 1971. It was necessary, according to the President, to modernize conventional forces, expand development of nuclear weapons and increase pay levels toward an all-volunteer armed force [see p. 69B3]. The President also reported an additional $6 billion in budget authority for national defense.

Service budgets for fiscal 1972 were. Navy $23.34 billion; Air Force $22.82 billion; Army $21.46 billion.

General-purpose forces were allotted $24.27 billion ($24.14 billion in fiscal 1971), strategic forces $7.63 billion in fiscal 1972 ($7.73 billion in fiscal 1971).

The budget included $3.32 billion for building new vessels and modernizing old ones, a rise from $2.59 billion in fiscal 1971.

Space—NASA's budget declined $200 million to $3.2 billion in fiscal 1972, but several new projects were covered which would involve increased spending in later years. The major such item was a space shuttle, or reusable rocket, for which $55 million–$60 million was requested for development of a 550,000-pound thrust engine and $100 million for an airframe.

The Nerva nuclear rocket program of NASA and the AEC would be cut back from an $86 million fiscal 1971 level to $15 million for each agency.

Budget Receipts
(In millions of dollars for the fiscal year)

	1970 actual	1971 estimate	1972 estimate
Individual Income taces	90,412	88,300	93,700
Corporation income taxes	32,829	30,100	36,700
Social insurance taxes and contributions:			
Employment taxes and contributions	39,133	42,297	50,225
Unemployment insurance	3,464	3,604	4,183
Contributions for other insurance and retirement	2,701	3,072	3,151
Excise taxes	15,705	16,800	17,500
Estate and gift taxes	3,644	3,730	5,300
Customs duties	2,430	2,490	2,700
Miscellaneous receipts	3,424	3,800	4,134
Total receipts	**193,743**	**194,193**	**217,593**

Budget Outlays
(In millions of dollars for the fiscal year)

	1970 actual	1971 estimate	1972 estimate
National defense*	80,295	76,443	77,512
International affairs and finance	3,570	3,586	4,032
Space research and technology	3,749	3,368	3,151
Agriculture and rural development	6,201	5,262	5,804
Natural resources	2,480	2,636	4,243
Commerce and transportation	9,310	11,442	10,937
Community development and housing	2,965	3,858	4,495
Education and manpower	7,289	8,300	8,808
Health	12,995	14,928	16,010
Income security	43,790	55,546	60,739
Veterans benefits and services	8,667	9,969	10,644
Interest	18,312	19,433	19,687
General government	3,336	4,381	4,970
Allowances for:			
Added amount for revenue sharing	-----	-----	4,019
Pay increase (excluding Department of Defense)	-----	500	1,000
Contingencies	-----	300	950
Undistributed intragovernmental transactions	-6,380	-7,197	-7,771
Total outlays	**196,588**	**212,755**	**229,232**
Budget deficit	**2,845**	**18,562**	**11,639**

*Includes allowance for all-volunteer force and civilian and military pay increases for Defense Department.

The projected final moon landing flight was set back five months to December 1972 in another economy move.

Planetary exploration was planned, with $180 million, a $145 million increase, going to the Viking project to send two unmanned spacecraft to land on Mars (by 1975) and $30 million requested for work to begin on development of a series of spacecraft to study the outer planets.

Revenue sharing—President Nixon's $16 billion revenue sharing plan was budgeted at $3.75 billion for general revenue sharing and $9.61 billion for special revenue sharing.

Part of the $9.61 billion was to fund existing grant programs, which were to be absorbed by the special revenue sharing project Jan. 1, 1972. An additional $269 million was to be applied during the six months as a "sweetener" for the program, which had already aroused important Congressional opposition.

The block grants were to include $2.11 billion for urban community development, covering urban renewal and Model Cities programs, among others; $954 million for rural development, such as in Appalachia; $2.9 billion for education, including all elementary and secondary education funds; $1.6 billion for manpower training; $408 million for law enforcement; and $1.91 billion for transportation.

Welfare reform—Nixon urged early enactment of a welfare reform plan that would set national eligibility standards, balance training and work requirements with training and work incentives, provide financial relief to the states and set a floor under benefit payments for "all needy families with children."

In companion requests, the President sought enactment of automatic cost-of-living adjustments in Social Security, which would require a 6% benefit retroactive to Jan. 1, plus increases in widow's pensions and proposals to put railroad retirement funds on a financially sound basis.

Education—Outlays by the Office of Education were to rise by $324 million to $4.7 billion in fiscal 1972. A major request was consolidation of 75 separate education grants. Student aid programs in higher education were to be reformed to focus more aid on lower-income pupils and more reliance on student loans.

Other proposals were for a federally chartered National Student Loan Association to provide a secondary market for federally guaranteed college loans and for a national foundation for higher education to finance research by colleges and universities.

Environment—Projected outlays for sewage treatment construction grants in fiscal 1972 totaled $1 billion, an increase from $422 million in fiscal 1971.

The Administration budgeted $129 million for air cleanup projects and $19 million for solid waste activity. In addition, some $85 million in supplemental funds were to be requested later for the Environmental Protection Agency (EPA). The projected outlays were much less than a total of $527 million authorized for the EPA under the new air and water statutes, which called for $375 million in fiscal 1972 for air research and enforcement activity and $152 million for solid waste treatment.

Manpower—These programs, including vocational rehabilitation and some veteran training programs outside the Labor Department, were budgeted at $3.76 billion, a 13% increase of $444 million over estimated fiscal 1971 spending. About $80 million of the increase was scheduled for the Work Incentive (WIN) program initiated in 1968 to train welfare mothers with school-age children for employment. Total WIN outlays were set at $201 million for fiscal 1972.

Manpower training programs under the Labor Department were allocated $1.44 billion in fiscal 1972 outlays. Under the revenue-sharing plan, these outlays were to be extended after Jan. 1, 1972 as block grants to state and local governments under a formula based on the size of the labor force and rates of unemployment and poverty in the state or locality involved.

Housing and 'Community' agency—Fiscal 1972 outlays for the Housing and Urban Development Department were budgeted at $3.9 billion, an increase of $552 million over fiscal 1971. Construction of housing for low and moderate income families was to be subsidized at a level of 516,000 units for fiscal 1972, an increase of 50,000. The Administration planned to renew its request for consolidation of housing programs administered by the department.

The department itself was to be revamped, under the President's reorganization plan, with the word "Community" replacing "Urban" and a new Community Development Special Revenue Sharing plan absorbing, after Jan. 1, 1972, Model Cities, urban renewal, rehabilitation loans and water and sewer grants. Spending for these four programs was estimated at $1.6 billion in fiscal 1971 and $2 billion for fiscal 1972 plus $150 million in revenue sharing funds.

To strengthen state and local planning efforts, the budget called for a $100 million commitment in fiscal 1972, double the previous year's amount.

Agriculture—Agriculture Department outlays were to increase in fiscal 1972 to about $10.5 billion from the previous year's $8.4 billion level. Much of the increase was to reimburse the Commodity Credit Corp. for farm subsidies, losses on commodity sales and food aid costs from previous years. It also covered a $460 million rise in food stamp outlays over fiscal 1971. The injection of funds into the food stamp program, expected to reach about 12.5 million persons by mid-1972, included an expected supplemental request for $120 million over the fiscal 1971 appropriation of $1.42 billion, plus about $2 billion more in fiscal 1972.

Some major programs were slated for revamping under the revenue sharing project: the 67-year Extension Service was to be absorbed into it with states using the funds at their discretion; the 34-year soil conservation program, recently renamed the Rural Environmental Assistance Program, was also to be absorbed. The Administration repeated its request for elimination of the special milk program, which Congress funded at the $104 million level for fiscal 1971.

Reflecting farm legislation enacted in 1970, direct payments to wheat, feed grain and cotton producers were tentatively funded at a $2.64 billion level, a $679 million (20%) decrease from the previous year.

Other programs—International development assistance was funded at a $1.5 billion level for fiscal 1972, a rise of $140 million. The military supporting assistance program was allocated about $1.7 billion. Total outlays for foreign aid and other international programs was estimated at $4 billion, a rise of $400 million.

The health program budget was to rise by $1.1 billion to $16 billion for fiscal 1972, including the $100 million increase in authority for cancer research. The budget provided more money for training health manpower and for family planning but proposed a reduction of funds for construction of health facilities under the Hill-Burton program.

In the civil rights field, the Administration planned to increase by more than 50% efforts to bar job discrimination and to increase nearly threefold federal assistance to desegregating school districts. Administration of the fair housing and equal opportunity laws was to be expanded and agencies were to receive 15% more funds to "assure nondiscrimination by recipients in their use of federal assistance."

The budget proposed a "substantial expansion in outlays for federally supported research and development" in science and technology. The budget for the National Science Foundation was to be increased from $506 million to $622 million in fiscal 1972.

Nixon recommended a doubling of the appropriation for the National Foundation on the Arts and the Humanities.

Law enforcement outlays were to rise from $1.2 billion to $1.5 billion in fiscal 1972, including $315.2 million for the Federal Bureau of Investigation, which received about $285.9 million the year before.

Economic report. In his annual economic report to Congress Feb. 1, President Nixon stressed "orderly expansion" as the key to economic policy in 1971 and set goals for lower levels of unemployment and inflation by mid-1972. The message was accompanied by the more detailed annual report of the President's Council of Economic Advisers (CEA).

President Nixon described 1970 as the year in which "we paid for the excesses of 1966, 1967 and 1968, when federal spending went $40 billion beyond full employment revenues." Noting that the end of those payments was near, the President forecast that 1971 would be "a better year, leading to a good year in 1972."

He tempered his optimism, however, by highlighting the twin problems of inflation and unemployment: "We are facing the greatest economic test of the postwar era. It is a test of our ability to root out inflation without consigning our free economy to the stagnation of unemployment."

The President set down as "our first task now" more rapid expansion of the economy as a means of reducing the unemployment rate while continuing the progress against inflation.

The President listed those forces currently present in the economy which made economic expansion in 1971. "probable": a 40% rate of increase in housing starts due to the greater supply and lower cost of mortgage money; improved financial conditions stimulating a strong increase of state and local spending; lower interest rates, including the banks' prime lending rate; increased after-tax incomes and higher savings of consumers; an economic boost in early 1971 as production lost during the 1970 auto strike was made up; and stronger export levels. Despite their strength, the President said, these positive factors were nevertheless not strong enough to assure the desired increase in the nation's output without supplementary fiscal and monetary policies.

Nixon said his full employment budget would do "its full share" in stimulating the economy. He said outlays would rise by $16.5 billion (about 7.5%) from fiscal 1971 to fiscal 1972, but would fall far short of the inflationary 15% average yearly increases that took place between 1965 and 1968. Receipts, he said, would drop $2.7 billion due to his business depreciation tax reform. Nixon forecast that federal expenditures in fiscal 1971 would be $212.8 billion, roughly equal to the revenues generated by an economy operating at full capacity.

Standing by his previous position that "a policy of free-for-all deficit financing would be an invitation to inflation and to wasteful spending," the President defended the Administration's

full employment bugdet as a means of providing necessary budget flexibility but avoiding waste and inflation.

The President did not discuss monetary policy and the amount of expansion that might be permitted by the independent Federal Reserve Board in terms of growth of the money supply or demand deposits and currency. (Speaking in New York Feb. 2, CEA Chairman Paul W. McCracken indicated that money supply growth would have to be at least 6% in 1971, and perhaps as much as 8%, for the Administration's target for the gross national product [GNP] to be attained.)

The formal report of the CEA, prepared by Chairman McCracken, Herbert Stein and Hendrik S. Houthakker, was more extensive than the shorter President's report and served to defend the Administration's "ambitious" economic goals and projections. However, the report departed from its usual detail in terms of supporting forecasts for major sectors of the economy, such as the numerical forecast of consumer spending. The report explained the lack of heavy statistical projections on the basis that the economy's vigorous or gradual recovery depended on variables over which the government had no control, such as the extent to which people and business preferred to save money rather than spending or investing it.

Noting the controversy surrounding the Administration's GNP projections, the council acknowledged that private forecasts placed the GNP for 1971 between $1.045 trillion and $1.050 trillion (a 7%-7.5% rise). In contrast, the government had forecast a 9% rise to $1.065 trillion. Commenting on the private forecasts, the CEA report said: "This is a possible outcome. However, it seems more likely that with present policies the outcome would be higher than that and could be as high as $1.065 trillion."

Concerning the international monetary scene, the CEA report increased the estimate of U.S. 1970 balance of payments deficit to $9.5 billion from $8 billion (on the official settlements basis which counts only the dollars mounting in foreign central banks), urged more currency-exchange rates in other countries, expressed concern over further farm export losses without a reduction in the European Economic Community's agricultural price supports before the entry of Britain into the EEC and indicated its view that the U.S. was needlessly losing price relief by restricting imports of goods subsidized by other countries.

The two topics of major concern discussed in depth by both the President and the council were:

The unemployment-inflation dilemma. In discussing the dual problems of unemployment and inflation, the President cited the two themes of (1) the transition to a less inflationary economy and (2) the transition from a wartime to a peacetime economy. The President said the Administration had accomplished its task of first halting the rate of inflation's acceleration and then getting "the rate down"; the President cited the annual rate of increase of the consumer price index in the last half of 1970, wholesale prices in the second half of 1970 and a lower increase in labor costs per unit of output.

Concerning the transition to a peacetime economy, the President noted that the release of about one million persons in military and civilian employment for defense during 1970 had swelled the ranks of the unemployed. Nixon noted that the two transitions were inevitably accompanied by some decline in output and rise in unemployment. He said that more expansive fiscal and monetary policies in early 1970 had helped to "get output rising again while the cost of living slowed its rise."

After giving its own account of the dual problems of inflation and unemployment, the CEA set two targets for the national economy to reach by mid-1972: a decline in unemployment to about 4.5% and in the rate of inflation to about 3%. The council said the targets provided a "feasible path" between the extremes of either permitting the present jobless rate to persist, with some benefit on the inflation front, or an effort to reach an unemployment rate of 4% by mid-1972.

The council admitted that the Administration's fight against inflation and unemployment in 1970 had been "dis-appointing," but added: "The policies of 1969 and 1970 set a ceiling to the mounting inflation and turned the inflation down; they set a floor to declining output and turned it upward." It also said the 6% unemployment rate had not been as large as in earlier transitions from inflation and war. The council suggested that 1970's persistent inflation despite rising unemployment might be attributed to the concentration of the economic slowdown in one sector of the economy—the defense sector. The council observed that while the reduction in defense spending had contributed to the rise in unemployment, it had had "little direct effect on the prices of most interest to consumers."

Wage & price curbs—The President and the CEA both firmly rejected a system of mandatory or voluntary restraints on wages and prices.

The President said: "I do not intend to impose wage and price controls which would substitute new, growing and more vexatious problems for the problems of inflation. Neither do I intend to rely upon an elaborate facade that seems to be wage and price control but is not."

Declaring that "free price and wages are the heart of our economic system," the President said his Administration would work "relentlessly" to stabilize costs and prices by guarding against pressures on market forces created by the government itself: "The government has a responsiblity to prevent misuses and imbalances of market power which impede an orderly operation of our free economic system." The President also pledged to "use all the effective and legitimate powers of government to unleash and strengthen those forces of the free market that hold prices down."

The President warned that business and labor must learn new patterns of behavior in that businesses "cannot expect to pass all cost increases along in higher prices" and that labor contracts and price lists "cannot embody the expectation that prices will continue rising at the peak rates of recent years." In cases where these lessons were not being learned, the President warned that the government "will act to correct the conditions" where normal competitive forces could be limited by "acts of commission or omission by the federal government." As an example, he cited the current reviews of the construction and steel industries, previous actions in lumber, copper and oil and the commitment to a liberal foreign trade policy.

The CEA stated its views accordingly: "There is now a great deal of experience to indicate that the superficially attractive route of voluntary controls is unlikely to lead to a solution. The basic deficiency in this approach is that it counts on a large number of people to acquiesce in conduct that they find contrary not only to their own interests but also to their view of fairness, propriety and efficiency. What is called for is a policy of doing what can effectively be done, wherever it can be done, and not pretending to do more."

Bank rates head down. Major New York banks initiated a reduction Jan. 6, that became industry-wide the next day in their prime lending rate from 6.75% to 6.5%. Chemical Bank was the first major bank to trim the prime (or minimum) rate charged on corporate loans, following the initial quarter-point reduction Jan. 4 by First Pennsylvania Banking and Trust Co., Philadelphia's largest bank. Chemical simultaneously announced an across-the-board cut of more than a half percentage point in consumer loan charges. The nation's largest bank, San Francisco's Bank of America, waited until Jan. 7 to make its reduction.

The cut was the banking industry's sixth in less than a year and scaled the rate downward from a record 8.5% in early 1970.

The Federal Reserve Board (FRB) Jan. 7 approved a cut—from 5.5% to 5.25%—made by 10 of the Reserve's 12 district banks in the discount rate on loans to commercial banks. It was the third reduction in less than two months and brought the rate to its lowest level since December 1968.

The reduction became effective Jan. 8 at reserve banks in Boston, New York, Philadelphia, Cleveland, Richmond, Chicago, St. Louis, Minneapolis, Kansas City and San Francisco. The Dallas and Atlanta Reserve Banks were expected to conform to the cut the following week.

The Reserve Board said its approval was based on a further decline in short-term interest rates. Short-term interest rates had fallen on a broad front Jan. 7 following the prime rate reduction by commercial banks. The cut also appeared to confirm a trend toward more frequent and smaller changes in the discount rate.

(Banking data issued by the New York Federal Reserve Bank Jan. 7 showed that the net reserve position of the nation's commercial banks was its easiest in three years in the week ended Jan. 6. Banks reported average free reserves [the difference between the surplus reserve of some banks and excess borrowings of others] were $174 million for that week, up from $68 million in the previous week. It was the largest free reserve average since the week ended Jan. 10, 1968 when free reserves totaled $384 million.)

There were fresh reductions Jan. 18 in both the prime and discount rates. The FRB trimmed by a quarter point to 5% its discount rate on loans to commercial banks.

Morgan Guaranty Trust Co., followed by two other large New York commercial banks, pared its prime lending rate for corporate borrowers to 6% just one business day after lowering the rate to 6.25% Jan. 15.

The Federal Reserve authorization permittted six (Boston, Philadelphia, Cleveland, Atlanta, Minneapolis and Dallas) of the 12 regional Reserve banks to cut their discount rates to their lowest levels since April 1968. It was the second reduction within an 11-day period, the shortest interval on record for rate changes. The FRB said it approved the reduction on the basis of further declines in short-term market interest rates.

The prime rate reduction was also significant in terms of the time space between cuts and brought to 2.5 points the total reduction in less than a year. However, the banking industry showed some reluctance in following the leads of Morgan Guaranty, Chemical Bank and Chase Manhattan Bank. By late afternoon Jan. 18, only eight of the nation's largest banks had lowered their rates. The chief heel draggers were San Francisco's Bank of America and Wells Fargo Bank which were more dependent than New York banks on personal savings accounts with their legally fixed maximum rates. When the two Pacific Coast banks finally lowered their key lending charges Jan. 19 from 6.5% to 6%, they also announced suspension of passbook savings accounts offering interest rates of 5.5% and 5.7% in favor of a maximum 5% rate. Bank of America said it was realigning its time deposit rates to correspond more closely with other market interest rates.

The changes in the two key banking rates paralleled a broad decline in short-term interest rates on the open market which included U.S. treasury bills, finance companies' commercial paper, banks' negotiable certificates of deposit and discount notes sold by the Federal National Mortgage Association.

The FRB Feb. 12 lowered its discount rate again—to 4.75%. Commercial banks Feb. 16 then pared their prime rate to 5.75%.

The Federal Reserve reduction was the fifth quarter-point cut since early November 1970. The board said the purpose of the action was to keep the discount rate in closer alignment with short-term market rates. The New York Federal Reserve Bank was the only district bank (of 12) which did not make a reduction, an apparent expression of the bank's concern over inflation and an excessively easy monetary policy.

Bankers Trust of New York initiated the cut in the prime rate before business hours Feb. 16. The reduction became general by late afternoon as other banks, and finally San Francisco's Bank of America, followed suit.

Bankers Trust said its action was based on current money market conditions and was in line with its policy to create a flexible rate system. The bank's reduction trimmed the prime rate to its lowest level since November 1967; it was the ninth reduction since March 1970, the fourth quarter-point cut for the year.

Mortgage ceiling cut. The interest rate ceiling on home mortgages backed by the Federal Housing Administration and Veterans Administration was lowered from 8% to 7.5% Jan. 12 and then to 7% Feb. 17, the latter cut being the third in three months.

George W. Romney, secretary of housing and urban development, said Jan.

12 that his decision to lower the ceiling was based on a continuing large inflow of funds to mortgage lending institutions and a further drop in market interest rates competitive with mortgages. Romney said the action should help spur housing production which, he said, was already "headed for a banner year in 1971."

The Feb. 17 cut would slice $8 a month off the cost of buying a home with a $25,-000 25-year mortgage.

The Federal Home Loan Bank Board reported March 24 that in February average interest rates on conventional home-loan mortgages had dropped below 8% for the first time since July 1969, falling to 7.8% from 8.08% in January.

Congressional Action

Hearings held by Congressional committees provided additional data on Nixon Administration policy, economic developments and non-Administration views.

Woodcock for wage-price board. In testimony before the Joint Economic Committee of Congress Jan. 26, Leonard Woodcock, president of the United Automobile Workers, detailed a plan for a wage-price review board to counter inflation. However, the main purpose of the board was to reduce excessive price increases in industries administering prices; unions would be required to participate in the hearings only if wage increases were a factor.

According to the plan, a consumer council would initiate hearings before the board, after which the board could use its power to subpoena records and marshal public opinion by holding hearings. The board would have no legal power to enforce wage-price rollbacks.

Woodcock's testimony stressed that the root of inflation lay in "administered" prices set by the nation's largest industrial corporations and not in contract settlements by the big unions. Woodcock said their prices were not only set in defiance of the laws of supply and demand but were often increased during recession periods to maintain a target rate of profit and offset falling sales. The labor union president added that earnings of unionized blue collar workers had grown less during the Nixon Administration than any other category of the working force.

Woodcock also castigated the Administration for "a most erratic economic policy." He said the business slowdown had been engineered by the Administration on a false premise—that of excess demand and an overheated economy. Woodcock argued that there had been no general excess demand since the Administration took office, when idle manufacturing capacity, Woodcock said, had already been rising for two years and unemployment was at a "shockingly high" level compared with other West European industrial democracies.

Administration defends forecasts. Administration officials appeared Feb. 5 and 8 before Congress' Joint Economic Committee to defend the economic projections of the annual economic reports to Congress by the President and the Council of Economic Advisers (CEA).

CEA Chairman Paul W. McCracken testified Feb. 5 in response to the charge of committee chairman Sen. William Proxmire (D, Wis.) that the CEA target of a $1.065 trillion gross national product (GNP) for calendar 1971 was "highly political" and had been ordered by "higher authority." McCracken conceded that the Administration figure exceeded private forecasts but said the projection was "probable" and "feasible."

He pointed out that private economists tended to underestimate strong advances by the economy. He also commented that the projected 9% growth in the economy was above average but not extraordinary when compared with other expansionary years since World War II.

In terms of policy instruments for attaining the Administration's goal McCracken said the President's budget would assist orderly economic expansion while a complementary monetary policy "should induce a rate of private expenditure" for goods and services that, when added to public purchases, would equal the projected GNP.

Acknowledging that the Administration did not know what monetary policy, the province of the independent Federal Reserve Board, would be implemented in 1971, McCracken estimated that anything below a 6% growth in the money supply (demand deposits and currency) would jeopardize the CEA's GNP target.

McCracken continued to reject mandatory wage and price controls or voluntary guideposts. However, he said, "It is clear that we now have in effect many elements of what has come rather loosely to be called an incomes policy. We are now considering ways to make these elements more systematic and comprehensive and to provide more adequately for their management. . . ."

George P. Shultz, director of the Office of Management and Budget, testified Feb. 8 that if private forecasts estimating a GNP of $1.045 trillion prevailed, there would be a $7.1 billion loss in revenue, producing a deficit of about $18.7 billion (depending on the distribution of corporate profits and personal income). Replying to Proxmire's criticism that the Administration had not provided a component breakdown of GNP in its reports to Congress, Shultz reported that the Administration forecasts were the product of a new econometric model* based on gross movements of the economy rather than the usual sector-by-sector "from the inside out" approach.

In response to Proxmire's objections to the Administration's deletion of the customary component breakdown of GNP,

---

*According to newspaper reports, Shultz's comment about a new formula on which GNP projections were based was an apparent reference to an econometric model developed in the Office of Management and Budget (OMB) by Arthur B. Laffer, 30, an associate professor on leave from the University of Chicago, where Shultz had also been faculty member before joining the Administration 1969. (An econometric model: a set of algebraic equations establishing relationships among certain past, current and future levels of economic activity and certain external events, such as monetary growth.)
According to the Laffer model, monetary policy changes exerted a "sharp" and "instantaneous" effect on the GNP, contradicting the view that monetary policy changes could not be felt until after a time lag. Thus, each one-percentage-point increase in the annual growth rate of the money supply, e.g. from 4% to 5%, would cause a simultaneous one-percentage-point acceleration in the annual growth rate of GNP (e.g. from 8% to 9%) during a calendar quarter. Using the Laffer model, OMB economists concluded that, based on a 6% money supply growth and federal expenditures of $212.8 billion in fiscal 1971 and $229.2 billion in fiscal 1972, GNP in calendar 1971 would average $1.075 trillion.

McCracken Feb. 13 released a letter to Proxmire detailing the major GNP sectors making up the total GNP forecast. The breakdown was as follows (all figures in billions of dollars):

	1970	1971 Estimate
Total	$976.5	$1,065
Business		
Fixed Investment	102.6	106
Residential Construction	29.7	41
Inventory Change	3.5	8
Net Exports	3.6	4
Federal Purchases	99.7	98
State and Local Purchases	120.9	135
Personal Consumption Expenditures	616.7	675

The large increase in personal consumption expenditures reflected a decline in the rate of personal savings from 7.3% to 6.9% which was anticipated because of "improving economic conditions and consumer confidence, rising consumer assets and liquidity, the effect of high residential construction on purchases of furniture and household equipment, some catch-up of automobile purchases deferred because of the 1970 strike and other factors."

A statement issued by Proxmire in connection with the letter labeled the consumer buying forecast "unbelievable" and said it would be the largest increase since 1948. Proxmire also questioned projections for state and local spending, and the inventory change category.

Gardner Ackley, former CEA chairman and currently chairman of the economic committee of the Democratic Policy Council, said Feb. 13 that the Administration's economic policies were "clearly inadequate" to attain its GNP employment targets. He called for deeper deficit spending, arguing that the Nixon full employment budget was not sufficiently stimulative to produce a sizable drop in the current 6% jobless rate; proper stimulation could only be provided by a full employment deficit. Ackley said the view that a balanced full employment budget would automatically produce full employment without inflation was "oversimplified and misleading." The Democratic economist said the economy needed a more expansionary monetary policy than it was likely to receive. He deplored the liberalization of business depreciation allowances as part of a "lamentable set of priorities."

Burns on economic policy. Arthur F. Burns, chairman of the Federal Reserve Board, testified before Congress' Joint Economic Committee Feb. 19. He said the Administration's forecast of a $1.065 trillion gross national product (GNP) in 1971 was "admirable" as a target but "optimistic" as a prediction.

Under questioning, Burns conceded that his "discriminating" staff of economists viewed the Administration projection as "very optimistic," indicating that the staff's figure was close to private forecasts of $1.045 trillion–$1.050 trillion. He said his own prediction ranged between the forecasts of his staff and the Administration.

In an apparent reference to the Administration's use of the Laffer model to project GNP growth, Burns derided as "simplified economic thinking" the idea that "the money machine would just grind out the GNP." He added: "There is no single, one-to-one relationship between the money supply . . . and the rate of increase of [national] output."

Burns indicated that the Federal Reserve was not planning an imminent change in monetary policy: "The banks are full of money and looking for customers. For a short time, we will continue [the present] policy and as the year goes by, we may be a little more restrictive or a little more stimulative."

Burns gave his assurance that the FRB would not "stand idly by and let the American economy stagnate for want of money and credit." However, he warned that further inflation could only be avoided as long as a clear distinction was made between "a shortage of confidence to use abundantly available money and credit . . . and an actual shortage of money and credit." Although Administration officials had indicated a money supply growth rate between 6% and 9% was needed to spur the GNP to its growth target, Burns advised that rates above 5% –6% historically had intensified inflationary pressures if continued for a long period.

Burns acknowledged that the money supply growth rate had slowed over the past few months, but said it did not reflect a change in FRB policy; instead, it mirrored the public's choice to hold additions to its deposit balances in the form of time accounts rather than demand deposits. He said that the money supply in December 1970 and January, with time and savings deposits taken into account, had shown an annual growth rate of more than 12%.

Burns, speaking broadly, said monetary and fiscal policies should remain stimulative, but with a cautious eye on possible rekindling of inflation. He backed the President's budget as "broadly consonant with the needs of an economy operating well below full employment."

Using the term "recession" instead of "downturn," Burns said there were signs the economy was heading toward a "real recovery." He said the actual strength of the recovery would depend upon "restoring the confidence of consumers and businesses in their own and the nation s economic future." He also underscored the weakness of defense spending and business expansion.

For the first time, Burns committed the full seven-man reserve board to an "incomes policy" which he described as measures "to improve the workings of our labor and product markets" to supplement fiscal and monetary policies in combatting inflationary pressures. Expanding on his initial suggestion for an incomes policy, Burns included such elements as stricter enforcement of anti-trust laws and their possible extension to labor unions, cancellation or enlargement of import quotas to widen competition and formation of local "productivity councils" to spur efficiency at the community, factory and store levels. Burns opposed extending for two years the President's standby powers to freeze wages and prices, scheduled to expire in March, as "dictatorial." However, he said a freeze limited to the construction industry for a short period would have the beneficial effect of showing other industries that the government was not powerless.

Federal budget hearings. The three top economic officials of the Nixon Administration appeared before the House Appropriations Committee Feb. 24–25 to review and defend the federal budget. All three—Treasury Secretary John B. Connally, George P. Shultz, director of the Office of Management and Budget, and Paul W. McCracken, chairman of the Council of Economic Advisers

(CEA)—strongly suggested a more expansionary monetary policy by the independent Federal Reserve Board.

The three officials argued that fiscal policy alone could not bring sufficient stimulus to the economy. McCracken advised that "since the money stock is now about in line with the volume of economic activity, economic expansion will require a complementary monetary expansion." Connally criticized as unsatisfactory the 1.1% annual rate at which the money supply (private demand deposits and currency) grew in January and the 3% annual rate increase it had averaged since September 1970.

Rep. George H. Mahon (D, Tex.), chairman of the House panel, chided the Administration for having had to revise its estimate for fiscal 1971 from a $1.3 billion surplus to an $18.6 billion deficit. Mahon warned that a similar miscalculation in the next fiscal year could mean a much larger deficit than the $11.6 billion forecast and greater inflation "than we have ever known before." Shultz acknowledged that the Administration would have to exercise care that spending did not exceed the full employment revenue ceiling "in any major way."

On the second day of the hearing, the Administration rejected suggestions for a bigger budget deficit to stimulate the economy, although Shultz conceded that a bigger deficit might be "a little bit helpful" at the present time. The officials reaffirmed the Administration decision not to seek any tax increases in 1971.

'Impounding'   charged—During   the hearings Shultz disclosed that the Administration was withholding an estimated $8 billion in appropriated funds. The disclosure drew fire from Sen. John J. Sparkman (D, Ala.) who charged March 3 that "impounding" the funds was a "serious breach of faith" with Congress. Sparkman, chairman of the Housing and Urban Affairs Subcommittee, voiced his criticism when he opened hearings into the withholding of about $1 billion from housing, transportation, public works and other urban programs. Mayors Thomas J. D'Alesandro (Baltimore) and Lee Alexander (Syracuse) testified that the cutbacks included $200 million for urban renewal, $200 million

for water and sewer facilities and $430 million for mass transit.

(Sen. Sam J. Ervin Jr. [D, N.C.] announced that the Senate Judiciary Subcommittee on Separation of Powers would hold hearings in March on the Administration action. Ervin said he was concerned about "the use of the impounding practice to avoid or nullify Congressional intent. All too frequently, when Congress votes substantially more funds for a program than the executive branch requested, the President signs the appropriation bill, then directs the Office of Management and the Budget not to release funds to the agencies designated to carry out the program in question.")

Caspar W. Weinberger, deputy director of the Office of Management and Budget, and George Romney, secretary of housing and urban development, appeared before Sparkman's subcommittee March 4 to testify that the funds had been withheld mainly as a means of combatting inflation. They said most of the impounded funds had been marked for construction, an area of central concern to the Administration because of spiraling wages and prices.

Democratic members of the subcommittee asserted that the Administration's explanation contradicted the purpose of President Nixon's expansionary "full employment" budget. They also argued that the high unemployment in the construction industry did not warrant a cutback in urban programs.

The $8 billion withheld by the Administration was broken down as follows: about $5 billion in highway construction funds, more than $1 billion in military construction, and the rest in other programs such as public works and urban renewal. Romney said funds for water and sewer facilities and urban renewal were not being used because the Administration did not want to "accelerate" programs "scheduled for termination."

Budget deficit. The Commerce Department reported March 18 that the federal budget deficit, measured on a "national income accounts basis," rose in the fourth quarter of 1970 to an annual rate of $17.6 billion—the highest in relation to the GNP since 1958's second quarter.

The national income accounts budget showed an $11.4 billion deficit for 1970, compared with a $9.3 billion surplus in 1969.

Federal receipts in the fourth quarter fell $2.7 billion to $192.2 billion; expenditures rose $3.2 billion to $209.9 billion. The fourth quarter budget deficit increase was largely ascribed to declining corporate profit tax receipts because of the auto strike.

Connally testimony. The Congressional Joint Economic Committee wound up its annual policy hearings Feb. 26 with the appearance of its last witness, Secretary of the Treasury John B. Connally. Connally testified on a wide range of issues and was praised by the committee for his detailed knowledge on all subjects, including the complex Tax Reform Act of 1969. Highlights of Connally's testimony:

■ Concerning the likelihood of a 9% gain in the gross national product (GNP) to reach the Administration target of $1.065 trillion in 1971, Connally said he was not "overly optimistic." He said: "I haven't seen enough elements of recovery which are sufficiently strong to lead me to relax very much, frankly." In contrast to previous official statements that the economy would rebound sharply in the first part of 1971, followed by slower growth in the second half reflecting the end of strike-related makeup output in the auto and steel industries, Connally said "a very very strong second half" would be needed to attain the Administration target.

■ On the question of possible tax relief to help stimulate the economy, Connally said the Administration was watching "constantly" a variety of alternatives. He indicated that he favored none of the 10 tax reform proposals sponsored by Rep. Henry S. Reuss (D, Wis.).

Concerning additional taxes on the oil and gas industry, Connally reminded the committee of the 1969 $700 million tax increase and said he did not believe the current situation warranted further increases. He said an extension of the holding period required for favorable long-term capital gains tax treatment from the current six months to one year would be a "deep depressant" to the nation's financial well-being. On merging estate and gift taxes, Connally said he favored a tax law that would encourage donors to give during their lifetime. He strongly opposed taxation of municipal and state bonds and warned against further cuts in depreciation allowances for oil and other "extractive minerals" industries.

■ Connally indicated that President Nixon would toughen his position against inflationary wage and price increases. He confirmed the President's lack of confidence in mandatory price and wage controls, generally voluntary guidelines and a wage and price review board. Nevertheless, Connally warned that the President would "start expressing himself in a very forceful manner."

■ Connally said he hoped all interest rates would be scaled down further, although he recognized the risk that short-term capital would be lured abroad by higher interest rates, thereby aggravating the U.S. balance of payments problem. Connally reasoned that most of the volatile short-term capital had "already flown the coop" and said the best payments policy was to strengthen the economy by offering better investment opportunities than outside the U.S.

(Prior to his confirmation by the Senate as secretary of the Treasury, Connally had told the Senate Finance Committee Jan. 28 that he favored easier money, lower interest rates and a greater degree of presidential "jaw-boning" on wages and prices.)

Meany scores Nixon on economy. AFL-CIO President George Meany, in a 48-page statement to the Congressional Joint Economic Committee March 7, denounced the Nixon Administration's economic policy as a "half-hearted exercise in success-through-optimism." He also reaffirmed organized labor's plans to seek much higher wage increases in 1971.

Meany argued his case for higher wage increases from the viewpoint that "wage and salary earners did not cause the inflationary rise of prices, nor have they been its beneficiaries." According to Labor Department figures, he noted, average hourly earnings of nonsupervisory workers on private nonfarm payrolls rose 5.9%, compared with the 6% increase in consumer prices. He also cited a 3.3% annual rate increase in output per manhour.

Meany rejected President Nixon's revenue sharing program because, he said, cutting back on other programs would not add to already available funds and would cancel out priorities for specific national problems. He disputed the Administration's view that state and local governments could better meet national priorities and use federal funds more efficiently. Meany called for full funding of existing categorical grants in aid and a complete takeover of welfare costs.

In suggesting measures to step up the economy, Meany called for an increase in the federal minimum wage to "at least" $2 an hour, tax reforms, a federal urban bank and land use policy, a capital budget separate from general operating expenses, creation of 500,000 public service jobs in 1971 to engage the unemployed, a comprehensive health program, full funding of government programs for public investment in education, health, housing and other projects to add at least $6 billion to the nation's "spending stream," a federal tax credit for state income tax payments and blockage of the Administration's business depreciation writeoffs which he termed "a tax bonanza to business."

Incomes-price board urged. The Democratic majority of the Joint Economic Committee, joined by one committee Republican, called March 29 for creation of a permanent incomes-price board to curb inflation. Their recommendation was contained in the committee's annual report on the President's annual Economic Report.

The Democrats were joined by Sen. Jacob K. Javits (R, N.Y.), who submitted 152 pages of "supplementary views."

According to the proposal, the board would consult with labor and management on voluntary wage-price guidelines aimed at checking inflation in gross national product terms within 2% annually. It would publish annually important wage and price decisions that exceeded the goal and make corrective recommendations to the parties involved.

In a bipartisan "statement of agreement," the committee members called for an overall budget review in Congress, welfare reform, expanded and improved manpower programs, environment protection, re-evaluation of transportation policy stressing competition and federal aid to state and local governments.

The Republican members backed the President's revenue sharing program; the Democrats offered alternatives of federalizing welfare and reforming existing categorical grants-in-aid.

Poll endorses wage-price curbs. The results of a Gallup Poll, released March 13, showed that 49% of those polled would support a wage-price freeze, while 38% would oppose such a freeze. Because of the "pinch on many family pocketbooks," the poll report said members of labor union families would just as likely back wage-price controls as members of non-union families. The report also found that older persons, in or near the fixed income bracket, were more favorable to a wage-price freeze than younger persons.

The poll canvassed 1,571 adults in 300 localities (13% of those polled had no opinion).

Strike against can companies ends. A 28-day strike against three major can manufacturers ended March 14 with acceptance of new three-year contracts calling for a package increase per worker of $1.50 an hour in wages and fringe benefits. The strike, by 33,000 workers represented by the AFL-CIO United Steelworkers of America (USA), began Feb. 15 against 125 plants of the Continental Can Co., the American Can Co. and the Crown Cork and Seal Corp. Negotiators reached agreement March 12 and it was ratified by the union's local presidents March 14.

The wage agreement was to provide increases of 50¢ an hour in the pact's first year, and 12½¢ more in each of the second and third years. An additional 12½¢ an hour was to be provided in each of the second and third years to offset anticipated increases in the cost of living. In addition, the workers were to receive 10¢ more an hour in increments between job classifications.

Pre-pact wages averaged $3.60 an hour.

A settlement with a fourth can company, the National Can Corp. with 4,000 workers, was reached Feb. 15 as the strike began against the other three companies.

Social Security, debt ceiling hikes. Legislation to provide a 10% increase in Social Security benefits and to raise the ceiling on the national debt was approved by both houses of Congress March 16. President Nixon signed the legislation March 17.

A planned increase in Social Security benefits had expired in the previous (91st) Congress after it had been tied to controversial legislation for welfare changes and trade provisions.

Wilbur D. Mills (D, Ark.), chairman of the House Ways and Means Committee, had initiated plans in the current Congress (92nd) to combine welfare and Social Security provisions in one piece of legislation. However, Democratic Congressional leaders decided to press for early action on the Social Security benefits by attaching it to the debt ceiling bill, which the House had passed March 3 by a 227–162 vote. It provided for a rise in the ceiling to $430 billion, the largest single increase since World War II. The existing ceiling of $395 billion was expected at the time to be exceeded by March 17.

Treasury Secretary John Connally had asked Congress Feb. 17 for an additional $40 billion in borrowing authority to raise the nation's permanent debt ceiling to $435 billion. Connally said the increase was prompted by the economic slowdown, spiraling spending in such areas as unemployment and welfare payments, and efforts to curb unemployment.

The Social Security rider was added to the debt ceiling bill in the Senate March 12. Both provisions were approved unanimously.

A Senate-House conference committee approved the final measure March 15 and it was passed the next day by votes of 358-3 in the House and 76-0 in the Senate. The projected date for breaching the old ceiling was shifted to March 19, permitting the President more time to consider signing without disrupting Treasury financing.

The debt ceiling section included authority for the Treasury to issue $10 billion in long-term bonds at interest rates above the 4.25% interest ceiling that had been in effect for 53 years.

The increase in Social Security benefits, retroactive to Jan. 1, would raise the minimum benefits to $70.40 a month for individuals and to $105.60 for couples. The maximum would rise to $213.10 a month for individuals (currently $193.70) and to $413.71 a month for couples (currently $376). A 5% increase was scheduled for the special payments extended to persons 72 and older not qualified for full Social Security benefits.

The cost of the increased benefits was estimated at $3.6 billion a year.

The conferees had eliminated from the bill a Senate-approved provision for new monthly minimums of $100 for individuals and $150 for couples, a provision opposed by Mills. The action reduced the estimated costs from $5.5 billion to $3.6 billion.

The payroll tax rate funding the Social Security trust fund, currently at 5.2%, was revised to go to 5.85% in 1976 and to 6.05% by 1987. The amount of individual income subject to the payroll tax was to rise from $7,800 to $9,000 effective in 1972.

Nixon urges financing speedup—The combination of retroactive benefits and future financing increases was criticized by President Nixon in his signing statement March 17. "Increasing Social Security benefits in a way that carries with it the seeds of a resumption of the inflation it has taken us more than two years to control would benefit no one," he said. He urged Congress to establish an escalator clause for Social Security benefits.

Brimmer on the economy. Andrew F. Brimmer, a member of the Federal Reserve Board, told a meeting of bank directors in Dallas March 20 that recent economic figures "indicate that a boom in economic activity is not likely to be generated in the near future." Referring to Administration forecasts of a gain in the gross national product (GNP), Brimmer said the results for the full year "may not come up to some of the more optimistic expectations."

Brimmer defended the Federal Reserve's policy of moderate monetary growth and contended that the "sharp decline in short-term interest rates and the greatly increased availability of credit certainly do suggest that the economy is not suffering from a shortage of money." He added that the "zone open to the Federal Reserve System within which to allow a further expansion of money and credit—without adding to inflationary pressures—is not very wide."

Echoing the testimony of Federal Reserve Chairman Arthur F. Burns before the Senate Banking Committee March 3, Brimmer suggested that additional fiscal measures would be a more favorable stimulus to the economy than an easier monetary policy. Burns had testified under questioning by the Senate committee that he did not favor an immediate tax cut, but added, "I wouldn't wait indefinitely" to actively consider tax relief steps.

Economic indicators. The Commerce Department's composite index of 12 leading economic indicators rose 1% in January but trailed the upward-revised 1.8% gain in December 1970. The increase, which brought the index to 117.9% of the 1957 average, was attributed to a "continuing rebound from the automobile strike and general strength among those indicators little affected by the strike."

Six of the eight available indicators rose—the average workweek in manufacturing, new durable goods orders, plant and equipment contracts and orders, the average price of 500 common stocks, the ratio of price to unit labor cost for manufacturers and the average weekly initial claims for state unemployment insurance (inversely treated). The two indicators reporting declines were new building permits and industrial material prices.

The composite index rose .6% in February. This was its fourth straight monthly rise. The increase, which brought the index to 118.6% of the 1967 average, partly reflected the rebound from the 1970 auto strike. However, a department official noted that the "sizable gains" in categories little affected by the strike (e.g. contracts and orders for plant and equipment, housing permits and stock prices) "show decisively that the economy is on a path of renewed growth."

Stock market hits peak. Volume on the New York Stock Exchange set a record 21.68 million shares Jan. 22 in the busiest trading day of the exchange's 179-year history. The Dow-Jones industrial stock average climbed 6.57 points to peak at 861.31, its highest level since closing at 863.05 Nov. 10, 1969. The bull market showing was ascribed to an unexpectedly optimistic annual earnings report Jan. 21 by General Electric Co. which projected profits at $3.60 a share, up from $3.07 a share in 1969.

Capital spending plans up. The business community revised upward its 1971 capital spending plans, according to joint projections issued by the Commerce Department and the Securities and Exchange Commission (SEC) March 8.

According to the latest quarterly survey, businesses were projecting a 4.3% increase over 1970 in outlays for plant and equipment to a total $83.1 billion. This contrasted with a 1.4% projection issued toward the end of 1970; nevertheless, the latest projection was still the smallest since the 3.4% increase in 1968.

Although a 6% rise in capital spending had been forecast for 1970, outlays rose only 5.5% from 1969 to $79.71 billion, mostly due to a sharp fourth quarter drop ascribed to the General Motors auto strike.

At seasonally adjusted annual rates, the survey reported the following figures for plant and equipment outlays: third quarter 1970 (actual)—$81.88 billion; fourth quarter 1970 (actual)—$78.63 billion; first quarter 1971 (planned)— $80.55 billion; second quarter (planned)— $82.54 billion; second half (planned)— $84.61 billion.

Price indexes rise. The Labor Department reported Feb. 19 that consumer prices rose a seasonally adjusted .3% (or at a 3.3% annual rate) in January, down from December 1970's .5% rise (or 6.6% annual rate). On an unadjusted basis, the consumer price index (CPI) edged up .1% to 119.2% of the new 1967 base period. It was the smallest monthly cost-of-living

increase since February 1967. The index stood 5.2% above a year earlier.

The department reported March 19 that consumer prices rose a moderate .2% in February both before and after seasonal adjustment. This was the slackest increase since August 1970. In the slimmest year-to-year increase in two years, the consumer price index at the end of the month stood at 119.4% of the 1967 base period, up 4.8% from a year earlier. The annual rate of increase over the past three months was 3.2%, compared with 5.2% for the previous three-month period.

The report noted that higher prices for food, apparel and most consumer services were moderated by declines in mortgage interest rates and prices of used cars and gasoline. The sharpest rise in food prices since May 1970 was paralleled by the first decline in non-food commodity prices since July 1965. The rise in consumer services' prices was the smallest since mid-1967.

In a related development, the Labor Department issued a short statement that it was abandoning the practice of press briefings held with technicians of the Bureau of Labor Statistics on consumer price and unemployment statistics. The department said one of the reasons for dropping the briefings was to avoid "the awkwardness of subjecting the professional staff of the bureau to questions with policy implications." House Speaker Carl Albert (D, Okla.) criticized the department decision: "The muzzling of those officials who for 20 years now— under Democratic and Republican administrations alike—have provided impartial interpretations of these statistics for newsmen is a most blatant attempt to impede the flow of government information to the public."

January wholesale prices were revised upward Feb. 17 to show a .7% increase before adjustment for seasonal factors and a .5% rise after adjustment. The Labor Department index recorded its sharpest unadjusted increase since a similar .7% gain in January 1970.

The January increase pushed the wholesale price index to 111.8% of the 1967 average.

In an unusual seasonal spurt, wholesale prices for food and farm products rose 1.7%. A sharp gain in food prices reflected marked increases for meat and poultry. The industrial commodities index, a key barometer of inflationary trends, climbed .4%, equaling the Decmber 1970 figure and exceeding the average for the last half of 1970.

Revised February wholesale price data, issued March 5, showed a seasonally adjusted .7% rise to 112.8% of the 1967 average, up 2.8% from a year earlier. Before seasonal adjustment the February gain was .9%, the sharpest advance since July 1953.

Most of the increase was centered in the volatile farm and food price category which climbed a seasonally adjusted 4.1% from January.

The industrial commodities index, regarded as the best indicator of overall price trends and excess demand, rose a scant .1% (seasonally adjusted), well below the .3% increases of the previous two months.

February jobless rate. The unemployment rate eased for the second straight month in February, dropping to 5.8% from January's 6%. The Labor Department March 5 attributed most of the decline to a decrease in the number of people seeking jobs rather than a rise in the number of available jobs. Among the highlights of the report, which department spokesman Harold Goldstein termed "sort of mixed:"

Most of the February decline was concentrated among persons looking for part-time work and young men between the ages 16–24.

Total employment fell to a seasonally adjusted 78,537,000 persons from 78,-864,000 in January.

Adjusted unemployment declined by 186,000 (115,000 of which were part-time job-seekers) to 4,847,000 persons. Unadjusted, the unemployment increase was 5,442,000, compared with 5,-414,000 in January.

The average duration of unemployment stood at 10.4 weeks, but the number of jobless unemployed for 27 weeks or more reached its highest level since September 1964.

Unemployment among Negroes was 9.6%.

Incomes up. Personal incomes rose by $9.2 billion in January and $2.2 billion in February to a seasonally adjusted annual rate of $828.9 billion. The January increase was the biggest since an $18.4 billion advance in April 1970. The Commerce Department said the January increase was "broadly based" and mirrored "rising employment, a longer workweek and higher hourly earnings." The February increase was the smallest since a $2 billion increase in October 1970. The department observed that the slow expansion was centered in wage and salary disbursements which rose only $1.6 billion after an $8 billion increase in January; although average hourly earnings were higher, total employment and average hours worked were lower.

Industrial output falls in February. The Federal Reserve Board reported March 15 that industrial output fell .4% in February, clouding Administration forecasts for an economic recovery in the first quarter of 1971.

The board's index of factory, mine and utility output, which had posted gains in the previous two months following the end of the auto strike, stood at a seasonally adjusted 164.8% of the 1957–1959 average, compared with the slightly downward-revised 165.4% recorded in January, when output rose .7%. The February decline put the index about 2.4% below its prestrike level in 1970 and 5.6% under the July 1969 peak. The February 1970 figure was 170.5.

Corporate profits down. The Commerce Department reported March 18 that corporate pre-tax profits had dropped almost $7 billion in 1970's fourth quarter to an annual rate of $77.5 billion. For all of 1970, pre-tax profits totaled $81.6 billion, down $9.6 billion (10.5%) from 1969, the lowest since 1965 and, relative to the gross national product (GNP), since World War II.

Corporate earnings after taxes in the fourth quarter of 1970 fell from an annual rate of $45.4 billion in the third quarter to $42.1 billion. On an annual basis, 1970 after-tax profits totaled $44 billion, compared with $48.5 billion in 1969.

Housing starts. Housing starts in January dropped more than 16% from December 1970's upward-revised seasonally adjusted annual rate of 2,028,000 units to 1,709,000 units. The January decline was the first in housing starts since August 1970, and occurred mostly in single-unit dwellings.

Housing starts in February inched up to a seasonally adjusted annual rate of 1,715,000 units.

Chase cuts prime rate to 5.25%. Chase Manhattan Bank in New York March 11 pared its prime (minimum) interest rate from 5.75% to 5.25%. The action spurred other commercial banks to cut their prime rates, but most only went as far as 5.5%. The foot-dragging by the other banks created a "split rate," an unusual situation in the banking industry which was expected to be only temporary.

Chase, the nation's largest lender to corporations, announced it was taking the action "to bring the prime rate into closer alignment with prevailing short-term rates," which had fallen sharply below the prime rate.

By March 12, most of the nation's major banks had adopted the quarter-point reduction to 5.5%. Two San Francisco banks—the Wells Fargo Bank and Crocker-Citizens National Bank—coupled their quarter-point reductions with a cut in the interest rate paid on passbook savings accounts to 4% from 4.5% effective April 1. Bankers indicated that the reduction in their time deposits interest rate was a logical sequence because of the direct relationship between interest banks received on loans and interest banks could "prudently" pay their savings depositors.

(The Federal Reserve March 11 reported the money supply averaged $217.7 billion in the four weeks ended March 3, representing a 7.3% annual growth rate over the past three months.)

San Francisco's Bank of America and two major Los Angeles banks—Security Pacific National Bank and United California Bank—March 15 announced half-point reductions in their prime rate to 5.25%. They also lowered their minimum rates on conventional home mortgages to 6.75% and interest on passbook savings to 4%.

The 5.25% prime interest rate became industry-wide March 19 when the last of the holdouts, led by First National City Bank in New York, conformed to the Chase level.

Albert focuses on aid to economy. House Speaker Carl Albert (D, Okla.) denounced the "do-nothing" economic policies of the Nixon Administration April 8 and said the House Democratic leadership accepted "the responsibility of providing the national leadership so urgently needed to end our prolonged economic slump."

"We do not believe," he said, "that inflation alerts, selective controls on single industries and the massive impounding of appropriated funds are the correct actions at this time."

In his statistical white paper, Albert cited discouraging economic statistics, among them: a nine-year high for unemployment over the past four months, the lowest (72%) manufacturing capacity utilization since 1958, a five-year low for corporate profits in 1970's fourth quarter, and the highest jobless rate since 1958 among professional technical workers, and the economy's low operating rate at an annual $70 billion below potential.

As for House action, Albert cited: (a) passage of a temporary extension of standby wage and price controls; (b) scheduling of floor action on a $2 billion emergency public works bill, plus extension of the Appalachian and other regional commissions; (c) completion of hearings on emergency public service employment; (d) introduction of legislation to raise the statutory minimum wage of $1.60 an hour to $2; (e) committee work on a bill for greater federal assumption of welfare costs; and (f) consideration of an Urban Development Bank to provide needy communities with low-cost federal loans.

Nixon Uses Stabilization Powers

Construction wage-price curbs. President Nixon signed an executive order March 29 setting up a primarily industry-regulated system of "constraints" to stabilize wages and prices in the construction industry. The order put into effect a plan recommended by the public sector members of the Construction Industry Collective Bargaining Commission after union leaders declined to submit their own proposals. Secretary of Labor James D. Hodgson had conveyed the commission's plan to the White House March 25.

With the executive order, the President also rescinded his Feb. 23 suspension of the Davis-Bacon Act, which required contractors on federally funded projects to pay union scale wages. The press reported that construction union leaders had made their cooperation conditional on reinstatement of the act.

The President issued the executive order under the Economic Stabilization Act of 1970 which gave him standby authority to use either general or selective wage and price controls. Just before Nixon signed the order March 29, the House approved a two-month extension of the wage-price control authority that had been passed by the Senate March 4. The action followed the defeat in a 183–143 vote of an amendment sponsored by Rep. Henry S. Reuss (D, Wis.) and other Democrats on the Banking Committee that would have prohibited presidential use of the authority against a lone industry.

The objective of the wage-price plan, according to Hodgson, was to keep wage increases in the construction industry in approximate alignment with annual increases given workers during the mid-1960s, or about 6%. First-year wage settlements in 1970 had averaged about 17% for the industry's three million union members. Other criteria would include productivity and cost-of-living trends, as well as allowances for "equity adjustments" to maintain traditional wage level differences among crafts in a single locality or with the same craft in nearby localities.

Under the order, monitoring machinery, in the form of 16 to 18 labor-management "craft dispute boards," would review collective bargaining agreements in each of the construction crafts. Any wage settlement found unacceptable by the boards would be further reviewed by the new tripartite Construction Industry Stabilization Committee, to be appointed by the secretary of labor. The committee would make the final decision within a 15-day period as to whether the particular wage settlement had violated the plan's criteria.

If a wage settlement or contract was ruled in violation of the government's criteria, violators would be subject to three sanctions: (1) the violation would be widely publicized; (2) the secretary of labor would be authorized to notify other government agencies of the violator's identity to discourage and possibly suspend government procurement in the area where the violation occurred; and (3) the secretary of labor would be empowered to take steps that would in effect suspend the Davis-Bacon Act on a selective basis. If the system failed altogether, the President might again suspend Davis-Bacon nationwide.

The order did not set criteria for price increases, salaries, bonuses and stock options, but left that function to an interagency committee to be appointed by the secretary of housing and urban development. Also not clearly defined were the weapons the government intended to use against construction company violators.

Administration officials denied that the wage-price plan represented controls or that the 6% measure for wage increases was similar to the "guidepost" of the Kennedy and Johnson Administrations. Hodgson said he did not regard the President's order as a policy switch, but as a signal that any industry which permits its wages and prices to range "far out in front" of others is "in danger of getting itself singled out by the government."

In an accompanying statement Nixon said the plan was supported by contractors and labor leaders who "indicated their willingness to cooperate with the government in fair measures to achieve greater wage and price stability." William E. Dunn, executive director of the Associated General Contractors of America, commented that while management would have preferred a stronger plan, "we are nevertheless completely and wholeheartedly behind the President's program." The President's order met with the resigned comment from 16 of the 17 building trades unions that "we have no choice but to obey." However, C. J. Haggerty, president of the AFL-CIO Building and Construction Trade Department, insisted that the 17 affiliated unions had not made a final decision to participate in the machinery. He said the department would put up a legal battle against the plan which he said was "fundamentally unfair in applying strict controls to wages and a vague procedure with respect to prices and profits." Union officials also protested that the plan included penalties not announced by the President but included in the Economic Stabilization Act under which the executive order was signed.

Labor Secretary Hodgson had repeatedly denounced the rising wage levels in the construction industry. He had said Jan. 8 that although the Labor Department had a "hands-off policy" against specifying which wage increases were "justified," he was personally dissatisfied with the construction situation.

Hodgson voiced the possibility of legislation to end the "chaos" in the industry's mode of collective bargaining. He pointed out that the small size of the bargaining units enabled striking workers to hold out against their employers indefinitely since they were able to seek jobs in nearby towns during a strike. Concerning possible action in connection with the Davis-Bacon Act, Hodgson pointed out that wage levels were set by private industry bargaining and thus that modification or repeal of the act would have little effect.

President Nixon had met Jan. 18 with his Construction Industry Collective Bargaining Commission and had asked it to devise a plan within 30 days to "seriously modify the wage-price spiral" in the industry. Hodgson, chairman of the commission, said the President was waiving various legislative proposals to deal with the "crisis situation" in the industry in favor of allowing the industry to work out its own solution. Hodgson observed that construction labor contracts signed during the first nine months of 1970 had provided for first-year median wage increases of 15.7%, in contrast to only 8% for settlements in manufacturing. He also stressed that unemployment in the industry had risen to 11% from 5.6% in 1968.

Nixon warned at his news conference Feb. 17 that he would take steps against the industry unless labor and management adopted some form of voluntary wage and price restraints. The President's warning came at the end of the 30-day deadline he had given the industry to come up with a proposal for self-regulation to control spiraling wages and prices in their sector.

The President commented that it was essential for the government to use its power to create "reasonable" wage and price stability in the construction industry. He noted that the federal government would be spending $14 billion on construction during fiscal 1972.

The President's warning came as talks between the Administration and construction union leaders reached an impasse.

A statement issued Feb. 11 on behalf of the presidents of 17 national construction unions affiliated with the Building and Construction Trades Department of the AFL-CIO had said the unions declined to propose a voluntary wage plan. The union leaders said they would "vigorously oppose any proposal or procedure that would erode, restrict or endanger collective bargaining."

One reason the union leaders refused to comply with the President's request was a reluctance to endorse a plan that singled out their industry. Opposition to a wage program for only the construction industry was voiced in other quarters. AFL-CIO President George Meany said at a news conference Feb. 15 that he would only support wage and price controls that affected all sections of the population equitably.

House Banking Committee Chairman Wright Patman (D, Tex.) said that controls applied "on a single-shot basis aimed solely at the construction industry" would violate "the clear intention of Congress" in its legislation giving the President wage-price authority.

Following the union leaders' Feb. 11 statement, John T. Dunlop, chairman of the presidential Construction Industry Collective Bargaining Commission and a Harvard University dean, made two trips to Miami in an effort to work out an accord with the unions, contractors and government. According to press reports, Dunlop, at a breakfast meeting with union leaders Feb. 15, had centered the discussion on federal controls, particularly a possible "wage-price freeze." Dunlop reportedly explained that a freeze might be necessary for a limited period to enable the government to set up machinery to insure "orderly" wage increases.

Secretary Hodgson formally reported to the President Feb. 16 that the construction industry had failed to come up with a voluntary program. The President asked Hodgson to extend the Administration's efforts by flying to Florida where the AFL-CIO executive council was holding its mid winter meeting.

House Democratic leaders—Speaker Carl Albert (Okla.), Hale Boggs (La.) and Thomas P. O'Neill (Mass.)—had urged Nixon Feb. 10 to exercise his authority to freeze wages and prices immediately to curb inflation.

George Romney, secretary of housing and urban development, reported to Congress' Joint Economic Committee Feb. 17 that the average hourly earnings of construction workers rose 41% during the last five years, compared with 29% for all manufacturing employes and 31% for private, non-farm workers.

Nixon Feb. 23 suspended Davis-Bacon Act provisions that required contractors on federal or federally assisted construction projects to pay prevailing wage rates, in effect, union rates. Hodgson had reported to the President earlier Feb. 23 on the industry's rebuff to the Administration's extended effort to gain a voluntary, anti-inflationary formula from both sides.

The President's move drew immediate criticism from labor and management. William E. Dunn, executive director of the Associated General Contractors of America, called it "disappointing, inadequate and totally ineffective." It would "not help in any way " he said, "to stop the demand for huge wage increases with 1,368 construction agreements set to expire this year."

AFL-CIO President George Meany said the action would have no real effect on halting inflation and was "an open invitation to unscrupulous employers to exploit workers by competitive undermining of fair wages and labor standards." In a later statement, Meany said Nixon's action "attempts

to correct the national economic problem—mass unemployment in a period of inflation—brought about by the unwise monetary and fiscal policies of the President and his economic advisers, by penalizing a single segment of the working population."

"What America needs," Meany said, "is full employment at fair wages and decent conditions, not punitive action against workers."

The President suspended the wage provisions of the Davis-Bacon Act under authority in the measure to so act if an "emergency" existed in the industry. Nixon said wage settlements had been twice as high as in manufacturing generally.

The President said "wage rates on federal projects have been artificially set by the law rather than by customary market forces." "Frequently," he said, "they have been set to match the highest wages paid on private projects. This means that many of the most inflationary local wage settlements in the construction industry have automatically been sanctioned and spread through government contracts."

As for the building trades worker, the President said, he was "caught in a vicious cycle" with his pay rate going up but his job opportunities declining, which often led to demands for higher wages which in turn further reduced available employment. Nixon. said by acting as he did he hoped to "break this cycle, expand employment and improve the overall position of the construction worker."

In a related development, Treasury Secretary John B. Connally Jr. appeared before the House Banking and Currency Committee Feb. 23 to support extension of 1970 legislation granting the President stand-by authority to impose wage and price controls. The Administration would not invoke the controls, Connally said, "short of an all-out national emergency."

Transportation Secretary John A. Volpe warned Feb. 24 that suspension of the Davis-Bacon provision was only a "first step" and that imposition of wage-price controls was a possibility.

The Nixon Administration implemented the suspension of the Davis-Bacon Act with letters to the states informing them that it regarded state laws governing construction wages on federal projects no longer in effect because of the suspension. Sen. Edward M. Kennedy (D, Mass.) protested the Administration's position March 21.

A majority of states had their own Davis-Bacon version requiring payment of the area prevailing wage on federally-aided construction projects. Nixon had suspended the federal provision, thus opening such projects to non-union labor, as an anti-inflationary move to counter increases in construction wages.

The letters interpreting the federal suspension as binding on states regardless of whether they had similar laws were sent to federal agencies as well as each state, and could lead to construction delays wherever the federal and state laws conflicted. The Federal Highway Administration, for example, informed regional offices that future contracts for roadbuilding could not be approved if they contained prevailing wage provisions in conformance with a state law.

In his protest, Kennedy March 21 condemned the Administration's "heavy-handed policy of federal domination." In a letter March 22 to George P. Shultz, director of the Office of Management and Budget, Kennedy said it was "unthinkable to use the President's proclamation to impose a blanket cutoff of all federal construction funds for states that fail to bring their own laws into compliance with the proclamation. It is equally unthinkable to rely on the dubious legal doctrine of preemption as a justification for this severe sanction."

Unions join wage board—The presidents of the 17 union affiliates of the AFL-CIO Building and Construction Trades Department April 5 announced their agreement to participate in President Nixon's wage stabilization plan for the construction industry. The unions said they were reversing their decision to fight the plan because they could find no "reasonable" grounds for a legal battle.

The union statement also said four union leaders would accept appointment to the 12-member White House stabilization committee "to protect the interests

of their memberships." The appointments to the committee, representing labor, management and the public and set up to review recommendations of individual craft boards, were announced April 5 by Secretary of Labor James D. Hodgson. Named were Hunter P. Wharton, International Union of Operating Engineers; S. Frank Rafferty, International Brotherhood of Painters and Allied Trades; John H. Lyons, International Association of Bridge, Structural and Ornamental Iron Workers; and Charles H. Pillard, International Brotherhood of Electrical Workers.

John T. Dunlop, secretary of the Construction Industry Collective Bargaining Commission, was appointed to represent the public and serve as chairman of the committee. Other public members were Clarence D. Barker, a member of the Department of Labor Wage Appeals Board; Stuart Rothman, also a member of the wage appeals board and a Washington lawyer; and Albert Rees, a professor of economics and director of industrial relations at Princeton University. Representing management were: John E. Healy II, president of the Associated General Contractors of America; Robert L. Higgins, executive vice president of the National Electrical Contractors Association; George A. Miller, executive vice president of Mason Contractors Association of America; and John E. Quinn, executive vice president of National Constructors Association.

12% construction wage pact approved—The Construction Industry Stabilization Committee announced its approval May 14 of a contract settlement for a painter's union in Little Rock, Ark. that provided an average wage increase of 12% a year over three years. Labor Secretary Hodgson had noted when President Nixon appointed the committee that the President's criteria for noninflationary wage increases were based on the 1961-68 period and said that this would be about 6% a year.

Committee Chairman Dunlop said May 14 that his panel was not using a percentage figure as a guideline but basing the painter's decision primarily on another presidential criteria calling for "equity adjustments" to restore "traditional relationships among crafts in a single locality."

First-year wage increases averaged about 17% in the construction industry in 1970.

Hodgson said May 17 the committee had approved 10–12 contract agreements in the industry thus far (the May 14 decision was its first formal opinion issued) and that while the wage increases ranged up to 13%, most were "clustered" in the 6%–9% area.

He said he considered it impossible, at least until 1973, to hold annual wage rises in the industry as low as 6%, and he stressed that the 6% "criterion" was only one of the critera in the presidential directive. He said the stabilization program for the industry had been "quite successful so far."

The Labor Department June 16 disclosed figures showing a sharp reduction of wage settlements in the construction industry since the government stabilization program went into effect. The report said the Construction Industry Stabilization Committee had approved 37 new contracts whose increases ranged from 5% to 9%. In 1970, increases had averaged about 18%.

Secretary of Housing and Urban Development George Romney June 25 announced proposed regulations to curb prices and management pay in the construction industry. The proposals of a panel headed by Romney, the Interagency Committee on Construction, would tie price and white-collar pay boosts to wage increases in contracts approved by the Construction Industry Stabilization Committee. The price controls would apply only in cases in which the wage panel had rejected a negotiated wage and fringe benefit increase.

■ I. W. Abel, president of the United Steel Workers of America, said March 30 that the 1.2 million member union would refuse to accept any wage limit similar to that imposed on construction bargaining. Abel, who held a news conference following a two-day meeting with the Basic Steel Industry Conference, said his talks with the 600 local presidents had persuaded him that the membership would reject any contract from the steel industry that was less than the settlement obtained from the can industry.

Burns opposes credit control change. Federal Reserve Board (FRB) Chairman Arthur F. Burns, in testimony before a Senate Banking subcommittee March 31, said the board's governors unanimously opposed strengthening their control over interest rates on bank deposits as a means of meeting social priorities. Burns spoke before the Subcommittee on Financial Institutions, which held hearings March 31, April 1 and 7 on bills (S1201, HR 4246) to extend for two years the government's authority to regulate bank interest rates, credit flow, and wages and prices.

The main thrust of Burns' testimony was directed at a proposal by the subcommittee chairman, Sen. William Proxmire (D, Wis.), to permit the seven-man board to apply variable reserve requirements against different types of bank assets (loans and investments) in order to more directly influence the flow of credit. The proposal, in the form of a rider to the Senate bill under discussion, would expand the power of the FRB, which could only set reserve requirements against bank deposits, or liabilities, by giving the board leeway to manipulate reserve requirements in a way to influence banks to favor certain borrowers. Thus, requirements could be lowered in one credit sector needing help, while raised in another to cool an inflationary situation.

In an opening statement to the hearing, Proxmire asserted that the Federal Reserve was the only major central bank which had refused to assume responsibility for allocating credit to socially important sectors of the economy. He said that under conditions of general restraint, market conditions did not distribute credit evenly or according to the public interest. As an example, he noted that the housing industry, representing only 3% of the total gross national product (GNP), bore 60%–70% of the credit curbs imposed by the FRB in 1969.

Burns countered that he opposed variable reserve requirements both on grounds of principle and practicality. He argued that the board was not equipped to determine social priorities and warned against putting the FRB "in the political arena in a big way," observing that European central banks had been "subverted to political ends" in their credit-allocating efforts.

Burns pointed out that operational difficulties were inherent in the Proxmire proposal. It would be difficult to administer and would complicate open market operations. It would also act as an incentive for more commercial banks to leave the Federal Reserve System in order to escape the additional controls. Already faced with declining membership, further declines would reduce the effectiveness of any reserve requirement changes, the chairman said.

Burns conceded there was sentiment in the Federal Reserve for some form of authority for a "supplemental reserve" requirement. It was well known that the basic idea of the Proxmire proposal had originated in an April 1970 speech by board member Andrew F. Brimmer. Brimmer apparently shared the rest of the board's concern over the proposal until it had been studied further.

As an alternative to the Proxmire rider, Burns suggested that other federal credit agencies be expanded in scope to help cushion monetary restraints in particular sectors of the economy.

Most of the additional testimony at the hearings revolved around the question of time limits to be imposed on Presidential authority over wages and prices. Proxmire and Burns favored tight limits, but Undersecretary of the Treasury Charls E. Walker asked Congress to be lenient in its time limit curbs. Burns favored a six-month cutoff of wage-price controls without specific Congressional authorization. Walker testified that the overall two-year extension was in the public interest "because of its applicability to specific industries."

Meany criticism—At the hearings April 7, AFL-CIO President George Meany delivered a scathing attack on the economic policies of the Nixon Administration and on FRB Chairman Burns. Meany said the time had come for the Administration to halt its misguided "game plans" and put an end to its double standard—one for workers, and one for banks and big business—in favor of more equitable policies.

He said: "Chairman Arthur Burns . . . and much of the Administration's leadership have been engaged in the shocking and blatant use of a double standard. To cover their record of failure in economic policy . . . they try to pin the blame on workers while providing subsidies and aid for the banks and big business."

Meany criticized the Administration's action against the construction industry workers because it gave "only a vague promise" of future construction price and profit curbs and made no mention of increasing land and financing costs. He said the AFL-CIO was still willing to cooperate with wage and price controls deemed necessary by the President if they were applied across the board to all industries and all kinds of income. Singling out one group of workers for wage restraints, he said, when prices of their food, clothing and other goods and services were free to rise "smacks of punitive action rather than a stabilization policy." Meany added that additional taxes on profits, dividends and capital gains should be imposed to round out any wage curbs.

Meany supported the Proxmire rider for supplemental and variable bank reserve requirements.

FRB vote on money supply. The Federal Reserve Board's Open Market Committee, at its meeting Jan. 12, voted 10–1 to further ease monetary policy into the first quarter in order to compensate for a money supply shortfall in the final quarter of 1970.

The directive to "promote accommodative conditions in credit markets and moderate expansion in monetary and credit aggregates" was made public April 12, allowing for the customary 90-day-period between the committee's meetings and publication of its directives.

Although the committee did not designate a target growth rate for the money supply (total currency in circulation plus demand deposits in banks), it said an annual growth rate of about 7.5% would be needed to make up for the 3.4% annual rate of the fourth quarter. Preliminary figures subsequently released in April indicated that the money supply actually expanded at about an 8.6% annual rate in the first period.

The lone dissenter on the 12-man committee was Darryl R. Francis, president of the Federal Reserve Bank of St. Louis, who argued for maintaining a 5% annual growth rate in order to produce "better" long-run performances in production and prices.

6% air fare hike. The Civil Aeronautics Board (CAB) April 12 authorized a 6% increase in domestic air fares as the first step of a tentatively approved 9% boost. The increase could provide $115 million—$400 million annually to the financially depressed industry in which six of the 11 major domestic carriers reported losses in 1970.

The authorization marked a two-fold break with past procedures by (1) requiring carriers to fill a certain percentage of their seating capacity and (2) setting the new fares as ceilings, permitting a new flexibility that could lead to price competition.

The board warned the airlines to continue excess cost and seating capacity reductions.

The industry had requested a 12%–24% increase. Industry leaders expressed doubts that fare increases alone could restore profits.

Two members of the five-man board dissented, G. Joseph Minetti and Robert T. Murphy, both Democrats. They said the increase was excessive and might drive away new passengers.

Third inflation alert. The Nixon Administration's third inflation alert, issued by the President's Council of Economic Advisers (CEA) April 13, warned the steel industry against exacerbating its competitive position by excessive wage or price increases.

It was the first alert to focus on future, rather than past, wage and price decisions, although the carefully worded statement did not make any threats or specify particular actions that the government might take. The two-part report also reviewed general wage and price developments and examined the freight transportation, New York taxicab, lumber, construction and meat industries.

The report was released with an eye to the forthcoming labor negotiations with the aluminum, copper and steel companies and the 13% first year wage increase already won by the steel workers from the can industry.

At a White House briefing, the CEA chairman, Paul W. McCracken, warned that extension of the can industry settlement, described as "excessive" in terms of long-term growth potential, to basic producers would impel the industry into "some combination" of three possible consequences: more inflation, added unemployment or further attempts by foreign competitors to "isolate or insulate" U.S. steel producers. Cheaper foreign steel imports would increase in the form of other finished products, causing unemployment in those related industries unless the steel industry was forced to meet "the full consequences of a deteriorating position in international competition," the report said.

The statement was an apparent reference to the expiration at the end of 1971 of voluntary steel import quotas and was interpreted as a hint that the Administration might loosen those import limits.

The CEA report cautioned the steel companies to keep down their prices for the sake of "long-term interests." The report noted that the companies could have "considerable discretionary pricing power" in view of the current high demand for steel in anticipation of a summer strike.

On the economy in general, the report said the rise in prices had been "distinctly more moderate" since the second alert in December 1970, but wage increases had not exhibited a comparable slackening. McCracken cited retail sales of autos and other goods [see below] as "some evidence that the pulsebeat of the economy is quickening" at the end of the quarter, but acknowledged it would "take a little time" before the improvement was translated into reduced unemployment. On balance, he said, "we have arrested the acceleration of inflation."

Among inflationary developments affecting other industries:

■ In anticipation of possible boosts in oil prices to counter oil tax and price increases negotiated in the Middle East and Venezuela, the report said those developments "should have no necessary effect on most U.S. petroleum prices."

■ The CEA would continue to consider "gradual deregulation" of the rail and truck industries to permit more competition. The report said freight rate increases far surpassed general increases in wholesale prices.

■ Rising lumber and plywood prices reflected heavy demand because of high 1971 housing starts forecasts, but further increases should be curbed.

■ McCracken explained that the 48% fare increase of the New York taxicab industry was cited as an example of "severe restriction on supply" in a regulated industry where the number of cabs had not been increased since 1937.

■ The report took note of the Administration's action in March to suspend quotas on meat imports as a means to moderate retail prices on meat. The report did not comment on the 6% domestic air fare hike authorized by the Civil Aeronautics Board April 13.

Reaction—I. W. Abel, president of the United Steelworkers of America, countered in Pittsburgh April 13 with a stinging indictment of the Administration's economic policies and a pledge for an "equitable settlement" in upcoming labor talks. The labor leader's statement said: "The average worker today is on the short end of the economic stick because of the disastrous economic policies of the present administration, which have given us both inflation and unemployment." Abel said the steelworker had been the victim, not the cause, of inflation.

In New York, where aluminum industry labor negotiations opened April 13, chief steelworker negotiator M. C. Weston Jr. said the union would press for an even higher settlement than the new three-year contract with the can industry.

AFL-CIO President George Meany, in a speech to the AFL-CIO Utility Workers Union of America April 14, supported the steelworkers. He denounced the inflation alert as a signal of a possible compulsory steel industry settlement. Meany said the steel labor union would demand a high wage increase to match the 16% drain on the

workers's purchasing power during the past three years of inflation.

R. Heath Larry, a vice chairman of the U.S. Steel Corp. and head of the bargaining team representing management, welcomed the CEA report. Larry said workers would not benefit from any union efforts to "follow or beat the last leader in the wage-inflation race," because of adverse business conditions in the industry, i.e. "very depressed profits and ... a serious cost disadvantage as compared with its lower-wage foreign competitors."

Chase raises prime rate to 5.5%. Chase Manhattan Bank in New York April 22 raised its prime (minimum) interest rate from 5.25% to 5.5%. Most of the nation's largest banks followed Chase's lead.

Chase announced it was taking the step to align the prime rate with rising short-term rates.

The increase was the first in the basic lending rate since June 1969. In the interim period, the prime rate had been cut in 10 successive steps from 8.5% to 5.25%.

Bankers said the key factor behind rising interest rates was a temperate firming of easy money policy in response to pressures on the dollar in foreign exchange markets and dollar outflows to foreign central banks.

Administration reaction to the banks' action was confusing. The afternoon following the Chase announcement, Treasury Secretary John B. Connally Jr. expressed disappointment and his opinion that loan demand did not justify the increase. Meanwhile, the President's Council of Economic Advisers formally stated that the change was consistent with interest rate developments and did not signal any trend in the "general structure of interest rates."

Nixon urges confidence in system. President Nixon spoke out April 26 for a sense of public confidence in the nation's future. Addressing some 3,000 businessmen attending a meeting in Washington of the U.S. Chamber of Commerce, the President put special emphasis on the need to have confidence that the free enterprise system would be maintained and not "dismantled and replaced by a system of bureaucratic controls."

The commitment to a "free economy" was under attack, he said, as was another of the basic American "principles"—the commitment to defend freedom "around the world."

Nixon told the businessmen some of the things they had "a right to be confident about"—"this nation will reject the counsel of the new isolationists," the U.S. would use its strength to build peace, the economy would continue its "vigorous" expansion without inflation, the private enterprise system would be preserved, the "dignity of work" would be preserved and not replaced by "the indignity of welfare," and the old American value of compassion for the dependent was not going to change.

In making these points, Nixon stressed that U.S. involvement in the war in Indochina was "ending" and that the U.S. goal was "total withdrawal" and "in a way that will assure the return of our prisoners of war and will give the South Vietnamese a chance to prevent a Communist takeover."

On the economy, the President asserted that "we are winning the fight against rising prices" and "the worst of inflation is behind us." "We are on our way to a period of solid, sustainable expansion—the kind of expansion the nation needs to provide new jobs for workingmen and new opportunities for businessmen," he said.

He cautioned against slipping back "into the bad habits of the past" and said government, labor and management must "keep their houses in order" —government "with a budget that does not exceed full-employment balance" and labor and management with "wage increases based primarily on increases in productivity and price increases kept to the absolute minimum."

There would be times "when economic freedom must be protected from its own excesses," he said, and he would continue to use his authority "to persuade business and labor to act responsibly in making further progress against inflation."

Nixon assured his audience "that the road to full employment with price stability . . . will be the road of free markets, free competition, free bargaining, free men." He would not cease to be amazed at those "who cry 'repression of freedom' at the drop of a hat but who, in the next breath, advocate total repression of the economic freedom of businessmen and workingmen."

Connally encourages investment—Treasury Secretary John B. Connally Jr. appeared before the Chamber of Commerce meeting April 27 to encourage the business executives not to postpone investments in new equipment. He assured them that his department's proposal to reduce business taxes by some $3 billion a year would go into effect as scheduled, retroactive to the beginning of 1971. The proposal, to permit tax deductions for depreciation of equipment to be taken over a 20% shorter time than permitted currently, had been attacked by prominent Democrats as a "giveaway" to business. Connally dismissed the criticism as arising from "political considerations."

The critics questioned whether the proposal would help the economy, with current plant equipment standing idle, whether business should receive tax relief while vital government programs suffered from underfunding, and whether it was legal because of the disparity between the periods during which the equipment was being used and for which the depreciation would be allowed.

The question of whether the proposal also infringed on Congressional tax-writing power was raised by Senate Democratic Leader Mike Mansfield (Mont.) April 23. He asked the Democrats on the Senate Finance Committee to find an answer.

Questions on domestic affairs. The majority of questions at President Nixon's domestic news conference May 1 concerned the economy and related topics.

Among Nixon's remarks:

"We are in the midst of a strong economic upturn." His Administration was achieving a strong economy, one that was prosperous, "but without having it at the cost of war." When the economy was "not moving as well as it should," he would take action, "on the tax front and other fronts," to stimulate it. Nixon did not think calling a national conference on unemployment was necessary. While there "may be zigs and zags" in the jobless rate, he believed "that what we are doing has now checked the rise in unemployment." (House Speaker Carl Albert [D, Okla.] had proposed April 29 a national conference on unemployment and inflation. A resolution embodying the proposal was introduced in the House by Rep. Carl D. Perkins [D, Ky.].)

Unemployment and inflation were the "two dangers," however, on the economic front. And inflation must be fought particularly on "the wage-price front" and "the government front." Wage-price decisions, he stressed, must be responsible. Referring to the upcoming steel negotiations, Nixon cited the declining share of world steel produced in the U.S. and the domestic industry's low profits "from a competitive standpoint." He cautioned that "a wage-price settlement must reflect the competitive realities in the world" or the domestic steel industry would find itself "noncompetitive in the world."

Nixon stressed the need to keep federal expenditures from exceeding "full employment revenues" and for him, "on occasion, perhaps, to veto those irresponsible spending proposals" from Congress.

He said he believed that "the long-term effect" of his policies would be to bring unemployment down. He tied the high unemployment rates in California and Washington state to "the change in defense spending" and the country's "turn from a wartime to peacetime economy." The entire West Coast, Nixon said, "has been highly dependent upon defense contracts and also on aerospace industry" and he promised that California and the Pacific Northwest will get special consideration.

A question about the business tax depreciation change was asked in relation to criticism from Sen. Edmund S. Muskie (D, Me.). Muskie had questioned whether the Administration had the authority to order the changes as planned. Nixon replied that he would "never comment on any political comments that are made in a conference that I hold as president of the United States." He conceded that there was a difference of opinion among lawyers within the

Administration as to presidential authority on the matter, but he had "practiced a good deal of tax law" himself and had decided it was "the correct legal view and the right view from the standpoint of the country" to order the depreciation allowances. It was "vitally important," he stressed, "to move this economy from a wartime to a peacetime basis" and incentives must be provided "for business to write off faster on a depreciation basis those kinds of expense that appropriately can be written off and that mean more jobs."

"Now any senator," he continued, "or any critic who wants to oppose a program that's going to mean more jobs for Americans—peacetime jobs, rather than wartime jobs—has a right to take that position. I don't agree with him."

Nixon pledges aid to farmers. President Nixon addressed himself to the problems of farmers in a radio talk May 2. Deploring the "perennially troublesome cost-price squeeze" on farmers, the President announced a number of federal initiatives to help the farmer reap more income from the "surging vitality of our agriculture."

Despite an anticipated higher total income for farmers in 1971 "than ever before in our history," he said, the farmer was confronted with "the fact that increases in total income are not always reflected in more net income" because of "the high cost of farming."

The President assured the farmers that definite progress was being made against inflation. He asserted that "the brightest future for agriculture lies in actions that stimulate new energy in the market system."

Nixon noted that farm exports were at their highest level and said, to aid that expansion, $1 million would be added to the $28.7 million funding for fiscal 1972 for the Foreign Agricultural Service.

1970 farm subsidy payments. Federal farm subsidy payments in 1970 totaled $3.7 billion, the Agriculture Department reported April 8. Of the total, 45.5% went to 137,000 farmers in payments of $5,000 or more; the remainder went to about 2.3 million smaller operators for acreage reductions and price supports.

Subsidy payments of $1 million or more were paid to nine large operators, the largest going to J. G. Boswell Co. of Corcoran, Calif., a cotton producer, which received $4.4 million, and to Giffen, Inc. of Huron, Calif., which received $4.1 million.

Of the nine producers receiving $1 million, six were in California and received a total of $14.4 million. Six other California growers were among the 14 receiving payments of from $500,000 to $1 million. The other farms receiving the largest subsidy payments were in Hawaii (4), Arizona (3), Florida (2), Mississippi and Montana.

Among those receiving $5,000 or more in farm subsidies were five members of Congress and close relatives of several members. The largest such payment went to Sen. James O. Eastland (D, Miss.), a senior member of the Senate Agriculture and Forestry Committee, whose plantation in Mississippi received $164,048, mostly in cotton price-support payments.

Only six of the 23 growers receiving more than $500,000 would be eligible for such large subsidies in 1971 because of the 1970 farm legislation limiting individual growers to subsidies of $55,000 for each crop of wheat, feed grain or cotton. The six not affected were sugar producers, who were not covered by the new legislation.

Wage-price control law extended. A bill extending the president's discretionary authority to impose wage and price controls through April 30, 1972, was approved by 67–4 Senate vote May 3 and House voice vote May 5. The authority would have expired June 1. President Nixon signed the bill May 18 and a spokesman reaffirmed the President's opposition to invoking the authority.

Wage-price board urged, inflation's toll assessed. Sen. William E. Brock (R, Tenn.) May 26 introduced a bill to establish a National Emergency Wage-Price Stabilization Board. He indicated the "heavy toll" that "inflation is taking on all Americans":

Workers in industry have been barely able to keep even despite fatter pay checks. Since 1965, when the inflationary spiral started shooting up, the average weekly wage has risen $29 while inflation has whittled the real gain down to $2.72.

Retired people on fixed incomes have been hard hit by rising expenses of housing, medical care, and other goods and services.

Young people, especially the newly married, find they are priced out of the market for single family homes. Many are forced to turn to small apartment units or to mobile homes.

Businessmen find profit margins shrinking. Efforts to control costs and boost productivity often lead to strikes or other labor difficulties.

And finally, homeowners are pinched by climbing property taxes, soaring costs of maintenance and service items.

A contributing factor in the dollar crises abroad has been our domestic inflation. Inflation has raised the price of our exports and made them less competitive. We have ended up with a balance-of-payments deficit and an excess of dollars abroad.

Brock urged Congress to help fight inflation by spending less:

First, on the list of measures that I feel are essential in the fight against inflation is fiscal responsibility. The Joint Congressional Committee on Reduction of Federal Expenditures reported that as of May 6, 1971, Congress has increased estimated outlays for fiscal 1971 and 1972 by about $610 million and $1,370 million, respectively, and has decreased estimated receipts for these 2 fiscal years by $157 million, and $2,657 million, respectively. The cumulative effect of congressional actions to date on outlays and revenues is to increase the estimated unified budget deficit for fiscal 1971 by $768 million to $19.3 billion and the estimated unified budget deficit for fiscal 1972 by $4,027 million to $15.7 billion. Most completed congressional actions directly affecting outlays and receipts affect outlays and receipts for the trust funds in which there is a projected surplus, so the projected deficits of $25.5 billion for fiscal 1971 and $23.1 billion for fiscal 1972 in Federal funds are not materially affected. These figures are very disturbing and point up the need for Congress to exercise greater restraint in authorizing Federal spending if we are ever to curb inflation.

Court refuses to bar mail hikes. Temporary postal rate increases went into effect May 16 after the federal courts rejected efforts by publishers and others to bar them.

The rate increases were 20%–33% for second-class and third-class mail, to 8¢ an ounce for first-class letters (formerly 6¢), to 11¢ an ounce for airmail letters (formerly 10¢) and to 6¢ for postcards (formerly 5¢).

Mohawk pilots get 21% raise. Arbitrator David L. Cole awarded pay increases averaging 21% over a three-year period to Mohawk Airline pilots May 14. Binding arbitration had been agreed upon March 19 to end a five-month strike. Pay for senior jet captains was to rise from $31,500 a year to $38,220 in 1973; wages of senior turbo-prop captains would go from $24,600 to $29,724.

Legislation ends rail strike. A two-day rail strike that virtually halted rail service on a national scale ended after enactment of emergency legislation May 18 providing more time for negotiations and an interim pay rise of 13½% for the strikers.

The strike, by 13,000 members of the AFL-CIO Brotherhood of Railroad Signalmen (BRS), began at 6:01 a.m. May 17 and effectively closed down rail operations by noon as other rail union members respected the signalmen's picket lines at commuter and intercity rail terminals. The major exceptions were the Long Island Railroad in New York and the South Shore Line in Chicago. Some 500,000 rail workers remained away from work.

A request for emergency legislation to end the strike was sent to Congress later in the day. Congress had worked out its own version by 9 p.m. May 18, President Nixon signed it shortly before 11 p.m. and BRS leader C. J. Chamberlain at 11 p.m. ordered picket lines removed. Restoration of service began immediately.

Negotiations with signalmen, who represented about 2% of rail workers, had been in progress for 19 months and the signalmen had been working without a contract since Jan. 1. The impasse had drawn Presidential intervention previously in March, when a strike had been threatened but a 60-day cooling off period had been imposed under the Railway Labor Act. This restriction expired May 15.

The signalmen were seeking to raise their $3.78 hourly wage by 54% over 36 months, retroactive to Jan. 1. They had rejected the recommendation of a Presidential emergency board for a 43% rise over 42 months, which was acceptable to the railroads and the pattern accepted May 13 by the rail engineers.

The signalmen cited their skilled-work status, low comparative wage base and the fact that their last wage increase had been a 3% boost in July 1969.

President Nixon's proposal May 17 was for a cooling-off period without a strike or lock-out extending to July 1 for continued negotiations. He also reminded Congress of his year-old proposal for stand-by emergency powers to intervene in major transportation labor disputes.

In the Senate, a substitute proposal by Sen. Jacob K. Javits (R, N.Y.) for a truce period to Oct. 1 and a 17½% wage rise gained favor. In the House, a truce to July 20 and a 13½% pay hike were considered, with House Interstate and Foreign Commerce Committee Chairman Harley O. Staggers (D, W. Va.) contending that the strikers should not gain more than the 13½% pay boost provided by Congress in 1970 to other rail unions in a similar situation. Three of four unions involved then in the dispute later signed pacts containing an additional 4% wage increase. The fourth union involved, the 160,000-member United Transportation Union (UTU), had not signed and thus had received only the 13½% hike. Staggers said it would be inequitable to give the striking signalmen 4% more than the UTU members.

The compromise, for the cooling-off period until Oct. 1 and the 13½% pay raise, was effected on the floor of each chamber to avoid a time-consuming joint conference.

Rail engineers' pact. An agreement on wages and work rules between the railroads and the Brotherhood of Locomotive Engineers was announced May 13. The new contract, covering from Jan. 1, 1970 through June 30, 1973, would provide a wage increase of about 42% over the 42-month period for the 38,000 engineers, whose pre-pact wage average was $12,000–$15,000 a year.

The work-rules reform agreed upon could not be carried out unless other operating employes went along with the changes.

Aluminum pacts provide 31% raise. Agreement was reached May 31 between the AFL-CIO United Steelworkers of America (USW) and four major aluminum companies on new three-year contracts that would provide wage increases of about 31% over the three-year period. The White House reported President Nixon was displeased over the size of the settlement.

One of the companies, the Aluminum Company of America (Alcoa), immediately announced it would raise the price of "nearly" all its fabricated products by an average of 6%, effective Sept. 1, as a result of the new contract and "the rising spiral" of costs of materials and services.

The aluminum settlement followed the pattern set by the USW in the can industry, which the Nixon Administration, in its April inflation alert, had found "excessive." It had warned against adoption of the pattern in the upcoming USW negotiations with aluminum, copper and steel industries.

White House Press Secretary Ronald L. Ziegler said June 1 that President Nixon was "disappointed" in the wage and price increases and would deplore further extension of the pattern, especially to the basic steel industry. Ziegler said Nixon felt that the aluminum pacts were "part of a pattern that must be broken to regain reasonable wage and price stability."

But Ziegler indicated that the Administration was not considering any restrictive action. It preferred not to interfere with the "free bargaining process," he said. "About all we can do at this time is to express a point of view."

The USW's aluminum contracts expired May 31. With Alcoa, the union represented 11,000 workers at nine plants. Other settlements also were reached May 31 with Kaiser Aluminum and Chemical Corp. (10,500 USW workers), Reynolds Metal Co. (8,700 workers) and Ormet Aluminum Co. (2,200 employes).

Similar contracts covering another 10,000 employes also were agreed upon May 31 by Alcoa and the Aluminum Workers International Union and two independent aluminum trade councils.

The new pacts' wage hikes included base wage increases ranging from 75¢ to $1.09 an hour over three years. The average hourly pay would rise from $3.67 to $4.22 in the first year. In addition, the union members were guaranteed cost-of-living increases totaling 25¢ an hour—12½¢ the second year and again in the third year of the contract. Additional increases were to be provided if the Consumer Price Index rose above the guarantee, the cost-of-living formula based on 1¢-an-hour wage rise for each .4 rise in the index.

Other features of the new pacts were vacation bonuses of from $30 to $50, a 38% increase in monthly pension payments (an employe with 30 years of service would get $270 a month) and a 25¢-an-hour pay differential for weekend work.

Telephone workers strike. About 532,-000 telephone workers walked off their jobs across the nation July 14 in a strike against companies of the Bell Telephone System (including two divisions of the Western Electric Co.) after a new contract offer was rejected by union leaders. Many other nonstriking workers honored picket lines and stayed off the job. Phone service was relatively unaffected as supervisory personnel took over the largely automated service.

The strike, called by Bell's largest union, the Communication Workers of America (CWA), was joined by the International Brotherhood of Electrical Workers (IBEW) in New Jersey and two large independent unions in Connecticut and Pennsylvania. CWA members across the nation had voted in May and June to authorize the strike. Their contracts had begun expiring April 30 and were extended on a daily basis until July 14.

After a contract agreement was reached between the CWA and the American Telephone & Telegraph Co., parent firm of the Bell System, July 20, CWA President Joseph A. Beirne ordered the members back to work. However, the labor picture remained confused as 80,-

000–90,000 workers resumed the strike July 21 after some local CWA leaders rejected the settlement.

In annoucing the tentative settlement at a Washington press conference July 19, Beirne said the total wage-benefit package amounted to more than a 33.5% increase. (AT&T announced a different figure of 31%.)

Beirne said basic wages, including cost-of-living increases, would rise about 29.5% over the life of agreement, beginning with a first-year increase of 12.8%. Other terms included unlimited additional pay for each increase in the Consumer Price Index (CPI), a big cities allowance of $5–$9 in extra weekly pay to compensate for higher costs of living, a "modified agency shop" requiring all employes on the job for 30 days to pay union dues, a reduction of "wage inequities" between male and female workers (one of the key issues originally blocking an accord), as well as improved pensions, health insurance, holidays and work schedules. Beirne said the contract would cost Bell about $4 billion.

Meanwhile July 21, the New Jersey Bell Telephone Co. reached tentative agreement on a new contract with the 12,000-member Telephone Workers Union of New Jersey, which included both CWA and IBEW members. The terms of the three-year, $48 million contract were nearly identical with those in the CWA contract.

In Philadelphia, the Pennsylvania Telephone Guild, an independent union representing some 2,660 employes of the Bell Telephone Co. of Pennsylvania, also agreed July 21 to a new three-year contract that provided for an immediate 12.3% pay increase. The increase was retroactive to May 9 when the old contract expired.

Brimmer on taxes. Andrew F. Brimmer, a member of the Federal Reserve Board, warned that more taxes might be needed to avoid a "serious deterioration" in public services at the state and local levels. Speaking at commencement exercises of Middlebury College in Middlebury, Vt. May 30, Brimmer conceded that higher taxes could result in more inflation and less economic growth but concluded that the cost was "worth paying."

Brimmer said the 1969 Tax Reform Act had given private consumption "a much higher priority over public spending than is consistent with our long-run requirements in the area of public service."

Brimmer said inflation had been the chief cause in 1955–1969 for increased spending by state and local governments which more than tripled from $39 billion to $132 billion. Inflation had accounted for more than 40% of that increase, he said.

Price indexes continue up. The Labor Department reported April 21 that consumer prices continued to rise at a moderate pace in March, increasing at a seasonally adjusted annual rate of 2.4%, and 2.7% for the first quarter. It was the slowest rate of increase for any quarter since the 1.7% of the first period of 1967.

The consumer price index rose .2% (seasonally adjusted) and .3% (unadjusted) in March to 119.8% of the 1967 average, standing 4.6% above a year earlier.

The report said more than two-thirds of the CPI increase was attributable to higher food prices, which climbed 1.1% in their sharpest monthly increase since late 1969. A substantial decline in mortgage interest rates lowered the CPI by about .2 percentage points. (A Federal Home Loan Bank Board report said mortgage interest rates in March dropped .25% to an average 7.66% nationwide. It was the lowest rate since May 1969.)

The Administration and one of its severest critics, Sen. William Proxmire (D, Wis.), hailed the report. Proxmire said: "This is the most encouraging indication in many months that the President's program of inflation control is beginning to work."

The Labor Department reported May 21 that consumer prices continued to rise moderately in April, increasing at a seasonally adjusted annual rate of 3.6%. Although it was the largest rise in three months, the consumer price index maintained the steady moderate pace of the previous three months, indicating some progress against inflation.

The index rose .3%, on both an adjusted and unadjusted basis, to 120.2%

of the 1967 average, standing 4.3% above a year earlier. It was the smallest year-to-year increase since August 1968.

The report said about three-fourths of the CPI increase was attributable to higher prices for food, apparel and used cars.

The report was greeted enthusiastically by President Nixon and other members of the Administration. However, their jubilation was dampened by news of a 2% drop in new durable goods orders, a leading economic indicator.

The Labor Department reported June 21 that consumer prices in May rose doubly as fast as in the first four months of the year. The CPI increased at a seasonally adjusted annual rate of 7.2%, the highest rate in 15 months. It rose .5%, on an unadjusted basis, and .6%, adjusted, to 120.8% of the 1967 average, standing 4.4% above a year earlier. A spokesman for the Council of Economic Advisers said the large and broad price increases in May were "disappointing." The report attributed half the increase to higher prices of apparel, used cars, homes and postage.

Wholesale prices continued to rise in March, but at a more moderate pace, the Labor Department reported April 1. The wholesale price index rose a seasonally adjusted .3% (and .2% on an unadjusted basis). The increase placed the index at 113% of the 1967 average, 2.8% above a year earlier. The slackened rate of increase was ascribed to sharp decline in the volatile farm produce category, which fell an adjusted .8% after climbing 4.1% in February.

The industrial commodities index, a key indicator of overall price trends and excess demand, rose a slim .2% (seasonally adjusted), mostly "due to price increases for commodities used in construction." The report said that for the first three months of 1971 the index rose at a mere 2.4% annual rate, seasonally adjusted.

At the Western White House in San Clemente, Labor Secretary Hodgson commented that wholesale and consumer price figures over the past two months were a "cumulative indication that our anti-inflationary fight is taking hold." He said the March wholesale price figure confirmed the Administration's view that the .7% increase in February was caused by "nonrecurring factors," particularly farm prices.

Wholesale prices continued to rise in April, accelerating for the third time in four months, the Labor Department reported May 6.

The wholesale price index rose a seasonally adjusted .4% (.3% on an unadjusted basis). The increase placed the index at 113.3% of the 1967 average, 3.1% above a year earlier.

The acceleration was ascribed to higher prices for industrial commodities measured by the key industrial-commodity index. The index climbed an adjusted .5% after a .3% increase in March. Nearly half the rise in industrial prices was attributed to higher prices of metals and metal products.

The Labor Department reported June 4 that wholesale prices had risen .3% (seasonally adjusted) in May.

The wholesale price index rose .4% on an unadjusted basis to 113.8% of the 1967 average, 3.4% above a year earlier. The report said that in the past six months the annual rate of increase was 4.3%, higher than any six-month period since that ending March 1970.

Productivity gain. The Labor Department said April 23 that productivity, rebounding from a sluggish two-year trend, rose sharply in the first quarter of 1971.

Productivity, or output per man hour, climbed at an annual rate of 5.3% for the entire private economy, 5.9% for the nonfarm economy and 8.7% in manufacturing. The Labor Department's figures reflected a sizable rise in production following the automobile strike.

GNP revised upward. The nation's Gross National Product for the first quarter of 1971 was revised upward to an annual rate of $1,020 billion, the Commerce Department reported May 13.

The nation's total output climbed a record $30.8 billion in the first quarter, $2.33 billion higher than previously estimated. The 13.1% dollar increase was the largest in 13 years.

Real GNP (expressed in constant 1957– 59 dollars), measuring physical output corrected for inflation, rose at a 7% annual rate to $732.7 billion, $1.1 billion higher than the original estimate.

The price index (the "deflator"), considered the best measure of inflation in the economy, exhibited a faster rate of inflation for the quarter, with a 5.6% annual rate, compared with the earlier estimate of 5.2%.

Most of the output gain was in the automobile-related sector, which accounted for $19.6 billion of the $30.8 billion gain.

Along with the GNP figures, the Commerce Department said that corporate pre-tax profits rose by $10.1 billion in the first quarter to an annual rate of $86.4 billion. The figure was higher than any quarter in 1970, but still fell below 1969 rates. Corporate earnings after taxes rose from an annual rate of $41.4 billion in 1970's fourth quarter to $47.5 billion. The profit figures were dominated by the car industry's recovery after the GM strike.

1970 family income unchanged. The median income of the average U.S. family failed to rise in 1970 for the first time in nine years because of inflation, the Census Bureau reported in its annual population survey May 20. The median income actually rose 4.7% ($440) to a total $9,870, but was offset by a 1.2% loss in purchasing power because of the 5.9% increase in consumer prices in 1970.

The survey was based on a sample of 50,000 persons.

1970 was a recession year. A set of charts issued July 2 by the Commerce Department in its publication, Business Conditions Digest, officially designated the period November 1969-November 1970 a recession year.

Unemployment rise resumes. The unemployment rate reverted to the January level of 6%, seasonally adjusted, after a two-month decline, according to a Labor Department report April 2. Total employment contracted to a seasonally adjusted 78,475,000 persons from 78,-537,000.

On a seasonally adjusted basis, total March unemployment climbed to 5 million from 4,847,000 in February. Before seasonal adjustment, unemployment declined from 5,442,000 to 5,175,000.

Most of the March increase was concentrated among persons 16-24, many of whom were new entrants or reentrants to the labor force. Jobless rates for other major labor force groups were mostly unchanged. However, the jobless rate for white-collar professional and technical workers reached 3.4%, the highest level since the statistic was first reported in 1958: the figure apparently mirrored the economic situation in the aerospace and defense industries.

The jobless rate for the first quarter of 1971 stood unchanged from the 5.9% level of 1970's fourth quarter.

Geoffrey H. Moore, commissioner of labor statistics, and two professional employment analysts from the Bureau of Labor Statistics appeared before the Joint Economic Committee at the request of the committee's chairman, Sen. William Proxmire (D, Wis.). Proxmire had called the hearing to take the place of press briefings on unemployment and cost-of-living figures at the Department of Labor which had been discontinued. Moore told the committee that the decision to end the briefings had come from President Nixon and Secretary of Labor Hodgson.

Five cities were added to the bureau's list of "substantial unemployment areas" March 25, bringing the number of major metropolitan areas in the category to 50 —the highest since June 1962. Added to the category of labor markets anticipating a 6% or more jobless rate for at least two months were: New Haven, Conn. (with a 6.5% jobless rate); Rockford, Ill. (6.7%); Terre Haute, Ind. (7%); Worcester, Mass. (7%); and Binghamton, N.Y. (6%).

Two areas, Muskegon, Mich. and Fresno, Calif., were added to the list of "persistent" unemployment areas whose jobless rate had been 6% or more for a year and had been at least 50% above the national average for several years. With the two additions, that category totaled six.

The unemployment rate rose in April to 6.1%, seasonally adjusted, the Labor Department reported May 7. The report said the job situation was "essentially unchanged" since March. Total employment inched up to a seasonally adjusted 78,698,-

000 persons in April. Total unemployment was 4,694,000 with seasonal adjustment, 5,-085,000 without seasonal adjustment.

Unemployment rates for most major labor force groups demonstrated little or no change from their high levels. However, the jobless rate for blacks spurted to 10% from 9.4% in March, the highest since the 10.4% of January 1964.

It was reported May 1 that three cities were added to the Bureau of Labor Statistics' "substantial unemployment" list, bringing the number of major metropolitan areas in the category to 52, the highest number since May 1962. Added to the category were Hartford, Conn.; Newark, N.J.; and Charleston, W. Va. New Orleans was dropped from the list.

The list of small labor markets hit by unemployment was increased to 687, after the addition of 25 cities.

The Labor Department reported June 4 that unemployment, rising in May for the third straight month, reached December 1970's seasonally adjusted 6.2%, a nine-year high. Employment climbed in May to a seasonally adjusted 78,961,000 from 78,-698,000 in April. Total unemployment after adjustment was 5,217,000.

Unemployment rates for most major labor force groups (men, women, blacks, whites, teen-agers) remained essentially unchanged from their high levels, except for a persistent rise in unemployment among women in the 20-24 age bracket. The jobless rate for the latter group registered 11.5%, the highest level in more than 10 years.

The category of persons jobless for 27 or more weeks reached its highest level since May 1963 as it rose to 580,000.

May economic indicators. The Commerce Department reported June 28 that its composite index of 12 leading economic indicators rose .6% in May, the index's seventh straight monthly rise. The advance, which brought the index to 124.9% of the 1967 average, was only half the 1.2% rise in April.

Four of the eight available indicators rose: the average workweek of manufacturing employes, new durable goods orders, new building permits and the ratio of price-to-unit labor cost among manufacturers.

The four indicators showing declines were plant and equipment contracts and

orders, industrial materials prices, the average price of 500 common stocks and the average weekly initial claims for state unemployment insurance (treated inversely in the index).

Industrial output. The Federal Reserve Board reported that industrial output had risen .2% in March to a seasonally adjusted 165.5% of the 1957-59 base period. While topping February's upward-revised 164.9%, it lagged behind January's 165.6%. The index also trailed the 168.8% of August 1970 before the General Motors strike, indicating that the auto industry had not fully caught up with pre-strike production levels.

Industrial output rose .3% in April to a seasonally adjusted 166.2% of the base and then climbed .7% in May, the highest rise since January, to a 167.3% level.

Housing starts. Housing starts rose 11.3% in March to a seasonally adjusted annual rate of 1,950,000 units. The advance was the sharpest since the nearly 18% increase in December 1970. The increase was welcomed by the Administration which was relying heavily on the housing sector to spur the economy. But housing starts declined 2.4% in April to a seasonally adjusted annual rate of 1,903,-000 units.

Machine tool orders at 11-year low. The National Machine Tool Builders' Association reported April 26 that new orders for U.S. machine tools had slipped to their lowest level in 11 years during the first quarter of 1971.

Machine tool orders, from sources both abroad and in the U.S., were viewed as a reliable indicator of business trends.

The new figures showed that the first quarter mark was at $176.4 million, the lowest since the third quarter of 1960. The new orders in March actually advanced 6.7% from the February total, but the totals for the first three months of 1971 were considerably lower than the orders taken in the same period a year earlier.

The association also reported that shipments of tools began to mirror the impact of the dipping new-order figures. The shipments of tools, which represented the actual sales of the machinery that brought money to the producers, dropped 33.2% in March and 32% through the first quarter of 1971.

The new orders for March were up from a total of $59.1 million in February, to $63 million. That was below the March 1970 new-order mark of $96.3 million.

1971 capital spending plans. Capital spending plans of U.S. businesses for new plant and equipment were projected at a modest 2.7% increase to $81.85 billion in 1971, according to a quarterly survey by the Commerce Department and the Securities and Exchange Commission reported June 1. The scheduled increase, the smallest in 10 years, contrasted sharply with a 4.3% projection in a similar survey three months earlier and the 5.5% gain recorded in 1970.

The downward revisions from the previous survey were mostly in the manufacturing industries, where spending plans were pared for aircraft and non-electrical-machinery goods, chemicals, food and beverages.

Stock prices dip. Prices on the New York Stock Exchange May 17 recorded their largest single-day decline in 11 months. The Dow Jones (D-J) industrial stock average toppled 14.76 points to close at 921.30 in the market's biggest setback since June 23, 1970, when the bluechip indicator plummeted 18 points to close at 698.11. Every major group on the exchange was hit by the decline.

The broad decline had not been unexpected, but it took rumors of an increase in the prime lending rate at major banks and a strike of railroad signalmen to be the final catalysts.

'Game Plan' Assessed & Reaffirmed

Administration dissatisfied. The Nixon Administration's dissatisfaction with its economic "game plan" was confirmed by Paul W. McCracken, chairman of the Council of Economic Advisers, in an interview June 17. McCracken said President Nixon would decide in July or August whether he would continue current policies.

Part of the discontent arose over the slow movement of the economy which forestalled any drop in the high rate of unemployment, one of the main targets of the Administration's economic expansion program. Nevertheless, McCracken said he believed that the economic performance for April, May and June, including the quarterly gross national product statistics, would show a "substantial, and a pretty good, expansion by historical standards."

Administration policy reaffirmed. President Nixon's decision not to change the "game plan" of his economic policy was announced by Treasury Secretary John B. Connally Jr. June 29. Connally, designated that day by Nixon as his "chief economic spokesman," said the President "has confidence we are on the right path" and reaffirmed the Administration's "twin goals" of controlling inflation and reducing unemployment, both persisting at high rates.

Four basic conclusions were drawn, Connally said, from a thorough review that weekend by the President and his advisers on economic and budget problems. They were to rule out at this time (1) a tax cut or (2) new spending to stimulate the still-sluggish economy, and also to rule out (3) a wage-price review board or (4) mandatory wage-price controls as a check to inflation.

In line with the decision not to increase fiscal spending, the President vetoed June 29 a bill to establish a $5.6 billion accelerated public works program on the ground the creation of jobs would be too far in the future and the spending inflationary.

The President, however, looked forward to enactment of another bill before Congress. This measure would create a $2.25 billion program to help state and local governments provide 200,000 jobs for the unemployed.

Connally, expressing the President's views on economic policy, acknowledged dissatisfaction with the 6.2% rate of unemployment but opposed stimulants on a short-range basis as jeopardizing future employment, even of those gaining jobs immediately, because of their added "thrust to inflation."

The Administration's current economic policies, he said, "must be allowed time to work." "Frankly," Connally said, "we are going to require some degree of patience on the part of the American people" before the policies, particularly with regard to unemployment, proved successful. An economy generating a gross national product in excess of a trillion dollars a year, Connally said, should not be moved up and down every morning "like a yo-yo."

As for the unemployment problem, he said the cuts in military services and defense spending had added 1.2 million persons to the job market and the jobless rate would be only 5.5% without the influx of the released servicemen. Describing the 4% jobless rate considered by economists as "full" employment a "myth," Connally said this had never been achieved in the past 25 years without war.

"I don't think," he added, "anyone wants to continue the war to achieve 4% unemployment." Connally declined to say whether the Administration retained its goal of reducing unemployment to a 4.5% rate by mid-1972.

The President was "acting to reduce unemployment," Connally said, and he cited statistics to indicate the economy was picking up—housing starts at a rate of 1.9 million a year, retail sales up to a level of $32 billion, industrial production rising, money supply growing and the 1971 budget deficit running "substantially in excess" of the projected $18 billion.

Public works bill vetoed—The accelerated public works bill vetoed by President Nixon June 29 had been passed in its final form by the Senate June 8 and House June 15.

The bill called for a $2 billion public works program, modeled after a Kennedy Administration program, later abandoned, to provide up to 80% federal grants to areas of high unemployment to build sewers, hospitals, public buildings and other facilities.

The bill also would have provided a four-year, $1.5 billion extension of the Appalachian Regional Commission and a two-year, $2 billion extension of the Public Works and Economic Development Act financing other regional commissions.

Nixon's veto was directed at the $2 billion accelerated public works program, which he described as a "costly and time-consuming method of putting unemployed persons to work." He also said it would stimulate construction jobs, which also had little immediate effect on joblessness, instead of helping "the broad spectrum of the presently unemployed."

The President urged Congress to reenact the other programs incorporated in the bill. He expressed support for another bill before Congress for a $2.2 billion program to provide public service jobs.

Senate upholds veto—The Senate failed July 14 to override President Nixon's veto of the $5.6 billion accelerated public works bill. The 57–36 vote in favor of overriding the veto fell five votes short of the two-thirds majority required to override a Presidential veto.

Fifty-one Democrats and six Republicans voted to override the veto. Sen. Harry F. Byrd Jr. (D, Va.) voted with 35 Republicans to uphold Nixon's veto.

Emergency job act signed. President Nixon signed into law July 12 the Emergency Employment Act (S31) authorizing $2.25 billion to provide public service jobs in the next two years for the unemployed at state and local levels.

Although Nixon had vetoed two other public service job bills in December 1970 and June 29, he said that the third bill removed his major objections to the earlier measures. He said that while the bill vetoed in December might have led to "dead-end" jobs, the new bill provided work that could lead to permanent employment. He added that the job opportunities opened up by the new bill would not lead to "entrapment in permanent public subsidy."

In signing the bill at the Western White House, Nixon estimated that it would provide 150,000 jobs. He said the new law would go into effect immediately in high unemployment areas such as those affected by layoffs in the aerospace industry.

The jobs provided by the new law would be similar to those envisaged under the two vetoed measures. A key difference, however, was that under the new law, state and local governments would be required in their applications to give the federal government assurances that the jobs would lead to permanent employment. In addition, the new law would expire in two years. The earlier measures would have been permanent.

June jobless rate. The Labor Department reported July 2 that the unemployment rate had dropped substantially in June, to a seasonally adjusted 5.6%. However, the department advised that the survey that provided the figures had been, for routine statistical reasons, taken unusually early in the month. The survey had been taken the week of June 6–12, before school and college graduations brought numbers of young people into the labor market.

Both the total number of people employed and the total unemployed rose, before seasonal adjustment, in June, but less than normally for the month.

Unemployment in the second quarter of 1971 averaged 6%, up slightly from the 5.9% of the two preceding quarters.

Education aid bill signed. President Nixon signed July 11 a $5.15 billion education appropriation bill (HR 7016), the largest of its kind in the history of the Office of Education. It was the first education aid bill passed by Congress that the President had not vetoed. Nixon praised Congress for voting the funds at an early date, permitting careful planning for the fall term.

The legislation was a compromise that had been worked out in conference and approved by both houses June 30 after the Senate had voted substantially more funds than the House. The final bill nevertheless hiked spending for the fiscal year that began July 1 by $375 million above the President's request in January. Nixon said the additional funds would have to be offset by cuts elsewhere in the federal budget in order to maintain fiscal stability.

Congress added $173 million to the President's request of $440 million for areas "impacted" by families from federal facilities, $138 million to his request of $1.85 billion for general aid to elementary and secondary education, $100 million to his request of $469 million for vocational and adult education, and $288 million to his request of $5 million for direct loans to students under the National Defense Education Act. The bill also provided funds for education of the handicapped, libraries and communications, research and development, overseas educational activities, salaries and expenses, and the Corporation for Public Broadcasting ($35 million).

School lunch aid. In response to a protest from 40 senators who had accused the Administration of reneging on a commitment to fund expanded summer free lunch for 2 million children in inner city areas, the Administration agreed to release an additional $15 million in funds. George P. Shultz, director of the Office of Management and Budget, made known the decision in a letter July 8 (published July 10) to Sen. Clifford P. Case (R, N.J.). Case had written a July 7 letter bearing the signatures of the bipartisan group.

The protest arose over an announcement by the Agriculture Department June 28 that it would operate the lunch program under an $18.1 million budget, despite requests from states that reportedly totaled $33 million.

Stock market drops. Stock prices on the New York Stock Exchange dropped sharply June 18 to their lowest level since June 23, 1970 at the time of the corporate liquidity crisis. The Dow-Jones (D-J) industrial stock average plunged 17.09 points to close at 889.16 against a background of concern over higher interest rates, a sluggish economy and steps by the Federal Reserve to slow money supply growth.

First Pennsylvania lifts prime rate. First Pennsylvania Banking & Trust Co. in Philadelphia raised its prime (minimum) interest rate from 5.5% to 5.75%, June 14. Although most of the nation's major banks were holding off until one of the large New York banks decided to take action, San Francisco's Bank of California went a notch higher than First Pennsylvania, boosting its key lending rate to 6% from 5.5% June 15.

The White House expressed disappointment over the prime rate actions. Rep. Wright Patman (D, Tex.) angrily called for a federal regulatory agency directly under the President to fix domestic interest rates. First Pennsylvania announced it had taken the action because of recent increases in money market rates and loan volume. The bank's total loans had risen about 20% from a year earlier, with more than half attributed to commercial loans.

6% prime rate becomes general. A nationwide boost July 7 in the prime interest rate charged by commercial banks standardized the 6% level.

Some banks had retained a prime rate of 5.5%, while others raised their rates to 6%. Although bankers generally had favored a hike in the rate, many had delayed action because of possible political repercussions.

The first major New York bank to raise its prime rate was Manufacturers Hanover Trust Co.

House Banking Committee Chairman Wright Patman urged President Nixon to use his standby credit-control authority to roll back the rate increases.

GNP target abandoned. In testimony at the Joint Economic Committe's midyear review of the economy July 8, Paul W. McCracken, chairman of the Council of Economic Advisers (CEA), indicated that the Administration was abandoning its gross national product (GNP) target of $1.065 trillion in 1971. Among his other conculsions: present economic performance was below the level necessary to attain the Administration's economic goals; the inflation at about 4% and unemployment just under 6% were exceeding expectations; further economic stimulus would accelerate inflation, and an incomes policy would be ineffective.

McCracken testified that it would be "irresponsible" and dangerous to try to push the economy to the $1.065 trillion GNP goal and run the risk of either reviving inflation or at least seriously delaying its abatement. McCracken said the chief reason for the slower-than-expected growth in GNP was a very small increase in inventories.

A statement by the CEA read by McCracken said the Administration would take no further steps to stimulate the economy. Its reasons were that it was unlikely that "even a very temporary gain"

against unemployment would result and that it might, in a nation so sensitive to inflation, "generate expectations which raise prices and interest rates and thereby retard, rather than advance, recovery." McCracken explained that the Administration was not halting economic expansion but was allowing already large expansionary influences to begin work. The chief expansionary forces he cited were an increased budget deficit and a 10.3% money supply growth rate in the first half of 1971.

McCracken disclosed that the Administration's projected $11.6 billion budget deficit for fiscal 1972, started July 1, would be revised upward by at least $7 billion. He said revenues would be $2 billion less than anticipated. Congressional spending had increased outlays by $3 billion, while "uncontrollable" outlays had added another $2 billion.

The moderately optimistic statement by the council forecast that economic output would expand and eventually begin reducing unemployment, while inflation would gradually begin to wane.

Both McCracken and the CEA statement rejected a broad incomes policy effort aimed at voluntary limits on private wage and price decisions. The council concluded: "There is no evidence to suggest that results can be achieved voluntarily, except very temporarily or in limited sectors of the economy." It cited the general failure of incomes policy in other countries, except for some limited success in a few small countries where social and economic sectors were highly organized.

In testimony before the committee July 7, both House Speaker Carl Albert (D, Okla.) and Majority Leader Mike Mansfield (D, Mont.) urged some form of incomes policy. Seeing no substantial progress against inflation, Mansfield called for temporary wage-price controls. Albert declared that if President Nixon refused to impose wage-price controls, he should "at least establish a wage-price review board as recommended by his own chief advisers as a minimal first step."

The Western White House in San Clemente July 9 said that press reports of McCracken's testimony had given too pessimistic an impression.

Postal Service contract. The new, semi-private U.S. Postal Service July 20 signed its first negotiated labor contract with seven postal unions, representing 640,000 postal workers. The contract provided for a $1,250 annual wage increase (paid out in installments of $250, beginning July 20), a limited cost-of-living increase and various retroactive payments.

In addition to the wage boosts, postal workers who had been on the job six months or more would receive a one-time $300 bonus not included in the wage base. Workers with less service would receive proportionately smaller bonuses. A cost-of-living provision provided up to $160 a worker.

James W. Hargrove, an assistant postmaster general, said the contract would cost the Postal Service about $630 million in the fiscal year ending June 30, 1972, plus an additional $330 million in the following fiscal year.

Western Union accord. The Western Union Telegraph Co. reached a settlement with the 17,000-member United Telegraph Workers union July 23. The union had initiated a nationwide strike against Western Union June 1.

A new two-year contract called for a 10% general wage increase and a 4% hike in fringe benefits.

Copper strike. The Nonferrous Conference, a 26-union coalition led by the United Steelworkers of America, reached tentative agreement in Salt Lake City July 25 on a new three-year contract with the nation's largest copper producer, Kennecott Copper Corp.

A strike had been called July 1 against the Big Four copper producers. It idled more than 35,000 workers in 11 states. The companies involved were Kennecott, based in Phoenix, Ariz.; Anaconda Co., in Salt Lake City; Phelps Dodge Corp. in Tucson, Ariz.; and American Smelting and Refining Co. (Asarco), in Denver.

Kennecott's three-year contract, conditional on resolution of a work rules issue, provided for a 92¢-an-hour wage boost over the life of the contract, about a 28% hike from the average $3.25 hourly rate. An unlimited cost-of-living escalator—one of the major obstacles to

a settlement—was to go into effect during the second year of the contract. Regular pension benefits were increased 50% to $7.50 a month for each year of employment.

The Kennecott settlement was similar to one reached with Miami Copper Co., a small producer and a unit of Cities Service Co., and also ratified by the conference. The Kennecott settlement covered about 8,500 strikers, the Miami accord about 650 strikers.

The Kennecott accord reinforced a pattern of terms won by the USW in earlier bargaining with the can and aluminum industries, except that it did not have guaranteed minimum payments under its cost-of-living clauses.

A similar 92¢-package with an unlimited cost-of-living escalator reached July 18 between Magma Copper Co. (a subsidiary of Newmont Mining Corp.) and seven striking unions in Tucson was rejected by the 250 conference delegates July 25. The unions were dissatisfied with the final wording of the contract, which union officials said would limit the application of benefits.

In Nevada, an accord covering Anaconda's Yerington mines was ratified July 31 by the Nevada Industrial Council, AFL-CIO. The pact called for an immediate 50¢-an-hour wage increase in the first year, followed by a 12.5¢-an-hour boost and cost-of-living adjustments in the second and third years.

Nixon meets with steel leaders. On the eve of steel industry labor negotiations, President Nixon addressed industry labor leaders and steel executives at the White House July 6. As outlined at a press briefing afterwards by George P. Shultz, director of the Office of Management and Budget, the President exhorted the negotiators to strive for a "constructive settlement" that took into account the competitive problems of the industry on the world market. The President refrained from issuing guidelines for the negotiations.

Attending the closed half-hour meeting were 13 steel industry executives and five union leaders.

Shultz said the President had expressed hope that the negotiators would weigh the industry's cost problems.

Shultz appeared to stress increased productivity as the "way in which high wages can be made compatible." He noted that the industry had spent more than $17 billion domestically in the past decade on capital improvements, but had shown no commensurate return in productivity.

The President used the meeting to make available a 66-page report on the industry prepared by a task force of the Cabinet Committee on Economic Policy headed by Hendrik S. Houthakker. The highly statistical and technical report apparently offered recommendations, but they were not made public. The report depicted a dismal situation grounded in declining profits and stock values, import inroads, "unfavorable" trends in output per manhour and labor force turnover, excess capacity in rolling mills, and the "almost invariably upward" trends in list steel prices that were "ineffectual in meeting import competition."

Also at the meeting, Deputy Undersecretary of State Nathaniel Samuels reported on plans to negotiate with trading partners a two-year extension of voluntary quotas on steel exports to the U.S.

(Later in the day, President Nixon reiterated his opposition to wage-price controls at a briefing for Midwestern media executives in Kansas City, Mo. He said controls that necessarily involved rationing could not work in peacetime and warned that they would "snuff out" the country's economic "dynamism.")

Steel pact reached; prices hiked. Agreement on a new three-year contract providing a total wage package increase of about 31% was reached Aug. 1 between the AFL-CIO United Steelworkers of America and nine steel companies. The accord was followed Aug. 2 by announcements from five of the companies that they would increase prices an average of about 8% covering nearly all products.

A White House statement Aug. 2 questioned whether the price rise was "in the industry's long-run interests." Administration reaction to the settlement itself, expressed Aug. 1 by Labor Secretary James D. Hodgson, was gratification "that the new contract contains a special provision to encourage productivity." Part of the agreement stipulated that

union and management would cooperate at the plant level to seek ways to improve productivity.

The settlement averted a strike of 350,000 workers scheduled for midnight Aug. 1. A strike had been set to begin 24 hours earlier but was postponed as agreement neared. The first firm economic offer by the companies reportedly had not been presented until July 28, and it was rejected by the union as "very stingy" July 30, the day J. Curtis Counts, director of the Federal Mediation and Conciliation Service, entered the dispute on his own initiative. Hodgson joined the negotiations late July 31.

The size of the wage package was expected, since the steel union had won a 30% increase in pay and benefits in earlier settlements with the can, aluminum and copper industries.

The basic wage increase for the steelworkers, who were getting an average standard wage of $3.50 an hour under the old contract, was 50¢ an hour in the first year and 12.5¢ an hour in each of the next two years. Other pay increments based on skill levels, Sunday pay and other extras would increase wages for skilled workers more than $1 an hour over the life of the contract.

A cost-of-living increase also was included in the new pact to provide a 1¢ increase for each rise of .4% in the Consumer Price Index. The contract guaranteed an annual 12.5¢-an-hour increase in the cost-of-living allowance in the last two years of the contract.

Pension improvements also were provided to raise the figure from $6.50 a month for each year of service to $8 for each of the first 15 years, $9 for the next 15 years and $10 for all additional years.

Union negotiators, led by USW President I. W. Abel, described the new pact as "the best ever." The chief industry negotiator, R. Heath Larry, vice chairman of U.S. Steel Corp., said the settlement was "certainly inflationary" and would cost the industry 15% more in wage costs in the first contract year. The industry reluctantly accepted the pact, he said, "because it is so important to the national economy that we not have a long and bitter strike at this time."

In addition to U.S. Steel, the negotiating companies were Bethlehem Steel Corp., Republic Steel Corp., National Steel Corp., Inland Steel Corp., Jones & Laughlin Steel Corp., Youngstown Sheet and Tube Co., Armco Steel Corp. and Allegheny Ludlum Industries, Inc.

Prices increased—The 8% price increases, to go into effect on a staggered schedule between Aug. 5 and Dec. 1, were first announced by U.S. Steel Aug. 2 and copied later in the day, with little variation, by Bethlehem, Republic, Armco and Youngstown. The pattern price rises extended to Inland, Wheeling-Pittsburgh Steel Corp. and Kaiser Steel Corp. Aug. 3. Together with previous price changes initiated in 1971, they would bring the total price increase in the industry for the year to about 15%, or larger than the total price rise for finished steel products during the previous decade.

The Nixon Administration statement, released Aug. 2 by Gerald Warren, deputy White House press secretary, said: "The Administration feels that in view of the already unfavorable competitive positions of the domestic steel industry, it is questionable whether the price increase is in the industry's long-run interests. Price increases of this magnitude at this time are bound to have an adverse effect on the tonnage of steel produced in the United States and on jobs in the steel industry. And it is questionable whether steel markets today will accept these increases. Both labor and management in the steel industry, let alone the general public, have a crucial stake in getting productivity up and costs and prices under control. The President urges labor and management to get to work on these central problems."

Another reaction, from Senate Democratic Leader Mike Mansfield (Mont.) Aug. 2, was that "it's too late for jawboning, two and one-half years too late. The time calls for drastic action. Otherwise the economic situation is going to get out of control." He urged the President to impose a temporary freeze on wages and prices.

Rail strikes. Selective and spreading railroad strikes by the AFL-CIO United Transportation Union ended Aug. 2 after

agreement on a 42-month contract with a 42% pay increase and on changes in some key work rules. The pact also provided for a permanent standing labor-management committee to handle economic and rules disputes.

The settlement was reached after President Nixon called both sides to a meeting at the White House July 30 to discuss the economic impact of the strike and urge "responsive bargaining" for a quick settlement.

Earlier July 30, the union had extended its strike action to six more carriers— the Atchison, Topeka and Santa Fe Railway; the Houston Belt & Terminal; the Alton & Southern Railway Companies; the Duluth, Missabe & Iron Range Railway; the Bessemer & Lake Erie; and the Elgin, Joliet & Eastern. It had initiated the strikes July 16 against the Union Pacific Railroad and the Southern Railway and extended it July 24 to the Southern Pacific Co. and the Norfolk & Western Railway.

Five of the 10 railroads shut down by the strikes were major carriers.

At the White House meeting July 30, Labor Secretary James D. Hodgson reported that 41% of the country's rail mileage had been idled by the strike and Paul W. McCracken, chairman of the Council of Economic Advisers, warned that if the strike continued against the selected targets through August, $50 billion "might be knocked out of the gross national product."

Agriculture Secretary Clifford M. Hardin had warned July 29 that the rail strike was causing "a rapid deterioration of the orderly movement of essential food products from farm to market." California farmers suffered a cash loss of $35 million on crops not moved to markets during the strike, the California Growers Council reported Aug. 3. Large amounts of grain also were piled on the ground near grain elevators in Kansas and Nebraska when the strike ended. Poultry farmers in the South and Southeast also were affected because of the loss of feed shipments, and 42,000 coal miners in Pennsylvania, the Virginias and Kentucky were laid off because of the strike.

President Nixon had intervened in the strike July 28 by dispatching Assistant

Labor Secretary W. J. Usery Jr. to UTU headquarters in Cleveland to meet with union President Charles Luna in an effort to break the negotiating impasse.

In Congress, Sen. Jacob K. Javits (R, N.Y.) introduced a resolution July 30 to empower the President to reopen or maintain service on the railroads if a national or regional emergency existed.

The 42% wage increase provided by the settlement consisted of hikes of 4% effective April 1; 5% Oct. 1; 5% April 1, 1972; 5% Oct. 1, 1972; plus 15¢ an hour more Jan. 1, 1973 and 19¢ an hour more April 1, 1973.

In addition, higher compensation was guaranteed if workers were idled because of work rule changes. Relocation allowances were authorized if necessitated by such changes.

Freight-rate increase foreseen—John C. Kenefick, chief executive officer of the Union Pacific Railroad, said Aug. 3 that the railroads "almost certainly" would have to institute a general freight-rate increase to help offset the cost of the strike settlement.

Nixon-Burns rift alleged. Testimony by Federal Reserve Board (FRB) Chairman Arthur F. Burns before the Joint Economic Committee July 23 fueled reports of a growing rift between President Nixon and his longtime friend over the means to curb inflation. Four days later it was widely reported that the Administration was considering a request for legislation to put the independent FRB in the executive branch of the government and to control it by doubling FRB membership (the new members would be Nixon appointees).

Speculation was rooted in a reported leak from the White House that described Nixon as "furious" over Burns' statement before that committee that "very little progress" had been made against inflation. Nixon was also said to have been exasperated by Burns' persistent suggestions, which Nixon consistently opposed, for a wage-price review board.

After some ambivalence concerning the reports by White House Press Secretary Ronald L. Ziegler, the White House formally and unequivocally denied July 30 that the President was considering changing the size and status of the FRB.

Burns' testimony. At a midyear review of the economy by the Joint Economic Committee, Burns said July 23 he was "cautiously optimistic" about the economy. However, he said that his confidence in the "vigor and curability" of the economic expansion currently under way would be "very considerably increased" by evidence of progress against inflation. The lack of progress, he testified, presented a "grave obstacle" to a rapid recovery in production and employment.

According to Burns, a key problem was the present economic picture's defiance of customary rules of economics: substantial unemployment and "extensive slack" in the economy had failed to check sharp rises in wages and prices. Burns said other countries, such as Britain and Canada, were experiencing a similar distortion of the rules.

Burns advised caution in the use of fiscal stimulation of the economy in view of the large federal budget deficit, its potential negative effect on private behavior and widespread fears of inflation. Burns said he continued to favor restoration of the business investment tax credit, but under more favorable conditions when the budget was not so massively in deficit.

Burns testified that he believed the FRB should have acted more firmly in the spring of 1970 to slow the rapid growth of the nation's money supply. He testified that present FRB policy was to "promote a more moderate rate of monetary expansion." He indicated that the FRB would cut back money supply growth if it continued to expand at the roughly 10% rate of 1971's first half.

Burns implied that credit had to be tightened because the Administration had not acted firmly enough to curb rising wages and prices, of which he saw no signs of moderation. He said lower interest rates were needed, but that was impossible until more progress was made against inflation. He added that the business and labor communities had much "goodwill and statesmanship" which could be used more fully by the Administration. He pointed out that the adjusted measure of wages rose slightly more in the first half of 1971 than in the previous two years. He reiterated his suggestion for a wage-price review board and urged compulsory arbitration of labor disputes in industries closely affecting the public interest. He conceded that the system of voluntary restraint might not work but said it should be tried.

Two days after Burns' testimony, Treasury Secretary John B. Connally Jr. and White House Press Secretary Ronald L. Ziegler said separately that the Administration was making "very good" and "very substantial" progress against inflation. Connally, appearing on the CBS program "Face the Nation" July 25, voiced confidence that the economy was in the midst of a substantial growth period. He denied that the Administration had made a "deliberate decision" to concentrate on the battle against inflation at the expense of economic expansion. He reaffirmed the Administration's opposition to tougher wage-price policies.

Nixon 'open' re wage-price boards. President Nixon said Aug. 4 that he would consider a recommendation on wage-price review boards, but only if Congressional hearings on the subject convinced him "that enforcing an incomes policy could be accomplished without stifling the economy."

He said at an unannounced news conference in his office, his first in nine weeks, that he had "an open mind" on the subject "in terms of examining the various proposals to see if there is a new approach which we may not have thought of."

Among Nixon's comments:

The President told reporters that he "would not sell the United States economy short at this point." There was "a lot of steam in the boiler" and his projection for the balance of 1971 was "that the economy will continue to move up as it has moved up in the first half. That doesn't mean that there will not be aberrations in the monthly figures. It does mean, however, that the economy has a great deal of strength in it."

"We are making progress against inflation, but it is going to require continued strong policies on the part of the Administration with the cooperation of the Congress in limiting our budget expenditures to full-capacity or full-employment revenues. That is the battle we will continue to wage, and it will also need cooperation from labor and management on limiting the wage price spiral." The President said the "unemployment curve" was down—from a high of 6.2% to below 6%—and he believed "it will continue, with monthly aberrations, on a downward course through the balance of the year. I believe that, as we go into 1972, I still stick with my prediction that we shall see unemployment continue to move downward and that 1972, for that year, will be a very good year."

Nixon said he opposed permanent wage and price controls because they "would stifle the American economy." While it was "essential that government use its power where it can be effective" against wage-price escalation, the problem was "how can we move without putting the American economy in a straitjacket?"

To another question, "how far will persuasion go?" Nixon replied that the record showed "that in most countries abroad that have tried it, except for very small countries that are tightly controlled, persuasion alone will work for only three to four months."

He said he would consider "a recommendation on wage-price boards" but would reject it if he found "that it would impose a new bureaucracy with enormous criminal powers to fasten itself on the American economy." He would consider such a recommendation favorably only if Congressional hearings to be held on the subject convinced him "that enforcing an incomes policy could be accomplished without stifling the economy."

As for numerical economic guidelines, the President said they "basically connote voluntary compliance and voluntary compliance goes on only for a brief time."

The Administration policy was to watch every forthcoming major wage-price negotiations and to "use the power of this office to the extent it can be effective to see that those negotiations are as responsible as possible." He would follow a selective approach, "to take those particular industries that are coming up for bargaining and to use our influence as effectively as we can to see that those settlements are responsible." He said he would "continue the policy of moving aggressively on individual settlements on a case-by-case basis."

Nixon conceded that the recent steel settlement followed by a price increase was "not in the interest" of the country, labor or industry, but "calling in the steel industry and getting them to change would not be effective" at a time when the industry's profits were at a 2½% level, "the lowest of any major industry." The steel settlement and price rise in the long run meant "less steel sold and less jobs, and that is why we are zeroing in on the productivity side, because increases in productivity can be the only answer where a wage increase of this kind takes place."

As another anti-inflationary step, the President revealed his intention to veto at this time any legislation to provide a wage increase for federal blue-collar workers.

The President took time "to set the record straight with regard to some greatly blown-up differences that I am supposed to have with my very good friend Arthur Burns," who had taken "the most responsible and statesmanlike" course in terms of monetary and fiscal policy "of any chairman of the Federal Reserve in my memory."

AFL-CIO criticizes Administration. The AFL-CIO Executive Council Aug. 9 deplored the Nixon Administration's economic policies.

While the council deplored the "economic mess" resulting from the Administration's "gross mismanagement," Meany called the Nixon economic program "a complete failure" and said referring to "a mess" was "an understatement."

The council reiterated its support of across-the-board wage and price controls as necessary to curb inflation, urged release of federal construction funds frozen by the Administration, recommended full funding of federal programs and called for an increase in the federal minimum wage to $2 an hour.

Nixon rating drops. The Louis Harris poll reported Aug. 9 that 73% of a cross-section 1,493 households, polled July 10–16, gave the Nixon Administration a negative rating on its economic policy; 5% were undecided. The 22% giving the Administration their approval represented a new low in contrast to 35% approving in May. On efforts to control unemployment, the Administration received a 77%-16% negative rating. The poll also showed that 62% believed the nation was still in a recession, 47% did not think things would improve in 1972 and 70% believed prices or the cost of living were rising faster than a year ago.

HUD, NASA, VA funds. An $18.3 billion, fiscal 1972 appropriation bill for the Housing and Urban Development Department (HUD), the National Aeronautics and Space Administration (NASA), the Veterans Administration (VA) and other independent agencies was given final approval in Congress by 363–30 House vote July 29 and Senate voice vote Aug. 2. President Nixon signed the measure Aug. 10.

The total was $882,721,000 more than the total requested by the Administration. One of the major differences was a full-year funding of $1.49 billion for Model Cities, urban renewal and rehabilitation loans. The Administration had requested only half-year funding of $640 million because it had budgeted its community development revenue-sharing proposal to go into effect for the second half of fiscal 1972. Since revenue sharing had not been enacted, and the prospect for passage was dubious, Congress allotted full funding for the programs.

Of the $18,339,738,000 in new budget authority provided by the bill, $3,274,-824,000 was for HUD, including $80,-323,000 for community planning and management and $1,652,750,000 for community development (Model Cities $150 million, urban renewal $1.25 billion, rehabilitation loan fund $90 million, neighborhood facilities grants $40 million, open space land program $100 million and salaries and expenses $22,750,000.)

In addition to the funds, the bill increased HUD's contract authority by $55 million for rent supplements, $170 million for home ownership assistance, $200 million for rental housing assistance and $9,300,000 for college housing. For the open space land program, the federal share was increased from 50% of the cost of land improvement to 75%.

Among the other agencies funded, the VA received $10,935,756,000, the Federal Communications Commission $31,454,000, the Securities and Exchange Commission $24,730,000 and the Selective Service System $82,235,000.

NASA's appropriations totaled $3,298,035,000. An attempt by Rep. Bella S. Abzug (D, N.Y.) to eliminate funding for the space shuttle had been rejected by the House June 30 and also June 3 during consideration of the NASA authorization. A similar attempt in the Senate June 29 by Sen. Walter F. Mondale (D, Minn.) had been defeated 64–22.

The NASA authorization, at a $3,354,950,000 level, was cleared by Congress by voice votes of the House July 27 and Senate July 28. Nixon signed it Aug. 6. The figure compared with total Administration requests of $3,300,635,000.

State, Justice, Commerce funds. The fiscal 1972 appropriation bill for the Departments of State, Justice and Commerce, the judiciary and some related agencies, was approved by 337–35 House vote Aug. 2, 46–44 Senate vote Aug. 3 and signed by President Nixon Aug. 10.

The bill's $4,067,116,000 of appropriations exceeded the previous year's total by $243,763,700 but fell below Administration budget requests by $149,686,000.

Labor-HEW funds. A bill appropriating $20,804,622,000 for fiscal 1972 for the Departments of Labor and of Health, Education and Welfare (HEW) and some related agencies was passed by 280–56 House vote Aug. 5 and 79–0 Senate vote Aug. 6. President Nixon, who had vetoed the fiscal 1970 Labor-HEW appropriations bill, signed the bill Aug. 9, although the total was $581 million more than his budget request and did not establish a ceiling favored by the Administration on federal payments to states for administrative costs of federal-state welfare programs.

The Congressional appropriations for HEW exceeded Administration requests by $605 million. The additional funds included $373 million more for health services, $156 million more for

the National Institutes of Health (NIH) and $78.6 million more for welfare.

The Labor Department appropriation —$1,315,913,000—was $24.2 million less than the budget request.

Other legislation. Among other measures involved in the inflationary situation:

■ A bill to provide a 10% increase in retirement benefits for railroad employes was approved by the Senate June 21 and House June 24 and signed by Nixon July 2. The increase was proportional to that provided in March to Social Security beneficiaries.

■ A $529,309,749 fiscal 1972 appropriations bill for the legislative branch was given final approval by the House and Senate June 30 and was signed by the President July 9. The total was more than the previous year's funds— by $86,405,430—and less than the budget request—by $6,039,858.

■ A $4,528,986,690 fiscal 1972 appropriations bill for the Treasury Department, U.S. Postal Service, the Executive Office and some independent agencies was approved by both houses of Congress June 30 and signed by President Nixon July 9. The total was slightly more than a billion dollars less than provided the previous year for the same departments and agencies and slightly more than $280 million less than the Administration's budget requests. The decrease from the previous year's funds reflected conversion of the Post Office Department into an independent government operation. The postal appropriation was $1,217,522,000 to make up the difference between postal receipts and costs for classes of mail for which rates returned less than handling costs.

$80 billion asked for defense. Defense Secretary Melvin R. Laird said Aug. 14 that he would ask for a defense budget of about $80 billion for fiscal 1973 (beginning July 1, 1972).

The $80 billion figure represented an increase of about $3 billion over the anticipated expenditures for fiscal 1972.

For fiscal 1972, the Defense Department had requested a budget of $76 billion but pay and pension increases authorized by Congress had swelled the figure closer to $77 billion.

Laird made his remarks to reporters en route to Norfolk, Va. for Navy ceremonies.

Laird said that even if the $80 billion were approved, "the expenditure level will still be lower than the pre-Vietnam period."

'71 budget deficit. The Commerce Department reported July 28 that the federal budget deficit reached $23.24 billion in the 1971 fiscal year ended June 30. It had been $2.85 billion in fiscal 1970. The deficit was the second largest since World War II. Revenue fell $6 billion short of Administration projections. For fiscal 1971, total budget outlays were $211.6 billion and receipts $188.3 billion. In a prepared statement accompanying the report, Treasury Secretary John B. Connally Jr. and George P. Shultz, director of the Office of Management and Budget, stressed that government spending in 1971 was below $214.1 billion—the hypothetical figure of "full employment" revenues.

The Commerce Department reported Aug. 20 that the federal budget deficit, measured on a "national income accounts basis," ran at a $22.5 billion annual rate in 1971's second quarter. This was the highest quarterly rate since World War II. The first-quarter deficit was at a $17.5 billion rate. Second-quarter federal spending rose to a $220.9 billion annual rate from the $213.2 billion rate of the first quarter; federal receipts ran at a $198.3 billion annual rate, up from the first quarter's $195.6 billion pace.

Jobless rate up in July. The unemployment rate rose .2% in July to a seasonally adjusted 5.8% pace after an abrupt drop in June to 5.6%. According to the Commerce Department Aug. 8, the increase was primarily among jobseekers who had re-entered the labor force; their numbers increased 206,000 to a seasonally adjusted total of 1,544,000.

The number of persons jobless 15 weeks or more rose 138,000 from June to an adjusted 1,311,000 (1.6% of the total labor force), the highest level for that category since August 1963.

On an adjusted basis, total employment jumped 498,000 from June to 78,-941,000 persons just behind the record 79 million total reported for March 1970.

Employment of adult men rose by 125,-000 to a record 45,888,000 (adjusted).

The narrower than expected increase in July was offset by concern that layoffs by steelmakers could push the rate higher in August. U.S. Steel Corp. had announced Aug. 4 it was recalling 19,000 of 38,000 steelworkers at two Chicago area plants. The New York Times reported Aug. 7 that tens of thousands of steelworkers had been laid off pending a pickup in steel orders. Many steel users were still drawing from inventories stockpiled in anticipation of a steel strike. In the Pittsburgh-Western Pennsylvania area, an estimated 47,000 workers had been laid off or temporarily idled; about 34,500 workers in the Chicago area were laid off.

Price indexes up. Wholesale and consumer price indexes rose in July:

Wholesale prices—Wholesale prices in July rose a seasonally adjusted .2% (a 2.4% annual rate) after having risen .4% in June. The Labor Department said Aug. 5 that on an unadjusted basis, wholesale prices gained .3% as opposed to a .4% rise in June. The wholesale price index stood at 114.6% of the 1967 average, 3.3% above a year earlier. The index's relatively favorable showing was clouded by a .7% jump in the key wholesale industrial price sector—the sharpest increase in almost 15 years.

Consumer prices—The Labor Department's Bureau of Labor Statistics reported Aug. 20 that its Consumer Price Index (CPI) rose only .2% in July, both with and without seasonal adjustment, to 121.8% of the 1967 average. On an annual rate basis, the July increase was at a 2.4% pace, in contrast to a 6% annual rate of increase in June. The annual rate of increase for the six months ended July 31 was 3.9%, compared with 5.5% for the same period of 1970. Food prices rose .1% on an adjusted basis, after a .5% increase in June. Nonfood items also rose an adjusted .1%, after rising .3% in June. In June, the CPI had risen .5% from May on an adjusted basis and .6% without adjustment to a record 121.5% of the 1967 average.

Leading indicators up. The composite index of leading economic indicators, foreshadowing future trends, picked up 1.4% in July, the Commerce Department reported Aug. 27. The July increase to 126.5% of the 1967 average followed a .1% decline (revised from a .5% decline) a month earlier. Four of the eight indicators (of 12) available rose: new durable goods orders, new building permits, the ratio of price to unit labor cost among manufacturers, and the average weekly initial claims for state unemployment insurance (treated inversely). The four declines were the average work-week for manufacturing employees, plant and equipment contracts and orders, industrial materials prices and the average price of 500 common stocks.

Other statistics. Among other statistics bearing on the inflationary situation:

GNP—The Commerce Department reported Aug. 20 that during the second quarter the gross national product (GNP) had risen to a seasonally adjusted annual rate of $1,041.3 billion—a $20.5 billion increase over the January-March period.

Real GNP (in constant 1958 dollars), corrected for inflation, rose at a 4% annual rate. The annual rate of inflation, measured by the price index (the "deflator"), was 4.1%.

Industrial output—According to Commerce Department figures Aug. 16, industrial production fell .8% in July, putting the index 1.4% below the year-earlier figure. Most of the decline was ascribed to cutbacks in steel inventories and strikes. However, the indicator was still 3.3% ahead of the November 1970 low.

Housing starts—Housing starts rose 1.2% in June to just under the government's target of 2 million units a year, the Commerce Department reported June 19. Housing starts during June reached a seasonally adjusted annual rate of 1,982,000 units, compared with an upward-revised rate of 1,959,000 in May and 1,393,000 in May 1970.

Building permits required by 13,000 localities slackened, as expected, from an exceptionally high 1,927,000-unit

pace in May to a still strong seasonally adjusted annual rate of 1,817,000.

For the first half of the year, housing starts were at an annual rate of 1,882,000 units, up 48% from the same period a year earlier. It was the fastest rate in 20 years.

Secretary of Commerce Maurice H. Stans said the June performance was evidence that the economy was moving forward strongly and that the Administration's economic plan was "proving out." He also said the figures showed a "powerful and sustained" expansion in home building.

Durables orders—Durable goods orders advanced in July for the third straight month, the Commerce Department reported Aug. 20. July's 3.5% increase to a seasonally adjusted $31.74 billion contrasted with June's .2% gain to $30.67 billion.

Consumer debt—Consumer debt grew in June by a seasonally adjusted $525 million the Federal Reserve Board reported Aug. 3. The June figures topped May's $493 million growth, but trailed April's $663 million rise.

Consumer debt picked up in July by a seasonally adjusted $761 million, the FRB reported Sept. 2. The increase represented the largest growth since the $793 million gain in June 1969. However, since the increase was entirely ascribed to a decline in repayments and did not reflect a rise in new credit, the report was not indicative of renewed consumer confidence.

Personal income—The Commerce Department said Aug. 19 that personal income in July dropped $11 billion from June to a seasonally adjusted annual rate of $859 billion. Income would have risen $2.25 billion had it not been for a large group of nonrecurring Social Security payments in June. June personal income was revised downward, to $870.1 billion.

Corporate profits—Pre-tax corporate earnings showed their third quarterly gain in the second quarter of 1971, but trailed 1968's record $89 billion annual rate, the Commerce Department reported Aug. 20. Second quarter pre-tax profits rose to a seasonally adjusted

$82 billion annual rate, up $3 billion from the first quarter's $79.1 billion annual rate and up $6 billion from the year-earlier quarter. Profit growth was concentrated in the durable goods sector, especially in the metals and machinery industries. The Commerce Department said the figures reflected effects of the liberalized depreciation rules issued in June retroactive to Jan. 1.

International Trade, Payments & Monetary Problems

Trade Accords, New Dollar Crisis

During early 1971 international trading partners continued efforts to reduce barriers to trade. Despite U.S. efforts to modify unfavorable trade terms, the U.S.' absolute trade surplus evaporated, there was a trade deficit in April, and U.S. monetary reserves continued to decline. Inflation and the deficits in the U.S. balance of international payments persisted, and a fresh wave of speculation against the dollar hit the currency markets in May.

Kennedy Round cuts. The fourth of the five annual installments of worldwide tariff cuts took place Jan. 1 in accordance with the Kennedy Round agreements reached in 1967.

The office of the General Agreement on Tariffs and Trade (GATT) had reported Dec. 23, 1970 that five nations had already completed, or virtually completed, their scheduled tariff reductions. Argentina was reported to have put its reductions into effect in 1967, Iceland in 1968, Canada and Ireland in 1969 and Switzerland in 1970. In general, their actions were taken to reduce import prices and to help counter inflationary pressures. GATT added that many participants in the Kennedy Round had speeded up their schedule of tariff cuts in actions designed to aid developing nations.

Comecon bank operational. The International Investment Bank, established in July 1970 by the Soviet bloc's common market organization, Comecon (Council for Mutual Economic Aid), began operations Jan. 1.

The bank, which called up $192 million of its total authorized capital, was expected to serve in the Soviet bloc the function served in the West by the World Bank. It would also borrow and lend for profit in the Eurodollar area and engage in common ventures with capitalist banks.

(The New York Times Jan. 1 reported that the International Bank for Economic Cooperation, Soviet bloc version of the International Monetary Fund, had increased its volume of operations from $2 billion in 1965 to $15 billion in 1969.)

IMF 2nd SDR allocation. The International Monetary Fund Jan. 1 made the second allocation of Special Drawing Rights (SDRs or paper gold), equivalent to $2.949 billion to 109 participants in the organization's Special Drawing Account. The first allocation, equivalent to $3.414 billion, had been made Jan. 1, 1970.

The 1971 allocation was computed at 10.7% of each participant's quota in effect Dec. 31, 1970. The U.S. was allocated the largest single amount—$716.9 million—following a Treasury Department announcement Jan. 1 that the necessary action for an increase in the U.S.' IMF quota had been completed. Other allocations included: Great Britain—$299.6 million; West Germany—$171.2 million; France—$160.5 million; Japan—$128.4 million; Canada—$117.7 million; Italy—$107 million; and India—$100.6 million.

The IMF revealed Jan. 7 that during the first year of operation of the Special Drawing Account, participants had used $857 million of the SDRs, or about ¼ of the initial allocation.

Payments gap narrows slightly. The Commerce Department reported Feb. 16 that the U.S. balance of payments deficit in the fourth quarter of 1970 showed only minimum improvement.

Measured on the overall "liquidity" basis, gauging potential pressures on the dollar, the seasonally adjusted payments deficit was $581 million, an insignificant improvement of $39 million over the $620 million deficit in the third quarter of 1970. The total deficit for 1970 dipped to $3.87 billion from $7.01 billion in 1969. The department pointed out that the "underlying" liquidity deficit in 1970 "probably wasn't much different" from the underlying deficit of $4.5 billion in 1969 because most of the improvement was due to short-term capital flows, $1 billion of special government transactions and the new special drawing right (SDR) allocation of $851 million issued by the International Monetary Fund.

Measured on the official settlements basis (an indicator of exchange market pressures), the payments balance showed deepening deficits both for the fourth quarter of 1970 and the year as a whole. The fourth quarter deficit widened from the third quarter's showing by $1.5 billion to a seasonally adjusted $3.3 billion. The deficit for 1970 reached a record $9.82 billion ($10.69 billion disregarding SDRs), compared with a $2.7 billion surplus in 1969. The official settlements measure, which did not take into account dollar accumulations by private foreign sources, reflected an

accelerating pileup of $7.61 billion in dollar holdings in foreign central banks.

Foreign dollar holdings up in 1970. The International Monetary Fund (IMF) reported Feb. 4 that industrialized West European nations, Canada and Japan had increased their holdings of foreign exchange by $10.8 billion in 1970, almost all of it in U.S. dollars.

The increase in foreign dollar holdings, the IMF said, was due to the large U.S. balance of payments deficit and developments in the Eurodollar market. The increase, which was unexpected, came in the year that the IMF made its first Special Drawing Rights (SDRs or paper gold) distribution, designed, in part, to take the place of dollars in international transactions.

OECD group urges harmonization. A working committee of the Organization for Economic Cooperation and Development (OECD) agreed to stress greater harmonization of West European monetary policies to guard against heavy and erratic outflows of dollars across the Atlantic. The two-day meeting of monetary experts, held in Paris March 25 and 26, also concluded that the U.S. should increase its anti-inflationary drive to cut the U.S. basic balance of payments deficit. The U.S. was also urged to curtail heavy dollar outflows into Europe.

1970 world trade figures. The General Agreement on Tariffs and Trade, in its annual report released Sept. 21, reported that the volume of world exports had risen by 8.5% during 1970, while the value of world exports had increased by 14% to $312.5 billion. The growth rate of world trade, measured in terms of exports, was 1.5% lower than in 1969 because of the low (2.5%) growth rate in the combined gross national product (GNP) of the industrial nations. The report said that the growth rate for world exports would not have had such a good showing without an "unexpectedly strong" import demand in the U.S.

In analyzing the trade patterns of developing nations, the report said their exports had deteriorated in 1970, raising their trade deficit from $2 billion to $3 billion, after a significant improvement in 1969. The report attributed the decline to the lower prices they received for primary products and the higher freight rates they paid.

The International Monetary Fund had reported March 1 that world trade in 1970 had increased in value but that inflation accounted for an unusually high portion of the increase. According to the IMF figures, trade in 1970, as measured by world exports, rose by 14.2% to $278 billion, with exports in the fourth quarter reaching a record annual rate of $301.6 billion. The report indicated, however, that "somewhat less than half" of the increase in 1970 was due to higher prices rather than higher volume.

1970 EFTA trade. The European Free Trade Association (EFTA) Reporter said March 10 that EFTA members' imports and exports had risen in 1970. Total commodity exports (f.o.b.) of the nine EFTA members reached $43.265 billion, an increase of almost 13% over 1969, while total commodity imports (c.i.f.) were $51.171 billion or 16% higher than 1969. Intra-EFTA trade (as calculated by exports, f.o.b.) reached $12.150 billion, an increase of more than 19% over 1969.

EFTA trade with the U.S. rose in 1970, with exports increasing by 4.2% to $3.870 billion and imports rising by 11.5% to $4.948 billion. Exports to the EEC also rose in 1970 by 15% for a total of $11.331 billion, while imports from the EEC rose more than 18% to a total of $16.159 billion. EFTA exports to Eastern European nations rose by 13.5% in 1970 to $2.097 billion, while imports rose by 16.7% to $2.351 billion.

U.S. trade surplus. The Commerce Department reported Feb. 26 that the U.S. surplus of exports over imports dwindled in January to its lowest level since June 1969. The January surplus, on a seasonally adjusted basis, totaled $49.1 million, compared with December 1970's downward-revised $165.9 million.

The January surplus resulted from an 8.3% rise in imports (at a seasonally adjusted $3,686,300,000) from December 1970, and a 4.6% increase in exports (at a seasonally adjusted $3,735,400,000).

Japan curbs textile exports to U.S. The Japanese Textile Federation announced March 8 that it would voluntarily restrict exports of textiles to the U.S. for a three-year period beginning July 1. The decision drew a critical response from American textile manufacturers and unions. The U.S. government expressed reservations.

The Japanese textile group hoped that its move would forestall trade-quota legislation pending in the U.S. Congress and would break the impasse in the U.S.-Japanese textile talks, in progress for two years. The export curbs would apply to cotton and wool textiles and man-made fiber textiles. Yarn and raw materials would be excluded. Exports during the first year of the restrictions would be 5% higher than the previous year, and there would be a 6% boost for each of the two following years.

The Japanese federation emphasized that if other textile-exporting countries, presumably South Korea, Taiwan and Hong Kong, did not enforce similar restrictions, Japan would not do so either. (South Korean government officials and Nationalist Chinese textile manufacturers said March 9 that they would not join Japan in voluntarily curbing exports to the U.S.)

The Japanese action was praised March 8 by Rep. Wilbur D. Mills (D, Ark.), chairman of the House Ways and Means Committee. Mills had played a leading role in the U.S.-Japanese textile negotiations and was regarded as a prime mover in the events leading to the Japanese announcement. He called on other Far East textile-exporting nations to impose similar restraints to eliminate the need for the U.S. Congress to impose quotas.

The International Trade Committee of the American Textile Manufacturers March 8 assailed the Japanese decision as "worse than no agreement at all." Institute President Frederick B. Dent called on President Nixon and Congress to "disavow and disregard the proposal and continue working for a real solution."

The heads of four major textile labor unions in the U.S. expressed similar opposition March 8 on the ground that the Japanese move placed no curbs by categories or product and thus would "lead to utter chaos in the American market." The unions were the Amalgamated Clothing Workers of America, the International Ladies Garment Workers Union, the Textile Workers of America and the United Textile Workers of America.

A White House statement March 9 called the Japanese plan a welcome step, but said "the better way to approach the problem would be" through a negotiated settlement.

Nixon rejects Japanese plan—President Nixon March 11 rejected the Japanese textile industry's plan to limit exports to the U.S. The President said the Japanese government's apparent ratification of the plan, which he described as a "maneuver" of the Japanese textile industry, precluded the bilateral government negotiations that he favored. As a result, the President said, he would give "strong support" to pending U.S. legislation to restrict textile imports by mandatory quotas. In addition, the President directed the secretary of commerce to immediately begin monitoring and analyzing textile imports from Japan on a monthly basis.

The President said that he objected to the Japanese plan because it (1) imposed "only one overall ceiling" on all Japanese textile exports to the U.S., with only a general understanding "to prevent undue distortions" of the present trade pattern, thus permitting specific categories to grow faster than the overall trade; (2) moved back the base date for the plan to March 31, 1972 instead of 1969 as proposed by the U.S. (the President noted that during the two years of negotiations with Japan, imports of man-made-fiber textiles had greatly increased and had reached a "record-breaking level" in January 1971); and (3) "magnifies the potential growth of the sensitive categories by including in the base exports of cotton products" which had already been limited by agreement and had been declining.

Peter Flanigan, an assistant to the President, said in a White House briefing March 11 that the President's decision to explore other solutions to the textile problem included possible negotiations for a restraint agreement

with the other three major textile-exporting nations—South Korea, Taiwan and Hong Kong.

Rep. Wilbur D. Mills said that he by the President's criticism of the Japanese plan. Mills implied he would not back legislation imposing quotas. Describing the Japanese plan as "a meaningful accommodation of the international textile problem," Mills said he knew of no other way to "obtain the protection which the textile industry is seeking and, at the same time, prevent other protectionist developments from accompanying that relief."

Mills' position was opposed, however, by the ranking Republican on his committee, Rep. John W. Byrnes (Wis.), who expressed support of the President at the White House briefing.

Japanese TV dumping ruling—The U.S. Tariff Commission ruled March 4 that Japanese television imports were damaging the domestic industry because they were being sold at less than fair value as defined in the Antidumping Act.

The commission ruling was the second part of a two-step procedure set down in the Antidumping Act to prohibit dumping (importation and sale of goods in the U.S. at wholesale prices lower than those in the home market or a third country). The first part of the procedure was completed Dec. 4, 1970, when the Treasury Department made the initial ruling that Japanese sets were being sold in violation of antidumping rules. The Treasury announcement had climaxed a three-year inquiry that was begun at the request of the Electronic Industries Association.

U.S.-British grain price pact. The U.S. Agriculture Department announced March 17 a new grain agreement between the U.S. and Britain. The pact would set a higher minimum British import price for U.S. corn, below which a levy would be imposed.

Under the accord, the minimum import price for corn would be increased in stages from $54.21 a metric ton to $63.19 a ton in the August-September 1972 period. No levy would be placed on corn imported for industrial uses—generally a third of all foreign corn consumption in Britain.

U.S. corn was sold in Britain at prices well above the new minimum prices. The pact was seen as an attempt, in the light of Britain's application for membership in the European Economic Community (EEC), to establish minimum corn prices below those used in the EEC.

The pact would be in effect from July 1 through 1972.

EEC farm price rises set. Agriculture ministers of the European Economic Community agreed March 25 on a controversial plan for higher farm prices, coupled with a $1.48 billion plan for modernization of the agricultural sector. Agreement came after three days of tense debate accompanied by a massive farmers' demonstration in support of higher prices March 23.

Under the plan, target prices (those set by the EEC as fair for farm goods) were increased for most cereals, milk and beef for the new agricultural year beginning April 1. Milk was to increase by an average 6%, while beef was to rise by 6% in 1971 and an additional 4% in 1972. Wheat and rye prices were increased by an average 3% and barley prices by 5%. The price increases were higher than those originally proposed by the EEC Commission, under the direction of Commission Vice President Sicco Mansholt, but lower than the average 15% increase demanded by farmers' organizations in the six member states.

At the insistence of Italy, which stood to gain little from the actual price increases, the ministers agreed on a $1.48 billion, four-year program to increase farm efficiency. (The current EEC plan alloted $285 million yearly for agricultural structural reform.) The reform plan, less extensive than the one suggested in the Mansholt plan, would offer farmers between the ages of 55 and 65 a pension of up to $600 per year if they would leave the land.

Preference plan set. The governments of the six European Economic Community (EEC) members agreed March 30 to introduce a system of generalized trade preferences for 91 developing countries beginning July 1. The decision authorized duty-free entry for manufactured and semi-manufactured goods from developing nations, while keeping the current tariffs on the same goods from developed nations.

The Common Market Executive Commission reported that the amount of trade involved would total about $1 billion yearly and that the six members would lose about $100 million in tariffs that they normally would have collected.

Generalized trade preferences had been approved in principle by most of the developed countries, following discussion in the United Nations Conference on Trade and Development and the Organization for Economic Cooperation and Development. The U.S. was currently preparing legislation authorizing trade preferences.

(The 91 countries involved were members of the so-called "group of 77" developing nations, which had grown to 91. Other developing nations not included in the group and thus not included in the EEC's plan were Cuba, Israel, Taiwan, Spain, Portugal, Greece, Turkey and Malta. France reportedly had refused so far to extend preferences to these eight countries, but discussions were continuing within the EEC and the OECD. Bulgaria and Rumania also wanted to take advantage of the preferences, but EEC had not yet acted on their requests.)

U.S. relaxes China trade bar. President Nixon April 14 took another step to ease U.S. relations with Communist China by relaxing a 20-year embargo on trade with that country.

Although the President's decision was understood to have been made several weeks before, it coincided with a Chinese invitation to a U.S. table tennis team to visit the mainland and with the team's friendly reception in Peking. The Chinese government admitted several Western newsmen to cover the event April 10 and resumed partial telephone contact with Britain and the U.S. April 14.

Nixon's announcement said he was asking the National Security Council for "a list of items of a nonstrategic nature which can be placed under general license for direct export to the People's Republic of China. Following my review and my approval of specific items on this list, direct imports of designated items from China will then also be authorized."

The statement also said that U.S. firms would be allowed to trade with China in dollars and that the U.S. was "prepared to expedite visas" for visitors or groups of visitors from China.

U.S. oil companies were to be allowed to supply fuel to ships or planes proceeding to or from mainland China with the exception of Chinese-owned or Chinese-chartered carriers going to or from North Vietnam, North Korea or Cuba. U.S. carriers were to be allowed to transport Chinese cargos between non-Chinese ports, and U.S.-owned carriers under foreign flags could call at Chinese ports.

According to the New York Times April 14, the President's order on currency transactions would not free some $100 million of mainland Chinese dollar assets frozen in 1950.

President Nixon June 10 released a list of 47 categories of items considered exportable to China and announced that Chinese exports to the U.S. would be treated in the same manner as items from other Communist countries.

The President's list included such nonstrategic goods as farm products, household appliances, automobiles and basic metals. Among items omitted were locomotives, trucks, high-grade computers, petroleum products and commerical aircraft. The announcement said, however, that "consistent with the requirements of national security" such items could be deemed exportable under special licenses following a review by the Commerce Department and other government agencies.

Ronald L. Ziegler, White House press secretary, said Nixon would "later consider the possibility of further steps" to "re-establish a broader relationship" with mainland China, whose total imports in 1970 were valued at $2 billion, of which 75% came from non-Communist countries.

In a related development, Nixon also lifted a requirement by which 50% of grain shipments to China, the Soviet Union and other Eastern European countries were to be carried in U.S. ships.

Oil and inflation. According to some observers, the growing world "energy crisis," and specifically the international oil situation, played an important role in aggravating balance-of-payments problems and inflation. These were points cited:

■ The Middle East and North Africa, with probably 560 billion barrels of the non-Communist world's estimated 660-billion-barrel petroleum reserve, was able to produce oil at a cost of from 6¢ to 20¢ a barrel and, in 1971, was commanding prices that were beginning to exceed $3 a barrel. By comparison, in the U.S., with reserves of about 40 billion barrels, the cost of producing petroleum was between $2.50 and slightly more than $3 a barrel.

■ The industrialized countries increasingly relied on Middle East/North African oil. Some 85% of the petroleum used in Western Europe came from the area, as did at least a similar percentage of the oil used in Japan. While less than 5% of the petroleum used in the U.S. as a whole came from the area, the U.S.' East Coast did depend on Middle East/North African oil to a great extent, and this dependence was growing.

■ The Middle East/North African oil-exporting countries, therefore, received tremendous and increasing revenues (about $5.9 billion in 1970), far in excess of costs and in greater quantities than they could spend on domestic development or on imports from the oil-importing countries. Their accumulation of such tremendous reserves of foreign currencies added to the tendency of these reserve currencies to drop in value.

The oil-exporting countries, therefore, were accumulating hoards of currency that depreciated in value while they were exporting (and thereby depleting) their reserves of a commodity that, when left in the ground, apparently increased in value. According to the observers, the oil exporters, therefore, ultimately devised a practical way of solving this problem: this was to cut oil exports but simultaneously to raise oil prices sufficiently (or more than sufficiently) to compensate for the decline in revenue that the lower volume would cause. The result was a further attack on the value of the currency they received for their oil.

Oil price raised—Representatives of 23 Western oil companies signed an agreement in Teheran Feb. 14 to pay the six oil-producing Persian Gulf states an additional $10 billion in revenue in the next five years. This would raise the countries' annual oil income from the current level of $4.4 billion to $7.4 billion in 1975.

The accord climaxed weeks of talks between the firms, 17 of them American-owned, and Iran, Iraq, Saudi Arabia, Kuwait, Abu Dhabi and Qatar. The pact provided increased payments by more than $1.2 billion in 1971, rising to $3 billion in 1975. The Gulf States reportedly had demanded $1.4 billion in increased payments in 1971, rising to $11.8 billion in 1975. The new annual increases were to start June 1, and were to be repeated at the beginning of 1973, 1974 and 1975.

The pact also included a fixed rate of 55% of the companies' net income, even if other oil producing nations gain higher rates, and an immediate boost of 35% a barrel in the posted prices for crude oil at Persian Gulf tanker terminals.

The 10-member Organization of Petroleum Exporting Countries (OPEC) had met with representatives of 17 Western oil companies in Teheran Jan. 12 and 21 and Feb. 2 to press new demands for higher payments.

The OPEC had first aired its new demands for higher revenue at a joint meeting in Caracas, Venezuela Dec. 28, 1970. The conferees issued a manifesto that included a demand that the oil countries' average oil-income tax rate of 55% become standard and that all posted prices be raised to the highest level. The posted prices normally were higher than the actual market prices and were used primarily to compute oil tax and royalty payments to the host country.

The OPEC members were Iran, Iraq, Saudi Arabia, Kuwait, Qatar, Abu Dhabi, Libya, Algeria, Indonesia and Venezuela. They accounted for about 85% of the world's oil production outside the U.S. and the Soviet Union. The oil companies had paid the 10 OPEC nations $6.2 billion in 1969.

The firms represented at the Teheran talks included British Petroleum, Standard Oil Co. (New Jersey), Iranian Oil Participants Ltd. and other American, Dutch and French companies.

In a memorandum submitted to the OPEC Jan. 16, a group of 15 oil firms, including 12 American companies, proposed to negotiate "simultaneously" with the 10 organization members to seek a single five-year "overall endurable settlement" of their demands. Previous oil contracts had been arranged between a company and a single nation. The Persian Gulf producers—Kuwait, Saudi Arabia, Iran, Iraq, Abu Dhabi and Qatar—sought a regional settlement in line with a resolution approved at the Caracas meeting. The memorandum of the 15 firms also expressed opposition to further dealings on an individual basis with Libya, which had attempted to increase its terms beyond those granted to the Persian Gulf producers.

Signing the memorandum were British Petroleum Co., the French Petroleum Co., Gulf Oil Corp., Mobil Oil Corp., the Royal Dutch Shell Group, Standard Oil Co. of California, Standard Oil Co. (New Jersey), Texaco Inc., Continental Oil Co., Marathon Oil Co., Occidental Petroleum Corp., Amerada Hess Corp., Atlantic Richfield Co., W. R. Grace & Co. and Nelson Bunker Hunt, a Dallas oil man.

Shah Mohammed Riza Pahlevi of Iran warned Jan. 24 that if the current talks with the Western companies collapsed in the next nine days "the question of cutting off the flow of oil" to the Western consumer nations "will be definitely considered." The shah promised observance of any agreement between the international firms and the Persian Gulf producers, but he scoffed at proposals for a wider regional settlement as suggested Jan. 16. The differences in geography and marketing factors made an overall global settlement a bad idea, the Iranian leader said.

The OPEC states had threatened to disrupt deliveries to the oil companies unless an agreement was reached by Feb. 3. But a decision to defer such action was taken at a ministerial meeting of the countries in Teheran Feb. 3-4. Major producers backed a suggestion by Shah Mohammed Riza Pahlevi of Iran Feb. 3 that legal or legislative measures be taken to realize their demands for increased revenue.

The new president of the OPEC, Iranian Finance Minister Jamshid Amougezar, said Feb. 4 "There is no question of further negotiation. It is simply a question of whether they [the oil companies] accept our terms or not." Amougezar's statement was made at the concluding session of the OPEC ministers' meeting. He said the substance of resolutions adopted at the conference provided for "very strong sanctions" against the companies if they refused to accept legislation raising prices.

A threat to cut off oil shipments to the West was reiterated by OPEC representatives at their European headquarters in Vienna Feb. 7. A resolution warned that "appropriate measures, including a total embargo on shipments of crude oil and petroleum products," would result from a Western company refusal to honor legislation providing for higher oil prices.

The Algerian government April 13 established the world's highest posted price per barrel for crude oil.

Algeria's oil price increase was announced at an agricultural gathering by President Houari Boumedienne, who set the new cost of a barrel of crude oil at $3.60. The old price was $2.85. The increase was retroactive to March 20.

Iraq and the Western oil companies June 7 signed an agreement raising the price of Iraqi oil from $2.41 a barrel to $3.211 and raising the tax rate on oil company profits from 50% to 55%. In addition, there would be an annual price increase of 2½% to compensate for inflation.

World gold output. The annual report of the Bank for International Settlements (BIS), covering the financial year April 1, 1970-March 31, 1971, estimated that world gold production rose from 40.6 million fine ounces in 1969 to a record 41.4 million fine ounces in 1970. At $35 per fine ounce, the value of the world output was $1.45 billion, compared with $1.42 billion in 1969. (The report did not include figures for the Soviet Union, other East European countries, Communist China or North Korea.)

South African gold output rose from 31.3 million fine ounces in 1969 to 32.1 million ounces in 1970. Canadian production declined by .2 million fine ounces to 2.3 million ounces. U.S. output rose to 1.79 million fine ounces from 1.72 ounces in 1969.

Official gold reserves held by various nations dropped by $1.95 billion to $37.18 billion, largely because of gold subscription payments to the International Monetary Fund (IMF) by member countries.

Gold holdings of international institutions were up by $2.22 billion to $4.1 billion, mainly reflecting the increase in gold reserves of the IMF.

The net amount of gold absorbed by the private market declined $135 million from $1.315 billion in 1969 to $1.18 billion, apparently because of lessened demand in European markets.

Burns plan to bolster dollar. Testifying at a closed Senate Banking Committee hearing April 19 on the recent international monetary crisis, Federal Reserve Board Chairman Arthur F. Burns rejected proposals to raise U.S. interest rates as a means of curbing the dollar outflow. He said that raising interest rates "would not meet our lasting needs at home or abroad."

Burns offered an alternative five-part plan to bolster the international position of the dollar: (1) restore price stability in the U.S. (the "overriding need" for the U.S. economy) in conjunction with an incomes policy; (2) continue restraints on private capital outflows; (3) persuade other countries to "relax promptly" curbs on imports and investments abroad by their citizens and make a greater contribution to defense of the free world; (4) work with other nations to minimize differences in monetary policies and make stronger use individually of national fiscal policies; and (5) adopt steps to offset effects of unavoidable short-term capital flows.

Burns also suggested that the international financial position of the U.S. would be strengthened by higher overseas investment earnings, increased foreign investment in the U.S. stock market and a continuing reduction of U.S. forces in Vietnam that would diminish the military drain on the nation's balance of payments.

Burns was optimistic about the future. He said various steps had already been taken to reduce capital outflow, such as encouraging banks to retain their Eurodollars (dollars on deposit abroad) and efforts by the Federal Reserve and Treasury to stem downward pressures on short-term interest rates. Along with his assessment that the "bulk of the short-term capital outflow is now behind us," Burns said the U.S. payments deficit on the official settlement basis (measuring dollars accumulated in foreign central banks) should begin to decline sharply.

U.S. trade deficit. The Commerce Department reported May 27 that in April the U.S. had suffered a $214.7 million trade deficit (or import surplus), representing its first unfavorable trade balance since the $405.8 million deficit in February 1969.

Imports rose 5.3% from $3.57 billion in March to a record $3.76 billion, while exports dropped 7.1% to $3.54 billion. The import rise was centered in agricultural products, steel and aluminum.

In the first four months of 1971, the surplus of merchandise exports over imports was $216.1 million, down from $755.1 million in the same 1970 period.

Dollar crisis, currency values revised. A massive wave of speculation against the U.S. dollar swept European money markets beginning May 4.

Before the speculation ebbed, five European currencies—chief among them the West German mark—were freed from fixed parity with the dollar or were revalued upward. The shifts amounted to a partial devaluation of the dollar.

Underlying causes of the crisis of confidence in the dollar were attributed to a variety of interrelated factors:

■ Continued and growing deficits in the U.S. balance of international payments, reaching $10.68 billion in 1970 when calculated on an official payments basis (excluding the U.S. special drawing rights [SDR] allocation of $851 million issued by the International Monetary Fund [IMF] in 1970; if the SDR allocation was included, the deficit totaled $9.82 billion). There had been repeated reports

that the payments deficit had grown substantially in the first quarter of 1971. This fact was confirmed May 17.

■ Monetary inflation in the U.S., coupled with declining interest rates in a recessive economy at a time when West Germany was raising interest rates in an effort to cope with its own inflationary pressures. The combined attraction of the mark's solidity and higher short-term interest rates pulled increasing amounts of U.S. dollars to West German money and capital markets. It was estimated that $6 billion had flowed from the U.S. to West Germany during 1970.

■ The spectacular recent growth of the market in Eurodollars—dollars held by Europeans and U.S. banks and firms doing business in Europe. The Eurodollar market had increased to an estimated $50 billion, most of this growth in the past three years. The Eurodollar pool, necessary for international liquidity, flowed relatively freely through the West's capital markets and added mass to the recent wave of speculation. Business Week estimated in its May 15 issue that $14 billion in Eurodollar funds had flowed to the U.S. during the tight money period ending in 1970 and that $11 billion had returned to Europe since the drop in U.S. interest rates.

■ Dwindling U.S. reserves of gold and foreign currencies. According to the May issue of the IMF publication International Financial Statistics, U.S. gold reserves declined from $16.057 billion in 1962 to $14.065 billion in 1965 and to $10.892 billion in 1968; grew to $11.859 billion in 1969, but dropped again to $11.072 billion in 1970 and stood at $10.963 billion in March. The West German Central Bank's holdings of U.S. dollars alone were reported to amount to close to $20 billion by May 5.

Some U.S. and European news sources (among them the New York Times, Le Monde and Time) attributed the latest run on the dollar to the publication May 3 of a group of West German economic studies urging that the mark be freed from its current dollar parity to float to a new and higher value. The studies, prepared jointly by West Germany's five leading economic institutes, drew widespread attention when the federal Economics Ministry commented later in the day that they were a "useful contribution" to the current debate in Bonn over the future of the mark. The Economics Ministry was considered to favor freeing the mark, but the Bundesbank—West Germany's central bank—was known to oppose it and reiterated in a statement May 3 that there was no immediate need for such action.

(All but one of the five economic institutes reported that they favored freeing the mark indefinitely from its fixed parity with the dollar even though this would create a major obstacle to economic cooperation with the other European Economic Community [EEC] nations and to efforts to form a European monetary union. The continued transfer of Eurodollars to the West German economy would wreck Bonn's anti-inflation program, they warned. The five organizations were Kiel University's Institute for World Economy, Munich's I.F.O. Institute, the Institute of Hamburg, Essen's Rhineland-Westphalia Institute for Economic Research and West Berlin's German Institute for Economic Research.)

The flood of dollars onto European markets forced European central banks to intervene and absorb them to prevent the dollar's value from falling below its "floor"—one per cent below its official fixed parity with the specific country's currency. The West German central bank alone was reported to have bought $1 billion in U.S. dollars May 4.

On the morning of May 5 West Germany's Bundesbank—followed by the central banks of Switzerland, Belgium, the Netherlands and Austria—unexpectedly withdrew support of the dollar and refused to accept more U.S. currency. The five countries suspended foreign exchange dealings for the rest of the week. Later in the day Portugal and Finland also closed their foreign exchange markets. The Paris and London markets remained open.

The Bundesbank acted after less than an hour of trading had swollen its dollar holdings by an additional $1 billion.

Also burdened with excess dollars were Switzerland, which took in $600 million May 5 and $110 million in the previous two days; the Netherlands, which bought nearly $240 million; and Belgium, which purchased over $50 million. Austrian purchases were not immediately disclosed.

The EEC monetary committee met May 6 to work out proposals to cope with the crisis and with the problems of inflation of its six members. The proposals were submitted to EEC finance ministers at an emergency Brussels meeting May 8.

Meanwhile, Chancellor Willy Brandt's Cabinet debated the differing proposals of Karl Klasen, Bundesbank president, and Economics Minister Karl Schiller. Klasen sought to keep the mark pegged at 3.63 to 3.69 marks to the dollar, while Schiller urged that the mark be allowed to float freely in foreign exchange markets subject to supply and demand. The Cabinet's decision not to unilaterally revalue the mark was announced May 6 by Bonn spokesman Conrad Ahlers.

West Germany won the grudging permission of its EEC partners May 9 to free the mark from its fixed parity with the dollar and to permit it to float within a certain range. Following a marathon 20-hour meeting of the EEC's finance ministers in Brussels, a compromise communique was issued that enabled the West German Cabinet to take independent action. The communique said that "certain countries . . . could enlarge for a limited period the fluctuation margins of their exchange rates compared with their current parities." The communique stipulated that measures to discourage disproportionate capital flows should accompany the expansion of currency margins.

The decision to float the mark, which went into effect May 10, freed the mark to find a new value in the competitive market, but within a predetermined and undisclosed range. The decision amounted to rejection of Schiller's proposal that the mark be completely freed. The secrecy of the new margins and their duration was intended to conceal from speculators the point at which the Bundesbank would intervene and sell marks to maintain the secret ceiling on its value.

In a supplementary action, the government introduced a series of tough new controls on capital movements designed to assist the Bundesbank in managing the float.

West Germany's close trading partners—Switzerland, the Netherlands, Austria and Belgium—all acted May 9 to control the tide of excess dollars in their countries. Switzerland raised the value of its franc 7% against the dollar and Austria raised the value of the schilling 5.05%. Belgium, the only EEC member with a two-tier (free and official) foreign exchange market, announced that it would float its franc in free market transactions (into which excess capital inflows would be funneled). The Netherlands floated the guilder.

The upward revaluations and flotations in effect devalued the dollar against these currencies.

(Switzerland's revaluation, the first parity change in the gold-backed Swiss franc since 1936, was taken as a protective measure against speculative investments from abroad seeking higher interest rates. Finance Minister Nello Celio May 9 blamed low U.S. interest policies for the flood of dollars. As of May 10, one U.S. dollar would be worth 4.08 francs, down from the former 4.37 parity.)

The International Monetary Fund formally approved the upward revaluation of the Austrian schilling at a meeting of its executive board in Washington May 9. In a separate announcement, the IMF noted the decision of Germany and the Netherlands to float their currencies, a violation of the IMF rule that the market price of a member's currency be held within one per cent—up or down—of its official parity. The two countries reportedly had assured the IMF that they would float their currencies only temporarily and would return to a fixed parity. No statement was issued about Switzerland, which was not a member.

As foreign exchange markets reopened May 10 in their first official day of trading since the suspension May 5, the mark's value rose by 3.3%. The rise was narrower than expected. Comparative calm prevailed in the markets. The dollar displayed firmness against the mark and most other currencies, and continued to regain strength in German markets May 11-12.

(The Japanese yen was in great demand and Japanese banks in London were forced to limit supplies May 11. The previous day, the Japanese government had ruled out a possible revaluation and flotation of the yen.)

EEC developments—At the EEC ministerial meeting May 8, West Germany's proposals to float the mark and seek joint EEC action encountered strong opposition from France and the EEC Executive Committee.

Schiller initially had sought agreement on a plan to float all of the EEC currencies together to create a new and flexible parity base that would result in common increases in value against the dollar. However, the French and Italians argued that such a plan could bring a devaluation of their currencies against those of other EEC members. Instead, they sought stiff controls by Germany to limit the dollar influx. Also involved was the community's monetary union plan. The first step of the plan—a reduction of the exchange rate margins between members' currencies—was to have become effective June 15.

Another issue arose over EEC farm policy. France, the Common Market's biggest farm producer and principal beneficiary of the farm program, feared that a change in the mark's parity would upset the whole system of farm finance. The system revolved around a pool of funds fed by members' contributions fixed in terms of the dollar.

West German farmers also stood to lose by their government's currency action, and Schiller asked controls against cheaper food imports from the rest of the EEC. He finally dropped the demand at the finance ministers' meeting but presented it again at an emergency meeting of EEC agricultural ministers in Brussels May 11.

The May 11 meeting turned into a 17-hour marathon in which the Bonn delegation threatened a walkout. France and West Germany finally reached a compromise early May 12 to keep the farm program intact. Under the compromise, whenever a member's currency floated 2.5% above its old fixed rate, it could tax imports and pay export rebates to equalize competitive market conditions in the home market. West Germany had sought a lower ceiling but relented after the French agreed to extend the tax to all products priced under the common farm policy. A monthly review of the measures was imposed.

U.S. reaction calm—The Nixon Administration maintained a calm attitude toward the dollar crisis.

Commenting on the suspension of dollar trading in Europe, Treasury Secretary John B. Connally told newsmen at a White House briefing May 6 that the problem was due primarily to the current 2% disparity in short term interest rates between the U.S. and Europe. However, Connally declared that the U.S. would not "sacrifice" its own economic programs to raise interest rates and narrow the gap. Conceding that national interests took precedence over the international monetary situation, Connally asserted that West Germany also had been unwilling to sacrifice domestic economic goals to international needs.

Speaking for the Nixon Administration in Hot Springs, Va. May 8, Vice President Spiro Agnew said in a speech to the Business Council that the U.S. could not allow "a transitory flare-up" in the international monetary system "to drive us into actions which are against the long-run interests of both this nation and our friends abroad." Agnew expressed confidence that the balance of payments would improve "as we move back towards wage-price stability." He also said an improvement would depend on "fair treatment by our trading partners abroad."

He added: "To be blunt, we are not, in my judgment, being treated fairly." Agnew said "the disproportionate responsibilities that we bear—and have borne for so many years—constrain our trading partners to work with us, cooperatively and constructively" toward more equal trading arrangements.

The Treasury reacted to the European currency shifts May 10 with a statement that foreign exchange markets "appear to be adjusting in orderly fashion" and that "no immediate action by the United States is called for." Otherwise, the Administration maintained silence. Privately, officials were optimistic that on

balance the U.S. would benefit from the currency adjustments.

In a related development, the Federal Reserve Board published May 10 the summary of a meeting of its Federal Open Market Committee three months earlier at which some members had voiced concern over "the undesirable consequences for international capital flows of further sizable declines in short term interest rates" in the U.S. However, the committee had taken no action to curb the decline in rates.

Huge payments deficit in '71—Commerce Department figures issued May 17 confirmed that the U.S. balance of payments deficit had reached a record $5.51 billion in the first quarter of 1971—an annual rate of more than $22 billion. The figures were seasonally adjusted and calculated on an official payments basis, which measured changes in dollar holdings in foreign central banks that could be used to claim gold from U.S. Treasury stocks at the official $35 per-ounce price. Calculated on a liquidity basis, which in addition took account of dollars held by private persons and firms abroad, the payments deficit amounted to a seasonally adjusted $3.08 billion for the quarter.

Testifying at a Senate finance subcommittee hearing on foreign economic policy, Treasury Secretary Connally said the first quarter deficit was "bad" and not "sustainable." Speaking shortly before the official figures were released, Connally reiterated that "the major cause of these extraordinary [dollar] outflows is transitory—interest rates here which are lower than those in Western Europe. That imbalance will be corrected as economies move back into phase." He again rejected any suggestion that U.S. interest rates be raised to match those of Europe. "The most damaging blow we could receive just now is an increase in interest rates," he asserted.

Connally said the recent wave of dollar speculation had amounted to a "disturbance" but not a crisis. "I regret the implication that the dollar has been weakened," he said. "I don't believe it has been." He conceded that foreign central banks held dollars amounting to many times the Treasury's gold reserve, but he held it unlikely there would be a raid on U.S. gold and he noted that U.S.

firms currently held $70 billion in foreign investments and assets. He urged redoubled efforts to improve U.S. productivity and competitiveness in world markets. He added that some relaxation of antitrust laws might be necessary to allow U.S. industries to compete abroad.

Gold prices rise—The monetary crisis spurred the free market price of gold to an 18-month high May 12 on the London bullion market. Gold closed at $40.45 an ounce.

A round of dollar conversions May 3–12 by the Netherlands, Belgium and France sapped a further $422 million from U.S. gold stocks and cut reserves to about $10.6 billion. France bought $282 million in U.S. gold May 11 to make a payment to the International Monetary Fund, instead of using its own gold stocks. Belgium May 12 exchanged $80 million in dollars for gold, explaining that its dollar reserves and its holdings of IMF special drawing rights were reaching their limits.

In Washington May 12, Sen. Jacob Javits (R, N.Y.) proposed a cutoff of Treasury gold sales and called for a "folding in" of U.S. gold to a new international reserve currency.

A report issued by the U.S. Treasury May 25 showed that U.S. gold stocks had declined in April for the sixth straight month. They dropped to $10.93 billion from $10.96 billion at the end of March, a sharp decline from the year-earlier $11.90 billion. Contributing to the drop was the transfer of $400 million to the Treasury's exchange stabilization fund, as well as withdrawals by France and Belgium. Other figures: total U.S. international monetary reserves—$14.31 billion (down from $14.34 billion in March), SDRs—$1.44 billion (unchanged) and convertible foreign currencies—$257 million (compared with $256 million in March).

U.S. gold stocks fell in May to about $10.57 billion, total international monetary reserves to $13.8 billion, SDRs to $1.24 billion; convertible foreign currencies rose to $318 million. International Monetary Fund automatic drawing rights declined from $1.682 billion at the end of April to $1.678 billion at the end of May.

Munich banking conference. Central bank governors and monetary officials met at the International Banking Conference of the American Bankers Association in Munich May 23–28, and representatives of the key nations appeared to draw closer to a consensus on some form of multilateral control of the Eurodollar market. They were divided, however, on the issue of controlling divergencies in interest rates, considered a main cause of the speculation against the dollar. European officials urged U.S. action to curb large dollar outflows, including a possible devaluation.

Some of the Europeans argued that devaluation was technically feasible and would be less disruptive than the huge amounts of dollars that had flowed to Europe and were nurturing inflation in their countries. The most conciliatory stand came May 25 from West Germany's foreign minister, Walter Scheel. Scheel called for an end to mutual recrimination and said the dollar should not be made a scapegoat for the monetary crisis. Scheel said the crisis had many causes, including "interest-induced and speculative movements of capital." He suggested it would be "useful" for the U.S. to reduce its balance of international payments deficit, but said the deficit "needn't endanger the world's currency order."

In a speech to the closing session of the conference May 28, Treasury Secretary John B. Connally declared that the U.S. would not devalue the dollar or change the price of gold. He pledged the U.S. would defend the strength of the dollar. Connally also made it clear that the U.S. expected Western Europe to grant it more equitable trading arrangements and to assume a larger share of the West's burden of defending the free world.

In calling for liberalization of European and Japanese trade restrictions, Connally commented: "The question is only—but the 'only' is important—whether those nations now more than amply supplied with reserves as well as with productive power should not now be called upon for fresh initiative in opening their markets to the products of others." "No longer does the United States economy dominate the free world.

No longer can considerations of friendship or need or capacity justify the United States carrying so heavy a share of the common burdens."

The West German delegation linked its demands for a reform of the international monetary system to return of the mark to a fixed exchange rate. Otmar Emminger, deputy governor of the Bundesbank, West Germany's central bank, reaffirmed at a news briefing May 25 his government's intention to return to a parity of 3.63 to 3.69 marks to the dollar. He said, however, that Bonn could not restore the fixed exchange rate if conditions persisted that could lead to renewed speculation and a new rush of dollars into West German capital markets. Emminger said the mark would not be restored to fixed parity unless (1) the U.S. again became an "island of stability" with a "better basic balance" in its international payments; (2) there was full restoration of "faith in the dollar's parity," and (3) there was a better alignment of U.S. interest rates with European rates.

West Germany's insistence on reform of the West's monetary system was elaborated May 27 by Wilhelm Hankel, assistant secretary for monetary and credit policy in Bonn's new Ministry of Economics and Finance. Hankel said the decision of West Germany and the Netherlands to withdraw support of the dollar amounted to "a first step towards changing the world monetary system." He said that domestic problems had forced the U.S. to shirk its role as world banker, leaving Europeans with no choice but to abandon their obligations to buy dollars under the dollar-parity system. Hankel said the floating of the mark "gives us the opportunity and time to prepare necessary reforms in the international monetary system."

The problem created by the disparity in short-term interest rates on the two sides of the Atlantic stemmed from (1) Europe's use of high interest rates to fight domestic inflation, and (2) the Nixon Administration's insistence on keeping U.S. interest rates low to fuel continued expansion of the economy and combat unemployment. The Europeans generally wanted the U.S. to raise interest rates to discourage the dollar outflow that was aggravating inflation in Europe.

The U.S. position had been elaborated May 19 by Federal Reserve Board Chairman Arthur F. Burns in a statement in Washington. Burns said that the U.S. would not raise its interest rates to improve its balance of payments position.

Other developments—The Belgian Cabinet decided after a nine-hour meeting May 11 not to float the Belgian franc or widen its permitted fluctuation from parity. The decision reportedly annoyed the Netherlands, which had floated the guilder and had pressed Belgium to follow suit.

The May issue of World Financial Markets, published by the Morgan Guaranty Trust Co., reported that the chief factors in the huge dollar outflow to Europe during April and early May were: (1) sales of dollars by U.S. corporations and subsidiaries of foreign firms anxious to limit currency risks, (2) withdrawal of funds by U.S. branches and agencies of foreign banks, (3) "leads and lags" in international payments that accelerated payments due in currencies believed likely to rise in value and delayed payments due in dollars because of a possible reduction in value, and (4) reduced investment by foreigners in U.S. securities.

French Finance Minister Valery Giscard d'Estaing met in Washington May 20 with Treasury Secretary Connally. He reiterated the French view that the fixed parity system should be retained by the international monetary system. He also told Connally that the monetary crisis had retarded moves for a monetary union within the EEC and had spurred a trend toward national curbs on capital flows.

BIS meeting. The Bank for International Settlements (BIS), located in Basel, Switzerland, drew central bankers from all over Europe to its annual meeting June 14.

Addressing the opening session, BIS Chairman Jelle Zijlstra announced an agreement by member central banks on joint action to control the Eurocurrency market (an unregulated pool of currencies on deposit, including an estimated billion in Eurodollars, held by institutions outside their country of origin). The Eurocurrency pool was believed to have been a primary source of the "hot money" capital flows that had fueled the recent run on the dollar. With about $3 billion of surplus BIS funds currently in the Eurocurrency market, the central bankers agreed to temporarily refrain from placing BIS funds in the market or to withdraw funds "when such action is prudent in the light of market conditions."

Zijlstra called on the central bankers for greater coordination of monetary policy, fiscal policy, and effective incomes policies to combat inflation,.

Both Zijlstra and the BIS Annual Report, released for the meeting, cited the payments deficit of the U.S., not a BIS member, as the chief cause of the latest monetary crisis. The report charged the U.S. with an "admitted absence of any program for a fundamental correction of the situation—unless the theory that other currencies were supposed to adjust to the dollar can be called a program."

U.S. monetary hearings. Two key Nixon Administration spokesman testified at hearings of Congress' Joint Economic Subcommittee on International Exchange and Payments that the U.S. payments deficit was not the chief cause of the recent monetary crisis. Citing U.S. measures to curb the dollar outflow, they rejected the BIS' allegation that U.S. had no plan to cure its payments problem.

Paul A. Volcker, Treasury undersecretary for monetary affairs, conceded June 17 that the persistent U.S. payments deficit (the net dollar outflow including all but short-term capital transactions) of $2.5 to $3 billion a year left the world "more vulnerable to monetary upsets." However, he said the immediate cause of the recent crisis was the unrestricted short-term capital flood permitted by the system of free and quick currency convertibility at fixed exchange rates. To restore international monetary stability, Volcker suggested such measures as limited mandatory controls on capital movements, a more flexible exchange rate system and an "international open market operation" in Eurodollars.

Hendrik S. Houthakker, an outgoing member (July 15) of the President's Council of Economic Advisers, expressed confidence June 22 that the disequilibrium in the U.S. and European balances of payments would gradually disappear. Asserting that recent crisis had a generally favorable outcome. Houthakker said the most unsettling result was the weakening of the fixed exchange rate system governed by the International Monetary Fund. As a remedy, he proposed that the IMF amend its rules to permit more flexibility without abandoning the fixed-rate principle. Houthakker said actions of West Germany and Canada had helped bring the dollar into equilibrium. He echoed the reported Administration view that the Japanese yen was undervalued and said that Japan's recent payments surpluses averaging $500 million a month were "unsustainable."

(The U.S. Treasury June 28 arranged for the Bundesbank to purchase up to $5 billion of special Treasury notes to give the Bonn central bank an outlet for some of its excess dollars.)

Federal Reserve Board (FRB) Member Andrew Brimmer, testifying June 16, disclosed that six major U.S. banks appeared to have sent $738 million abroad in the week ending May 12, at the height of the monetary crisis.

C. Fred Bergsten, a former economic specialist on the National Security Council staff in the White House, said June 28 that the present monetary system was workable and that the U.S. balance of payments was not in "disequilibrium" if properly analyzed. He proposed a plan under which the "reserve currency" role of the dollar would be altered and diminished, but not altogether abolished.

The subcommittee's chairman, Rep. Henry S. Reuss (D, Wis.) failed to win support for a proposal to cease Treasury gold sales to float the dollar temporarily in world exchange markets.

Second monthly trade deficit. The U.S. ran a trade deficit for the second straight month in May, the Commerce Department reported June 28. The seasonally adjusted $205 million deficit (or import surplus) marked the first time since August-October 1950 that imports substantially exceeded exports over a consecutive two-month period. The two monthly deficits nearly erased the surplus of 1971's first three months.

The first five months of 1971 showed a slight trade surplus of $11.1 million, well off the $1.08 billion level of the comparable period in 1970. The slow rate of increase in exports was ascribed to weak demand abroad for industrial materials and equipment.

Imports in May rose 6.1% to $3.99 billion; exports rose 6.8% to $3.78 billion.

European Unity Advances

Britain to be EEC member. After 12 months of intensive negotiations in its third bid for entry into the European Economic Community (EEC), Great Britain reached final agreement with the EEC at 5 a.m. June 23 on the remaining major obstacles to market membership.

Earlier, a major obstacle had been removed when Britain and the EEC ministers agreed June 7 on the gradual phasing out of sterling's role as an international reserve currency.

In a Luxembourg negotiating session with the EEC Council of Ministers, chaired by French Foreign Minister Maurice Schumann, Britain's negotiator Geoffrey Rippon pledged London's commitment to "an orderly and gradual rundown of official sterling balances" after Britain's entry into the market. He also agreed that, after entry, Britain would be ready to discuss appropriate measures geared toward "progressive alignment" of sterling with the other market currencies aimed at achieving "economic and monetary union in an enlarged community." Meanwhile Britain pledged to "stabilize" the current sterling balances to accommodate the long-term objective of monetary union. The latter statement was viewed as a promise to discourage a rise in official balances prior to entry.

France had opposed the sterling reserve role because it gave Britain special trading privileges and exposed Britain to world monetary crises that might involve the EEC.

The British government launched its campaign to win public approval of Britain's entry into the EEC with the presentation July 7 of a White Paper to the House of Commons.

Emphasizing the disparity between Britain's limited economic progress over the past decade and the far better performance of EEC members, the 20,-000 word paper said "there is no alternate grouping" to provide Britain with a sufficiently large market to stimulate economic expansion. To reject entry, the paper declared, would be to "maintain our interests from the narrow—and narrowing—base" of recent years. It added that such an action would be "a rejection of an historic opportunity and a reversal of the whole direction of British policy under successive governments during the last decade . . . In a single generation we should have renounced an imperial past and rejected a European future."

The paper urged the nation to "accept the challenge, seize the opportunity and join the European Communities."

Estimating the cost of EEC entry to the British public, the government said the rise in average retail food prices during the transitional period would be about 15%, resulting in a cost of living increase of 0.5% annually for six years. (The food price estimate was lower than that suggested by market critics.)

The EEC foreign ministers July 12 accepted a five-year plan, proposed by Britain's chief market negotiator, Geoffrey Rippon, for ending London's existing controls on movements of capital to EEC nations. The plan would give Britain two years to remove restrictions on direct investments in EEC countries by British companies, 2½ years to lift the restrictions on personal capital movements, and five years to end restraints on portfolio investments in EEC countries.

Europeans deadlock on reform. Two days of French-West German summit talks July 5–6 in Bonn failed to break a deadlock over monetary reform that had brought a meeting of Common Market finance ministers to a standstill July 2. The disagreement centered on West Germany's refusal to comply with a French demand that the German mark be returned to fixed parity prior to any joint agreement on Common Market monetary reform.

The impasse was not broken by the Bonn meeting of President Georges Pompidou and Chancellor Willy Brandt. Separate talks were held simultaneously by Finance Minister Valery Giscard d'Estaing and Economics and Finance Minister Karl Schiller.

According to a spokesman, Brandt promised only that the floating of the mark from parity would not continue indefinitely. Brandt expressed support for monetary and economic union within the Common Market. He said that West Germany was prepared to cooperate in controlling capital flows, as long as the measures adopted conformed to German law and free-market principles.

Chancellor Brandt, in an interview published by the Paris newspaper Le Monde July 6, said his ultimate goal was the creation of a "rationally organized European government which can take decisions in common policy fields, and which is under parliamentary control." As he saw it, a European government would not eliminate national identities.

Brussels stalemate—The Brussels talks of the Common Market finance ministers had been halted July 2 by the abrupt departure of French Finance Minister Giscard d'Estaing. The meeting had been called to discuss proposals by the European Economic Community's Executive Commission for widening permissible bands of exchange rate fluctuation to curb surplus capital flows and enhance flexibility of members' currencies.

The opposing Bonn-Paris viewpoints took shape in discussions July 1.

Giscard d'Estaing made it clear that France would only back greater currency flexibility on the condition that Germany and the Netherlands detail the date on which they would return their currencies to a fixed parity. Schiller balked at setting a deadline on the ground that it would generate renewed speculation on foreign exchange markets.

Schiller made it clear the next day that the mark would continue to float until the IMF adopted new rules widening the permissible margins of fluctuation on exchange rates to 2% or 3% either side of parity from the now authorized 1% (Common Market currencies were generally held within bands of .75%). The French finance minister reminded Schiller that the May 9 Common Market directive authorizing Germany to float the mark had stipulated that no member could add supplementary conditions to the commission's proposals.

E-W trade developments. The Soviet Union July 14 signed a trade agreement with Benelux—the economic union of Belgium, the Netherlands and Luxembourg—providing for most-favored-nation treatment. The pact, believed to be the first between the Soviet Union and a Western economic group, was signed in Brussels by Nikolai S. Patolichev, Soviet minister of foreign trade, and his Belgian counterpart, Henri Fayat, and by the Dutch and Luxembourg ambassadors.

British Prime Minister Edward Heath confirmed July 2 that the U.S. had withdrawn its opposition to sale of two British computers to the Soviet high-energy physics institute at Serpukhov, 60 miles south of Moscow. The U.S. was said to have blocked the sale, by International Computers Ltd., for more than a year in a NATO committee which passed on strategic exports to Communist nations. It reportedly approved the sale on the basis of Soviet promises not to use the computers in nuclear weapons programs and to allow their regular inspection by British technicians.

Poland and British Petroleum Ltd. signed July 1 a 10-year agreement valued at $500 million for the supply of three million tons of crude oil a year to a processing plant to be built in Gdansk by 1975. The agreement was signed for BP by Lord Strathalmond, the company's chairman, and for Poland by Antonu Poniatowski, director of a government enterprise in charge of foreign trade in chemicals.

Nixon to visit Peking. Disclosing a major revision of U.S. foreign policy expected to have wide economic as well as political repercussions, President Nixon announced July 15 that he would visit Peking before May 1972 to confer with Communist Chinese leaders "to seek the normalization of relations between the two countries and to exchange views on questions of concern to the two sides." A follow-up announcement July 16 said the President would confer with both Communist Party Chairman Mao Tse-tung and Premier Chou En-lai. No American President had ever been received by a Chinese government.

In his address, broadcast from Los Angeles, Nixon disclosed that arrangements for the projected meeting with Chinese leaders had been worked out in secret talks held in Peking July 9–11 by Henry A. Kissinger, his national security affairs adviser, and Chou En-lai. Kissinger, on a fact-finding tour of Asia, had made the secret flight to Peking from Pakistan, one of his stopover points.

Nixon said the plan for the proposed trip was being announced simultaneously in the U.S. and Peking. Alluding to the Nationalist Chinese government on Taiwan, the President emphasized that "our action in seeking a new relationship with the People's Republic of China will not be at the expense of our old friends." Nixon called his forthcoming visit "a major development in our efforts to build a lasting peace in the world." He said it was in accord with his oft-stated belief that "there can be no stable and enduring peace without the participation of the People's Republic of China and its 750 million peoples."

Nixon said that Chou had extended the invitation to him to come to Peking in response to his [Nixon's] expression of interest in a visit to China. The Chinese premier was reported to have confirmed to a visiting French group July 17 that it was the President who had suggested the trip.

Export expansion bill signed. The Export Expansion Finance Act of 1971 was passed by Senate voice vote Aug. 2 and 219-140 House vote Aug. 5. It was signed by President Nixon Aug. 17.

The legislation extended the life of the Export-Import Bank to June 30, 1974 and liberalized East-West trade provisions by removing current restrictions against Export-Import Bank credits to nations giving aid to another country in armed conflict with the U.S. A ban against bank-financed trade for countries in armed conflict with the U.S.—i.e. North Vietnam—was retained, as well as a ban against exports to any country of

items of war-related material that could be sent to North Vietnam.

The ban against financing exports to Communist-bloc countries supplying North Vietnam had been in effect three years. The final House vote represented a reversal of a 207–153 House vote July 8 to retain such a ban, and there was protest in the House Aug. 5 that relaxation of the trade barrier, originating in the Senate and adopted by House-Senate conferees, represented a flouting of the House will. Republican Leader Gerald R. Ford (Mich.), however, pointed out that such trade would still come under presidential discretion and could be barred if it was determined to be against the national interest.

Balance of payments deficit. The U.S. balance of international payments deficit for the second quarter, ended June 30, was the worst on record, according to figures released by the Commerce Department Aug. 16. On an "official settlements" basis—measured by dollars mounting in foreign central banks—the deficit was a seasonally adjusted $5.77 billion (a $23.08 billion annual rate). On the overall "liquidity" basis, the deficit was a seasonally adjusted $5.85 billion (a $23.4 billion annual rate).*

*New balance of payments measurements. The Commerce Department July 6 published a new set of measures for U.S. balance of payments statistics. The department warned that none of the new statistics provided a precise gauge of whether the payments balance was in "equilibrium." The chief innovations were a "balance on current account and long-term capital" and a "net liquidity balance." The revisions were intended to remove the two major distortions in previous statistics—Eurodollar and special Treasury dealings.

The current account of the balance of payments measured transactions in goods (exports and imports), services (including net investment income and overseas military spending), remittances and other transfers to foreigners (e.g. pensions) and U.S. government nonmilitary grants to foreign countries.

The balance on current account and long-term capital comprised all forms of government and private, long-term capital flows into and out of the U.S., including direct investment, securities purchases and long-term government loans.

The new net liquidity balance included some short-term capital flows, bank lending to foreigners and the erratic "errors and omissions" category.

The department retained the volatile "official reserve transactions balance" ("official settlements") which added the remainder of U.S. short-term, private, capital outflows and reflected fluctuations of foreign central bank dollar holdings. The category omitted dollars acquired by private foreigners.

Trade deficit—According to the Commerce Department report on the Gross National Product, issued Aug. 20, U.S. overseas trade (including goods and services, such as shipping costs) for the second quarter was sharply revised to show a net export deficit at a $2.2 billion annual rate. On a seasonally adjusted basis, total exports of goods and services were running at an annual rate of $64.2 billion, imports at an annual rate of $66.4 billion. It was only the second time since the end of World War II that the U.S. had failed to show a quarterly surplus of exports over imports on a goods and services basis.

The department's merchandise trade figures disclosed a running deficit for May, June, July and for the second quarter: −$205 million in May, −$363 million in June, −$304 million in July and −$803 million for the second quarter. Imports were up 6.1% to $3.988 billion (seasonally adjusted) in May, up .09% to $4.023 billion in June, down 5.6% to $3.799 billion in July, and up 8.9% to $11.669 for the second quarter. Exports rose by 7.4% to $3.983 billion in May and then declined by 3.2% in June to $3.661 billion, by 5.6% in July to $3.799 billion and by 2.4% in the second quarter to $10.966 billion.

Record low for U.S. gold stock. U.S. gold stocks plunged $61 million in June to $10.507 billion, the Treasury Department reported July 26. The drop reflected a $50 million purchase by the Swiss central bank. The eighth consecutive monthly decline brought the gold stock down a total $565 million in 1971 and down $1.38 billion from June 1970.

The Treasury report said that total U.S. international reserve assets fell $298 million in June to $13.5 billion—$2.8 billion below June 1970 and the lowest for any month since August 1938.

The report said that as of the end of April, foreign governments held $27.29 billion in U.S. currency and private foreigners held $18.61 billion.

The U.S. gold stock was further drained by France's exchange Aug. 9 of $191 million of surplus dollars for gold to repay debts to the IMF.

U.S. reserve assets fell an additional $221 million in July, the Treasury reported

Aug. 25. $54 million of the decline was from the nation's gold stock. Total U.S. monetary reserves at the end of July were $13.283 billion, $10.453 billion in gold.

France checks dollar intake. The Bank of France inadvertently touched off a burst of speculation against the dollar Aug. 4 when it became known that the bank had issued instructions the previous day banning all purchases of dollars except for commercial transactions. Rumors of an impending revaluation of the franc, fanned by the central bank's action, sent European currencies soaring and the dollar falling on the Zurich, Frankfurt and London money markets. The dollar dropped below its floor in Brussels and Paris. On receiving news of the French bank's action, the "Big Three" of Swiss banking—the Swiss Bank Corp. in Basel, and the Union Bank of Switzerland and Swiss Credit Bank in Zurich—temporarily suspended dollar dealings.

The French central bank took stronger measures Aug. 6 to stem the inflow of dollars by announcing that French banks would no longer pay interest on foreigners' deposits of French francs for less than 91 days. Banks were also expected to adhere unofficially to a proposed $500,000 ceiling for deposits not requiring authorization.

The pressure on the dollar subsided Aug. 6.

Dollar weakens, gold soars. A congressional report urging effective devaluation of the dollar was blamed for a new round of speculation against the dollar and a sharp rise in the price of gold on European exchange markets Aug. 9. The Swiss central bank suspended convertibility of the dollar to stem a speculative tide of "hot money" into Switzerland. In Frankfurt, the dollar closed at 3.4090 marks to the dollar, in effect a 7.5% devaluation of the dollar in terms of the mark's value before it was floated May 10.

Early Aug. 9, the Swiss franc climbed to 4.060 to the dollar, the support level set by the Swiss National Bank, causing the central bank to intervene in the market. Although the Swiss bank would not say how many dollars it was forced to absorb, press reports described the amount as "hundreds of millions of dollars." The bank announced later Aug. 9 that it was freezing payment on francs purchased with dollars for 10 days. The suspension was intended to last until Aug. 20, when a "gentlemen's agreement" between the central bank and the Swiss Bankers Association was to become effective. The agreement, concluded in July, would empower the central bank to fix reserve requirements as high as 100% on foreign-owned franc deposits in excess of normal business transactions and to limit or forbid interest payments on funds entering Switzerland.

The dollar briefly dropped through its floor of 620.50 lira in Milan Aug. 9. In Brussels and Tokyo, central banks intervened to keep the dollar from falling below its limits. In Paris, the dollar fell to its floor of 5.5125 francs to the dollar.

On the London bullion exchange, gold rose Aug. 9 from $42.90 an ounce to $43.95, its highest level since the two-tier system for gold dealing was introduced in March 1968. By the close of trading, the price dropped back to $43.10.

Subcommittee proposes revaluation. The Congressional Joint Economic Subcommittee on International Exchange and Payments, in a report Aug. 7 based on hearings held in June, in effect recommended devaluation of the dollar. The report said that international exchange rates should be readjusted to compensate for the dollar's overvaluation. It urged the International Monetary Fund (IMF) to pressure certain of its members to revalue their currencies upward against the dollar.

It warned: "If the membership of the Fund fails to confront this issue and does not specify a mechanism through which dollar exchange rates can be promptly restructured, the United States should then promptly consider a unilateral initiative to achieve this same result, perhaps by floating the dollar within specified limits."

The report made no estimate of the dollar's overvaluation.

The subcommittee chairman, Rep. Henry Reuss (D, Wis.), said at a news conference Aug. 7 that a total devaluation of the dollar by raising the price of gold would be unacceptable; he said it would give gold producing countries "windfall profits," but would not assure a shift in the dollar's relative exchange rates with other currencies.

Reuss said that the persistently large U.S. balance of payments deficit, expected to reach $6.5 billion–$7 billion in the second quarter, was evidence that the dollar was overvalued.

The Treasury Department rebuffed the report Aug. 7. It said it planned no discussion in the IMF on exchange rate realignments. Conceding a serious balance of payments problem, the Treasury said a strong trade and payments position depended on a "healthy, noninflationary domestic economy."

Two leading economists, Milton Friedman and Robert V. Roosa, opposed the report as impractical in separate interviews Aug. 10. Friedman, a professor at the University of Chicago, said unilateral devaluation of the dollar could not work without the cooperation of other countries.

Americans Under Economic Control

Nixon Freezes Wages & Prices, Ends Dollar's Tie to Gold

After resolutely resisting wage and price controls for more than two years in the face of growing inflation and despite increasing demands for economic action, in mid-August 1971, the Nixon Administration abruptly banned further wage or price increases. This unexpected reversal of the President's "game plan" ushered in "Phase One" of a stabilization program designed to halt the upward rush of prices and wages, to end the overseas attacks on the value of the U.S. dollar and to reverse the growth of deficits in the U.S.' balance of international payments.

Emergency measures imposed. President Nixon announced without warning Aug. 15 that he was ordering an immediate 90-day freeze on wages, rents and prices and was ending the traditional convertibility of the dollar into gold, in effect freeing the dollar for devaluation against other currencies.

These were the two major points in a program that included a 10% surcharge on dutiable imports, a $4.7 billion reduction in federal expenditures, a reduction in federal personnel, and a request for Congressional action to end automobile excise taxes and enact tax incentives for industry.

The price-wage freeze was the first to be imposed in the U.S. since the ceiling ordered by the Truman Administration Jan. 26, 1951 to cope with the inflationary spiral generated by the first six months of the Korean War.

The suspension of the dollar's ties to gold, ordered after massive speculation against the dollar and deficits in the U.S. balance of payments, ended the world monetary system based on the dollar and its convertibility into gold at a fixed $35 an ounce.

Major elements of the new policy—especially the wage-price freeze—had been advocated by Nixon's principal Democratic opposition (with increasing force as it became clear that economic problems would be a major issue in the 1972 Presidential elections) but had been rejected by the Administration as steps toward a controlled economy.

The President disclosed his decision in a nationally televised address from the White House.

Nixon described his actions as a "new economic policy for the United States," one whose "targets are unemployment, inflation and international speculation." He said that the nation's current economic difficulties stemmed in part from the difficulties of transition from a war economy to one of peaceful prosperity. These problems, he said, demanded decisive action to solve them.

233

Among elements of his program that Nixon discussed in his address:

Wage-price freeze—"I am today ordering a freeze on all prices and wages throughout the United States for a period of 90 days. In addition, I call upon corporations to extend the wage-price freeze to all dividends." Nixon said he had appointed a government Cost of Living Council, headed by the secretary of the Treasury, "to work with leaders of labor and business to set up the proper mechanism for achieving continued price and wage stability after the 90-day freeze is over."

He stressed the temporary nature of the freeze:

"Let me emphasize . . . First, it is temporary. To put the strong, vigorous American economy into a permanent straightjacket would lock in unfairness; it would stifle the expansion of our free enterprise system. And second, while the wage-price freeze will be backed by government sanctions, if necessary, it will not be accompanied by the establishment of a huge price control bureaucracy. I am relying on the voluntary cooperation of all Americans . . . to make this freeze work."

Texts of Nixon's Orders on Wage-Price Freeze and Surcharge

Stabilization Order

Whereas, in order to stabilize the economy, reduce inflation, and minimize unemployment, it is necessary to stabilize prices, rents, wages and salaries; and

Whereas, the present balance-of-payments situation makes it especially urgent to stabilize prices, rents, wages and salaries in order to improve our competitive position in world trade and to protect the purchasing power of the dollar:

Now, therefore, by virtue of the authority vested in me by the Constitution and statutes of the United States, including the Economic Stabilization Act of 1970 (P.L. 91-379, 84 Stat. 799), as amended, it is hereby ordered as follows:

Section 1. (A) Prices, rents, wages and salaries shall be stabilized for a period of 90 days from the date hereof at levels not greater than the highest of those pertaining to a substantial volume of actual transactions by each individual, business, firm or other entity of any kind during the 30-day period ending Aug. 14, 1971, for like or similar commodities or services. If no transactions occurred in that period, the ceiling will be the highest price, rent, salary or wage in the nearest preceding 30-day period in which transactions did occur. No person shall charge, assess, or receive, directly or indirectly in any transaction, prices or rents in any form higher than those permitted hereunder, and no person shall, directly or indirectly, pay or agree to pay in any transaction wages or salaries in any form, or to use any means to obtain payment of wages and salaries in any form, higher than those permitted hereunder, whether by retroactive increase or otherwise.

(B) Each person engaged in the business of selling or providing commodities or services shall maintain available for public inspection a record of the highest prices or rents charged for such or similar commodities or services during the 30-day period ending Aug. 14, 1971.

(C) The provisions of Sections 1 and 2 hereof shall not apply to the prices charged for raw agricultural products.

Section 2. (A) There is hereby established the Cost-of-Living Council, which shall act as an agency of the United States and which is hereinafter referred to as the council.

(B) The council shall be composed of the following members: the Secretary of the Treasury, the Secretary of Agriculture, the Secretary of Commerce, the Secretary of Labor, the Director of the Office of Management and Budget, the Chairman of the Council of Economic Advisers, the Director of the Office of Emergency Preparedness, and the Special Assistant to the President for Consumer Affairs. The Secretary of the Treasury shall serve as Chairman of the council and the Chairman of the Council of Economic Advisers shall serve as Vice Chairman. The Chairman of the Board of Governors of the Federal Reserve System shall serve as Adviser to the council.

(C) Under the direction of the Chairman of the council, a Special Assistant to the President shall serve as Executive Director of the council, and the Executive Director is authorized to appoint such personnel as may be necessary to assist the council in the performance of its functions.

Section 3. (A) Except as otherwise provided herein, there are hereby delegated to the council all of the powers conferred on the President by the Economic Stabilization Act of 1970.

(B) The council shall develop and recommend to the President additional policies, mechanisms and procedures to maintain economic growth without inflationary increases in prices, rents, wages and salaries after the expiration of the 90-day period specified in Section 1 of this order.

(C) The council shall consult with representatives of agriculture, industry, labor and the public concerning the development of policies, mechanisms and procedures to maintain economic growth without inflationary increases in prices, rents, wages and salaries.

(D) In all of its actions the council will be guided by the need to maintain consistency of price and wage policies with fiscal, monetary, international and other economic policies of the United States.

(E) The council shall inform the public, agriculture, industry and labor concerning the need for controlling inflation and shall encourage and promote voluntary action to that end.

Section 4. (A) The council, in carrying out the provisions of this order, may (I) prescribe definitions for any terms used herein, (II) make exceptions or grant exemptions, (III) issue regulations and orders and (IV) take such other actions as it deter-

Ending dollar-gold link—Nixon asserted that the primary causes of the dollar's difficulties in international money markets were a recurrent wave of monetary crises and the speculation that resulted—created in part, he said, by the "international money speculators" who benefited from them.

"In recent weeks," he said, "the speculators have been waging an all-out war on the American dollar." However, Nixon added: "The strength of a nation's currency is based on the strength of that nation's economy—and the American economy is by far the strongest in the world."

The President said he had taken the following action "to defend the dollar against the speculators":

"I have directed [Treasury] Secretary [John B. Jr.] Connally to suspend temporarily the convertibility of the dollar into gold or other reserve assets, except in amounts and conditions determined to be in the interest of monetary stability and in the best interests of the United States."

Nixon conceded that the dollar would float downward in value against some other currencies and that foreign goods and travel would cost Americans more, but, "lay[ing] to rest the bugaboo

---

mines to be necessary and appropriate to carry out the purposes of this order.

(B) The council may redelegate to any agency, instrumentality or official of the United States any authority under this order, and may, in administering this order, utilize the services of any other agencies, Federal or state as may be available and appropriate.

(C) On request of the Chairman of the council, each executive department or agency is authorized and directed, consistent with law, to furnish the council with available information, which the council may require in the performance of its functions.

(D) All executive departments and agencies shall furnish such necessary assistance as may be authorized by Section 214 of the act of May 3, 1945, 59 Stat. 134 (31 U.S.C. 691).

Section 5. The council may require the maintenance of appropriate records or other evidence, which are necessary in carrying out the provisions of this order, and may require any person to maintain and produce for examination such records or other evidence, in such form as it shall require, concerning prices, rents, wages and salaries and all related matters. The council may make such exemptions from any requirement otherwise imposed as are consistent with the purposes of this order. Any type of record or evidence required under regulations issued under this order shall be retained for such period as the council may prescribe.

Section 6. The expenses of the council shall be paid from such funds of the Treasury Department as may be available therefore.

Section 7. (A) Whoever willfully violates this order or any order or regulation issued under authority of this order shall be fined not more than $5,000 for each such violation.

(B) The council shall in its discretion request the Department of Justice to bring actions for injunctions authorized under Section 205 of the Economic Stabilization Act of 1970 whenever it appears to the council that any person has engaged, is engaged or is about to engage in any acts or practices constituting a violation of any regulation or order issued pursuant to this order.

Import Surcharge

Whereas, there has been a prolonged decline in the international monetary reserves of the United States, and our trade and international competitive

position is seriously threatened and, as a result, our continued ability to assure our security could be impaired;

Whereas, the balance-of-payments position of the United States requires the imposition of a surcharge on dutiable imports;

Whereas, pursuant to the authority vested in him by the Constitution and the statutes, including, but not limited to, the Tariff Act of 1930, as amended (hereinafter referred to as "the Tariff Act"), and the Trade Expansion Act of 1962 (hereinafter referred to as "the TEA"), the President entered into, and proclaimed tariff rates under, trade agreements with foreign countries.

Whereas, under the Tariff Act, the TEA, and other provisions of law, the President may, at any time, modify or terminate, in whole or in part, any proclamation made under his authority;

Now, therefore, I, Richard Nixon, President of the United States of America, acting under the authority vested in me by the Constitution and the statutes, including, but not limited to, the Tariff Act, and the TEA, respectively, do proclaim as follows:

(A) I hereby declare a national emergency during which I call upon the public and private sectors to make the efforts necessary to strengthen the international economic position of the United States.

(B) (1) I hereby terminate in part for such period as may be necessary and modify prior Presidential proclamations, which carry out trade agreements, insofar as such proclamations are inconsistent with, or proclaim duties different from, those made effective pursuant to the terms of this proclamation.

(2) Such proclamations are suspended only insofar as is required to assess a surcharge in the form of a supplemental duty amounting to 10 per cent ad valorem. Such supplemental duty shall be imposed on all dutiable articles imported into the customs territory of the United States from outside thereof, which are entered, or withdrawn from warehouse, for consumption after 12:01 A.M., Aug. 16, 1971, provided, however, that if the imposition of an additional duty of 10 per cent ad valorem would cause the total duty or charge payable to exceed the total duty or charge payable at the rate prescribed in column 2 of the tariff schedules of the United States, then the column-2 rate shall apply.

(Also included in Nixon's orders were temporary modifications to implement Section B of the import surcharge proclamation.)

of what is called devaluation," he said, ". . . if you are among the overwhelming majority of Americans who buy American-made products in America, your dollar will be worth just as much tomorrow as it is today. The effect of this action, in other words, will be to stabilize the dollar."

Import surcharge—"I am taking one further step to protect the dollar, to improve our balance of payments," the President said. "As a temporary measure, I am today imposing an additional tax of 10% on goods imported into the United States. This is a better solution for international trade than direct controls on the amounts of imports. . . . It is an action to make certain that American products will not be at a disadvantage because of unfair exchange rates. When the unfair treatment is ended, the import tax will end as well."

Tax, budget & personnel cuts—The President said that although "our unemployment rate today is below the average of the four peacetime years of the 1960s," it had become necessary to deal forcefully with it and "to embark on a bold new program of investment in production for peace." He said that he would ask Congress to act on the following measures immediately after its summer recess:

■ Passage of the Job Development Act of 1971.
■ A 10% one-year tax credit to industry for investment in new equipment, to be continued at a 5% rate the second year.
■ Repeal of the current 7% federal excise tax on automobiles, with the saving (about $200 per car) passed on to customers.
■ A speedup in the rise in personal income tax exemptions from $650 to $750 on Jan. 1, 1972, a year early.

Nixon said: "To offset the loss of revenue from these tax cuts which directly stimulate new jobs, I have ordered today a $4.7 billion cut in federal spending. . . . To check the rise in the cost of government, I have ordered postponement of pay raises and a 5% cut in government personnel. I have ordered a 10% cut in foreign economic aid. In addition, since the Congress has already delayed action on two of the great initiatives of this Ad-

ministration, I will ask Congress . . . to postpone the implementation of revenue sharing for three months and welfare reform for one year."

In conclusion, the President called on Americans to help him make the program work and restore confidence in the economy. He urged them to meet the challenge of foreign competition in peacetime, saying, "Every action I have taken tonight is designed to nurture and stimulate that competitive spirit, to help us snap out of the self-doubt, the self-disparagement that saps our energy and erodes our confidence in ourselves." "Our best days," he said, "lie ahead."

Executive orders issued. The major parts of the Administration's new economic policy became effective Aug. 16 when the President signed two documents—Executive Order 11615, entitled Executive Order Providing for Stabilization of Prices, Rents, Wages and Salaries, and Proclamation 4074, entitled Proclamation Regarding Imposition of Supplemental Duty for Balance of Payments Purposes.

The Executive Order, which set specific conditions for administration of the 90-day wage-price freeze, was issued under authority given the President by the Economic Stabilization Act of 1970.

Administration explains plan. The ramifications of the new Nixon economic policy were explained by senior Administration officials at a special White House press briefing shortly before the President's address Aug. 15 and at a televised press conference held by Treasury Secretary Connally Aug. 16.

The White House briefing was led by Connally, George P. Shultz, director of the Office of Management and Budget, and Paul W. McCracken, chairman of the President's Council of Economic Advisers. (These three, plus Arthur F. Burns, chairman of the Federal Reserve Board, had spent Aug. 14–15 with the President at his Camp David, Md. retreat, for final discussion of the new policies.)

Addressing the White House press corps, which had been assembled and informed of the content of the President's speech, Connally said that the problems dealt with by the new policy had been under study for months but "I think all of the decisions he is announcing tonight were made this weekend." Connally conceded that he had "express[ed] a high degree of confidence" about the policy now abandoned by the Administration, but, he said, increased difficulties with the balance of trade and instability on the foreign monetary markets "reached a point where it was felt desirable to act . . . in a concerted, integrated fashion to try to solve those difficulties."

Asked whether the ending of the dollar's convertibility into gold was in effect a devaluation, he said: "No, I would not use the word 'devalue' simply because I don't know what's going to happen. . . . for all I know the dollar may rise with respect to certain countries. . . . It may go down in relation to other currencies." Connally insisted that Nixon had only ended convertibility, that he had not changed the price of gold nor altered the dollar's official gold evaluation. The dollar, he said, remained "interchangeable with other currencies" and its flotation to new rates of exchange depended entirely on the other governments concerned. He added: "I don't know how long it will float."

Connally made it clear that the Administration's intention was to force other countries to revalue their currencies on a realistic basis and to begin "new negotiations for a basically new international monetary system that will permit us to continue to assume the burdens and the duties and the obligations that we have assumed over the years and yet not go broke doing it from a [poor] trade balance."

With respect to the duration of the wage-price freeze, McCracken told the newsmen that "any wage-price freeze can last only for a relatively short period. The problem of the procedures and the . . . program that will be devised in order to go from there on through ultimately to a free pricing system again, at the same time maintaining price stability, these are matters to be worked out by the [Cost of Living] Council." McCracken refused to say whether a wage-price board was envisaged after the expiration of the 90-day freeze.

Connally, questioned about his past objections to a wage-price freeze because of the difficulties in enforcing it, said: "I don't think either he [the President] or I have ever said that we were not for a wage-price freeze. He and I both have said that we were not for wage and price controls. As I interpret those two phrases, they mean entirely different things. . . . He put on a wage-price for a limited period of time, 90 days, with the idea that this would be voluntarily adhered to by the American people. . . . It is a different animal entirely from wage-price controls as we normally speak in those terms."

Shultz stressed the Administration hope that as a result of the freeze it would "have a new situation emerge," one that could be dealt with without controls. He said it was "conceivable" that the freeze might be continued in some form after the 90-day period, but he did not indicate what sort of mechanisms would be involved.

Connally on details—In his televised meeting with newsmen at the Treasury Aug. 16, Connally provided further details on the Administration's new program and the ways in which it would be applied.

Beginning with a strong statement of support for the program, Connally said: "I personally believe the President's program contains the most sweeping, courageous and important economic proposals made in the last 40 years in this country." Connally rebuffed reporters' suggestions that the program was an admission of the failure of the Administration's past policies: "I don't think we did it in terms of an admission of anything," he said. "I would characterize it as a new policy . . . designed to solve the really hard-core basic problems that this nation faces here and abroad."

The 90-day wage-price freeze was total, Connally asserted. Except for a very few cases in which the government might grant "hardship" adjustments, "it will affect all individual raises, all merit raises, affect all raises under contract" and cost-of-living increases. None would be permitted, he said, not even those raises negotiated previously to take effect after Aug. 14. He said that new contract increases could be negotiated but none could become effective during the 90-day period.

Connally made it clear that no price increases were permitted, not even those previously announced, unless they were in effect "to a substantial degree . . . prior to Aug. 14." Asked about enforcement, he said that "the Justice Department will be immediately authorized to take action both in the form of injunctive relief . . . and to prosecute those who willfully violate [the freeze]." When a reporter remarked that the $5,000 penalty would not be a deterrent to large businesses, Connally said it was "inconceivable" that a large firm would violate the freeze and "incur the wrath of the American people."

Connally said interest rates had not been frozen because the Administration felt it would be "counter-productive." "We want to make it abundantly clear . . . that we think lending institutions have to assume the responsibility for making available . . . money at reasonable rates so it will not stifle the expansion that's necessary." Asked whether the Administration hoped that interest rates would remain at current levels, Connally said: "No, it is my hope that interest rates will come down."

Connally was asked why the President had not acted to freeze corporate dividends or profits. He replied: "Well, . . . there was no authority to freeze dividends, although as you heard the President say last night, he's calling on . . . business to observe the spirit and the letter of it. Again, we felt that to try to . . . make it apply to profits over a 90-day period was not a practical matter of proceeding. . . . As a matter of fact, profits generally in American businesses have declined over the last several years to unacceptable levels, where, frankly we felt that by controlling prices during this freeze period would take care of that problem."

Commenting on a reporter's observation that the import surcharge had raised the question of American industry's ability to compete on world markets without protection, Connally said: ". . . he [Nixon] is going to say to all of the nations of the world that we believe in fair trade as well as free trade. . . . Now the truth of the matter is that we basically feel that barriers, administrative and otherwise, have been raised against American products by many countries around the world." When these barriers are removed by negotiation, he said, "we're willing to compete with any nation in the world on any commodity."

Connally predicted that the international financial community would be "delighted that the United States has faced up to reality, and that we are setting about . . . to do something about the basic disequilibrium that exists in our relations with our trading partners around the world. It can't do anything but breed confidence."

Connally concluded with an expression of hope that the new policy would not lead to greater government intervention in the economy. He said: "There are people in this country who call for a mandatory controlled wages and prices. Dr. [John K.] Galbraith is the leading disciple of this theory. This Administration is committed to the opposite concept, that the progress of this nation as a democracy, the success of this system as conceived, has been the ingenuity, the imagination, the vitality of the private sector of this economy." Connally said that the President has made it "abundantly clear that he's not willing to supplant the private initiative . . . vigor and vitality with government and the dead hand of government."

Revenue breakdown. According to Administration estimates issued shortly after Nixon's announcement, the government would realize a net gain of $500 million as a result of the President's new program.

The Administration's calculations showed a preliminary reduction of $6.3 billion in federal revenues due to the program. These were the reductions: $3 billion in accelerated investment tax credit, $1 billion in the anticipated accelerated increase in personal exemptions and $2.3 billion in elimination of the 7% excise tax on automobiles.

A preliminary revenue increase of $2.1 billion was expected from the import surcharge on dutiable imports.

The Administration calculated that $4.7 billion would be saved in expenditure reductions. This was broken down to show the following savings: $1.3 billion due to the freeze of federal pay increases, $1.1 billion from deferral of general revenue sharing plans, $500 million from reduction in federal employment, $700 million from deferrals of some special revenue sharing programs and $1.1 billion from deferral of welfare reform and other federal programs.

Plea to Congress. President Nixon called Congressional leaders to a White House meeting Aug. 17 and urged them, according to Press Secretary Ronald L. Ziegler, to approach the economic proposals in a "bipartisan spirit."

Pointing out that parts of his package had been proposed by Democrats, Nixon told the group "there should be plenty of credit for everyone." In particular, Rep. Wilbur D. Mills (D, Ark.), chairman of the House Ways and Means Committee, was cited, according to Ziegler, as being "responsible for several parts of this package."

Mills was on record as advocating reinstatement of the investment tax credit, imposition of an import surcharge and other elements of the Nixon program, such as tax relief for individual taxpayers, a cut in federal spending and some form of wage and price controls.

Mills Aug. 16 had described Nixon's new economic program as "excellent" and predicted early House approval. He did indicate that Congress might prefer further tax reduction than proposed by the President and, at the White House meeting Aug. 17, Mills suggested substituting an increase in the minimum standard deduction for Nixon's proposal to provide an across-the-board increase in personal exemptions.

For his part, the President was reported to have assured the Congress members he did not expect them to "rubber stamp" his proposals. He coupled this with an appeal against enlarging the program into a "Christmas tree package" of larger benefits.

Congressional reaction—Immediate reaction to President Nixon's new economic policy was mixed. Some key Congressional leaders—notably Senate Democratic Leader Mike Mansfield (Mont.) and Rep. Mills—were receptive to the new economic proposals and predicted favorable action in Congress.

Many of the Democratic senators considered contenders for the 1972 presidential nomination, however, were critical, with Sen. George McGovern (S.D.), the only declared Democratic candidate, calling Nixon's speech "sheer bunk, irrelevancy and mystery."

Mansfield's reaction to Nixon's new program Aug. 15 was "delight" that the President's patience finally ran out. The wage-price freeze he considered "harsh but very necessary." After attending the Presidential briefing Aug. 17, Mansfield predicted a majority of the Senate would "go all the way with the President" in approving the program.

Other favorable comment came from Sen. Russell B. Long (D, La.), chairman of the Senate Finance Committee. He said Aug. 16 that he agreed "with most, but by no means all, of the President's recommendations" and that the program as a whole was one "the nation had a right to expect." After attending the White House meeting Aug. 17, he indicated that he might initiate action to reduce interest rates if the Administration did not. Several questions on this issue at the meeting with Nixon were answered by Treasury Secretary Connally, who expressed reluctance to freeze interest rates at their current high levels and concern that such a freeze might freeze credit activity as well.

House Republican Leader Gerald R. Ford (Mich.) reported after the meeting that "the President said we were moving into a decade of peace and that if the full tax package is approved, along with the actions he already has taken, we can have a full year of prosperity without the plague of inflation."

Senate Republican Leader Hugh Scott (Pa.) was vacationing and did not attend the meeting but in a broadcast to his constituents Aug. 14 had warned that a wage-price board was "becoming more and more necessary." He said it should set limits "on how much wages and prices should increase over a period of time."

Democratic contenders comment—McGovern's criticism of the new Nixon economic program was the harshest coming from the Democratic senators. In addition to terming Nixon's speech "bunk," McGovern said Aug. 15 the wage-price freeze was "four years overdue," the plan for a 5% reduction in the federal employment in a period of high unemployment was "absurd," the job development credit "looks like another handout to big business" and the "backdoor devaluation" of the dollar "a disgrace." For "a great nation like ours to end in this way the convertibility of the dollar," he said, would severely damage the dollar "along with our credit and credibility around the world" and make the U.S. "the economic pariah of the world."

Sen. Henry M. Jackson (D, Wash.) Aug. 16 said the Nixon program was "much too little and too late" and the proposed tax cuts, if counterbalanced with the proposed budget reductions, "inadequate" to provide the necessary stimulus to the economy.

Sen. Fred R. Harris (D, Okla.) focused criticism Aug. 16 on the amount of tax reduction granted to business, which he estimated, by adding the investment credit to the new depreciation allowance, concentrates $8 billion in this one sector of the economy. He said Aug. 17 the President's program bore a "pro-business bias."

Sen. Hubert H. Humphrey (D, Minn.) Aug. 16 criticized Nixon for failing to act for two years and said his action now had been prompted only "under pressure from Congress and the public."

Sen. Edmund S. Muskie (D, Me.) issued his first statement Aug. 18 on the new economic proposals, which he said represented a confession that the old "do-nothing" policy had failed. He faulted the President for waiting too long to act, hoped the wage-price freeze would work and cautioned that it should be implemented with "tough consistent action."

Joint panel urged action—The Joint Economic Committee, hours before Nixon revealed his economic program, released a report Aug. 15 criticizing the Administration's "do-nothing" approach to the economy and recommending stimulative tax cuts and a wage-price review board to administer voluntary "guideposts" to counter spiraling.

The report urged the Administration to release $1 billion in housing and urban development appropriations it had frozen and advocated doubling the $1 bil-

lion recently enacted for public service employment. Another $7 billion in stimulation was recommended from tax cuts —acceleration of personal income tax cuts scheduled for 1972 and 1973 and delay of a scheduled increase in the income base from which Social Security taxes were taken.

Another suggestion was for states and cities beset by falling tax revenues because of high unemployment to be relieved under a federal grant program. The report said payments to state and local governments "should be related to the unemployment rate."

Of the Republicans on the committee, six of eight opposed stimulative measures advocated by the majority; four signed a statement saying the economy was "recovering."

After the Administration program was announced, Committee Chairman William Proxmire (D, Wis.) issued a statement Aug. 17 saying the test of the new policies would be whether prices and wages were held down after the 90-day freeze period. Proxmire recommended a permanent set of guideposts to counter the inflationary spiral.

Labor denounces wage freeze. Opposition to President Nixon's Aug. 15 wage freeze developed immediately within the ranks of organized labor.

AFL-CIO President George Meany Aug. 16 denounced the 90-day freeze as "patently discriminatory" against workers. "In the absence of effective machinery to insure enforcement on the price front and equity to the workers on the wage front," he said, "the entire burden is likely to fall on workers covered by highly visible collective bargaining contracts."

AFL-CIO Textile Workers Union President William Pollock the same day called the freeze "unjust" because it "slams the door" on hundreds of thousands of textile workers anticipating "long-overdue wage increases to compensate them for the 4% cut in real wages" resulting from the rising cost of living between July 1969 and June 1971.

Vice President William W. Winpisinger of the AFL-CIO International Association of Machinists, negotiator for 22,000 railroad workers, declared

Aug. 16 he would not "take it laying down."

Paul Jennings, president of the AFL-CIO International Union of Electrical Workers, Aug. 16 described President Nixon's general approach as "the outmoded and discriminatory trickle-down theory" of giving direct benefits to business to provide "crumbs for the people at some later stage."

United Mine Workers President W. A. (Tony) Boyle, whose contracts were to expire Oct. 1, declared his intention Aug. 16 "to negotiate on the basis of no wage freeze" and "make up for past inflation and . . . win our full equity in our industry and the national economy."

The confrontation stiffened Aug. 17 when Labor Secretary James D. Hodgson accused Meany of being "out of step" with his union members. Meany's comments "on the President's historic initiatives are saddening," he said. "The President's freeze is a forthright step to protect the American worker's earnings."

The same day J. Curtis Counts, director of the Federal Mediation and Conciliation Service and chief federal labor mediator, called upon the workers involved in strikes—estimated at about 150,000 employes in 350 strike actions —to return to work during the 90-day wage-price freeze period. He asked organized labor not to begin any new strike action. About 900,000 workers were covered by contracts due to expire within the three-month period. Counts said "we are not going to hold a club over them" but pointed out the possibility of a $5,000 fine against unions striking during the freeze.

Hodgson issued a statement Aug. 18 saying that "we intend to continue our policy of urging strikers to go back to work and negotiate, but we have no intention at the present time of using sanctions."

Labor's defiance mounted Aug. 18. United Automobile Workers President Leonard Woodcock warned that the UAW would terminate contracts with the auto companies if the wage-price freeze were extended and workers denied wage increases due under the new pacts Nov. 22. The union then, he said, would consider itself "free to take any action we want."

"If this Administration thinks that just by issuing an edict, by the stroke of a pen, they can tear up contracts," Woodcock said, "they are saying to us they want war. If they want war, they can have war."

Woodcock extended some blame to the Democrats, saying while "Mr. Nixon's hand wielded the dagger" it had been "put there by the leading Democrats in Congress, who advocated a law to put in the restraints."

In San Francisco Aug. 18, Harry Bridges, president of the International Longshoremen's and Warehousemen's Union, revealed he had sent a telegram to Nixon Aug. 17 declaring the union's opposition to the wage freeze and its intention to "continue in full force" its strike of West Coast docks. "By your action," the wire read, "the burden of fighting inflation is placed on the backs of the working people." Nixon's order, it said, "favors the rich, creates a new tax bonanza for United States corporations, allows interest rates to run scot free and hurts millions of American workers and small businessmen."

Other unions sent telegrams to the White House Aug. 18. One from the AFL-CIO State, County and Municipal Employes asked exemption from the freeze. Its president, Jerry Wurf, said "there is great doubt whether the federal executive has the legal authority to impose freeze conditions on local and state government bodies."

Another, from AFL-CIO Sheet Metal Workers President Edward J. Carlough, said "construction workers already wear one straitjacket" from a previous wage stabilization plan and asked, "Must they wear another one?"

David Selden, president of the AFL-CIO American Federation of Teachers, which was in convention, said Aug. 18 it was "inconceivable" that his union's negotiations currently under way and "coming to a climax" should be halted. The union's executive council called the wage freeze "blatantly discriminatory" in that it exempted profits, dividends and interest rates.

In New York, Mayor John V. Lindsay Aug. 16 ordered suspension of collective bargaining with municipal labor unions and authorizations of rent increases. The wage and price controls, he said, were "very late but still needed" although there were "innumerable questions about federal enforcement and regulation" which could not be answered without "clear and specific guidelines" from Washington. Lindsay said Aug. 17 he was "deeply troubled" by the impact of the wage-price freeze on the city's uniformed services.

Business applauds move. The business community reacted favorably to the President's economic measures. As W. P. Gullander, president of the National Association of Manufacturers, saw it Aug. 16: "The bold move taken by the President to strengthen the American economy deserves the support and co-operation of all groups." The American Bankers Association Aug. 16 called the move "courageous" and affirmed its "resolve to cooperate in the national effort."

Arch N. Booth, executive vice president of the U.S. Chamber of Commerce, Aug. 16 said businessmen would support the 90-day freeze on wages and prices and the period would "give us time to consider longer-run measures to achieve stability."

Some stressed the importance of the President's move as a way to change the prevailing economic mood. Thus, "An important aspect of his program," according to an Aug. 16 statement by Charles B. McCoy, president and chairman of E. I. duPont de Nemours & Co., Inc., "is the elimination of uncertainty. Widespread concern about such matters as wage and price controls and the price of gold have held down consumer spending in this country and encouraged foreign speculation against the dollar."

Gabriel Hauge, chairman of Manufacturers Hanover Corp. and a former economic adviser to President Eisenhower, said Aug. 16 the President's action "lanced the boil of pessimism."

The automobile industry also responded affirmatively. General Motors Corp. (GM) chairman James M. Roche said Aug. 16 he was "pleased with the President's approach" to the nation's economic troubles. The company Aug. 16 rescinded price increases announced Aug. 5 for its 1972 cars and said the new models, which would have cost about $200 a car more, would be sold at 1971

prices during the 90-day price freeze period.

A similar expression of full cooperation came Aug. 16 from Ford Motor Co. Ford the next day dropped its plans for price increases on 1972 models. Chrysler Corp. made an announcement Aug. 18 to retain 1971 prices on 1972 models during the freeze.

Mixed review from economists. Leading economists gave a mixed review Aug. 15 to the President's new economic policy.

Arthur Okun and Paul Samuelson generally reacted favorably, while John Kenneth Galbraith and Milton Friedman expressed disfavor.

Okun, former chairman of the Council of Economic Advisers with the Johnson Administration, praised the domestic moves as "a leap forward into realism" and predicted that the international moves would result in some kind of devaluation.

Samuelson, with the Massachusetts Institute of Technology, expressed approval of the entire package except the federal spending cutback.

Friedman of the University of Chicago, who at times served as an unofficial adviser to Nixon, denounced the wage-price freeze as "pure window dressing which will do harm rather than good." He considered the 10% tax on imports "undesirable."

Galbraith of Harvard University said the program was not expansive enough. "It would have been much better," he said, "if the President increased grants to the cities to reduce unemployment." He viewed the wage-price freeze as a step forward and the investment tax credit and international action as two steps backward. On the tax credit, he said, "A lot of that goes to people who will save it rather than spend it." "The Administration," he continued, "is reducing the federal budget, postponing revenue sharing, postponing welfare reform—all expenditures that are highly efficient, that are certain to be spent. I think there will be a net reduction in jobs."

Stock market reacts sharply. President Nixon's announcement sent the New York stock market rocketing upward

Aug. 16 as the exchange recorded its biggest single-day gain in history in record-shattering volume.

Two days later, what was called the "Nixon rally" subsided as stock prices retreated in profit-taking and consolidation.

The initial upsurge Aug. 16 sent the Dow-Jones industrial stock average up 32.93 points to close at 888.95. The surge eclipsed the old mark of 32.04 points recorded May 27, 1970. Volume on the floor of the New York Stock Exchange climbed to 31.72 million shares, surpassing the former peak of 28.25 million shares set Feb. 9.

The market continued to rise Aug. 17, but the gains were less dramatic than the previous day. With automobile stocks showing the way, the Dow-Jones industrial average gained 10.95 points to close at 899.90. Volume totaled 26.79 million shares, third heaviest turnover in the market's history.

Consolidation and profit-taking blunted the surge Aug. 18. The Dow-Jones average dropped 13.73 points to 886.17, the lowest level of the session. The decline continued Aug. 19, but then the market reversed itself and the D-J average rose to 880.91 Aug. 20. The average continued to rise—by 11.47 points Aug. 23, by 11.57 points Aug. 24 to 904.13 (passing 900 for the first time since mid-July) and by 4.24 points Aug. 25 to 908.37.

Nixon makes 5-state tour. In his first public comments since he announced his new economic policy, President Nixon Aug. 17 appealed for a moral re-awakening, a revival of "the heritage of a hard working people."

Nixon opened a five-state tour en route to the Western White House in San Clemente, Calif. for a two-week working vacation with an address in New York before the Supreme Council of the Knights of Columbus, a Roman Catholic fraternal organization.

(While in New York, he was visited Aug. 18 by Gov. Nelson A. Rockefeller who emerged from the conference praising Nixon's new policy as "the most exciting and significant" proposed "in the history of our country.")

In his address, Nixon cited "a new prosperity with full employment and

without war" as the "highest ideals of America."

The President said his "new economic policy" was based on three goals:

(1) To generate more jobs—"everyone who wants to work in America should have the chance to work. In the next 10 years we must create 20 million new jobs" and "we can do it."

(2) To halt the rise in the cost of living, which was "the inevitable legacy of war."

(3) To "defend the American dollar against the attack of international speculation." He expressed determination "that the American dollar must never again be hostage to the world's money manipulators."

The President said it would be "not easy" for the working man to forego wage increases, for the federal employe to cope with an increased work load because of reduced personnel and for investors to forego dividend increases. But, he said, "if the temporary sacrifice of each of these groups of America will result in stopping the rise in the cost of living for all Americans, this is a great goal and this is worth sacrificing for."

(In his speech, President Nixon also promised support for parochial schools. At a time when private and parochial schools were closing "at the rate of one a day, we must resolve to stop that trend and turn it around—and you can count on my support to do that," he said. "We must see to it that our children are provided with the moral and spiritual and religious values so necessary to a great people in great times.")

The President flew to Illinois Aug. 18 for a visit to the state fair and the Old State Capitol in Springfield, where he signed a bill to make Abraham Lincoln's family home a national historic site. In brief remarks, he referred to his new international policy on the dollar as a way to meet "the need to revalue the currencies of the world."

Later Aug. 18, Nixon stopped off in Idaho Falls, Ida. where he told a crowd of 5,000 that he was going to Communist China in search of "a full generation of peace." He appealed for a renewal of the "competitive spirit" to make his new economic policy a success.

Concluding his five-state tour with an address at the annual convention of the Veterans of Foreign Wars in Dallas, Nixon called on the nation's veterans Aug. 19 for their "whole-hearted support" of his economic program.

The President asked them to accept "short-term sacrifices" to help the Administration's effort to stop inflation.

"I know what it means for some of you to forego a pay raise you deserve for a time, for others to wait a little longer for dividends your invested dollar has earned," Nixon said. These sacrifices were necessary for the good of the country, he asserted.

Nixon gains in polls. In a Gallup Poll conducted one week after announcement of the new economic program and reported Sept. 5, President Nixon's rating showed a clear lead over three top potential Democratic challengers. Nixon was favored 43%–38% over Sen. Edward Kennedy (Mass.), 43%–37% over Sen. Hubert Humphrey (Minn.) and 42%–36% over Sen. Edmund Muskie (Me.). Gov. George Wallace (D, Ala.), included in each trial contest as a possible third-party candidate, registered 10%–11%.

A Gallup poll reported Aug. 19 that 91% of 537 adults interviewed had heard of Nixon's new economic program and that 70% approved. Nearly three times as many felt they would be "helped" rather than "hurt" by the program.

The Harris Poll reported Sept. 7 that the wage-price freeze was supported by 73% of those interviewed and the proposed business investment tax credit by 45%, the only part of the new program failing to receive less than majority support in the survey.

Economic Controls in Action

1st COL order on public employes. The Cost of Living Council, authorized by President Nixon to oversee the wage and price freeze, decided Aug. 17 that the nation's 13 million federal, state, county and municipal employes and 2 million teachers were subject to the 90-day order.

The decision announced by the council reversed a statement issued Aug. 16 by the Office of Emergency Preparedness (OEP) saying that state and local government employes would be exempt from the freeze on wages.

News of the council's decision was made in a brief announcement at the Treasury Department. At the same time, the council issued a series of 29 answers to frequently asked questions about the 90-day freeze.

The council, headed by Treasury Secretary John B. Connally Jr., included: Paul W. McCracken, chairman of the Council of Economic Advisors; George P. Shultz, director of the Office of Management and Budget; George A. Lincoln, director of the OEP; Virginia H. Knauer, assistant to the President for consumer affairs; Agriculture Secretary Clifford M. Hardin; Labor Secretary James D. Hodgson and Commerce Secretary Maurice H. Stans. Dr. Arthur Burns, chairman of the Federal Reserve Board, served as an adviser.

In its decision on government salaries, the council ruled that the wages of firemen, policemen, civil servants and other state and local government employes "are subject to the freeze just as are all wages in private industry."

The council said increases in teachers' salaries would be allowed only if the contract period began before Aug. 15, the date the President announced the freeze.

If the terms of new contracts for teachers were to begin after Aug. 15, the council said, the increase would not be allowed.

In its series of questions and answers, the council dealt with a broad range of issues involving prices, wages, taxes and rents.

Some of the council's directives issued Aug. 17:

■ Wages of federal government employes were frozen under the President's order.

■ The price freeze applied to increases announced before Aug. 15.

■ The council confirmed an OEP ruling that previously announced tuition rates for the 1971–72 academic year were not covered by the freeze.

■ Stock and bond prices were not included in the freeze.

■ Interest rates were not affected by the order.

■ Any increase in surcharges or other sales or excise taxes would be paid by the consumer in addition to the base price of any item. This ruling, the council said, applied to imported goods as well as other goods which were directly taxed.

■ Bona fide promotions that constituted an advancement to an established job were allowed. Increases in certified apprentice and learner's rates under programs established before Aug. 15 were allowed. Merit and longevity raises were not permitted.

■ State and local taxes were not frozen by the President's order.

The council did not say whether the freeze on wages for federal employes affected scheduled military pay increases. A spokesman for the OEP said current interpretations of the freeze permitted the pay raises for servicemen. The Defense Department said Aug. 18 that the scheduled increases would be paid.

OEP opens centers. The Office of Emergency Preparedness, the operating arm of the Cost of Living Council, began setting up Aug. 16–18 the organizational superstructure responsible for smoothing out the wrinkles of President Nixon's 90-day price and wage freeze.

In its first move, the OEP opened "regional service centers" in Atlanta, Boston, Chicago, Dallas, Denver, Kansas City, Mo., New York, Philadelphia, San Francisco and Seattle. The OEP maintained its key command post in Washington.

An OEP spokesman said the regional centers would place "very heavy emphasis" on responding to inquiries from the public. As of Aug. 18, the regional centers had begun investigating complaints about violation of the order for wage and price control.

(The OEP was created in 1962 as an arm of the executive branch to coordinate civil defense planning after natural disasters and to oversee the "stabilization of the civilian economy" in event of nuclear attack. Before the President's freeze order, OEP had a staff of 325. George A. Lincoln was the OEP director.)

To help the OEP administer the wage and price freeze, other government experts were shifted from their agencies to work with OEP personnel. Under the expanded OEP setup, each of the 10 offices would be under a regional director and would have two or more public information specialists and one or more economic stabilization experts.

The OEP began spelling out details of the freeze in a series of directives issued Aug. 16. Among them:

■ Previously announced increases in tuition rates for the 1971–72 academic year would be permitted to stand.

■ Price increases subject to take effect in the future were covered by the freeze.

■ No cost-of-living increases would be permitted during the 90-day freeze.

■ Increases in pensions would be permitted to stand.

The OEP also issued an "information sheet" Aug. 17 of questions and answers giving policy guidance on the wage-price freeze. An OEP spokesman said official guidelines would be issued later.

Among the guidelines was a decision to exempt from the freeze unprocessed raw foods sold at the retail level, such as fresh fruit and vegetables. OEP officials said processed foods, such as pasteurized milk, frozen orange juice and butter, would be subject to the freeze.

The exemption for unprocessed raw foods meant that prices for those products would be allowed to fluctuate in their normal pattern.

The OEP also said in its "information sheet" that apartment rents were covered by the freeze.

(The OEP, clarifying its Aug. 17 statement on rents, said Aug. 18 that the 90-day freeze applied to housing rents even if landlords and tenants had agreed on an increase before Aug. 15.)

Among some of the other directives issued Aug. 17:

■ Insurance rates would be frozen by the President's order.

■ The freeze covered the prices of used commodities, such as used cars.

■ Fees for professional services, such as those performed by doctors and lawyers, were subject to the freeze.

Freeze apparatus altered. The government continued Aug. 18–25 to reshape the apparatus being assembled to administer the President's freeze on wages and prices, adding several new units to it.

One of the newly formed units was a Policy Committee, placed just beneath the Cost of Living Council in the organizational structure. The Policy Committee was headed by Arnold R. Weber, executive director of the council, and George A. Lincoln, director of the Office of Emergency Preparedness (OEP), and included representatives of the Departments of Commerce, Labor, Agriculture, Housing & Urban Development and Treasury.

The Policy Committee was to review recommendations submitted by a 45-man staff of specialists drawn from departments and agencies throughout the federal bureaucracy and headed by Weber. The committee reviewed the suggestions of Weber's group, refined them and sent them on to the council for final approval or further revision.

Under the original machinery set up in the first week of the freeze, the OEP was responsible for coordinating the government's efforts on wage and price controls, but under the revised setup, Weber's group assumed that responsibility.

(There was no official comment on why Weber's group had replaced the OEP as the chief coordinating unit, but there were published reports that Connally was dissatisifed with the low response by OEP personnel to policy directives.)

Weber's staff had already begun to tackle some of the tasks formerly assigned to the OEP. The 45-man group began to draw up recommendations for policy rulings and make clear interpretations of the President's wage-price freeze order.

Under the new format, the OEP served primarily as a backup unit to Weber's specialists. The OEP also provided the main channel for disseminating the Cost of Living Council's decisions through its 10 regional centers. The OEP was also responsible for the work of 3,000 offices of the Agriculture Department's Stabilization and Conservation

Service and 360 district and subdistrict offices of the Internal Revenue Service (IRS), all of which were to be ready to answer specific questions about the wage-price controls.

The agriculture agency units were to handle questions in rural areas. The IRS tax offices were to answer questions in urban areas.

The Treasury Department was responsible for drawing up legislation which President Nixon called for in announcing his program. Treasury also provided staff support to the Cost of Living Council.

The Labor Department was charged with seeking union compliance with the freeze. The Agriculture Department sought compliance from farmers and from producers of foodstuffs. The Department of Housing & Urban Development sought compliance on rents. All legal action was being handled by the Justice Department.

COL Council directives. The Cost of Living Council continued to clarify and amplify the 90-day order.

The second set of answers to frequently asked questions was released Aug. 19. Among them:

The 7% excise tax on autos remained in effect until such time as Congress rescinded it. The President had requested authority to rescind the excise tax retroactive to Aug. 15. If this authority was approved, rebates would be made to auto purchasers.

Rent agreements with an increase signed Aug. 1 but with an effective date after Aug. 15 were frozen and the rent increase was disallowed.

The 10% import tax surcharge could not be applied to goods already in stock.

The wage freeze did not terminate bargaining for wage changes during the 90-day period of the order. However, no wage increase negotiated during the 90-day period could go into effect during the freeze period.

Unions and management could not negotiate pay raises to be effective after the date of the freeze but also retroactive to cover the freeze period.

The third set of guidelines was issued Aug. 20. Among them:

A partial list of foodstuffs exempt from the freeze were live animals and poultry, shell eggs, raw milk, sugar cane, all fresh fruit, all fresh vegetables, fresh seafood and fresh fish. Included in the freeze were slaughtered animals, dressed poultry, pasteurized milk, raw and refined sugar, canned and frozen fruits and frozen vegetables.

Puerto Rico was covered by the freeze. The U.S. Customs Zone was the boundary for the freeze. Trust territories outside the customs zone were not included in the freeze.

Teachers could not receive an increase negotiated in contracts scheduled to go into effect Sept. 1.

Businesses could not reduce services and maintain the same price inasmuch as that would represent an increase in price for a product.

Merchants could not pass on to consumers the cost of an increase in state and local taxes.

The fourth set of guidelines was issued Aug. 23. Among them:

Service charges and other fees charged by banks were subject to the freeze.

Fees or charges which a state or local government charged for services provided by the government (water, gas, sewage) could not be increased. But fees for licenses or legal penalties, such as traffic tickets, could be increased.

Previously planned increases in pension benefits for those who retired before the freeze or those about to retire were allowed.

The fifth set of guidelines was issued Aug. 24. Among them:

Welfare payments were not covered by the wage-price freeze.

Companies could not increase fringe benefits (such as profit-sharing) during the freeze.

The prices of school lunches which were supported by the Agriculture Department were covered by the freeze.

Tenants whose leases expired could not have their rent raised to the level paid by new tenants in similar developments.

The sixth set of guidelines was issued Aug. 25. Among them:

State payments to persons disabled in job-related accidents under workman's compensation were not subject to the freeze.

Profits from family-owned businesses were not covered by the freeze.

Employers could not increase the number of days off inasmuch as this constituted an increase in fringe benefits.

Americans working abroad for companies which were incorporated in the U.S. were subject to the freeze.

College and school board rates were not exempt from the freeze. (The council said tuition increases could be allowed only in cases where "there were substantial transactions during the base period (confirmed by deposits.") If there was not a substantial volume the increase was not allowed.

Landlords would be violating the freeze if they attempted to evict tenants for refusal to pay rent in excess of the ceiling rent applicable to their rental apartment or house.

Among decisions issued in the days that followed:

Aug. 26—Employer contributions to a pension fund could be increased to finance a benefit increase which was granted and became effective before Aug. 15. . . . Professional athletes who had not entered into new contracts prior to the freeze could not negotiate contracts during the freeze which called for increases in salary to cover their services during the freeze. . . . A new rate for

teachers was permissible if the teacher either performed work prior to Aug. 15 under a new contract calling for a wage raise or if the teacher was eligible to have earned a salary at the new rate prior to Aug. 15. In the case of systems negotiating a systemwide contract, all teachers may receive increased payments under such contracts if any one teacher either performed work or was accruing pay prior to Aug. 15. . . . No exceptions from price ceiling would be granted companies which did not raise prices prior to Aug. 15 even though they paid higher wages under new labor pacts before that date. . . . Retailers would not be permitted price raises for merchandise bought for higher prices during the base period but not raised in price prior to the freeze. . . . Commodity futures markets, except for raw agricultural products, were covered by the freeze. The ceiling price for all futures prices maturing during the period would be based on "spot" (or cash) prices during the 30-day period ending Aug. 14. Where spot prices were not available the ceiling would be the price at which a substantial volume of the most recent futures contract was traded during the base period.

Aug. 27—The import surcharge should be shown in dollars and cents on the sales ticket or invoice when the charges were passed on to the consumer.

Aug. 28—Prices, wages and rents which normally fluctuated in distinct seasonal patterns would be adjusted during the freeze under certain conditions, among them that a large and distinct fluctuation must be shown at a specific, identifiable point in time which must be a documented and established practice that had taken place in each of the past three years. . . . Dues were subject to the freeze because they were a fee for service (examples: professional associations, trade associations, unions, country clubs).

Aug. 30—A fish or other denizen of the seas was not covered by the freeze until shelled, gutted, shucked, skinned or scaled.

Aug. 31—If a labor agreement had been reached prior to Aug. 14 but had not been placed in effect, the new wage rate could be paid if both sides had reached an agreement and work was performed or wages accrued prior to Aug. 15 at the new rate.

Sept. 1—A company required by antipollution laws to purchase more expensive fuel during the freeze than it purchased in the base period could not adjust its prices to reflect the higher cost of the fuel.

Sept. 4—A sale of stock or a sale of an equity interest in a going concern was not covered by the freeze. . . . Cash or stock dividends on the common stock of corporations should remain at a rate not exceeding the effective rate declared in the most recent divided period prior to Aug. 15 (a telegram asking that dividends be frozen according to this guideline was sent Sept. 3 by Commerce Secretary Maurice Stans to chief executives of the large corporations).

Other government action—In addition to the policy-making guidelines issued by the Cost of Living Council, other government agencies and departments announced decisions in response to the President's 90-day freeze. Among those decisions:

The Interstate Commerce Commission reported Aug. 16 that it was freezing at present levels rates charged by railroads, trucking lines and bus companies. The ICC also suspended all pending proposals for rate increases by transportation industries falling under the commission's jurisdiction.

The Treasury Department indicated Aug. 16 that the freeze applied to all representatives of professional sports teams. Thus holdouts—players who had not signed contracts in the hope of negotiating for more money—could sign only for their previous year's salary.

The U.S. Postal Service said Aug. 17 that the freeze would delay an increase in third-class mail rates scheduled Sept. 15.

Government officials said Aug. 18 that they assumed that the freeze covered commodity futures trading in soy bean oil and meal, frozen orange juice and pork bellies. The same officials indicated that they assumed trading on future markets such as corn, wheat and soybeans would not be subject to the 90-day order. These were raw agricultural products which were previously exempt.

Treasury Secretary Connally said Aug. 19 that the freeze would mean servicemen would have to wait to get military pay increases.   Connally said "the military are not going to get a raise. They are going to be treated like everybody else."

The Federal Home Loan Bank Board announced Aug. 23 that the government would move against further increases in mortgage interest rates.

Home mortgage action. The federal government took action Aug. 9–24 to curb high mortgage interest rates. Pressure to take action became apparent June 7, when Housing & Urban Development Secretary George Romney announced he would not act to raise the 7% interest rate ceiling on government-backed mortgages until a "more realistic assessment of the basic strength of the mortgage market" could be made.

The same day, the Bank of America in San Francisco raised its minimum rate on home mortgage loans from 7% to 7½%. In the federal housing market, large discounts, or "points," were being utilized to equate the difference between rates in the conventional (non-federal) and federal markets, each point representing an amount equal to 1% of the mortgage and absorbed by the seller or by raising the selling price.

Romney rejected a shift upward in federal ceiling rates because of the "volatility" of long-term rates and the "artificially high level" of corporate bond yields.

But he announced Aug. 9 that President Nixon was releasing $2 billion of special housing funds to maintain the mortgage interest rate of 7% for the Federal Housing Administration (FHA) and Veterans Administration (VA). Points then were at 8%–10% of the mortgage.

The Federal Home Loan Bank Board Aug. 19 authorized savings and loan associations to make conventional home loans with down payments as low as 5%. Heretofore, federal savings and loan associations could put no more than 30% of their assets in loans in excess of 80% of the value of the real estate being purchased, and only 10% of assets in loans in excess of 90% of value. The new policy applied only to single-family homes or condominiums and had a limit for a maximum loan of $30,000.

Board Chairman Preston Martin described the 95% conventional loan as "an idea whose time has arrived." He pointed out that the board's program was not designed to compete with the FHA and VA programs but "to supplement" them.

Further action was taken Aug. 24, when the average interest rate on a conventional mortgage for a new home was reported to have risen to 7.65% in July from 7.5% in June. The Federal Home Loan Bank Board reduced the "liquidity requirement" for savings and loan associations from 7½% to 7% of their assets, freeing $800 million formerly required to be held in "liquid" form.

A second action was taken Aug. 24 by the Federal Home Loan Mortgage Corporation, which raised the price it would pay in purchasing mortgages, reduced the number of points to be paid by three, and allocated $300 million to the program for a six-month effort.

In a related development, following President Nixon's imposition of the wage-price freeze, and a letter from Treasury Secretary John B. Connally Jr. urging no increase in interest rates, Lewis S. Eaton, president of the U.S. Savings and Loan League, announced Aug. 24 that member associations had been informed "that the federal government expects no increases in interest rates for the duration of the 90-day freeze."

Texas bows to wage freeze. Gov. Preston Smith (D, Tex.) Aug. 19 defied the federal government's wage freeze as it applied to state employes and teachers, finding it in conflict with state law, but he accepted Texas Attorney General

Crawford C. Martin's ruling Aug. 23 that the President's authority in the matter susperseded that of the governor.

Martin, however, sought an exemption for Texas state workers and teachers from the President's Cost of Living Council, and he conferred with the council's executive director, Arnold R. Weber, the next day.

Similar requests to exempt state employes and teachers from the wage freeze were sent to the council by Gov. John McKeithen (D, La.) Aug. 20 and Gov. John C. West (D, S.C.) Aug. 24.

Smith had ordered a scheduled 6.8% pay raise for state workers into effect Sept. 1 under a state fund bill, and he also ordered scheduled automatic pay raises for teachers into effect. He said Aug 19 the question of whether the President had the authority to overrule Texas law was "more important" to the state than the wage freeze.

White House Press Secretary Ronald L. Ziegler, in Dallas Aug. 19 with the President on tour, expressed disbelief that Smith "would put himself in a position to deliberately flaunt" a policy which would "benefit all Americans."

President Nixon's comment later Aug. 19 was that "Gov. Connally can take care of him." The reference was to Smith, who served as lieutenant governor six years when Connally was Texas governor. Connally had backed another candidate for governor in 1968 and Martin had become attorney general with Connally's support.

The Cost of Living Council Aug. 20 requested the Justice Department to "take prompt action" to insure Texas compliance with the wage freeze, and the department shortly afterwards announced plans to initiate court action. Smith said Aug. 22 that he would abide by a court decision but felt the issue "ought to be carried to the Supreme Court."

Martin's decision Aug. 23 was that the federal order flowed from an expressed Congressional authorization while the state order was "merely directive" and not mandatory.

Labor's defiance eases. Organized labor's defiant opposition to President Nixon's economic policy changes softened somewhat Aug. 19–25. While not abandoning its opposition to what it considered the anti-labor bias of the wage-price freeze, labor focused its efforts on Congress, where there were indications of support for revision of the program. Senate Democratic Leader Mike Mansfield (Mont.) said Aug. 25 that he expected an extended debate in Congress over Nixon's tax proposals and an effort to increase tax relief for the average worker.

These were the major moves:

AFL-CIO states position—The focus on Congress became apparent Aug. 19 in a statement by the AFL-CIO Executive Council calling on Congress to create a more "effective, equitable and enforceable stabilization program." "We have absolutely no faith," it said, "in the ability of President Nixon to successfully manage the economy of this nation for the benefit of the majority of its citizens."

Citing labor's repeated pledges of cooperation with across-the-board controls on corporate profits and executive benefits as well as on wages, prices and rents, the statement said, "The President's program simply does not meet that test of equity."

The council supported the President's actions on the dollar but accused him of "playing word games with the American people." It would have been better, it said, "if the President had admitted that his actions amounted to a devaluation of the dollar on the international money market."

Support also was expressed for the repeal of the automobile excise tax, but the 10% import surtax was termed a "temporary stopgap." The statement criticized the President for having "studiously avoided" taxes on licensing and patent agreements and on overseas profits of U.S. firms.

The council's position was sharpened by AFL-CIO President George Meany, who told newsmen Aug. 19 "we're not advocating defiance," "we're just not cooperating. If they can put it over without our cooperation, I guess they will."

If the President took action to enjoin strikes during the 90-day freeze, he said, "we will not abide by any such dictate." Contracts would be considered to have been "nullified" by the President if benefits were denied or delayed by the freeze, and labor would feel free to walk off the job, he said.

The proposed business investment tax credit was denounced by Meany as "a blatant tax giveaway to big business." He urged Congress to reject it and force the Administration to pay $600 million in frozen wages to federal workers.

The labor council meeting Aug. 19 was visited by George P. Shultz, director of the Office of Management and Budget, and Labor Secretary James D. Hodgson, who said they had appealed for "a moderate kind of support" for the new economic program. Labor's opposition, particularly a refusal to renounce strikes and return to work, could do "great damage" to the program, Hodgson said.

Meany Aug. 19 expressed "delight" with a pledge of cooperation from the unaffiliated United Automobile Workers (UAW).

In announcing Aug. 21 that the AFL-CIO headquarters was calling labor union attorneys to a meeting Aug. 26 to consider legal action in its dispute with the Administration, a spokesman said there had been "increasing pressure from our people in the field" for a nationwide general strike.

Teamsters, UAW position—A surprise endorsement of the President's new economic program came Aug. 19 from the International Brotherhood of Teamsters, whose president, Frank E. Fitzsimmons, called the program "a bold measure to preserve the economy." "We in the Teamsters," he declared, "intend to cooperate fully with the President's order."

But Fitzsimmons also called for controls on profits, dividends and interest rates and asserted the union's right to strike during the freeze over noneconomic issues.

UAW President Leonard Woodcock, in a statement issued Aug. 25 after meeting with Meany, declared that the UAW would try to "accommodate" itself to the 90-day freeze "as a practical matter." Woodcock, whose first reaction had been that the Administration could "have war" if it wanted it, said his union would join with the AFL-CIO effort to get Congress to reject proposals

for tax incentives to big business. The justifications for investment in new plants and equipment were "fraudulent," he said, because a quarter of the nation's industrial capacity was currently idle.

Woodcock, who conferred Aug. 25 with Fitzsimmons as well as with Meany, said the differences among them over the new economic program were only "rhetoric" and they were united in opposition to the ban on wage raises and strikes.

Woodcock expressed concern that the real problems would come after the 90-day freeze, and that the Administration had not provided any "on-going plan."

Court action planned—Plans to initiate court action challenging the President's power to suspend negotiated wage increases were announced Aug. 20 by the AFL-CIO Amalgamated Meat Cutters and Butcher Workmen.

The National Education Association and the AFL-CIO American Federation of Teachers also announced the same day they were considering a court test of the wage freeze.

Labor's stance decried—Statements denouncing organized labor's position against the President's program were issued Aug. 19 by the National Association of Manufacturers (NAM) and the U.S. Chamber of Commerce. The NAM considered the AFL-CIO stand to be "defiance of the national interest and certainly not in the real interest of millions of union members . . . [and] unbelievably irresponsible." The Chamber said "it ill behooves union leaders who have had the major part in causing inflation to throw a monkey wrench into the machinery designed to stop it."

Agnew sure of Meany support—Vice President Agnew said Aug. 25 he believed AFL-CIO President Meany would eventually support Nixon's 90-day freeze order.

In a speech to the American Society of Association Executives in Miami Beach, Agnew said that Meany was a partisan Democrat and a hard bargainer for the people he represented, "so we have to read his resounding excoriations in the light of these two extenuating circumstances."

Agnew said, however, that Meany "is a patriotic American, and when it comes to the crunch, I am sure he will put the interests of all Americans ahead of any group—because the public interest is the workers' interest."

Agnew also assailed some leading Democrats—among them Sens. Edmund S. Muskie (Me.), George McGovern (S.D.) and Henry M. Jackson (Wash.)—for what he described as their "nitpicking [against the Nixon policy] for the sake of political advantage."

Labor's cooperation sought—Labor Secretary James D. Hodgson told AFL-CIO President George Meany Aug. 26 that organized labor would be consulted on any controls retained after the 90-day wage-price freeze. The pledge was made during a surprise visit to AFL-CIO headquarters in Washington.

Hodgson said in an interview Aug. 29 he would be meeting formally with labor leaders soon "in order to have something ready" for the post-freeze period. Similar "formal consultations" were planned with business, consumer, agriculture and state and local government leaders, he said.

Meany indicated Aug. 27 that he favored creation of a board representing labor, management and the public to deal with wage and price issues on a continuing basis after the current freeze period.

As for the Administration's new economic program, the federation still had "no intention of cooperating" with it, he said.

United Automobile Workers President Leonard Woodcock said Aug. 29 he would cooperate with a tripartite board and, like Meany, urged Congress to enact legislation establishing a wage-price review board "on a permanent basis."

Other labor developments—Agriculture Secretary Clifford M. Hardin Aug. 30 denounced labor leaders "who for selfish reasons oppose the freeze."

■ The AFL-CIO American Federation of State, County and Municipal Employes Aug. 30 approved a policy of "non-cooperation" with the wage freeze.

■ The Boston Police Patrolmen's Association Aug. 31 sought a federal court ruling against applying the wage freeze to government employes.

■ The Gallup Poll reported Aug. 28 that the new economic program was supported by 65% of labor union families interviewed and 75% of nonunion families, indicating a wide divergence between the view of union leadership and that of rank-and-file members.

Democrats attack program. The Democratic National Committee Aug. 21 attacked President Nixon's economic policy changes as an "economic crisis package" that "clearly favored corporate interests over those of the average American family."

It said the requested investment tax credit and the already authorized accelerated depreciation schedule would produce "an $8 billion tax bonanza in one year for big business." It charged that there was a "serious imbalance" between the amount of tax relief proposed for business and the relief proposed for individuals, estimated at $2-$3 billion.

It declared that the President's "new economic game plan" showed it was "distinctly Republican in character" by denying wage increases to public employes and military personnel but doing "nothing about the windfall profits being accumulated on Wall Street."

The Democrats said the wage-price freeze and action on the dollar were "long overdue and welcome" but offered "no solution to inflation or the disastrous United States balance of payments deficit." "They merely provide the Nixon Administration," the statement said, "with an opportunity to develop solutions." Furthermore, it said, the wage-price freeze "discriminates heavily against salaried and hourly workers" by exempting profits, dividends and interest rates from its provisions.

As for the 10% surcharge on dutiable imports, the Democrats cautioned that while it could improve the balance of payments status, it "might easily be retained for purely protectionist reasons," resulting in higher consumer prices, a shielding of inefficient American business and a world trade war of retaliation against the U.S.

In its recommendations, the party renewed its call for wage-price guidelines and a wage-price review board and proposed increasing individual tax relief, postponing a Social Security tax rate rise scheduled for 1972 and substituting the investment tax credit for the liberalized depreciation schedules.

McGovern for profits tax—Sen. George S. McGovern (S.D.) suggested Aug. 21 an extension of the freeze on wages and prices to cover profits as well. He proposed enactment of an 82% tax on all profits in excess of 1970 levels.

The only announced candidate for the Democratic presidential nomination, McGovern, addressing a group of financial writers in Washington Aug. 24, said that the economy had replaced Vietnam as his main issue.

Like the Democratic National Committee, he gave qualified support to the wage-price freeze and the dollar action. But he said the freeze should cover corporate dividends as well as profits and that the floating of the dollar should have been accomplished with international cooperation and not with a surprise announcement.

McGovern expressed opposition to the import surcharge, reduction of federal employment, the investment credit for business and cancellation of the automobile excise tax.

McGovern Sept. 6 called the Nixon program "the most unfair economic package ever designed by a President." "The new economic game plan is an admission that the old economic game plan was a complete failure," he said. And the new plan "was a bonanza for the rich and no help at all for those really being hurt by inflation."

As for the wage-price freeze, McGovern said it should have been made a selective one so that it could be enforced.

Criticism by Muskie—Sen. Edmund S. Muskie (Me.) said Sept. 6 he would not support the Administration's new economic program because it would benefit "the comfortable few" at the expense of others. In California, opening a 32-state tour as an undeclared candidate for the Democratic Presidential nomination. Muskie proposed an alternative economic program of temporary consumer tax credits ($7 billion), direct emergency relief to state and local governments ($3.5 billion) and increased unemployment benefits.

Urging replacement of the Nixon plan for investment tax credits with the consumer credit, Muskie said "what business needs today is markets not tax gimmicks." He denounced the Administration's approach to economic issues as "sadly typical" of its approach to "the broader question of economic justice."

Muskie said after the current 90-day freeze on wages, rents and prices, there would be "no excuse" for "less restraint on corporate prices than on workers' wages," for "abrogating union contracts already negotiated in good faith," for "letting dividends go scot free" or for "a rise in interest rates." But the "most unfair" part of the Nixon plan, he said, was the proposed delay for welfare reform and revenue sharing.

Muskie also attacked Nixon for failure to consult labor in formulating the economic program.

'Phase Two' planning begins. Treasury Secretary John B. Connally Jr. said Aug. 19 that "with all our problems of the next 90 days" of the wage-price freeze period, "we're directing most of our attention at this moment to what follows it." The Cost of Living Council had met that day, he said, to plan "how we can best act and proceed to be sure that we don't have a revival of inflation and of inordinate demand."

He said the extent of the action necessary after the current freeze would be determined largely "by the spirit that permeates the country at that time and how well people settle down and are willing to stabilize themselves."

Connally made the remarks on the NBC-TV "Today" program. In reply to a question, Connally said he thought "at some point in the not too distant future we're going to have to take a look at the capacity of big business and big labor to abuse power in this country."

Labor Secretary James D. Hodgson told newsmen Aug. 19 that Herbert Stein, a member of the Council of Economic Advisers, was in charge of "Phase Two" planning and that the goal would be a "steady, phased growth" with inflation under control.

Commerce Secretary Maurice H. Stans said Aug. 20 the Administration did not believe it would be possible to "drop the controls and do nothing" at the end of the 90-day freeze. Only two options were excluded, he said —either ending controls entirely or establishing permanent wage-price controls. A selective wage-price freeze was an option being considered.

Connally, on an ABC-TV news program Aug. 23, confirmed that it was "highly unlikely" that all anti-inflationary measures would be dropped after the 90-day period. "I would think there would have to be more than that," he said, but "what it will be, how intensive it will be, how pervasive it will be, what it will be called, I don't know."

Stans said Aug. 24 he felt that "Phase Two" restraint would "have to be mandatory rather than voluntary." Speaking to newsmen after meeting with 11 prominent businessmen, Stans defended the business aspects of the President's economic program by saying business was at a "considerable disadvantage" in that profits would have to be sacrificed because wage and material price increases made before the freeze could not be recouped.

Profits tax discussed—Three high Administration officials broached the possibility of imposing some form of restraint on profits in the post-freeze period. Housing and Urban Development Secretary George Romney, a member of the Cost of Living Council, asserted Aug. 27 that restraints imposed after the current freeze period "cannot exclude profits." He suggested establishing a wage-price review board backed up by Justice Department enforcement through the courts.

Emphasizing that he was expressing his personal views rather than those of the council, Romney said: "We have permitted business and union organizations to develop power that enables them to increase prices and wages without sufficient regard to productivity, monetary policy, fiscal policy, demand, the market, unemployment or the impact of imports. As a result, price and wage actions are increasingly being imposed on con-

sumers in a way and on a scale that represent an abuse of power."

(In an interview published by the New York Times Aug. 29, Treasury Secretary John B. Connally Jr. was quoted as asserting that "we are at the end of an era in our economic policy. . . . It would be unwise to think we can go back to where we were before. American business and labor may have to get used to the idea of living within certain parameters.")

Labor Secretary James D. Hodgson and Commerce Secretary Maurice H. Stans, in separate interviews Aug. 29, said controls on corporate profits and dividends would have to be considered for the "Phase Two" period and might be necessary. Pointing out that profits were not covered under the law invoked to impose the wage-price freeze, Hodgson said a restraint on profits "certainly" would have "to be one of the things we consider in Phase Two."

Stans said unless inflation abated quickly, such measures as controls on profits "certainly might be necessary in order to provide equity."

Congressional hearings. Hearings on the President's new economic program were opened by the Joint Economic Committee of Congress Aug. 19.

The first witnesses, economists Walter Heller and Otto Eckstein, former members of the Council of Economic Advisers, supported much of the program but advocated revision of the tax proposals to provide more relief to consumers.

They agreed there was need, in view of the plant capacity idle currently, for increased consumer spending rather than more industrial plant construction.

Both favored the dollar action and wage-price freeze while advising quick decision during the freeze on long-term restraint policies.

Heller questioned the import surtax because of the inconsistency of raising prices while trying to slow rising costs.

Consumer advocate Ralph Nader told the panel Aug. 20 the dollar action and proposal to accelerate an increase in the personal income tax exemption were creditable but the remainder of the Administration's program was "grossly inequitable" because it aided big business at the expense of the consumer.

Nader charged that "a number of corporate leaders knew in advance of portions of the package" and that General Motors Corp. (GM) in particular had been alerted in advance and "tried unsuccessfully to slide under the deadline." Conceding that his evidence for the charge was circumstantial, Nader said GM "knew what was coming" when it had notified dealers 10 days before the President's program was announced to start selling 1972 model automobiles with the new price increases immediately upon receipt of the cars. Normally, new car sales were delayed until late September and the official start of an advertising sales campaign.

GM denied the charge later Aug. 20 and again Aug. 23, when Chairman James M. Roche said his first inkling of the new program came in a telephone call from Connally the afternoon of the President's Aug. 15 announcement. Roche said Connally had asked about the industry's pricing and profit status and the possible effect of controls on them.

Commerce Secretary Maurice H. Stans challenged Nader Aug. 22 to substantiate his charge against GM, but Nader rebutted later that day it was "time for the burden of proof to be put on the government and industry" rather than on those "without access to the inner councils of business."

At a Joint Economic Committee session Aug. 23, three former wage-price administrators—Paul Porter, Michael V. DiSalle and George W. Taylor—advocated long-term controls on basic industry and big unions before the end of the current freeze.

Paul W. McCracken, chairman of the Council of Economic Advisers, predicted Aug. 30 that the new economic program would produce a net gain of $15 billion in the gross national product (GNP) in 1972 and create about 500,000 new jobs. Testifying before the joint committee, McCracken said the program would produce a "positive impact" of $24 billion on the GNP. However, he said, reduced federal spending would lower the net gain by $9 billion. An "abnormally large part" of the GNP gain would come from productivity gains, he said, and some $8 billion would accrue from "a substantial shift in consumer confidence as a result of the President's program."

McCracken told the committee of the Administration's intention to follow the current 90-day freeze on wages and prices with a "less severe" economic program but one with enough legal "clout" to prevent new inflation. "Some kind of quantitative guidance is desirable," he said.

He cautioned the committee that Congressional revision of the package toward more tax reductions could result in "overshooting" the goals of the program.

McCracken viewed a possible curb on profits with disfavor. While the only practical way to control profits was through taxation, he said, this would be a "disincentive" to increased economic activity.

Another witness before the Joint Economic Committee Aug. 30 was Arnold Weber, executive director of the Cost of Living Council. In discussing enforcement of the current freeze, he said the government was considering imposing a $5,000 fine for each specific violation rather than against each violator, or a $5,000 fine, for example, for each can of peas sold in violation rather than a single $5,000 fine against the canner.

Gardner Ackley, a former chairman of the Council of Economic Advisers and an economic strategist for the Democratic Party, told the committee Aug. 31 that he opposed any curb on profits, which were running at a low level and should be permitted to rise. A tax on excess profits, he said, was "a lousy idea."

He praised the wage-price freeze as a "vital first step" and urged that it be replaced in the second phase "with an effective incomes policy." "Beyond that," he said, "an incomes policy must be buttressed by a whole range of further institutional changes."

Ackley suggested a "social compact" among business, labor and other groups for implementing a wage-price stabilization program after the current freeze expired. The ingredients for the post-freeze program should include, he said, "tough control on further price increases; the spreading out over time of cost-of-living catch-ups; and the superseding of deferred wage increases that exceed productivity gains."

He suggested a selective freeze for phase two, with the current freeze suspended for retail prices, except for "big-ticket" items. Other exemptions should be allowed, he said, for rents, personal services, wage rates " in low-wage industries" and other areas not requiring a transition period.

Ackley said an effective incomes policy could be built with wage-price "guideposts" or a wage-price review board backed by the "modest use of legal sanctions." He said permanent controls would be too troublesome and a voluntary system "would not work." He cautioned that even a compulsory system would not work without the support "or tolerance" of the general public, and further, that this was not an item to be taken for granted in peacetime.

The panel heard from economists Edward M. Bernstein and Arthur M. Okun Sept. 1. Bernstein, a former U.S. Treasury and International Monetary Fund official, said an average 12% depreciation of the dollar, in relation to other currencies, would be needed to bring the U.S. international payments into balance. In the interest of smoothing the way toward agreement on a new pattern of exchange rates, he suggested the U.S. itself devalue the dollar by 7%–8%.

Okun, a former chairman of the Council of Economic Advisers in the Johnson Administration, said the U.S. "should never again buy an ounce of gold for monetary purposes." "Our first aim," he said, "is an adjustment of exchange rates that would put a realistic price tag on the dollar in world markets."

Bernstein opposed the new 10% import surtax as "very deflationary for the world." Okun said it should be dropped after the goal of more favorable exchange rates was "clearly achieved."

Okun recommended removal of all direct controls on wage and prices after the 90-day period and institution of guidelines. For wage increases, he proposed a "rule" of about 5% in the first year, approximating the average 3% increase in productivity plus half the increase in consumer prices over the past year. For prices, he suggested a rule averaging 1%–2% with business absorbing without a price rise the first 1%

increase in total labor and nonlabor costs for each unit produced.

Okun opposed a control on profits, including an excess profits tax. He called the Administration's tax package "unbalanced" between business and individual reductions and said it would "make a major long-term sacrifice of precious federal revenues."

AFL-CIO President George Meany, in a letter to the panel Sept. 1, declined to testify and reiterated his position that "if sacrifice is necessary, it must be equal."

In testimony before the Joint Economic Committee Sept. 13, Professor Arthur S. Miller considered the wage-price freeze unconstitutional and subject to invalidation if challenged in the courts. Former Supreme Court Justice Arthur J. Goldberg said selective controls were unworkable and across-the-board controls were required, regardless of the possible concomitant requirement for a large bureaucracy to administer them.

Economic growth forecast. The Commerce Department's mid-year report on the economy, published Aug. 26, forecast a steady economic growth period for the remainder of 1971 and into 1972. Of the 23 industries sampled in the report, 15 were expected to exhibit gains in 1971 of 5% or more, five were to advance by lesser amounts and three to decline. Only one industry, aerospace, was expected to have reduced sales through 1972.

Key indicators down. The government's composite index of key economic indicators dropped .1% in August. The dip came after the index had reached a new peak in July following a steady climb since the fall of 1970.

The index usually foreshadowed general economic trends.

The decline brought the index to 125.9% of the 1967 average. It was the second drop in the past three months. Six of the eight indicators used declined while two rose.

Declines were recorded in the average workweek for manufacturing employes, new durable goods orders, new building permits, the average price of 500 common stocks, the ratio of price-to-unit-labor cost among manufacturers, and the average weekly initial claims for state unemployment insurance (treated inversely). The increases were in plant and equipment contracts and orders and in industrial materials prices.

Wholesale prices continue rise. Based almost totally on prices before the Aug. 15 wage-price freeze, the August wholesale price index rose a seasonally adjusted .7% (an 8.4% annual rate) to 114.9% of the 1967 average. The Labor Department report Sept. 2 showed that industrial prices continued to rise sharply and farm prices failed to reflect their normal seasonal decline.

The August rise for the index as a whole was the largest monthly gain since February and exceeded the .2% adjusted gain of July. On an unadjusted basis, the index rose .3%, matching the July increase.

The key industrial price sector rose an adjusted .5% from July at a 6% annual rate. The report said that over the past six months, the key sector had risen at an annual rate of 5.7%, the largest half-year pace in more than 15 years.

Consumer prices up. Consumer prices rose .3% in August, according to statistics released Sept. 22 by the Labor Department. After adjustment for normal seasonal changes, the rise in the consumer price index was .4%. That brought the index from 121.8% to 122.2% of the 1967 average.

The Labor Department emphasized that the impact of President Nixon's 90-day freeze on prices and wages could not be gauged accurately in the August figures because certain data reflected price changes before the Aug. 15 freeze.

Both the .3%-unadjusted and .4%-adjusted figures were higher than in July, but less than in May and June.

Jobless rate up in August. The Labor Department's monthly unemployment report showed that the jobless rate in August rose .3% for the third straight month to 6.1% of the labor force. The August figures reflected data collected before President Nixon's economic policy speech Aug. 15. Labor Secre-

tary James D. Hodgson said the figures showed the necessity for the stimulative actions of the President's new program.

Employment in August rose 260,000 persons to a record 79,197,000 on a seasonally adjusted basis. The rise in the jobless rate had been caused by a heavy increase in the civilian labor force which climbed 483,000 in August to a seasonally adjusted 84,312,000.

Unemployed persons, on a seasonally adjusted basis, totaled 5,115,000, an increase from 4,888,000 in July. Most of the rise took place among adult men and teenage boys, all in the white worker category.

8 areas added to 6% jobless list—Eight additions were made Aug. 30 to the Labor Department's list of metropolitan areas with unemployment of at least 6% of the labor force. Raising the total to 62 areas, the highest in nine years, were Philadelphia, Boston, Fort Worth, Dayton, Ohio, Shreveport, La., Wilkes-Barre-Hazelton, Pa., Charleston, S.C., and Davenport, Iowa-Rock Island-Moline, Ill.

Personal income registers rise. Personal income showed a strong rise in August, increasing by $8.8 billion. The increase, announced by the Commerce Department Sept. 16, was viewed as an unusually large one.

It was not, however, attributed to President Nixon's new economic policy. The department noted that Nixon's new economic moves had only "a very minor effect" on August income figures.

Part of the rise was laid to a pay increase for employes of the U.S. Postal Service, which totaled $2 billion on an annual rate.

The August increase followed a July decline of $10.9 billion which set the total personal income level at a seasonally adjusted rate of $859.2 billion. The upswing in August brought the total personal income mark to a seasonally adjusted level of $868.9 billion. In August 1970, the total personal income mark had been $809 billion.

Consumer debt up. The Federal Reserve Board reported Oct. 4 that consumer debt rose in August by a seasonally adjusted $827 million, the largest gain since May 1969, when it increased $846 million.

The rise, following a $761 million increase in July, was the ninth consecutive increase in consumer installment credit.

Total installment credit outstanding at the end of August was a seasonally-adjusted $104.06 billion and non-installment credit was $25.64 billion, bringing total consumer credit outstanding to an adjusted $129.7 billion.

Housing starts up. New housing starts climbed in August to a record level for the second consecutive month. According to statistics released by the Commerce Department Sept. 17, new housing starts rose 13,000 units to a seasonally adjusted rate of 2,228,000 units.

The previous high for new housing starts was set in August 1950.

Building permits, which the Nixon Administration saw as a more significant indicator of housing activity, dropped 44,000 units to a seasonally adjusted annual rate of 2,008,000 permits.

Bank loan rates steady—A survey by the Federal Reserve Board of 279 banks showed that interest rates on bank loans before the Aug. 15 freeze and two weeks after it began were substantially the same. Those findings were made public Oct. 14 in a letter from Arthur F. Burns, chairman of the Federal Reserve Board, to Rep. Wright Patman (D, Tex.), chairman of the House Banking and Currency Committee.

Burns said the "changes in effective rates between the two weeks are, almost without exception, very small, and decreases substantially outweigh increases."

The biggest changes were shown in construction loans where the average interest rate dipped from 8.74% to 8.67% and two-year non-automotive consumer loans where the rate fell from 13.17% to 13.11%.

Administration Defines Policy

Nixon stresses 'work ethic.' President Nixon stressed the American "work ethic" and increased productivity in a Labor Day radio address Sept. 6. He called upon Americans to dedicate themselves to "a new prosperity without war and without inflation."

The work ethic, or competitive spirit, "the inner drive that for two centuries has made the American workingman unique in the world," he said, was "ingrained in the American character" and "that is why most of us consider it immoral to be lazy or slothful—even if a person is well off enough not to have to work, or deliberately avoids work by going on welfare."

The President referred to "the overwhelming response" to his recent call, in launching his new economic program, for "some degree of sacrifice." While there had been complaints, "counter-suggestions" and "criticisms by special interest groups," he said, "the most heartening reaction was the surge of national confidence, the reaffirmation of our competitive spirit, the willingness to make a personal sacrifice in pursuit of worthy goals by the man in the street, the worker on the job, the homemaker trying to balance the family budget."

Nixon called for exploration of "the new needs of today's wage earners," which he identified as (1) "more responsibility" for the individual worker, "more of the feeling that his opinion counts"; (2) better recognition and reward for "extra effort"; (3) opportunity for growth in a job; and (4) more respect for work "that is all too often considered 'menial.'"

Referring to his father, who worked as a streetcar motorman, an oil-field worker, a farmer and in a filling station, the President emphasized that "no job is menial in America if it leads to self-reliance, self-respect and individual dignity."

He said an effort should be made to provide workers "the chance for a new variety" in work, or "second careers," and to reinstill a pride in craftsmanship and "good service." He urged a further effort to "make sure that technology does not dehumanize work but makes it more creative and rewarding."

"The most important part of the quality of life is the quality of work," he stressed, "and the new need for job satisfaction is the key to the quality of work."

As the American economy moved to meet these "new needs" of the worker, he said, it could expect, in return, productivity, which, he said, "really means getting more out of your work." Citing the four elements of productivity as investment in new technology, job training, good management and high employe motivation, Nixon said, "taken together, they raise the amount each worker actually produces."

Promise to farmers—President Nixon held out the promise of "a new prosperity . . . without inflation and without war" to a group of 40,000 dairy farmers Sept. 3. They were meeting in Chicago for a convention of the Associated Milk Producers, Inc., an organization for marketing and political purposes of dairy cooperatives in 22 states.

"Our new economic policies," he told them, offer relief from the cost-price inequity with which farmers had been burdened for the past 20 years. During that time, he said, the prices of items paid for increased 52% and the prices of farm products rose only 8%.

The President praised the farmer for being "an exciting exception" to the lower national rate of productivity, and he said a higher standard of living without inflation and a stronger position in world trade could be achieved by the U.S. "only by increasing productivity."

Productivity Commission statement. President Nixon Sept. 7 authorized publication of a policy statement by the National Commission on Productivity that called for increased productivity in terms of output per man hour. The report by the 23-member panel was presented at a White House news conference by George P. Shultz, director of the Office of Management and Budget.

The report said the first prerequisite to higher productivity was "an expanding economy, with maximum employment and maximum utilization of plants and machines." Other suggested "targets of opportunity" for stimulating productivity included more serious

discussion between management and labor on issues related to worker output such as work rules, work schedules, group incentives and job safety.

Shultz said the rate of productivity since 1966 had fallen below the average for the prior 20 years.

Federal pay freeze. President Nixon formally submitted to Congress Sept. 1 his proposal to delay federal pay raises six months as "an example for the American people in our striving to achieve prosperity in peacetime."

Nixon told Congress "a significant reduction" in federal expenditures was needed to balance his proposed tax cuts, which would provide "a powerful stimulus to the economy" but one that should not be inflationary.

The Administration's intention to impose a six-month wage freeze on the Civil Service, applying to 1.3 million white collar workers and 2.9 million military employes, had been part of the new economic program announced by the President Aug. 15.

In a separate directive Sept. 1, Nixon extended the pay freeze to the 600,000 federal blue collar workers.

Nixon warned in an Oct. 2 statement that his economic program would be "torpedoed" if Congress gave in to "political pressure" and vetoed the raise deferral.

The deferral was upheld by 207–174 House vote Oct. 4 and 51–32 Senate vote Oct. 7.

Six firms called on dividends. Four members of the Cost of Living Council met Sept. 7 with executives of six companies called to Washington to explain why they raised dividends after the wage-price freeze had been invoked Aug. 16. Within days all six had either agreed to make adjustments or had showed that they had not violated the guidelines.

Paul W. McCracken, vice chairman of the COL Council, described the discussion as a "full, problem-centered" session during which the business executives expressed their support for the President's economic program and pledged their cooperation.

A day after telegrams were sent to the executives requesting the meeting, the council issued guidelines Sept. 4 suggesting that dividends be held at their level before the wage-price freeze. President Nixon had requested curbs on dividends on a voluntary basis.

The executives summoned to Washington represented Briggs & Stratton Corp. (Milwaukee), which raised its quarterly dividend Aug. 17 to 35¢ a share from the equivalent of 30¢; Martin Yale Industries Inc. (Chicago), which said its 3¢ dividend on stock outstanding after a six-for-five split (the same rate paid before the split) did not represent an increase; National Propane Corp. (New Hyde Park, N.Y.), 89% owned by DWG Corp., which hiked its dividend from 15¢ a share to 50¢ to "regularize" payments resulting from special dividends paid in 1970; Selas Corp. of America (Dresher, Pa.), which effectively increased its dividend by 20%; Florida Telephone Corp. (Ocala), which boosted its quarterly dividend by 1¢, effective, the company noted, Dec. 20 after the wage-price freeze; and Volume Shoe Corp. (Topeka, Kan.), which in effect raised its quarterly payout on presplit shares by .5¢.

The COL Council announced Sept. 9 that three of the companies—Briggs & Stratton, Martin Yale and Selas—had agreed to retract the increases by reducing the dividends paid in the next quarter.

In addition, the council excused from censure two other companies summoned, conceding that the dividend declared by National Propane Corp. was "in fact lower than the dividend declared in the previous quarter," and that Volume Shoe Corp. "had announced a dividend increase but had not in fact declared the increase."

The sixth company involved, Florida Telephone Co., was cited Sept. 9 by Treasury Secretary Connally for its "demonstration of recalcitrance" for refusing to compensate a dividend increase or communicate with the council. However, Connally announced Sept. 13 that Florida Telephone had agreed to adjust its dividend in the first quarter of 1972 to offset the infraction.

2 firms rescind increases—In response to the COL Council's guidelines Sept. 4 asking dividend restraints, two companies announced dividend rollbacks Sept. 7. The Citizens and Southern Corp., parent company of the Citizens and Southern National Bank of South Carolina, said it was rescinding a 5¢ increase in its quarterly dividend. L. L. Ridgway Enterprises Inc. voted in Houston to rescind a 10% stock dividend.

Nixon seeks Congress' support. President Nixon addressed a joint session of Congress Sept. 9 to request bipartisan support for his new economic program. Nixon announced that the 90-day freeze on prices and wages would not be extended beyond 90 days. He said he would confer with representatives of Congress, business, labor and agriculture to help plan the next phase. The Cost of Living Council would meet with representatives "of all other interested groups," the President said.

While giving assurance that he would "take all the steps needed to see that America is not again afflicted by the virus of runaway inflation," Nixon cautioned that "nothing would be more detrimental to the new prosperity in the long run than to put this nation's great, strong free-enterprise system in a permanent straitjacket of government controls. Regimentation and government coercion must never become a way of life in the United States of America. That means that price and wage stabilization, in whatever form it takes, must be only a way station on the road to free markets and free collective bargaining in a new prosperity without war."

The President urged Congress to enact his tax proposals and to "be responsible" in "the area of budget restraint." Tax cuts should be accompanied by spending cuts, he said, and spending increases should be accompanied by tax increases. Since his welfare reform and revenue sharing plans had not yet been enacted, he recommended delaying the effective date of revenue sharing for three months and of welfare reform for a year. He said there was insufficient time "to get the administrative machinery in place" by the previously scheduled effective dates.

In the next session of Congress, the President planned to present new proposals for tax incentives to create new jobs and "new programs to insure that America's enormous wealth of scientific and technological talent is used to its fullest in the production for peace."

As for his current tax proposals, Nixon asked Congress to consider them on a "first priority" basis. They would, he said, "create 500,000 new jobs in the coming year" and reduce taxes paid by individuals by $3.2 billion and provide $2.7 billion in incentives to companies to invest in job-producing equipment. The proposals were to remove the 7% excise tax on automobiles and the business investment tax credit, which he called the "job development credit," and to anticipate by a year a planned $50 increase in the personal income tax exemption (to make it effective Jan. 1, 1972). By ending the 7% car tax, he said, sales would be stimulated, and "every 100,000 additional automobiles sold will mean 25,000 additional jobs."

The President spoke of "meeting the challenges of peace," which he invoked in his appeal for bipartisan support of his new economic program. There were three immediate problems, he said: jobs would have to be found for the veterans returning to civilian life and those unemployed because of defense plant cutbacks, the rise in the cost of living must be stopped, and the value of the dollar must be protected so it was again "competitive in the world."

Abroad, "America has entered a new era in its economic relationships," he said, and while it "will remain a good and a generous nation, . . . the time has come to give a new attention to America's own interests here at home."

Nixon cautioned against making "the mistake of disparaging and undermining 'the system' that produces America's wealth." "As we correct what is wrong in this nation," he said, "let us always speak up for what is right about America."

"Let the challenge of competition," he said, "give a new lift to the American spirit. . . . To build a full generation of peace is a great enterprise.

"To help the poor and feed the hungry, to provide better health and housing and education, to clean up the environment, to bring new dignity and security to the aging, to guarantee equal opportunity for every American—all these are great enterprises.

"To build the strong economy that makes all these possible—to meet the new challenges of peace, to move to a new prosperity without war and without inflation—this truly is a great enterprise, worthy of our sacrifice, worthy of our cooperation, and worthy of the greatness of a great people."

End-of-freeze remark criticized—The President's announcement that the wage-price freeze would be ended after 90 days drew criticism Sept. 9 from Rep. Wilbur D. Mills (D, Ark.) and Sen. Henry M. Jackson (D, Wash.).

Mills, chairman of the House Ways and Means Committee, said "it was a mistake" for Nixon "to announce he was going to lift the freeze before he has an alternative plan to replace it." Mills thought "it might have been necessary to extend the freeze for a short time to give us a chance to work out an alternative."

Jackson considered the announcement "a major blunder" and said "the net effect of the President's speech could be inflationary" when the freeze ended.

Connally offers to cooperate. Treasury Secretary John B. Connally Jr. testified before Congress Sept. 8 on behalf of President Nixon's new tax program and indicated a willingness to cooperate in revision of certain items.

Appearing before the House Ways and Means Committee, Connally sought to rebut criticism that the program was too heavily weighted with business benefits, as opposed to individual benefits. He appealed to Congress not to revise the package into "a Christmas tree" with tax gifts for everyone.

Connally disclosed that the federal budget deficit for fiscal 1972, projected at $11.6 billion in January and $7 billion higher in July, had further escalated to the $28 billion range, and said total federal outlays, originally estimated at $229.2 billion, were rising to $232 billion.

In defending Nixon's tax proposals, Connally estimated that tax reductions provided by the Nixon Administration, including those of the 1969 Tax Reform Act and proposed depreciation easements, would total $34 billion through 1973 for individuals and only $1 billion for corporations.

Although the proposed business investment tax credit would mean $3.8 billion less federal revenue next year, Connally said, it was needed to modernize industry, spur capital formation and create new jobs. He pointed out that current profits were the lowest since 1938, measured as a percentage of the gross national product, and that total wages and salaries increased 37% in the past five years while corporate profits declined more than 10%.

He opposed a tax on excess profits, saying there were no excess profits. (President Nixon's opposition to such a tax, because it was "a poor form of taxation" that would be "counterproductive" to business efficiency, had been made known by White House officials Sept. 3.)

Citing the decline in interest rates since initiation of the wage-price freeze, Connally said imposing a limit on them would have been unwise.

However, he said, the President would not be reluctant to invoke profit and interest curbs if necessary.

Connally indicated his willingness to reach accommodation when Committee Chairman Wilbur D. Mills (D, Ark.) suggested adding to the tax package an early increase in the minimum standard deduction. Connally suggested limiting the benefit to families with the lowest incomes to substantially reduce the federal revenue loss.

Shultz sees jobless rate decline. George P. Shultz, director of the Office of Management and Budget, told the House Ways and Means Committee Sept. 9 he expected the unemployment rate to fall below 5% by July 1972 as a result of the Administration's new economic program (the rate in August was 6.1%). Shultz made the prediction in response to probing by Committee Chairman Wilbur D. Mills (D, Ark.) about whether the Administration's tax reduction program was extensive enough if the unemployment situation did not improve.

Shultz also revealed during his testimony, as Treasury Secretary John B. Connally Jr. had the day before, disturbing data about the fiscal 1972 budget. Federal revenues, he said, "could be perhaps $13 billion–$14 billion lower" than the estimates in January, and an $8 billion deficit was now projected for the "full employment" budget (spending and tax collections compared on the basis of a 4% unemployment rate, the so-called full-employment figure).

Shultz also broke down for the panel the President's proposed $5 billion reduction in federal spending—$1.3 billion from a six-month postponement of federal pay increases, $800 million from a reduction in federal jobs, $1.1 billion from a three-month deferral of general revenue sharing, $500 million from deferral of special revenue sharing for transportation and urban development, $600 million from postponement of welfare reform for a year, $300 million from sale of HUD mortgages and private refinancing of urban renewal projects, $200 million from a 10% cut in foreign aid, and $100 million from other actions.

Other testimony—AFL-CIO President George Meany told the Mills committee Sept. 13 the Phase Two controls on wages and prices should be voluntary or "we might as well go to Hitler's system, or Mussolini's."

Meany denounced as "deceptive and cruelly misleading" the Administration's labeling of the business investment tax credit as a "job development" tax credit. He said it was likely not to create a single job while costing the taxpayers $4 billion annually. He objected to the onetime benefit proposed for the individual taxpayers on the increased personal exemption and standard deduction as against the corporation "tax break," that, he said, "would go on and on and on." By 1980, he said big business would have received a $70 billion windfall from the Administration's program while individuals would have received only $2.3 billion.

Corporate witnesses Sept. 13 backed the investment tax credit proposal. Union Pacific Chairman Frank E. Burnett said it would help the railroads obtain freight cars in chronic shortage. Air Transport Association of America President Stuart G. Tipton said it promised relief for the troubled airlines, which lost $200 million in 1970. American Bankers Association Vice President Allen P. Stults said the Administration tax package had his group's "unqualified endorsement."

Other testimony was heard Sept. 14 by the committee from business organizations in support of the Administration program and from consumer advocate Ralph Nader and Rep. Henry S. Reuss (D, Wis.) in opposition.

Tax break agreement—Mills and Rep. John W. Byrnes (Wis), ranking Republican on the committee, indicated Sept. 14 in separate interviews reported by the New York Times that they were in agreement about repealing part of a depreciation tax break for business, effected earlier in 1971, and applying the recouped funds—$1 billion–$2 billion—to tax relief for poor persons. Both favored reinstatement of the investment tax credit for business but not at the rate proposed by the President—10% the first year and 5% thereafter. A single rate was suggested, 7% by Byrnes, Mills reserving opinion on a firm figure.

The House Ways and Means Committee concluded its hearings on the Administration's tax proposals with testimony Sept. 17 from Taxation With Representation, which represented itself as "a public interest tax lobby," and the Nation-Wide Committee on Import-Export Policy.

Labor, business, farm leaders consulted. President Nixon held separate consultations at the White House Sept. 10–14 with seven labor leaders, 11 business executives and five farm leaders on Phase Two of his anti-inflation program.

After the President had met with the business and labor leaders, it became apparent there was a key difference of opinion between labor and business on the type of agency to curb price and wage increases in Phase Two.

Labor favored a tripartite board representing labor, management and the general public without government interference. Such a board would make its own rules on wages and prices to be controlled and administer regulation, if any. Labor offered its cooperation in Phase Two but conditioned it on an equitable program that applied to profits as well as to wages and other sectors. The labor officials reported that union members expected to receive after the freeze any wages due by contract but denied by the freeze.

On the other hand, the businessmen favored federal administration of wage-price policy with the private sector relegated to no more than an advisory role. General Motors Chairman James M. Roche, one of the participants, said "policy decisions should be in the hands of the government." Another participant, Archie K. Davis, president of the U.S. Chamber of Commerce, suggested continuation of the current Cost of Living Council, headed by Treasury Secretary John B. Connally Jr., for basic decision-making in Phase Two with no role for the public sector.

Meany calls U.S. board 'fascist'—AFL-CIO President George Meany, one of those conferring with the President Sept. 10, had said during a television interview Sept. 5 that he considered creation of a federally enforced wage-price control board "the first step toward fascism."

In a pre-Labor Day interview Sept. 2 with labor reporters (reports released Sept. 5), Meany had elaborated this view by drawing a distinction between "a voluntary setup" outside the government and a wage-price board backed up by government power and the courts. The latter, he said, was "the road to fascism. If you ever get into that one, you will never turn back—where labor-management situations and where wages and hours and everything are controlled by the courts."

He rejected as "some sort of window-dressing" a board where power was retained by the Justice Department or the Cost of Living Council. "That we won't buy," he said, "because we are not going to go into that sort of a swindle. If there is going to be government control, it is going to be direct. It is not going to be camouflaged by saying we have a labor-management setup there."

On the TV program Sept. 5, Meany said he was "quite sure" organized labor would agree to a "no-strike" pledge if it had a part in setting up an acceptable system for controls. But the labor representatives conferring with the President Sept. 10 relayed their consensus that a no-strike pledge was "not feasible" for Phase Two.

In his Labor Day message, Meany Sept. 6 had denounced the Nixon economic program as "a form of socialism for big business." He said it was "incomprehensible" that the President "would at this point in time propose the same kind of 'trickle down' economic program that has been discredited so often before."

Meany criticized the President for "proposing to hand over the people's money to industry" in order to stimulate industrial development at a time when "industry can find no use for 27% of the industrial capacity that already exists."

The President's new proposals were, he said, "part of his continuing lack of concern for the public interest" and "in the tradition of every big-business-oriented Administration this nation has had."

Meany favored instead an economic program oriented toward the problem of unemployment and "the backlog of unfinished business" in housing, education and health. He recommended increased tax relief for individuals to expand consumer purchasing power and more public investment in schools, hospitals, new housing and transportation.

Another of participants at the Oct. 10 meeting, United Automobile Workers President Leonard Woodcock, announced Sept. 11 that his union was initiating action to press in Congress for the tripartite board favored by organized labor.

The other labor leaders meeting with the President Sept. 10 included AFL-CIO Secretary-Treasurer Lane Kirkland and union presidents I. W. Abel, AFL-CIO United Steelworkers of America; Frank Fitzsimmons, International Brotherhood of Teamsters; John H. Lyons, AFL-CIO International Association of Ironworkers; and Joseph A. Beirne, AFL-CIO Communications Workers of America.

Business leaders attending the Sept. 13 White House meeting, in addition to Roche and Davis, were Wilson Johnson, president, National Federation of Independent Businessmen; Robert C. Bassett, National Association of Small Businessmen; Stephen D. Bechtel Jr., president, Bechtel Corp.; Berkley Burrell, president, National Business League; Edward W. Carter, president, Broadway-Hale Stores; Edward J. Dwyer, president, ESB, Inc.; William M. Batten, chairman, J. C. Penney, Inc.; R. Heath Larry, vice chairman, U.S. Steel Corp.; and Walter

B. Wriston, chairman, First National City Bank.

Farm leaders for productivity peg— Leaders of five major farm organizations who met with President Nixon Sept. 14 pushed for higher federal supports for farm prices and for curbing wage and price increases unjustified by productivity increases.

An opening statement, read by John W. Scott, master of the National Grange, declared that "the power of both labor and management to set the costs of labor inputs and prices received—unrelated to efficiency or productivity—must be controlled if we are to have a stabilized economy and progressive economic growth."

The other farm organization presidents attending the meeting were Oren Lee Staley, National Farmers Organization; Robert C. McInturf, National Council of Farm Cooperatives; Tony T. De Chant, National Farmers Union; and William J. Kuhfuss, American Farm Bureau Federation.

White House briefings continued. The White House continued its series of meetings with interested groups on Phase Two plans. Commerce Secretary Maurice H. Stans and other Administration aides conferred Sept. 15 with officials of the American Apparel Manufacturers Association. President Nixon met with Congressional leaders Sept. 17 and with a group of consumer advocates Sept. 21. He also met with a group of governors Sept. 16.

Members of the business delegation meeting with Stans Sept. 15 reported afterwards he had informed them, while no exact formula had been devised for Phase Two control, productivity gains would be the "essence" of any formula applied. Stans also was said to have indicated that President Nixon was more inclined toward continued government control during Phase Two than toward the tripartite board (labor, management, public) favored by organized labor. The performance of the tripartite stabilization board in the construction industry was reportedly cited, with Stans pointing out the reduction in annual construction wage increases from 17% to 10%, while the board was operative, would be "totally unacceptable" if applied to the entire economy.

The business officials said Stans reported the President's opposition to applying controls on dividends or profits in Phase Two, as well as Stans' comment that "sonner or later the Administration will have to confront labor on this issue."

(President Nixon said at his news conference Sept. 16 remarks attributed to Stans "represented what is a strongly felt view primarily in the business community. It does not represent that we have foreclosed the matter as far as our own thinking is concerned.")

After the President's meeting with Congressional leaders Sept. 17, Rep. Wright Patman (D, Tex.), who attended as chairman of the House Banking and Currency Committee, cited the need to extend the legislative authority for the wage-price freeze beyond April 30, 1972 to isolate the legislation from politics during the election year. Another participant, Sen. Jacob K. Javits (R, N.Y.), also said the stabilization legislation would have to be extended for a considerable period.

Others attending the meeting were Senate Democratic Leader Mike Mansfield (Mont.), Senate Republican Leader Hugh Scott (Pa.), House Speaker Carl Albert (D, Okla.), House Republican Leader Gerald Ford (Mich.) and House Democratic Whip Hale Boggs (La.).

The consumer advocates told President Nixon Sept. 21 an "equality of sacrifice" was called for in Phase Two, with controls extended to profits, dividends and interest rates. They urged stricter enforcement of consumer laws governing packaging, labeling and lending and asked to be included in the make-up of any Phase Two enforcement group. They warned that monitoring was needed to check on product quality and market practices, such as withdrawal of low-priced items, during the stabilization program.

The consumer's viewpoint was presented to the President by Don S. Willner, president of the Consumer Federation of America, and Colston E. Warne, president of the Consumers Union. Other groups represented at the meeting were the California Consumer Affairs Department, the American Association of Retired Persons, the National Federation of Business and Professional Women's Clubs, the Neighborhood Consumer Information Center, the National Retired Teachers Association and the National Association of Retired Civil Employes. (Consumer advocate Ralph Nader was not invited.)

Orders for Phase Two. Treasury Secretary John B. Connally Jr. disclosed Sept. 11 that President Nixon had instructed the Cost of Living Council (CLC) to devise by Sept. 30 recommendations for Phase Two of the wage-price stabilization program.

Connally commented at a press conference after a meeting of the CLC with the President at the White House.

Retention of some form of controls against inflation following the 90-day wage-price freeze was indicated by Connally Sept. 13 when he issued an advisory note to businessmen, through the CLC, about entering into long-term purchase contracts for goods and services to be shipped after the current freeze. "Parties that enter into such contracts," he cautioned, "should do so with full regard both for the conditions created by the wage-price freeze now in effect and for any further step that may be undertaken."

A complementary cautionary note about collective bargaining agreements scheduled to take effect after the freeze was issued Sept. 14 by Labor Secretary James D. Hodgson, also a member of the CLC. The statement said the freeze was not intended as a "moratorium" on collective bargaining but cautioned that if settlements were reached the parties should be advised that subsequent revisions of these terms may be needed depending on what policies will prevail following the 90-day freeze."

Hodgson also reported that 170 work stoppages involving 75,000 workers were ended during the freeze period so far and, "in addition, many potential disputes have been averted by special agreements between the parties to extend the terms of their old contracts and in some cases to resume or to continue collective bargaining on unsettled disputes."

'Strong' Phase Two program planned. President Nixon said at his news conference Sept. 16 that "there will be a strong, effective follow-on program" after the 90-day wage-price freeze expires.

The freeze, he said, was "overwhelmingly" supported by the American people, who "want it followed" and "don't want to have a freeze followed by a thaw where you can get stuck in the mud." Phase Two "will be strong," Nixon pledged, and "will deal with the problem of wages and prices and will restrain wages and prices in major industries."

Phase Two "will require the cooperation of labor and management" and "will have teeth in it," he added. "You cannot have jawboning that is effective without teeth."

Curbs to cover entire economy. President Nixon disclosed his intention Sept. 23 to have Phase Two restraints after expiration of the 90-day freeze on wages and prices "cover the whole economy." In a question-and-answer session before the Economic Club of Detroit, Nixon said it was his intention to focus primarily on large industries "where there is the greatest possibility of inflationary tendencies," but he added that "all of the economy will be covered."

The President also indicated for the first time that "it may be necessary in some areas" to impose export subsidies for U.S. industries to enable them to compete in foreign markets by selling their products more cheaply.

In other comment on his new economic policy, Nixon displayed a reluctance to impose controls on corporate profits. Questioned about the possibility of action to curb profits in such fields as banking and the drug industry, where there were "fantastic" profits, according to the questioner, Nixon disclaimed any desire to "penalize" any sector of the economy "for being successful." In reply to a suggestion about launching a campaign to "educate the public" on the need for corporate profits, Nixon declared "I am for profits because I believe that more profits mean more jobs."

Stans rebuts pro-business charges. Commerce Secretary Maurice H. Stans Sept. 28 accused critics of the Administration's tax proposals of "partisan political obstruction."

In rebuttal to charges that the proposals were a "bonanza for business," Stans said business would receive $3.4 billion in tax relief from the program next year, and individuals $2.2 billion. He pointed out, however, that since 1960 individuals had received $27 billion in tax relief compared with $9 billion for corporations.

Stans said corporate profits, at 4% of the total national output of goods and services, were at the lowest level in 25 years. If new jobs were to be created, he said, profits would have to improve and they "would have to go up considerably before we would have to control excess profits."

He said he had received pledges from 1,211 of the nation's largest corporations that they would not increase dividends during the wage-price freeze. Telegrams from the department had been sent to 1,250 firms, with only eight, he said, responding that they were unwilling "to comment" on the matter. Replies from another 31 companies had not been received.

Stans also rebutted a charge the nation was headed for a depression. There was "strong evidence of strength in the economy," he said.

(Rep. Wright Patman [D, Tex.], chairman of the House Banking Committee, had said Sept. 26 the country was "not dealing with inflation and unemployment in a satisfactory way" and warned "we're liable to have a depression . . . before we know it if we don't do something and do it quickly.")

Congressional hearings. Harold R. Sims, acting executive director of the National Urban League, told the Joint Economic Committee Sept. 17 the Administration's new economic program "does little to help the blacks and the poor." He said the wage freeze was especially hard on poorly paid workers. He cautioned that "any more dramatic domestic policies which favor the rich over the poor will not be tolerated by the general public, which has to support the program if it is to work."

The committee Sept. 21 took testimony from Sen. Philip A. Hart (D, Mich.), chairman of the Senate Antitrust and Monopoly Subcommittee, and from two economists favoring taxes on excess profits during Phase Two.

Hart, contending that "the real pricing power was in the executive suites of our major industries," told the panel he planned to present legislation for the purpose of "beating back corporate giantism."

The economists were Professors Henry C. Wallich of Yale University and Lawrence R. Klein of the University of Pennsylvania. Wallich suggested establishment of a benchmark for "nonexcessive profits," based on a national average of all corporate profits as a ratio of the gross national product (GNP). A surcharge would be levied on profits. whenever the profits-to-GNP ratio exceeded the benchmark.

Klein proposed pegging increases of both wages and profits to productivity.

Wage-price role for Congress urged. A Congressional role in the wage-price stabilization program was urged by Sen. William Proxmire (D, Wis.) Oct. 1 and AFL-CIO President George Meany Oct. 4.

Proxmire, chairman of the Joint Economic Committee of Congress, said Congress should have a role in shaping the Phase Two program. He said Congressional action would probably be necessary because he considered the president's power under the 1970 Economic Stabilization Act "too broad" in some areas and too limited in others, such as "lack of authority to roll back prices."

Proxmire called attention to the act's proscription against wage or price sanctions imposed on a particular industry or sector of the economy.

Presenting his recommendations based on hearings by his committee, Proxmire proposed separate wage and price boards "under the umbrella of the super"-stabilization board, which would have on it representatives of the public interest.

He suggested basing wage increases on the "average productivity gain in the economy plus some portion—say one-half—of the annual increase in the cost of living." He estimated the increase would be 5%–5½%. Proxmire favored retroactive application of wage gains that were due but denied during the freeze.

It was impractical to "vitiate" negotiated contracts, he said.

Proxmire suggested that the stabilization board should receive advance notification of price raises by industries "characterized by extraordinary pricing power or . . . resource shortages."

He opposed a curb on profits, saying the "key to the profits question is effective price restraint."

Meany, testifying Oct. 4 before the House Banking and Currency Committee, said, "In view of the Administration's record of unkept promises, disastrous policies, sudden flip-flops and utterly lopsided programs, it is our considered contention that Congress must reassert control over the economy." Congress gave the President "a blank check in the Economic Stabilization Act," he said, and "he has proved unworthy of that trust." He urged the committee to draft a stabilization policy "defining" the national emergency and "insuring" effective and equitable controls.

The committee, which had originated the freeze legislation and was opening hearings on operation of the freeze, also heard economist Leon H. Keyserling, former chairman of the Council of Economic Advisers, who said Oct. 4 the government should "forget about wage-price controls" and should "concentrate the entire weaponry of its traditional powers upon restoring maximum employment and production as soon as possible."

Meany appeared before a Washington conference Oct. 5 of the federation's Industrial Union Department to reassert his contention the President did not have the power to nullify collective bargaining contracts by a freeze.

The department had initiated a "save our jobs" conference Oct. 4 by picketing Congress for action to "freeze profits, not wages." Department President I. W. Abel, head of the United Steelworkers of America, opened the conference with an assertion that the American worker was "drowning in a flood of imports."

House votes modified tax program. The House passed by voice vote Oct. 6 a modified version of President Nixon's tax proposals for his new economic policy.

The House debated the bill one hour 39 minutes Oct. 5 under a rule barring floor amendments. The version approved was the one reported Sept. 29 by the House Ways and Means Committee, which had modified the Administration's proposals.

President Nixon praised the House action Oct. 6 as reflecting "an overwhelming national will for prompt legislative measures to stimulate the economy, create jobs and halt inflation."

Organized labor, however, called it "a giant raid on the federal treasury that would transfer billions of dollars in public funds into the private treasuries of big business." This view, and an appeal to reject the bill, were contained in AFL-CIO letters to all members of Congress Oct. 5.

The committee revised the Administration program to a total tax revenue reduction of $25.6 billion over a three-year period, calendar 1971-73, compared with the Administration's $27.3 billion total for the same period. During the three years, individual taxes would be reduced by $5.7 billion compared with the Nixon program's $2.2 billion, and business taxes (not including the automobile excise tax repeal) would be cut by $14.1 billion, compared with the Administration's $20.1 billion figure.

The committee approved shifting tax relief for individuals from the Administration's program for 67% of the total relief to those with incomes of $10,000 or more, to a program where 62% of the relief would go to those with incomes of $10,000 or less.

One of key labor objections was the continuing tax relief for business, which the AFL-CIO estimated would amount to $80 billion over the next 10 years.

Among the House bill's major provisions:

■ The tax credit for business investment would be reinstated at a 7% rate, retroactive to April 1. It would not apply to equipment manufactured overseas unless the President granted an exemption for specific reasons—if there were a monopoly of American production of the item, if there was no other source except the foreign one, of if the import was for the purpose of initiating production of the item in the U.S.

■ The 7% excise tax on new automobiles would be repealed, as would be the 10% tax on trucks weighing up to 10,000 pounds.

■ The liberalized depreciation rates put into effect previously by the Treasury would be incorporated into the bill but without authority to advance the effective date for claiming depreciation.

■ Tax liability for businesses receiving a large part of their receipts from export sales would be deferred according to the amount exports were increased over previous years.

■ The $650 personal exemption for individual taxpayers would rise to $675 in 1971 and to $750 in 1972.

■ The standard deduction would rise in 1972 to 15% of income or $2,000, whichever was lower (currently 13% or $1,500).

■ The minimum standard deduction would rise to $1,300 in 1972 (currently $1,050) and a phaseout, reducing the amount as income increased, would be eliminated.

Suits filed to bar freeze violations. The Justice Department initiated court action Sept. 23 to enforce the wage-price freeze imposed by President Nixon Aug. 15. The suit was filed in U.S. district court in New Orleans to bar raises of about $400 to 2,800 teachers employed in Jefferson Parish, La.

Three other suits were filed—Sept. 24 against a San Antonio apartment owner for raising rents, Sept. 27 against the owner of the Atlanta Falcons professional football team for increasing ticket prices and Sept. 28 against a Corvallis, Ore. property owner for raising apartment rents.

Proxmire for gas price rollback—Sen. William Proxmire (D, Wis.), chairman of the Joint Economic Committee, called upon President Nixon Sept. 20 to roll back a "clearly inflationary" gasoline price increase established just prior to the price freeze. Proxmire said the price increase stemmed from an Administration decision, relayed to "several oil reporters" for trade publications, not to carry over into 1972 allocations of foreign oil not used in 1971.

Gas prices rolled back—The Cost of Living Council announced Sept. 24 that 144 oil firms found in violation of the price freeze had agreed to roll back the increases, most of them in the pump price of gasoline.

The council also announced that two natural gas firms in Texas had agreed to retract or compensate for dividend payments exceeding the freeze level.

Court rolls back rent rise—U.S. District Judge Adrian Spears in San Antonio Oct. 5 granted the Justice Department's suit for an injunction barring an apartment rent increase. A refund was ordered. It was the first legal enforcement of the 90-day freeze.

American Motors raises prices—American Motors Corp. began selling some of its 1972 model cars Sept. 22 at prices above the 1971 levels with the approval of the Office of Emergency Preparedness, which held that the overall model price had not increased since some optional equipment was made standard on the new models.

Pay up, profits down 1965–71. According to a Wall Street Journal article Sept. 13, wages and salaries rose 60% while profits dropped 4% during the period 1965–71. The rise in family incomes exceeded the increase in the cost of living during this period, and weekly earnings rose at a greater rate than consumer prices. The article presented this table of annual consumer price (cost of living) indexes and median family incomes (1971 not then available):

Year	Cost of living	Median family income
1965	94.5	$6,957
1966	97.2	7,500
1967	100.0	7,974
1968	104.2	8,632
1969	109.8	9,433
1970	116.3	9,867

What these figures add up to, over the five-year span of inflation, is—
Cost of Living: up 23%.
Family Income: up 42%.

It presented this table to compare the indexes of producer prices of consumer goods with weekly wages (1971 figures for June):

Year	Consumer goods prices	Average weekly earnings
1965	96.1	$95.06
1966	99.4	98.82
1967	100.8	101.84
1968	102.7	107.73
1969	106.6	114.61
1970	109.9	120.16
1971	113.1	127.57

Consumer Goods Prices: up 17.7%.
Average Weekly Earnings: up 34.1%.

The total wages-and-salaries and profits as compared with gross national product (all totals in billions, 1971 figures are second-quarter annual rates):

Year	GNP	Wages, salaries	Corporation profits
1965	$685	$359	$46.5
1966	750	394	49.9
1967	794	423	46.6
1968	864	465	47.8
1969	929	509	44.5
1970	974	541	41.2
1971	1,041	572	44.6

Gross National Product: up 52%.
Wages and Salaries: up 60%.
Corporate Profits: down 4%.

Wholesale prices drop. The Wholesale Price Index registered its sharpest drop in five years in September, the Labor Department reported Oct. 7.

The index declined a seasonally adjusted .4%, or at a 4.8% annual rate. In August, the price index rose .7%.

The September decline, the first drop in 10 months, was the biggest since the adjusted .5% drop in October 1966. Analysts laid the decline to President Nixon's wage-price freeze.

The decline brought the index of all commodities to 114.5% of the 1967 average. At the same period in 1970, the index was at 111.3% of the 1967 average.

The index of wholesale prices of industrial commodities alone dropped .1%. Many analysts considered that index a more accurate measure of the basic price trends in the economy.

Consumer prices. Consumer prices rose .2% in September in contrast to the average monthly increases of nearly twice that much in the previous six months, the Department of Labor reported Oct. 22. The consumer price index was 122.4 of the 1967 base period.

Despite the relative improvement, government findings indicated serious violations of the Aug. 15 wage-price freeze. Paul W. McCracken, chairman of the President's Council of Economic Advisers, listed items that would be investigated by the Internal Revenue Service for "possible violations" of the freeze; they included: women's and girls' clothing, frozen orange juice, beef, margarine and salad oil.

Jobless rate steady. The Bureau of Labor Statistics monthly unemployment report, made public Oct. 8, showed that the jobless rate in September remained virtually unchanged from the August level.

The seasonally adjusted unemployment rate slipped from 6.1% in August to 6% in September. Such small changes, however. were not regarded as statistically significant.

The total number of jobs rose 325,000 in September, 130,000 of them in the manufacturing sector. The rise in employment in manufacturing jobs was the first such rise since May and was the largest gain in a single month in more than five years, except for those months in which major strikes were ended.

The increase of 325,000 jobs brought the number of persons employed to 79,-522,000 on a seasonally adjusted basis.

Unemployed persons, on a seasonally adjusted basis, totaled 4.8 million. Of these, 1.8 million were adult men, 1.8 million were adult women and 1.2 million were youths of both sexes between 16 and 19.

2 more areas on 6% jobless list—Two more areas were added Sept. 30 to the Labor Department's list of metropolitan areas with unemployment of at least 6% of the labor force, raising the total to 64.

The addition of the San Francisco-Oakland and Gary-Hammond-East Chicago, Ind. areas raised the total to the highest level in a decade.

(In March and April of 1961, there were 101 major cities on the list.)

At the same time, the Labor Department announced that it had added six areas to its list of smaller cities with a jobless rate of 6% and above. The department also removed four cities from the small-city list leaving 776 cities on the list.

Poor urban jobless rate—The Labor Department announced Oct. 18 that unemployment in poor urban areas rose from 10.1% to 10.4% during the July-September period because of a sharp increase in joblessness among Negroes that reached 14.1%. The jobless rate for whites fell from 9.1% to 8%.

The department also announced temporary suspension of these statistics in 1972 during a changeover from 1960 to 1970 census data.

Personal income. Personal income rose a moderate $3.25 billion in September after a strong gain in August, the Commerce Department reported Oct. 21. Income stood at a seasonally adjusted annual rate of $870.8 billion, as wages and salaries showed no change from August's $580.9 billion annual pace. The income increase, traced mostly to farming and higher pensions, was described as reasonable in view of the Aug. 15 wage-price freeze which was a depressive factor.

Housing starts. The government also announced Oct. 18 that seasonally adjusted housing starts dropped 12.5% in September from the record annual rate of more than 2.2 million units reached in August.

3rd quarter plant outlays. The National Industrial Conference Board reported Nov. 20 that outlays for plant and equipment improvements increased 12% in the third quarter to $6.1 billion. Martin R. Gainsbrugh, the board's chief economist, said the expenditures by 1,000 of the nation's biggest manufacturers were the first important sign of an upturn in new investment decisions over the past two years.

He said the results indicated "industry's belief that sales and profits in 1972 will be substantially higher; secondly, the need to tool out rising labor costs through technological innovation; and thirdly, the desire to protect a share of the market."

Phase Two Pattern Emerges

New administrative machinery set up. In a nationally televised address Oct. 7, President Nixon outlined his plans for Phase Two economic controls to fight inflation following expiration of the 90-day price-wage freeze.

He asserted that the current freeze had been "remarkably successful" and "the primary credit" for its success belonged "to the American people," who had "shown a willingness to cooperate in the campaign against inflation."

The program of wage and price restraint would be continued after the end of the freeze, he said, and he announced new administrative machinery for Phase Two—a Price Commission, a Pay Board and a Government Committee on Interest and Dividends. The Cost of Living Council (CLC) established in Phase One of the stabilization program would continue to operate under the chairmanship of Treasury Secretary John B. Connally Jr.

Nixon asked Congress for a one-year extension of the Economic Stabilization Act, due to expire April 30, 1972, in order to have the government prepared to act against those not cooperating with the stabilization program. Phase One experience so far proved, he said, that "the vast majority of Americans will cooperate wholeheartedly with a system of voluntary restraint." The need for cooperation from everyone and every sector of the economy was a recurrent theme of the President's address. "What is best for all of us is best for each of us," he said.

The President set no calendar deadline for ending Phase Two controls but pledged not to make controls "a permanent feature of American life. When they are no longer needed, we will get rid of them." "We began this battle against inflation for the purpose of winning and we're going to stay in it 'till we do win it," he said.

Nixon also spoke of the need for "some price reduction psychology." "We've lived too long in this country with an inflation psychology," he said.

Regarding general goals for Phase Two, he said some adjustments of prices and wages would be permitted and the stabilization effort would be focused primarily on "those major portions of the economy that are the primary causes of inflation," although "we will not hesitate to take action," he added, "against any part of the economy that fails to comply."

New machinery explained—Nixon said the Price Commission would be made up "of persons outside of government, all public members, not beholden to any special interest group." It would develop yardsticks and be empowered "to restrain prices and rent increases to the necessary minimum and to prevent windfall profits."

The Pay Board would be made up of representatives of labor, management and the public, and both it and the Price Commission would seek voluntary cooperation from business and labor and would be "backed by the authority of

law to make their decisions stick." Their staffs would be small, Nixon said.

The CLC was to have the power to back up the Pay Board and the Price Commission "with government sanctions where necessary." Donald Rumsfeld, a counselor to the President, was named a member of the CLC to "spend full time as the director of operations."

The Government Committee on Interest and Dividends was appointed "to apply a yardstick" to these areas. It would be headed by Dr. Arthur Burns, chairman of the Federal Reserve Board. Nixon said he was confident that the effort to hold interest rates down could be accomplished "on a voluntary basis," but, "as a safeguard," he was requesting Congress to provide "standby controls over interest rates and dividends."

As for profits, the President said "all Americans will benefit from more profits" because they led to more jobs, more competitive goods and more tax revenue. But he drew the line against "windfall profits," which he described as profits flowing directly from the stabilization program. "In the few cases where this happens," he said, "rather than tax such excess profits, the Price Commission's policy will be that business should pass along a fair share of its cost savings to the consumer by cutting prices."

'Progress' on international front—President Nixon reported there had been "substantial progress in our campaign to create a new monetary stability and to bring a new fairness to world trade." The U.S., he said, "welcomes foreign competition" but had "a right to expect that our trading partners abroad will welcome American competition."

It was "a healthy development," he added, "that the world has come to understand that America believes in free trade as long as it is fair trade. This will mean more sales of American goods abroad and more jobs for American workers at home."

Goal & further details. The White House Oct. 7 provided further details of the Phase Two program. It revealed that the CLC proposed an interim goal of a 2%–3% inflation rate by the end of 1972, about half the pre-freeze rate.

It also disclosed additional Phase Two machinery:

■ A committee on health services, with representatives of the medical professions, the insurance industry, consumer interests and the public, to advise the CLC on ways to apply Phase Two standards in this area and to enlist "the full voluntary cooperation" of the industry. The committee's advice also would be available to the pay and price boards.

■ A committee on state and local government cooperation to advise the CLC, assist the pay and price boards and stimulate voluntary cooperation "by both the state and local governments and by individual citizens." The committee, appointed by the President, would have membership from these governments and employe organizations.

The Construction Industry Stabilization Committee would continue to operate within the standards issued by the Pay Board.

The Productivity Commission, established in 1970 with members from labor, management, the federal government and the public, would be expanded to include representatives of agriculture and state and local governments. It would consult with the CLC "on the contributions of productivity to the economic stabilization program."

A task force within the CLC was to be set up to recommend steps to assure that the stabilization program was "not unnecessarily prolonged."

A national system of regional and local service and compliance centers was to be established, primarily drawn from the Internal Revenue System, to support administration of the Phase Two program. It would provide information to the public, investigate complaints, monitor activities and review requests for exemptions in accordance with guidelines from the Price Commission and Pay Board. The system would operate under the policy guidance and control of the price and pay agencies while reporting to the CLC, which would be responsible for "the effective functioning and coordination of the system." All enforcement cases were to be handled by the Justice Department.

The CLC had authority to subject to review the programs of the special panel established to obtain voluntary restraint on interest rates and dividends. General guidelines and procedures of the Price Commission also were subject to review by the CLC, but the decision of the commission on individual appeal cases was to be final and not subject to appeal to the CLC.

The Pay Board and the Price Commission were to formulate standards of "permissible" compensation, prices and rents, the standards subject to review by the CLC "for consistency with the anti-inflation goal." If either pay or price agency was unable to develop continuing standards in time to take effect at the end of the current freeze, it could propose interim standards. If none were forthcoming, the CLC would issue interim standards.

Major economic units would be required to give advance notification to the Pay Board or Price Commission of proposed wage or price increases. Other economic units of less critical importance would be required to "report promptly on their prices, costs, profits, employe compensation or such other matters as may be specified." Price and wage activity in the remainder of the economy would be monitored.

The Pay Board's members—five each from management, labor and the public— would be appointed by the President. The chairman would come from the public members and would serve on a full-time basis. The Price Commission would have seven public members appointed by the President, who would designate one of them chairman to serve on a full-time basis.

The statement, in outlining the Phase Two program as a projection from the 90-day freeze, asserted that "the post-freeze program, to achieve its objectives, must give more attention to equity and economic efficiency, must be more participatory, must not initially demand zero inflation and . . . must not involve a vast and intrusive bureaucratic machinery." However, it said, the first requirement was "to hold down the rate of inflation and none of these other conditions can be allowed to dominate that."

Executive Order sets up boards—An Executive Order establishing other Administration machinery for Phase Two, such as the Pay Board and Price Commission and extending the life of the CLC and providing for the new post of executive director (Rumsfeld), was issued by President Nixon Oct. 15.

Connally clarifies Phase Two. Treasury Secretary John B. Connally Jr. said at a news conference Oct. 8 the freeze would remain in effect after the initial 90-day period, "subject to whatever standards and criteria" were set in the meantime by the Pay Board and Price Commission. Rulings of the CLC, he said, would remain in effect until changed by the two boards.

Asked about the duration of Phase Two in relation to the goal of reducing the inflation rate to 2%–3% by 1973, Connally said there would have to be a public consensus "that the inflationary psychology" had been halted and broken.

The wage and price boards, he said, would have the authority to set standards for balancing equities, alleviating inequities and hardships and granting exemptions. He stressed that the CLC did not anticipate, want, nor would it accept, the boards' "passing the buck up" to it. Their decisions in the pay and price fields were "going to be final," Connally said, and would not be appealed to the CLC, which, he reiterated, was "not going to veto" the boards' actions.

While it was an "arm of the President" and would "continue to function as it is now constituted," Connally said the CLC would have "an overall responsibility in the field for the President" and "an overall review" of the boards' actions. The government "is going to continue to be in this picture" and if it became apparent that actions of the boards were "not in consonance with the President's announced goal of holding inflation down," he said, "then frankly some action will have to be taken."

Since the boards would make decisions "case by case," he said, the government probably would not know for several months whether the decisions would "indeed produce the desired results." So the government would study the situation as it developed, Connally explained. But the Administration did not intend

"to first give the authority and responsibility to the Pay Board and Price Commission and then withhold it."

Connally conceded that it would be "extremely difficult" to operate Phase Two without the support of labor, but he said "there's no point in that. We all have the same objectives" to hold down cost-of-living increases and to halt inflation.

Asked about the policy on deferred wage increases, Connally said they were "a matter for the Pay Board to determine" in light of its responsibility and the goal for a 2%–3% inflation rate by 1973. He also said it would be the "business of the Pay Board to decide" on maximum amounts to any particular wage increase.

He did not anticipate that a conflict on standards between the Pay Board and the CLC would appear since "there is no divergence of objectives"—increases permitted would result from labors and productivity increase and therefore be "real increases and paid in real value."

'Some progress' internationally—In the international area of the Administration's new economic policy, Connally saw "some progress" but cautioned that "it's not an easy problem . . . for the simple reason that we want our balance of payments improved. The only way they can be improved, in a sense, is to the detriment of other nations. Other nations have to give up something in order that we might gain something."

As for trade barriers, he anticipated elimination over the next several months of "certain restrictions" either on a unilateral basis or by bilateral negotiations. There were "certain specific changes and corrections," Connally said, that could be brought about "in a very brief period of time."

Nixon gets labor support. Organized labor agreed Oct. 12 to support the Phase Two mechanism after receiving President Nixon's personal assurances that the Pay Board—as the AFL-CIO Executive Council interpreted the assurances—would be "completely autonomous" and that the Cost of Living Council would not have veto power over its decisions either as to standards or cases.

Organized labor indicated its cooperation and willingness to sit on the proposed Pay Board immediately after Nixon's announcement of the Phase Two mechanism. But a problem arose over the role of the Pay Board and the CLC.

AFL-CIO President George Meany said Oct. 8 there was a "conflict" in interpretations presented the day before by the White House in separate briefings for the labor leaders and later for newsmen. United Automobile Workers President Leonard Woodcock said Oct. 8 that he would not sit on the Pay Board unless it was given total autonomy. He said two Cabinet-level officials had given conflicting interpretations of the roles of the Pay Board and the CLC—Labor Secretary James D. Hodgson asserting the board had the final power, Budget Director George Shultz saying the council had veto power.

The confusion persisted despite Treasury Secretary Connally's explanations at his news conference Oct. 8 and appeal for labor cooperation. Later Oct. 8, Meany announced that the federation's Executive Council would meet to decide the issue.

At the meeting Oct. 12, which was attended by Woodcock and Frank Fitzsimmons, president of the International Brotherhood of Teamsters, the group received from Nixon an initialed statement outlining the "different" roles of the Pay Board, Price Commission and the CLC.

The statement said the CLC would "serve as a policy review group for the post-freeze program" to "assure" that actions and decisions of the board and other units in the program were "of such a pattern and impact as to achieve stated goals and objectives." It would not, the statement said, "approve, disapprove or serve as an appeal level for case decisions" made by the Pay Board and Price Commission and would not "approve, revise, veto, or revoke specific standards or criteria" developed by the two boards.

Other functions of the CLC were to determine the coverage of the Phase Two program and to monitor, evaluate and coordinate the policy conduct of the program's units. It would also recommend any enforcement cases it deemed necessary to pursue to the Justice Department.

The statement outlined the functions of the Pay Board and Price Commission: (a) establishment of standards, criteria and procedures for their implementation; (b) rendering final decisions on individual cases; (c) recommending legal action to assure compliance to the Justice Department; and (d) providing mediation as needed to augment federal mediation.

After the Executive Board meeting, Meany said the federation would serve on the Pay Board. Woodcock and Fitzsimmons also pledged their support. The White House later released a statement by Nixon welcoming the action and praising the labor leaders for having "acted in the best interest of their own members and of the country."

The Executive Council's statement, released by Meany, said the federation would serve on the Pay Board and "help try to make the President's mechanism to control the cost of living work." It also said the federation would establish its own "watchdog units" to monitor prices, it would "continue to oppose the President's tax measures" before Congress and would continue the "fight for full employment, which is the key answer to America's problems."

Too ambitious, Meany says—At his news conference Oct. 12, Meany described the Administration's goal to reduce inflation to 2%–3% by 1973 as "a little too ambitious." He said a 4% goal would be reasonable. Asked about his position concerning pay increases deferred by the 90-day freeze, Meany pointed out the Pay Board would determine policy but his own position was "that money is coming to the workers and they should get it."

Some wage, price rises seen. Herbert Stein, a member of the President's Council of Economic Advisers, predicted Oct. 15 some wage and price increases would be permitted after the 90-day freeze period ends.

The move, Stein said, would be widespread enough so that "a temporary upsurge in prices is possible in the first weeks or even months after the end of the freeze." He cautioned that the temporary period of price rises "would not be a sign of what may be expected during a longer period in Phase Two," which he indicated the Administration expected to last about two years.

Stein presented his views during an appearance before a Business Council meeting in Hot Springs, Va.

Stein told the business executives they could not expect the stabilization policy to be "designed or executed in the image of the business community." The program would "not survive long enough to do much good," he said, "if the business community insists on its particular version of reasonableness, if it tries too hard to get the program converted to its interests, if it helps to make the program a battleground between business and labor and contributes to pollution of the psychological atmosphere which will retard the economic recovery."

Stein's expectation of some price and wage increases after the freeze ended was shared by Presidential assistant Peter M. Flanigan and CLC Director Arnold R. Weber, who also appeared before the Business Council Oct. 15. They both considered the immediate post-freeze period a time for "equitable adjustment," as Weber put it.

(Commerce Secretary Maurice H. Stans was a fourth top Administration official attending the meeting Oct. 15 to discuss Phase Two at closed sessions.)

Stein cautioned Oct. 15 that it was "essential" to recognize that "some wage rates will obviously have to rise more than the average and some less" and "some sellers will be allowed to rise more, and some less, depending on circumstances. In fact, many prices must not rise at all and some must decline." The goal of a 2%–3% inflation rate, he said, "cannot be translated into a standard of permissible price increases which allows everyone to raise his prices 2%–3%.".

A council panel of economists reported to the group Oct. 15 its prediction that the inflation rate would not fall to 2%–3% but probably to a 3%–4% range in 1972 and that the unemployment rate would fall to 5%–5.5% by the final quarter of 1972 in contrast to the Administration forecast of a rate near 5% by mid-1972.

Conally's views. Treasury Secretary John B. Connally Jr. addressed the Business Council Oct. 16. He said he thought Congress "has gone too far in reducing individual income taxes $36.4 billion over the last five years while raising corporate taxes $3.2 billion." Connally said he had appeared before Congress "without fear, embarrassment or shame" to tell it "I think profits are too low in this country."

At a news conference Oct. 16, Connally made these points:

■ He "would assume" that the new Pay Board would establish a "general standard" for acceptable wage increases during Phase Two and that the standard would be applied with some flexibility.

■ The U.S. was under "no compulsion" to have the international monetary problem "settled this month or this year," and it was unlikely that agreement would be reached at the November meeting of the Group of Ten financial ministers "because they're not ready to make an agreement." He indicated that the delay was caused primarily by the political hazards inherent in the program and not by the lack of financial merit in the U.S. stance.

■ He was not troubled by threats of retaliation on trade restrictions or a trade war because retaliation was "a two-way street" and the U.S. "the biggest market of all." But the U.S. was ready to consider other selective removal of the 10% import surtax as it had done for textiles and specific U.S. requests for removal of European trade barriers would probably be offered at a meeting of international financial experts and the Group of Ten deputies. Connally said the West Germans "have much on their side" in suggesting removal of the surcharge on their products.

Congress gets Phase Two plans. The Nixon Administration's proposed legislation to carry out Phase Two of its anti-inflation program was sent to Congress Oct. 19.

The proposals would:

■ Give the President authority to regulate prices, rents and wages until April 30, 1973 (current authority was to expire April 30, 1972), plus new authority to hold down interest rates and dividends;

■ Authorize civil penalties of up to $2,500 in addition to the $5,000 criminal fine provided under the current legislation;

■ Establish a Temporary Emergency Court of Appeals, to be selected by the chief justice of the Supreme Court from among federal district or circuit court judges, to review federal court injunctions in wage-price cases and to hear appeals from decisions of the Pay Board and the Price Commission. President Nixon's intention to seek formation of such a court had been disclosed by Administration sources Oct. 11.

At a White House briefing on the proposed legislation Oct. 19, Treasury Undersecretary Charls E. Walker said while the Administration was requesting authority to stabilize interest rates and dividends at "levels consonant with orderly economic growth," the new economic program was expected to "cause interest rates to decline" and he did not expect interest controls actually to be imposed.

Walker also said the Administration would "strongly oppose" a move in Congress, by Sen. William Proxmire (D, Wis.), chairman of the Joint Economic Committee, among others, to require Senate confirmation of presidential appointments to the Pay Board and Price Commission.

Walker was questioned about a provision of the proposed legislation declaring the rules and regulations issued by the Cost of Living Council (CLC) during the 90-day freeze "approved, ratified and confirmed." Organized labor was reportedly concerned that the provision would bar recovery of pay increases deferred during the freeze. (White House officials had said Oct. 7 the Administration regarded the 90-day freeze as absolute with no provision for retroactive benefits, wage or price increases, during that period.)

Walker denied that the provision would prevent the Pay Board from ruling on the issue. CLC Operations Director Donald Rumsfeld, also at the briefing, said the thrust of the provision was that the CLC's current rules were "legal [and] not that it must remain chipped in concrete forevermore."

Labor's concern over the court provision of the proposed legislation also was reported. Patrick E. Gorman, president of the AFL-CIO Amalgamated Meat Cutters and Butcher Workmen, which was challenging the freeze as a "Gulf of Tonkin resolution for the economy" without adequate safeguards for individuals, said Oct. 20 that the judicial review provision could vitiate legal challenges to the freeze.

Court upholds legality of freeze. A three-judge federal district court in Washington Oct. 22 upheld the constitutionality of the law authorizing President Nixon's wage-price freeze.

The challenge was brought by the AFL-CIO Amalgamated Meat Cutters and Butcher Workmen on the grounds that the law constituted an improper delegation of power by Congress to the President and violated the separation of powers doctrine.

The decision conceded that the court "cannot blink at the broad discretion being given to the President by the act," but it said the law "does at least contain a standard of broad fairness and avoiding gross inequity—leaving to the future the implementation of that standard." The statute was not unconstitutional, it held, "as an excessive delegation of power by the legislature to the executive for the limited term of months contemplated by Congress to follow the initiating general freeze."

Administrative & judicial action. The Cost of Living Council refused Oct. 18 to grant a request by the state of Hawaii that prices be allowed to go up there because of higher shipping costs as a result of a strike by West Coast longshoremen.

A spokesman for the CLC said the exemption could not be granted because the group had ruled that increased costs did not justify price increases.

In another decision, the CLC said Oct. 19 that it would investigate propane price increases announced by seven major oil companies. One of the companies announced Oct. 20 that it would roll back its prices, and all seven companies actually did so by Oct. 27.

Enforcement of the freeze also moved ahead in the courts. The government said Oct. 15 that a U.S. district court in Portland, Ore. had ordered a Portland landlord to stop charging increased rents. It was the government's second successful court case for compliance with the freeze.

Freeze felt widely. The Cost of Living Council Oct. 15 released the results of a survey conducted by the Census Bureau showing that many Americans had already been affected by the 90-day freeze on wages and prices. Almost 21% of those questioned said the freeze had either kept them or someone living with them from getting a raise. An additional 4.4% said the freeze would affect them by mid-November.

The survey indicated that many Americans were skeptical about the effectiveness of the President's order. Only 33% said the freeze had effectively stopped price increases. Sixty per cent, however, said the freeze had halted wage increases.

Pay, Price Boards appointed. President Nixon's appointments to the new Pay Board and the Price Commission were announced Oct. 22.

Donald Rumsfeld, the new executive director of the Cost of Living Council, said the President had told the appointees that the post-freeze controls would require decisions "that are fair and just and will invoke public support."

Outgoing CLC Executive Director Arnold R. Weber was named as one of the public members of the Pay Board. His resignation from the CLC post was announced at the same time. The position for the duration of Phase One, the 90-day freeze period, would be filled by Edgar R. Fiedler, who was head of the CLC's policy review staff. Rumsfeld would assume direction of the CLC operation for Phase Two.

U.S. District Court Judge George H. Boldt of Washington state was named chairman of the Pay Board. C. Jackson Grayson Jr., dean of Southern Methodist University's school of business, was selected as chairman of the Price Commission.

Other public members of the Pay Board, in addition to Boldt and Weber, were Kermit Gordon, president of Brookings Institution and former director of the Budget Bureau; William G. Caples, Kenyon College president and a former vice president for industrial relations for Inland Steel Co.; Dr. Neil H. Jacoby, professor of business economics and policy at the University of California, Los Angeles, and a member of the Council of Economic Advisers under President Eisenhower. He was also a former U.S. representative on the United Nations Economic and Social Council.

The five business members of the Pay Board were Rocco C. Siciliano, president of the T. I. Corp., a holding company, and a former Commerce Department undersecretary; Virgil B. Day, vice president for business environment of the General Electric Co.; Robert C. Bassett, chairman and president of Bassett Publishing Co. and Vertical Marketing, Inc.; Leonard F. McCollum, chairman of the Continental Oil Co.; and Benjamin F. Biaggini, president of the Southern Pacific Co.

The Pay Board's labor members were AFL-CIO President George Meany; Leonard F. Woodcock, president of the United Automobile Workers; I. W. Abel, president of the AFL-CIO United Steelworkers; Frank E. Fitzsimmons, president of the International Brotherhood of Teamsters; Floyd E. Smith, president of the AFL-CIO International Association of Machinists and Aerospace Workers.

The seven-member Price Commission, composed of public members only, included one black, William T. Coleman Jr., a partner in a Philadelphia law firm, and one woman, Dr. Marina von Neumann Whitman, professor of economics at the University of Pittsburgh. Other members, in addition to chairman Grayson, were William W. Scranton, president of the National Municipal League and former governor of Pennsylvania; John W. Queenan, retired as a managing partner in the accounting firm of Haskin & Sells; J. Wilson Newman, vice chairman of the National Bureau of Economic Research; Robert F. Lanzillotti, professor of economics and dean of the college of business at the University of Florida.

Women seek bigger representation— The naming of only one woman to the pay and price boards was protested Oct. 24 by the National Women's Political Caucus, which urged expansion of the membership to include more women.

The caucus Oct. 24 also protested on the same ground President Nixon's handling of the recent Supreme Court appointments and sought permission from Congress to testify at hearings on the nominations.

Deferred pay raises upheld—Support for the granting of pay raises deferred by the 90-day freeze was expressed Oct. 24 by CLC Director Donald Rumsfeld and Leonard Woodcock, head of the United Automobile Workers.

In an Associated Press interview, Rumsfeld said the Pay Board had authority to permit retroactive collection of frozen pay increases.

Woodcock, on the ABC "Issues and Answers" broadcast, spoke of the overwhelming case for granting such deferred increases. He cited the benefit of stability in honoring existing contract terms.

Labor concerned over contracts—Reports from labor sources after the Pay Board's first working session Oct. 28 said that the labor members' major concern was validation of the existing contracts providing for wage increases that had been blocked by the Aug. 15 freeze. Labor's disgruntlement over composition of the Pay Board, its view that the board was "stacked" against labor with public members inclined toward the business or Administration viewpoint, also was reported. The labor members were described as particularly opposed to the appointment of Arnold Weber, former executive director of the Cost of Living Council, as a public member of the Pay Board.

Freeze on mergers proposed—Rep. Wright Patman (D, Tex.), chairman of the House Banking and Currency Committee, proposed Oct. 24 a freeze on corporate mergers on the grounds economic concentration produced many price problems and "it would be foolhardy" to permit further concentration during the freeze period. He advocated rigorous enforcement of antitrust laws. "Unless we have a strong anti-monopoly program," he said, "we will find ourselves back in the same economic mess shortly after the controls are removed."

Farm subsidies increased. Agriculture Secretary Clifford M. Hardin announced a program Oct. 18 designed to increase farm subsidies in 1972 to reduce surplus production of corn and other livestock feed grains. The program called for more acreage to be taken out of production and higher subsidies to farmers idling the acreage. The new program was designed as a result of a record 1971 corn crop of 5.4 million bushels, almost one-third more than in 1970, when the corn blight cut output. The blight was not a factor in 1971.

The new program was expected to cost $1.5 billion–$1.75 billion compared with costs of $1.2 billion in 1971. The goal was to reduce acreage by 38 million acres for feed grains, including corn, grain sorghums and barley. This would compare with an idling of 18.2 million acres in 1971 for farmers to qualify for federal price support loans.

Some of the mechanics of the new plan: (a) The amount of land idled to qualify for price supports would be increased from 20% to 25% of a farmer's acreage; (b) the federal payment for idling the land would be increased from 32¢ to 40¢ for each bushel that would otherwise have been produced on the idled land; (c) voluntary options were permissible for a farmer to set aside from production an additional 10% of his corn land, with payments of 52¢ a bushel, and an additional retirement of another 5% or 10% of corn or sorghum acreage, with payments of 52¢ a bushel; (d) the current basic price support loan guarantee of $1.08 per bushel of corn would be continued; (e) price supports on grain sorghum would be raised from $1.73 per 100 pounds to $1.79; supports on barley from 81¢ a bushel to 86¢; (f) the federal support program for cotton would remain basically the same; price supports for soybeans would remain at $2.25 a bushel.

Bank adopts floating rate. The First National City Bank, the nation's second largest and New York's largest bank, announced Oct. 21 it would replace the fixed prime rate with a weekly floating "base rate." The bank said the new rate would be keyed half a point above the effective rate for 90-day commercial paper (unsecured corporate notes sold over the counter to investors in the open market).

Edward L. Palmer, chairman of the bank's executive committee, gave the following explanation for the base rate, which would begin at 5.75% Oct. 25: "We feel there is a need . . . for a bank commercial loan rate that is more immediately sensitive to market forces than the existing prime-rate system [in effect since 1934]. The new base-rate concept should respond more quickly to changes in the demand and supply of credit as determined by competitive market forces."

Irving Trust Co. (Oct. 21) and the First National Bank of Boston (Oct. 29) adopted the floating rate concept. The Boston bank, however, did not tie adjustment of its base rate mechanically to any single rate, or combination of rates, but let it float freely against general market forces.

Foreign car prices raised. Volkswagen of America Inc. and Nissan Motor Corp. in U.S.A.—two of the largest foreign car importers in the U.S.—announced a second round of price increases Oct. 13 for most 1972 models. Earlier increases had covered the 10% import surtax imposed by the U.S. Aug. 15, and new increases reflected currency upvaluations in Germany and Japan. German-owned Volkswagen announced it was raising prices for the small VW another 6.8%, following a 4%–5% increase Aug. 25. The Japanese firm said it would boost prices on most 1972 Datsuns by 7%, compared to the earlier 10% increase. Nevertheless, the two foreign companies were confident of a steady sales momentum.

(Ford Motor Co., it was reported Oct. 17, had raised by $24 retail sticker prices on Pinto models sold outside the Midwest to cover the 10% surtax on engines and transmissions imported from Ford plants in Europe.)

Composite index rises. The composite index of 12 leading economic indicators rose a brisk 1.2% in October, based on 8 available indicators, and .2% in September on the basis of revised figures, the Commerce Department reported Nov. 26. The index for October was 128.6% of the 1967 base period.

Harold C. Passer, assistant commerce secretary for economic affairs, described the advance as a "decisive uptrend" that was "consistent with private forecasts of a vigorous expansion of the economy in 1972."

Of the available indicators, three declined: stock market prices, industrial material prices, and plant and equipment orders. The largest increase was in new housing permits. Other increases were recorded for new durable goods orders and the average workweek. Initial claims for unemployment insurance (treated inversely) declined and the

ratio of price to unit labor costs was unchanged.

Wholesale prices hold steady. The Wholesale Price Index held steady in October, the Labor Department reported Nov. 4. The index declined .1% on a seasonally adjusted basis—or at a 1.2% annual rate—and rose .1% at a seasonally adjusted rate.

The October decline brought the index of all commodity wholesale prices to 114.4% of the 1967 average, 3.1% above the year-earlier period.

Treasury Undersecretary Charls E. Walker commented that the figures "provide encouraging evidence that the wage-price freeze is putting the brakes on inflation" and were evidence of widespread compliance with the freeze. The seasonally adjusted increase was attributed almost fully to higher prices for foods that were not covered by the freeze.

The key index of wholesale prices of industrial commodities dropped .3% on an adjusted basis—the sharpest decline since 1962. On an unadjusted basis, the index stood at a steady 115% of the 1967 average.

Consumer price rise slows. Consumer prices rose .2% (without seasonal adjustment) in October, the Labor Department reported Nov. 19. After seasonal adjustment, the Consumer Price Index (CPI) rose only .1%, the smallest adjusted monthly increase since April 1967. The index was 122.6 of the 1967 base period—3.8% above a year earlier and the smallest year-to-year change since February 1968.

Ezra Solomon, a member of the Council of Economic Advisers, hailed the consumer price figures as further evidence that "the 90-day freeze brought a virtual halt to price and rent increases." October's .2% overall increase represented a 2.4% annual inflation rate.

The October index included both prices on items collected monthly and those gathered on a three-month basis. The department report said that if the index had been based only on items priced monthly, the index would have shown no change. The department also noted that, in a special check on 10,250 items in the tri-monthly category to uncover any changes in the September-October period (when the wage-price freeze was in effect), only 75 items showed increases.

Jobless rate down. The unemployment rate dropped for the second straight month in October, down .2% from 6% in September to a seasonally adjusted 5.8%, the Labor Department reported Nov. 5. The downward trend was an improvement, but still not firm enough to be more than "marginally significant," according to Geoffrey H. Moore, commissioner of labor statistics.

Despite the general downturn, black unemployment reached 10.7%—its highest level since November 1963 when the black jobless rate was 11.2%. The category also inched back to the traditional 2-1 ratio of black unemployment to white unemployment, widening the gap between blacks and whites to that ratio for the first time since August 1969. The white rate declined from 5.4% to 5.3%.

Total employment grew 320,000 to a record 79,845,000 (seasonally adjusted), a million persons higher than during the May–July period and an increase of 1,400,000 over the past five months. Total unemployment dropped 270,000 to 4,570,000 persons and, on a seasonally adjusted basis, was down 135,000 to 4,938,000.

3 more areas on 6% jobless list—Three more areas were added Oct. 28 to the Labor Department's list of metropolitan areas with unemployment of at least 6% of the labor force, raising the total to a 10-year high of 65. The total was 68 in October 1961.

The three additions were all in Ohio—Canton, Lorain-Elyria and Youngstown-Warren. Two cities in Indiana—South Bend and Terre Haute—were removed from the list.

At the same time, the Labor Department announced it had added eight areas to its list of smaller cities with a jobless rate of 6% or more. Three areas were dropped, leaving 785 areas on the small-city list.

Personal income. Personal income in October rose a moderate $800 million to a seasonally adjusted annual rate of $872.3 billion, the Commerce Department reported Nov. 17. The October rate was about $750 million more than September's upward-revised $871.5 billion.

On a monthly basis over the first nine months of 1971, personal income had been rising at an average $5.7 billion.

Industrial output up. The Federal Reserve Board (FRB) reported Nov. 16 that industrial production rose a modest .2% in October.

The October index was a seasonally adjusted 106.3% of the 1967 average, compared with September's upward-revised 106.1% and August's revised 105.3%. The August and September revisions were based on more recent data on output of business and defense equipment and industrial materials.

Beginning of Phase Two

The 90-day wage-price freeze ended at midnight Nov. 13, and Phase Two of the Nixon anti-inflation program went into effect Nov. 14. Earlier in November the Administration had issued additional Phase Two guidelines and had continued putting together the machinery designed to make the new "game plan" work.

Dividend guideline of 4% set. The Committee on Interest and Dividends announced Nov. 2 a guideline limiting increases in corporate dividends to 4% during Phase Two of President Nixon's economic stabilization program. The panel, headed by Federal Reserve Board Chairman Arthur F. Burns, said the 4% guideline was "the general principle" to be observed voluntarily by corporations in paying dividends after Jan. 1, 1972. Dividends paid before that fell under the Administration's request for no increases.

The base for the 4% ceiling could be taken from dividends paid in any of the fiscal years 1969–71.

There were indications that the Administration was hopeful that the dividend guideline would be a precedent for some of the other stabilization units, in particular the Pay Board, in setting similar percentages for wage and price increases. Commerce Secretary Maurice H. Stans expressed hope Nov. 2 that "this initial guideline will shape the post-freeze program."

In testifying Nov. 1 before the House Banking and Currency Committee, Burns had said that increases in dividends during Phase Two should be "limited in such fashion that expansion of dividend income will be equitably related to increases in the incomes of wage earners."

Appearing before the Senate Banking Committee Nov. 2, Burns said uncertainty over the stabilization program was "slowing down the economic recovery."

As for interest rates, Burns said Nov. 2 that his panel was not considering adopting a guideline for them because the marketplace should be the determinant. His unit, he said, would "prod sluggish rates" that were unresponsive to market forces toward lower rates. (He had told the House panel Nov. 1 that he viewed his stabilization unit "as a new instrument for jawboning," or appealing for voluntary compliance.)

Burns Nov. 2 urged quick enactment of the Administration's request for extension of the stabilization legislation to remove some of the uncertainty over the Phase Two program.

The Administration's proposals for extended controls, however, were criticized at the hearings Nov. 2. David Ginsberg, former general counsel of the Office of Price Administration during World War II, told the Senate unit that the proposed controls had "more restraints and fewer safeguards than any piece of legislation I have ever seen." It was, he said, "a total grant of authority without hearings, without consultation and without review." Consumer advocate Ralph Nader told the House panel the legislation was "far broader than is necessary" and contained "potential abuses," such as prosecution of "only violators of wage standards and not violators of price standards, or vice versa, or any politically attractive combination thereof."

The Committee on Interest and Dividends said Nov. 15 that mutual funds panies would be exempt from its general guideline to hold dividend increases to no more than 4%. Companies that paid little or no dividends in the base period (any year fiscal 1969–71) would be allowed to pay 1972 dividends of up to 15% of earnings after taxes and after payment of dividends on preferred stock.

Pay Board sets 5½% guideline. The Pay Board, charged with responsibility for setting wage increase standards during Phase Two, adopted a 5½% guideline for new raises Nov. 8. The board vote was 10–5, with the labor members unanimously opposed.

In a broad policy statement, the Pay Board ruled on:

(1) Future pay increases set under existing contracts, which would be permitted unless challenged by "a party at interest," presumably management, or by at least five Pay Board members. In that case the increase would be reviewed to determine whether it was "unreasonably inconsistent with the criteria established by the board";

(2) Retroactive increases for pay raises denied during the freeze, which would be approved only in a limited number of carefully defined circumstances. Such increases could be condoned if (a) prices were raised in anticipation of wage increases scheduled to occur during the freeze; (b) retroactivity was "an established practice or had been agreed to by the parties" to a post-freeze wage agreement replacing one that expired before the freeze (a provision applicable to settlements in the current dock and soft coal strikes); (c) the increases were covered by future criteria established by the board "to remedy severe inequities."

In setting the 5½% guideline for pay increases concluded "on and after Nov. 14," the beginning of Phase Two, the board defined "permissible annual aggregate increases" as "those normally considered supportable by productivity improvements and cost of living trends."

The 5½% figure was referred to as an initial one, whose "appropriateness" would be subjected to periodic review by the board, "taking into account such factors as the long-term productivity trend of 3%, cost of living trends and the objective of reducing inflation."

In reviewing new and existing contracts and pay practices, the board said it would consider "ongoing collective bargaining and pay practices and the equitable position of the employes involved, including the impact of recent changes in the cost of living upon the employes' compensation."

Labor's opposition posed a potential problem for continued operation of the board as constituted. "They abrogated our contracts," AFL-CIO President George Meany commented after emerging from the board's meeting Nov. 8.

Prior to adoption of the initial criteria, which were proposed by the public members, the board had rejected—also by a 10–5 vote—labor's proposal to establish a 6% guideline for future wage increases and to honor existing contracts except those providing for wage increases open to a challenge of inconsistency with the board's criteria or were in excess of 8% annually.

Labor objected to the 5½% formula because it fell well below the 7.2% total supportable, according to the board's own criteria, by the 3% productivity rate plus the consumer price increase of 4.2% over the past 12 months.

Another potential problem for labor was whether the 5½% guideline included fringe benefits. When the question was

Text of Pay Board Policies Issued Nov. 8

[1]
Millions of workers in the nation are looking to the Pay Board for guidance with respect to permissible changes in wages, salaries, various benefits and all other forms of employe total compensation. It is imperative to have a simple standard with as broad a coverage as possible at as early a date as possible. There is probably a need for exceptions and for individual consideration of special situations as soon as practical, and guidance to the millions whose pay relations are relatively simple as an early essential.

[2]
This general pay standard is intended, in conjunction with other needed measures, to meet the objectives which led to the establishment of the board.

[3]
The general pay standard should be applicable to:
(1) Changes that need approval before becoming effective;
(2) Changes that must be reported when they become effective, and
(3) All other changes requiring compliance but not requiring specific approval or reporting.

[4]
Effective Nov. 14, 1971, the general pay standard shall be applicable to new labor agreements and, where no labor agreement is in effect, to existing pay practices. The general pay standard would provide:

On and after Nov. 14, 1971, permissible annual aggregate increases would be those normally considered supportable by productivity improvement and cost of living trends. Initially, the general pay standard is established as 5.5 per cent. The appropriateness of this figure will be reviewed periodically by the board, taking into account such factors as the long-term productivity trend of 3 per cent, cost of living trends, and the objective of reducing inflation.

In reviewing new contracts and pay practices, the Pay Board shall consider ongoing collective bargaining and pay practices and the equitable position of the employes involved, including the impact of recent changes in the cost of living upon the employes' compensation.

(B) Existing contracts and pay practices previously set forth will be allowed to operate according to their terms except that specific contracts or pay practices are subject to review, when challenged by a party at interest or by five or more members of the board, to determine whether an increase is unreasonably inconsistent with the criteria established by this board.

In reviewing existing contracts and pay practices, the Pay Board shall consider ongoing collective bargaining and pay practices and the equitable position of the employes involved, including the impact of recent changes in the cost of living upon the employes' compensation.

(C) Scheduled increases in payment for services rendered during the "freeze" of Aug. 16 through Nov. 13, 1971, may be made only if approved by the board in specific cases. The board may approve such payments in cases which are shown to meet any of the following criteria:
(I) Prices were raised in anticipation of wage increases scheduled to occur during the "freeze."
(II) A wage agreement made after Aug. 15, 1971, succeeded an agreement that had expired prior to Aug. 16, 1971, and retroactivity was an established practice or had been agreed to by the parties.
(III) Such other criteria as the board may hereafter establish to remedy severe inequities.

[5]
Following approval of special procedures by the Pay Board with respect to hearing "prior approval" cases and other special situations, application may be made for an exception to the general pay standard and for hearing on such matters as inequities and sub-standard conditions.

[6]
No retroactive downward adjustment of rates now being paid will be required by operation of the general pay standard unless the rates were raised in violation of the freeze of the general pay standard.

[7]
Provisions may be considered for vacation plans, inplant adjustments of wages and salaries, in-grade and length of service increases, payments under compensations plans, transfers and the like.

posed at a news conference Nov. 8, public members of the board referred to a paragraph of the policy statement saying, "Provisions may be considered for vacation plans, in-plant adjustment of wages and salaries, in-grade and length of service increases, payments under compensation plans, transfers and the like."

House panel OKs contracted raises— The House Banking and Currency Committee Nov. 4 approved payment of wage increases in current contracts, including those deferred during the 90-day freeze. The committee would bar such raises only if President Nixon determined, with the burden of proof on the government, that a specific raise was "grossly disproportionate" to pay increases in general.

The committee also approved amendments to the Administration's proposed stabilization legislation to require imposition of interest rate controls, to exempt

Text of CLC Rulings on Control-Exempt Items

Exemption of Certain Segments of the Economy From the Controls of the Post-Freeze Program

The Cost of Living Council has determined that certain economic sectors shall be exempt from control during Phase Two of the economic stabilization program, effective Nov. 14. The immediate exemption of these sectors is consistent with the President's objective of removing price and wage controls as quickly as conditions warrant. The principal reasons for these decisions are as follows:

1. Certain economic sectors are characterized by a large number of sellers and frequent price fluctuations with a minimum of inflationary pressure. Example: Raw agriculture.

2. In certain other sectors there is no clear basis for establishing a fair and equitable ceiling price because of the nature of the product and the selling process. Examples: handicraft objects, antiques, and art objects.

3. Certain transactions are not being controlled because they are not United States transactions. Examples: Exports, imports and international shipping rates.

4. Certain prices are self-assessed or characterized by a strong element of mutuality. Examples: Dues of nonprofit organizations.

In addition, it should be noted that certain economic transactions cannot be characterized as wages, salaries, prices or rents and are therefore not included in the program. Examples are: taxes, workmen's compensation, welfare payments, child support and alimony.

Price Coverage

The following were exempt from controls during the freeze and will continue to be exempt during the post-freeze period:

1. Raw unprocessed agricultural products.

2. Raw seafood (a more liberalized definition of "raw seafood" will be adopted during the post-freeze period which will permit shelling, shucking, skinning, scaling, eviscerating, removing heads and icing).

3. Financial securities.

4. Exports and first import transaction.

The following were not exempt during the freeze, but will be exempt during the post-freeze period:

1. All used products (includes all second-hand goods that have provided some prior service to the previous owner).

2. Disposal sales.

A. Sales of abandoned or confiscated property by the United States Government or other Government agencies pursuant to court decree.

B. Sales of real and personal property by the United States Government.

C. Sales and deliveries of damaged commodities by insurance companies, transportation companies, or agents of the United States Government, or by any other person engaged in reconditioning and selling damaged commodities received in direct connection with the adjustment of losses from insurance companies, transportation companies, or agents of the United States Government.

3. Custom services and products made to individual order as follows:

A. Leather goods.

B. Wigs and toupees.

C. Clothing.

D. Fur apparel.

E. Dressmaking service on material owned by individual customers.

F. Taxidermy services.

G. Framing pictures and mirrors.

H. Jewelry.

4. Miscellaneous, as follows:

A. Antiques.

B. Art objects: paintings, etchings, and sculpture.

C. Collectors coins and stamps.

D. Precious stones and mountings into which precious stones are set.

E. Rock and stone specimens.

F. Handicraft objects.

5. Royalties and copyrights for materials furnished for publication.

6. International shipping rates.

7. Dues to nonprofit organizations.

8. Real estate as follows:

A. Unimproved real estate and improved real estate with improvements that are not newly constructed.

B. Real estate with newly constructed improvements in those cases (I) in which the sales price is determined after completion of the construction, or (II) in which wage rate costs are known and pertinent wage rates are not subsequently altered by actions of the Pay Board after the sales price is set.

9. Rents, as follows:

A. Commercial, industrial, and farm property.

B. Newly constructed or substantially rehabilitated dwellings offered for rent for the first time after Aug. 15, 1971. "Substantially rehabilitated" means a rehabilitation cost of at least one-third or more of the total value (including costs of rehabilitation of the rehabilitated property).

10. Raw sugar.

poor workers from wage controls and to permit consumers to sue merchants violating price ceilings.

The panel's changes were denounced later Nov. 4 by President Nixon as "damaging and clearly inconsistent with the effort to achieve price stability." Nixon stressed that one segment of the economy should not get "special treatment" but disclaimed any intention "to prejudge how these particular issues should be decided."

Committee Chairman Wright Patman (D, Tex.) in turn accused Nixon Nov. 4 of turning "a bipartisan economic stabilization program into a political attack on the Democrats."

Mills upholds contract validity—Rep. Wilbur D. Mills (D, Ark.) said Nov. 7 the Pay Board should honor the validity of wage contracts negotiated before the freeze. The chairman of the House Ways and Means Committee said "Congress cannot abrogate such contracts" and could not delegate the authority to the Pay Board.

Pay raises averaged 8%—The Labor Department reported Nov. 2 that union pay increases for the year ended Sept. 30 averaged 8.1% for each year of major collective bargaining agreements reached in that period. The year earlier average had been 9.9%.

Phase Two monitoring, exemptions.

The Cost of Living Council (CLC) announced Nov. 10 a "three-tiered" system for monitoring Phase Two pay and prices. Certain exemptions from controls in Phase Two also were announced. CLC Director Donald Rumsfeld characterized the categories and exemptions as broad guidelines under which the pay and price boards would work in promulgating their specific regulations.

Price monitoring—Companies in the first price tier—those with sales of $100 million or more—were required to notify the Price Commission of proposed price increases and get approval for them. Some 1,300 firms, accounting for 45% of total sales in the U.S., were in this category.

The second tier encompassed companies with sales in the $50–100 million range. Advance approval was not required for price increases but quarterly reports on prices, costs and profits were required, as they were of first-tier firms. Some 1,100 companies fell in the second category, their sales accounting for about 5% of total sales.

All other companies, some 10 million accounting for 50% of total sales, were included in the third tier, where no regular reports were required. However, all Price Commission regulations would be applied and spot checking would be performed for adherence to the regulations. Maintenance of "adequate records of price, cost and profit changes" would be expected from most companies in the third tier, with leniency granted to smaller concerns with gross sales below $100,000.

Wage monitoring—First-tier wage monitoring, with advance approval from the Pay Board required for increases, applied to pay adjustments affecting 5,000 or more workers. The category was expected to cover some 500 employe units accounting for 10% of all employes, or about eight million workers.

The second tier, where notification was required when wage raises became effective, covered pay adjustments affecting 1,000–5,000 workers, about 7% of the U.S. work force in an estimated 4,000 labor units.

Third-tier pay adjustments were required to comply with Pay Board standards and be subject to spot checks. The category, groupings of fewer than 1,000 workers, comprised about 83% of the work force.

Panels on health, government named.

President Nixon Nov. 10 named the members of two advisory panels to the Cost of Living Council on implementation of the stabilization program. Those appointed:

Committee on the Health Services Industry (21 members): Mrs. Barbara Dunn, commissioner of Connecticut's Department of Consumer Protection, chairman.

Karl D. Bays of Chicago, head of the American Hospital Supply Corporation.

Dr. Earl W. Brian of Sacramento, director of the State Department of Health Care Services.

Brooks Chandler of Chattanooga, senior vice president of Provident Life and Accident Insurance Company.

Jane Claflin of Boston, a Voluntary Services officer at Massachusetts General Hospital.

Dr. James R. Cowan of Maplewood, N.J., State Health Commissioner.

Theodore E. Cummings of Beverly Hills, head of the Pacific Coast Properties, Inc.

Martin S. Feldstein of Belmont, Mass., economics professor at Harvard.

Miss Rosamond C. Gabrielson of Phoenix, Ariz., director of nursing services at Good Samaritan Hospital.

Dr. James W. Haviland of Seattle, former acting dean of the University of Washington School of Medicine.

John A. Hill of Nashville, president of the Hospital Corporation of America.

Mrs. Alice K. Leopold, a San Francisco lawyer.

Dr. William E. Lotterhos of Jackson, Miss., president of the American Academy of General Practice.

Kenneth M. McCaffree of Seattle, professor at the University of Washington School of Public Health.

J. Alexander McMahon of Durham, N.C., president of the state Blue Cross-Blue Shield plan.

C. Joseph Stetler of Bethesda, Md., president of the American Pharmaceutical Manufacturers Assn.

William Thoms of Nashua, N.H., administrator of the Greenbriar Nursing Home.

Samuel John Tibbitts of San Marino, Calif., president of the Lutheran Hospital Society of Southern California.

John F. Tomayko of Bethesda Park, Pa., director of insurance for the United Steelworkers of America.

Dr. Donald G. Walden, a Denver dentist.

John Colman Whitwell of Princeton, former acting chairman of the Princeton Department of Chemical Engineering.

Committee on State and Local Government Cooperation (17 members): Raymond W. DeWeese, businessman of Portland, Ore., chairman.

Lester L. Bates, board chairman of the New South Life Insurance Company, Columbia, S.C., a former mayor there.

Dr. Eleanor Beard of Lake Oswego, Ore., a member of the State Board of Education.

John E. Burton, retired vice president for business at Cornell University, Ithaca, N.Y.

William J. Conner of Wilmington, Del., county executive New Castle County and president of the National Association of Counties.

John H. Connolly of Waukegan, Ill., a five-term Republican representative in the State General Assembly.

Robert N. Davies, an Indianapolis lawyer.

Samuel G. Hanson of Sacramento, executive director of the National Assembly of Governmental Employes.

Charles J. Irwin of Mountainside, N.J., director of the State Division of Consumer Affairs.

Abe Lavine of Albany, director of the New York State Office of Employe Relations.

Jack D. Maltester, mayor of San Leandro, Calif.

Robert E. Merriam of Chicago, chairman of the United States Commission on Inter-governmental Relations.

Gov. Thomas J. Meskill (R, Conn.).

Dr. John D. Millet of Columbus, chancellor of the Ohio Board of Regents.

Donald E. Morrison of Washington, president of the National Education Association.

Gov. Calvin L. Rampton (D, Utah).

Asa T. Spaulding of Durham, a founder of the North Carolina Mutual Life Insurance Co.

Price guideline set at 2½%. The Price Commission announced Nov. 11 a guideline to limit price increases to an average of 2½% a year. In its policy statement, the commission outlined general guidelines, to be implemented with specific regulations later, to restrain prices as part of the Administration's stabilization goal to reduce the national rate of inflation to not more than 2%–3% by the end of 1972.

The commission also acted to curb profits accruing from price increases, ruling out any increase in pre-tax profit margins (as a percentage of sales) as a result of price adjustments. There was no limit of the total amount of profits, such as those accumulating from an increase in sales volume and remaining within the allowable profit margin based on the profit average of any two of the last three fiscal years that ended before imposition of the 90-day freeze.

As for prices, the commission held they "may not exceed" freeze period levels except as changed by the commission's regulations or orders. The basic policy, it said, was "that price increases will not be allowed" except those justified by cost increases in Phase Two and reduced to reflect productivity gains, or output per manhour. Price increases would not be granted to provide retroactive relief for the impact of the freeze.

The commission noted that its policies relied "heavily on voluntary compliance" but that "close supervision" would be imposed "on those segments of the economy which substantially affect price levels."

It also stressed that its 2½% price increase limit would be applied in the aggregate, that some individual pricing would be less and some more, and that its standards could be modified "by considerations of equity."

The commission statement covered:

■ Retailers and wholesalers, who were permitted price increases reflecting increased costs of merchandise but not permitted increases in their "customary initial percentage markups." Retailers also were not permitted price increases until their freeze period prices on food and other items, to be specified in later regulations, were posted prominently, and such lists in any event were to be posted by Jan. 1, 1972.

■ Public utilities and regulated industries, where decisions on rate adjustments would have to be submitted by regulatory agencies to the commission, which retained the right to "implement more stringent decisions."

■ Rents, which would continue to be frozen in Phase Two, with the exception of change for hardship cases, pending new rent guidelines.

■ Doctors and other professionals, who were subject to the rules barring price increases except those justified by increased costs.

■ Service industries also were covered by the guidelines, including the rule to keep price raises within the pretax profit margin as a percentage of sales as established during the base period.

Text of the Price Commission's Nov. 11 statement:

The policies of the Price Commission announced herein are designed to achieve a goal of holding average price increases across the economy to a rate of no more than 2.5 per cent per year. This is in line with the President's goal to stabilize the economy, reduce inflation and minimize unemployment, and with the Cost of Living Council's objective of reducing the rate of inflation to not more than 2 to 3 per cent by the end of 1972.

These policies rely heavily on voluntary compliance, but they impose close supervision on those segments of the economy which substantially affect price levels. Specific regulation implementing these policies will be issued in the next few days.

Prices may not exceed their freeze period levels except as changed by published regulations or on orders of the commission.

The basic policy is that price increases will not be allowed except those that are justified on the basis of cost increases in effect on or after Nov. 14, 1971, taking into account productivity gains. While price increases, in the aggregate, must not exceed 2.5 per cent a year, many adjustments will be below 2.5 per cent, and some will be above 2.5 per cent as justified on the basis of cost increases and other factors. Price increases will not be granted to any individual or firm to provide retroactive relief for the impact of the Aug. 16-Nov. 13, 1971, freeze.

Reporting procedures for price increases vary depending on the amount of annual sales or revenues reported by a firm in its most recent fiscal year.

[A]

Firms with sales of $100 million or more must prenotify the Price Commission on proposed price increases. Unless the commission advises otherwise within 30 days after the notification is received, the notified price changes may take effect.

[B]

Those firms with sales of between $50 million and $100 million must make quarterly reports to the Price Commission on changes in prices, costs and profits.

[C]

All other firms are not required to prenotify or report on a regular basis, but will be subject to the standards and criteria that the Price Commission will establish.

Different economic sectors will be subject to different rules and regulations. These sectors are: (a) manufacturers; (b) wholesalers, retailers, and similar commercial enterprises; (c) service industries and the professions; and (d) others.

Manufacturers

Prices charged by manufacturing companies may not be increased over freeze period levels, except as the following provisions may apply:

[1]

Allowable cost increases in effect on or after Nov. 14, 1971, reduced to reflect productivity gains will serve as a basis for price adjustments:

[2]

Price adjustments shall not result in an increase in a firm's pretax profit margins (as a percentage of sales) as established during its base period.

Retailers/Wholesalers

Retail and wholesale prices are to be controlled on the basis of customary initial percentage markups which are applied to the cost of the merchandise or service. These customary inital percentage markups cannot be higher than those in the base period. Moreover, a firm may not increase its prices beyond that amount which would bring its net profit rate before taxes (as a percentage of sales) to a level greater than that in the base period.

Retailers are to post prominently their freeze prices for all covered food items and for many other selected items other than food as will be specified in the regulations. Until all such selected prices are posted, retailers are not permitted to increase any prices. In any event, such freeze prices must be posted no later than Jan. 1, 1972.

Service Industries and the Professions

Prices charged for services may not be increased over freeze period levels, except:

[1]

As a result of allowable cost increases in effect on or after Nov. 13, 1971, reduced to reflect productivity gains.

[2]

In any event, price increases shall not result in any increase in a firm's pretax profit margin (as a percentage of sales) as established during its base period.

The commission recognizes there is a multitude of different service industries, characterized by widely varying types of costs and market conditions, possibly warranting more specific forms of regulation. The commission is considering more specific regulations.

Until the commission publishes specific regulations for nonprofit organizations and governmental units, the prices of services supplied by such organizations may be adjusted for allowable cost increases in effect on or after Nov. 14, 1971.

Base Period

For purposes of these regulations, base period shall mean the average of any two of the past three fiscal years of the firm ending prior to Aug. 15, 1971.

Rents

Guidelines for rents will be developed after consultations with the Rent Board. In the interim, the freeze will continue with some rule changes amending freeze-period definitions which resulted in hardships. Landlords are required to record and make available upon request both the unit-by-unit freeze period rent and the basis for any adjustments. The Rent Board will develop basic rent guidelines for consideration by the commission.

Regulated Industries

For prenotifying firms the relevant regulatory agencies shall submit all existing and new requests for rate increases to the Price Commission. These regulatory bodies will also notify the Price Commission upon approval of rate adjustments which will be reviewed by the Price Commission. For reporting firms, the regulatory bodies will report approved rate adjustments for review by the Price Commission. The Price Commission will retain the right to implement more stringent standards.

Some regulated firms' proposed rate increases have been approved by regulatory authorties, but were not allowed to become effective because of the freeze. Such increases may go into effect; however the appropriate regulatory authority shall review such increases for consistency with the goals of the economic stabilization program.

Corrections of Inequities

Inequities arising as a result of certain definitions and rules promulgated under the freeze or for other exceptional reasons will be handled as follows:

[1]

Changes will be made to amend certain definitions and to correct inequities created by the operation of rules promulgated under the freeze, but none of these changes will permit retroactive price increases. On or after Nov. 14, freeze-period prices may be adjusted pursuant to such changes. Specific price adjustments are subject to review by the commission. In such cases, the commission will determine whether the increase is significantly inconsistent with the goal of reducing the rate of inflation.

[2]

Prenotification firms must file with the commission any proposed price increases based on the modification of freeze-period rules.

[3]

Firms which can demonstrate a continuing gross inequity not ameliorated by the rules of the Price Commission may request an exception through local I.R.S. offices.

[4]

Firms must retain records supporting price increases that are made pursuant to the modified rules, and reporting firms must file reports of these changes with the commission.

Windfall Profits

Windfall profits refer to those profits which would not have existed except for unique conditions created by the operation of the economic stabilization program. The Price Commission is determined to take those measures necessary to achieve the goal of reducing the rate of inflation of 2–3 per cent by the

end of 1972. Therefore, in the administration of the stabilization program the commission will at certain times issue such regulations as necessary to cause windfall profits to be converted into price reductions.

Other Considerations

Notwithstanding the foregoing, in making determinations based on the standards sets forth in this statement, the Price Commission will take into account whatever factors it considers relevant to an equitable resolution of that case and considers necessary to achieve the over-all goal of holding average price increases across the economy to a rate of no more than 2.5 per cent per year.

FRB cuts discount rate. The Federal Reserve Board Nov. 10 approved the requests of seven of the 12 regional Reserve banks to lower their discount rates from 5% to 4.75%, effective Nov. 11. The seven banks were Boston, Philadelphia, Cleveland, St. Louis, Minneapolis, Dallas and San Francisco. The other banks were expected to follow suit.

The Federal Reserve said the change was made "in recognition of reductions that have taken place in other short-term interest rates and is intended to bring the discount rate into better alignment with short-term rates generally."

Approval of a lower discount rate followed general reductions of the commercial banks' prime rate from 6% to 5.75% Oct. 20 and 5.75% to 5.5% Nov. 4.

Burns reassures Wall Street. Federal Reserve Board Chairman Arthur F. Burns met in New York Nov. 11 with members of the Wall Street community and the press to sketch the prospects for economic recovery under the Administration's Phase Two controls. The meeting was arranged by New York Stock Exchange (NYSE) Board Chairman Ralph DeNunzio at the suggestion of the Administration.

Burns told the group that there were "powerful reasons for expecting economic recovery to accelerate and corporate profits to rise."

Responding to questions Burns said he expected the 5.5% guidelines for wage increases during Phase Two to be lowered as price increases leveled off in 1972. Burns said that "in view of the wide support the President's program has in the population and in the ranks of organized labor," it seemed to him "just speculation" that labor leaders would withdraw from the Pay Board. If they did walk out, he said, the President could restore the wage freeze or reconstitute the Pay Board with public members.

Burns assured his audience of investment bankers and stockbrokers that the Federal Reserve Board did not envisage a credit squeeze and there would be an ample money supply to spur "orderly" economic expansion without inflation. (The Federal Reserve System published banking figures Nov. 11 showing that the money supply declined at a 4% annual rate during September and October. Milton Friedman, University of Chicago economist and proponent of the theory that money supply was the major influence on economic growth, held Nov. 10 that FRB money supply policy was "sharply contractionary," but he said he believed the slowdown was only temporary.

Burns' trip to Wall Street coincided with the Price Commission's announcement of new price standards and a sharp retreat in stock prices Nov. 11. The Dow Jones industrial average dropped 11.24 points to close at 814.91—its lowest point since Dec. 3, 1970, when it closed at 808.53.

More pay, price decisions. Further pay and price decisions applicable to Phase Two were made by the Cost of Living Council (CLC) and the Pay Board Nov. 12–13.

The CLC approved Nov. 12 the $2.4 billion military pay boost scheduled to go into effect Nov. 14 to provide 2.6 million uniformed personnel pay raises averaging 15%. The ruling exempted all federal employes from wage controls except the six-month deferral of general pay increases for white-collar workers imposed by the Administration.

The CLC also exempted from Phase Two controls workers earning less than $1.60 an hour, the federal minimum wage, and prices on new life insurance and annuities.

The CLC also sanctioned scheduled pay increases due more than 100,000 autoworkers Nov. 23 as well as price increases to account for the increased labor cost to the car companies. It held that pay increases already set to go into

effect between Nov. 14 (beginning of Phase Two) and Jan. 1, 1972 would not need prior federal approval, and that companies involved "will be allowed to make necessary price adjustments" subject to Price Commission regulations.

Ford Motor Co. Nov. 13 raised the price of its Pinto small car almost 6%, the first major price hike on new cars in the industry. The company said the increase had been reviewed with federal officials. But the Price Commission later Nov. 14 disclosed it had asked the CLC to rescind its ruling permitting raised prices to offset wage increases due before the end of the year. Automobile officials requesting guidance on the issue as the 90-day freeze ended Nov. 14 were told that day that the higher prices on new cars could be set but would probably be rolled back at least for 72 hours.

The Price Commission also clarified Nov. 13 its reporting requirement for wholesalers and retailers with more than $100 million in annual sales. Such firms would not be required to obtain advance approval of price increases, such as firms that large in other sectors, but would be required to file notification of increases.

In another ruling, the commission Nov. 13 said companies sustaining a loss and projecting a loss for the current fiscal year could raise prices as much as necessary to eliminate the loss. If the allowable markup margin were exceeded, however, the additional markup would not be permitted to go high enough to produce a projected profit.

The Pay Board exempted from its guidelines Nov. 13 pay increases and other benefits due workers for length of service. Such longevity benefits, such as in-grade raises, would not be counted against the board's 5½% annual pay raise limit applied to future contracts.

The Pay Board Nov. 12 issued a stipulation that the Construction Industry Stabilization Committee, established prior to the freeze, would have to conform to Pay Board regulations.

Phase Two begins. President Nixon said Nov. 12 that "some bulge" on the price-wage front was possible after the 90-day freeze ended at midnight Nov. 13 and the nation entered Phase Two of the economic stabilization program. But, the President stressed, the decisions of the Pay Board and Price Commission had been "very sound" and he expected their effort to succeed, especially with the impetus of "the enormous" public support for the stabilization program.

Nixon conceded there was an element of uncertainty concerning Phase Two but said it was "inevitable" in a free-enterprise system, which, he pointed out, was "the major advantage" the U.S. had "in its competitive position in the world."

The President made the remarks at a news conference.

Some of the immediate major decisions facing the stabilization boards involved the automobile industry, which was considering price hikes to offset contracted pay increases due early in Phase Two, teachers, coal miners and rail workers.

According to a survey conducted by the National Education Association, which released the results Nov. 16, 63% of the nation's teachers lost raises during the 90-day freeze and another 7% were in the process of negotiating increases when the freeze began.

Nixon confronts AFL-CIO. President Nixon appeared before the AFL-CIO in convention at Bal Harbour, Fla. Nov. 19 and appealed for support of Phase Two. The confrontation came a day after the federation had adopted a policy of non-cooperation on Phase Two and after AFL-CIO President George Meany had denounced the President's economic policies and had challenged Nixon personally on the issue.

Policy of noncooperation adopted—The policy of noncooperation adopted by the convention Nov. 18 called on the three AFL-CIO representatives of the Pay Board, the Phase Two wage-control unit, not to vote on issues before the board unless their votes were decisive for labor's side. The policy also would encourage strikes by affiliated unions to gain contracted pay increases denied during the wage freeze.

Their representatives were to remain on the Pay Board "only so long as a reasonable hope exists of securing recognition of the validity of contracts and of achieving justice for working people gen-

erally—including most particularly, those with low or substandard incomes and those without the protection of strong bargaining representatives."

Until these objectives were assured, the policy statement said, "labor cannot associate itself with the actions of the board or encourage cooperation with their administration or enforcement." The resolution recommended "that the unions of the AFL-CIO insist at every level on the validity of their contracts in all their terms and in all their particulars, and that they take every lawful action at their command to insure that their contracts are honored."

The federation also would continue its legislative effort in Congress "to protect the validity of contracts."

Meany challenges Nixon—In his speech to the convention Nov. 18, Meany attacked the President for his "fat-cat" economic philosophy and individual members of the Pay Board, which he considered "a stacked deck" against labor with "not a hope or very little hope, for equity."

He charged that the board had tried to goad labor into quitting and to divide its five members by offering separate "under-the-table deals" (two non-AFL-CIO labor representatives were on the board for teamsters and auto workers).

Nixon's "innate philosophy," Meany said, "is based on the idea that if you make the fat cats a little fatter, somewhere along the line the poor simpletons are going to profit by it. His slogan is 'profits, profits, profits.' "

Meany suggested the odds were 20–1 against success for Phase Two, and if it did not work labor would be the "scapegoat" whether "we help or don't help," and "the next step would be more stringent and oppressive measures that could destroy our American institutions."

In commenting on the federation's resolution of noncooperation, Meany directly challenged President Nixon. "If the President of the United States doesn't want our membership on the Pay Board on our terms," he declared, "he knows what he can do."

Nixon takes up challenge—In his speech Nov. 19, Nixon referred to Meany's remark and gave his rejoinder: "Well, you know, President Meany is correct. I know exactly what I can do and I'm going to do it."

He wanted a controls program that was fair to organized labor and all elements of society, Nixon said, and "a great majority of the American people and a majority of union members want to stop the rise in the cost of living and that's what we're going to do." In order to accomplish that, the Administration wanted the participation of business, labor, consumers and "all the other areas of the society," Nixon said, but "whether we get that participation or not," it was his obligation as President "to make this program of stopping the rise in cost of living succeed, and to the extent that my powers allow it, I shall do exactly that."

Appealing for labor's support, Nixon said:

". . . This isn't like an ordinary collective bargaining dispute where labor wins and management loses. If we fail in this venture America will lose and all of us will lose and I say to you we can't let that happen. It means that we must work together."

A cool reception—Nixon himself told the labor delegates some of his advisers had questioned the wisdom of his appearance before them since a majority of them were "against you politically."

The reception given him was cool, labor's opposition obvious. Some phrases in Nixon's speech evoked derisive laughter, such as his reference to the "remarkable success" of the wage-price freeze, and his plea to the delegates to ask their wives about the recent slowdown in the rise of consumer prices.

Shortly after the President's speech, the convention heard from Sen. George McGovern (S.D.), a candidate for the Democratic presidential nomination, who attacked Nixon's economic policy, citing the high unemployment, and urged Nixon's defeat in 1972.

Connally deplores Meany action—Treasury Secretary John B. Connally Jr. Nov. 22 attacked Meany over the President's reception at the convention. Meany's actions, Connally said, "reflected an arrogance and a boorishness and a discourtesy that ill become a leader of the American labor move-

ment." It must be made clear, he said, "that we cannot permit one man to put himself above the interest of all of the working people of this country . . . He does not represent all of these people."

Connally said Phase Two could not function as well as it should without organized labor's cooperation, but that it was "inconceivable that a responsible group of people would not cooperate."

He also deplored the $20,000 increase in Meany's annual salary (to $90,000) voted by the convention Nov. 19. This was "flagrant contempt" for the anti-inflation program, he said.

Teamsters promise Nixon respect—The White House disclosed Nov. 20 that President Nixon had received more than 1,000 telegrams in 24 hours supporting the President on his stand before the AFL-CIO convention. Among the telegrams was one from Teamsters President Frank Fitzsimmons inviting Nixon to visit Teamster conferences on the Pay Board and assuring him he would be "afforded the sincerest respect and courtesies that you and your office deserve."

UAW favors remaining on Pay Board—President Leonard Woodcock of the United Automobile Workers told a special convention of his union in Detroit Nov. 13 that labor had done well in protecting workers' benefits for Phase Two. Existing contracts and future bargaining were "protected" by board decisions, he said, and the only doubtful issue of interest to labor was the problem of pay increases denied during the freeze.

Woodcock advocated labor's continuing role on the Pay Board.

Retroactive increases denied. The Pay Board Nov. 17 voted 9–5, with management and public members lined up against labor, to rule out retroactive payment of raises deferred by the freeze, except in special cases or unless challenged by five or more members of the board.

The board issued a clarifying statement Nov. 22, specifying that special cases involved those of "severe inequity," which it said existed in "tandem relationships." The board spelled out the following criteria under which employes could claim a "tandem" situation:

A "tandem relationship" means a well-established and consistently maintained practice whereby the precise timing, amount and nature of general increases in wages, salaries and other compensation of a given appropriate employe unit have so followed those of another such unit of employes of the same employer or of other employers within a commonly recognized industry (such as SIC two-digit category) that a general increase, in the normal operation of the practice, would have been put into effect and have been applicable to work performed on or before Nov. 13, 1971, but for the operation of the freeze.

1. The basic contract to which tandem is claimed must have been completed before Aug. 15.

2. The tandem relationship was clearly established either for five years or in the last two bargaining agreements.

3. The agreement for which retroactivity is sought expired no more than 30 days after the basic agreement.

4. It can be shown that retroactivity was either an established practice or had been agreed to prior to the end of the freeze.

Employes who would have become eligible for a new or increased benefit during the freeze and who otherwise cannot become eligible for the benefit may be granted the benefit retroactively.

Low-wage employes who would have become eligible for a pay increase during the freeze and whose rate of pay prior to the freeze was $2 per hour or less.

In a related development, the Senate Banking Committee Nov. 18 voted 14–0 to allow retroactive payment of most frozen wage increases.

Pay Board approves miners' raise. The Pay Board, with its public members strongly objecting, voted 10–3 Nov. 19 to uphold the first-year pay raise of a three-year soft coal contract signed Nov. 13 by the United Mine Workers of America (UMW). No ruling was made on the second and third yearly raises.

The contract, covering 100,000 soft-coal miners, on strike in 25 states since Oct. 1, called for an average package increase in wages and benefits of 30% over the three-year period, or 39% if an increase from 40¢ to 80¢ per ton royalty payment for the miners' pension fund were figured in, the first increase in the royalty payment since 1952.

The Administration's chief spokesman on economic policy, Treasury Secretary John B. Connally Jr., commented on the coal pact during an appearance before the Economic Club of New York Nov. 16. He said if the Pay Board approved the pact "it will hurt, no question about it" and somebody else would have to be

squeezed "awfully hard, down the road" to keep within the guideline of an average 5½% wage increase set for Phase Two.

The contract had come under board scrutiny Nov. 18 because the first-year increase, defined as 15% by the board's management members and 16.8% by its public members, exceeded the 5.5% guideline for new pay increases. The board earlier had classified the settlement as an "existing" contract and not subject to the wage guideline since it had been signed a half hour before the end of the wage-price freeze. However, the board decided to review the contract informally under its authority to roll back increases that the board determined were "unreasonably inconsistent" with other wage scales.

The business members of the board said the increase was justified on the basis of a needed 4% increase in the UMW health and welfare fund, the relative wage position of miners, difficulties of their work and a need to attract new workers to the industry.

A stiff dissenting statement by the five public members warned: "It is highly improbable that the rate of inflation will be reduced sufficiently to meet the goal of the stabilization effort if increases of this magnitude are permitted." The statement said the miners' raises in the first year should be held at 12.5%, enough to take into account the 5.5% guideline, the 4.1% increase in the health and welfare fund, and "further adjustment to reflect inter-industry relations." The two public members who abstained from voting were Chairman George A. Boldt, who voted only in event of a tie, and Neil H. Jacoby because of a possible conflict of interest.

There was also a strong reaction from members of the Congressional Joint Economic Committee Nov. 20. The committee chairman, Sen. William Proxmire (D, Wis.), said he was "shocked, astonished and surprised" at the decision, which he said, "must seem to be very soft to most Americans." Rep. Henry S. Reuss (D, Wis.) criticized the Pay Board's failure to explain the impact of the decision on coal prices. Boldt, who was testifying before the committee, replied that coal prices were an issue for the Price Commission.

The seven-member Price Commission, without mentioning the soft-coal settlement, warned business Nov. 22 that it would not be allowed to pass on the increased costs of wage raises approved by the Pay Board.

Coal price request cut—The Price Commission Dec. 1 allowed a coal company to pass on to consumers only 60% of the 15% wage increase approved by the Pay Board for soft-coal miners. It approved a 3.78% price increase for the Old Ben Coal Co. (a subsidiary of the Standard Oil Co. of Ohio), which had requested 6.71%.

Price Commission Chairman C. Jackson Grayson Jr. used the Old Ben ruling to serve notice on business that the commission would not condone prices increased to cover inflationary wage rises, even if the latter were approved by the Pay Board. In general, he said, if a price was increased to absorb a wage rise that exceeded the Pay Board's 5.5% guideline, the commission would consider the pricing inflationary.

In explaining the ruling for Old Ben, Grayson said the firm was permitted to pass on 5.5% of the pay rise plus about 4.1% of pension costs for miners, whose welfare fund was in financial distress. As for the technical matter that the mine contract had been agreed upon before the 90-day freeze ended, Grayson said it had been signed after Phase Two guidelines had been announced and were known.

The ruling was criticized as "shortsighted" Dec. 8 by Carl E. Bagge, president of the National Coal Association. Bagge said the policy would close some mines and "destroy the incentive" to open new ones.

Construction pay hikes—The Construction Stabilization Committee announced Nov. 26 approval of 48 contracts containing pay increases, many of which exceeded the 5.5% annual increase guideline established by the Pay Board. Some of the raises: 16% for glaziers of Great Falls, Mont. (current wage $5.11 an hour), 20% for sheet metal workers in 30 counties in Iowa, and 24% for plasterers in Wichita, Kan.

Construction panel summoned—The Construction Industry Stabilization Committee (CISC) was told Dec. 2 by Pay Board Chairman George H. Boldt to postpone approval of new construction settlements until its representatives consulted with the board. CISC announced Dec. 3 approval of more settlements—ranging from 9.9% over 12 months for Philadelphia bricklayers to 56.2% over two years for Delaware plasterers.

The consultation between the construction panel and Pay Board was held Dec. 8.

Statement on merit increases—The Pay Board said Dec. 3 in a statement on merit pay increases that "an aggregate increase in wages and salaries under any merit or salary administration plan, where no labor agreement exists, is subject to the 5.5% standard." The board noted that merit increases generally were substantial in fields not usually covered by union contracts while such increases generally were small under union contracts.

44% in survey to hold price line. The Price Commission said Dec. 13 that 44% of large firms responding to its survey gave assurances they would try to "hold the line" on price increases.

About 40% of the respondents indicated they planned to seek price increases. About 1,000 of 1,500 companies surveyed responded.

Medical charges limited. The Price Commission Dec. 15 imposed ceilings of 2.5% on increases in doctors' fees and of 6% on increases in hospital charges. The guidelines, applying to whatever rates were in affect as of Dec. 15, were designed to bring the rate of increase in health costs, currently running at 12.9%, down to 6.45%.

Medical services were also required to maintain price lists revealing any changes and to make them available to patients.

The 2.5% guideline would apply to physicians, dentists, osteopaths, chiropractors, medical and dental laboratories and convalescent and rest homes. Any increase would have to be justified by higher costs.

The 6% rule covered hospitals, nursing homes and mental institutions, which could increase charges of up to 2.5% on their own and increases between 2.5% and 6% after reporting them to the Internal Revenue Service. Increases above 6% required an "exception" obtained from a State Advisory Board, to be appointed by governors, or a district director of Internal Revenue or the Price Commission, the final step in the exemption process.

The commission also required these institutions to base any cost increase on aggregate wage and salary increases within the 5.5% guideline, non-wage expense increases within a 2.5% guideline and expenditures for new equipment within a 1.7% annual guideline.

Union waives raises. Workers at Frigidaire (a division of General Motors Corp.) appliance plants in Dayton, Ohio voted Nov. 21 to waive a 3% wage increase due Nov. 22 and a similar raise scheduled a year later. They also relinquished a cost of living increase in December and similar raises falling later within the current contract. The workers, members of the International Union of Electrical Workers (IUE) Local 801, currently earned $4.34 an hour.

In return for the wage concessions GM agreed to recall some of 3,400 workers laid off since the fall of 1970 when the most recent IUE contract was signed—200 workers Dec. 6 and 650 by Feb. 1. It was rumored that GM was considering closing down its Dayton plants because of lagging sales.

Frigidaire announced Dec. 10 that it would reduce prices on refrigerators and laundry appliances.

Price Commission decisions. The Price Commission Nov. 17 approved a request by American Motors Corp. to raise prices on 1972 models by 2.5%.

The Commission said the AMC request was justified on the basis of "allowable costs, taking into consideration productivity and the manufacturer's price changes will not increase" profits as a percentage of sales over the base-period level.

The Price Commission also:

■ Approved Nov. 22 price increases for food wholesalers and retailers in Puerto Rico on perishable items flown to the island because of the continued dock strike.

■ Permitted rent increases authorized by state or local control agencies to take effect. The Nov. 22 decision did not apply to public housing or subsidized housing subject to "rent formulas in the financing programs." State and local authorities would be required to inform the commission of control methods, regulation changes and "aggregate rent increases."

■ Approved Nov. 23 steel price increases about triple the commission's 2.5% target and insisted the decisions would not set a precedent. The commission granted the requests of Bethlehem Steel Co. for a 7.6% increase and that of National Steel Co. for a 7.2% hike, both on tinplate products. Tin mill products made up 10% of Bethlehem's sales and 25% of National's volume. The increases covered higher labor costs effective from Nov. 14 to Jan. 1, 1972. (CF & I Steel Co., 88% owned by Crane Co., said in N.Y. Nov. 23 it had been granted a 8% boost on steel rails.) The commission said the increases were granted because they would not exceed the companies' permissible profit margins (the increase would raise National's total income 1.8%). C. Jackson Grayson, the commission's chairman, insisted that the approved increases would not set a precedent for higher prices on sheet products, the industry's most important product category.

■ Approved Nov. 23 a 3.9% price increase, as requested by Western Electric Co. (the manufacturing unit of the American Telephone and Telegraph Co.), on telecommunications equipment. The increase, affecting 55% of the company's volume, represented a 2.1% price boost in terms of total volume.

■ Rejected a request by United Illuminating Co. of New Haven for retroactive recovery of more than $600,000 paid for more costly low-sulphur fuel during the wage-price freeze.

Car price increases approved—The Price Commission approved price increases for the Big Three auto manufacturers Nov. 24–30.

Chrysler Corp., which had requested a 5.3% increase on its 1972 model cars, was permitted a 4.5% rise Nov. 24 but announced it was imposing only a 3% increase for "competitive reasons." General Motors Corp. had requested a 3% increase Nov. 23. The 3% Chrysler hike was expected to add $95 to the price of an average model, with a $30 additional increase probable for optional equipment.

Ford Motor Co., which had originally requested a 2% price rise but upped it to 4.4% Nov. 24, was granted an average price increase of 2.9% for cars, trucks and equipment Nov. 29. The commission said the 4.4% increase would have put Ford over the guideline by exceeding the profit margin of its base period—any two of the three previous fiscal years. (Ford announced Dec. 10 that it would raise prices only an average 2.6% for competitive reasons.)

The commission Nov. 30 approved a 2.5% average price increase for General Motors, which announced that the higher prices, expected to average $113 per automobile, would be effective immediately.

(The Japanese automobile manufacturer Toyota announced Nov. 23 a 1.6% price increase on its passenger cars sold in the U.S. This was on top of its 8.9% price hike on 1972 models announced in October. The hikes were attributed to the upward valuation of the Japanese yen, higher tariff charges and higher production costs.)

Other price decisions—The Price Commission took these additional actions:

Nov. 24—It approved, on the grounds labor costs would be covered and total revenues increased by 1.3%, a 3.8% price increase on newspaper advertisements sold by Field Enterprises, Inc., publisher of the Chicago Sun-Times and Chicago Daily News.

Nov. 26—It rejected, citing lack of productivity-gain estimates, a request by the Bassett Furniture Co. of Bassett, Va. for a 1.8% price increase.

Nov. 29—It denied, because the 1971 profit margin to date was higher than in the company's base period, a request by the Oscar Mayer Co. for a 1.31% increase on its line of processed meat products.

The commission announced it would review all rate increases of public utilities and require regulated companies with revenues of $50 million or more a year to submit reports and state and federal regulatory agencies to certify that approved rate rises were consistent with guidelines.

Dec. 1—It approved: a 3.71% increase on advertising for the Washington Post, which had sought 4.02%; a 4.1% rise on publication grade paper and a 3.4% rise on newsprint for the International Paper Co. (the government estimated the total revenue rise at less than 1%); increases ranging from 1.3% to 4.7% for 12 plants of the American Bakeries Corp. (a 2.52% increase in total revenues).

Rent Advisory Board appointed. President Nixon announced Nov. 23 the appointment of 14 persons to the Rent Advisory Board to assist the Price Commission on stabilization of rents.

Public members

Thomas B. Curtis (chairman) of St. Louis, vice president and general counsel of Encyclopaedia Britannica, former congressman (R, Mo. 1950–69).

Charles J. Urstadt, Bronxville, N.Y., commissioner of Housing and Community Renewal for the state of New York.

George E. Sternlieb, Short Hills, N.J., professor and director of the Center for Urban Policy Research, Rutgers University, Newark.

Murray L. Weidenbam, Creve Coeur, Mo., professor at Washington University, St. Louis; former assistant secretary of the Treasury for economic policy.

Ronald C. Morgan, Cincinnati, lawyer; formerly associate director of Cincinnati Lawyers for Housing.

Industry members

Fred C. Tucker Jr., Indianapolis, chief executive officer, F. C. Tucker Company, realtors and developers; president-elect of National Association of Real Estate Boards.

Harvey M. Meyerhoff, Owing Mills, Md., president, Monumental Properties, Inc., Baltimore; honorary life director, National Association of Home Builders; president, Home Builders Association of Maryland.

Robert H. Pease, Hinsdale, Ill., senior vice president, Draper & Kramer, Inc., Chicago; former president of the Mortgage Bankers Association of America.

Robert Ross, San Antonio, Tex., president, Ross Real Estate Company; president, National Apartment Association.

Bruce P. Hayden, West Hartford, Conn., vice president, mortgage and real estate department, Connecticut Life Insurance Company.

Consumer members

Mrs. Rossetta Wylie, Philadelphia, chairman, National Tenants Organization; president, Resident Advisory Board (public housing organization), Philadelphia.

Mrs. Mary Elizabeth C. Sowards, Pikeville, Ky., chairman, Citizens Commission for Consumer Protection in the office of the Governor; member, President's Consumer Advisory Council.

Pete Vasquez Villa, Rancho Mirage, Calif., compliance officer, Riverside Economic Opportunity Board, Riverside, Calif.

Robert D. Blue, Eagle Grove, Iowa, lawyer; member, Older Americans Advisory Committee to the secretary of health, education and welfare; member, executive committee of the planning board, White House Conference on Aging; governor of Iowa 1944-1948.

Price Commission Chairman C. Jackson Grayson Jr. Nov. 30 asked landlords to continue the freeze on rent increases on residential properties to allow the commission and the new advisory board to develop guidelines. The government reportedly had received some 70,000 inquiries on rents during the first two weeks of Phase Two.

The National Association of Real Estate Boards, at its 64th annual convention in Miami Beach, Fla., heard its president, Bill N. Brown of Albuquerque, N.M., call Nov. 14 for removal of all controls on rents during Phase Two. George Romney, secretary of Housing and Urban Development, told the convention Nov. 17 that temporary control of rents was "a small price to pay if inflation can be curbed and costs brought under control."

Landlords cautioned. The Internal Revenue Service issued a statement Dec. 3 cautioning landlords not to raise rents, even within current guidelines, unless they had complete records on rental practices and made them available to tenants facing increases. Tenants were advised to be "vigilant" and told they were legally entitled to withhold rent increases from landlords refusing to produce the records. The service said it would "vigorously investigate" complaints. Landlords were requested to make available to tenants prices for units and "the reason for any increase" over the amount charged during the 90-day freeze.

Wholesale prices rise. The Labor Department reported Dec. 3 that the wholesale price index rose a slight .1% in November. Herbert Stein, member and chairman-designate of the President's Council of Economic Advisers (CEA), said the negligible increase, all attributed to raw farm products not subject to the wage-price freeze, was "the best evidence we have so far" that the freeze was working.

The seasonally adjusted .1% increase over October brought the index to 114.5% of the 1967 base period, 3.2% above a year earlier. The department said the combined index fluctuations for the September-November period amounted to an .8% decline at a seasonally adjusted annual rate.

The key industrial commodities index was 114.9%, showing no change on an adjusted basis from October and down an unadjusted .1% ("almost entirely the result of decreases for controlled items.")

Consumer price rise moderate. Continuing its moderate rise, the consumer price index rose .2% in November at a 2.4% annual rate, the Labor Department reported Dec. 22. Combined with rises in September and October, spanning the three-month wage-price freeze period, consumer prices rose at a seasonally adjusted 1.7% annual rate. It was the smallest three-month increase since 1967.

Jobless rate up. The unemployment rate in November rose to 6% from 5.8% in October, even though total employment (seasonally adjusted) hit the 80 million mark for the first time in history, the Labor Department reported Dec. 3.

Seasonally adjusted unemployment rose 212,000 to 5,150,000 persons, with most of the increase occurring among white adults in the 20-24 age group who had lost their jobs. On an unadjusted basis, total unemployment was 4,815,000. Total employment expanded 177,000 to an adjusted 80,022,000 persons.

Black unemployment in November dropped to 9.3% from 10.7% in October.

TOTAL OFFICIALLY MEASURED UNEMPLOYMENT, 1969-71			
[Thousands of persons]			
	1969	1970	1971
Unemployed	2,832	4,088	4,993
Discouraged [1]	574	638	774
Part-time unemployed [2]	852	1,010	1,143
Total	4,258	5,736	6,910
Unemployment rate [3] (percent)	5.2	6.9	8.1

[1] Those not in labor force because they think they could not find a job.
[2] Full-time equivalent of part-time unemployment of those who work part time because of slack work, material shortages, or inability to find full-time job. "Full-time" defined as 40 hours per week.
[3] Unemployed plus discouraged plus full time equivalent of part-time unemployed as percent of civilian labor force adjusted to include discouraged.

Source: Bureau of Labor Statistics.

Joblessness for white workers rose from 5.3% to 5.7%.

5 fewer areas on 6% jobless list—Seven areas were dropped and two were added Nov. 29 to the Labor Department's list of metropolitan areas with unemployment of at least 6% of the labor force, reducing the total from the 10-year high of 65 to 60. The department also announced that, according to preliminary figures, 17 smaller areas were added and three were removed from its list of smaller cities with a jobless rate of 6% or more. The changes brought the list to an all-time high of 803.

Industrial output. Industrial output gained significantly in November, the Federal Reserve Board reported Dec. 15. The board's index of industrial production rose .8% to a seasonally adjusted 107% of its 1967 base period.

U.S. Steel, other price rulings. The Price Commission Dec. 7 approved an average price increase of 3.6% for products of the U.S. Steel Corp. The company originally had sought an 8.6% increase on certain products only, but withdrew the request when the commission decided against a product-by-product approach. The commission opted in favor of granting an aggregate increase within which prices on individual products could vary.

The commission indicated that it intended to extend the principle to other "homogeneous" concerns. Commission

Chairman C. Jackson Grayson Jr. said the system would give firms more flexibility in pricing, and, "in a major basic industry should help to stabilize the general price structure."

Although specific figures were not released, U.S. Steel said the price rise granted would not fully cover its increased costs for labor and materials. Commission sources confirmed that the firm was entitled under the guidelines to a slightly larger price rise than it was given.

(U.S. Steel Dec. 10 announced a 7.7% rise in the prices of tin mill and sheet and strip products used to make tin cans, automobiles and appliances. The firm said the increases, affecting about 25% of its steel products, would have an impact on its entire range of steel mill products of less than the 3.6% average price increase approved by the Commission Dec. 7.)

The commission approved Dec. 3-8 a series of price increases based on increased labor and material costs and adjustments for productivity. Some of the requests were reduced to account for productivity increases. Among the price increases approved:

Dec. 3—N.Y. Times Magazine, Book Review and special advertising, 4.5% increase, same as request. Chrysler Corp.-MoPar Division (auto parts), 3.7% increase, 4.4% requested. Levi Strauss Co. (selected cotton products), 2.84% increase, same as request.

Dec. 6—J. P. Stevens (cotton materials), 3.95% increase, same as request. Fibreboard Corp. Paperboard and Packaging Division, 3.6% increase, 5.4% requested.

The Cost of Living Council announced Dec. 8 that companies experiencing steep, unexpected shifts in the price of raw materials need not obtain approval from the Price Commission before passing the new costs along in price raises.

Both boards criticized. Both the price and pay boards came under attack Dec. 8 from Henry Ford 2d, chairman of the Ford Motor Co. Ford assailed "the depressing effect of continuing uncertainty over the effects and the duration of Phase Two. There is uncertainty as to whether or not overall wage and price levels—as opposed to some wages and some prices—will in fact be controlled." There was "a real risk," he said, "based on the Pay Board's decisions thus far, that the economic program will do little to limit underlying cost pressures."

Ford said if Phase Two policies were reasonably effective, "we believe that the present recovery from the 1969–70 recession will build to a faster pace."

Ford's remarks were made in a year-end company statement revealing that the firm planned to increase its capital spending by 24%, from $645 million in 1971 to a record $800 million in 1972. Of the increase, $102 million would be spent outside the U.S., $53 million in the U.S.,

Pay Board defended. The Pay Board was defended Dec. 8 by Labor Secretary James D. Hodgson. He said the Administration had been aware it would have to "swallow" very large wage settlements in coal, aerospace, railroads and some other industries at the beginning of Phase Two. It was "no surprise," he said, that such settlements were being granted for industries signing new contracts at the end of the 1971 collective bargaining cycle. The stabilization program "has to stand" some high initial wage settlements, he said, and retroactive payment of frozen wages would not cause many problems for the program. As for AFL-CIO President George Meany, who had staked out a policy of noncooperation with the Pay Board, Hodgson said Meany had a "real problem" to decide whether or not to put the success of the stabilization program ahead of "politics."

Rail pact approved by Pay Board. The Pay Board approved Dec. 9 the railroad signalmen's contract provisions providing "catch up" wage increases comparable to those granted other rail unions before the wage freeze. The signalmen's pact, called for increases of about 46% over 42 months, retroactive to January 1970.

The Pay Board held it had no authority to challenge the early increments —5% in January 1970 and 6.9% in November 1970, which were ordered by Congress, and 2.6% and 2.9% in January and April of 1971, which were recommended by a presidential emergency board.

The pact's next increment of 5% retroactive to Oct. 1 was approved by the board on the "catch-up" reasoning since the agreement, the board said, "conforms in most of its features to contracts already in effect with railroad unions representing some 320,000 of the nation's 485,000 railroad employes." But the board announced Dec. 17 that this approval was a "mistake" because the policy of retroactive payment of frozen wages was undergoing review.

Future increments provided by the pact, two in 1972 and the last in April 1973 and amounting to 15.4% of the 46% contained in the pact, remained subject to later approval by the board.

The decision on the signalmen's wages was supported by the board's five labor members and four of the business members. (Three public members reportedly voted against the approval, another was absent and the chairman, also from the public sector, did not vote except to break a tie. The fifth business member was represented by an alternate, who abstained.)

Douglas Aircraft strikers return. United Auto Workers President Leonard Woodcock issued a back-to-work order Dec. 11 to 4,000 strikers at Douglas Aircraft of Canada Ltd. at Malton, and cut off strike benefits of up to $40 a week as of Dec. 13.

The order was unprecedented in the history of the union in Canada and came after a five-hour meeting at UAW headquarters in Detroit.

Although the international union originally sanctioned the strike, Woodcock said McDonnell Douglas, the parent U.S. firm, had made a settlement offer Nov. 13 which had agreed to the demands by the union. However, local membership had rejected the offer in a secret ballot Nov. 18. International officers complained their efforts to defend the settlement had been blocked by organized heckling and "anarchist groups."

The new settlement provided increases of 80¢ an hour over three years, plus improvements in pensions and other fringe areas.

9-year Florida rail strike ends. An agreement to end a strike begun Jan. 23, 1963 against the Florida East Coast Railway was given preliminary approval by a federal district court in Jacksonville Dec. 17. The line, with outside help, continued operating except for the first week of the strike.

The agreement called for an out-of-court settlement in which 11 non-operating unions would be paid $1.5 million in damages and strikers' salaries would be increased 31% Jan. 1, 1972 and 6% more a year later. The old wage paid union employes was $2-$2.50 an hour.

Phase Two court suits. The Justice Department filed suit Dec. 17 against the Cincinnati Transit, Inc. to have its 5¢ fare increase rescinded, bus riders compensated and an 11% reduction in service restored.

The suit was the third filed by the government under Phase Two. The first, against a one-unit landlord in El Paso, Tex., resulted in an injunction Dec. 1 barring an eviction. The second was filed Dec. 15 against a Wilmington, Del. landlord seeking redress on rent increases for 289 of 342 tenants.

Discount, prime rate cuts. The Federal Reserve Board (FRB) lowered its discount rate again Dec. 10 from 4.75% to 4.5%. Morgan Guaranty Trust Co. and Chase Manhattan Bank pared their prime rates from 5.5% to 5.25% Dec. 13. However, many banks were reluctant to cut their prime rate, saying they were studying the situation.

The FRB reduction, effective Dec. 10, was approved for the Reserve banks of Boston, St. Louis, Kansas City and San Francisco.

Economic control authority extended. Both houses of Congress Dec. 14 approved a bill to extend through April 1973 the president's authority to control wages, prices and rents. President Nixon, signing the measure Dec. 22, said that with the enactment of the bill, plus other steps taken, the "major elements of our New Economic Program are now in place."

"We can now confidently say that 1971 is ending on a most encouraging eco-nomic note and that 1972 will begin as a year of great economic promise," he said.

Nixon said, while the legislation extended his authority to exert economic controls until April 30, 1973, he hoped and expected that controls would be ended before then and the economy returned to "reliance on free-market forces."

The bill, the Economic Stabilization Act, made subject to federal guidelines all rent-controlled apartments, such as in New York, where there were 1.4 million rent-controlled residential units, and Boston. (Under a Price Commission ruling Nov. 22, rents under state or local control were exempted from federal guidelines.)

The bill contained a plan to provide retroactive pay increases that had been scheduled to become effective after Aug. 15 but were barred by the freeze—as long as the increases were not "unreasonably inconsistent" with federal guidelines and prices, taxes or appropriations, or productivity had not been increased in anticipation of the pay raises.

The bill also called for federal civilian and military employes to receive a 5.5% pay raise as of Jan. 1, 1972 instead of the raise being deferred until July 1, 1972, as requested by President Nixon.

In addition, the bill required:

■ The president to establish controls on increases in interest rates and dividend payments unless he affirmed on a category-by-category basis that they were not necessary.

■ Mass transit systems not subject to federal or state regulation to seek permission of the Price Commission before raising fares.

■ Senate confirmation within 60 days of the pay and price board chairmen, and confirmation of future appointments to the boards.

Other provisions (a) gave subpoena power to the pay and price boards for witnesses and documents, (b) permitted consumer suits against merchants or landlords increasing prices or rents above guidelines, with triple damages allowed on the amount of overcharge, (c) set fines of $5,000 for willful violation of the federal economic control regulations, civil penalties of $2,500 for other violations, and (d) called upon the Pay Board not to include fringe benefits in decisions on pay raises.

A Senate provision to exempt the press and other publishing and information media from wage or price controls was eliminated by Senate-House conferees. The Senate had passed its version of the bill Dec. 1, the House its version Dec. 10 by 324–33 vote. The provision on rent-controlled apartments originated in the House on an amendment written by Rep. Bella S. Abzug (D, N.Y.) and offered by Rep. Frank J. Brasco (D, N.Y.).

The House provisions on retroactive pay called for back payment of raises if covering increases had been effected by a company in prices or a government in taxes or if productivity were increased.

Tax bill enacted. The $25.9 billion tax relief bill was passed by both houses of Congress Dec. 9 and signed by President Nixon Dec. 10. Final passage came on a 320–74 vote in the House and a 71–6 vote in the Senate.

At the signing ceremony, the President called the bill, which was an integral part of his new economic policy, a "responsible" one.

Appropriations. A $70,518,463,000 defense appropriations bill, the second largest defense appropriation in U.S. history, was passed by Congress Dec. 15 and signed by President Nixon Dec. 18. The total was $3 billion less than requested by the Administration. Nixon's chief legislative aide, Clark MacGregor, expressed concern Dec. 18 over the reduction and said Nixon would ask Congress for "a substantially strengthened defense budget" in 1972.

A $3,406,385,371 fiscal 1971 supplemental appropriations bill was cleared by Congress Dec. 10. This total was $151,461,000 more than the Administration requested. Among the funds were: Manpower Administration $802,924,000; Health Manpower $492,980,000; Office of Child Development $376,317,000; Programs for the Aging $55,250,000; Office of Economic Opportunity $741,-380,000; Public Works $119,010,000; Economic Development Assistance $30 million; Minority Business Enterprise $40 million; Federal Aviation Administration $17,033,000; Postal Service $200 million.

Pay Board decisions. The Pay Board Dec. 17 announced rules governing increases in pay for executives, stock options and exceptions allowable from the 5.5% wage increase guideline.

Increases in compensation for executives were to be bound by the same 5.5% guideline applied to other wage earners. The guideline encompassed executive salaries and benefits, such as bonuses and incentive pay.

As for stock options, those granted before Phase Two began Nov. 14 could be exercised, new ones could be granted if the number of shares and the option price were not less than 100% of market value. The total number of stock options granted could not exceed the average granted over the last three years.

The rule for exceptions would permit some wage raises to exceed the 5.5% guideline up to a ceiling of 7%. The exceptions could be justified under certain circumstances, (a) if a "tandem" arrangement existed where wages levels were closely related to others in the same industry (b) if there were a lot of jobs unfilled and difficulty in filling them at the set wage level, and (c) if aggregate pay rises of the last three years averaged less than 7% annually.

In another action Dec. 17, the board authorized the Construction Industry Stabilization Committee to continue passing on labor contracts settled in the 90-day freeze period that ended Nov. 14, but the board deferred any action on retroactive payment of frozen wages pending policy on construction raises.

Pay Board Chairman George H. Boldt told newsmen Dec. 17 that the board was "over the hump and on the way to being an effective agency" and that there was "no indication at all that labor members of the board are not cooperating" in its activities. In other internal movement within the board, labor members Dec. 17 criticized the 7% ceiling for exceptions on raises as "excessively narrow" while the five business members Dec. 22 announced separately that they would challenge every contract with scheduled pay raises exceeding 7% a year. Boldt later

Dec. 22 ruled out a blanket challenge on such raises and said specific challenges would have to be submitted.

Phase Two directives. Phase Two economic stabilization directives applying to rent, insurance, dividends, federal purchasing and mail rates were issued by various stabilization units and federal officials Dec. 20–28. Among the details:

Rents—The Price Commission reaffirmed Dec. 20 its decision to leave rent control with existing local control agencies but stressed that rent-controlled units were not exempt from the Price Commission regulations and that rent increases were subject to review.

New rent regulations were issued by the commission Dec. 22 indicating that controlled rent increases of 3%–3.5% annually would be permitted. Landlords with units not covered by state or local controls would be permitted to raise base rents 2.5% to cover operating costs plus an additional amount to offset state and local property taxes and fees (not counting city-provided gas and electricity). This additional allowable increase was expected to fall within an overall range of $\frac{1}{2}$–1%, according to Price Commission Chairman C. Jackson Grayson Jr. The increases for taxes and fees were to be applied on a weighted basis with expensive units in a building paying more than the others.

Increases also were allowable for capital improvements. The improvements would be subject to a strict interpretation by the commission, and increases of more than 10% for such a reason would be subject to prior approval by the Internal Revenue Service.

Tenants would have to be given 30 days' notice of rent increases.

In defining base rent, the commission specified that units rented on a week-to-week or month-to-month basis would have a base rent of the amount paid during the 90-day freeze period that began Aug. 15. If rents were increased during this period under previous Phase Two rules, they would be rolled back without refunds. For leases running more than a month, landlords could average increases, decreases and unchanging renewals made during the 30-

day period prior to the freeze for their base rent. If no new leases were signed in that period, the previous 30-day period would be used, and if no new leases were signed during that second 30-day period, base rent would be the rent on May 25, 1970 plus 5%.

Insurance premium rates—A guideline to limit insurance premium rate increases was issued by the Price Commission Dec. 22. It applied to all insurance except life, which had been previously exempted from controls. The guideline would be applied by a formula with factors for the insurers' past losses on the insurance involved, administrative expenses, which would be held to a 2.5% annual increase guideline, and allowance for inflation, which would be held to 62.5% of the current prediction for that premium.

Companies would be required to get approval of increases from state insurance departments, subject to the final authority of the Price Commission.

Blue Cross-Blue Shield decision—In its first application of its insurance guidelines, the commission Dec. 23 reduced a requested rate rise on health and medical coverage for 1.6 million federal workers from 34.1% to 22%. The ruling applied to Blue Cross-Blue Shield, which had requested an increase on rates for federal civilian employes. Its original request of 53% had been cut to 34.1% by the Civil Service Commission.

Dividends—The Committee on Interest and Dividends revised its rules Dec. 21 to exempt from its 4% guideline companies newly turning to public ownership (with 500 or more common stockholders) and companies with fewer than 500 common stockholders. Another revision would permit companies that declared a higher regular dividend in 1971 prior to the freeze period Aug. 15 to count the higher dividend as its base for calculating the additional 4% allowed in 1972.

Federal purchasing—Federal purchasing officials were informed Dec. 28 that "a decisive factor" in placing government contracts for goods and services would be "whether contractors are in compliance with the economic stabilization program in all of their transactions." This directive to agency heads was issued by Caspar W. Weinberger, deputy director of the Office of Management and Budget, as chairman of the Regulations and Purchasing Review Board.

Mail rates—Donald Rumsfeld, executive director of the Cost of Living Council, said Dec. 23 that the Postal Service would be required to certify to the Price Commission that its rate increase proposals were justified by increased productivity and the necessity to maintain adequate services and cover future expansion. They were not expected to reflect any anticipated inflation.

The Postal Service Dec. 23 issued notification of its intention to increase 3rd class mail rates by an average 23.9% Jan. 24, 1972.

Price lists—The Internal Revenue Service informed retailers Dec. 27 that base-price lists would have to be posted "prominently" for the convenience of customers before Jan. 2, 1972. The lists were to be readily accessible. Base prices were those in effect when the 90-day freeze began Aug. 15.

Interest rates—President Nixon Dec. 23 determined that controls were not needed at this time on interest rates. The presidential finding was required, or control would have had to be exercised, under the new stabilization act.

Local government fees—Cost of Living Council Executive Director Rumsfeld announced Dec. 23 that fee increases by state and local governments for services (such as garbage collection) would not require prior approval but would be subject to federal monitoring to hold them within the average 2.5% guideline.

'Uneasiness' under Phase Two? Sen. Hubert H. Humphrey (D, Minn.) warned in a statement inserted in the Congressional Record Dec. 17 that "the same uneasiness that accompanied Phase One is now present in Phase Two":

Industry is still operating at 75 percent plant capacity;

Consumer savings still hovers around 8 percent;

Unemployment is still over 5 million;

The largest balance-of-payments deficit, $48.4 billion on an official reserve transaction basis for the third quarter of 1971;

For the first time in this century we are running a deficit in our balance of trade with other nations;

The Consumer Price Index is still abnormally and unacceptably high;

There has been total loss to GNP of approximately $126 billion in 1970 and 1971;

Minority group unemployment is shockingly high;

Farm parity is lowest in years; and

Thousands of workers exhaust their unemployment compensation benefits every week....

We have been told over and over again that one of the prime purposes of the freeze was to get business moving again. The results, though, speak otherwise. Business is not moving. Even the Secretary of the Treasury has complained about the reluctance of business to invest, to step up production, to hire....

Labor is not certain that contracts will be approved. Business does not know whether pass-through costs will be allowed. Landlords do not know whether they can raise rents. Consumers are in a quandry whether or not to spend. Teachers do not know if they will get increases. Families cannot plan on legitimate wage increases that will allow them to catch up from last year....

Stock market. The New York Stock Exchange concluded its trading year Dec. 31 with the Dow Jones industrial index at 890.20, up 51.28 points for the year. 1971 was a record year for volume turnover—3.89 billion shares—contrasted with 1970's previous record of 2.93 billion.

International Problems

World Unprepared for Phase One

The Nixon anti-inflation policy announced Aug. 15 came as a surprise to the overseas commercial, financial and diplomatic community. There was bewilderment and in some cases anger in the reaction to the U.S. decision to end the dollar's tie to gold and to impose a 10% surtax on imports.

IMF informed of U.S. action. The U.S. formally notified the 118-nation International Monetary Fund (IMF) Aug. 16 that it "no longer freely buys and sells gold for the settlement of international transactions." This meant that the U.S. would no longer honor its agreement to pay out gold for foreign-held dollars at the rate of $35 an ounce. According to the Treasury's Public Affairs Department, U.S. gold reserves stood at $10,132,144,053.74 when payments were suspended Aug. 16.

The Treasury was instructed to limit further use of all reserve assets to settlement of outstanding obligations and, in cooperation with the IMF, "to other situations that may arise in which such use can contribute to international monetary stability and the interests of the U.S."

In another move, the Federal Reserve Board (FRB) was asked by the White House to suspend use of its "swap" network for converting dollars into other foreign currencies. (The FRB July 12 had increased its swap lines in order to temporarily borrow back excess dollars from other countries.) The White House said the two-tier gold pricing system (referring to the March 1968 agreement by major nations to refrain from gold dealings with private parties) should not be affected by the suspension of convertibility.

Foreign exchanges closed. President Nixon's unexpected policy reversal left foreign bankers, politicians and tourists bewildered amid an atmosphere of turmoil and confusion. Most European governments acted quickly Aug. 16 to close their foreign exchange markets with no clear idea of when normal currency dealings would resume. Dollars from U.S. tourists abroad were greeted coldly as some foreign banks, hotels, and shops refused to accept them. In some cases, currency exchange rates were arbitrarily set, making tourists' purchases 10% higher. In unofficial transactions the dollar consistently weakened against strong European currencies, especially the mark and Swiss franc.

The Swiss national bank announced Aug. 17 that foreign exchange markets in Switzerland would probably be closed for the rest of the week, but it would allow currency dealings between large com-

301

mercial banks at floating rates. In limited trading, the dollar sank to a price of 4 Swiss francs, 1.5% below the last supported price Aug. 13.

The free gold exchanges reopened Aug. 17 in London and Zurich, but without panic buying and little change in the price of gold. In Zurich, the ruling price was $43–$43.50 an ounce, compared with $43.12 Aug. 13. The London price was $43.05, compared with the last quoted price of $43 Aug. 12.

Revaluation of Japanese yen—Japan stressed its determination not to revalue the yen by keeping the Tokyo foreign exchange market open. Japan's policy to continue supporting the dollar at the "support" level of 357.37 yen to the dollar forced the Bank of Japan to absorb $1.4 billion in a three-day period Aug. 16–18, pushing its dollar holdings over the $10 billion mark for the first time.

After telling an emergency cabinet meeting Aug. 17 that a decision on possible revaluation of the yen should await developments in Europe, Finance Minister Mikio Mizuta declared: "We will not yield to the mounting international demand for yen revaluation." However, with the 10% surtax dampening the argument that revaluation would keep Japanese exports from becoming more expensive, the Japanese government and industrialists indicated they would prefer revaluation of the yen to the costly burden of the surtax.

The Bank of Japan was forced to absorb $2.7 billion in dollars during the week following the U.S. suspension of convertibility. In order to curb massive dollar purchases, the central bank banned further borrowing of dollars by Japanese banks from foreign banks Aug. 19, but Japan continued to support the official yen-dollar parity.

Reaction abroad to 10% surtax. Announcement of the 10% import surtax brought bitter reaction abroad and caused a severe slump in foreign stock markets.

Concern in Europe—Although U.S. Treasury Undersecretary Paul A. Volcker, sent by the President to Paris and London Aug. 16–17 to explain his trade

and dollar moves, said Europeans "understand and even welcome" the trade package, reports from abroad reflected otherwise. European industrialists expressed concern over a U.S. retreat to protectionism and economic leaders were disturbed because the U.S. failed to consult in advance with its trade partners. According to the Washington Post Aug. 18, high-level sources in Brussels said the Volcker trip conveyed an uncompromising posture by the U.S. and failed to clear up concern over the duration of the surtax or the conditions for lifting the levy.

In Germany, trade organizations and corporations were sharply critical of the U.S. action. Otto Wolff von Amerongen, president of West Germany's Chamber of Commerce, said the 10% surtax was "unbearable" and would "ruin" German trade with the U.S. However, Karl Klasen, president of the Bundesbank (central bank), saw no danger of a trade war between the U.S. and other countries.

The Common Market's European Commission said Aug. 18 the surtax had wiped out all U.S. trade concessions since 1932. The commission said it would send a delegation to Geneva Aug. 24 to ask for a ruling on the surtax from the General Agreement on Tariffs and Trade (GATT). If GATT ruled that the surtax was not necessary, foreign governments would be free to retaliate against U.S. exports. Ralf Dahrendorf, the Market's commissioner for external affairs, said the import measure was not good sportsmanship, but the commission would not seek retaliation endangering the U.S.-Common Market trade account of about $15 billion.

Canada seeks exemption—Finance Minister Edgar J. Benson announced in Ottawa Aug. 18 that Canada would seek exemption from the surtax which, he said, was unfair to Canada. The day before, Acting Prime Minister Mitchell Sharp had announced Canada would send a ministerial delegation to Washington to lodge a "vigorous protest" against the surtax.

Benson said the decision was based on grounds that Canada's dollar, which had been floating for 15 months, had not damaged U.S. imports unfairly and that Canada had not undervalued its dollar in relation to the U.S. dollar.

(About one-fourth of Canada's exports to the U.S.—$3 billion of a total annual sales of $13 billion—could be affected by the surtax.)

After a three-hour emergency cabinet meeting Aug. 17 Sharp said: (1) Canada feared that its dollar would be driven higher by the affect of the surtax on Canadian exports throughout the world; (2) the surtax would chiefly hit and increase unemployment in the second-industry product sector, where Canada's jobless rate of over 6% was concentrated, and (3) the U.S. and Canadian economies were too tightly integrated for the surtax not to also adversely affect the U.S.

Japanese stock market plummets. The Japanese stock market reacted sharply to news of the 10% import surtax with four days of continuously falling prices. The Dow-Jones Tokyo stock average closed Aug. 19 at 2,190.16 yen, a total drop of 20% since prices first began to plummet Aug. 16. The sliding stock prices reflected Japan's position as the U.S.' second largest trading partner. The impact of the surtax could cut Japan's exports to the U.S. by as much as $1.5 billion annually.

Stock prices fell a record 210.50 points Aug. 16. They fell sharply again the morning of Aug. 17, recovered slightly in the afternoon, then closed at 2,440 yen marking a decline of 89.66 points. The D-J average slid another 112.54 points Aug. 18 to close at 2,328.28 yen.

(The Washington Post reported Aug. 13 that, according to diplomatic sources, Secretary of State William P. Rogers had warned Japan several weeks earlier that the U.S. would penalize Japanese imports unless Tokyo removed barriers against U.S. trade at a faster pace. The warning had since been renewed by State Department officials in talks with Japan's ambassador, Nobuhiko Ushiba.)

(The State Department disclosed Aug. 17 that both Japan and Canada had been given brief advance notice of the U.S. dollar and trade measures. About an hour before the President's speech Aug. 15, Rogers telephoned both Japanese Prime Minister Eisaku Sato and Canada's acting prime minister, Mitchell Sharp.)

Canada fails on surtax plea. A Canadian delegation sent to Washington to seek exemption for Canada from the 10% import surtax carried home Aug. 19 only a U.S. promise to "consider" the request. Canadian Finance Minister Edgar J. Benson and Trade Minister Jean-Luc Pepin led a group that met with Treasury Secretary John B. Connally Jr. and Commerce Secretary Maurice Stans.

Just prior to the meeting Aug. 19, Connally had said in a television interview on NBC that he did not think the Canadian position was strong. He said he would remind the delegation of "when they imposed a surcharge in 1962 and we went up there to ask for relief for American products, they said no. . ."

Benson said there had been no discussion of a partial exemption or lower surtax.

In a nationwide broadcast Aug. 20, Prime Minister Pierre Trudeau said that thousands of Canadians might lose jobs as a result of the surtax. However, he rejected any idea of a trade war because "everyone would be a loser in those circumstances."

IMF recognizes dollar float. The International Monetary Fund (IMF) in Washington Aug. 20 broke its official silence on the U.S. monetary measures and recognized the U.S. dollar as a floating currency. It also released a cablegram from the IMF's managing director, Pierre-Paul Schweitzer, warning the 118 member nations that only prompt action to restore an orderly world monetary system could prevent "disorder and discrimination" in world currency and trade relations.

The IMF statement noted that suspension of the gold-dollar link by the U.S. was a violation of its obligations to maintain the dollar at fixed par value in international transactions. It urged the U.S. "to collaborate with the Fund to promote exchange stability, to maintain orderly exchange arrangements with other members, and to avoid competitive exchange-rate alterations."

(Leakage of an IMF staff report forecasting currency realignments, including a 13%–14% upvaluation of the German mark against the dollar, caused European money markets to react nervously and the dollar to continue weakening Aug. 24–25. Schweitzer acknowledged Aug. 24 that the IMF had prepared informal estimates of some possible future currency alignments.)

Israel devalues pound. Finance Minister Pinhas Sapir, with IMF approval, announced Aug. 21 a 20% devaluation of the Israeli pound, from 3.50 to 4.20 pounds to the U.S. dollar. The action followed an emergency cabinet session at which devaluation was approved. Sapir, who said that Israel was acting to prevent President Nixon's economic measures from widening Israel's already huge trade deficit, said devaluation should improve Israel's balance of payments and prevent growth of unemployment.

(In other currency developments outside Europe, Indonesia Aug. 23 devalued its currency, the rupiah, by 10% from 378 to 414 rupiahs per dollar. Greece kept the parity of the drachma, but said it would buy other currencies based on fluctuating quotations for the dollar, in effect devaluing the drachma against rising currencies. South African money markets remained closed Aug. 23; the government said it would maintain the rand in relation to the dollar.)

Common Market divided. The Common Market Council of Ministers, at a 16-hour meeting in Brussels Aug. 19–20, agreed to the reopening of their exchange markets Aug. 23 but not on a joint policy toward the newly freed dollar. Consequently, each member nation was to decide for itself how much the dollar would be allowed to depreciate against its currency.

Fourteen hours of talks failed to resolve the conflict begun between France and West Germany when Bonn decided to float the mark in May. Just prior to the council's meeting, two separate meetings of the European Commission and the Monetary Committee had also ended in an impasse Aug. 18.

The conflict centered on Germany's proposal for joint flotation of the six EEC currencies. Under the plan, the six currencies would fluctuate against each other within narrow margins but would move up or down freely against the dollar. France refused to allow its franc to float or be revalued. After an emergency cabinet meeting Aug. 18, France proposed the system it adopted Aug. 23, a two-tier exchange system with one market for commercial transactions and one for speculation. Germany had traditionally opposed the system, currently operating in Belgium, because government intervention would be required in the free market.

(After a special meeting in Stockholm Aug. 18, Sweden, Norway, Denmark and Finland announced jointly they would seek a common front to deal with the monetary crisis. The meeting comprised the finance ministers and central bank chiefs of the four nations.)

Money markets reopen. European foreign exchange markets reopened Aug. 23 after a week's suspension. The European governments and their central banks took a variety of measures to cope with the newly floating dollar, and on the first day of trading it showed surprising strength against other currencies.

None of the major nations followed President Nixon's proposal Aug. 15 that they raise the fixed value of their currencies against the dollar. Instead, the various methods they adopted included controlled floats, widened bands of fluctuation on either side of the fixed parity, two-tier systems, and in Israel's case, outright devaluation.

Britain, Switzerland, Belgium and Italy allowed their currencies to find their own market parity with the dollar. It was the first time since war was declared on Sept. 3, 1939 that the pound sterling was allowed to float. In trading Aug. 23, the pound recorded a de facto upvaluation of about 2%.

Swiss money markets remained officially closed Aug. 23, but in interbank trading where the Swiss franc was allowed to float unofficially, the dollar was quoted at just below the official lower support level of 4.01 francs to the dollar. A cabinet meeting Aug. 23 failed to reach a decision on policy toward the monetary crisis. (An agreement between the Swiss National Bank and the Swiss Bankers Association, originally set for Aug. 20, to fix bank reserve requirements at 100% on foreign funds in excess of those on deposit July 31 went into effect Aug. 13. Another decree by the central bank banned interest payments on deposits made by nonresidents after July 31, except for those that could not be withdrawn before six months. The measures were intended to halt a new influx of dollars.)

Belgium permitted its franc to float against the dollar in both parts of its two-tier system. In the Brussels commercial market, the dollar closed at 48.75 to 48.90 Belgian francs, a more than 2% upvaluation for the franc. According to an agreement reached by Belgium Aug. 21 with its Benelux partners, Holland and Luxembourg, the three countries formed a provisional monetary bloc within the Common Market to coordinate a common float against the dollar (the Luxembourg and Belgian francs were already united by joint statute of the Belgian-Luxembourg economic union). In Amsterdam, the guilder, which had been floating since May, rose about 3.9% in relation to the dollar, quoted at 3.475 to 3.48 guilders.

In Milan, the Italian lira was permitted to float above the mandatory support level of 620.50 lire to the dollar for a rise in value of just over 1%.

France, with the approval of the IMF Aug. 21, reopened its monetary exchanges with a two-tier system, made up of a financial market in which the franc could fluctuate freely and a commercial market where the franc would be supported within 1% of the official rate, 5.55419 francs to the dollar. The commercial franc closed above the mandatory intervention level at 5.5237; the floating financial franc was 5.46 francs to 5.48 francs to the dollar, representing just over a 2% rise in value to the dollar.

West Germany continued to float its mark. In Frankfurt, the dollar picked up strength and closed at 3.4250 marks to the dollar.

Austria waited until Aug. 24 to reopen its money markets. It supported the official parity of 26 schillings to the dollar, but widened the margins on either side of parity.

Norway's central bank Aug. 23 floated the crown in relation to the dollar. The Bank of Sweden announced Aug. 22 it would not alter the exchange rate of the krona, but would let the dollar decline without imposing a lower limit.

Japan asks dollar devaluation. Japan parried U.S. demands for a revaluation of the yen by reportedly proposing that the U.S. devalue the dollar by a 5% rise in the price of gold. Finance Ministry envoy Yusuke Kashiwagi, according to Kyodo News Service, made the proposal when he met with Paul A. Volcker, Treasury under secretary for monetary affairs, during a trip to Washington Aug. 20–21.

Buoyed by the relative stability of money markets in Europe Aug. 23, a newly formed seven-member Cabinet Council of Economic Ministers held out against revaluation of the yen until after multilateral talks on an international realignment of currencies. The council ruled out bilateral negotiation of the yen's parity with the U.S.

The Japan Chamber of Commerce and Industry Aug. 26 called on the government and the Bank of Japan to revalue the yen moderately as soon as possible.

U.S. rejects devaluation. White House Press Secretary Ronald L. Ziegler Aug. 23 rejected suggestions that the U.S. devalue the dollar by a slight rise in the price of gold. Ziegler said: "It is not our intention to change the price of gold either up or down."

Press reports quoted high Administration officials Aug. 19 as saying a resumption of the dollar's convertibility into gold depended on concrete assurances by other governments that they would take steps to institute higher exchange rates for major currencies, revise "unfair" trade restrictions and take a greater share of the West's defense burdens.

Japan floats yen. Following an emergency meeting at the Finance Ministry Aug. 27, the Japanese government announced it would float the yen within undisclosed parity bands against the U.S. dollar. Finance Minister Mikio Mizuta said Japan would ask the U.S. to remove its 10% import surtax on Japanese products.

The Finance Ministry statement said the present par value of 360 yen to the dollar would be maintained, thus avoiding outright revaluation of the yen. The float was accomplished by a temporary suspension, effective Aug. 28, of International Monetary Fund (IMF) rules setting a 1% fluctuation margin on either side of a currency's parity.

The Ministry acknowledged that it was reversing its past compliance with IMF rules, but observed that it was acting in an international monetary situation that had "become markedly fluid with exchange rate fluctuation of most of the major currencies exceeding" the prescribed margins. The statement noted that the competitive strength of the yen had become so "enhanced" during the past two decades that the IMF margins were "no longer wide enough to ensure the smooth functioning of trade and other external transactions."

Both Mizuta and Tadashi Sasaki, governor of the Bank of Japan, declined to specify the limits of the float. However, Sasaki's statement that the Bank of Japan would intervene in the market to buy dollars if the yen rose too high indicated that the float would be strictly controlled.

The decision was made after a hectic day of trading unloaded $1.25 billion in dollars on the Tokyo foreign exchange, most of which the Bank of Japan was forced to absorb in supportive actions. In the 12-day period since the U.S. monetary and trade actions Aug. 15, the central bank had intervened on the market to absorb nearly $4 billion as the dollar frequently struck the lowest margin permitted under IMF rules—357.37 yen to the dollar.

White House Press Secretary Ronald L. Ziegler, at the Western White House in San Clemente, Calif., described the Japanese float as a "useful step" toward realignment of the exchange rate. A Treasury Department statement also referred to Japan's decision as a "further step" toward a "more realistic" realignment of international exchange rates.

In 2½ hours of Saturday trading Aug. 28, the yen floated as high as 341.30 yen to the dollar, an effective upvaluation of 5.47%.

Currency controls tightened—Japan tightened its currency exchange controls Aug. 31 against a runaway rise in the yen's value. The controls were imposed after the yen floated upward to a quotation of 339 yen to the dollar, representing a 5.8% upvaluation. The measures prohibited advance payments for Japanese exports, sharply restricted "free yen" accounts by non-Japanese residents and insured strict observance of unofficial guidelines set down by the Bank of Japan requiring each foreign exchange bank to have on reserve a certain number of dollars.

■ Japan Aug. 31 conveyed through its embassy in Washington a request for removal of the 10% surtax. The note spelled out Japan's view that its decision to float the yen was sufficient grounds for removal of the surtax.

■ U.S. Assistant Secretary of State Philip Trezise, visiting Tokyo Aug. 31 at the request of Japanese officials, informed foreign and economic ministers that the surtax would remain for some time. Trezise told the Japanese that the U.S. would lift the surtax only after currency revaluations by surplus trade nations were accompanied by looser import curbs and specific proposals, worked out by the nations themselves, to assure a stronger dollar.

■ Nippon Steel President Yoshihiro Inayama, representing the Japanese steel industry, reached a tentative agreement in Washington Aug. 30 with Deputy Undersecretary of State Nathaniel Samuels to extend for three years Japan's voluntary curbs on steel exports to the U.S. The agreement would limit Japanese exports to increases of 2.5% annually.

U.S. Policy Under Attack

GATT criticizes U.S. trade measures. The U.S. withstood a barrage of criticism directed at its 10% import surtax during an emergency meeting in Geneva Aug. 24–26 of the 54-nation council of the General Agreement on Tariffs and Trade (GATT). The meeting, called to determine possible violation by the U.S. of GATT's fair trade rules, established a committee to further study and report on the effects of President Nixon's Aug. 15 protective trade measures.

The chief line of argument revolved around the Common Market's contention that the U.S. balance of payments deficit was not the result of an unfair trade balance and thus would not be cured by the steps taken, and U.S. insistence that the surtax was needed to assure its economic health.

Deputy Undersecretary of State Nathaniel Samuels, leading the U.S. delegation, opened the meeting Aug. 24 with the explanation that since most European nations were operating with a trade surplus, "The time has come for us to have some reasonable surpluses." He said the U.S. had decided on a "temporary" surtax to restore the U.S. balance of trade and payments over the emergency quantitative curbs sanctioned by GATT because of the "need for prompt action and the desire to avoid the administrative complications and the greater restrictiveness of import quotas."

Samuels said repeal of the surtax depended on "collective" action by U.S. trade partners to correct the imbalance that led to its imposition. He refined his position later Aug. 25 by saying the U.S. was seeking a "lasting improvement" in its balance of payments before lifting the surtax.

Common Market Trade Commissioner Ralf Dahrendorf blamed the U.S. balance of payments deficit on direct overseas capital investments and "accidental causes," such as "numerous social conflicts or threatened social conflicts in the ports and in various economic sectors," slower economic expansion on foreign markets, speculative actions tied to monetary uncertainty and the threat of U.S. "protectionist measures involving imports or limits on foreign suppliers." Dahrendorf cited Market statistics showing that U.S. investment in the six member nations had increased from $1.9 billion in 1958 to $10.2 billion in 1969 and an estimated $13 billion in 1970. During 1969 the Six had only invested $3.3 billion directly in the U.S.

Dahrendorf rejected as completely unacceptable U.S. refusal to devalue the dollar in terms of gold and use of the surtax as a lever to pressure its trade partners to revalue their currencies instead.

Dahrendorf protested that the surtax, which affected 88% of the Market's exports to the U.S., was "totally incompatible" with GATT rules and called for its early removal. At France's insistence, the Common Market reserved the right to invoke Articles 23 of GATT to seek redress for damages to its trade from U.S. action.

Dahrendorf's arguments were fortified by the British and Japanese delegations. Sir Max Brown, the British delegate, warned Aug. 24 that the surtax might block the general currency realignment the U.S. sought. Mexico Aug. 24 accused the U.S. of violating the Punta-del-Este accords of 1961, which, Mexico claimed, should have exempted Latin American nations from the U.S. surtax.

The U.S. was again bitterly denounced Aug. 25 by 15 speakers representing developing countries who argued that the surtax would prevent them from diversifying their economies.

The White House Aug. 25 reiterated that the surtax was justifiable and "totally consistent" with GATT rules. White House Press Secretary Ronald L. Ziegler commented: "The existing set of circumstances would suggest that it's not to the benefit of anyone for other nations to retaliate."

(The Commerce Department reported Aug. 26 that the total trade deficit for the first seven months of 1971 was $674.4 million, a sharp contrast with the almost $2 billion surplus for the same period in 1970.

Import surtax exemptions. The U.S. Treasury reversed itself Sept. 1 and exempted from the new 10% import surtax about $1.5 billion to $2 billion worth of merchandise in transit to the U.S. or on the docks by Aug. 16, the effective date of the surcharge. The exemption was expected to relieve importers of up to $200 million in additional duties.

The exemption extended to goods enroute to the U.S., tied up by the West Coast dock strike, and in bonded warehouses or foreign free trade zones in the U.S. (A bonded warehouse was under bond to the government for payment of duties and taxes on stored goods. A free trade zone was one in which merchandise might be stored and processed free of tariffs.) The Treasury's new order required withdrawal of imported goods from bonded warehouses by Oct. 1 as a condition of the exemption.

Less than a week earlier, the Treasury had specified that merchandise on the way to the U.S. or halted by the dock strike would be subject to the surcharge.

The Treasury's announcement Sept. 1 justified the exemption on the basis of claims by many small importers that they faced bankruptcy without it.

Latins criticize U.S. economic policy. An emergency meeting of the Special Commission for Latin American Coordination (CECLA) was convened in Buenos Aires Sept. 3-5 at the request of Argentine President Alejandro Lanusse. Lanusse had proposed the meeting Aug. 21, urging other Latin nations to adopt a common front to combat recent U.S. economic policies that "gravely affect" the economies of Latin American nations.

The session, attended by representatives of 20 Latin American and Caribbean nations, ended Sept. 5 with the adoption of a document, the "Manifesto of Latin America," that asked for exemption from the new U.S. 10% surcharge on imports and outlined the position of Latin America in the face of U.S. economy measures. The document also dealt specifically with the "unilateral" American measures of the suspension of convertibility of the dollar into gold and reduction of financial aid to developing countries.

In the manifesto, the Latin nations declared "unjust" the "consequences" of corrective measures of the U.S. balance of payments deficit, since they were not responsible for the causes" of the deficit. They criticized the U.S. policy as a "serious threat to the growth of world trade and its effects, in particular, for the developing nations in which the increase of exports is an important element of their development' strategy."

The document pointed out that Latin America should be exempted from the surcharge payment since "the balance of payments of the Latin nations with the U.S. has traditionally been favorable to that country." (It was reported Sept. 3 that the U.S. surplus in its trade with Latin America exceeded $350 million in the first half of 1971.) The delegates also argued that the 10% surcharge "constitutes a violation of the promises in force that the U.S. has assumed in forums and that are found in such international documents as GATT, UNCTAD..."

Group of Ten meeting. Deputy finance ministers of the Group of Ten industrial nations ended two days of consultations in Paris Sept. 4 on the trade and currency measures introduced by the U.S. Aug. 15. The meeting was called for an exchange of views among its members—the U.S., Britain, France, Belgium, the Netherlands, Italy, Canada, Japan, West Germany and Sweden.

No concrete measures were presented at the meeting, either by the U.S. or its trade partners. Paul Volcker, Treasury undersecretary for monetary affairs, said the U.S. did not have a plan for solving the monetary crisis at present favored "consultation, not negotiation." He said: "Any solution will necessarily have to be a multilateral solution, but how any particular groupings of countries come to agreement among themselves is up to them, not us."

Rinaldo Ossola, vice governor of the Bank of Italy and moderator of the meeting, had opened the session Sept. 3 with an expression of understanding of the U.S. position. He described the U.S. balance of payments situation as one of "fundamental disequilibrium"—the term used in Article 4 of the Bretton Woods agreement of 1944 to describe a balance of payments condition under which a signatory might alter its currency's parity. Ossola said currency exchange rates needed realignment "in order to remedy the deterioration of the relative competitiveness of American products." However, he warned the U.S. that its 10% import surtax was an obstacle to currency realignments.

Ossola also implied that the U.S. was not solely responsible for its unfavorable trade predicament. He said: "When there is a payments deficit somewhere, at least two nations are involved."

A report presented to the meeting indicated that since the new U.S. economic program was announced Aug. 15, the dollar had undergone a 6% devaluation. The West German mark and Canadian dollar were said to have been upvalued by about 8% against the dollar; the Dutch guilder by 5%; the British pound, Italian lira and Belgian franc by 3%; and the controlled French franc used in commercial transactions by 1%.

At a news conference following the meeting, Volcker rejected suggestions of a devaluation of the dollar by an increase in the price of gold in exchange for revaluations of other currencies. (On the free market, gold bullion was quoted Sept. 6 at about $41 an ounce.) Volcker was firm on U.S. intentions to maintain the official $35-an-ounce gold price.

Italian Treasury Minister Mario Ferrari-Aggradi had proposed an outright devaluation of the dollar in terms of gold at the meeting Sept. 3. Otmar Emminger, vice governor of the West German Bundesbank (central bank), had suggested Sept. 1 raising the price of gold by 5%–6%; Edward M. Bernstein, a former IMF research director currently a private consultant in the U.S., had testified before the Congressional Joint Economic Committee Sept. 1 that the U.S. should seek the desired 12%–15% depreciation of the dollar by a direct 7%–8% devaluation in terms of gold.

Soviet ruble devalued. The U.S.S.R. State Bank disclosed Sept. 1 a devaluation of the ruble against 15 floating currencies that had drifted to higher rates. The adjustment, made known in the bank's monthly announcement of exchange rates for the ruble, averaged about 1% and reportedly was the most extensive devaluation for the ruble in 10 years. Since the ruble was not a convertible currency, the new rates mainly affected tourists and foreigners resident in the Soviet Union. The official exchange rate of one ruble to $1.11 U.S. was maintained.

Europe tightens money curbs. Among recent actions taken by European gov-

ernments to cope with speculative inflows of dollars:

■ Following a record $1.56 billion capital inflow in August, Britain Sept. 2 lowered its bank rate—the interest rate at which the Bank of England lends to financial institutions—from 6% to 5% to discourage further transfers. Britain's gold and foreign exchange reserves rose in August by $937 million to $4.8 billion.

Britain had also imposed controls Aug. 27, effective Aug. 31, prohibiting interest payments on new pound holdings by nonresidents.

■ The Netherlands introduced a series of currency controls Sept. 6 in order to curb speculative capital inflows into the country. The curbs were directed at foreigners, who were channeling money into Dutch bonds and debentures. Nonresidents were required to buy bonds with what were designated as "O" guilders obtained from a revolving pool of "O" guilders fed by the sales of the bonds. If foreign demand became heavy, the "O" guilders could only be obtained at a premium, making them progressively more expensive for speculators.

Common Market urges devalued dollar. The six European Common Market countries reached agreement Sept. 13 on a joint trade and monetary policy intended in part to win formal devaluation of the U.S. dollar and revocation of the 10% U.S. surtax on imports.

It was the first time the six—France, Italy, West Germany and the Benelux countries—had been able to agree on a unified response to the new Nixon policy.

The agreement was reached by the six countries' finance ministers at a Brussels meeting called to set Common Market policy for forthcoming meetings of the Group of Ten industrial nations and of the World Bank and International Monetary Fund (IMF). The joint statement, based on a draft proposal made public in Brussels Sept. 10 by the Common Market's Executive Commission, indicated that the European community countries would not passively accept the burdens offered them by the new U.S. economic policy.

The joint statement accepted the U.S. contention that it was time to restructure the world monetary system to take account of changed conditions. It proposed the following as basic preconditions:

■ Official devaluation of the dollar by raising the price of gold for intergovernmental transactions above the $35 an ounce in effect since 1934.

■ A gradual end to reliance on "national currencies [the dollar]" as reserve units in world trade and monetary relations.

■ Retention of gold as the principal common denominator of international monetary relations, with increased emphasis on the "paper gold" Special Drawing Rights issued by the IMF or other international instruments of a similar nature.

■ Realignment of the world's major currencies, "including the dollar," to restore equilibrium to the system of international payments.

■ Restoration of fixed parities among the major currencies, with greater flexibility in exchange rates to inhibit future speculation.

■ Revocation of the 10% U.S. surcharge on imported goods as part of the agreement to reform the international monetary system.

U.S.-Japan talks fail. Two days of talks led by U.S. Secretary of State William P. Rogers and Japanese Foreign Minister Takeo Fukuda failed to produce acceptance by either side of the other's trade and monetary demands. The U.S. was pressing Japan for an immediate and substantial revaluation of the yen against the dollar. Japan wanted revocation of the 10% surtax imposed by the U.S. on dutiable imports.

The meeting, the regular annual consultation of the U.S. and Japanese Cabinets, was held in Washington Sept. 9–10. Participants included Treasury Secretary John B. Connally Jr., Finance Minister Mikio Mizuta, Commerce Secretary Maurice H. Stans, Trade Minister Kakuei Tanaka, and the members of both Cabinets responsible for agriculture, labor, transportation and economic planning.

Although the question of revaluation of the yen was not formally on the agenda, it was the central point of Rogers' address to the opening session, a draft of which was transmitted to the Japanese government and was leaked to the Japanese press Sept. 6–7. Fukuda raised the fundamental Japanese demand at a news conference on his arrival in Washington Sept. 8. He warned that "frictions" over trade could harm the postwar U.S.-Japanese relationship and that lengthy retention of the 10% import surtax "may well bring about retaliatory measures" from other nations.

The disagreements were made clear at press briefings following the first day of talks Sept. 9.

The State Department said Rogers had told the Japanese that the U.S. needed "a major realignment of the dollar against other currencies, including the yen, in order to establish a realistic exchange-rate structure." Rogers said "projections for the year ahead are for Japanese trade and current account surpluses of massive proportions that are clearly incompatible with the position of Japan's trading partners." Rogers further demanded "elimination of remaining Japanese import restrictions, especially on items of trade interest to the United States," and "a substantial, indeed dramatic increase in Japanese official development assistance to developing countries."

Fukuda's statement did not allude directly to revaluation of the yen. It said that Japan would join in consultations on exchange rates but that "the success of such consultations depends on the essential condition that all countries concerned should share the burden." Fukuda rejected Rogers' basic contention, saying "I do not think that our current balance of payments is in basic disequilibrium." Fukuda blamed the existing surplus on a slowing of the Japanese domestic economy and ineffective sales efforts by U.S. exporters. He asserted that in many cases "they are not doing enough to explore business opportunities" in Japan.

(State Department officials released figures Sept. 9 showing that the U.S. trade deficit with Japan was currently running at an annual rate of $2.8 billion, up about $1 billion from a year earlier.)

The final communiqué issued when the talks ended Sept. 10 made it clear that the two sides differed on the reasons for the current trade crisis and had not agreed on any measures to deal with it. The Japanese were said to have offered to ease quota restrictions on imports of U.S. computers, light planes, petroleum and some foodstuffs, but the U.S. delegation reportedly rejected the concessions as insufficient.

At a Washington press conference Sept. 10, Fukuda commented that the two sides occasionally had used "loud voices" to make known their views. He said one of the loudest was that of Treasury Secretary Connally.

Finance Minister Mizuta told newsmen Sept. 10 that no bilateral agreement was possible on revaluation of the yen. He said that Japan could help the U.S. in many ways but "upward revaluation . . . is not one of them."

Japan-Canada 'alliance.' Following his talks in Washington, Fukuda flew to Ottawa for two days of meetings Sept. 13–14 with External Affairs Minister Mitchell W. Sharp. The talks, attended by the other members of the two Cabinets, centered on the two countries' shared problem as the two main exporters to the U.S. They supplied 42% of the total U.S. imports.

Meeting with newsmen Sept. 14, Fukuda declared that Japan was "ready to assume a leadership role to defend and protect free trade and to fight against protectionism." He proposed that Japan and Canada form an "alliance" to fight the U.S. import surtax and to seek a new round of trade liberalization talks.

Sharp confirmed that Canada would work with Japan in "pressing hard" for such talks. Sharp added that Canada was opposed to a formal devaluation of the U.S. dollar and considered the current parity of the U.S. and Canadian dollars ($1 Canadian = $.98½ U.S.) to be "realistic."

Japanese surplus, yen rates. The Finance Ministry announced in Tokyo Sept. 14 that Japan's preliminary payments balance for August had shown a surplus of $3.3 billion, up strikingly from the $495 million surplus in July and the record $1.183 billion in May, when the West German mark was floated and Japan experienced heavy inflows of dollars. The Ministry attributed the huge surplus, more than the $2 billion recorded for all of 1970, to prepayments by foreign importers. However, the August trade surplus was at a record level, $850 million. Receipts from exports totaled $2.04 billion and payments for imports totaled $1.19 billion.

Japan's foreign reserves were said to amount to $12.514 billion at the end of August, making them, after West Germany's, the second largest in the world.

The dollar fell on the Tokyo market Sept. 14, reaching a low of 337.75 yen. This was 6.2% below the dollar's old official value of 360 yen.

$9 billion U.S. deficit seen. In testimony Sept. 13 before the Senate Finance Committee's Subcommittee on International Trade, Treasury Undersecretary Paul A. Volcker disclosed that the basic U.S. balance of payments deficit had reached an annual rate of $9 billion during the first half of 1971. This would be three times the $3 billion deficit recorded for 1970, according to the New York Times. The basic balance ignored distortions introduced by short-term capital flows.

The Times said Volcker had informed the Group of Ten that the deficit might be running at an annual rate of $11 billion and the U.S. hoped to reverse this and attain a $2 billion surplus with its new policies. The Europeans were reported to fear the dislocation that would follow a payments shift as large as $13 billion in one year.

(Testifying before the Senate subcommittee Sept. 14, Robert V. Roosa, former Treasury undersecretary for monetary affairs, opposed a formal devaluation of the dollar against gold. He said there was no need "to glue back together some pieces of the broken idol through a hastily contrived 'return to gold' at some slight change in its dollar monetary price." What was truly necessary, Roosa said, was to depreciate the dollar against "a handful" of leading currencies.)

U.S. confronts Group of 10. A full ministerial meeting of the Group of 10 in London Sept. 15–16 provided the backdrop for the first top-level confrontation of the U.S. and its trade partners since President Nixon introduced his controversial trade and currency measures Aug. 15. The meeting ended in a deadlock after the participants—the U.S., Britain, the six Common Market countries, Canada and Japan—stated their positions but failed to compromise their differences.

A brief communiqué Sept. 16 said the only agreement reached was that "a substantial adjustment is required . . . of the present payments imbalance in the world . . . and that measures to bring about this adjustment should be taken on a wide front and should include an appropriate realignment of currencies." Deputy finance ministers of the Group were instructed to prepare an agenda for its next meeting, in Washington Sept. 26.

The differences that emerged at the meeting were hardened by the U.S. delegation's insistence on the other nations' acceptance of the entire U.S. package for curing its payments imbalance. The package, as presented by Treasury Secretary John B. Connally Jr. Sept. 15, called for an upward revaluation of certain foreign currencies to spur U.S. exports, removal of "unfair" trade barriers and more sharing among allies of America's worldwide defense burdens.

Connally specifically challenged other countries to help the U.S. achieve a $13 billion turnaround in its balance of payments deficit by attainment of a $7 billion–$8 billion annual trade surplus. Connally commented after the meeting Sept. 15: "We had a problem and we're sharing it with the world, just like we shared our prosperity. That's what friends are for." Connally said that the $13 billion figure was not inflated for bargaining, but was a "conservative" figure that did not cover short-term money movements or net increases in long-term capital flows. Federal Reserve Board Chairman Arthur F. Burns, who also attended the meeting, said the U.S. objective was to achieve "equilibrium in our balance of payments with a certain margin of safety."

(The Commerce Department reported Sept. 16 that the U.S. "basic" payments deficit [covering all transactions with foreign nations with the exception of short-term capital movements] rose to a record annual rate of more than $12 billion in the second quarter of 1971.)

The $13 billion figure drew objections from Italian Finance Minister Mario Ferrari-Aggradi, chairman of the Common Market Finance Ministers group, who rejected the projection as "too ambitious" and dangerous to world economies if achieved too quickly. Ferrari-Aggradi said the U.S.' immediate goal should be a moderate deficit with a mid-term objective of a zero balance rather than a surplus. Indirectly referring to U.S. rejection of outright devaluation of the dollar by increasing the price of gold, Ferrari-Aggradi declared that "deficit" countries ought to participate in any currency realignment.

Japanese Finance Minister Mizio Mizuta reportedly told the meeting Sept. 15 that the Japanese economy could not withstand a substantial revaluation of the yen.

The atmosphere at the meeting reportedly became strained Sept. 16 when Connally refused to commit the U.S. to a three-step program proposed by Pierre-Paul Schweitzer, managing director of the International Monetary Fund, with modifications by Anthony Barber, Britain's chancellor of the exchequer.

The program, reportedly favored by a majority of the delegates, proposed as a first step negotiations on changes in currency parities, a return to fixed parities with wider, more flexible bands, a rise in the price of gold (thereby directly devaluing the dollar), and removal of the U.S. 10% import surtax. A second round of talks would discuss ways of assisting the U.S. in correcting its balance of payments deficit, restoring the dollar-gold link and capital controls to prevent inflationary movements of speculative money. The third round of discussions would center on fundamental reform of the world monetary system and the development of new monetary instruments.

Persistent demands for a U.S. commitment on the gold-price issue and a timetable for removal of the 10% surtax reportedly evoked an irritated response from Connally that "I am authorized to say only I will not change our position one iota." He insisted that the U.S. had no intention of devaluing the dollar by raising the price of gold. Connally was also said to have been angered by what he called undue concern over the surtax. In an apparent reference to Japan and West Germany, Connally said there were members of the Group who could absorb losses from the surtax and still maintain a trade surplus.

At a final press conference Sept. 16, Canadian Finance Minister Edgar J. Benson, chairman of the meeting, said he did not regard the meeting as a failure because no one had expected a solution to emerge. French Finance Minister Valery Giscard d'Estaing declared that the meeting had ended "without any narrowing of the different viewpoints." He depicted Connally's tough presentation at the meeting as a display of U.S. intransigence. He said Connally had "answered all the questions negatively."

$13 billion U.S. goal clarified. Projected trade figures for 1972, released by the Nixon Administration Sept. 17, showed that the $13 billion figure cited by Treasury Secretary Connally at the Group of 10 meeting in London Sept. 15 was calculated by adding a projected $11 billion payment deficit and a $2 billion safety margin sought by the Administration.

The $11 billion deficit forecast was reached by combining a projected $5 billion trade deficit, or a $4 billion deficit on current account (goods, financial services and remittances), with an assumed $6 billion in net long-term capital outflows (comprising $4 billion in government disbursements and $1 billion–$2 billion in private capital). The forecast implied that the U.S. must seek an $8 billion trade surplus, or $9 billion on current account, in order to offset the $6 billion long-term capital outflow with an added $2 billion margin of safety.

5th straight trade deficit. The U.S. suffered its fifth consecutive monthly trade deficit in August. According to figures released by the Commerce Department Sept. 27, merchandise imports exceeded exports by a seasonally adjusted $259.7 million.

That deficit was slightly less than in July, when the deficit totaled $304 million. But the total deficit for the first eight months of 1971 stood at $936.1 million, in contrast to a $2.2 billion surplus

at the same time in 1970. The August deficit represented the fifth consecutive month in which the U.S. balance of trade ran in the red.

Officials said the temporary 10% tax surcharge, which President Nixon hoped would restore a more favorable balance of trade, had not had any significant effect on the August import-export figures.

September trade surplus. The U.S. balance of trade reversed itself in September, after five months of deficits, and recorded a seasonally adjusted $265.4 million surplus, the Commerce Department reported Oct. 28. The turnaround was the result of a 22.6% one-month increase in exports to $4.51 billion. Imports rose 7.8% to $4.25 billion.

Assistant Commerce Secretary Harold C. Passer said the effect of actual and threatened dock strikes had inflated the figures and made them unreliable as a "clear basis for appraising trends." Furthermore, import figures were recorded according to merchandise value at the foreign port of export, giving the U.S. a more favorable showing than if they had been recorded according to their landed cost. Passer concluded that the impact of the Aug. 15 economic measures was not yet apparent.

The U.S. trade deficit for the first nine months of 1971 was a seasonally adjusted $670 million, compared with a $2.4 billion surplus in the same period of 1970.

3rd quarter payments deficit soars. The Commerce Department, on the basis of preliminary figures, reported Nov. 15 the largest balance of payments deficit in U.S. history in the third quarter—a staggering $12.1 billion after seasonal adjustment. The resulting $23.4 billion payments deficit for the January-September period topped any annual deficit, including the $9.8 billion in 1970, and was the equivalent of a $31 billion annual rate for 1971 as a whole.

The $12.1 billion deficit, measured on the "official settlements" basis, occurred mainly in July and early August, and, according to Assistant Commerce Secretary Harold C. Passer, was one of the chief reasons for the Administration's

10% import surtax and halting gold sales to other governments.

The broader "net liquidity deficit" measure also deepened in the third quarter to a record $9.3 billion, seasonally adjusted, from $5.72 billion in the second quarter. Officials ascribed the increase to currency speculation before the Aug. 15 economic measures, and "leads and lags" in commercial and financial payments and receipts that occur when a company, anticipating that the dollar would decline in value and another currency rise, speeded up dollar payments to a foreigner for imports. The liquidity deficit was restrained from growing even deeper by a $420 million rise in net foreign purchases of securities and a $125 million decrease in U.S. net purchases of foreign securities.

U.S. foreign exchange reserves. The Treasury said Oct. 28 that U.S. foreign exchange reserves had edged up to about $12.1 billion in September. The U.S. gold stock remained essentially constant at $10.2 billion and foreign convertible currency reserves stood at $250 million. The Treasury also reported that Switzerland had helped the U.S. finance its international balance of payments deficit in September through the net purchase of $270 million worth of special Treasury securities.

Nixon on trade measures. Addressing a Washington news conference Sept. 16, President Nixon touched on the impact abroad of his new economic policy. The President said one question being asked of the U.S. was how long the "temporary" surcharge would be kept on imports. His answer was "that if all we were seeking was a temporary solution, 'temporary' would be very brief, but we are not seeking a temporary solution. . . . What we are seeking is a permanent solution, and that is why the length of the temporary surcharge will be somewhat longer, because we need to address ourselves not only to the matter of monetary policy and exchange rates, we have to address ourselves to burden-sharing and we have to address ourselves also to trade restraints, including nontariff barriers."

"This is a time for our friends around the world—and they are all competitors —to build a new system with which we

U.S. Gold Holdings, Total Monetary Reserve Assets & Liquid Liabilities to Foreigners			
[In billions of dollars]			
	Gold holdings	Total assets	Liquid liabilities
End of World War II	20.1	20.1	6.9
1957	22.8	24.8	15.8
1970	10.7	14.5	43.3
August 1971	10.1	12.1	[1] 46.0

[1] Estimated figure.

Source: U.S. Treasury Department.

can live so that we don't have another crisis in a year."

As for Japan, Nixon said that the U.S. and Japan "inevitably are going to be competitors because we are both strong economies. . . . What we are trying to do is work out a new system that will recognize the realities so that we can reduce these tensions that have developed, the number of crises that have come up over and over again in the international field."

GATT opposes U.S. surtax. The 55-member Council of the General Agreement on Tariffs and Trade (GATT), meeting in Geneva Sept. 16, adopted a report demanding that the U.S. rescind its 10% surcharge on imports "within a short time." The report, approved by a working party of 24 nations Sept. 11, declared that the surtax, "to the extent that it raised the incidence of customs charges beyond the maximum rates bound under Article Two [of the agreement], was not compatible" with GATT rules.

The report said that the surtax, if not removed quickly, would have "far-reaching effects on world trade and trade liberalization." The report warned that GATT's position was not negotiable and that members affected by the surtax were entitled to take retaliatory measures.

The U.S. delegate, Herbert F. Propps, joined in the unanimous decision to issue the report but made it clear that his concurrence did not signify a change in the U.S. position. The U.S. held that its balance of payments deficit made a "temporary surcharge appropriate and compatible with its GATT obligations."

Propps argued that the surtax was less harmful than quantitative curbs he said were permissible in view of a secret International Monetary Fund (IMF) report confirming the seriousness of\ the currency crisis. The IMF report, contained in an unpublished portion of the GATT statement, asserted that the proper remedy for the crisis was a readjustment of currency parities.

The GATT report said that the unfavorable U.S. balance of payments was only "temporary and accidental" and the surtax was an "inappropriate" cure.

Among the items in the report that were not published but were leaked to the press: a protest by the developing nations that the surtax contravened a recent endorsement by GATT and the U.S. of preferential tariffs on exports from their countries, condemnation, by the 24-nation working group, of two other provisions of the Nixon economic program —the disqualification of foreign-manufactured equipment from proposed tax credits for equipment improvements and the tax incentives for exports under the Domestic International Sales Corporations (Disc) proposal.

(Canada's external affairs minister, Mitchell Sharp, said Sept. 21 that the Disc plan and the job-development tax credit "pose an even greater threat to Canada as an industrial and trading nation" than the 10% surtax. Addressing the Center for Inter-American Relations in Washington, Sharp added, "These proposed permanent protectionist measures call into doubt the basic assumption of our trading relations with the United States and indeed of world trading arrangements generally.")

Also withheld from publication were annexes to the working group's report that included a U.S. paper reportedly showing that GATT had not retaliated against 10 members who had imposed import surtaxes in the past—Great Britain (a 15% surtax in 1964), Canada (a 5% surcharge, later increased to 10% in 1962), and France, Ceylon, Chile, India, Israel, Peru, Uruguay and Yugoslavia.

Monetary & Trade Revision Planned

IMF/Bank meeting on reforms. The governors of the 116-nation World Bank Group and the 118-country International Monetary Fund met in Washington Sept. 27-Oct. 1 for their 26th joint annual conference. The meeting, attended by most of the world's finance ministers and central bank chiefs, centered on the need to restructure the world monetary system and to deal with the dislocations stemming from the new U.S. economic policy.

Despite an early atmosphere of divisiveness, the IMF governors reached agreement Oct. 1 on broad outlines of the measures needed to reform the monetary system and deal with the differences between the U.S. and its trade partners.

Declaring that "the present international monetary situation contains the dangers of instability and disorder in currency and trade relationships but also offers the opportunity for constructive changes in the international monetary system," the board voted a resolution calling on member governments to:

"Establish a satisfactory structure of exchange rates, maintained within appropriate margins, for the currencies of members, together with the reduction of restrictive trade and exchange practices, and

"Facilitate resumption of the orderly conduct of the operations of the fund."

Collaborate in efforts to bring about "A reversal of the tendency in present circumstances to maintain and extend restrictive trade and exchange practices, and

"Satisfactory arrangements for the settlement of international transactions which will contribute to the solution of the problems involved in the present international monetary situation."

IMF Managing Director Pierre-Paul Schweitzer, announcing the resolution, hailed it and the "constructive atmosphere" of the meeting. He cited a general belief that the U.S. import surtax would be removed as quickly as possible.

U.S. Treasury Secretary John B. Connally Jr. and Karl Schiller, West Germany's economics and finance minister, who served as chairman of the meeting, opened the session Sept. 27 with addresses stressing the meeting's "historic" opportunity to begin a lasting reform of the world monetary system. Connally called on the governors to build a new financial system for "the next quarter century." At the same time he declared that the U.S. "must insist" that decisions at the meeting be "fair" to the U.S. Schiller said the first priority of the meeting was "avoiding international conflict in trade and payments and an escalation of restrictive and protectionist policies."

The meeting's first day was taken up with speeches by Robert S. McNamara, president of the World Bank Group (the International Bank for Reconstruction and Development, International Development Association and International Finance Corporation), and IMF Managing Director Schweitzer.

McNamara said that the World Bank was not directly involved in currency problems but was nonetheless deeply concerned because of their impact on the developing nations. He noted that the currency problems of industrial nations often reduced foreign aid (current aid targets envisaged a rate of increase from $8 billion yearly in 1970 to $12.5 billion annually in 1975) and disrupted trade and capital flows upon which the poorer countries' economic growth was "critically dependent."

Schweitzer urged an early return to "rules of law providing for orderly and just international economic relations." He said the monetary uncertainty created by floating currencies and protective measures was damaging international trade and investment planning, and especially the domestic economies of smaller countries.

Schweitzer appealed to the finance ministers and central bank governors assembled at the meeting to make "every effort to cooperate" with the U.S. in curing its balance of payments deficit. Schweitzer insisted that the U.S. 10% import surtax end with the creation of new parities for major currencies.

(Federal Reserve Board Chairman Arthur F. Burns testified before the House Banking Committee Sept. 27 that the U.S. could not abandon the surtax "until we get a reasonable realignment of exchange rates and our trade agreements with other countries change so that American products are not at their present disadvantage in the world.")

Italy's Treasury Minister Mario Ferrari-Aggradi Sept. 28 joined Schweitzer in urging that the U.S. end the surtax "simultaneously with the realignment of parities." He warned that the U.S. faced an "escalation of retaliatory measures."

President Nixon, at a White House reception honoring the IMF governors Sept. 29, defended the surtax. He said, "If the U.S. is to play a world role and not turn inward, it must be strong economically and not be weak." "A weak U.S.," he said, "will be isolationist without question, while a strong U.S. will continue to play a responsible role in the world." Nixon explained further that "permanent" reform of the monetary system would take time, which might mean the surtax would remain in effect for some time.

Earlier in the day, Nixon met with Schweitzer for a briefing on the world monetary situation before he met with the governors. With Connally and Burns sitting in on the meeting, the White House said Nixon had told Schweitzer he was encouraged that IMF members understood the U.S. balance of payments problem. Nixon also reportedly told Schweitzer, who had taken a tough position on direct dollar devaluation, that the U.S. would not change its position on the matter.

The highlight of the conference was Connally's conditional offer Sept. 30 to remove the surtax if other nations (1) made "tangible progress toward dismantling specific barriers to trade" (he did not specify the nations or items involved) and (2) allowed "market realities freely to determine exchange rates for their currencies for a transitional period."

Connally presented his offer as a "more timely and constructive" way to remove the surtax than as part of lengthy and arduous negotiations over specific new currency exchange rates. A government official later said the proposal was submitted as an "alternative" to, but not necessarily a substitute for, direct negotiations. The proposal was warmly applauded at the meeting as the first U.S. step toward breaking the international economic stalemate.

Connally proposed a "clean float" be authorized to permit currency rates to fluctuate in response to market forces uncurbed by intervention or restrictive measures by national governments and central banks. Connally's argument for a truly free float echoed complaints voiced by Schweitzer Sept. 27 that most countries were not freely floating their currencies, but were influencing them by market operations and by "expedients and restrictions that are growing daily" and "may become progressively harder to dismantle."

Although Connally's speech implied flexibility on issues of immediate negotiation and did not repeat the demand that removal of the surtax be tied to defense burden-sharing, it expressed determination to secure a binding solution to the inequities of the U.S. position abroad. He said, "We are committed to ending the persistent deficit in our external payments. Indeed, at this point in time, the only question can be the means to that end, not to the end itself." He insisted that the U.S. would not engage in a trade war—"We don't want it, nobody wants it." Connally called for adequate exchange rate flexibility and wider parity margins to help maintain reasonable payments balances.

Concerning longer-term reform, Connally implied that the U.S. was willing to accept a less central role for the U.S. dollar in place of a "different and more symmetrical balance of opportunities and responsibilities" between the U.S. and other leading economies.

Connally did not rule out a small change in the official gold price as part of a currency realignment bargain. Connally sought to play down the "contentious" gold price issue as economically insignificant and retrogressive "in terms of our objective to reduce, if not eliminate, the role of gold in any new monetary system." He said, "We differ from the French. We don't want to protect the role of gold. Gold makes great jewelry."

French Finance Minister Valery Giscard d'Estaing was one of several delegates who called for a devaluation of the dollar as part of a general currency realignment. The argument used by Giscard d'Estaing and Ferrari-Aggradi Sept. 28, Schiller Sept. 27, and Schweitzer Sept. 25 and 27, was that all currencies without exception should participate in the general realignment. Schweitzer, providing a new rationale for a gold price change Sept. 27, said an increase in the price of gold was necessary to maintain the value of the IMF's Special Drawing Rights (SDRs or paper gold) which were fixed in terms of gold and thus were rising and falling in value as the dollar fluctuated against other currencies.

France, Italy, Canada, Japan, India, Belgium, Holland and Australia, led by Schiller and Schweitzer Sept. 27, supported proposals for replacing the dollar with Special Drawing Rights as the major reserve unit. Although most of the world's speakers only endorsed the concept, British Chancellor of the Exchequer Anthony Barber presented a detailed plan to implement it Sept. 28.

The core of the Barber plan was to phase out national currencies, including the dollar and British pound, as reserve currencies in order to create a system not dominated by a national currency. The three central points of the plan were: (1) use of SDRs as the pivotal measure of the monetary system and its main reserve unit, (2) controls for adequate but not excessive world liquidity without reliance on the deficit position of one or more countries and (3) expanded use of national currencies for trading and market intervention.

OECD, Group of ten meetings. The world's leading central bankers and finance ministers met in Paris under a shroud of secrecy for a meeting of the Working Party Three of the Organization for Economic Cooperation and Development (OECD) Oct. 18–19. They switched hats to become deputy ministers of the Group of Ten industrial nations Oct. 19–20. The meetings were intended to work out an acceptable method of counteracting the massive U.S. balance of payments deficit and lay the groundwork for a full-scale ministerial meeting of the Group of 10 in November. The working party focused on the $13 billion turnabout the U.S. said it needed to improve its balance of payments, followed by a Group of Ten consultation on the agreed contributions the U.S.'s trading partners would make to implement the turnaround in terms of parity changes.

At the conclusion of the OECD meeting Oct. 19, Otmar Emminger, chairman of the Working Party Three and vice chairman of the West German Bundesbank (central bank), said no agreement had been reached on an appropriate adjustment of the U.S. balance of payments deficit, although he disclosed that some member nations were willing to accept an $8 billion–$9 billion turnaround.

An OECD staff paper presented to the Working Party Three Oct. 18 predicted that the U.S. gross national product (GNP) would rise 6.3% in the first half of 1972 from the current half, even after the effects of inflation were eliminated. The report forecast a combined real GNP gain of 4.8% for Canada, Japan, France, West Germany, Italy and Britain.

Rinaldo Ossola, chairman of the Group of 10 deputies and deputy director of the Bank of Italy, said Oct. 20 that the deputies tentatively agreed to permit a 3% swing either side of parity in any new or temporary package of exchange rates. He reported that the delegates had deliberated on an "average weighted realignment" to implement an agreed-upon turnaround of the U.S. deficit.

Japan signs cotton pact extension. The General Agreement on Tariffs and Trade announced Oct. 13 that Japan had signed the three-year extension of the agreement regulating the international cotton textile trade. Japan had been one of two nations of 30 that had refused to sign the extension pact. The eight-year agreement, known as the Long Term Agreement, had been extended by GATT for three years in 1970.

The agreement enabled a country besieged by cotton imports to request an exporting country to restrain shipments and, failing agreement, to impose import restrictions.

Japanese-U.S. textile accord. Under heavy pressure from Washington, Japan initialed a three-year agreement with the U.S. Oct. 15 to limit its exports of man-made and woolen textiles to the U.S. The three-year dispute over Japan's textile exports to the U.S. had strained relations between the two nations and had culminated in an ultimatum by President Nixon that the U.S. would impose unilateral quotas if agreement was not reached by Oct. 15.

The agreement would allow an annual growth rate of about 5% for exports of man-made fibers and 1% for woolen goods. In return, the U.S. agreed to remove—retroactive to Oct. 1—its 10% surcharge on the categories of textiles covered by the agreement. The textile surtax would be removed for all nations.

The agreement, called a "memorandum of understanding," was initialed in Tokyo by David Kennedy, President Nixon's ambassador-at-large and special negotiator on textiles, and Kakuei Tanaka, Japan's minister of international trade and industry. Kennedy said the accord "will remove an issue that has contributed in very large measure to misunderstanding between our two countries." Tanaka said that with the accord, the "textile matter . . . has been practically solved."

The agreement replaced a voluntary control program enforced by the Japanese textile industry since July 1.

Hong Kong, Taiwan, Korea accords —Agreements to curb man-made and woolen textile exports were reached between the U.S. and Hong Kong, Nationalist China and South Korea, the U.S. government announced Oct. 15.

The agreements were for five years and were said to permit an annual growth of 7½% in synthetic exports and 1% for woolens. The accords were concluded under the threat of unilateral quotas by the U.S.

(Nationalist China had reached agreement earlier in October. Y. T. Wong, Nationalist China's director of the Board of Foreign Trade, had confirmed Oct. 4 that his government had accepted an accord in talks with Anthony Jurich, special assistant to Ambassador-at-Large Kennedy, in Taipei Oct. 2.)

The agreement was denounced Oct. 16 by Philip Haddon-Cave, Hong Kong's financial secretary, as "highly unsatisfactory from Hong Kong's point of view." He protested that the negotiations were conducted under a threat of unilateral import restrictions and within "an unreasonable time limit."

The commerce and industry minister of South Korea, Lee Nak Sun, Oct. 16 expressed dissatisfaction with the agreement, but said it was "not unfavorable compared with those signed by other countries."

Denmark votes 10% import surcharge. The Danish Folketing (parliament) Oct. 20 approved, by a vote of 90–88, a temporary 10% import surcharge proposed the previous day by the new Social Democratic government of Premier Jens Otto Krag.

The surtax would be applied to all imports except most raw materials and unprocessed foods, newsprint, fuel oils, medicines, fresh fruit and vegetables, tea, coffee, cocoa and a few other products.

Government officials explained the action was taken to strengthen the nation's currency and improve the balance of payments before Denmark's entry into the European Economic Community, expected in 1973.

The surcharge would be reduced to 7% in June 1972, to 4% in January, 1973, and abolished at the end of March 1973.

Denmark was the first nation to follow the U.S. example of imposing an import surcharge to improve its economic situation.

U.S.-EEC talks. U.S. and European Economic Community (EEC) officials failed to resolve their differences over terms for lifting the U.S. 10% import surtax during a two-day meeting in Washington Oct. 21–22. At separate news conferences, an optimistic assessment for early removal of the levy by the two EEC officials was flatly negated by Undersecretary of State for Economic Affairs Nathaniel Samuels as a "misunderstanding."

Samuels insisted that there had been no change in the U.S. position—that conditions for lifting the surtax remained: "satisfactory progression on the monetary problem" and "tangible progress" on removal of certain short-term trade barriers. He added that the U.S. would also demand a commitment from the EEC nations to negotiate long-term trade problems.

The EEC was represented by Sicco Mansholt, vice president of the Commission of European Communities, and Ralf Dahrendorf, a commissioner and expert in trade policy.

■ As European demands for retaliation against the surtax intensified, the U.S. embarked on its own counter-offensive against the EEC's special trade pacts with Spain and Israel. Through its delegate in Geneva, William K. Miller, the U.S. protested Oct. 6 that the EEC's trade pacts violated the rules of the General Agreement on Tariffs and Trade (GATT) and claimed its right to some recourse—first through special consultations with the EEC, Israel and Spain, and if those failed, to present its case before the 79-nation trade organization.

■ In response to reports of a U.S.-West German agreement in principle to exempt West Germany from the surtax, the EEC Commission requested a secret meeting of the EEC's six foreign ministers Oct. 19. Following the meeting, the six, including West Germany, issued an affirmation of solidarity that trade and monetary negotiations with the U.S. would be held on a community, not a national, basis. Prompting the meeting. was Treasury Secretary Connally's disclosure Oct. 16 that the U.S. was considering selective removal of the surtax and a London Financial Times report Oct. 17 that Connally and West German Economy and Finance Minister Karl Schiller had made a deal during the September International Monetary Fund meeting in Washington.

Connally, in a speech Oct. 20 at the annual meeting of the American Bankers Association in San Francisco, reaffirmed the U.S. position that the surtax would be retained until other nations made sufficient strides toward ending monetary and trade practices, which he said denied "equality of opportunity" for U.S. goods.

Britain's EEC entry approved. The British House of Commons Oct. 28 approved the principle of Britain's membership in the European Economic Community (EEC) on terms negotiated by the Conservative government. The vote was 356–244. The unexpectedly large majority—112 votes—was a historic turning point in Britain's 10-year effort to join the Common Market.

Connally-Japanese talks. Treasury Secretary John B. Connally Jr. ended two days of talks in Tokyo Nov. 11 on Japan's role in helping the U.S. reverse its balance of payments deficit.

On his return to Washington Nov. 13, Connally said the Tokyo talks were held in an atmosphere of understanding, but that no specific commitments had been sought or reached. The Administration apparently had decided to abandon a prepared package of demands in the face of a stiffening Japanese position.

Connally told newsmen in Tokyo Nov. 11 that instead of "coming to Japan as 'Typhoon Connally,' I assure you that I came as gentle as a breeze." He said the purpose of his trip was to suggest, not demand, ways in which Japan could help the U.S. reverse its unfavorable trade deficit with Japan. He noted that, with a 25% increase in Japanese exports in 1971, the deficit was expected to total $3 billion —the largest U.S. deficit with another nation ever recorded. Japanese assistance, he said, could take the form of "revaluation of currency, realignment of currency, . . . lifting restraints and restrictions and tariffs . . . contributions to mutual security [or] it can be part of all these."

Connally met privately with Finance Minister Mikio Mizuta and Foreign Minister Takeo Fukuda Nov. 10. On Nov. 11, he met with Premier Eisaku Sato on overall issues, Minister of International Trade and Industry Kakuei Tanaka on trade questions, Minister of Agriculture Munenori Akagi on Japanese food import curbs and the director general of the Economic Planning Agency, Toshio Kimura.

On the topics covered:

Revaluation of the yen—According to Japanese officials cited by the New York Times Nov. 12, Mizuta told Connally Nov. 10 that Japan was unwilling to realign the yen with the dollar without an overall settlement that included the European Economic Community (EEC). (Japanese officials said it was their impression that the U.S. wanted to use an agreement with Japan to pressure the European nations to agree to a general realignment of currencies.) Mizuta reportedly asserted that Japan was in economic "recession" and could not raise the official value of the yen without substantial concessions from the U.S., most important a removal of the 10% surtax. Connally reportedly countered that recession was a relative matter and he did not believe Japan was in a real recession.

At a news conference Nov. 11 following the two-day talks, Connally denied reports that he was seeking an upvaluation of the yen by 15%–30%; Japanese officials confirmed that he had not specified a figure.

On his return to Washington Nov. 13, Connally said Japan was convinced that, although "politically difficult," revaluation of the yen was necessary and unavoidable.

Devaluation of the dollar—Mizuta, according to Japanese officials cited by the New York Times Nov. 12, did not insist on devaluation of the dollar against gold but said Japan would support the Europeans if they demanded it as part of a general monetary settlement.

At the Nov. 11 news conference, Connally pointed out that the dollar in effect had been devalued against almost every major currency when the U.S. suspended gold convertibility. This, he commented, was "humbling oneself to the ultimate degree."

Import surtax—During their talks Nov. 10, Mizuta insisted on a commitment from the U.S. to remove the surtax simultaneously with a realignment of currencies. Connally upheld the position that the surtax would be dropped when the U.S. balance of payments regained equilibrium. Connally commented sarcastically Nov. 11, "I would be happy if many countries of the world would limit their tariffs to 10%." He noted that Japan's removal of import quotas on cattle had been accompanied by a new tariff of $135 per head—"roughly equivalent to the total value of the animals."

U.S.-Japan trade agreements. Following talks by U.S. and Japanese officials in Honolulu Dec. 11–12, Japan announced Dec. 13 it would remove its import quotas on four agricultural items and cut tariffs on 30 industrial items. The discussions were part of the continuing negotiations on an international currency realignment.

Twenty-seven of the 30 items whose tariffs would be cut were on a list of 28 agricultural and 12 industrial products the U.S. had demanded concessions on in return for lifting its 10% import surtax. Japan also pledged to reduce its automobile tariff from 10% to 8% in exchange for removal of the U.S. surtax from Japanese cars.

The discussions were led by Japan's ambassador to the U.S., Nobuhiko Ushiba, and President Nixon's special trade representative, William D. Eberle, who had just ended similar talks with the Common Market nations in Brussels.

Common Market rebuffs U.S. The Council of Ministers of the European Economic Community (EEC) Dec. 11 refused to give the market's executive commission a mandate to continue talks with the U.S. on trade and currency realignment. The EEC foreign ministers also canceled plans for further trade talks prior to a Group of 10 meeting to be held in Washington later in December on the currency problem.

The rebuff was at French insistence. Foreign Minister Maurice Schumann said France did not want to negotiate while the U.S. held "a knife at the Common Market's throat"—an apparent reference to a list of demands for short-term trade concessions presented by the U.S. Dec. 9.

William Eberle, the U.S. trade representative, had submitted the demands to Ralf Dahrendorf, the EEC commissioner for foreign trade, at a meeting in Brussels. The U.S. demands were not disclosed, but were described as "overwhelming" and "unexpectedly tough."

Press sources said the demands included a freeze on import duties on farm products if the dollar was devalued (since EEC tariffs were fixed in terms of gold, devaluation of the dollar against gold would penalize U.S. exports), a grain stockpile agreement to help U.S. sales, special concessions for U.S. citrus fruit and tobacco and compensation for trade lost from preferential agreements between the EEC and four candidate members—Britain, Ireland, Denmark and Norway.

The Wall Street Journal Dec. 10 quoted Dahrendorf as objecting to what he interpreted as a U.S. demand for "fundamental changes in all policies as a condition for realignment." According to sources cited by the Washington Post Dec. 10, Eberle told the EEC it should renounce its plans to extend industrial free trade to four more European non-candidate states nations and attacked EEC association (preferential) agreements with less developed nations. Dahrendorf reportedly felt that a U.S. demand for a freeze on EEC grain prices and abolition of levies on farm imports attacked the market's common farm policy.

The EEC foreign ministers Dec. 11 issued a declaration of intent that trade concessions should be reciprocal and negotiations should not begin until after currencies were realigned and the U.S. devalued the dollar against gold.

(Sicco Mansholt, EEC commissioner for farm policy, told a group of U.S. newsmen Dec. 13 in Brussels that Western Europe would increase farm prices 4%–6% after a world currency realignment, weakening the competitive advantages the U.S. would gain from devaluation of the dollar. He said it would be "politically impossible" for the West German coalition government to freeze farm prices as demanded by the U.S.)

Group of 10 meets on currencies. The Group of 10 nations' finance ministers and central bank chiefs held a closed session in Rome Nov. 30–Dec. 1 to discuss a general realignment of major currencies as a solution to the present international monetary uncertainty.

The meeting's chairman, U.S. Treasury Secretary John B. Connally Jr., reported at a post-meeting news conference in Rome Dec. 1 that "no offers were made and no acceptances taken," but enough progress had been made to schedule a December meeting in Washington. Press sources reported that progress included a dramatic reversal of the U.S.'s refusal to devalue the dollar with a "hypothetical" offer of a 10% devaluation. Without mentioning this, Connally said the talks had focused on "many hypothetical situations and figures relating to a multitude of currency realignments and their distribution." He stressed that the "complexity and sensitivity of the problems" extended beyond the U.S. dollar. "Some countries," he said, "are more concerned about their parities with relation to their neighbors than with the U.S."

According to the press, the reference to a 10% devaluation of the dollar arose Dec. 1, when the finance ministers and bank chiefs were in a closed executive session at the Palazzo Corsini. Asked what its contribution would be to a general currency upvaluation, the U.S. delegation caused a hasty recess when it asked what the other nations would do if the dollar was devalued by 10%. When the talks resumed later that day, the U.S. was reportedly told that 10% would be too high.

U.S. willingness to even consider devaluation was regarded as a major step toward substantive negotiations. In a discussion Nov. 30 of specific "percentages and figures" acceptable to the participating nations, the other delegates had rejected a U.S. proposal for an overall 11% upvaluation of major currencies (not including the dollar) in exchange for removal of the U.S. 10% import surtax. The proposal, advanced by Treasury Undersecretary Paul A. Volcker just before the session Nov. 29, also called for 3% fluctuation margins in any new parity system (as opposed to the 1% permitted under the old system). The U.S. apparently altered its position after the delegates of the European Economic Community (EEC) and Britain refused to present their proposed parity changes unless the U.S. accepted dollar devaluation "in principle."

(Morgan Guaranty Trust Co. reported Dec. 1 that an effective 7.23% devaluation of the dollar had taken place since the U.S. suspended the dollar-gold link Aug. 15. The figure was based on the currency quotes of the U.S.'s 14 chief trading partners, weighted according to the amount of trade each had with the U.S. in 1970 and measured from parities that existed before May. Other figures measured on the same basis showed a 6.96% rise for the Japanese yen against other currencies, a 5.52% increase for the West German mark, a 1.15% devaluation of the British pound and a 5.98% devaluation of the French franc.)

France tightens exchange controls. French Finance Minister Giscard d'Estaing announced strict new foreign ex-change controls Dec. 3 to block, beginning Dec. 10, the conversion back to other currencies of non-resident franc holdings accumulated from Nov. 30. The move was designed to prevent foreigners from speculating in the commercial franc—the franc maintained at the old parity rate.

The Bank of England the same day, unexpectedly and without explanation, withdrew its support for the dollar on the foreign exchanges, resulting in a 56-point rise in the sterling rate to a high of $2.4986. It was the first time the rate had been permitted to pierce the $2.4940 barrier.

World Currencies Realigned, U.S. Dollar Devalued

After months of tedious and often acrimonious negotiation, the U.S. and its world trading partners agreed on measures that, it was hoped, would help end the U.S. trade and payments deficits and the recurring monetary crises. Despite previous reluctance to devalue the dollar and revoke its import surtax, the U.S. agreed to both of these steps as part of a general realignment of major currencies.

Agreement on U.S. devaluation. President Nixon and French President Georges Pompidou conferred personally Dec. 13-14 and reached an agreement paving the way for a formal devaluation of the dollar along with a general realignment of the world's major currencies. The accord envisaged an early settlement of the international monetary crisis and looked toward the "imminent opening" of trade negotiations between the U.S. and Europe on outstanding trade problems. The agreement was reached during a summit meeting held on Terceira Island in the Portuguese Azores.

In a communiqué issued Dec. 14 after about 12 hours of talks, the two presidents agreed to "work toward a prompt realignment of exchange rates through a devaluation of the dollar and revaluation of some other currencies." The U.S. agreement in principle, which openly committed the Nixon Administration to the first official change in the dollar value of gold since 1934, marked a major concession to Europe—and to France in particular—which had long insisted on the move as a way to alleviate the world monetary crisis.

The two presidents agreed that the realignment could "be accompanied by broader permissible margins of fluctuation around the newly established exchange rates." This marked a concession by France to the U.S., which had recently called for a 3% fluctuation margin in a new parity system, compared to the old 1% figure. France previously had insisted that the existing exchange rate margins remain untouched.

Pompidou did not agree to revalue the franc. He told newsmen Dec. 14 that "perhaps the franc will be absent" from the revaluation scene. An unidentified U.S. official said, however, that Pompidou had at least promised not to devalue the franc along with the dollar, an action that would have eroded the U.S. trading advantage stemming from devaluation.

France's main concession in the summit accord was to agree to work with other members of the European Economic Community (EEC) to prepare "a mandate which would permit the imminent opening" of trade negotiations with the U.S. Previously, France had refused to let the EEC open negotiations pending U.S. concessions toward a monetary settlement.

The communiqué also said Nixon had underscored the importance of restoring wage-price stability and productivity growth in the U.S.

Reaction to devaluation decision. The commitment by Nixon to devalue the dollar was greeted with general approval by Congressional leaders Dec. 14. Senate Majority Leader Mike Mansfield (D, Mont.) said a moderate dollar devaluation would "do no harm and probably would do some good." Rep. Henry Reuss (D, Wisc.), a member of the House Banking Committee and one of the co-sponsors of legislation introduced in November to authorize devaluation, said the agreement was "glorious" and called for immediate action on the bill.

France's five co-members in the European Economic Community received the news without surprise since the U.S. had already signaled its intention to devalue at the Group of 10 meeting in Rome.

Dollar weakens sharply. The Nixon-Pompidou announcement that the dollar would be devalued sent the dollar plunging on most international money markets Dec. 14–15.

The French central bank intervened in the country's two-tier system to support the dollar against the commercial franc but then withdrew, letting the dollar slip to 5.51 francs to the dollar. The floating financial franc rose to 5.29–5.31 francs to the dollar Dec. 15, up from 5.38–5.39 francs to the dollar Dec. 14—in effect a 3.14% upvaluation of the franc.

After quiet trading, the dollar closed in Frankfurt Dec. 14 and 15 at 3.25 marks to the dollar, a de facto upvaluation of more than 12% for the mark from its old official parity of 3.66 marks to the dollar. The German central bank had also intervened both days to prevent the dollar from dropping any lower.

In London, the pound held Dec. 15 at about $2.51, almost 5% above the parity of $2.41 to the pound.

The Japanese yen reached a 12% upvaluation since it was floated Aug. 28 as the dollar fell to a low of 321.39 yen Dec. 15.

Gold prices on European bullion markets showed little reaction to the decision to devalue the dollar.

Dollar devalued, currencies realigned. The U.S. agreed Dec. 18 to devalue the dollar.

Finance ministers and central bank governors of the Group of 10 nations meeting in tight security in Washington, D.C. Dec. 17–18, reached agreement on a general realignment of currency exchange rates that included an 8.57% devaluation of the dollar against gold.

The agreement—said to be the first genuinely multinational negotiation of exchange rates—ended the flotation of major currencies that had existed since the U.S. suspension Aug. 15 of the dollar's convertibility into gold.

The accord was announced by President Nixon Dec. 18 in a surprise visit to the Smithsonian Institution, where the financial officials and their aides had been meeting for the past two days and nearly 400 members of the world press had gathered. Flanked by the ministers and bank governors, Nixon declared that he was privileged to announce on their behalf "the conclusion of the most significant monetary agreement in the history of the world." The President confirmed that for its part, the U.S. had agreed to official devaluation of the dollar and swift removal of the 10% surtax on imports.

Nixon said that all of the governments involved in the negotiations would be asked "who won and who lost?" The answer was that "the whole free world has won," he said. The agreement, he said, would bring "a more stable world with more fair competition and more true prosperity."

The President's comments were echoed at a news conference held by Treasury Secretary John B. Connally Jr. later that day in the company of Federal Reserve Board Chairman Arthur F. Burns and Treasury Undersecretary Paul A. Volcker. Connally described the negotiations as "difficult and tense" and at times "heated." Referring to past U.S. opposition to devaluation of the dollar, he conceded that "we've come a long way." He added, "But we're pleased it's settled—everyone's pleased it's settled. We will return to a degree of stability."

Volcker said no plans had been formulated for a de facto devaluation of the dollar and the matter would be "held in suspense" until Congressional action on the gold price. He also said the U.S. would not intervene in foreign exchange markets to stabilize the dollar's value.

Neither Connally nor Volcker would give a precise assessment of how the average weighted depreciation of the dollar would affect the U.S. balance of trade and international payments.

Terms of realignment—The agreement included a proposed increase in the official price of gold from $35 an ounce to $38. The Group of 10 communiqué, however, stated that the U.S. Congress would be asked to authorize the new rate only when undisclosed short-term trade concessions to the U.S. (presum-

ably from Japan, Canada and the European Common Market) were "available for congressional scrutiny." Restoration of the dollar's convertibility into gold was not immediately envisaged. In the interim, exchange rates would be fixed as if the new gold price were already effective. (The International Monetary Fund Dec. 19 waived reporting of the working exchange rates as formal "par values," identifying them instead as "central rates.")

The higher gold price formally devalued the dollar by 8.57% in terms of converting dollars to foreign currencies, or 7.89% when converting foreign currencies to dollars. The devaluation and realignment amounted to an average depreciation of 12% in the dollar's value when weighted for differing parities and the varying levels of trade with the other countries concerned.

Most of the member nations, plus Switzerland (a participating observer at the Group of 10 meeting), agreed to further revalue their currencies by varying amounts. The exceptions were France and Great Britain, whose rates remained unchanged in terms of their relation to gold but not the U.S. dollar, and Canada, whose dollar continued to float. Although the new rates were not officially disclosed by the Group of 10 communiqué in order to permit individual announcement by the members, it was revealed that, compared with the rates prevailing before May 1971, they would include upvaluations of the German mark by 12.89%, of the Japanese yen by 16.89%, of the Belgian franc by nearly 11%, and of the Swiss franc by 14.89%. Upward revaluations for the British pound and the French franc would be 8.57%—the equivalent of the U.S. devaluation. The Italian lira and Swedish kroner would be devalued by 1%–2%.

IMF approves agreement—The chief monetary aspects of the agreement were approved by the executive directors of the International Monetary Fund (IMF) in Washington Dec. 19. (The IMF directors had conferred Dec. 16 with the deputies of the Group of 10 ministers.) The directors approved the new pattern of exchange rates set by the Group of 10 negotiators.

New exchange rates of major foreign currencies in terms of their unit value to one U.S. dollar:

Currency	New Value	Old Value*
	(number of foreign currency units)	
Japanese yen	308	360
British pound	.383774	.416667
German mark	3.223	3.66
French franc**	5.116	5.55419
Italian lira	568.4	625
Belgian franc	44.81	50
Dutch guilder**	3.245	3.62
Swiss franc**	3.85	4.37
Swedish krona	4.813	5.17

*Before May 1971. **Unofficial.

The Group of 10 communiqué had acknowledged that the group's agreement did not include all members of the International Monetary Fund, who "will need urgently to reach decisions with respect to their own exchange rates." The communiqué warned that "it is particularly important at this time that no country seek improper competitive advantage through its exchange rate policies. Changes in parities can only be justified by an objective appraisal which establishes a position of disequilibrium."

The IMF directors approved an agreement by the Group of 10 meeting permitting wider fluctuation margins of 2.25% above and below the new currency parities instead of the former system's permissible fluctuation of 1%.

Surtax, tax credit lifted—Carrying out the commitment given by the U.S., President Nixon removed the 10% import surtax Dec. 20 and Treasury Secretary Connally simultaneously announced the ending of the 7% investment tax credit on U.S.-made goods. The U.S. had committed itself at the October meeting of the Group of 10 deputies to lifting of the tax credit on the removal of the surtax. Nixon signed the proclamation ending the surtax while in flight to Bermuda for talks with British Prime Minister Edward Heath, a bitter foe of the surtax.

3rd quarter payments deficit. Devaluation of the dollar was expected to help reverse the largest balance of payments deficit in U.S. history. On the eve of the Group of 10 negotiations, the Commerce Department Dec. 16 reported that the "basic" balance of payments deficit—

U.S. Balance of Trade & Payments

	Trade balance on census basis	Balance of payments
1960	$4,579,000,000	$4,806,000,000
1961	5,467,000,000	5,538,000,000
1962	4,533,000,000	4,361,000,000
1963	5,262,000,000	4,583,000,000
1964	7,082,000,000	4,002,000,000
1965	5,222,000,000	4,292,000,000
1966	3,872,000,000	3,379,000,000
1967	4,141,000,000	3,557,000,000
1968	†37,000,000	660,000,000
1969	1,289,000,000	660,000,000
1970	2,699,000,000	†10,000,000
1971	2,047,000,000	†2,906,000,000

† Deficit.

formally the balance on a current account and long-term capital basis—had amounted to $3.1 billion in the third quarter. The figure was just below the $3.2 billion deficit of the second quarter.

The "balance on current account," covering all transactions except capital flows, showed a $921 million deficit in the third quarter, the deepest since 1959. The current account balance reflected the reversal of the traditional surplus of exports over imports in July and August.

U.S.-British consultations. President Nixon and British Prime Minister Edward Heath expressed determination Dec. 21 after two days of talks in Bermuda to pursue "close and continuing consultation" on world problems although a changed relationship between the two countries was implicit in Britain's entry into the European Economic Community (EEC).

The Atlantic alliance "is, and must remain, the cornerstone of the defense of the free world," they declared in a joint communiqué, and British entry into the EEC would "reinforce the strength" of the alliance.

Their joint statement also affirmed that the current goal of statesmanship was "to lift the sights beyond the problems of immediate urgency to those major political and economic issues which in the longer term will determine the shape of the world in which we all live."

A "new balance" had to be struck between the European community, the U.S. and Japan, Heath said, and the immediate problems were to achieve monetary reform and the removal of trade barriers.

Nixon said it was essential for "the new Europe and the new America" and the other nations of the world, particularly Japan, to "work together." "We will compete," he said, "but it is also indispensable that that competition be constructive and not destructive."

Index